MW01505673

Sri Sarada Devi
and Her Divine Play

Sarada Devi (1853–1920), known respectfully and affectionately as "Holy Mother." This reproduction was made from the original photograph taken in Calcutta, November 1898.

Sri Sarada Devi
and Her Divine Play

Swami Chetanananda

Vedanta Society of St Louis

Copyright © 2015 Vedanta Society of St. Louis

Library of Congress Cataloging-in-Publication Data

Chetanananda, Swami.
  Sri sarada devi and her divine play / Swami Chetanananda. -- First edition
    pages cm
  Includes bibliographical references and index.
  ISBN 978-0-916356-99-6 (hardcover : alk. paper) 1. Sarada Devi,
1853-1920. 2. Hindus--India--Biography. 3. Spiritual life--Hinduism. I.
Title.
  BL1175.S36C44 2015
  294.5'55092--dc23
  [B]
                    2015027983

FIRST EDITION 2015
Second printing 2016

Cover design by Diane Marshall
Printed in Canada

*Those who wish to learn in greater detail about the
teachings contained in this book may write to:*

Vedanta Society of St. Louis
205 S. Skinker Blvd.
St. Louis, MO 63105, U.S.A.

www.vedantastl.org

Contents

Illustrations

Preface

*S*ri *Sarada Devi and Her Divine Play* is a biography of Sarada Devi, the wife and spiritual companion of Ramakrishna Paramahamsa, the spiritual phenomenon of this age. Nowadays, Sarada Devi is affectionately and respectfully referred to by her devotees as Holy Mother. When we study her life in depth, we find that she enacted her divine play in three parts.

First was her Adi Lila, or early lila, which comprises events from 1853 to 1886. She grew up in rural Jayrambati, a small village in West Bengal, and was married to Ramakrishna while still a child. At the age of 18 she joined Ramakrishna in Dakshineswar, near Calcutta, and lived with him off and on until his passing away in 1886.

Second was her Madhya Lila, or middle lila, which includes events from 1887 to 1908. During this period she went on pilgrimages, passed through various ordeals, and slowly began to conduct Ramakrishna's spiritual ministry.

Third was her Antya Lila, or final lila, comprising events from 1909 to 1920. She revealed her divinity by showering her spiritual treasures on everyone who came to her.

Though we have made this classification, we understand that it is not completely possible to divide Holy Mother's life chronologically, because some events occurred in more than one period. But in a general way, readers will observe in chapters 1 through 9 how she initiated her divine play by preparing herself to be a world teacher; in chapters 10 through 28, how she enacted her drama by demonstrating the four yogas in her ideal life; and in chapters 29 through 35, how her drama gradually came to a close. Through her spontaneous outpouring of love and compassion, she revealed her true nature and bestowed fearlessness upon her disciples and devotees.

Holy Mother's simple and pure life inspires us; her modesty and humility overwhelm us; her love and compassion conquer our hearts; her struggle and suffering strengthen us to face all ordeals and crises of life; her contentment and indifference to poverty make us ashamed when we complain and become disgruntled over small things; her forbearance and acceptance of various ailments — dysentery, malaria, rheumatism, and kala-azar — encourage us to endure our illnesses silently; her grace and forgiveness convey her divinity to us; her truthfulness and steadiness convince us that we can rely on her; her common sense and presence of mind show us how to be practical; her unselfish service and complete self-surrender are models for our own lives. She demonstrated the highest truths of Vedanta in her daily life, and harmoniously reconciled the contemplative life with the active life. The Mother's divine life is a beacon for lost and weary souls in this world. Her life and her message help the downtrodden and depressed as well as those who have lost hope in trying to find meaning in life. Innumerable people are receiving peace and bliss, solace and succour from her simple life and practical teachings.

Truly, while Ramakrishna's life was one of condensed spirituality that may be compared to the snow in the Himalayas, Holy Mother's life was one of flowing spirituality, like the water of the Ganges. Melted snow turns to water, but they are the same substance: one is solid; the other is liquid. We cannot see the physical forms of Ramakrishna or Holy Mother, but their lives and teachings are living in the hearts of countless people all over the world. Millions and millions of people in the East and the West now think of and meditate on them daily. Every great religious personality gives shelter, rest, and peace to all. Referring to those great souls, Jules Michelet wrote in *The Bible of Humanity*: "Man must rest, get his breath, refresh himself at the great living wells, which keep the freshness of the eternal."

There are many biographies and reminiscences of Holy Mother in Bengali, and three important biographies in English. Swami Tapasyananda wrote *Sri Sarada Devi: The Holy Mother* in 1940. During the centenary of Holy Mother (1953–54), Swami Gambhirananda wrote an exhaustive biography in Bengali under the title *Srima Sarada Devi*, which he translated into English in 1954 as *Holy Mother Sri Sarada Devi*. Finally, in 1962, Swami Nikhilananda wrote a beautiful biography entitled *Holy Mother*. Since that time, however, more information about Holy Mother has come to light. Some of my brother monks and Western devotees have asked me to write an updated biography of Holy Mother. After translating Swami Saradananda's *Sri Ramakrishna Lilaprasanga* (*Sri Ramakrishna and His Divine Play*), I felt my work was half done. Just as a theatre audience becomes irritated and begins shouting if an interesting drama ends midway, so I thought the devoted followers of Ramakrishna and Holy Mother might be annoyed with me if I did not complete the whole drama. To this end, I started *Sri Sarada Devi and Her Divine Play*. It took me almost seven years to complete this volume, but I deeply felt that this project would help me accomplish two goals: First, it would engage my mind in meditating on Holy Mother for a long period; second, her sublime life and practical teachings would inspire people in this joyless world.

In the 1950s and 1960s, I had an opportunity to associate closely with many monastic and householder disciples of Holy Mother and to hear many stories from them. Those reminiscences of the Mother are my treasure trove. Years ago I edited 49 reminiscences of Holy Mother, which were published in Bengali by the Udbodhan Office in Calcutta under the title *Matri Darshan*.

The following are the main source materials for this new biography, *Sri Sarada Devi and Her Divine Play*:

1. *Sri Sri Mayer Katha* by Holy Mother's Disciples
2. *Matri Sannidhey* by Swami Ishanananda
3. *Sri Sri Mayer Smritikatha* by Swami Saradeshananda
4. *Sri Sri Ma O Jayrambati* by Swami Parameswarananda
5. *Srima* by Ashutosh Mitra
6. *Bharatiprana Smritikatha*, edited by Pravrajika Nirbhayaprana
7. *Matri Darshan*, compiled and edited by Swami Chetanananda
8. *Sri Sri Mayer Padaprante* (in four volumes), compiled and edited by Swami Purnatmananda
9. *Srima Sarada Devi* by Swami Gambhirananda
10. *Sri Sri Sarada Devi* by Brahmachari Akshaychaitanya
11. *Sri Srima Saradamani Devi* by Manada Shankar Dasgupta
12. *Sri Srimayer Jivankatha* by Swami Bhumananda
13. *Sri Sri Ramakrishna Lilaprasanga* by Swami Saradananda
14. *Holy Mother* (in English) by Swami Nikhilananda

Apart from the above sources, I collected materials from many other books and magazines, which are listed in the references at the end. I tried to make this book authentic by using eyewitness accounts and reminiscences of the Mother's disciples who lived with her for many years. In addition, I translated the Mother's own words as far as possible instead of paraphrasing them.

Most of the valuable information and eyewitness accounts in this biography have been collected from *Sri Sri Mayer Katha*, so I will present a brief history of that work here to satisfy the curiosity of the reader.

Swami Arupananda, a disciple and attendant of Holy Mother, began to record his conversations with her in Jayrambati and Udbodhan House on 1 February 1907. After the Mother's passing away, he collected reminiscences about Holy Mother from other monks and devotees. Sarajubala Sen, a close disciple of the Mother, recorded her conversations with Holy Mother in her diary beginning in 1911, and she gave this record to Arupananda. The swami was very happy to have so much intimate information about Holy Mother, but he was hesitant to publish his manuscript. After a couple of years, Swami Shuddhananda, a disciple of Swami Vivekananda, went to Varanasi and stayed there for a while. At that time he read Arupananda's manuscript and was delighted with it. After returning to Calcutta, Shuddhananda asked Swami Saradananda to publish those reminiscences and teachings of Holy Mother.

In 1924 (Vaishakh 1331) Ramananda Chattopadhyay wrote a short biographical sketch of Holy Mother for *Pravasi* magazine and requested her close disciples to publish more stories about Holy Mother's life. When Shuddhananda pointed this out to Saradananda, he agreed to publish Arupananda's manuscript on the condition that it would be edited so that readers would understand the Mother's teachings correctly. Arupananda was asked to come to Udbodhan with his manuscript. When he arrived, it was decided that every evening the manuscript would be read in the presence of Saradananda and Shuddhananda for review. Thus the whole manuscript was revised. Udbodhan published it in Bengali, in two volumes (Volume 1 in 1926 and Volume 2 in 1936), under the title *Sri Sri Mayer Katha*. Then Ramakrishna Math, Chennai, translated it into English and published it in one volume as *The Gospel of the Holy Mother*.

Undoubtedly, we are indebted to all those who recorded so much valuable information about the Mother. Brahmachari Akshaychaitanya was the first biographer of Holy Mother in Bengali, and his book, *Sri Sri Sarada Devi*, was published in 1937. But the Mother's biography by Swami Gambhirananda is the most exhaustive and authentic account, and I relied upon it heavily while writing the present biography. He once told me that he had collected material from the written reminiscences of the Mother's disciples, verbal testimonies from senior monks and devotees, printed books and magazines, and M.'s diary. When I asked whether he had saved those precious documents, he replied that when the book was published he did not feel any need to preserve them. This is a great loss.

I am especially grateful to Swami Gambhirananda because his book was the source of my inspiration. I must also acknowledge my indebtedness to Swami Nikhilananda, as I used some of his translations in this book.

I have tried to avoid repetition as much as possible, but in some places it was unavoidable. For example, two or three disciples of Mother narrated her daily routine in Jayrambati and Udbodhan, and described her journey from Jayrambati to Calcutta. I included all of these accounts, because each person had something new to contribute. This will help the readers view and meditate on Holy Mother from various perspectives. Although Calcutta, Madras, Bangalore, and Bombay have since been renamed as Kolkata, Chennai, Bengaluru, and Mumbai, respectively, we have used the former names in this book, as these are the names that were current in Holy Mother's day.

Generally, biographers focus on the important events in the lives of great people and skip the insignificant details, but I included both in an attempt to inform the reader of even the smallest aspects of Holy Mother's life. In the eyes of a lover, everything related to the beloved is sweet and precious. I feel inadequate and incompetent to interpret the Mother's life, so I have simply presented all the facts and figures, stories and episodes to the reader, who may interpret them in their own way. Some quotes have been used more than once for continuity of thought and narration.

I have tried to make this biography of the Mother as chronological as possible, as well as readable and understandable. The Mother's disciples were happy in her company; they did not pay too much attention to dates and years, which are important for biographical history. Regarding the chronology of the Mother's life, I had a greater advantage than the earlier biographers because through the efforts of different researchers over the last fifty years many new materials have come out.

I wish to express my gratitude to my proofreaders, my typesetter, my designer, and those who corrected the manuscript on the computer. I also gratefully acknowledge the help that I received from my editors: Kim Saccio-Kent, a freelance editor in San Francisco; Pravrajika Shuddhatmaprana, a nun of the Vedanta Society of Southern California; Linda Prugh, an English teacher in Kansas City; Janice Thorup, a former adjunct professor of writing at Washington University, St. Louis; Chris Lovato, professor, University of British Columbia, Vancouver. Margy Olmstead, a devotee in Portland, made the index, and Linda Prugh prepared the glossary.

I know my limitations very well. I frankly want the reader to know that I am not worthy of writing this biography of Holy Mother. But this verse of the *Shiva-mahimnah Stotram* (31) induced me to undertake this project: "O Lord, where is my ill-developed mind, subject to misery, and where is your boundless divinity, endowed with infinite virtues? The very thought of your vastness scares me; but my devotion made me fearless and forced me to offer this garland of words at your feet."

Finally, I feel blessed that Holy Mother used my body and mind, as a writer uses a fountain pen, to write her biography. If her children can visualize her divine play through the pages of this book, I will be happy.

Chetanananda
Vedanta Society of St. Louis
4 July 2015

Introduction

Doubt is a demon that arises from ignorance and false knowledge, destroying happiness and peace of mind. Can there be any peace in a home where the husband and the wife distrust each other? Doubt is horrible, but it can be uprooted by true knowledge and by the grace of God.

Many people are like Doubting Thomas, mentioned in the New Testament, who doubted the resurrection of Christ even after hearing from other disciples that they had seen Christ. Once a devotee from Kalma (now in Bangladesh), doubted the divinity of Sarada Devi, or Holy Mother, the spiritual consort of Ramakrishna. This uncertainty was tormenting his mind and ruining his spiritual life. In search of a solution, he went to the Udbodhan House in Calcutta to see Swami Saradananda, an attendant of Holy Mother.

The devotee from Kalma said, "Swami, I believe that Sri Ramakrishna was an avatar, but I don't consider Holy Mother Sarada Devi to be Bhagavati [the Divine Mother]."

Saradananda replied, "Well, if you believe that the Master was God, then why do you have such doubts about Holy Mother?"

"The Master had samadhi frequently," said the devotee, "but we don't witness that in Holy Mother. Moreover, she didn't practise intense sadhana as the Master did."

"Then you are not convinced that the Master was God," Saradananda said.

The devotee humbly replied, "No, Swami, I wholeheartedly believe that the Master was God."

Saradananda responded, "Then you believe that God married the daughter of a poor woman who made her living collecting and selling cow-dung patties?"

Without saying anything further, the devotee bowed down to Saradananda and said joyfully, "My doubt is gone."[1]

This book is the story of Sarada Devi (1853–1920), the wife of Ramakrishna (1836-1886). Ramakrishna, the God-man of the nineteenth century, is well known all over the world for demonstrating acceptance and respect for all religious traditions. He was truly a spiritual phenomenon.

After he passed away, his disciple Swami Vivekananda was among the first to bring the wisdom of yoga and Vedanta to the West. Romain Rolland, a French Nobel Laureate, wrote: "The man [Ramakrishna] was the consummation of two thousand years of the spiritual life of three hundred million people."

According to Indian religious tradition, an avatar, or Divine Incarnation, does not come alone. He comes with his Shakti, his female counterpart, as well as a group of great souls who propagate his message. Ramachandra came with Sita, Krishna with Radha, Buddha with Yashodhara, Chaitanya with Vishnupriya, and Ramakrishna with Sarada. Swami Nikhilananda wrote:

> The wife is called *sahadharmini*, the copartner of the husband in spiritual pursuits. Marriage does not imply the superiority of the husband or the inferiority of the wife. The one is incomplete without the other. This concept is symbolized by the Hindu deity Ardhanārishwara, of which one half is female and the other half male. When a man regards his wife only as an object to satisfy physical desire, disaster befalls the family. A Hindu scripture says: "She is the Goddess of Fortune for the righteous and force of evil for the wicked."[2]

This book describes how Ramakrishna's wife, Sarada Devi, carried out her husband's spiritual ministry for 34 years after his passing away, and inspired the monks and devotees of the Ramakrishna Order. Her life is a glowing example of Vedanta in practice. She demonstrated how to commune with God while living in the world; how to lead a life that is both active and contemplative; how to adjust one's actions through forbearance and forgiveness; how to cultivate peace and joy in one's daily life through love, compassion, humility, selfless service, detachment, and devotion. Her final message was: "My child, if you want peace of mind, do not find fault with others. See your own faults. Learn to make the world your own. No one is a stranger, my child; the whole world is your own."

People usually seek a role model to guide and shape their lives. We enjoy seeing a person who practises what he or she preaches. We are not perfect, but we want perfection in others. Sarada Devi was a perfect role model in her various relationships as daughter, sister, wife, and mother, as well as householder and nun. From the Hindu point of view, the culmination of womanhood is being a mother. As a mother, a woman commands the highest respect in the family because of her unselfish love and self-sacrificing service. Moreover, she is regarded as a veritable goddess.

She is the embodiment of the Motherhood of God. Children are usually freer with their mother than with their father; they never hesitate to make demands upon her. According to a Bengali proverb, there may be a bad child, but never a bad mother.

Only a jeweller knows the value of a gem. We really don't know the true nature of Holy Mother, although we hear about her greatness from the words of Ramakrishna, Vivekananda, and some other close disciples of the Master and Holy Mother. Ramakrishna said of Holy Mother: "Sarada is an incarnation of Saraswati [the goddess of learning]. She was born to bestow knowledge on others. She has hidden her physical beauty lest people look upon her with impure eyes and thus commit sin."[3] In 1894, Swami Vivekananda wrote from America to Swami Shivananda:

> You have not yet realized how precious Holy Mother is. People will not understand her now, but they will, gradually. Brother, there will be no salvation of the world without the help of the Divine Power. Why is it that our country is the weakest and most backward of all countries? Because *Shakti* is held in dishonour here. Holy Mother has been born to revive this wonderful *Shakti* in India; and making her the nucleus, once more will Gargis and Maitreyis be born into the world. Without the grace of *Shakti* nothing will be accomplished. What do I find in America and Europe? The worship of *Shakti*, the worship of Power. Yet they worship Her ignorantly, through sense gratification. Imagine then what a lot of good they will achieve when they worship Her with purity, looking upon Her as their Mother![4]

It is natural that when God assumes a human form, people consider Him to be one of their own. Krishna said in the Gita (9:11): "Fools disregard Me when I assume a human form; for they are unaware of My higher nature as the Supreme Lord of all beings." It is a great mystery when Divine Incarnations descend to earth and we see them eating, sleeping, walking, and acting as we do. They cover themselves with the veil of *Yogamaya* so that ordinary people cannot recognize them. If they do not reveal themselves out of their grace, no one can know them. The villagers of Nazareth knew only that Jesus was a carpenter's son. They could not recognize his divine aspect. In every age avatars are misunderstood; only their close disciples recognize who they are.

Once a woman devotee asked Holy Mother, "Mother, why can't we comprehend that you are the Divine Mother?"

Holy Mother replied: "How can everyone recognize divinity, my child? There was a big diamond lying at a bathing ghat. Considering it to be an ordinary stone, people rubbed their feet against it to smooth their soles. One day a jeweller came there and immediately recognized it as a large and precious diamond....In fact, the Master was God. He assumed a human form to mitigate the sufferings of humanity. He came to this world incognito, like a king who visits the city in disguise. I am Bhagavati [the goddess]."[5]

From the 1950s onward, I was fortunate enough to come in contact with several disciples of Holy Mother; I heard many stories about her from them. In 1969, I asked Swami Ishanananda: "Swami, you were an attendant of Holy Mother for 11 years. Could you tell me, what was the most striking characteristic that you witnessed in Holy Mother? What is the difference between Holy Mother and our mothers, sisters, aunts, and other women in our families?"

The swami kept quiet for a while and then said: "Have you seen any man or woman who is devoid of desire? Holy Mother was completely free from desire. Every human being is subject to desire, which originates from ignorance. Only God is desireless. Holy Mother was the Divine Mother Herself."

In 1977, I asked Swami Saradeshananda, a disciple and attendant of Holy Mother: "Swami, you served Holy Mother for several years in Jayrambati. Please tell me, what impressed you most about her life?"

"Humility," answered the swami. "Mother was completely egoless."

We are not born in this world with friends or enemies. We make friends or enemies mainly through what we say and how we behave. Human relationships can become torn apart instantly by heartrending words. Swami Satyaswarupananda was a disciple of the Mother. In 1986, in Varanasi, he told me about one of her most wonderful characteristics: "The Mother never used harsh words to hurt anybody. She spoke in a gentle and tactful way that would not cause any pain to others. For example, once she gave some money to someone who was shopping for her. He did not return the change. She then said to that person, 'My son, do you need any more money for those purchases?'

"Embarrassed, he replied, 'Mother, I am sorry, I forgot to return the change.' He then returned the change."

Swami Prabhavananda once told me that Holy Mother was the embodiment of purity; her mind never went below the *vishuddha chakra* (throat centre).

Regarding the difference between other women and Holy Mother, one of her disciples, Swami Vishuddhananda, said: "I gave a name to Holy Mother: *Gandi-bhāngā Mā*—the Barrier-breaking Mother. The mothers that we see around us have barriers or limitations. Their affection is limited to their respective children. But the affection of Holy Mother was limitless and had no barrier. She was the Mother of the Universe."

When Ram is ill, Ram's mother is upset, but not Shyam's mother. When Shyam is ill, Shyam's mother suffers, but not Ram's mother. Each mother knows that her child came from her body and she is therefore attached to him or her. Holy Mother, on the contrary, was the mother of all beings — the Cosmic Mother. Holy Mother saw all children, all men and women, and even birds and beasts emerge from her cosmic body. She had infinite love and affection, compassion and forgiveness for each and all.

Many fascinating stories of Holy Mother relate that she appeared to her devotees as Kali, Jagaddhatri, Bagala, or some other goddesses. Some devotees lost consciousness upon seeing her divine form. Ramakrishna experienced all beings as manifestations of the Divine Mother. He knew that Sarada Devi was that Divine Mother, and when he departed, he left her to demonstrate the Motherhood of God to the world.

Swami Saradananda dedicated to Holy Mother his book, *Mother Worship in India*, with these words: "By whose gracious glance the author has been able to realize the revelation of Divine Motherhood in every woman — to her lotus feet the work is dedicated in all humility and devotion."[6]

It is true, we have neither the eyes nor the experience of Ramakrishna or Saradananda, but nevertheless we have a deep desire to know our beloved Holy Mother. We need her grace to know her. Our only hope is her assurance: "Those who are my children are already free. Even Providence cannot do any harm to them."[7]

Holy Mother was the embodiment of Shakti, the cosmic energy of God. In this book, the reader will be able to visualize how that divine energy manifested in this world over a period of 67 years. Henry Thomas and Dana Lee Thomas noted in *Great Philosophers* that when we study the living biographies of the world, "Our world becomes wider, our imagination richer, and our life more coloured and more zestful as the result of our companionship with the travellers of the spirit and the pioneers of thought."[8]

Human beings do not live by bread alone; they are sustained in this world mainly through the cultivation of three virtues: faith, hope, and love. In this biography, *Sri Sarada Devi and Her Divine Play*, I have tried to show how the compassionate Holy Mother nourished humanity with these life-giving virtues — faith, hope, and love.

1
Jayrambati:
An Idyllic Village in Bengal

Ittham yadā yadā bādhā dānavotthā bhavishyati;
Tadā tadā avatiryāham karishyāmi arisamkshayam.
   —*Chandi, 11:54-55*

Whenever the demoniacal powers try to disrupt or destroy this world, I shall incarnate and destroy those enemies of divine beings.

The birthplace of an avatar or a great soul becomes an eternal place of pilgrimage. Ayodhya, Mathura, Bethlehem, Navadwip, Kamarpukur, Jayrambati — the birthplaces of Ramachandra, Krishna, Jesus, Chaitanya, Ramakrishna, and Sarada Devi respectively — are forever marked on the world map. In the nineteenth century, Kamarpukur and Jayrambati were insignificant villages of Bengal, almost unknown to the outside world. Now people from all over the world visit the birthplaces of Ramakrishna and Sarada Devi, or Holy Mother.

Jayrambati is a *shaktipith,* a place where the Cosmic Energy — the Divine Mother — took a human form. This small village is situated in the southeastern part of the Bankura District in Bengal, 64 miles northwest of Calcutta and four miles northwest of Kamarpukur. In the nineteenth century, approximately 100 families lived there in mud huts with thatched roofs, without running water, electricity, or sanitary facilities.

Jayrambati: A Rural Haven

Imagine a village with verdant plants and trees, and abundant fruit and flowers. It is surrounded by vast meadows, and beautiful lakes and ponds, with a murmuring river flowing nearby. Imagine rustic huts and temples, a blue sky above, green rice fields below, bright sunshine all around, colourful red-dust roads, birdsongs, and a pure and gentle breeze cooling the meadows. During the monsoon season, the farmers plough with their bullocks under a sky full of clouds. At other times the cowherds play their flutes under a banyan tree as their cows graze. Imagine nightfall in a Bengal village: women wave oil lamps to the

Village of Jayrambati, ca. 1930.

Cosmic God at the altar in the courtyard and blow conches; mothers and grandmothers tell stories from the Ramayana and the Mahabharata to children gathered around them as flames of oil lamps flicker on the wall. Throughout the entire village the sound of vesper bells and gongs from the temples reverberate. Scenes such as these thrill the imagination, which at least temporarily uplifts human minds from the mundane world. This description, however, is not fictional: this idyllic village was Jayrambati, the birthplace of Sarada Devi, 162 years ago.

In Sarada Devi's time, Jayrambati was a small village surrounded by fertile agricultural land. The villagers grew rice, wheat, lentils, potatoes, beans, chilies, sugarcane, and cotton, among other crops. Most of the villagers supported themselves by farming and fishing; a small group of brahmins taught and officiated as priests. Sarada Devi was born into one of these brahmin families.

As a young girl, Sarada was not confined to her small village. The Amodar River runs along a meadow north of the village. Sarada considered it to be the Ganges and bathed there with her brothers during the rainy season when there was sufficient water. There is a cremation ground on the southern bank of the river and the village Deshra lies to the north. To the east of Jayrambati is the village of Haldi; to the south, Jibta; to the southwest, Masinapur; and to the west, Sihar. The village of Sihar, half a mile from Jayrambati, is the birthplace of Sarada Devi's mother and also of Hridayram Mukhopadhyay (known as Hriday), a nephew of Ramakrishna. North of Sihar is Shiromanipur, a poverty-stricken village that was predominantly inhabited by Muslims. In later years Holy Mother hired workers from Shiromanipur to construct a house. Four miles northwest of Jayrambati is Koalpara Ashrama, where Sarada Devi would rest when she travelled from Vishnupur to her village, a journey of 28 miles by bullock cart.

When Sarada Devi was young there was no market in Jayrambati. Though the villagers were more or less self-sufficient, they sometimes journeyed to Kotalpur, a small town nine miles away, to buy clothes, salt, spices, kerosene, matches, utensils, and other necessities. They could buy sweets and groceries from markets in Kamarpukur and Kayapat-Badanganj, six miles away. There was a grocery shop in Sihar, within a mile of Jayrambati. In Jayrambati there lived a barber family, a blacksmith family, a family of confectioners, and a few families who sold milk from their cows.

Banerjee's Pond is located to the south of Jayrambati. The villagers used its water for bathing, cooking, and drinking. To the west of the village is Aher Lake (now called "Mother's Lake"), which was used to irrigate the village fields. A small pond called Punyapukur is in the centre of the village. The villagers used its water to wash clothes and utensils. Sarada Devi's house is located to the west of Punyapukur, and Kalupukur, another small pond, is just southwest of her ancestral home.

The people of Jayrambati were either poor or middle class, and they were very devout. Religious festivals, performances of religious plays, recitals from Hindu mythology, kirtan, and devotional Baul singing brought relief from the monotony of their daily lives.

There are four temples in that small village. The presiding deity of the village is the goddess Simhavahini. In her temple, the deity is flanked by her two companions, Chandi and Mahamaya. A separate temple for the goddess Shitala is located in the southeast corner of the village; Sarada Devi's family worshipped at this temple. In autumn, Durga Puja was held in the Shitala temple, and many people from other villages attended. To the northwest of Punyapukur, two thatched huts were used as temples: one was dedicated to Lord Sundarnarayan (Sarada Devi's ancestral deity) and the other to Mother Kali. This hut was later used as a children's school when Kali worship was discontinued. On the west side of the village are temples to Jatra-siddhi and Birkant Dharma-thakur. The villagers of Jayrambati did not just visit their own temples, however. For example, at the time of Shiva-ratri (the spring festival to Shiva), they would flock to the Shantinath Shiva temple in Sihar to attend the 24-hour kirtan.

Travel between Calcutta and Jayrambati

In the latter part of the nineteenth century, it was difficult to reach Calcutta from the Kamarpukur-Jayrambati area. The journey took three to four days. People generally made the journey in a group because the extensive meadows and secluded roads were often infested with bandits. Travellers between Jayrambati and Calcutta had to walk 64 miles and cross five rivers — Amodar, Dwarakeshwar, Mundeshwari, Damodar, and Ganges. Those who could afford the expense travelled by palanquin or took the train from Burdwan, nearly 34 miles from Jayrambati. Nowadays one can drive from Calcutta to Kamarpukur-Jayrambati in just three hours. (The distance between Kamarpukur and Jayrambati is 4 miles.)

2
Birth
and Early Life of Sarada Devi

Prakritim paramām abhayām varadām
   nararupa-dharām janatāpa-harām;
Sharanā-gata sevaka-toshakarim
   pranamāmi parām jananim jagatām.
—*A hymn by Swami Abhedananda*

O Divine Nature Supreme! Remover of all fears, giver of boons, who has taken a human form, who removes the miseries of humanity, who confers joy on those who take refuge in you, O Supreme Mother of the Universe! I bow down to you.

Sarada Devi was born into a pious brahmin family. Her father, Ramchandra Mukhopadhyay, was devout, truthful, and upright. Although poor, he would not accept gifts from just anyone. Ramchandra had three brothers: Trailokya, Ishwar, and Nilmadhav. Trailokya was a Sanskrit scholar, but he died in his youth. Nilmadhav was a bachelor. Ishwar earned a very small amount of money by performing rituals in some homes in Calcutta. The brothers all lived together, and Sarada grew up in a large extended family. Her mother, Shyamasundari Devi, was deeply spiritual and came from the Majumdar family of Sihar. Sarada's maternal grandfather was Hariprasad Majumdar, who had five sons (Rambrahma, Tarak, Kedar, Sripati, and Vaikuntha) and two daughters (Shyamasundari and Dayamayi).

Sarada later described her parents: "My father was a righteous man, a sincere devotee of Ramachandra. He had such a good heart and amiable nature that anyone passing by his house would be invited to share a smoke. He greatly enjoyed smoking tobacco and would prepare the smoke himself. My mother was kind and guileless and loved to feed people. She carefully managed every detail of the household and collected the things that were necessary for the whole year. She would say, 'My household is for God and His devotees.' How could I have been born in that family if my father and mother had not practised religious austerities?"[1]

The bel tree where Shyamasundari Devi had a vision of the Divine Mother in the form of a little girl. The girl embraced her, announcing that she was joining her family.

The birth of an avatar or a saint is often associated with supernatural phenomena. For example, as Ramakrishna's mother, Chandramani, once stood in front of the Yogi Shiva temple in Kamarpukur, she was surrounded by light and later felt that she had conceived a child. At the same time, Ramakrishna's father, Kshudiram, was in Gaya. Lord Vishnu appeared before him and said he wanted to be born as his son. Other examples: Kaushalya became pregnant with Ramachandra when she ate sacrificial cake; Lord Vishnu himself entered the womb of Devaki, Krishna's mother; and Jesus was born of the Virgin Mary, as the angel Gabriel had foretold.

A mystical event is also associated with Sarada's birth. One day as Shyamasundari was on her way to visit her family in Sihar, she felt an urge to answer the call of nature. As she squatted in the bushes under a bel tree on the east side of Ella Pond, which was close to a potter's kiln, she heard jingling sounds from the kiln and saw a little girl of six climbing down from the bel tree. The little girl put her tender arms around Shyamasundari's neck, and she fell down unconscious. She had no idea how long she remained in that condition. Later, her relatives found her under that tree and took her home. From then on she felt that she was pregnant.[2]

Later Holy Mother recounted this incident: "My birth was like the Master's. My mother went to Sihar to see the deity. On her way home, she suddenly felt an urge to answer the call of nature, and she went into the bushes under a nearby tree. It was a false urge. She felt as if air entered her womb, making her feel very heavy. She remained in that condition. Then my mother saw a beautiful girl of five or six years, clad in a red sari, descending from the tree. She put her tender arms around my mother's neck and said: 'Here I come to your home, Mother.' My mother fell down unconscious and had to be carried home. That girl entered my mother's womb and thus I was born."[3]

At that time Sarada's father, Ramchandra, was in Calcutta, but before he left Jayrambati he had an extraordinary experience. One day when he was napping after his noon meal he had a vivid dream in which an exquisitely beautiful young girl appeared. She had a golden complexion and was wearing precious jewellery. As she tenderly embraced his neck, he asked who she was. She replied in a musical voice: "You see, I have come to your family." Ramchandra was convinced that this was an auspicious omen and his interpretation of the dream was that Mother Lakshmi had revealed herself to him so that he could make money performing rituals in Calcutta. When he returned from Calcutta, Shyamasundari told him

Shyamasundari Devi (d. 1906), mother of Sarada Devi.

about her vision. The simple couple had no doubt about the authenticity of their visions; they were certain that a divine child would be born to them. Ramchandra kept away from his wife until the birth of the child.

Sarada Devi, the first child of Ramchandra and Shyamasundari, was born on Thursday evening, 22 December 1853. As was customary, as soon as she was born a conch shell was blown to announce the good news. Her family name was Saradamani, or Sarada.* In course of time this holy couple had six other children: a daughter named Kadambini and five sons, Prasanna, Umesh, Kalikumar, Barada, and Abhay. Kadambini was married to Sudharam Chakrabarty in Kokanda Village but she died young without having any children. Umesh died when he was 17 or 18 years old and was unmarried. Abhay died while in medical school, leaving Sarada Devi to look after his wife, Surabala, and daughter, Radhu, who was born after his death.

Almost all past avatars, except Ramachandra and Buddha, began their lives in sorrow and hardship. It seems that their personal experiences of suffering helped them to understand the sufferings of humanity and their role in relieving them. The avatars' primary mission is to replace degraded and corrupt religious practises with life-giving eternal religion. The huts of the poor, not the palaces of the rich, allowed these great souls to become intimate with genuine religious traditions. Generally it is the poor who hold fast to God and His dispensation. Perhaps that is why the great teachers of the world are drawn to take birth in poor families.

Sarada faced dire poverty from the very beginning of her life. This gave her strength of character, forbearance, practical wisdom, common sense, perseverance, and the ability to adapt to outward circumstances. Her father owned some agricultural land on which he grew rice and cotton, but it was not productive enough to feed the whole family. He had to supplement his income by performing worship in private homes. Shyamasundari and little Sarada would pick cotton from the field and with it make the sacred threads worn by brahmins, thus contributing to the family income.

Later Sarada recalled: "I would wade neck-deep into the water to cut grass for the cattle. I used to carry puffed rice to the field as refreshment

---

*Once Swami Gauriswarananda asked Holy Mother who had given her name. The Mother replied: "My mother wanted to give me the name Kshemankari. Before I was born, my mother's sister came to see her. She had a daughter named Sarada, who died very young. I was born after her death. My aunt said to my mother: 'You change your daughter's name and give her the name Sarada. Then I will think that my Sarada has come to you and I shall forget my daughter, seeing her.' So my mother gave me the name Sarada."

for the workers. One year the paddy crop was destroyed by locusts, and I gleaned rice stalks from one field after another. I would accompany my brothers to bathe in the Amodar River, which was the Ganges to us. After bathing, we would sit on the bank and eat puffed rice before returning home. I was always attracted to the Ganges."[4]

When divine beings assume a human form, guardian angels accompany them. Reminiscing about her early life, Holy Mother once said: "A young girl resembling me used to walk with me and help me in my work. We had great fun together, but she would disappear as soon as anyone else approached. This experience continued until I was 10 or 11 years old. When I entered a pond to cut grass for the cattle, this girl went with me. As I cut and took one bundle to the bank and returned to the water for more grass, I found she already had another bundle ready for me."[5]

Sarada learned how to read and write, but it was not considered important to educate girls in those days. Later she described her struggle to learn:

> I accompanied my brother Prasanna and cousin Ramnath to our village primary school and learned the alphabet. In Kamarpukur [probably in 1867], Lakshmi [Ramakrishna's niece] and I read *Barna Parichay — Part One* [the first primary book by Ishwar Chandra Vidyasagar], but Hriday, the Master's nephew, snatched away my book. He said: "Women should not learn to read and write. Are you going to read dramas and novels later on?" Lakshmi was the favourite daughter of the family, so she did not have to give up her book. I secretly paid one anna for another copy. Lakshmi would study in the school and then teach me when she returned. While I was in Dakshineswar, I actually learned well. When the Master had to go to Shyampukur for treatment [in the fall of 1885], I was left alone. A girl from Bhava Mukherjee's family would come to bathe in the Ganges daily and she would sometimes stay with me for a long time. She used to give me lessons and then test me on what I had learned. I shared vegetables with her and other things that I received from the temple authorities.[6]

Sarada and Lakshmi studied up to *Barna Parichay — Part Two* (the second primary book by Ishwar Chandra Vidyasagar) with Sharat, a young son of Pitambar Samanta, the store manager of the Dakshineswar temple. Ramakrishna arranged this so that they could read the Ramayana and other holy books.[7] Sarada also learned how to write.[8] People learn more about life through observation and experience than in a classroom. Little Sarada's earliest training began in her village, where she studied the people around her. Her observations eventually helped her to become a great teacher.

Sarada Devi's old thatched cottage in Jayrambati has an earthen floor, mud walls, one door, and one window. Dimensions: 12' 6" x 7' 0"; ceiling 7' 3"; veranda 4' 10" wide.

Sarada's lack of formal education did not stunt her intellectual development. She was born with divine qualities such as purity, humility, self-control, self-sacrifice, nonviolence, truthfulness, modesty, detachment, compassion, courage, forgiveness, and fortitude. Her parents taught her how to love and serve others, and how to be content with an austere life. She also received practical lessons while helping her father during his worship, cooking and cleaning with her mother, and helping to raise her younger siblings. In addition, she became acquainted with the spiritual culture of India by listening to devotional songs sung by minstrels and religious mendicants. She participated in the religious festivals of her village and watched dramas based on the Ramayana, the Mahabharata, and the lives of saints, which left a deep impression on her young mind. She received firsthand experience of reality as she shared the simple life of the villagers — their struggle for existence, their poverty and their deaths. This helped her develop a loving and deep understanding of humanity.

Aghoremani Devi, Sarada's village companion and playmate, said: "Sarada was straightforward, the embodiment of simplicity. She never quarreled with her playmates. Indeed, when they fell out with one another, she acted as a mediator and peacemaker. She loved to make images of Kali and Lakshmi and worshipped the goddesses with flowers and bel leaves."[9] Other villagers remarked: "From her very childhood, Sarada was extremely intelligent, quiet, and well-behaved. She always worked enthusiastically. It was never necessary to remind her of her duties because she thoughtfully anticipated them and performed them cheerfully."[10]

It is inspiring to visualize Sarada's early life. She helped her mother husk paddy by operating the husking machine. Sometimes she cooked when Shyamasundari was busy. The rice pot was so big and heavy that Sarada could not lift it, so she had to ask her father for help. Sarada collected water from Banerjee's Pond and carried it home, balancing a pitcher on her hip like the other village women. While bathing, she learned how to swim by holding the empty pitcher upside down and using it as a float.

Sarada later recalled a heartbreaking incident that happened in 1864 when she was 11 years old:

> Once there was a terrible famine in Jayrambati. Many starving people came to our house for food, as our previous year's surplus rice was stored in a bin. My father arranged to have several potfuls of khichuri made with that rice, mixing it with lentils. He said: "All the members of the family will eat this simple food and share it with others, but a little good rice should be cooked for my Sarada." Sometimes the hungry people came in such

Banerjee's Pond, or Talpukur, in the southwest section of Jayrambati. Sarada Devi bathed here.

numbers that the khichuri would run short and a fresh supply had to be cooked. When the fresh hot khichuri was served on the leaf plates, I used to fan it to cool it off quickly. Ah! People suffered unbearable hunger pains as they waited!

One day a low-caste woman with shaggy hair and bloodshot eyes came to the house. Unable to bear her hunger, she rushed to the cowshed and began to eat the soaked rice-powder from a tub meant for the cattle. We repeatedly told her to come inside the house and eat khichuri, but she was too impatient to wait. Only after eating some rice powder did she listen to our calls. What a terrible famine! After experiencing that suffering, people began to garner paddy during the harvesting time....Is hunger a small thing? Hunger and thirst remain as long as a person has a human body.[11]

This terrible scene of hunger and poverty became deeply imprinted on little Sarada's mind. Later she herself experienced both. Only one who has experienced hardship understands another's suffering. She learned to feel for others during the early days of her life, and this empathy is the basis of religion. Despite the advancement of civilization, science, and technology, millions of people go to bed every night with an empty stomach; this is true even in the richest countries of the world.

Sarada learned from Ramakrishna that the practice of religion is not possible on an empty stomach. Throughout her life, Sarada enjoyed feeding people. She cooked for her husband and later cooked for her disciples and devotees.

3
Marriage
and Early Years

Svanushthita svadharmāya sāradā-griha-medhine;
Svardhuni-vāri-nirdhuta dakshineswara-vāsine.
— *A hymn by Swami Vimalananda*

O Ramakrishna, you acted well by performing the dharma as a householder with Sarada Devi. You made your dwelling place in the temple garden of Dakshineswar, sanctified by the heavenly river Ganges.

According to the Hindu tradition, the Impersonal God is Existence-Knowledge-Bliss Absolute. Brahman, or the Impersonal God, is formless; but the Personal God has form — and He is omniscient, omnipotent, and omnipresent. He is ever-free, ever-perfect, and ever-pure. The Personal God is endowed with the power to create, preserve, and destroy. This Power is called Shakti, or Mahamaya, the Divine Mother. Shiva and Shakti — the male principle and the female principle — are inseparable, like fire and its power to burn, or milk and its whiteness. Both are necessary for creation.

When the Personal God takes a male form as a human being, He comes with His Shakti to fulfill His mission. Even though born as a human being, an avatar is endowed with divine qualities. God is beyond all limitations: He is neither a monk nor a householder. Maya cannot bind Him. Marriage is considered to be a bondage for others, but it is not so for an avatar. Some avatars were married, such as Ramachandra and Krishna; some renounced their wives and became monks, such as Buddha and Chaitanya; some were lifelong monastics, such as Jesus and Shankara. Ramakrishna married and then took monastic vows, but he did not renounce his wife. He accepted a woman (Bhairavi Brahmani) as his guru, and he preached the Motherhood of God. His Chosen Ideal was the Divine Mother. His wife became his first disciple.

The village of Sihar is the birthplace of Ramakrishna's nephew Hriday and also of Sarada's mother, Shyamasundari. It is famous for the

Sarada Devi, Calcutta, November 1898. This is the first of three photos taken at that time.

Shantinath Shiva temple, where pilgrims from neighbouring villages regularly go for worship. When Ramakrishna came to Kamarpukur from Calcutta, he invariably visited Sihar and stayed some days with Hriday. Once a famous singer came to Sihar and gave a performance at Hriday's house when Ramakrishna was visiting. Shyamasundari was then at her father's home with Sarada, who was three years old at the time. The mother and daughter went to listen to the performance. When the performance was over, a village woman teasingly asked Sarada whom among the boys she would like to marry. With a tiny finger she pointed at Ramakrishna.*

While Sarada was growing up in rural Jayrambati, Ramakrishna was practising intense sadhana in Dakshineswar. After having his first vision of the Divine Mother in 1856, his longing increased for uninterrupted communion with God. Completely god-intoxicated, he became indifferent to food, sleep, clothing, and other necessities of life. He spent day and night in meditation and prayer. His restless longing for God expressed itself in agonizing cries for the Divine Mother. He shunned the company of worldly people, and he was incapable of functioning like an ordinary person. Because of his god-intoxicated state, he could not continue to perform the temple worship at Dakshineswar where he was a priest, and people said he had gone mad. The owners of the temple considered his ecstatic state to be a mental illness and arranged for him to be treated.

There is a saying in Bengal: "Words walk through the ears." The news of Ramakrishna's condition and his inability to continue his job as a priest reached his mother and brother Rameswar in Kamarpukur. They were very concerned, and in September 1858 they brought him home. Chandramani was very distressed when she saw her son's indifference to worldly matters and his seeming madness for God. She tried various remedies, including medicine, rites performed to propitiate the gods, and charms and incantations to exorcise evil spirits. However, Chandramani soon realized that her son was actually normal, to a great extent. Without Ramakrishna's knowledge, she and Rameswar began to search for a suitable bride. For various reasons, this was not so easy. Noticing that they were growing frustrated and anxious, Ramakrishna told them one day in an ecstatic mood: "Why are you fruitlessly looking for the girl here and there? Go to Ramchandra Mukherjee's house in Jayrambati and you will find the girl there, tied, as it were, with a straw."**

*Swami Saradeshananda wrote in his *Sri Sri Mayer Smritikatha* (p. 135) that this incident took place at Sarada's maternal uncle's house in Sihar during a picnic.
**The allusion is to a local custom. The stem of a particular fruit destined to be offered to the deity is often tied with a straw to set it apart from other fruits.

Ramakrishna in Calcutta, 10 December 1881.

Someone went to Jayrambati and returned with the news that the prospective bride was only 5 years old. Ramakrishna was then 24, so this was not considered an ideal match. Nonetheless, Chandramani decided to arrange the marriage. The negotiations were settled in a few days. Rameswar paid 300 rupees for the dowry, and an auspicious day was chosen for the wedding in May 1859.

Swami Nikhilananda explained the mystery of this marriage:

> Early marriage for a Hindu girl, especially one living in a village, was not then uncommon. But such a marriage was really in the nature of a betrothal. The actual marriage took place after the wife attained maturity, when she and her husband lived together. Ramakrishna's marriage was, however, a strange one. Here was a bride in whom the consciousness of sex was not awakened and who remained free from it all through her life. And the bridegroom regarded all women as his own mother and the embodiment of the Divine Mother of the Universe — an attitude which he maintained as long as he lived. At that time, because of his absorption in spiritual practices, he was oblivious of both his body and the world, and was guided in every action by the Divine Mother Herself, with whom he had established a most intimate relationship. Therefore it may be presumed that in his marriage he was guided by the finger of God. It served no human purpose for either of them. But it fulfilled a divine mission; for Sarada was destined to continue, after his death, his unfinished work of spiritual ministration.[1]

On the day of the wedding, the village women clothed the handsome bridegroom with a dhoti and a chadar, decorated him with dots of sandal paste on his forehead, and placed a garland around his neck. Shakambhari, Rameswar's wife, was a little sad. Because of their poverty, they could not afford to hire a musician for the bridegroom's marriage procession. To cheer his sister-in-law, Ramakrishna imitated the sounds of a drum with his mouth and danced, slapping his hands on his hips like the village musicians. Thus he created a joyful atmosphere, and everyone laughed.

Rameswar also could not afford to hire a palanquin, so Ramakrishna and his companions walked the four miles to Jayrambati. The traditional wedding ceremony was performed in the old mud cottage of Sarada's family. To satisfy Sarada's parents and to maintain appearances, Chandra borrowed some jewellery from the wealthy Laha family for the bride to wear during the ceremony.

Although Sarada's parents were poor, they tried their best to conduct the ceremony according to the scriptures. The whole family and many villagers were present. The priest repeated the mantras and, as was customary, the village women walked around the bride and bridegroom in a circle, holding 27 burning sticks. A piece of thread dyed with turmeric was tied between the groom's and the bride's wrists to symbolize the bond between two human beings. Accidentally a burning stick burnt the connecting thread, which was extremely inauspicious. But who can change the will of Providence? Undoubtedly marriage is a kind of bondage, but the Divine Mother destroyed that bond of ignorance and made it an extraordinary spiritual partnership. Sarada was a little girl of five who had almost no concept of marriage; and Ramakrishna was an illumined soul who had transcended the sense plane.

When the ceremony was over, the bride's father was busy feeding the bridegroom's party. The feast was arranged in the courtyard and Sarada's old mud cottage was prepared for the bridal chamber. According to tradition, the village women and bride's friends assembled in the bridal chamber to tease and joke with the bridegroom. Seeing so many women in that room, Ramakrishna thought of the playful Divine Mother. Immediately he began to sing a song about the Divine Mother in his melodious voice. The women were all surprised and charmed as they gazed at the bridegroom's beaming face, and they forgot to play practical jokes on him. Ramakrishna was completely possessed by a divine mood that night. Blessed are the women who witnessed the spiritual union of Hara and Gauri — Ramakrishna and Sarada.[2] It was an unusual wedding.

The day after the wedding Ramakrishna returned to Kamarpukur with Sarada, but as she was so young, her Uncle Ishwar accompanied her, carrying her on his shoulders. Chandramani welcomed the new bride with due ceremony and arranged a small feast for friends and family members. Sarada later recalled: "I was married when the dates ripen. I don't remember the month. During my 10 days' stay there, I would pick up ripe dates from the ground. One day Dharmadas Laha [the village landlord] came and seeing me asked, 'Is this the newly married girl?'"

Chandramani was anxious when the time came to return the borrowed jewellery to its owners. She had affectionately made the new bride her own, and now she would have to take the jewellery away. This thought filled the old woman's eyes with tears. Although she did not express her sorrow, it did not take long for Ramakrishna to perceive it. He consoled his mother, and then while Sarada was sleeping he himself took the jewellery away so deftly that she was unaware of it. The jewellery was immediately sent to the Lahas. But when the intelligent girl awoke, she asked, "Where is my jewellery?" Chandramani took Sarada on her lap and consoled her, saying, "My darling, later Ramakrishna will give you better

Ramakrishna's family home in Kamarpukur, ca. 1930s.

jewels than those." The matter did not end there. Sarada's Uncle Ishwar came to see her that day. When he learned of this incident he was offended and took Sarada back to Jayrambati at once. Chandramani was terribly hurt. To ease her pain Ramakrishna said playfully, "Whatever they say or do, they can't annul the marriage now!"

After the marriage ceremony, Ramakrishna stayed in Kamarpukur for one year and seven months. He visited Jayrambati sometime in December 1860, when Sarada was 7 years old. When Ramakrishna arrived in Jayrambati, Sarada washed his feet and fanned him, which amused her friends. Sarada was extremely bashful and always tried to hide herself when in public. One day Hriday brought some lotuses and, to Sarada's great consternation, worshipped her feet with those flowers.

After spending a short time in Jayrambati, Ramakrishna went back to Kamarpukur, taking Sarada with him. Ramakrishna stayed in Kamarpukur for only a few days although Chandramani begged him to stay longer. He returned to Dakshineswar and plunged once more into spiritual practices, forgetting all about his young wife. Sarada returned to Jayrambati and resumed her family duties.

Sarada visited Kamarpukur twice more during her childhood. She later recalled: "When I was 13, I went to Kamarpukur; the Master was then in Dakshineswar. I stayed there for a month and then returned to Jayrambati. After five or six months I returned to Kamarpukur and stayed a month and a half. I lived with my brother-in-law [Rameswar] and sister-in-law [Shakambhari] and others.* I used to think: I am a new bride. How shall I go to the Haldarpukur and bathe by myself? One day I left the house by a back door and was worrying about the matter when eight young maidens suddenly appeared, apparently from nowhere.** As I started for the tank, four of them walked in front of me and four behind. Thus guarded, I walked to the water and all of us bathed together. Afterwards they brought me home. This continued every day during that visit to Kamarpukur. I wondered who those girls were, but I could not figure it out."[3]

After Ramakrishna's visit to Kamarpukur with the young Sarada, he did not return for nearly six and a half years. During this period, he practised various sadhanas, including Tantra, Vatsalya bhava, Madhura bhava, Vedanta, and Islam. After that strenuous spiritual journey, his health broke down and he contracted dysentery. In 1867, to recuperate and regain his health, Ramakrishna returned to Kamarpukur

* Chandramani was then living with Ramakrishna in Dakshineswar.
** According to Hindu mythology, the Divine Mother of the Universe has eight maidens as attendants.

accompanied by Hriday and his tantric guru, Bhairavi Brahmani. The family then sent a message to Sarada asking her to come to Kamarpukur. She was then 14 years old.

Swami Saradananda wrote about Sarada's visit and spiritual training under Ramakrishna's guidance:

> During this visit to Kamarpukur the Master earnestly attended to a noble duty. Although he was initially indifferent to his wife's coming to Kamarpukur, when she arrived to serve him, he began to educate and train her for her well being. Knowing that the Master was married, Tota Puri had once said to him: "What does it matter? He alone is firmly established in the knowledge of Brahman who can keep intact his renunciation, detachment, discrimination, and self-awareness even while living with his wife. He alone has attained supreme illumination who can always look upon man and woman alike as the Atman and deal with them accordingly. A person who is aware of the differences between the sexes may be a good aspirant, but that person is still far from having the knowledge of Brahman." Remembering Tota Puri's words, the Master now began to test the Self-knowledge that he had achieved after his long sadhana and to train his wife for her own spiritual development.
>
> The Master could not neglect any action or leave it half-finished if he considered it to be his duty. The same applied to the present situation. The Master came forward to thoroughly train his adolescent wife, who solely depended on him in every respect relating to both secular and spiritual matters. He taught her how to serve God, the guru, and the guest; how to perform household work skillfully and spend money discreetly; and most important, how to surrender everything to God and become expert in dealing with people according to place, time, and circumstance. We have hinted elsewhere how far-reaching was the result of the teaching that the Master imparted to her by setting the example of his ideal life endowed with unbroken chastity. It is enough to say that Sarada was fully satisfied with the Master's chaste and pure love. Throughout her life she worshipped the Master as her Chosen Deity and built her own life by following his example.[4]

The Master loved his birthplace and the simple village people there. Sarada recalled the Master's light-hearted mood in Kamarpukur:

> The Master was suffering from stomach trouble. I was then quite young. Early in the morning he would wake up and tell me, "Please cook these items for lunch." My sister-in-law [Lakshmi's mother] and I cooked accordingly. One day there was no *panchphoran** in stock for seasoning. My

---

*A combination of five spices: caraway, fennel, cumin, black cumin, and fenugreek.

sister-in-law asked me to cook it without those spices. The Master heard her words and said: "How can that be? If you do not have spices in the house, get a pice worth from the village shop. It is not proper to cook a dish without the proper seasoning. I left behind the rice pudding and the gourmet dishes of Dakshineswar temple and came here just to enjoy egg-plant curry seasoned with panchphoran, and you want to deprive me of it. That can't be!" Another day he said to me: "Please prepare lentil soup with five kinds of lentils and season it in such a way that it will make a hog grunt!"*

One morning he got up and said, "Today I shall eat this particular spin-ach. Please cook it for me." My sister-in-law and I collected that spinach and prepared it for him. After a few days he said: "What a nice fix I am in! The moment I leave the bed, I speak of nothing but food. Good God! Now I have lost all relish for food and shall eat whatever you cook."[5]

Thus Ramakrishna lost all interest in his body and paid no heed to it.

Ordinary people marry to fulfill their legitimate desires for children, for having a companion with whom they share their happiness and misery, or for practising *garhasthya dharma* — that is, fulfilling the duties of a householder. The householder's life is the bedrock of society. The *Mahanirvana Tantra* says: "Householders should connect their lives with Brahman and try to realize Him. Whatever actions they perform, the results should be offered to Brahman." It is edifying to reflect on the spiritual marriage of Ramakrishna and Sarada.

Sarada later recalled:

One day the Master was eating and asked for a little salt. I said, "There is no salt in the spice rack." Irritated, the Master said: "What do you mean there is no salt? Never say the word 'no'. Always be positive and collect the things that are necessary for the household." When my mother visited Kamarpukur, the Master received her cordially and asked her to make some pickle for him.

During my stay in Kamarpukur, Ramlal's father would ask me to sleep with his brother [Ramakrishna], and the Master would smile. At that time we used to sleep in the same bed, and he would tell me stories the whole night. He taught me how to do housework and behave with people. One should know that God is one's very own, the eternal substance.[6]

Ramakrishna addressed Bhairavi Brahmani as "Mother," so Sarada

---

*The allusion is to a certain way of seasoning. Strong spices and red chili are thrown into hot oil in a deep pan and then the soup or stew is poured into it. This gives out a pungent smell and makes a noise that is heard from a distance. Ramakrishna liked this kind of seasoning.

regarded her as her mother-in-law. However, the Brahmani was hot-tempered, and Sarada was afraid of her. Sarada later recalled: "She was fond of chilies and cooked her own food, which was excessively hot. She would share her food with me. I silently ate it, always wiping away my tears. When she would ask, 'How is it?', I answered fearfully, 'Very nice indeed!' My sister-in-law commented, 'Uh, it is terribly hot.' The Brahmani would be angry at such criticism of her cooking and exclaim: 'My daughter says that it is tasty. Nothing can please you. I will not give you what I cook anymore.'"[7]

The Brahmani became very jealous of Sarada because the Master was paying attention to her. At that time the Brahmani also had a disagreement with Hriday regarding the village's caste rules. When she realized her mistakes, she repented and begged forgiveness from the Master, and then left for Varanasi. Sarada later recalled: "One day the Brahmani decorated the Master like Gauranga with garlands and sandal paste. The Master was in an ecstatic mood. She called me to see him. As soon as I went there, the Master asked, 'How do I look?' 'Wonderful,' I said. I then bowed down to him and left. One day the Brahmani left without informing anybody."[8]

Ramakrishna was witty and full of fun. Sarada recounted the following incident:

> At Kamarpukur, Lakshmi's mother and I would prepare the meals. She was a good cook. One day the Master and Hriday were taking their meals. He tasted the food prepared by Lakshmi's mother and said in praise, "O Hriday, the person who cooked this dish is Vaidya Ramdas, an expert physician." He then tasted what I cooked and commented, "The one who has prepared this is Srinath Sen, a quack doctor."
>
> "That may be true," said Hriday, "but this quack will always be at your service, even ready to give you a massage. All that you have to do is to summon her. But Vaidya Ramdas is a very expensive physician; he is not always available. People first consult the quack; he is always your friend."
>
> "That is true, that is true, she is always available," the Master replied, smiling.[9]

Ramakrishna knew that Sarada would be a spiritual teacher one day, so he taught her about the insubstantial nature of the world and warned her about its sorrows and pitfalls. He trained her to cultivate detachment from transitory objects and develop devotion to God, who alone is real and eternal.

Lakshmi later recalled the following incident, which she witnessed in Kamarpukur:

One day the Master pointed to Aunt Sarada and said: "What good is there in giving birth like dogs and jackals to a whole brood of children? You raised your young brothers and sister tenderly; you witnessed how deeply your parents lamented when two of them died, and you also grieved for them. How miserable life in the world is! Why should you bother with it? Without any such trouble, you look like a goddess now and will always remain a goddess."

One morning the Master was brushing his teeth with a twig and Aunt was mopping the mud floor, mixing mud and cow dung with water. Pointing to Aunt, the Master jokingly said: "Bedecked with jewellery, you may dance and sing at the rice-eating ceremony for your son, but you will fall on the ground crying when he dies." Hearing the Master harping on death, Aunt Sarada asked gently, "But do they all die?"

Perhaps the Master felt that Aunt had the innate longing for mother-hood that is present in all women. At once he loudly called out to the other ladies: "See, I have stepped on the tail of a cobra. Goodness gracious! I often said to myself: 'She is such a simple soul, unaware of the ways of the world.' But see how much she keeps inside her. Did you hear what she said? 'Do they all die?'" Aunt ran away.[10]

Once a religious play was being performed in a neighbouring village. Sarada and the other women of the family wanted to see it, but the Master would not permit them. The ladies were hurt. The Master consoled them, saying that he would see the play and recount it to them. After seeing the play he returned home and reenacted the whole show in minute detail. He had a sweet musical voice, a remarkable memory, and a wonderful talent for acting. The ladies forgot their disappointment as they enjoyed his performance.

People generally think that a spiritual person is supposed to be austere and serious, but Sarada always saw her husband free and frank, happy and cheerful. She later recalled: "I never saw his face sad and sour. He always radiated joy — whether he was absorbed in samadhi or in the company of an older person or with a 5-year-old child. Never did I see him gloomy."[11] He conquered the heart of his young wife with pure love and then poured his spiritual wisdom into it. Sarada later described how the Master established divine bliss within her heart: "At that time I always felt as if a jar of bliss, full to the brim, was set in my heart. It is impossible to describe that divine joy."[12]

In the evenings the Master often talked to Sarada and her companions for hours about spiritual matters and his own inner experiences. He also entertained them with stories and jokes. Tired after a whole day of housework, the teenaged Sarada would fall asleep on the floor. Her

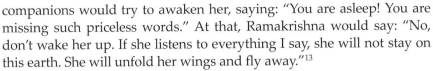

companions would try to awaken her, saying: "You are asleep! You are missing such priceless words." At that, Ramakrishna would say: "No, don't wake her up. If she listens to everything I say, she will not stay on this earth. She will unfold her wings and fly away."[13]

Later Sarada recalled her days in Kamarpukur:

After my marriage I stayed mostly in Jayrambati. When the Master visited Kamarpukur from Dakshineswar, my mother-in-law would send someone to bring me there. I was then a little girl and I did what they asked me to do. They taught me how to serve my mother-in-law and husband. My mother-in-law loved me deeply. In the evening many men and women of the village would come to the Master to listen to his talks and singing. He would talk about God or tell humorous stories, and sometimes entertain them with singing. Sitting in a corner I would listen and then fall asleep. If someone would try to wake me up, the Master would say: "Don't call her. Let her sleep."[14]

Sarada had great love and respect for her husband's family members because they were deeply spiritual. Although she never met her father-in-law, Kshudiram, or brother-in-law, Ramkumar, and his wife, Sarvajaya, she would later praise them:

My father-in-law was a pious and spirited brahmin. He never received gifts from anyone. He even prohibited his people from accepting any gift brought to his house in his absence. But as regards my mother-in-law, if anyone privately made a gift of food to her she would accept it, cook it, offer it to Raghuvir [the family deity], and then give it to others as prasad. My father-in-law used to get angry if he happened to find out about it. He possessed burning devotion. The Divine Mother Shitala would walk with him. He had a habit of picking flowers in the early hours of the morning. One early morning he went to pick flowers in the garden of the Lahas. Then a girl of 9 or 10 [Mother Shitala] came and addressed him, saying: "Father, come to this side. There are many beautiful flowers on this branch. Let me bend the branch down so you can pick the flowers." He asked, "Who are you, here at this time of day, my child?" She replied, "I belong to the Haldar family." He was so deeply spiritual, and that is the reason God was born in his family.[15]

God comes down from Vaikuntha, the heavenly abode of Vishnu, to where the devotees call Him. On the night of Kojagari Purnima [the full-moon night in autumn], Lakshmi [the goddess of wealth] comes down to the earth from Vaikuntha. She visits and accepts the worship of those people on whom She wants to bestow Her special grace. In Kamarpukur my mother-in-law saw the goddess Lakshmi as a fair-complexioned girl of 14 or 15, adorned with earrings made of conch shells and diamond-cut bangles around Her arms. She talked to my mother-in-law under the ba-kul tree in front of the house. My mother-in-law asked, "Who are you, my dear?"

Lakshmi replied, "I have just come here."

My mother-in-law asked: "Have you seen my son Ramkumar? He has gone to perform worship. It is quite late and he has not returned yet."

Lakshmi replied: "Yes, he is on his way back with his gifts. I am now coming from that house to visit your house."

My mother-in-law said: "No, my child, there is nobody at home. Please do not come now." Considering Her to be a stranger, my mother-in-law repeatedly refused to receive Her. Lakshmi then said, "All right, my gra-cious gaze will remain on your family." She then disappeared. Just see, their financial condition never improved to a great extent. Somehow they got by with plain food and ordinary clothing.

My mother-in-law saw the goddess Lakshmi come from the direction of the Lahas' granaries. My brother-in-law returned and after hearing the story from his mother, he exclaimed: "Mother, you did not recognize that the goddess Lakshmi Herself came. Today is Kojagari Purnima, the day of Lakshmi Puja." He could foretell things, and verified this incident by astrological calculations.[16]

The wheel of time is always turning. Every union ends in separation. After spending seven months in Kamarpukur, Ramakrishna left for Dakshineswar and Sarada returned to Jayrambati. Saradananda wrote about the transformation that took place in Sarada after living with her husband:

By the time the Master left Kamarpukur for Calcutta a few months later, Sarada was endowed with an infinite wealth of joy that she carried back to Jayrambati with her. We can easily guess that this blissful experience had effected a transformation in all her movements, speech, and conduct, and in how she worked. But it is doubtful whether ordinary people noticed this. She was now gentle and not fickle, thoughtful and not impertinent, and her love was not blinded by selfishness. Moreover, her experience had eradicated all kinds of worldly desires from her heart, made her infinitely sympathetic to the pain and suffering of others, and gradually transformed her into an embodiment of compassion. Due to the influence of this inner bliss, she neither felt any physical suffering nor was she disappointed if the loving care she gave to her relatives was not reciprocated. Content in every respect and absorbed within herself, she passed her days at her father's house. Although her body was in Jayrambati, her mind was with the Master at Dakshineswar. At times she felt an intense desire to see the Master and be with him, but she carefully controlled herself and waited patiently. She believed that since the Master had graciously loved her so much at their first meeting, he would not forget her. When the right time arrived, he would call her to him. Thus, days passed one after another as she waited for that auspicious day, all the while holding to her firm faith within.[17]

Union and separation are part of human life. The joy of union is intensified a thousandfold after a long period of separation and intense longing. Mental union is higher than physical union, and spiritual union is higher than mental union. While studying the lives of the avatars, we find that for a certain period of their lives they were separated from their spiritual consorts — Rama was separated from Sita, Krishna from Radha, Buddha from Yashodhara, and Chaitanya from Vishnupriya. Is there any meaning to this? We do not know. Perhaps it was part of their divine play to teach humanity how to be detached from family ties and shun attachments. In the 26 years of their married life, Ramakrishna lived with Sarada in Kamarpukur, Jayrambati, Dakshineswar, Shyampukur, and Cossipore for a total of approximately 10 years.

Dakshineswar Temple Garden as seen from the Ganges, ca. 1930s.

4

Journey
to Dakshineswar

Charan vai madhu vindati charan swādum udumvaram;
Suryasya pashya shremānam yo na tandrayate charan.
—*Charaiveti*
  —*Rigveda*

To march along is to gain immortality; marching by oneself is the
sweet fruit of the journey. Look at the sun—the ever glorious and
eternal traveller—who once having started on his journey has
never felt drowsy. Hence, O traveller, march along.

The more often gold is rubbed with a touchstone, the more it glit-
ters. A fire burns more brightly when the wood is stirred, and a
snake raises its hood high when it is struck. Similarly, a human
soul awakens when a person is challenged. The lives of the divine women
who accompanied the avatars in every age were full of suffering and tragedy. Enduring all forms of hardship, they demonstrated how to overcome
suffering through strength of will and how to surrender to Providence.
Suffering on top of suffering made the divinity of those great women
shine forth. This is why, in the Indian tradition, we pay respect to the
Shakti or the female counterpart of God first: we say Lakshmi-Narayan
and not Narayan-Lakshmi; similarly, we say Gauri-Shankar, Sita-Ram,
and Radha-Krishna. It sounds poetic, sweet, and melodious when the
name of the Shakti comes first.

Although the life stories of the avatars' spiritual consorts are full of
pain and suffering, their love for their husbands shines forth unparalleled.
They represent the ideal of womanhood. Their lives were brightened
by their love and purity, patience and forbearance, contentment and
service, self-control and renunciation, devotion and faith, gratitude and
unselfishness, poverty and austerity, sacrifice for humanity and reliance
on God. They were established in their own greatness and glory by virtue
of these noble qualities.

From 1867 to 1871 Sarada lived with her parents in Jayrambati and continued to serve her relatives. Four long years passed. Though her body was in Jayrambati, her mind dwelled on her sweet memories of the Master. Sarada grew into a beautiful young woman of 18. Every day she expected to hear from her husband, but no message came. Sometimes she would say to herself: "He was very kind to me during our last meeting. How can he ever forget me? In good time he will, of his own accord, call me to his side. Let me patiently wait for that happy moment."[1]

There is a saying: "Gossip spreads faster than the gospel." In the absence of any word from her husband, Sarada became a victim of terrible village gossip. Gossip breaks hearts and ruins lives. Its victims are helpless and it causes innocent people to pass sleepless nights and makes them cry into their pillows. Reports came from Dakshineswar that Ramakrishna had gone completely insane and that he wandered around naked, crying to the Divine Mother. The villagers mistook Ramakrishna's god-intoxicated state for insanity.

At the bathing ghat, the village women chattered and gossiped. One woman pointed at Sarada and said, "There is the madman's wife." Another woman added with mock sympathy: "Ah, poor Shyamasundari! She has married her daughter to a lunatic. How sad!" There is a saying: "Rumour has a thousand tongues."

Even at home, Sarada had no peace. She heard her mother lament: "I have married my daughter to a madman. It is as if I have thrown her into deep water with her hands and feet tied!" Sarada was stung by these remarks and avoided people as much as she could. She found relief in keeping herself busy with household duties day and night. When it was unbearable to be at home, she visited her Aunt Bhanu, a widow who lived nearby and was very loving and sympathetic. This woman had insight and understood the divine personality of Ramakrishna. She once told Shyamasundari: "Your son-in-law is Shiva Himself, and Krishna too. You may not understand this now, but you will in the future. Mark my words."[2]

Referring to this difficult time, Sarada later said: "One must always be busy. Work keeps the body and mind in good shape. During my young days at Jayrambati, I was active day and night and did not visit anyone's house. If I ever did, I heard people say, 'Shyama's daughter has been married to a madman!' I avoided people so that I might not hear such remarks."[3]

Later Sarada related to some women devotees her days of suffering during that period:

I was then in Jayrambati. I was a mature young woman. I heard that the Master had rubbed his face on the bank of the Ganges and cried, saying, "Mother, Mother! Do thou reveal thyself to me." People could not understand him, so they spread rumours that he had become mad. When I heard this, I was terribly hurt, but out of shame I could not express my feelings to anyone. Seeing my tearful eyes, only Aunt Bhanu understood. She would console me, giving me a hug and caressing my head, saying: "Why do you make yourself miserable listening to gossip? Your husband is Lord Shiva Himself. I recognized him in the bridal chamber on the very day of your marriage. Don't worry. You will see, one day that very madman will conquer the hearts of all. He is mad in the name of the Divine Mother — and that very Mother will make everything right."[4]

The villagers' ridicule went on unabated. There is a saying: "The funeral pyre burns a human being only once, but agony and anxiety burn all the time." Sarada burned with anxiety, constantly doubting her husband's sanity. Again and again she deliberated within herself: "Is my husband no longer the same person? People are saying he has become mad. Is this true? If this has indeed happened by the decree of Providence, I should not stay here. I must take care of him."[5] At last her patience reached its limit: she decided to go to Dakshineswar and see for herself.

Sarada later said: "It was March 1872. Some of our village women were going to bathe in the Ganges [in Calcutta] on an auspicious occasion.* I said to one of them, 'I want to go to Dakshineswar to see how my husband is doing.' She reported this to my father. I was shy and afraid to talk to him. My father agreed, saying, 'It is fine if she visits Dakshineswar.' He accompanied us."[6]

Sometime after the middle of March 1872, Sarada, her father, and several women started their journey to Calcutta. During those days the long roads through the fields were frequented by robbers, so people always travelled in groups. Most people walked, except for the wealthy, who used palanquins. It was a strenuous journey of 64 miles that crossed five rivers: the Amodar, Dwarakeshwar, Mundeshwari, Damodar, and Ganges. Travellers passed through the panoramic scenery of vast paddy fields and beautiful lotus ponds. Sometimes they rested under the shade of peepul and banyan trees along the road, and at night in a roadside inn.

Sarada and her companions walked happily for two or three days, but then Sarada's legs and feet began to hurt. She had never undertaken such a long journey, and she was barefoot. Her feet swelled with blisters

*It was Dol Purnima, the swing festival of Krishna and the birthday of Chaitanya, which fell on 25 March 1872.

and bruises. Moreover, life in a malaria-stricken village had not given her robust health. Sarada had a terrible attack of malaria on the way, and she developed a high fever. Ramchandra was very worried. He took shelter in a wayside inn with his daughter. After covering Sarada with a chadar so that she would not shiver with chills and fever, he went to collect food and water.

Sarada was terribly distressed that she had fallen ill. That night, however, she had a wonderful vision that greatly reassured her. She later recalled:

> I was lying almost unconscious with fever, without any sense of decorum. Just then I saw a girl come and sit down beside me. She was black in complexion.* I had never seen such beauty before. She began passing her hand over my head and body; it was so soft and cool that the burning sensation of my body began to subside. I asked, "Where do you come from?'"
>
> She replied, "I come from Dakshineswar."
>
> Amazed, I said: "From Dakshineswar! That's where I long to be — to see my husband and to look after him. But now I have this fever, and perhaps I shall never see him again."
>
> "What are you saying?" said the girl. "Of course, you'll get to Dakshineswar. As soon as you're better, you shall go to him. I've been taking care of him there for your sake."
>
> I said: "How good you are! Tell me — are you one of our relatives?"
>
> "I am your sister," she told me.
>
> I said, "Ah — so that's why you've come to me!" I then fell asleep.[7]

Many years later Sarada told the same story with more detail:

> Once when I was young, I was travelling to Dakshineswar. On the way I was seized with high fever. I was lying unconscious when I saw a girl with a very black complexion and feet covered with dust enter my room and sit by my bedside. She began to stroke my head. Noticing that the girl's feet were covered with dust, I asked, "Mother, didn't anybody give you water to wash your feet?"
>
> She replied, "No, Mother, I shall be leaving right now. I have come to see you. Why do you fear? You will get well." From the next day I gradually recovered.[8]

The next morning Ramchandra found that his daughter's fever had subsided. He thought it would be better to continue on slowly rather than to stay in the inn. Encouraged by her vision, Sarada eagerly agreed. Luckily, after walking a short distance, they found a palanquin for her.

---

* It was evidently the goddess Kali who appeared to her in this vision.

Ramakrishna's room at Dakshineswar, ca. 1930s.

Her fever returned, but it was not as severe as on the previous day, so she said nothing about it. They arrived at Baidyabati and then took a boat to Dakshineswar. Sarada, her father, and the other women reached the temple garden at nine o'clock that evening.

As Sarada alighted from the boat, she heard the Master say to Hriday: "O Hriday, this is her first visit. I hope the hour is auspicious." The Master's first words, laden with tenderness, were to encourage Sarada to go straight to his room. Her companions waited outside.

As soon as the Master saw Sarada, he said: "So you have come. Very good. I am very happy." He then told someone, "Spread a mat for her on the floor." She and her father sat on the mat. When the Master heard that she was ill, he expressed his concern. In an apologetic tone, he said: "You have come so late. Alas, my Mathur* is no longer alive to look after you. With his death I feel as if I have lost my right arm." After that introductory conversation, Sarada wanted to go to the nahabat (concert tower), where her mother-in-law was staying. The Master said: "Oh no, stay in my room. It will be inconvenient for the physician to see you there."[9] It was almost ten o'clock at night and dinner was over; there was no cooked food available. At that time Dakshineswar was a remote village and there were no restaurants. Hriday brought two or three baskets full of puffed rice to Sarada and her companions for supper. A separate bed was made for Sarada on the floor in the Master's room, and it was arranged that one of her companions would spend the night with her. Her father and other companions stayed in the nahabat and other rooms in the temple complex.

One can imagine what was going on in her mind while lying in her husband's room. Although Sarada was exhausted by the fever and the long journey, she must have been relieved to find that her husband was not insane. He seemed normal and rational, loving and caring. His cordial welcome eased her anxiety and uncertainty. Her godlike husband had not forgotten her, and he was as gracious as before. For the past four years, ignorant and worldly people had spread vicious rumours. Although Sarada had been tormented by the village gossip, she now realized that some good had come of it: it had ultimately led to a happy reunion with her husband.

Moreover, Sarada must have been apprehensive about how the Master would receive her. She knew that he had taken monastic vows from Tota Puri in 1864. A monk renounces his family and his wife. She had

---

*Mathur was a son-in-law of Rani Rasmani and caretaker of the Dakshineswar temple. He died on 16 July 1871, eight months before Sarada arrived.

perhaps expected to be rejected, which would have been unbearable for a devout and faithful wife. This apprehension disappeared when she found that the Master let her sleep in his room and intended to arrange for medical treatment. Overwhelmed by her husband's love, compassion, and kindness, Sarada joyfully fell asleep.

With good medical treatment and a special diet, Sarada recovered within three or four days. The Master himself supervised her medical care and diet, and then arranged for her to stay with his mother in the nahabat during the day. At night she slept in his room. Sarada was now entirely reassured. She immediately decided that her duty was to serve the Master and his mother. Sarada's father was pleased by his daughter's happiness and he returned home without her after a few days.

Later, Sarada told the devotees: "The Master thought so much about my welfare. He always looked after my comfort and saw to my needs. What an intense love he had for me! People had circulated a rumour that he was mad and my parents were anxious about me. Afterwards, they were relieved and happy observing the Master's normal behaviour and his loving relationship with me."[10]

Ordinary people may wonder why Ramakrishna did not bring his wife to Dakshineswar earlier. Saradananda explained the situation: "Undoubtedly an ordinary person would have done that [brought Sarada to Dakshineswar earlier], but the Master was not such a person — so he did not behave in that manner. Those who are accustomed to performing every action while depending solely on God at every moment of their lives do not make any plans. For the good of themselves and others, they depend on the assistance of God's cosmic intelligence and wait for a signal rather than resorting to their own limited, puny intellects as we do.... In addition, we can say that the Master knew through his yogic vision that this was the will of God."[11]

Providence has its appointed hour for everything. After finishing his sadhanas, Ramakrishna waited to share his hard-earned spiritual treasures with his wife. Sarada also waited for the right time, when she achieved her maturity, to act the next part of her divine drama with her husband. Providence set the stage for this act in the temple garden of Dakshineswar.

Basalt image of Bhavatarini Kali at Dakshineswar.

5
Awakening
of Divinity

Evam bhagavati devi sā nityāpi punah punah;
Sambhuya kurute bhupa jagatah paripālanam.
　—*Chandi, 12:36*

Sage Medha said to Surath: O King, the Supreme Goddess, although eternal, manifests Herself again and again for the protection of the worlds.

Ramakrishna was a world teacher and Sarada was his first disciple. He knew the mission that Sarada would carry out when he was gone, so he wanted to transmit to her the spiritual treasures that he had accumulated over his many years of sadhana. When Ramakrishna had visited Kamarpukur in 1867, he had begun to train Sarada in spiritual disciplines, but he could not finish the task. At that time she was only 14 years old, and moreover, he was there for only a short time. It was not his nature to leave anything unfinished. Whenever he started a spiritual practice he devoted himself to it completely, followed his teacher's instructions implicitly, and did not rest until he attained success.

In 1872 Sarada was a mature woman of 18 years, so Ramakrishna resumed her training. He also wanted to test himself. He remembered his guru Tota Puri's statement: "He alone is firmly established in the knowledge of Brahman who can keep intact his renunciation, detachment, discrimination, and Self-awareness even while living with his wife. He alone has attained supreme illumination who can always look upon men and women alike as the Atman and deal with them accordingly."[1]

Ramakrishna now began to teach Sarada not only the lofty goal of human life, but also how to perform mundane household duties. In addition, he taught her about meditation, prayer, samadhi, and the knowledge of Brahman. But his method of teaching was not limited to verbal instruction; he also closely watched her to see whether she was carrying out his instructions. While training his disciples, he normally kept them near him and through affection made them his very own. One day he told Sarada: "As Uncle Moon is the dear uncle of all children, so God is dear to all beings. Everyone has a right to call on God. Out of His grace He reveals Himself to all who call upon Him. You too will see Him if you but call on Him."[2]

Recalling her early days in Dakshineswar, Sarada once said: "On moonlit nights I would look at the reflection of the moon in the placid water of the Ganges and piteously pray to God with tearful eyes, 'O Lord, there are stains even on the moon, but let my mind be absolutely stainless.'"[3]

The relationship of a young married couple is usually centred more on the physical plane, but throughout their lives Ramakrishna and Sarada demonstrated an ideal spiritual relationship. Each tested the other. One night when Sarada went to Ramakrishna's room to sleep, he said to her, "Tell me if you have come here to drag me down the road leading to the worldly life."

"Certainly not," Sarada replied without a moment's hesitation. "Why should I drag you into the world? I am here to help you to realize your spiritual ideal."

Sarada challenged Ramakrishna as well. One day she asked him as she was massaging his feet, "How do you regard me?"

He replied by pointing to himself and saying: "The Mother who is worshipped in the temple, and the mother who gave birth to this [pointing to his body] and is now living in the nahabat — the same mother is now stroking my feet. Really and truly I always regard you as the embodiment of the blissful Mother of the Universe."[4]

The Master's experience is supported by the scriptures: "O Goddess, You are the embodiment of knowledge and You are manifest in all higher and lower forms of conceptual knowledge. You are embodied in every woman in the world. O Mother, You alone are present everywhere in this universe, pervading everything. You are incomparable and beyond expression. Who can describe Your infinite glories by singing hymns?" (Chandi, 11:6)

Ramakrishna was firmly established in Truth. Now he decided to use his relationship with his wife to test his purity and spiritual integrity. Swami Saradananda described the Master's deliberations: "One night as he watched Sarada lying asleep beside him,* the Master began to discriminate addressing his own mind: 'O my mind, this is the body of a

---

* Yogin-ma recalled: "This I heard from Holy Mother's lips that during her first visit to Dakshineswar, the Master asked her to stay with him at night. In those days the Master and the Mother slept in the same room. The Master occupied the larger bed and the Mother the adjacent small cot." — *Mayer Katha*, 134

woman. Men look on it as an object of great enjoyment and they always lust after it. But if one possesses this body, one must remain confined within the flesh; one can't realize God. O my mind, let there be no theft [hypocrisy] in your inner chamber. Don't be thinking one thing inwardly and pretending another outwardly! Be frank! Do you want this woman's body, or do you want God? If you want the body, here it is in front of you. Enjoy it.' Discriminating in this way, the Master was about to touch Sarada's body when his mind suddenly recoiled and lost itself so deeply in samadhi that he did not regain normal consciousness all night. The next morning after considerable difficulty he was brought back to the conscious plane when the Lord's name was repeated in his ear."[5]

During the prime of her youth, Sarada slept in a bed next to her husband's for eight months. Her mind, like her husband's, constantly soared to a higher plane and she never had any desire for physical pleasure. Such events are unheard of in the lives of other great religious teachers. Many years later, referring to his wife's innate purity, Ramakrishna said to a disciple: "If she had not been so pure, and if she had lost her self-control and made demands on me — who knows? Perhaps my self-control would have given way. Perhaps I would have come down to the physical plane. After I married, I implored the Divine Mother, 'O Mother, eradicate lust completely from my wife's mind.' While living with her at that time I realized that the Mother had truly granted my prayer."[6]

It is wonderful to hear about the human play of divine beings in this world. Their minds may dwell in the transcendental plane, but they behave like the rest of us. Monks look at women as daughters, sisters, or mothers, but not as wives. Although Ramakrishna had a wife, it was not possible for him to maintain any kind of worldly relationship with her. For him, all women were manifestations of the Divine Mother, and he never deviated from that attitude all through his life.

After repeated tests, Ramakrishna became convinced of Sarada's absolute purity, and he now became eager to awaken her innate divinity. Purity and renunciation are the two wings of spiritual life: they help spiritual aspirants reach their destination. Christ said: "Blessed are the pure in heart, for they shall see God."

Shodashi Puja

According to Tantra, the Divine Mother has ten forms: Kali, Tara, Shodashi, Bhuvaneshwari, Bhairavi, Chinnamasta, Dhumavati, Bagala, Matangi, and Kamala. Shodashi is also called Rajrajeshwari and Tripurasundari. According to the *Lalita-sahasra-nama*, Shodashi is the most benign and purest form of the Divine Mother. One can worship this deity in a clay image or in a young girl about the age of 16. According to the *Narada Pancharatra*, one day Kali became mad at Shiva and took the form of Shodashi — literally, a 16-year-old girl and a paragon of beauty. The Divine Mother takes various forms according to time and situation. Creation, preservation, and destruction are all Her play. When killing demons, She takes a destructive form, but She assumes a benign form for Her devotees.

On 5 June 1872, the night of Phalaharini Kali Puja, Ramakrishna worshipped Shodashi, the third form of the Divine Mother, in Sarada. Years before, he had begun his sadhana by worshipping *Adyashakti*, or the Primordial Power, in the image of Bhavatarini Kali of Dakshineswar. Finally, on that new moon night in 1872, he worshipped the same Adyashakti in the living form of Sarada. Thus he completed his sadhana by offering to her the results of all his spiritual practices.

This important event awakened Sarada's divinity, manifested his own spiritual relationship with Sarada, and made clear the role she would play in the future. By performing the Shodashi Puja, Ramakrishna signified that the Adyashakti had taken form as Sarada Devi. When Sarada was worshipped as Shodashi she was 18 years old, in the prime of her youth. The scriptures do not require that the girl who participates in this worship be exactly 16 years old, but she should be young and beautiful.

The short meditation mantra of the Goddess Shodashi is:

Bālārka-mandalā bhāsām chatur-bāhum trilochanām;
Pāsha-ankusha-sharān-chāpam dhārayantim shivam shraye.
— The form of Shodashi, the beloved of Shiva, is crimson like the rising sun. She has four arms and three eyes and She holds four weapons — noose, goad, arrows, and bow — in her four hands.[7]

The worship mantra of Shodashi is:

Hring tripurasundaryai namah.
— Salutations to the Mother Tripurasundari.

Swami Saradananda described the occasion:

It was the new moon night, an auspicious occasion for the Phalaharini Kali Puja. This special festival is also observed in the Kali temple of Dakshineswar. The Master made a special arrangement for privately worshipping the Divine Mother as Shodashi in his room rather than performing it in the temple. At the right side of the worshipper's seat, a low wooden seat, beautifully painted with rice powder pigment, was placed for the Goddess to sit on during the worship. The sun had set

Above: Painting by an unknown artist depicting the Shodashi Puja.
Below: Wooden seat used by Sarada Devi during the puja.

and the new moon night arrived in a veil of deep darkness. Hriday was performing the worship in the Kali temple that night, so he helped with the preparations for the Master's worship as much as possible and then left for the temple. After the priest Dinu had finished the evening worship service in the Radha-Govinda temple, he came to help the Master prepare for the worship, and then he left. It was nine o'clock in the evening when the preparations for the mystical worship were complete. The Master had sent a message to Sarada beforehand to be present during the worship, and now she arrived in the Master's room. The Master sat for worship.

The Master finished the preliminaries and sanctified the articles of worship by repeating the mantras. He then beckoned Sarada to sit on the decorated wooden seat. While she was watching the worship, Sarada had already entered a semiconscious spiritual state. So without fully knowing what she was doing, she moved like one who is spellbound and sat facing north on the right side of the Master, who was seated facing east. According to the scriptural injunctions, he repeatedly sprinkled sanctified water on her from the pitcher installed in front of him. He then uttered mantras and invoked the Deity with the following prayer:

"O Divine Mother Tripurasundari! O Eternal Virgin, possessor of all power! Please open the gate of perfection. Purify her body and mind, and manifest Yourself through her for the welfare of all."

He then performed the ceremony of *nyasa** in accordance with the injunction of the scriptures, and worshipped her with sixteen items as a veritable manifestation of the Devi. After offering food, he took some of it and put it in her mouth. Sarada lost outer consciousness and went into samadhi. While uttering mantras in a semiconscious state, the Master also went into deep samadhi. Thus, the worshipper and the worshipped became fully united and unified in the Atman, Existence-Knowledge-Bliss Absolute.

Some time passed in this way. It was long after midnight when the Master gradually regained partial consciousness of the world. In that semiconscious state he offered himself to the Devi manifest in the person of Sarada, and then forever surrendered at her feet himself, the results of his sadhanas, his rosary, and everything else. He then bowed down to her with this prayer:

"O Consort of Shiva, the most auspicious of all auspicious beings! O Doer of all actions! O Refuge of all! O three-eyed** Goddess of golden complexion! O Power of Narayana, I salute You again and again."

---

*Nyasa consists of touching different parts of the body with appropriate mantras and mentally identifying them with the different parts of the Deity.
**The third eye, placed on the forehead between the eyebrows, denotes the eye of wisdom.

The worship was completed. The Master's sadhana culminated in this worship of the Divine Mother in the body of a woman who was an embodiment of spiritual wisdom. Both his divine and human aspects had achieved ultimate perfection.[8]

Sarada later recalled the events of that night:

The Master performed the Shodashi Puja a month and a half after my arrival in Dakshineswar. It was the night of the Phalaharini Kali Puja. People were excited by the festive singing and music in the temple. At about nine at night, he sent for me to come to his room. Hriday had made all the necessary arrangements for the worship. Dinu, one of the Master's distant nephews, picked the flowers and bel leaves for the worship. The Master was alone in the room. He asked me to sit on a low wooden seat. I sat facing the jar of Ganges water, which was in the northwestern corner of the room. The Master sat near the western door facing eastward. All the doors were closed. The articles for worship were to my right. First he painted my feet with *alta* [a red dye], put vermilion on my forehead, and clad me in a new cloth. He then fed me with sweets and a betel roll. I saw him doing all this, but had no desire to utter a word. I was in an ecstatic state and completely oblivious to the external world. Hence I did not know exactly how the worship proceeded. Finally I bowed down to him mentally and returned to the nahabat.[9]

This ceremony was significant for both Ramakrishna and Sarada for four reasons:

First, although both were divine, when they incarnated as human beings their minds were covered with a thin veil of maya. If they were always aware of their true nature, they could not have functioned in the world. When they were young, they were not fully aware of their divinity. Because Ramakrishna had attained illumination by performing sadhana, he decided to awaken his young wife's divinity.

Second, their souls became one with pure consciousness and transcended the idea of sex, which originates from body consciousness. Just as Ramakrishna saw the Divine Mother in Sarada, she also saw the Master as the embodiment of all gods and goddesses. Sarada later said to one of her disciples: "Know that the Master and I are identical." Ramakrishna said of her, "She is my Shakti [Power]." The scriptures say: *Shakti shaktimān abheda* — Shakti and the possessor of Shakti are inseparable.

Third, in this ceremony the Master gave Sarada a taste of divine love. By worshipping Sarada as the goddess Shodashi, Ramakrishna paid the highest respect to all womankind. He then empowered Sarada to teach the Motherhood of God after his passing, thus demonstrating that women are not inferior to men. They can also be world teachers.

Fourth, Ramakrishna offered to Sarada the results of his many years of sadhana. By doing so he empowered her to conduct his ministry without her having to practise those sadhanas herself, and he made her the full partner in his spiritual glory. She attained the exalted position of a spiritual teacher without needing to endure the usual austerities practised by saints. The spiritual disciplines that she did perform were not for her own illumination, but for the benefit of her disciples.

Later a woman devotee asked Holy Mother,* "Well, Mother, how did you feel when the Master worshipped you as Shodashi?"

She answered with a bashful smile: "What can I say? I couldn't understand the mystery. I was not myself then. Perhaps the Divine Mother Bhavatarini possessed me, so I was not aware of what was going on. I saw that the Master dressed me, applied red paint to my feet, worshipped me, bowed down to me, but nothing made any impression on my mind. I sat still, and the Master finally made a full prostration, touching my feet. Afterwards, when I regained my normal consciousness, I mentally bowed down to him again and again and begged for forgiveness."** Saying this, she closed her eyes and remained quiet.[10]

After the Puja

After the Shodashi Puja, Holy Mother continued her daily routine of cooking, cleaning, and serving her husband and mother-in-law. She slept in the Master's room for another six months. She later vividly described those nights to her disciples:

> It is impossible to describe his spiritual moods in those days. In his god-intoxicated state he would sometimes say words incomprehensible to me, sometimes laugh, sometimes weep, and sometimes remain motionless in samadhi, like a corpse. The whole night would pass that way. My body trembled with fear and I eagerly awaited the break of day. At that time I knew almost nothing about samadhi.
>
> One night his mind did not come down to the ordinary plane of consciousness for a long time. I was frightened and sent for Hriday. He came and repeated the Lord's name for a while into the Master's ear. Only then did the Master regain his normal mood. After that day the Master taught me various mantras and also told me how to use them for different

*The name by which Sarada Devi was known among the devotees. Henceforth, we shall use the term "Holy Mother" or "the Mother" in lieu of "Sarada".
**Because the Master bowed down to her. According to the custom in India, a wife bows down to her husband but not a husband to his wife.

Left: The concert tower, or nahabat, where Sarada Devi lived on the ground floor; Chandramani Devi, her mother-in-law, lived upstairs. Right: The semi-circular porch of Ramakrishna's room, ca. 1930s.

kinds of samadhi. Thus I gradually got rid of my fear and also succeeded in bringing his mind down from samadhi. But as I did not know when he would go into samadhi, I kept awake all night. Coming to realize my plight, he asked me to sleep in the nahabat.[11]

There are two nahabats in the temple garden of Dakshineswar — one in the south, the other in the north. Holy Mother lived with her mother-in-law in the northern nahabat, Chandramani staying upstairs and Holy Mother downstairs. Her tiny octagonal room was 7'9" long and 7'9" wide; its ceiling was 9'3" in height. Its door was 2'2" wide and 4'2" high — too low for Holy Mother, who was approximately 5'6" tall.

Holy Mother recalled: "The door to the nahabat was so low that at first I would always bump my head against the upper frame. One day I got a cut on my head. Then I became accustomed to it. My head bent of itself as soon as I approached the door. Many aristocratic women from Calcutta frequently came there. They would stand at the door, peep inside, and remark: 'Ah, what a tiny room for our good child! She is in exile, as it were, like Sita.'"[12]

In our minds we can see Holy Mother, busy with her housework and forgetting herself in her service to her husband and mother-in-law. Her head bumps against the door frame and tears trickle from her eyes. Covering her wound with her veil and ignoring the pain, she serves her husband and mother-in-law. Chandramani was so infirm that she could hardly move, and she depended on her daughter-in-law for everything. If anyone cautioned Holy Mother not to hurry, she would reply: "My respected mother-in-law is now old. She needs me, so when she calls I must rush to her."[13]

During this first visit, Holy Mother stayed at Dakshineswar from March 1872 to October 1873. At that time the Master considered himself to be a maid or a female confidante of the Divine Mother. Holy Mother helped him to dress accordingly and also cooked for him. Some women from Dakshineswar who used to visit the Kali temple became close to Holy Mother. Prompted by these women, one day Holy Mother said to the Master: "Well, if there is no child, how will the family continue?"

The Master replied: "What good is there in having just one son? In the near future you will have so many sons and daughters that you will be exhausted looking after them."[14]

Holy Mother recalled: "The Master didn't talk about anything other than God. He told me: 'Look, this body exists one moment and dies the next. People undergo so much suffering and pain in this world! Why would this body beget more children? God is the eternal reality; it is better to call on Him. As soon as you assume a body, you have endless troubles.'"[15]

A year after the Shodashi Puja, Holy Mother developed stomach problems. Shambhu Mallick, a devotee of the Master, brought Dr. Prasad to treat her, but it did not help. As she did not want the Master to be worried about her, she left for Kamarpukur and Jayrambati in October 1873. There she slowly recovered with the change of diet and climate.

Holy Mother in Kamarpukur and Jayrambati

Human life never goes smoothly. Undoubtedly poverty is painful, but it has a positive side: it helps the inner power of the soul to manifest; it turns the mind so that it surrenders to God; it teaches one how to fight through ordeals; and it helps one recognize a true friend. Like other people in the world, Holy Mother faced disease, bereavement, and poverty. In December 1873, while she was in Kamarpukur, her brother-in-law Rameswar died. She then moved to Jayrambati, where her father died a few months later, on 26 March 1874. As a result, her mother suffered dire poverty. With her husband's death, the income from his priestly duties came to an end. Her children were young and there was no one to look after the farm. Fortunately, Shyamasundari was strong and steadfast, and she took up work husking paddy for the family of a well-to-do neighbour. She received one fourth of the rice she husked in exchange for her labour. Holy Mother began to help her mother by working the husking machine. Even with Holy Mother's help, Shyamasundari could not manage the household and also raise her young children on such a small income, so she sent her sons to different relatives to be educated. Holy Mother did not want to burden her mother, so she decided to return to Dakshineswar.

Second Visit to Dakshineswar

During Ramakrishna's lifetime, Holy Mother travelled between the Jayrambati-Kamarpukur area and Dakshineswar nine times.* The

---

*Holy Mother lived with Ramakrishna at Dakshineswar, Shyampukur, and Cossipore during the following periods:
First visit: March 1872 to October 1873 = 1 year 7 months
Second visit: April 1874 to September 1875 = 1 year 5 months
Third visit: 17 March 1876 to November 1876 = 9 months
Fourth visit: March 1877 to August 1877 = 7 months
Fifth visit: March 1881 = 1 day
Sixth visit: January 1882 to June 1883 = 1 year 6 months
Seventh visit: January 1884 = 1 day
Eighth visit: January 1884 to July 1884 = 7 months
Ninth visit: March 1885 to August 1886 = 1 year 5 months

distance between the Jayrambati-Kamarpukur area and Dakshineswar is 60 miles via the Telo-Bhelo route. (*See route map on p. 807.*) Holy Mother would walk 52 miles, cross four rivers by ferry, and finally take a boat across the Ganges from Baidyabati to Dakshineswar. She had no shoes and wore only a sari. She walked through the sun and rain without an umbrella, ignoring her discomfort. On her long journeys she would carry a cloth bundle either on her head or held against her waist under her right arm. The bundle contained all her belongings: a couple of saris, her jewellery, a thin towel (*gāmchā*), a cloth bag filled with puffed rice, a few chunks of hard molasses, and some bananas or other fruit. She would tie a few coins into one of the upper corners of her sari to pay the ferrymen.

Holy Mother was extremely intelligent and practical. When she travelled she hid her jewellery inside the puffed rice to protect it from robbers. Holy Mother always travelled in a group to protect herself from highwaymen. When she and her companions were tired, they rested along the side of a road under a tree. They bathed in their saris in a pond or lake near the road, and then let their clothes dry on their bodies. They passed their nights on rope cots or on straw beds in roadside inns that provided a resting place for pilgrims or passersby. The owners of inns often ran grocery shops. The travellers who could not afford to buy a meal could buy rice and dal to cook their own meal.

It probably took Holy Mother three or four days to reach Dakshineswar from Jayrambati or Kamarpukur. She arrived in Dakshineswar in April 1874 for her second visit. She again took up residence in the nahabat and began serving the Master and his mother.

Shambhu Mallick was a wealthy devotee of the Master who had a garden house near the Dakshineswar temple. When he saw the Mother's tiny living quarters in the nahabat, he decided to build a cottage for her. Swami Saradananda described the situation:

> It was probably in 1874 that Holy Mother came to Dakshineswar for the second time. She lived with the Master's mother in the nahabat as before. Shambhu felt that the tiny room was inconvenient for Holy Mother to live in, so he acquired on lease a piece of land near the Dakshineswar temple for 250 rupees and decided to build a spacious thatched cottage for her there. Captain Vishwanath Upadhyaya, an officer of the Nepalese government, was then visiting the Master and became devoted to him. When Vishwanath heard about Shambhu's building project, he promised to supply all of the timber needed. As the *sal* wood business of the Nepal Government was under his control, it was not expensive for him to secure the timber. When the construction started, Vishwanath sent three big

logs of *sal* wood from the warehouse located in Belur Village across the Ganges. But that night a strong high tide carried away one of the logs. Believing it to be a bad omen, Hriday was annoyed and remarked that Holy Mother was unlucky. When the Captain heard this, he sent another log, and the cottage was completed. Holy Mother lived there for nearly a year. A woman was then appointed to be with her and to help her with the household work. Every day Holy Mother cooked various dishes for the Master in that cottage, carried them to the Dakshineswar temple, and returned to her cottage after he had finished his meal. Sometimes during the day the Master would visit the cottage to look after her and make sure she was happy. He would stay with her for a while and then he would return to the temple. There was only one exception to this routine: One afternoon as soon as the Master arrived at Holy Mother's cottage, a heavy rain started falling. It continued until midnight, making it impossible for him to return to the temple. He was compelled to stay there overnight, and Holy Mother cooked rice and soup to serve him.*

After living in that cottage for a year,** Holy Mother had a severe attack of dysentery. Shambhu took special care for her recovery, arranging for Doctor Prasad to treat her. When she recovered a little, she left for her native village of Jayrambati, probably in September 1875. Shortly after her arrival there, she had a severe relapse and was bedridden. Gradually that disease worsened so much that her condition became critical. Holy Mother's father had passed away by then, so her mother and brothers served her the best they could. We heard that when the Master was told of her severe illness, he said to Hriday: "Well, Hriday, just think — if she should die now! Her coming into the world would have been in vain. She would have failed to achieve the main purpose of human life."[16]

We can visualize the Mother during the second visit of her stay in Dakshineswar. She was a young woman, 21 years old. Forgetting her abdominal pain and discomfort from dysentery, she continued her daily routine for a year. Over and above that, she endured verbal abuse from Hriday, who considered her to be his rival in caring for the Master. She returned to Jayrambati in September 1875, when she finally recovered her health to some extent.

Soon after her return Holy Mother again was attacked by dysentery and became bedridden. The disease took such a serious turn that her life

---

*The Master humorously said to Holy Mother: "This is as if I have come home like any priest of the Kali temple going home at night." — *Srima Sarada Devi*, 52
** Swami Saradananda mentioned that Shambhu Mallick built the cottage for Holy Mother probably in 1874. But according to the Mother's account, she stayed in the cottage during her third visit to Dakshineswar. According to M.'s diary, Shambhu transferred the property as a gift on 11 April 1876 and died in 1877.

was in danger. When Ramakrishna heard of her illness, he was extremely concerned.

Only one who has suffered from dysentery knows how horribly painful it is. Holy Mother had to answer the call of nature frequently, but there were no toilets in Jayrambati. She would go into the bushes near Kalu Pond, close to her hut, and sometimes lie down near the ghat. She later described this period: "I suffered from dysentery for a year. The body became a mere skeleton. I would go to answer the call of nature near Kalu Pond, but as I had to go there frequently, I would lay myself down near the pond. One day I saw my reflection in the water and noticed that all that remained of my body was only a few bones. I thought: 'Dear me, what is the use of this body? Let me give it up. Let me leave it here.' Seeing me in that condition, Nibi [a neighbour woman] said: 'My goodness! Why are you lying down here? Come, come to your room.' She then held me as I walked to my bed. Oh, what a terrible disease I had! It wouldn't leave me."[17]

When human effort fails, people take refuge in Providence. Holy Mother's suffering and struggle encourage us to fight against the diseases and difficulties in life, and her triumph over them gives us a ray of light in the midst of our darkness and hopelessness. She described how her suffering came to an end by the grace of the Divine Mother:

My body then was swollen all over. My nose, eyes, and ears were running profusely. My brother Umesh said, "Sister, will you take a vow to fast in front of the village goddess Simhavahini?"* I agreed and he supported me as I walked to the temple. The full moon was then a new moon to me, as my sight was blurred from the continuous discharge of fluid. Over and above this, my dysentery continued. I lay down in front of the temple, and then crawled nearby to answer the call of nature. That night my godmother, who lived nearby, grunted loudly from time to time so that I might not be frightened. Soon Mother Simhavahini appeared to my mother in the form of a blacksmith girl of Radhu's age [12 or 13] and said: "Go and bring your daughter back. She is so ill that she should not be left alone. Bring her back right now. Give her this medicine and she will be cured." She also told me: "Make juice by crushing a squash [lau] flower and mixing it with a little salt. Apply this to your eyes and they will clear up." I then took the medicine that my mother had received and applied the squash flower juice to my eyes. This almost immediately cleared the mucous from my eyes and they began to stop watering. My normal vision came back the same day. Gradually the swelling of my body disappeared and I recovered. I told people about the medicine I had received from Mother Simhavahini.

*A custom often followed by people in order to recover from a difficult illness.

The goddess Simhavahini's temple in Jayrambati.

The deities inside Simhavahini's temple.

From that time on the power of the goddess became known far and near, and people in large numbers began to visit Her. I received medicine and the world was also blessed....Mother Simhavahini is a living goddess. I keep some earth from that temple ground in a container. I eat a little of that earth every day and give some to Radhu to take also.[18]

The human condition constantly fluctuates between fortune and misfortune, and neither state is permanent. Holy Mother was unfortunate in her health. Hardly had she recovered from dysentery when she had an attack of malaria, accompanied by an enlargement of her spleen.

At that time villagers relied on local remedies when they were ill. In those remote villages of Bengal, modern medical facilities were not available, so poor villagers would seek divine help and apply folk remedies to cure their diseases. Holy Mother went with her mother to the Kayapat-Badanganj Shiva temple, six miles from Jayrambati, for a traditional treatment that was as bizarre as it was painful. The patient bathed and then was made to lie down on the temple floor. A piece of banana leaf was placed on his or her abdomen. Three or four people held the patient's hands and feet tightly, and then the patient's abdomen was branded with a burning branch from a plum tree. Holy Mother watched other patients undergoing this cruel treatment and heard their piteous cries. When her turn came she would allow no one to touch her, but lay quietly down on the ground and was branded. Silently she endured the excruciating pain, and her spleen gradually returned to normal.

Sometimes we wonder why great souls endure so much suffering. Human life consists of happiness and misery, comedy and tragedy. When divine beings take human forms, they must obey this law of maya. Because happiness and misery are inevitable, avatars accept this reality when they take on a human life — but they are not affected by it. Rather, their minds dwell in their divine nature beyond the pairs of opposites. They take human birth to teach ordinary people how to face difficulties and suffering, maintain peace and harmony, and experience divine bliss by leading a God-centred life.

Third Visit to Dakshineswar

In 1876 Holy Mother journeyed to Dakshineswar via Telo-Bhelo with two villagers, Gosain Das and an unidentified woman. They arrived on 17 March.

This time Holy Mother stayed in the cottage that Shambhu Mallick had built instead of at the nahabat. Holy Mother later said to M.'s wife, Nikunja Devi: "My daughter, Shambhu Mallick built that cottage for me, but I was reluctant to live there alone. One day I mentioned that to the Master. He then said to Hriday, 'Hride, you bring your wife.'"[19] Thus Hriday's wife from his second marriage came to stay with the Mother at Dakshineswar. On 22 May 1876 Holy Mother observed the Savitri-vrata* in Dakshineswar.

In an article entitled "Glimpses of Pages from an Account-Book," in *Amritarup Sri Ramakrishna*, Swami Prabhananda supplied some new information regarding Holy Mother's cottage that is based on the Chatterjee family account book covering two years: 1283 B.E. (1876–1877) and 1287 B.E. (1880–1881). He received the account book from Anil Gupta, a grandson of M.

Prabhananda wrote:

> Shambhu Mallick leased a piece of land for 250 rupees to build a cottage for Holy Mother. Vishwanath Upadhyaya supplied the necessary timber for its construction. A thatched hut was built there. In the account book we find that on 3 May 1876, worship and other rituals were performed there, and the priest was paid four annas. On the same day a door was installed at the house at a cost of two annas and two paisa. Then on 12 June a wooden cot was bought for three rupees and eight annas from someone named Ramteli. A maidservant named "Kali's Mother" was also appointed at a monthly salary of one rupee to help Holy Mother with her household work and to stay with her. Lakshmi, Sri Ramakrishna's niece, lived in this cottage for a few days, and Hriday's second wife also came there to live with Holy Mother. Either Kali's Mother or Gupi, a temple employee, did the marketing for them. Of course Holy Mother did not live there long, but Hriday's wife continued to live in that cottage even after Holy Mother returned to the nahabat.[20]

Shambhu Mallick and his wife were extremely devoted to the Master and Holy Mother. Shambhu's wife regarded the Master as God. Whenever Holy Mother was at Dakshineswar, she would invite Holy Mother to her home on Tuesdays, an auspicious day for Mother worship, and worship her with sixteen items.

Holy Mother stayed in the new cottage, close to Ramlal's house, with Hriday's wife and a maid, but she did not live there for long. Soon after she

---

*This vrata, or vow, is observed by married women on the full moon day in the month of Jaishtha (mid-May to mid-June). On this day it is believed that princess Savitri brought back her husband Satyavan from the clutches of Yama, the god of death, through her devotion and prayers.

moved there, the Master was stricken with a severe attack of dysentery and could not go to the pine grove to answer the call of nature. Holy Mother later recalled:

Is blood dysentery an ordinary disease? During the rainy season the Master suffered from dysentery. A commode was made by making a hole in the centre of a wooden box and putting an earthen pan below, and this was kept on the northern veranda. I used to clean it in the morning, and others did it in the afternoon. At that time a woman came from Varanasi to nurse the Master. One day she brought me from that cottage to the nahabat and said: "Mother, the Master is so sick and you are living away from him?"

I replied: "What can I do? How can Hriday's wife live here alone, and moreover Hriday is with the Master."

She said: "It does not matter. They will find a companion for her. It is not right for you to stay away from the Master."

I took her advice and came to the nahabat to look after the Master. When the Master got well, that woman left and I never met her again. She really helped me a lot. I later inquired about her in Varanasi but could not locate her. Strangers came to Dakshineswar whenever the Master needed them, and afterwards they disappeared.[21]

This woman from Varanasi not only encouraged Holy Mother to nurse the Master, but also encouraged her to give up her shyness in front of the Master. Yogin-ma later said: "Previously the Mother had felt bashful and kept her veil on in front of the Master, but that woman from Varanasi removed the Mother's shyness. One night she escorted the Mother to the Master's room and removed the Mother's veil in front of the Master. Then the Master began to talk about God to them and they listened spellbound. They were so absorbed in listening to him that they did not notice the sun rise."[22]

After serving the Master for a few months, Holy Mother returned to Jayrambati via Burdwan on 8 November 1876 with Hriday's brother Rajaram. Swami Prabhananda quoted from the account book of the Chatterjee family: "Eleven rupees were spent for travelling expenses for two people. The expenses incurred on the journey included boat fare from Dakshineswar to Howrah, eight annas; train fare from Howrah to Burdwan, four rupees and 12 annas; fare for a bullock cart from Burdwan to Kamarpukur, four rupees; plus miscellaneous expenses on the road including food, one rupee and 12 annas."[23]

Perhaps this was the part of the play that Holy Mother had to go back and forth between Kamarpukur-Jayrambati and Dakshineswar. She was dependent either on her husband or on her mother, and dependence always brings misery. After her father's death, her family in Jayrambati was passing through hardship. Her uncle, Ishwar Chandra, was performing rituals for people in Calcutta but could not make enough money to send back to the family in Jayrambati. The Mother's younger brother Prasanna learned to perform rituals and left for Calcutta to earn some money. Holy Mother did not get any financial help from her husband or from his family, as they were also poor, so whenever she had any difficulties she took shelter with her mother at Jayrambati. She helped her mother with cooking, cleaning, washing, and other household work. Shyamasundari had a strong body, indomitable willpower, and steadfast faith in God.

Fourth Visit: Encounter with the Robber

Ramakrishna's mother, Chandramani, passed away at Dakshineswar on 13 February 1877.* The Master had tremendous love and respect for his mother. When she died, he cried aloud, saying, "Mother, Mother." Hriday reprimanded him, saying, "Uncle, you are a monk and now you are crying for your mother?"

The Master replied: "You rascal, keep quiet! I may have become a monk, but that does not mean I am a heartless beast."[24]

Holy Mother later told Nikunja Devi: "When my mother-in-law was dying, the Master said: 'O Mother, blessed you are — you who carried me in your womb! Mother, you looked after me in this form; henceforth please do the same.' Another day, after his mother's passing away, he told me before lunch, 'Please wait, let me go to the Panchavati and cry for my mother.'"[25]

At the time of Chandramani's death, Holy Mother was in Jayrambati. When she heard the news, she left for Dakshineswar. On this occasion she encountered a robber in the field of Telo-Bhelo. She was travelling on foot, accompanied by the Master's niece Lakshmi and nephew Shivaram, as well as two village women, Satyavama and Saukhuni, who wanted to bathe in the holy Ganges. During her journey she hid her jewellery in the bundle of Lakshmi's puffed rice[26] as a precaution against robbery. The Master had taught Holy Mother: "Adjust yourself according to time, place, and person." Although Holy Mother lived

* When Chandramani was about to die, she was carried to the Bakul-tala ghat for the *antarjali* rite, which involves immersing the lower part of a dying person in water. According to the *Lilaprasanga*, the Master asked his nephew Ramlal to perform the last rites as he was a monk and not allowed to perform such rites. In the account book of the Chatterjee family, there is a reference to gifts bestowed on the fourth day after Chandramani's death for *agradani*, a rite in which a brahmin ceremonially receives the first gift in memory of a deceased person.

Above: Mother Kali of Telo-Bhelo, known as the "Robber's Kali."
Below: The field of Telo-Bhelo, where Sarada Devi encountered a robber in 1877.

behind a veil of modesty, if necessary she could fearlessly cast off her habits and customs to deal appropriately with any situation. During this incident she showed exceptional courage, intelligence, and self-control.

Swami Saradananda narrated the story:

> In those days Holy Mother usually travelled from Jayrambati and Kamarpukur to Dakshineswar on foot because she had no money, or little of it, or for some other reason. People travelled from the Jayrambati-Kamarpukur area to Jahanabad (Arambagh) and then crossed the ten-mile-long field near Telo and Bhelo to reach Tarakeswar. From there they had to traverse a similar field, Kaikala, to reach Baidyabati, and finally cross the Ganges by boat to Dakshineswar. Those two vast fields were inhabited by highwaymen. Even now people say that many travellers lose their lives at the robbers' hands in the morning, at noon, and in the evening. Telo and Bhelo are two small villages situated almost side by side. In a field, a couple of miles away from these villages, is a temple with a fierce and dreadful form of Kali, known as the Robbers' Kali of Telo-Bhelo. People say that robbers worship this Kali before proceeding to rob and murder travellers. In those days people travelled in groups to traverse those two fields in order to protect themselves from robbers.
>
> Once Holy Mother was walking from Kamarpukur to Dakshineswar with the daughter and younger son of Rameswar and a few other men and women. After reaching Arambagh, her companions thought they had enough time to cross the field of Telo-Bhelo before dusk, so they were unwilling to pass the night there. Although the Holy Mother was exhausted from the journey, she said nothing and walked on with the party. But they had scarcely walked four miles when she found she could not keep up with them and began to lag behind. They waited for her for a while, then asked her to walk faster and moved on. When they reached the middle of the field, they noticed that she was then quite far behind and was walking slowly. They waited for her again and when she caught up they said: "If we walk this slowly, we shall not cross the field before 9:00 p.m., and we may be attacked by robbers." The Holy Mother knew that she had inconvenienced the others and caused them alarm, so she asked them not to wait for her. She said: "You go on to the inn at Tarakeswar and rest there. I shall meet you as soon as possible." Seeing the approach of sunset and taking her at her word, without further delay they began to walk faster and were soon out of sight.
>
> Holy Mother then continued along as fast as she could, but she was terribly exhausted. After a while the sun sank below the horizon of the field. Extremely anxious, she wondered what to do. Just then she saw a tall, dark, fiercesome-looking man with a staff on his shoulder rapidly approaching her. Another person, probably his partner, was behind him.

She realized that it was useless to run away or to shout, so she stood still and awaited their arrival with great fear.

Within a few moments the man reached her and asked harshly: "Who are you, standing here alone at this hour of the evening?" To placate him, Holy Mother surrendered to him completely, addressing him as "Father": "Father, my companions have left me behind, and it seems I have lost my way. Kindly accompany me to where they are. Your son-in-law lives at the Kali temple in Dakshineswar. I am going to him. If you accompany me there, he will certainly appreciate your kindness and show you proper courtesy." No sooner had she said this than his companion arrived. Holy Mother noticed that it was not a man but a woman, his wife. When Holy Mother saw her, she was greatly reassured. Holy Mother then took her hand and addressed her as "Mother," saying: "Mother, I am your daughter Sarada. My companions have left me behind and I was in great danger. It is sheer luck that you and Father have come; I do not know what I would have done otherwise."

Holy Mother's unhesitating and simple behaviour, her complete trust, and her sweet words melted the hearts of the Bagdi highwayman and his wife. Forgetting social customs and caste, they accepted her as their own daughter and consoled her. Aware of her physical exhaustion, they would not allow her to go farther that night, but they took her to a small shop near the villages of Telo-Bhelo and arranged for her to stay the night. The woman made a bed for Holy Mother with some of her own clothes and other things, and the man bought puffed rice and sweetened parched rice for her to eat. Thus with parental love and care they let her sleep, guarding her throughout the night. They woke her up the next morning and accompanied her to Tarakeswar about an hour after sunrise. There they took shelter at an inn and asked her to rest. The woman told her husband: "My daughter practically fasted last night. Finish your worship at the Shiva temple quickly and buy some fish and vegetables. I would like to feed her well."

While the man was carrying out his errands, Holy Mother's companions came to the inn in search of her and were delighted to see that she had arrived safely. When the man returned, Holy Mother introduced her adopted parents to her companions, saying, "I don't know what I would have done last night if they hadn't taken me under their protection." Everyone performed worship in the Shiva temple, cooked and ate together, and had a little rest. When the party prepared for their journey to Baidyabati, Holy Mother expressed her gratitude to the Bagdi couple and took her leave of them. Holy Mother told us later: "In one night we had become so close that when we parted we began to weep profusely. I repeatedly invited them to visit me at Dakshineswar when they could, but even when they agreed, I parted from them with great difficulty. They accompanied us for a considerable distance. The woman picked some green peas from a nearby field, tearfully tied them in a corner of my cloth, and said plaintively, 'Sarada, my child, when you eat puffed rice tonight, please have these peas with it.' They kept their promise and visited me a few times at Dakshineswar, bringing sweets and other gifts. I told the Master the whole story, and he received them warmly, treating them as kindly as if they were his own relatives. Although my robber-father is simple and well behaved now, I believe he used to commit robbery before we met."[27]

One can imagine the deep impression that Holy Mother made on the bandit's mind. Did he and his wife get a glimpse of her real nature? She once asked them: "Why do you show me such kindness and affection?"

They replied: "You are not an ordinary human being. We saw you as Mother Kali."

"How is that?" she said. "What did you see?"

They firmly replied: "No, child, we have really seen you as Kali. You hide that form from us now because we are sinners."

"You may say so," Holy Mother said in a detached tone, "but truly I know nothing about it."[28]

Travelling with the Master

During the rainy season, when the water of the Ganges became saline, Ramakrishna suffered from stomach trouble from drinking that water, and the damp climate was not good for his health. Accordingly, during the rainy season, he would spend a few months in Kamarpukur. In July 1877 the Master went to Kamarpukur, accompanied by Holy Mother and Hriday. They went by steamer from the Armenian Ghat in Calcutta to Bandar, and via Ghatal in the Midnapore District, and then took a boat to Bali-Dewanganj. From there they either walked or were conveyed by palanquin for the final eight miles. When they arrived at Bali-Dewanganj in the evening, it was raining incessantly and they needed to find shelter. Banshidhar Modak and his wife, Giribala, a righteous and wealthy couple, came forward to receive these unknown guests in their newly built cottage. The next morning Hriday wanted to continue their journey but Banshidhar asked them to stay at his home for three days.

When the identity of the visitors became known, the villagers flocked to Banshidhar's house to listen to the Master's immortal words. As the rain continued, the Master, Holy Mother, and Hriday stayed for three days and then left for Kamarpukur. As far as we know, this was the only occasion that Holy Mother travelled with the Master.[29]

The Mother later recalled: "Once we went together to Kamarpukur by boat via Bali-Dewanganj. We ate wonderful prasad and the Master sang many songs on the way. Ah, what a great mood he was in! He said to me: 'I know who you are, but I will not tell you now.'[30] He pointed to himself and said, 'Everything is inside this place.'"

After staying in Kamarpukur for a couple of months, Ramakrishna returned to Dakshineswar in September 1877. Holy Mother then went to Jayrambati. Shyamasundari loved to have her daughter's company, as she would get both physical and spiritual help. That year, despite her poverty, Shyamasundari had managed to save some rice to offer at the village's public worship of Kali. Holy Mother later recounted the story:

> Once during the Kali Puja in Jayrambati, Nava Mukhopadhyay did not accept our rice because of a village feud. My mother had sincerely prepared rice and other things as our contribution to the public worship, but he refused to take those from our home. As a result, my mother wept bitterly the whole night. She lamented with great agony: "I made rice for Mother Kali and he has rejected it. Who will eat this rice now? Indeed, it is Kali's rice, and none else can eat it." That night she had a vision of Jagaddhatri [the Mother of the Universe] with a red complexion, sitting cross-legged near the door. We had only one room, which belonged to my brother Barada. When the Master would come, he lived in that room. Mother Jagaddhatri roused her from sleep by patting her and then said: "Why are you crying? I shall eat Kali's rice. You don't need to worry." My mother asked, "Who are you?" Jagaddhatri replied: "I am the Mother of the Universe. I will accept your worship in the form of Jagaddhatri."
>
> The next morning my mother said to me: "Sarada, who is that Deity with a red complexion who sits cross-legged? I will worship Jagaddhatri." She became very excited and resolved to worship Jagaddhatri. She borrowed 13 maunds of paddy from the Biswas family to prepare rice. The rain was incessant. Then my mother prayed: "O Divine Mother, how can I perform Your worship? I can't dry the paddy to husk it." Finally, it so happened that by the grace of Mother Jagaddhatri there was rain all around but bright sunshine in our courtyard where my mother had spread the paddy on a mat. The sculptor dried the clay image near a fire, and then painted it.
>
> My brother Prasanna went to Dakshineswar to invite the Master for the celebration. When he heard the news of the Jagaddhatri Puja, the Master said: "The Mother will come — the Mother will come! Very good. Oh, your family has suffered so much poverty!"
>
> Prasanna said: "Please come. I have come to take you."
>
> The Master replied: "My approval is as good as going to your place. Go home and perform the worship. It will bring you prosperity."

Jagaddhatri Puja was performed nicely [14 November 1877], and all the villagers were invited and fed. Moreover that extra rice helped to meet all the expenses. During the immersion ceremony, my mother whispered into the ear of the image: "Mother Jagai, please come again next year. I will collect everything for Your worship all year round." The next year my mother said to me, "You also contribute something and my Jagai will be worshipped."

I replied: "I don't want to get involved with all this trouble. You have performed the worship once. That is enough. Why are you inviting more trouble? It is not necessary."

My goodness! That same night I had a vivid dream in which Jagaddhatri and Her two companions — Jaya and Vijaya — appeared and said, "Shall we go away then?"

"Who are you?" I asked.

One of them said, "I am Jagaddhatri."

I then said: "No, Mother. Where will you go? Please stay. I didn't ask you to leave."

From then on I have been coming to Jayrambati every year during Jagaddhatri Puja. We did not have too many members in our family, so I used to clean and wash the worship vessels and look after Puja preparations by myself.[31]

After 12 years Holy Mother thought that it would not be necessary to continue the worship. But on the very night that she decided to discontinue the worship, Mother Jagaddhatri again appeared in a dream and said to her: "Sadu, Madhu Mukhopadhyay's aunt, wants to worship Me. Shall I go there?" When She asked three times, "Shall I go?" Holy Mother held Her feet and eagerly said: "Mother, I won't let you go. I shall worship You at our house every year."[32] Later the devotees bought three and a half acres of rice fields in the name of the deity, so that the worship of Mother Jagaddhatri could continue. Later Swami Yogananda bought wooden plates and utensils so that Holy Mother would not have to scrub those metal utensils.

Fifth Visit

In March 1881 Holy Mother travelled to Dakshineswar from Jayrambati with her mother, her brother Prasanna, her niece Lakshmi, and some neighbours. They travelled via Telo-Bhelo. On the way to Dakshineswar they stopped at Tarakeswar to perform a special ceremony in which Holy Mother made an offering of her nail clippings and hair to Lord Shiva in gratitude for her recovery from a recent illness. They then went to an apartment that Prasanna had rented in Calcutta.

Holy Mother recalled:

The next day we all went to Dakshineswar. No sooner had we arrived than Hriday, for some unknown reason, began to ask: 'Why have they come? What have they got to do here?' He was rude and discourteous. My mother did not respond. Hriday was from Sihar, and my mother came from the same village. Nonetheless, Hriday did not show any respect to my mother. My mother said: "Let us all return home. With whom shall I leave my daughter?" For fear of Hriday, the Master remained quiet. We left the same day. Ramlal called a boat so that we could cross the river. While we were leaving, I mentally prayed to Mother Kali: "Mother, if you bring me here again, I shall come."[33]

Hriday used to treat Holy Mother rudely; he probably wanted to control the Master by serving him and did not want any rival. The Master cautioned him, saying: "Look here. You may insult me, but don't hurt her feelings. If He who dwells in this [meaning himself] hisses, you may somehow get by; but if He who dwells in her hisses, no one — not even Brahma, Vishnu, or Shiva — will be able to protect you."[34]

There is a saying: Pride must have its fall. Within two months of this incident, Hriday arranged his own downfall. Trailokya, a son of Mathur, came to Dakshineswar with his wife and children to attend the annual Snanyatra festival in May 1881. Hriday was conducting the worship in the Kali temple, and Trailokya's 8-year-old daughter was there without her parents. Suddenly Hriday was seized with a desire to worship the goddess in the person of this little girl, and following Tantric rites he offered flowers and sandal paste at her feet. It was the sandal paste that betrayed Hriday. Trailokya's wife noticed it as soon as her daughter returned from the ceremony. When she heard what Hriday had done, she was horrified, for it was believed that if a brahmin worshipped a girl of a lower caste, she would be widowed soon after her marriage. When Trailokya saw his wife crying and learned the cause, he became furious and ordered Hriday to leave the temple precincts immediately.

Ramlal then became the main priest of Kali. Puffed up with pride, he began to neglect the Master, who often remained unconscious due to ecstasy. His food would dry up on his plate and there was no one to look after him. The Master sent repeated messages to Holy Mother asking her to return to Dakshineswar. Finally, he sent the following message to her through Lakshman Pyne of Kamarpukur: "I am experiencing great difficulty here. After becoming a priest in the Kali temple, Ramlal has joined the group of other priests. Now he pays no heed to me. Please come by all means, any way you like — in a litter or a palanquin. I shall bear the expenses — be it ten rupees or twenty."[35]

Sixth and Seventh Visits

In January 1882 Holy Mother returned to the Master via Telo-Bhelo, probably travelling by palanquin up to Baidyabati and then by boat to Dakshineswar. She served the Master till June 1883 and then returned to Jayrambati.

In January 1884 she returned to Dakshineswar. After putting her cloth bundle in the nahabat, she went to the Master's room and bowed down to him. A few days before, in a state of samadhi, the Master had fallen and fractured a bone in his left arm. The Master asked her when she had left home, and learned that it was a Thursday afternoon, which is inauspicious according to the Bengali almanac. Bowing before tradition, he said: "This is why I have broken my arm. Please return home and start your journey again at an auspicious hour." Holy Mother was ready to leave then and there, but the Master said: "Please stay today. You may go tomorrow." The next day she left for Jayrambati.

Eighth and Ninth Visits

After spending a few days in Jayrambati, in January 1884 Holy Mother returned to Dakshineswar. A few months later, in July 1884, the Master sent Holy Mother to Kamarpukur to attend the wedding of his nephew Ramlal.

Yogin-ma recalled:

The day that Holy Mother was leaving for Kamarpukur to attend the wedding of Ramlal, I went to Dakshineswar. I was very sad at the thought that I would not see her for many days. Before her departure, Holy Mother went to bow down to the Master. He came out of his room and stood on the northern veranda. Holy Mother bowed down and took the dust of his feet. The Master said to her: "Go carefully. See that you don't leave behind any of your belongings in the boat or railway compartment." This was the first time I saw the Master and Holy Mother together.[36]

The Master also said: "Maintain good relationships with the neighbours. If someone is sick, please visit that person or make inquiries through somebody."[37]

During this trip Holy Mother went with others by train from Howrah to Burdwan, and from there to Kamarpukur by bullock cart via Uchalan. The distance between Howrah and Burdwan is 67 miles and between Burdwan and Kamarpukur, 30 miles. After Ramlal's marriage ceremony

Holy Mother stayed in Kamarpukur and Jayrambati for a few months and then returned to Dakshineswar via Burdwan in March 1885. This was her last visit to the Kamarpukur-Jayrambati area during the Master's lifetime.

Ramakrishna in Jayrambati

Before 1881 Ramakrishna visited Kamarpukur several times to recover from his broken health, especially during the rainy season. Hriday accompanied him on these journeys. The Master was fond of the people in his village and entertained them with songs and stories. He would visit Jayrambati, Sihar, and Vishnupur also. Following are some incidents that took place during some of those visits:

Once in Jayrambati the Master went to bed after supper and then he went into ecstasy. He felt terribly hungry and asked for some food. Holy Mother told him that there was nothing except for some rice soaking in water.* The Master said, "Serve it to me."

"But there are no vegetables," she told him.

The Master replied: "Why don't you look more carefully? Today you made a hot fish curry. See if any of that is left."

Holy Mother went to the kitchen and found that a tiny fish and some sauce were left at the bottom of a bowl. The Master was happy when she brought it to him. He ate three pounds of soaked rice with that fish and was satisfied.[38]

Some people in Jayrambati often ridiculed the Master by calling him the "mad son-in-law." Now and then he would jump up from his seat and exclaim: "This time everyone will be liberated, including the Muslims and untouchables. None will be left behind." At this, villagers would remark: "What a madman!" When village women came to see him, he would make witty remarks, sometimes off-colour. This would make them laugh and cause many of them to run away in embarrassment. The Master would tell those who remained: "The weeds have been removed. Now be seated and I shall talk to you."[39]

Aunt Bhanu, a neighbour of Holy Mother, had previously had a glimpse of Ramakrishna's spiritual intoxication and became very fond of him. Swami Nikhilananda, who met Aunt Bhanu, recalled:

Once she made a garland and wanted to put it around Sri Ramakrishna's neck. Hiding it under her sari, she went to the Master but felt shy about

---

*As there was no refrigerator in the villages at that time, people would soak leftover cooked rice in water instead of throwing it away. They would then eat that rice, mixed with coconut, yogurt, salt, and green chili, for breakfast.

offering it to him in the presence of other women. The Master somehow came to know of her intention and told a naughty joke that made the women laugh and leave the room. When Bhanu was alone with him he asked her to offer the garland. As soon as it was put around his neck he went into deep samadhi. Bhanu was frightened, thinking he might have been stung by a poisonous insect hidden in the flowers. Presently Hriday arrived and brought the Master back to the normal state of consciousness with the help of a mantra. After that incident, Shyamasundari tried to keep women away from his presence.[40]

Once when Holy Mother was at Jayrambati, the Master also went there. He asked her to wash his feet with fuller's earth [saji-mati]. Seeing her loving service to her husband, some women commented: "Look, what has happened to Sarada! She has no physical relationship with her husband, yet still she has so much love for him!"[41]

Swami Subodhananda related this incident: One night in Jayrambati, the Master went to bed after supper. Afterwards Holy Mother had her supper and finished the housework. When she entered the Master's room, she found a blazing light shining on the bed, but the bed was empty. She stood there the entire night with folded hands. At daybreak the Master emerged from the light and bowed down to Holy Mother, saying: "You have appeared in this form — very good."[42]

6
With Ramakrishna
in Dakshineswar

Nityotsava bhavet teshām nitya shrih nitya mangalam;
Yeshām hridistho bhagavān mangalāyatanam harih.
— *Pandava Gita*

Those who install the auspicious Lord in their hearts always enjoy festivity and attain prosperity and blessedness.

Holy Mother first came to Dakshineswar in March 1872 when she was 18 years 3 months old, and lived with the Master off and on for approximately 8 years in Dakshineswar and 9 months in Shyampukur and Cossipore. She considered her time living with the Master in Dakshineswar to be the glorious period of her life. She later joyfully recalled: "Those were my blissful days. The Master put a pitcher of bliss in my heart."

Austerities in the Nahabat

Whenever we think of Holy Mother's hardships in the nahabat,* we cannot control our tears. Chapter 5 described the nahabat where Holy Mother lived in Dakshineswar. This two-storey brick structure still stands. It is about 75 feet north of Ramakrishna's room on the bank of the Ganges. The upper level of the nahabat commands a panoramic view of the sacred river, the temple complex, and the flower gardens. Holy Mother lived on the ground floor in a tiny octagonal room that is about 50 square feet.

*The following is a detailed description of the nahabat as it was in Holy Mother's time given by Swami Gambhirananda in his biography of Holy Mother: The room downstairs, where Holy Mother lived, is octagonal in shape, each wall measuring 3'3" in width. The distance between the walls across the floor is 7'9". The floor area is a little less than 50 square feet. The only opening door in the southern side is 4'2" X 2'2". There are two vents. There is another door in the southeast corner of the veranda for the kitchen. The width of the veranda is 4'3". The height of the room is 9'3".

Probably later, the vents were sealed up and two doors were added — one on the north and the other on the west.

Nahabat in Dakshineswar with the bamboo screens that shaded the lower veranda where Sarada Devi stood to listen to the kirtan in Ramakrishna's room.

All around the room is a narrow veranda, about four feet wide, with two doors leading into the room. The room has two vents but no windows. For the sake of privacy, the veranda was surrounded by plaited bamboo screens, which offered privacy but blocked sunlight and fresh air. At the northeast corner of the veranda is a staircase leading upstairs. Under the stairs in the southeast corner, there is a low space that Holy Mother used for cooking.

That tiny room in the nahabat was her bedroom, living room, shrine, workplace, and storage room. It also served as a guest room when Rama-krishna's niece Lakshmi and women devotees visiting from Calcutta would stay at night. After the Master's passing away, Holy Mother remi-nisced about her days in the nahabat:

> I used to live in the nahabat. Oh, how much hardship I had to go through to live in that tiny room! I had to store all my belongings and groceries in it. From the ceiling hung a pot in a sling containing live fish, used for the Master's meals. They splashed in the water all night. The Master had a weak stomach; he could not digest the oily and spicy food offered to Mother Kali. So in the nahabat I cooked for him and for the devotees. Surendra Mitra provided 10 rupees every month for household expenses, and Senior Gopal would buy the groceries. I had to make chapatis from six to eight pounds of flour. The Master brought Latu, who worked for Ram Datta, and said: "This boy is good. He will help you knead the dough." Ram Datta came by carriage and said, "Today I shall eat chana dal and chapati." No sooner had I heard this than I started cooking. When Rakhal stayed with the Master, I often cooked khichuri for him. I spent many hours cooking.
>
> Sometimes I lived alone in the nahabat, and from time to time Lakshmi, Yogin, Golap, Gaurdasi, and others stayed with me. I used to bathe at four o'clock in the morning. When there was a little sunshine on the steps in the afternoon, I would dry my hair. I then had very thick hair. The fisherwomen were my companions. When they came to bathe in the Ganges, they kept their baskets on the veranda of the nahabat and went down for their dip. They would tell me many stories, and then collect their baskets and leave. At night I used to hear the fishermen sing as they caught fish in the Ganges.
>
> Many devotees came to the Master, and there was continuous singing, dancing, kirtan, bhava, and samadhi in his room. I made a hole in the bamboo screen and stood behind it to watch what was going on in the Master's room. Because I stood for long periods of time, I developed rheumatism. While listening to the kirtan, I thought that if I were a devotee, I could stay with the Master and listen to him speak.[1]

Above: Early photo of the Bakul-tala ghat where Sarada Devi bathed in the Ganges. The nahabat is visible on the right.
Below left: Exterior staircase of the nahabat ascending to Chandramani Devi's room. Below right: The kitchen under the stairs used by Sarada Devi.

Another painful aspect of Holy Mother's life in the nahabat comes to mind. There were no bathing or toilet facilities in the nahabat; moreover, the temple garden was a public place that offered very little privacy. Holy Mother was so modest that she kept herself veiled to hide her face from people she did not know. During the dark hours of the morning she would go to the jungle on the bank of the Ganges to answer the call of nature and then would bathe in the Ganges. Later she recalled her sad plight: "I suffered terribly by suppressing the urge to answer the call of nature and thus developed intestinal problems. If I felt the urge during the day, I controlled it till evening and prayed to the Lord to spare me embarrassment. Only during the dark hours of night could I go out."[2] What discomfort! Later, Yogin-ma (a woman devotee of the Master) realized Holy Mother's predicament and arranged to have an outhouse built near the nahabat.

Holy Mother recalled:

> One day the Master said to Hriday: "You see, I was a little anxious about her. She is a village girl and not accustomed to living in this place where there is no toilet. I would be embarrassed if someone saw her going to ease herself in the bushes and made a comment. But she is so discreet that no one knows when she goes to answer the call of nature — even I have never seen her." I was anxious when I heard this and thought: My goodness! The Divine Mother shows him whatever he wants. Now if I go to the bushes, he may see me. I then earnestly prayed to the Divine Mother, "O Mother, please protect my modesty." My loving Mother always shielded me as if with her wings. I stayed in Dakshineswar so many years, but no one saw my private affairs.[3]

Regarding her natural shyness and modest habits, the manager of the temple garden once remarked: "Yes, we have heard about her living here, but we have never seen her."

Lakshmi's eyewitness account helps us to visualize Holy Mother's daily life in the nahabat:

> At Dakshineswar we stayed in the nahabat. When the Master wished to indicate the Mother to his visitors, he would make a circle with his finger at the tip of the nose. This was because the Mother wore a nose ring. He used to refer to the nahabat as a cage and to us as Shuk-Sari.* When fruits and sweets that had been offered to the Divine Mother were brought to the Master, he would remind Brother Ramlal: "Don't forget that there are two birds in that cage. Give them some fruits and peas." Newcomers would

*She is referring to two birds in Indian folklore that love to proclaim Krishna's glories.

take the Master's words literally. Even Master Mahashay [M., the recorder of *The Gospel of Sri Ramakrishna*] did so at first.

Village women would come to visit the Mother, and sometimes the Master overheard their conversations. Once he said to the Mother: "These women come and stroll by the goose pond. When they see me they talk among themselves and I hear what they are saying. They say: 'This man is good, but one thing is strange! He does not sleep with his wife at night.' Please don't pay any heed to their talk. They are worldly women. They may convince you to use tricks or medicines to divert my mind towards the world. Please don't follow their advice. I have given myself completely to God." The Mother was embarrassed and reassured the Master: "Oh, no, no. I won't pay any attention to them."

How we managed in that tiny room of the nahabat, I sometimes wonder. It was the Master's divine play! Usually it was shared by Holy Mother, another girl, and me. Sometimes Gopal-ma, who was a large woman, or other women devotees from Calcutta also stayed with us. Moreover, we had to store our groceries, cooking vessels, dishes, and even the water jar in that room. Since the Master had a weak stomach we also stored the food for his special diet.

The Master did not sleep much at night. When it was still dark outside he would move around the temple garden, and while passing near the nahabat he called: "O Lakshmi, O Lakshmi. Get up. Ask your aunt to get up also. How long will you sleep? It is almost dawn. The crows and cuckoos are about to sing. Chant the name of the Divine Mother."

Sometimes in the winter, when the Master called for me, Mother, lying under her quilt, would whisper: "Keep quiet. He has no sleep in his eyes. It is not the right time to get up, and the birds have not yet started singing. Don't respond." But if the Master didn't get a response, he would pour water under the doorsill, and since we slept on the floor we had to get up without delay. Even so, sometimes our beds got wet.

The Master lost some hair from the front of his head because of excessive heat in his body, and some of his hair and beard turned grey. He did not care to live long, to be an old man. He would say, "I don't want to hear people saying that there is an 'old monk' in Rasmani's temple garden."

"Don't say that," the Mother replied. "You are not old. Do you think you are old enough to leave this world? Moreover, if you live here as an old monk, people will say a 'wise monk' lives in Rasmani's Kali temple."

The Master replied: "Pooh! Who is going to call me a wise monk? Anyhow, I can't bear it if anybody calls me 'old fellow.'"[4]

Yogin-ma recalled: "Holy Mother used to live in the nahabat like a shy bride. She wore a sari with a broad red border. Her hair was black, thick, and long, and she wore a vermilion mark on her forehead. She also wore a necklace, a nose ring, earrings, and bracelets.* Her company gave me immense joy. She liked the way I braided her hair very much, and I was delighted to do it for her."[5]

Once in the early morning Holy Mother went to bathe at the Bakul-tala ghat,** which is near the nahabat. It was still dark, so she did not notice that a crocodile was lying on one of the steps. Fortunately, at the sound of her approach, it slid into the river before she got too close. Holy Mother screamed and ran back to the nahabat. Holy Mother's companion Gauri-ma held her, trying to comfort her, and joked: "It was not a croco-dile, Mother. It was Lord Shiva. He came to touch your feet."

"Set aside your fun," replied Holy Mother. "I am about to die of fear."

"You are the embodiment of fearlessness, Mother. How can you be afraid?" said Gauri-ma.[6]

Holy Mother's Daily Routine

Every day Holy Mother got up at three o'clock in the morning, before other people awoke. After bathing in the Ganges, she spent about an hour and a half in worship and meditation, after which she started cooking for the Master and his devotees. If the disciples were not in Dakshineswar to perform the task, she would rub the Master's body with oil before his bath. Afterwards she would prepare betel rolls for the Master and his devotees.

Generally the Master took his lunch before noon, so when he returned from his bath, Holy Mother carried his food tray to his room and personally watched over his meal. She often diverted his mind with light talk so that he would not fall into samadhi while eating, which frequently happened without warning. At one o'clock, when a nearby factory blew its whistle, Holy Mother took her lunch. After a short rest, she would sit on the steps of the nahabat and dry her hair.

The Master was concerned about Holy Mother's health. He told her, "If a wild bird is kept within a cage day and night, it gets rheumatic." While the temple officials were resting in the early afternoon, the Master often sent Holy Mother to visit some neighbours who lived near the north gate. She returned to the nahabat during evening vespers when no one was around. Then she would light a lamp, burn incense, and sit for meditation. Afterwards she began cooking the evening meal. After feeding the Master

---

*These bracelets were given by Mathur Babu to the Master while he was practising the spiritual discipline of *madhura bhava*.
**This bathing ghat was constructed mainly for the women of Rasmani's family and the women from neighbouring villages.

and his mother, Holy Mother took her own supper and then retired to bed at about 11 o'clock.

M. described how Holy Mother lived in the nahabat:

Sri Ramakrishna's mother used to live in the upper room of the northern nahabat, and Holy Mother lived in the lower room. Holy Mother lived there like a caged bird. She cooked for the Master in a tiny kitchen under the stairs of the nahabat. [*M. pointed to the steps leading to the upper floor of the nahabat.*] Holy Mother would sit here and repeat her mantra as she cooked. As a result of her limited movement, she developed rheumatism that caused suffering all through her life. Her little room was filled with groceries and other things, and sometimes women devotees also stayed there. Oh, what superhuman patience, perseverance, and self-control! Her self-sacrifice and service were incomparable.[7]

One should not think that Holy Mother only suffered; she also experienced spiritual ecstasy in the company of Ramakrishna. She later reminisced: "What a unique man he was! How many minds he illuminated! What unceasing bliss he radiated! Day and night his room echoed and reechoed with laughter, stories, talking, singing, and music. The Master sang, and I listened hour after hour, standing behind the screen of the nahabat. What joyous days we passed through! People poured in day and night, and there was no end to spiritual talk."[8]

Service to the Master

In spiritual life, service to others is vital because it effaces the ego. There is a Hindi saying: *Sevā, bandi, āur adhinatā, aise mili raghurāi*: "Service, worship, and humility are three important disciplines for God-realization." Krishna says in the Gita (4:34): "Learn it by prostration, by inquiry, and by service. The wise, who have seen the Truth, will teach you that Knowledge." Ramakrishna taught his disciples practical Vedanta, that is, to serve human beings as God. According to Vedanta philosophy, Brahman, or God, dwells in all beings. Service to others is the easiest and quickest way to conquer the hearts of others. One can tame even ferocious wild animals with loving care. In Ramakrishna's household in Dakshineswar, Holy Mother took the position of the mother of the house. Disregarding her own health and comfort, she served the Master, his disciples, and his devotees day and night. She demonstrated the ideal of service throughout her life.

Yogin-ma reminisced about how Holy Mother cared for the devotees: "One day Holy Mother was preparing betel rolls in the nahabat, and I was watching her. She prepared some rolls with cardamom and other spices, and other rolls with only lime and betel nut. I asked: 'Mother, will you not add cardamom and spices to all of them? For whom are the good spicy ones and for whom are the ordinary ones?'

"She replied: 'Yogin, the good ones are for the devotees. I have to make them my own by taking special care of them. These ordinary ones are for the Master, as he is already my own.'"[9]

Cooking consumed a great deal of Holy Mother's time and energy. Now and then she received help from a maidservant. During the early days in Dakshineswar, she cooked for only a few people: the Master, his mother, and occasionally some relatives and guests. But from 1880 onward the number of the Master's devotees increased. On the occasion of the Master's birthday, she cooked for as many as 50 or 60 people.

It was not possible for her god-intoxicated husband to buy groceries, nor could Holy Mother perform this task because she was too shy to appear in public. Also, she did not know how to count money. Senior Gopal, who was older even than Ramakrishna, bought groceries. Sometimes Holy Mother sent the maidservant to get something from the local market. The temple manager probably provided staples like rice, dal, and oil from the temple store.

The Master was not indifferent to Holy Mother; he noticed that she was overworked. One day he saw Latu meditating in the Panchavati. On his way to the pine grove, where he went to answer the call of nature, he said to him: "O Neto, the one on whom you are meditating is here now cooking and cleaning the dishes in the nahabat. Do you know that?"* Then he took Latu to Holy Mother and said, "This boy will help you with the housework."[10] From then on, Latu washed dishes, prepared spices, kneaded dough, and did other chores.

Ramakrishna's stomach was very delicate, so he depended on Holy Mother to prepare special meals for him. In July 1884, when Holy Mother went to Kamarpukur to attend Ramlal's wedding, the Master jokingly told Balaram Basu one of the purposes of his marriage:

> The Master (*pointing to Balaram*): "Well, can you tell me why I married? What is the purpose of having a wife? I cannot even take care of the cloth on my body — it just drops off. Why then do I have a wife?"
>
> Balaram smiled and kept quiet.
>
> The Master: "Oh, I understand (*taking a little curry from the plate and showing it to Balaram*) — for this reason I married. Otherwise, who else would

---

*Evidently Ramakrishna meant Holy Mother, whom he regarded as identical with Mother Kali. Latu had been meditating on Kali.

cook for me with such care? (*Balaram and the other devotees laughed.*) Truly speaking, who else would look after my food? They all left today — (*seeing that the devotees did not understand who had left*) along with Ramlal's aunt. Ramlal is going to be married, so everyone left for Kamarpukur today. I watched her departure impassively. It was truly as if someone else had left. Then I grew anxious when I thought about who would cook for me. You see, some kinds of food do not agree with my stomach, nor am I always conscious enough to eat. She [*Holy Mother*] knows what kind of food suits me and makes various preparations accordingly. So I asked myself, who will cook for me?"[11]

Orthodox Hindus consider a woman to be unclean for three days during her monthly period. At that time she cannot cook and perform other household duties. When Holy Mother could not cook for the Master, he got his meals from the kitchen of the Kali temple. But that oily and spicy food did not agree with him. One day when his stomach was upset, he sent for Holy Mother and asked her why she had not prepared his meal. When she explained, the Master said: "Who told you that a woman cannot cook for those three days? You must cook for me as usual. There is nothing wrong with it. Please tell me: what is impure in a person — the skin, the flesh, the bones, the marrow? It is the mind that makes one pure or impure. There is no impurity outside the mind."[12] From then on Holy Mother always cooked for the Master, and he did not suffer from an upset stomach.

The Master was not a big eater; he became nervous if he saw a large quantity of rice on his plate. He refused to eat it for fear of upsetting his stomach. But Holy Mother tricked him by compressing the rice into a small mound. She also boiled down his milk to make the quantity seem smaller. She cooked bitter squash curry; prepared soup with gandal leaf; and made dishes with raw figs, green plantain, eggplant, and other vegetables that the Master liked. Because the Master had no body consciousness, she watched how he ate and rested, and she protected him from disturbance.

A madwoman sometimes came to Dakshineswar and disturbed the Master. One day she acted immodestly, and the Master scolded her sharply. When Holy Mother heard about it, she said to Golap-ma: "See what he has done. If the girl acted foolishly, why didn't he send her to me? Why did he scold her?" Then she sent for the woman and said to her: "My child, if he is annoyed by your presence, don't go to him. Why don't you come to me?"[13] Holy Mother took care of her with love and compassion, thus protecting the Master. Holy Mother later recalled how she handled the temple maidservant who cleaned Ramakrishna's room:

Brinda was by no means an easy woman. A fixed number of luchis [fried bread] were set aside for her refreshment. She would be extremely abusive if that was found wanting. She would say: "Look at these sons of gentlemen! They have eaten my share also. I do not get even a few sweets."

The Master was afraid lest those words should reach the ears of the young devotees. One day, early in the morning, he came to the nahabat and said: "Well, I have given Brinda's luchis to others. Please prepare some for her. Otherwise she will become abusive. One must avoid wicked persons."

As soon as Brinda came I said to her: "Well, Brinda, there is no refreshment for you today. I am just preparing luchis."

She said: "That's all right. Please do not take the trouble. You may give me raw foodstuffs." I gave her flour, butter, potatoes, and other vegetables.[14]

Once when the Master was ill, an ayurvedic doctor from Calcutta named Gangaprasad Sen treated him. The doctor prescribed some medicines that would become ineffective if the patient drank water, so he forbade the Master to drink even a drop. The childlike Master began to ask everyone, "Well, shall I be able to live without water?"

Holy Mother assured him, "Of course, you will be all right without drinking any water."

The Master replied: "Look, you will have to remove water even from the washed pomegranate seeds."

Holy Mother said: "Everything will happen by the grace of Mother Kali. I shall do my best."

He took the medicine and resolved not to drink any water.

Holy Mother recalled:

Every day I gave him three to four seers [1 seer = four cups] of milk to drink — later on even five to six seers. The man who milked the temple cows used to give me milk in large quantities. He would say to me: "If I give all this milk to the temple, the priests will take it home after worship and give it away to anyone and everyone. But if I leave the milk here, the Master will have it." He used to give me up to five or six seers of milk a day. He was a good man, full of devotion. I used to give him sweets. I would boil the milk down to a seer and a half.

The Master would ask me, "How much milk is there?"

I would say, "A seer or a seer and a quarter."

He would remark: "Perhaps more. I see such a thick scum."

One day Golap was there. He asked her, "How much milk is there?" And she told the truth. "Ah! so much milk," he exclaimed, "that is why I get indigestion. Call her, call her." I came in, and he told me what Golap had said about the milk. I pacified him, saying: "Oh! Golap does not know the measurement. How can she know how much the pot contains?"

Another day he asked Golap about the milk and she said in reply, "One full bowl from here and another from the Kali temple." At this the Master got nervous again. He sent for me, and began to ask about the exact measurement of the bowl as to how many *Poas* and *Chataks* it contained. I replied: "I do not know about Poas and Chataks. You will drink milk. Why all these enquiries about measurements? Who knows about all these calculations?"

He was not satisfied. He said: "Can I digest all this milk? I shall get indigestion." Really, that day he did get indigestion. He did not take anything that night, except a little sago water.

Golap said to me afterwards, "Well, Mother, you should have told me about it before. How could I know? His whole evening meal is spoiled." In reply I said to her: "There is no harm in telling a lie about food. Thus I coax him to eat." In this way his health got better and he was almost cured of his illness.[15]

Many years later when Mrs. Sara Bull, an American devotee, asked Holy Mother about her attitude towards Ramakrishna, she replied: "In spiritual matters, absolute obedience; in other things I used my own common sense."[16]

In the early days, when the Holy Mother lived in Dakshineswar, a maid would stay with her in the nahabat at night. One night there was torrential rain and the maid could not come, so the Master asked Holy Mother to sleep in his room so she would not have to be alone. When she arrived, the Master asked: "Where is your jewellery? Bring it here."

Holy Mother replied: "I can't go back now. It will be all right."[17]

This little incident shows the love and concern that Ramakrishna had for his wife, although most of the time he was in an ecstatic state.

In the early days, Holy Mother did not have many companions except some fisherwomen and a maid who stayed with her for a short time. Occasionally she had some women visitors from Calcutta. An elderly woman who had led an immoral life in her youth often visited Holy Mother. Noticing her a few times, the Master asked Holy Mother, "Why do you allow her in the nahabat?" He told her of the woman's past.

She replied: "That may be, but now she talks only about God and spiritual matters."

"But," the Master insisted, "whatever she may say now, she was once a prostitute. Why should you speak to her? Goodness gracious!" Thus he forbade her from even speaking with that woman lest she have an adverse influence on her.[18]

Holy Mother's open-mindedness and compassion emerged with the awakening of motherhood in her. She felt that she was a mother to everyone who came to Ramakrishna, and she acted accordingly. In this aspect of her life she could not bear outside interference. She could not turn away anyone who addressed her as "Mother." One day she was carrying the Master's food to his room. A woman begged her, "Mother, please allow me to carry the tray to the Master." Holy Mother agreed. That woman took the food to the Master's room, placed it before him, and left. Holy Mother sat down to watch him eat, but he could not touch the food. He said to her: "What have you done? Why did you allow her to touch the tray? Don't you know she leads an immoral life? Now how can I eat food she has touched?"

Holy Mother said: "I know all about it. Please eat."

The Master still could not touch the food. At her repeated requests, he said, "Please promise not to allow that woman to carry my food again."

Holy Mother humbly replied: "Master, I can't make any such promise, but I shall try to bring your food myself. If someone addresses me as 'Mother' and asks to carry the tray, I cannot refuse. You must not forget that you are not only my Lord; you are the Lord of all."[19] The Master was pleased with this response and ate his meal.

Golap-ma was a simple and guileless woman who had lost her husband and only daughter, and she came to Ramakrishna for consolation. After a few visits, the Master introduced Golap-ma to Holy Mother, saying: "You should feed this brahmin girl well. Sorrow is assuaged when the stomach is full." The Master knew that when he was gone Holy Mother would need a companion. One day he talked to Holy Mother about Golap-ma: "Keep your eye on this brahmin woman. She will live with you permanently." Golap-ma began to stay with Holy Mother in the nahabat from time to time.

During one of Golap-ma's visits the Master asked her to bring him the food that Holy Mother had cooked at the nahabat. After that she carried his food to his room every day. This meant that Holy Mother could no longer see the Master at mealtimes as she was used to. In addition, in the evenings Golap-ma would spend long hours in the Master's room, and Holy Mother had to wait with Golap-ma's supper, sometimes until 10 o'clock at night. When the Master realized Holy Mother's inconvenience, he asked Golap-ma not to stay in his room so long. But Golap-ma did not understand. She said: "No, no. Mother loves me very much and regards me as her own daughter. She calls me by my first name."[20]

Although Holy Mother was deprived of visiting the Master for some time, she nonetheless allowed others to serve him. She maintained a low profile so that the jealous women who used to visit him would have no chance to criticize her. Some days Holy Mother would see the Master only when he went to the pine grove. The Master was forgetful of the world and his body, yet he was not indifferent to Holy Mother's welfare. He always kept a close watch on her health and comfort. One day, when he learned that she had a headache, he repeatedly asked Ramlal: "Why does she have a headache?"

The Master also kept a watchful eye over the young men who would one day be his monastic disciples. He gave them spiritual instructions and would send them to different areas in the temple garden at night to practise meditation. He generally kept Baburam and Rakhal near him. He even told the Holy Mother how many pieces of *chapati* (unleavened bread) should be given to each disciple: Rakhal six pieces, Latu five, and four each for Senior Gopal and Baburam. Even though Baburam was supposed to have four, Holy Mother would give him six. When the Master came to know about it, he immediately went to the nahabat and complained that her indiscreet affection might hinder Baburam's spiritual development. Holy Mother firmly replied: "Why are you so worried because he had two extra chapatis? I shall look after his future. Please don't make an issue about his food." The Master understood that Holy Mother was exercising her motherly prerogative towards her children.[21]

A student of M.'s named Sarada Prasanna, who later became Swami Trigunatitananda, visited the Master in secret because his family disapproved. Whenever he came, the Master gave this sincere young disciple spiritual instructions, fed him, and sent him to Holy Mother for his carriage fare. As soon as Holy Mother heard that Sarada had come, she would put one anna for the carriage fare on the porch of the nahabat so that he would not have to ask for the money.

Once the Master sent Sarada to Holy Mother for spiritual instructions, calling attention to her infinite power by quoting a Bengali couplet:

Radha's infinite power of maya is beyond description,
Millions of Krishnas and Ramas evolve, abide, and dissolve in it.

Although Sarada was Ramakrishna's disciple, Holy Mother later gave him formal initiation.[22]

Sometimes Narendra and other disciples spent the night with the Master. On these occasions Holy Mother cooked khichuri (rice and dal) especially for Rakhal. One day the Master said to Holy Mother: "Narendra will eat here tonight. Please cook some nice food." She made some chapatis and thin moong dal. After supper the Master asked Narendra, "How was the meal?"

Narendra replied: "Very good. It was like an invalid's diet."

The Master then asked Holy Mother: "Why did you prepare such plain food for him? Please make rich chana dal and thick chapatis for Narendra." Afterwards, Holy Mother cooked rich food for Narendra, which made him happy.[23]

Aghoremani Devi, a great devotee of the Master, was called Gopal-ma because she had visions of baby Krishna. She used to call Ramakrishna "Gopala" because she saw baby Krishna in him. Sometimes she stayed with Holy Mother in the nahabat. She was an extremely orthodox Hindu widow and would not eat food that others had touched. When she came, Holy Mother had to wash the kitchen area so that Gopal-ma could cook her own food.

Devotees often brought sweets and fruits for the Master. Holy Mother would set aside some for him and distribute the rest to the devotees. One day Holy Mother distributed all the sweets. Gopal-ma told her, "My daughter-in-law, you have given away everything and did not keep anything for my Gopala [Ramakrishna]." Holy Mother was embarrassed. Luckily Nistarini Devi came from Calcutta with a basket of sandesh and saved the situation.

No rules or laws can bind a mother's heart. Holy Mother continued to give away things as usual. One day the Master expressed his disapproval, asking her, "How can you successfully run a household, if you give away things like this?" Holy Mother said, "All right," and abruptly left the room. Greatly distressed, Ramakrishna said to Ramlal: "Go at once and placate your aunt. If she gets angry then all my spirituality will come to naught."[24]

Sometimes so many devotees came to Dakshineswar that there was not enough food in stock to feed them all. Holy Mother had some difficulty cooking for large groups of people. One day she asked Senior Gopal to buy a large quantity of vegetables from the market. When the Master saw this, he asked Holy Mother, "Why did you ask for so many vegetables?"

"I have to feed many people," she replied.

The Master objected: "The temple authorities are supposed to supply the groceries. It is not good to spend so much money. Moreover, if you cook for long hours, you will get sick from the heat. You will not have to cook so many dishes anymore. I shall not eat them." The Master did not eat any of the dishes that she made with those vegetables.

Holy Mother wept bitterly, and Ramakrishna consoled her: "Look, I admonished you because you suffer when you cook so many dishes over

the fire twice a day! I have decided that I will not ask you to cook particular dishes anymore. I shall eat what chance may bring. If you have any
desire to cook something for me, please do. Don't ask me about it."[25]

Holy Mother's Training

Ramakrishna trained Holy Mother in social customs as well as in
spiritual practices. It is amazing how he made her a role model for other
women. He used to say: "Women must be active. They should not sit
idle; otherwise useless and injurious thoughts will fill their minds." In
addition to her arduous household duties, Holy Mother had many other
tasks. One day the Master gave her some jute fibre and asked her to plait it
into slings for hanging pots of sweets in his room. She made a pillow with
the left-over fibres. She slept on a hard mat under which she spread some
burlap. Referring to this austere bed later on, she said to her devotees:
"Now I use a soft pillow and a mattress — how different from the hard
bed I slept on at Dakshineswar! But I slept as well then as I do now. I don't
notice any difference."[26]

Ramakrishna considered Rakhal to be his spiritual son. When Rakhal
married, his wife, Vishweshwari, visited Dakshineswar. The Master
looked at her and realized that she represented an auspicious aspect of the
Divine Shakti. He then sent word to Holy Mother to give Vishweshwari
a rupee and unveil her face. This is the traditional ceremony by which a
mother welcomes her daughter-in-law.

Girish Ghosh's friend Kalipada Ghosh was a terrible drunkard. He
refused to give money to his family, instead spending it on wine. His
wife, Vishnupriyangini, was very pure and devout. She went one day
to the Master, seeking some kind of medicine to change her husband's
habits. The Master sent her to Holy Mother, saying: "There is a woman
who lives in the nahabat. She knows all those things. She will give you the
medicine." Holy Mother was then performing her daily worship. She sent
the woman back to the Master, saying: "He knows everything. Please go
to him." He again sent her back to Holy Mother, and this exchange went
on three times. At last, Holy Mother wrote the Master's name on a bel leaf
that had been offered to the Lord and gave it to Kalipada's wife, saying:
"My child, save this in an amulet. Then chant the Lord's name and your
wish will be fulfilled."

After Kalipada's wife had chanted the Lord's name for 12 years, Kalipada
came to visit the Master. As soon as he came, the Master remarked, "This
man has come here after tormenting his wife for 12 years."[27] Kalipada
was transformed and he became a great devotee of the Master.

Gauri-ma regarded Ramakrishna and Holy Mother as her own parents, and she was very free with them. She recognized the Master to be an avatar and believed that he and Chaitanya were the same. One day Ramakrishna was talking to Holy Mother and Gauri-ma in the nahabat, and he started teasing Gauri-ma. He had noticed that she was very fond of Holy Mother, so he asked: "Whom do you love more? Her or me?" Gauri-ma answered with a song:

O Flute Player, Krishna, you are never greater than Radha;
When people are in trouble, they call for you;
But when you are in trouble, your flute sounds the name of Radha.

Holy Mother was very embarrassed, and she squeezed Gauri-ma's hand. The Master laughed and left the room.[28]

Ramakrishna and Holy Mother demonstrated an ideal marriage based on mutual love and respect. Later Holy Mother described the Master's thoughtfulness: "How kind was the Master's behaviour to me! He never spoke a single word that could hurt me. One day at Dakshineswar I carried his food to his room and, thinking I was Lakshmi, he said, 'Shut the door as you go out,' addressing me familiarly as tui.* I replied, 'All right.' When he heard my voice, he was startled and cried out: 'Oh, it is you! I thought it was Lakshmi. Please forgive me for addressing you as *tui.*' I answered, 'What does it matter?'"

The next morning, the Master went to the nahabat and apologized again to Holy Mother: "You see, I couldn't sleep the whole night. I felt very bad for addressing you so disrespectfully."[29] He had no peace until Holy Mother reassured him.

The Master saw all women as manifestations of the Divine Mother, so he was always respectful to them. He taught Holy Mother how to massage his feet, but whenever she did it, he always bowed down to her. Although the Master was a *paramahamsa sannyasin,* a holy man whose mind always dwelt in a higher realm, sometimes he would consult with Holy Mother when making decisions. He said: "Once I wanted to go to a certain place. I asked Ramlal's aunt** about it. She forbade me to go, so I could not."[30]

* In the Bengali language there are three forms of the second personal pronoun. When addressing a revered elder, *apani* is used. To a person of equal rank and age, one says *tumi.* But the familiar form, *tui,* is used only when speaking to juniors or servants. Thus it would have been considered disrespectful had the Master knowingly addressed Holy Mother in this manner.
** According to an old Bengali custom, out of respect, the wife does not call her husband by name; she uses such words as "Aryaputra" or "Thakur." The husband may call his wife by name. Ramakrishna, however, respectfully referred to Holy Mother as "Ramlal's aunt."

During his sadhana, Ramakrishna renounced money, saying, "Money is clay and clay is money."[31] Later, he could not touch it. The temple manager would give the Master's salary to his nephew Hriday, who kept it in a box. Years earlier, when Ramakrishna had taken the borrowed wedding jewellery from the child Sarada, Chandramani had promised her that Ramakrishna would give jewellery to her later. The Master fulfilled that promise when Holy Mother came to Dakshineswar. He instructed Hriday: "See how much money there is in your box. Have a pair of diamond-cut gold bangles made for her."[32] These would have cost 300 rupees at that time. The Master also gave her all the jewellery that Mathur had made for him when he practised madhura bhava, a sadhana in which he saw himself as Radha. He said: "Her name is Sarada. She is Saraswati, the Goddess of Learning. That is why she loves to adorn herself."[33]

Swami Prabhananda provides this information regarding the jewellery that was given to Holy Mother:

Hriday copied on a page in the account book from an old list thus:

"In 1271 B.E. [1864] Sriyukta Kartababu Mahashay [Mathur] asked Sriyukta Bhattacharya Mahashay [Ramakrishna] to make a set of gold jewellery.* This is the copy of that list."

Thereafter the particulars of the jewellery are given: 1 necklace (weighing 3 bharis 4 annas and 2 pai); 1 pair of chokers (weighing 3 bharis and 14 annas); 1 pair lotus earrings (weighing 1 bhari 7½ annas). Some more jewellery were made in a second installment: 1 pair of bell-shaped earrings (weighing 1 bhari 7½ annas: price 22 rupees); other jewellery (2 bharis and 6½ annas). The total weight of the jewellery came to 12½ bharis of gold costing 171 rupees 8 annas and 1 paisa. [1 bhari = 180 grains; 15.43 grains = 1 gram]

On 7 October 1875, it is mentioned in the account book, "An armlet [baju] was bought for the younger aunt [Holy Mother]."

We can safely presume that after Holy Mother's arrival at Dakshineswar, she started wearing this jewellery, and that Sri Ramakrishna was relieved at fulfilling his Mother's promise to little Sarada [at Kamarpukur in 1859]. At that time Chandramani Devi was living at Dakshineswar and this must have made her happy, too.

There is another entry in the account book on 17 March 1881: "The cost of repairing the nose ring of the younger aunt's maidservant is 1 rupee." And again, "The cost of silver jewellery for the younger aunt's maidservant is 2 rupees." So Holy Mother not only wore jewellery herself but also arranged for her maidservant to wear it.[34]

---

*It seems this jewellery was made in 1864 for Sri Ramakrishna when he was practising madhura bhava sadhana.

Swami Prabhananda also supplied this information about the Mother:

We know from the biography of Holy Mother that in 1876, she lived some of the time at the thatched cottage in Dakshineswar which Shambhu Mallick had built for her. Only occasionally did she live in the nahabat. But in 1880-81 she mainly lived in Jayrambati. She led a very simple life, and her needs were few. In June 1876 she bought a sari for 10 annas, a packet of vermilion for 2½ annas, a comb for 5 paisa, a box for 9 annas. Then on 8 November 1876 when she left for Jayrambati, she bought a bottle of coconut oil for 5 annas. It is also recorded that in 1880 two saris were sent to Jayrambati for her from Dakshineswar. Once while staying at Dakshineswar she took 4 annas for personal expenses. On another occasion Holy Mother gave to her maidservant 4 annas for the observance of the Savitrivrata (a vow sometimes taken by married women), 4 annas for a pillow cover, and 4 annas for her household expenses. Thus we get a glimpse of Holy Mother's feeling for others, as also of her lifestyle.[35]

Although the Master led a god-intoxicated life and was often in samadhi, he was extremely practical. Like other men, he was concerned about how his wife would be supported after his death. One day he asked her how much money she needed for her monthly expenses. She told him that five or six rupees should be enough. Evidently this did not satisfy him. He asked again: "How many chapatis do you eat at night?" The shy Holy Mother blushed at the mention of eating. However, when the Master repeatedly asked, she replied, "Five or six." After thinking a while, the Master said: "Then five or six rupees should be enough." He deposited sufficient money to yield that much in interest with Balaram, a wealthy householder disciple. Balaram invested that money and sent Holy Mother 30 rupees every six months after Ramakrishna's passing.[36]

Although Holy Mother was brought up in a rural village and could scarcely read and write, she possessed keen intelligence, strong common sense, and farsightedness. Once a Marwari devotee saw a dirty sheet on the Master's bed. Intending to help with the Master's household expenses, he offered to invest 10,000 rupees in the Master's name, which would be sufficient for the Master's food, clothing, bedding, and other necessities. The moment the Master heard this proposal, he developed a terrible headache. He prayed to Mother Kali tearfully: "Mother, why are you tempting me again at this stage of my life?" The Master refused the devotee's offer. When the devotee insisted, the Master decided to test Holy Mother. He sent for her and said: "Look, a devotee wants me to accept this money, which is utterly impossible for me. Now he wants to leave the gift with you. Why don't you accept it?"

Holy Mother immediately replied: "What are you saying? How can that be? The money must not be accepted. If I take it, it will be as good as your taking it, because even if it is kept with me, the money will be spent for you. People show you respect for your renunciation. You must refuse the gift." Ramakrishna was relieved that Holy Mother passed the test.

Holy Mother said that the Master trained her in all domestic matters, such as how to place a wick in a lamp and how to recognize the character of various family members and deal with them appropriately. He also taught her spiritual disciplines, singing, meditation, samadhi, and even the knowledge of Brahman.

When Holy Mother was living in Dakshineswar, Ramakrishna often asked for her opinion on various matters. Holy Mother would always reply: "Please excuse me. I would rather not answer right now. I shall give you my opinion later."

"Why not now? With whom will you consult?" the Master would insist.

But Holy Mother's reply would invariably be: "Oh, no. Let me think a little and then I shall talk with you about it."

Returning to the nahabat, Holy Mother would pray fervently to the Divine Mother: "Please tell me, Mother, what to say."

In response to her prayers, Holy Mother received the answers to the Master's questions, which she would then share with him.[37]

Spiritual Practices

When divine beings assume a human form, they usually act like ordinary people, although their minds dwell in two planes: the divine and the human. Sometimes they remain absorbed in God-consciousness, and other times they function in the world like the rest of us. They eat, sleep, do their duties, and also practise spiritual disciplines.

Swami Saradananda wrote:

Avatars [Divine Incarnations] do not have even the slightest trace of selfish desire. They have no wish to enjoy sensual pleasures here or hereafter, nor any intention of enjoying infinite bliss by liberating themselves while disregarding the fate of others in the world. The primary object of their quest is to investigate the unknown divine power that has helped them from their birth.

Their compassionate minds are therefore solely absorbed in the question of how they can gain full control over that divine power, ascend to higher and higher planes of consciousness at will, and stay there as long as they want, and then teach that technique to all people so that they too can attain peace. For this reason, the two powerful currents of sadhana and compassion are seen constantly flowing side by side in their lives.[38]

Although the Master had transmitted the results of his sadhana to Holy Mother during the Shodashi Puja, he continued to train her in the practice of spiritual disciplines. To her he was guru, father, mother, companion, husband, and God Himself. Holy Mother witnessed her husband's complete conquest of lust and greed. She learned from him how to become a world teacher.

The divine and the human manifested side by side in Holy Mother's life also. She demonstrated how the active life and the contemplative life can coexist. In the early hours of the morning she was absorbed in samadhi on the veranda of the nahabat. During the day she was busy cooking and serving the Master and others. While the rice or dal was cooking, she would sit on one of the steps leading to the upper floor of the nahabat and repeat her mantra. She later said: "My child, it is a great fortune to have a human birth. One must call on God wholeheartedly. One should practise hard. Is it possible to achieve anything without intense discipline? One should make time for spiritual practices in between household chores."[39]

It is wonderful to visualize Holy Mother sitting on the western veranda of the nahabat, absorbed in deep meditation in the dark hours of early morning. She recalled:

At Dakshineswar I used to get up at three o'clock in the morning and sit in meditation. Often I totally forgot my body and the world. Once on a moonlit night I was repeating the mantra sitting near the steps of the nahabat and the whole area was quiet. Generally when the Master went to the pine grove to answer the call of nature, I would hear the sound of his sandals; but that day I did not hear anything. I was absorbed in deep meditation. In those days I used to wear a red-bordered sari and jewellery. As I meditated, a gentle breeze blew the upper corner of my red-bordered cloth off my back, but I did not know it. The boy Jogin [later Yogananda] was carrying the water pot for the Master and he saw me in that condition. Ah, those were unforgettable days!...Another day while I was in meditation, the maidservant Brinda shoved a brass plate in front of me with a bang. The sound hit me and penetrated as it were into my heart, and I cried out.[40]

Patanjali listed nine obstacles to spiritual life: disease, laziness, doubt, lack of enthusiasm, lethargy, clinging to sense enjoyment, false perception, difficulty attaining concentration, and difficulty maintaining concentration. All seekers face those obstacles to some degree in their spiritual journey, even Holy Mother. She said: "One should shun laziness and practise japa and meditation regularly. Once in Dakshineswar I was unwell and did not get up at three o'clock. I felt lethargic. The next day I got up even later. This happened on several successive days. Gradually I felt that I no longer had the inclination to get up early. At once I realized that it was a trick of the mind and that laziness had possessed me. I then forced myself to get up at the usual time and resumed my previous habit. One cannot succeed in spiritual life without firm determination."[41]

Later, one day Holy Mother said to her niece Nalini: "When I was your age, I worked very hard — and in spite of that, I used to repeat the mantra 100,000 times every day."[42]

When the Master was practising sadhana at Dakshineswar and Holy Mother was in Kamarpukur, she and Lakshmi received initiation with a Shakti mantra from a monk named Swami Purnananda. When Holy Mother later came to Dakshineswar, the Master wrote a mantra on her tongue and initiated her. He asked her to offer that previous mantra at the feet of her Ishta.[43]

He also taught her mantras for different gods and goddesses and transmitted his spiritual experiences to her so that she could conduct her spiritual ministry. Later when Holy Mother initiated her disciples, she told them: "The mantras I give were taught to me by the Master. These are siddha-mantras."[*44]

After receiving her mantra from the Master, Holy Mother told Lakshmi: "The Master wrote a mantra on my tongue. Why don't you go to him and ask for a mantra." When Lakshmi went to the Master, he wrote on her tongue a seed mantra of Radha-Krishna, which was a Vaishnava mantra. When Lakshmi informed him that she had already been initiated with a Shakti mantra, the Master replied: "It does not matter. I gave you the right mantra."[45]

Whenever an opportunity arose, the Master would give spiritual instructions to Holy Mother and Lakshmi. One evening he spoke at length to them about the gopis' love for Krishna. At the end of his talk, he said to Lakshmi: "Discuss what you have heard from me with your aunt tonight. You have seen the cows eating grass in the field during the day-time; at night they chew the cud. Similarly, you should go over with your aunt what you have learnt now. Then you will not forget my words."

Many years later, when someone read *The Gospel of Sri Ramakrishna* to Holy Mother, she said: "The Master used to give me such fine instructions. If only I had known how to write, I would have noted down his words."[46]

---

* Holy Mother means that one can attain God by repeating these mantras.

On another occasion the Master drew a diagram of the six centres of the kundalini on a piece of paper and gave it to Holy Mother. Unfortunately it was lost. She later lamented: "Ah, how could I have known then that so many things would happen in connection with the Master? I lost that diagram of the six centres of the kundalini and could not trace it anywhere."[47]

Once a young woman came from Calcutta. When she was in the nahabat, she was overwhelmed with spiritual emotion and accidentally kicked over and broke the water jar. The all-forgiving Mother was not upset. On the contrary, she asked the Master, "Well, why could I not have ecstasy like her?"

The Master consoled her, saying: "They are city girls. They indulge in excitement and are shameless. They are like one who has one leg on a banyan tree and the other on a bel tree. They chew the entire goat and then swallow it. Why do you want to be like them? You will achieve everything. Please wait. You have a bashful nature. You belong to a higher realm. Compared to you, those women are in a lower state. Have you not heard about the subterranean river*?"[48]

One day Narendra came to Dakshineswar and the Master asked him to sing a song. Narendra tuned the *tanpura* [a stringed instrument] and began to sing:

> Thou art my All in All, O Lord! — the Life of my life, the Essence of essence;
> In the three worlds I have none else but thee to call my own.
> Thou art my peace, my joy, my hope; thou my support, my wealth, my glory;
> Thou my wisdom and my strength.
> Thou art my home, my place of rest; my dearest friend, my next of kin;
> My present and my future, thou; my heaven and my salvation.
> Thou art my scriptures, my commandments; thou art my ever-gracious Guru;
> Thou the Spring of my boundless bliss.
> Thou art the Way, and thou the Goal; thou the Adorable One, O Lord!
> Thou art the Mother tender-hearted; thou the chastising Father;
> Thou the Creator and Protector; thou the Helmsman who dost steer
> My craft across the sea of life.[49]

*According to the Ramayana, when Dasharatha died, Rama, Lakshmana, and Sita were in exile near the shore of the Phalgu River in Gaya. Rama and Lakshmana went to take a bath. Meanwhile Dasharatha appeared to Sita and asked for a pinda, or sacrificial cake. Sita asked him to wait, but he insisted on having a pinda from her and so she offered it to him. When Rama came, Sita told him what had happened, but he did not believe it. The Phalgu River was a witness. Sita requested it to testify, but it remained silent. Then Sita cursed the river: "Henceforth you will go below the sand and flow invisibly."

Above: Yogin-ma (Yogin) and Golap-ma (Golap).
Below: Gopal-ma (Aghoremani) and Gauri-ma (Gauri or Gaurdasi).

The Master went into samadhi as he listened to this song. In the nahabat, Holy Mother and Yogin-ma listened to Narendra's devotional singing and they were greatly moved. Later the Master told Holy Mother: "Let me tell you this: You have heard Narendra's song 'Thou art my All in All, O Lord!' Please meditate on that song for a few days."[50]

A spiritual attitude towards work evolves from "work *and* worship" to "work *as* worship," and finally to "work *is* worship." Holy Mother never felt any difference between work and worship. Despite her heavy household work, she made time for japa and meditation. During her spare time she picked flowers from the garden to make garlands for the image of Mother Kali.

Holy Mother could also sing well. One night she and Lakshmi were singing in low voices, and the Master heard them from outside. The next day he said to Holy Mother: "Last night I heard you singing, and you seemed to be absorbed. That's very good."[51]

The Mahabharata says (3:28:31): "Gentleness conquers the hearts of the cruel as well as the kind. There is nothing in this world that gentleness cannot conquer. So gentleness is a powerful virtue." Holy Mother was an embodiment of gentleness and modesty. Because she lived in the temple garden of Dakshineswar, a public place, the Master always protected her from the gaze of outsiders. That is why there was a bamboo screen around the nahabat. He even forbade his nephew Ramlal to visit the nahabat without a purpose, in order to give Holy Mother privacy. Once Hriday brought prasad from the Radhakanta temple to Holy Mother and Lakshmi and chatted with them for a long time. The Master scolded him: "When you go to the nahabat, return immediately after finishing the errand. Be careful! Do not spend a long time there indulging in jokes and laughter."[52]

A musician named Nilkantha often came to Dakshineswar and sang for the Master. The Master was very fond of his singing, and he knew that Holy Mother and Lakshmi loved to hear kirtan. He therefore told Ramlal: "Please keep the north door of my room open. There will be a current of ecstasy and devotion here, with singing and dancing. They must hear and see; otherwise how will they learn?" As the women stood behind the bamboo screen of the nahabat, they watched the Master sing and dance through a hole in the screen. When he saw the hole, the Master humorously remarked: "O Ramlal, the hole in your aunt's bamboo screen is becoming larger and larger!"[53]

Holy Mother was an eyewitness to the Master's god-intoxicated life. Perhaps he was trying to share with her his divine intoxication, vision, and samadhi. At the same time he was trying to evaluate her understanding of spiritual ecstasy. One day the Master was returning from the Kali temple when Holy Mother was sweeping his room and making his bed. As he walked through the paved courtyard, his eyes were bloodshot and his legs unsteady. He looked like a drunkard. When he entered the room, he touched Holy Mother and asked, "Hello, have I drunk wine?"

Surprised, Holy Mother immediately replied: "No, no, you have not drunk wine."

The Master then asked: "Then why am I tipsy? Why can't I talk properly? Am I drunk?"

"No, no," she assured him. "Why would you be intoxicated like an ordinary drunkard? You are drunk with ecstatic love for the Divine Mother." The Master calmed down and then joyfully replied, "You are right."[54]

In those days in Dakshineswar, many spiritual aspirants would visit the Master and he would introduce the women aspirants to Holy Mother. One day a bhairavi, or Tantric nun, came to Dakshineswar. The Master said to Holy Mother: "Today a bhairavi will come. Please dye a cloth with ochre for her and I shall present it to her." The bhairavi came after worshipping Mother Kali and had a long conversation with the Master. She stayed at Dakshineswar for a few days. She looked after Holy Mother, but she had a hot temper and she was sometimes intimidating. Once she told the Mother: "Keep some rice soaked in water [which has a cooling effect] for me or I will pierce you with this trident." When Holy Mother expressed her fear to the Master, he replied: "Don't be afraid. She is a real bhairavi; that is why her temper is a little hot."[55]

During meditation, Holy Mother would forget time and space, but a desire came to her to experience ecstasies as Gauri-ma did. One day she asked the Master through Lakshmi to fulfill her desire. The Master said in reply: "Why does she wish to have ecstasies? Gauri is a girl from Kalighat with a masculine nature. She can withstand public criticism. It is good for her [Holy Mother] to suppress spiritual emotions." Then quoting a proverb he said: "'A female with a calm and sweet nature develops strength and attains success.' A woman should lead a life of steadiness and humility. Modesty is her religion. If she loses it, people speak ill of her."[56]

All sincere spiritual seekers covet ecstatic moods, spiritual visions, and samadhi. They want to enjoy that blissful state. Holy Mother witnessed the Master's frequent samadhi and the spiritual moods of his devotees, so it is quite natural that she wished to experience samadhi. She knew that the Master had the power to impart samadhi, but he did not encourage outer manifestations of spiritual feelings in Holy Mother. Another day when she complained that she was not having ecstasy, the Master told her: "What will happen if you fall into ecstasy? Your clothes will fall off and you will cut capers. Who will look after your clothes?"[57] During samadhi the Master was completely oblivious of the external world and could not keep his clothes on his body. Moreover, Hriday and the disciples had to support him so that he would not fall.

Yogin-ma recalled:

A few days after I became acquainted with Holy Mother, she said to me: "Please tell the Master that I would like to experience a little spiritual ecstasy. I don't find him alone to speak about this matter myself."

The next day I found the Master seated alone on his cot. I bowed down and informed him of Holy Mother's wish. He listened but remained silent and grave. When he was in a serious mood like that, no one dared talk to him. I sat there silently for a while and then left after bowing down to him. Returning to the nahabat, I found that Holy Mother was performing her daily worship. As I opened the door, I noticed she was laughing ecstatically and she then began to cry profusely. Tears streamed from her eyes. This continued for a while. Then she became still and went into samadhi. I shut the door and came away.

After a long while, when I returned to her room, she asked, "Have you just come from the Master's room?"

I said: "Well, Mother, you say that you do not experience ecstasy!" Abashed, Holy Mother laughed.

Afterwards, from time to time I used to spend the night in Dakshineswar with Holy Mother. One night someone was playing a flute. As Holy Mother listened, she went into an ecstatic mood and began to laugh off and on. I sat on the corner of her bed with great hesitation. I restrained myself from touching her in that state as I was a householder. She regained her normal state after a long time.[58]

Holy Mother later said: "When I lived in Dakshineswar, someone would play the flute at night. I thought it was God playing the flute. That sound would create such an intense longing for God that my mind would merge into samadhi."[59]

One day Holy Mother was meditating when someone loudly called out to her. Her meditation broke and she cried out. The Master rushed to the nahabat when he heard this and gradually Holy Mother became calm. The Master said to others: "When someone is in meditation, one should neither call nor make any noise near that person."[60]

Swami Nikhilananda wrote:

Sarada Devi did not outwardly practise austerities or observe rituals to the extent Sri Ramakrishna did. Her life was one of quiet prayer and meditation, and she never neglected the performance of her daily duties. She appeared to others more like a householder than a recluse or ascetic. Yet the ocean of her spiritual experience was as bottomless as his. This shows that she was not just a saint or a mystic, but, like her husband, a manifestation of Divinity.

Sri Ramakrishna was fully aware of Sarada Devi's future. Referring to her one day, he said to a woman disciple: "She is Saraswati. She has assumed a human body to impart wisdom to men; but she has hidden her celestial beauty lest people, by looking at her, should befoul their minds with sinful thoughts." Both before and after his death, the Master often reminded her of her future role. He gave her detailed instructions about awakening the spiritual power of her future disciples.[61]

The Master trained Holy Mother to reveal the Motherhood of God in this age. Her maternal instinct had already developed when she was very young, and she was endowed with purity and renunciation, love and devotion, unselfishness and compassion. Although she did not have any biological children, she saw all beings as her children and she served them like a loving mother. She later said: "The Master regarded all creatures as manifestations of the Divine Mother. He left me behind to give expression to this Motherhood."[62]

One day Holy Mother carried food to the Master. He was lying on his bed in samadhi, but he looked so devoid of life that Holy Mother began to weep because she thought he had left the body. She had long been worried about his health. Then she remembered he had once said to her that if she ever found him in this state she was just to touch his feet and that would bring him back. So she began to rub his feet. Rakhal and the others heard her weeping and hurried into the room. They also began to rub him vigorously.

This brought the Master back to consciousness. He opened his eyes and asked with surprise what was wrong. When he realized their fears, he smiled and said: "I was in the land of the white people. Their skin is white, their hearts are white and they are simple and sincere. It is a very beautiful country. I think I shall go there."[63]

Holy Mother's Companions in Dakshineswar

A devotee called "Pande's wife" was an elderly woman who was very fond of the Master and the Mother and lived nearby. Sometimes she supplied milk for the Master. Occasionally Holy Mother visited her in the afternoon and carried some cooked food to her. The Mother often told Pande's wife stories of her village. Once she said to her: "People in our part of the country quarrel and fight over their property. They haven't enough patience to settle their matters amicably. The possession of land and property is so temporary, and still they are so proud of their ownership! It is only a play for a few days! This body has a form, but the mind is boundless. It can be expanded like the vast space, but it is bound by maya. People do not know this mystery of maya, so they suffer and inflict suffering on others."[64]

Binodini Dasi, or Brinda (or Brinde), was a maidservant for the Dakshineswar Kali temple. Brinda was a widow with no children, and her home was in Alambazar. She was very faithful to Rani Rasmani and Mathur Nath Biswas, Ramakrishna's first patron. One night during Kali Puja, Mathur's wife, Jagadamba, lost her necklace in the crowd. Fortunately Brinda found the necklace and returned it to Jagadamba. Although she was busy with her duties in the temple, she served Rasmani's family when they visited Dakshineswar.

Mathur and Jagadamba gave Brinda enough money to support her for the rest of her life. She served the Master and the Mother with great devotion. After the Master's passing away, Brinda gave up her work in the Kali temple.

Brinda later recalled:

I helped the Mother with her household work in the nahabat. There were not too many devotees at that time. I accompanied the Mother to the temple and also on her visits to the neighbours. When she went to answer the call of nature at night in the jungle, I escorted her. She was extremely shy and did not talk to the men devotees. Once she had terrible dysentery and frequently went to the bushes, but did not say anything to anyone. Seeing her condition, I told her: "What is this, Mother? Why did you not tell me about your physical condition?" I immediately went to the Master and reported everything. He asked Hriday to call a doctor. Hriday brought a kaviraj [an ayurvedic doctor], and later two more doctors came to treat her. After recovering from her illness, she said to me: "Brinde, you have saved my life. May the Lord bless you." I told her: "Mother, from now on if you are not well, just tell me. Then everything will be taken care of." I served Holy Mother and received her blessings. She loved me very much. When I stayed with her for a long time, the Master teased us: "I see your conversations do not end." Those days were wonderful and joyful. It was all the grace of the Divine Mother.[65]

Panchanani Dasi, who was called "Jadu's mother," was another maidservant for the Dakshineswar temple. She was a young widow who lived in Kamarhati; her son, Jadu, had died at an early age. Her duty was to wash the worship utensils used in the temple. Sometimes she stayed with the Mother at night in the nahabat. When the Master's devotees began to arrive, Jadu's mother helped Holy Mother clean the dishes, pots, and pans. She recalled:

> We belonged to a low caste. My duty was to clean the utensils of the temple. I noticed that many people bowed down to the Master and the Mother, and I had a desire to bow down to the Mother and touch her feet. But she was a brahmin and so I did not dare touch her. But the Mother fulfilled my desire. One day while cutting vegetables, the Mother cut her finger and it was bleeding. As soon as she saw me, she said: "Jadu's mother, my finger has been cut. Please quickly bring a piece of torn cloth and bandage my finger." I found a piece of cloth nearby and bandaged her finger. Then I bowed down and touched her feet. The Mother said, "Your desire is fulfilled now?" I replied, "What do you say, Mother?" She said, "Nothing," and kept quiet. It seems she read my mind and fulfilled my desire.[66]

There was a Muslim community in Dakshineswar and some of its members would come to the Gazi-tala, a Muslim shrine located in the Dakshineswar temple compound. Ramakrishna practised Islamic sadhana there. Jahida Bibi was a poor Muslim woman who had no close relatives, but she raised an orphan boy named Sheikh Khatir, who was a distant relative. She survived by begging for alms. One day she hadn't received anything, so she approached Holy Mother in the nahabat for help. The Mother gave her rice, vegetables, and a cloth. During the Muslim festival, the Mother would send offerings to the Gazi-tala. Holy Mother was fond of the Muslim children who came to the nahabat for sweets.[67]

A group of fishermen lived at Malpara in Dakshineswar near the Deva-mandal ghat. They would sing while catching fish in the Ganges at night, and in the morning they would sell the fish in the market. Their wives would sell fish from door to door. Kshanta Dasi, Patal Dasi, Kshirod Dasi, Narayani Dasi, Padma Dasi, Golapi Dasi, and other women used to sell fish in Dakshineswar, Ariadaha, Kamarhati, and Alambazar. Patal Dasi recalled:

> We used to go in a group to the temple ghat of Dakshineswar to bathe. We then met the Mother in the nahabat and talked to her. I was young then. The whole Panchavati area was full of trees and bushes. In the beginning the Mother inquired about us and later we became very close to her. We talked to her frankly about our homes, husbands, children, in-laws, and even our quarrels with our husbands. Once Kshirod had a fight with her

husband and he pushed her to the ground; as a result one of her teeth was broken. This made the Mother angry and she said: "How badly these men treat their wives! Without women they cannot function, yet they oppress their wives and show their brute force. Kshirod, stop talking to your husband, but do all your household duties. Serve food to your husband but don't show your affection voluntarily. Let him think that everyone in this world is equally valuable." Kshirod followed the Mother's advice and later her husband was remorseful and apologized to her.

Once Mokshada's daughter had a bad fever and the medicine of a kaviraj could not cure her. When the Mother heard about it, she gave an offered flower to Mokshada and instructed her to place it on her daughter's head, which cured her. The Mother asked about what we cooked at home and we learned that she was fond of *sajina* [a kind of vegetable], bitter leaves of the patal plant, and *kamranga* [a kind of sour fruit]. Yashoda would catch small fish and oysters. When the Master was sick in Cossipore, the doctor prescribed oyster soup for him. We knew that the Mother would hurt herself opening the oysters, so we helped her to do that.

Now most of our companions are gone except Golapi and me. Golapi was quite young, so the Mother was fond of her. The Mother gave us sweets and fruits, and invited us to attend kirtan or yatra in the temple. We were illiterate women and had no idea how great she was. But we felt that she was an embodiment of compassion. The Mother also gave us clothes, vermilion, and oil. Once Kshirod was possessed by a spirit. A kaviraj, a sorcerer, and a maulavi all tried but could not give her any relief. Finally, the Mother sent a bottle of oil and asked her to rub it all over her body. This cured her, but Kshirod did not live long. At that time the Charak Fair [the last day of the Bengali year] was held in the fishermen's area. One of us bought a palm leaf fan for the Mother, which made her very happy. She showed our small gift to others. It is not possible to forget the Mother.[68]

These unsophisticated women loved Holy Mother with innocent hearts, and the Mother poured her affection upon them. After the Mother left Dakshineswar, Golapi regularly came to the Ganges for her bath. On her way back home she would carry a jug of water to wash the step of the nahabat where Holy Mother would sit. Shashi Samanta, a son of a temple official, wrote: "One day I asked Golapi why she was washing that place. She replied: 'Sir, the Mother lived here for a long period and blessed us. I wash this spot where she sat. This will do me good for my next life.' I was dumbfounded observing her devotion."[69]

Golapi told two stories about the Mother:

Once my husband was suffering from fever. There was no hope for his life. The ayurvedic doctor said that he was now in the hands of God. He told me to pray to Him. We all began to cry. I was young then. Patal Dasi came and consoled me. That night I was seated near the head of my husband; I was not fully awake or fully asleep. I heard someone say to me, "Touch this flower, offered to Mother Kali, to his head." My dream broke. I did not see anyone around. I was scared to think that my husband would die. In the morning I went to the temple. I entered through the north gate and came near the nahabat. I saw the Mother standing in the veranda with a small bundle in her hand. My goodness! In my dream I had seen a similar bundle. When I bowed down to her, the Mother said: "It is good that you have come. I was waiting for someone from your area who could take this bundle to you. There is a flower offered to Mother Kali in it. Touch it to your husband's head. Let the doctor continue his treatment. There is a piece of rock candy in it also. Make rock candy syrup and give it to your husband." When the Mother handed over the bundle to me, I cried and asked, "Mother, will my husband live?" The Mother replied: "My child, birth and death are not in human hands. God knows everything. Pray to Him." I touched that flower to my husband's head, and he continued taking that ayurvedic medicine. His fever was gone within a few days. From time to time after that the Mother sent some fruits for my husband.[70]

My aunt came from the Midnapore district to see the Kali temple of Dakshineswar and to bathe in the Ganges. One night there was a yatra performance at the Kali temple and I took my aunt there. On our way we stopped at the nahabat, as I had a desire to introduce my aunt to the Mother. When we entered the nahabat veranda, I saw the Mother moaning on the floor. She told me that she was suffering from an excruciating stomachache. There was nobody to look after her. I told her: "Mother, I have brought my aunt to watch the yatra performance in the temple."

"Very good," replied the Mother.

Then we left. I helped my aunt to find a seat in the natmandir to watch the yatra, and I returned to the nahabat. I couldn't find the Mother there. The room was empty. I presumed that she had gone to answer the call of nature. I began to search for her near the bank of the Ganges and found a kerosene lantern at a distance, which gave me the clue that she must be there. I waited for some time and then went to the light. I saw her lying on the ground. I lifted her up and brought her to her room in the nahabat. I asked, "Mother, did you not tell anyone about your condition?"

She replied: "Yes, I did. They gave me some medicine in the afternoon."

Seeing her condition, I didn't go to see the yatra; instead, I stayed with her. When the yatra was over, I took my aunt home. The next day I came to see the Mother and learned that she was feeling a little better. The ayurvedic doctors suggested drinking some juice of *amrul* spinach [an antidote for dysentery]. I collected *amrul* spinach from our garden and took it to her. She took the soup of *thankuni* spinach that I also gave her.

The Mother was very fond of me and she always gave me something when I visited her. Once, she gave me a bottle of oil and told me: "Golapi, when you use this oil your head will remain cool. Anger is very bad. Never lose your temper." It was by the grace of the Mother that I got rid of my bad temper.

When the Master became sick, he left for Calcutta for treatment. The day the Mother left Dakshineswar, we all went to see her off and cried. She consoled us, saying: "You have many friends here. May the Lord keep you well." It was the last time that I saw the Mother. I really had great fortune to come into contact with such a great soul. Now I think of the Mother and wait for the day when she will deliver me.[71]

Despite her uncomfortable living conditions and occasional illnesses, Holy Mother considered her time with the Master in Dakshineswar to be her golden days. Although she had no biological children, she became a true mother to the virtuous and the wicked, the rich and the poor, the literate and the illiterate. Even the weak, neglected, unsophisticated, afflicted, and low-caste women of the Dakshineswar area found a safe refuge in her, and the Mother bound them to her with a cord of motherly love.

7
Holy Mother's
Reminiscences of the Master

He rāmakrishna madhuram tava satcharitram,
  tvat punya nāma madhuram madhuram tvad angam;
Sambhāshanam cha madhuram madhuram cha gānam,
  tat kim nu yanna madhuram bhavati tvadiyam.
— *Sri Ramakrishna Karnamritam by Ottur Bala Bhatta*

O Ramakrishna, your life story is sweet; your holy name is sweet; your divine body is beautiful; your conversation is sweet, and so is your song. O Lord, is there anything in you which is devoid of sweetness?

Memories are precious. One's life will not end if a hand, leg, or eye is lost, but it is disastrous if memory fails. People live on their memories. Joyful memories bring smiles, and sorrowful memories give rise to tears. Some unimportant memories fade from the mind, but the sweet ones remain forever. Holy Mother never forgot the golden period of her life when she stayed with the Master in Dakshineswar. Later, she would recount stories concerning the Master to her disciples and devotees. These incidents depict various facets of Ramakrishna's life and also the mutual love and appreciation they had for each other.

The rest of this chapter consists of Holy Mother's reminiscences as recorded by her disciples on different occasions. These reminiscences were first published in the Bengali book *Sri Sri Mayer Katha* and later translated into English and published in *Ramakrishna As We Saw Him.*

The Source

The Master used to say that his body had come from Gaya. When his mother passed away he asked me to offer *pindam* [funeral cakes] at Gaya. I replied that I was not entitled to perform those rites when the son himself was alive. The Master replied: "No, no, you are entitled to do it. Under

121

Ramakrishna in samadhi at Dakshineswar, February 1884.

no circumstances can I go to Gaya. If I go, do you think it will be possible for me to return?"* I did not want him to go there, so later on I performed the rites at Gaya.

An Ideal Husband

The Master was interested in nothing but God. When I asked him what I should do with the saris, conch shell bracelets, and other things with which he had worshipped me when he performed the Shodashi Puja, he said after a little thought, "Well, you can give them to your mother, but be careful that when presenting the gifts, you don't look upon her as your personal mother but as the Mother of the Universe." I did so. Such was his teaching.

My mother would grieve, "I have married my Sarada to such a crazy husband that she can't enjoy ordinary married life or have any children and hear them call her 'Mother.'" One day the Master heard her and said: "Don't grieve over that, Mother. Your daughter will have so many children, you will see, that her ears will ache at hearing the cry of 'Mother.'" He was quite right. Everything he said has come to pass.

Ramakrishna's Vision and Samadhi

During the years of his sadhana [spiritual practices], the Master would shrink through fear at the sight of various objects of temptation; he shunned all those allurements. One day in the Panchavati he suddenly saw a boy approaching him. Startled, he began to wonder: who is he? Then the Divine Mother explained to him that a cowherd of Vraja would join him as his spiritual son. When Rakhal came, the Master asked, "What is your name?" "Rakhal." ['Rakhal' means cowherd boy.] The Master exclaimed: "Yes, yes, that's right." Rakhal looked exactly like the boy whom the Master had seen in the Panchavati.

One day Hazra said to the Master: "Why do you think so much about Narendra, Rakhal, and the others? Why don't you immerse yourself in the thought of God all the time?" The Master said, "Look, how I become absorbed in God." Saying so, he merged into samadhi. His hair and beard stood on end. He remained in that state for an hour. Ramlal then began to chant the names of various gods and goddesses. Hearing those divine

---

*Tradition has it that Sri Ramakrishna's birth was preceded by a vision his father had at Gaya of Vishnu, who announced that he would be born as his son. Hence, the spiritual association Sri Ramakrishna had with Gaya was likely to overwhelm him if he went there. Gaya is also associated with Buddha and Chaitanya as a turning point in their lives.

names, the Master slowly regained his normal consciousness. After coming down from samadhi, he said to Ramlal: "Just see, when I remain absorbed in God, I lose outer consciousness. That's why I keep my mind in a lower plane thinking of Narendra, Rakhal, and the others." Ramlal said: "Uncle, don't listen to Hazra. Stay in your own mood."[1]

Ramakrishna's Childlike Nature

When the Master was staying at Dakshineswar, Rakhal [Swami Brahmananda] and other devotees were very young. One day Rakhal came to the Master and said that he was very hungry. The Master went to the Ganges and cried out: "O Gaurdasi, come here! My Rakhal is hungry." At that time there was no refreshment stall at Dakshineswar. A little later a boat was seen coming up the Ganges. It anchored at the temple ghat. Balaram Babu,* Gaurdasi, and some other devotees got off the boat with some *rasagollas* [sweet cheese balls]. The Master was very happy and shouted for Rakhal. He said: "Come here. Here are sweets. You said you were hungry."

Rakhal became angry and remarked, "Why are you broadcasting my hunger?"

The Master said: "What is the harm? You are hungry. You want something to eat. What is wrong in speaking about it?" The Master had a childlike nature.

Rakhal's Parents

To please Rakhal's father, the Master would say, "A good apple tree begets only good apples." When Rakhal's father came to Dakshineswar the Master would carefully feed him delicious things. The Master was afraid that he would take the boy away. When Rakhal's stepmother came to Dakshineswar, the Master used to tell Rakhal: "Show her everything. Take good care of her so that she will think her son loves her dearly."

The Red Flower

Once at Dakshineswar a girl named Asha picked a beautiful red flower from a bush that had very dark leaves. As she held the flower she wept and kept saying: "What is this! Why should such a lovely red flower have such dark leaves? O Lord, how strange is your creation!"

When the Master saw her crying, he asked: "What is the matter? Why are you weeping?" She was quite unable to explain but continued to cry until the Master comforted her with many words.

* Balaram Basu. "Babu" is a courtesy title given out of respect.

The Master's Appreciation

One day I made a big garland of seven strands with some jasmine and red flowers [rangan or ixora]. I soaked the garland in water in a stone bowl and the buds quickly turned into full blossoms. I then sent the garland to the Kali temple to adorn the image of the Divine Mother. The ornaments were taken off Kali's body and she was decorated with the garland.

The Master came to the temple. He at once fell into an ecstatic mood seeing the beauty of Kali so enhanced by the flowers. Again and again he said: "Ah! These flowers are nicely set off against the dark complexion of the Divine Mother! Who made the garland?" Someone mentioned me. He said, "Go and bring her to the temple." As I came near the steps I found some of the men devotees there — Balaram Babu, Suren Babu, and others. I felt extremely shy and was anxious to hide. I took shelter behind the maid Brinda, and was about to go up to the temple by the back steps. The Master noticed this and called out: "Don't use those steps. The other day a fisherwoman was climbing those steps and slipped. She had a terrible accident and fractured her bones. Come by these front steps." The devotees heard those words and made room for me. I entered the temple and found the Master singing, his voice trembling with love and devotion.

The Master's Compassion

One day a woman who had been a man's mistress came to the Master and said with repentance: "That man ruined me. Then he robbed me of my money and jewellery." The Master was aware of the innermost contents of people's minds, but still he wanted to hear everything from their lips. He said to the woman: "Is it true? But he used to give us grand talks about devotion." In the end, the woman confessed to him all her sins and was thus released from their evil effects.

God and Mammon

What is there in money, my child? The Master could not touch it. His hand would recoil from it. He said to Ramlal: "This world is illusory. Had I known it to be otherwise, I would have covered your Kamarpukur village with leaves of gold. But I know the world is impermanent. God alone is real."

A Ghost Story

One day the Master went to Beni Pal's garden house [in Sinthi] with Rakhal. He was strolling in the garden when a spirit came to him and said: "Why did you come here? We are being scorched. We cannot endure your presence. Leave this place at once." How could it stand his purity and blazing holiness? The Master walked away with a smile and did not tell anyone about the incident.

Immediately after supper he asked someone to call for a carriage, though it had been previously arranged that he would spend the night there. A carriage was brought and he returned to Dakshineswar that very night. When I heard the sound of the carriage near the gate, I strained my ears and heard the Master speaking with Rakhal. I was startled. I thought: "I do not know if he has taken his supper. If not, where can I get food at this late hour?" I always kept something in store for him, at least farina. He sometimes asked for food at odd hours. But I was quite sure he was not coming back that night and so my store was empty. All the gates of the temple garden were barred and locked. It was one o'clock in the morning.

He clapped his hands and began to repeat the names of God, and after a while someone opened the gate. Meanwhile I was anxiously thinking about what to do in case he was hungry. As he came in he shouted to me: "Don't be anxious about my food. I have finished my supper." Then he narrated to Rakhal the story of the ghost. Rakhal was startled and said: "Dear me! It was really wise of you not to have told me about it at that time. Otherwise my teeth would have been set on edge through fear. Even now I am seized with fear."

The Photograph of Ramakrishna

Several prints were made of the Master's first photograph [in the shrine pose]. The brahmin cook took one of them. The first picture was very dark, just like the image of Kali, so it was given to the brahmin. When he left Dakshineswar for some place — I do not remember where — he gave it to me. I kept the photograph with the pictures of other gods and goddesses and worshipped it. At that time I lived on the ground floor of the nahabat. One day the Master came there, and at the sight of the picture he said, "Hello, what is all this?" Lakshmi and I had been cooking under the staircase. Then I saw the Master take in his hand the bel leaves and flowers kept there for worship and offer them to the photograph. He worshipped the picture. This is the same picture. That brahmin never returned, so the picture remained with me.*

What Did the Master Look Like?

His complexion was like gold, like *harital* [a yellow mineral]. It blended with the colour of the gold amulet that he wore on his arm. When I rubbed

* This picture is now in the shrine of Holy Mother's house, Udbodhan, Calcutta.

him with oil I could clearly see a lustre coming out of his entire body. People looked at him wonderstruck when he went with slow, steady steps to the Ganges to take his bath....When he came out of his room at the temple, people stood in line and said to one another, "Ah, there he goes!" This also happened at Kamarpukur. Men and women looked at him with mouths agape whenever he chanced to come out of his house. One day he went for a walk in the direction of the canal known as Bhutir Khal. The women who had gone there to fetch water stared at him and said, "There goes the Master!" The Master was annoyed and said to Hriday, "Well, Hridu, please put a veil over my head at once."

The Master was fairly stout. Mathur Babu had given him a low wooden seat on which to sit. It was rather wide, but it was not quite big enough to hold him comfortably when he sat cross-legged on it to eat his meals.

I never saw the Master sad. He was joyous in the company of everyone, whether a boy of five or an old man. I never saw him morose, my child. Ah, what happy days those were!

Ramakrishna's Renunciation

Once there was a mistake in the accounts relating to the Master's salary. I asked him to talk to the manager of the temple about it, but he said: "What a shame! Shall I bother myself about accounts?"

Once he said to me: "He who utters the name of God never suffers from any misery. You don't need to worry about it!" These are his very words. Renunciation was his ornament.

You will gain everything if you but take refuge in the Master. Renunciation alone was his splendour. We utter his name and eat and enjoy things because he renounced all. People think that his devotees also must be very great, as he was a man of such complete renunciation.

Ah, me! One day he came to my room in the nahabat. He had no spices in his small bag. He used to chew them now and then. I gave him some to chew there and also handed to him a small amount packed in paper to take to his room. He then left, but instead of going to his room, he went straight to the embankment of the Ganges. He did not see the way, nor was he conscious of it.

He kept repeating, "Mother, shall I drown myself?" I became restless with agony. The river was full to the brim. I was then a young woman and would not leave my room, and I could not see anyone around. Whom could I send to him? At last I found a brahmin belonging to the Kali temple coming in the direction of my room. Through him I called Hriday, who was then eating his meal. He left his plate, ran to the Master, caught hold of him, and brought him back to his room. A moment more and he would have fallen into the Ganges.

Because I put some spices in his hand he could not find his way. A holy man must not lay things by. His renunciation was one hundred percent.

Once a Vaishnava monk came to the Panchavati. At first he showed a great deal of renunciation. But, alas, like a rat he began to gather various things — pots, cups, jars, grain, rice, pulses, and so forth. The Master noticed this and said one day: "Poor thing! This time he is going to be ruined!" He was about to be entangled in the snare of maya. The Master advised him strongly about renunciation, and further, asked him to leave the place. Then he went away.

The Master's Love for His Devotees

Once Balaram's wife was ill. The Master said to me, "Go to Calcutta and visit her."

"How can I go?" I said. "I don't see any carriage or other conveyance here."

The Master replied in an excited voice: "What? Balaram's family is in such trouble and you hesitate to go! You will walk to Calcutta. Go on foot." At last a palanquin was brought and I set out from Dakshineswar. Twice I visited her during her illness. On another occasion I went on foot at night from Shyampukur.

The younger Naren used to visit the Master. He was thin and dark, with pockmarks on his face. The Master was very fond of him. When Patu and Manindra came to see the Master, they were very young, about 10 or 11 years old. Once at the Cossipore garden during the Holi festival [a spring festival associated with Krishna] everybody had gone out to play with *abir* [red powder], but these two would not go. They began to fan the Master, changing hands frequently. They were so young that they could not manage it. They also massaged the Master's legs. The Master had a cough, so his head ached and he needed constant fanning. He kept saying to them: "Go away now. Go downstairs and play with *abir*. Everybody has gone."

But Patu said: "No, sir, we are not going. We are staying here. How can we go away and leave you?"

They refused to go. The Master could not check his tears. He said: "Oh, my dear, they are my Ramlala [the child Ramachandra], here to take care of me. They are mere children, but they will not leave me, even to enjoy themselves!"

The Meaning of the Master's Suffering

At the time of his illness, the Master said that he wanted to eat an amalaki fruit. Durgacharan procured some after searching for three days without eating or sleeping. The Master then asked him to eat his meal, and he himself took some rice so that the food would be prasad. I said to the Master: "You are taking rice quite well. Why, then, should your meal consist only of farina pudding? You should eat rice rather than pudding."

"No, no," he said. "I would rather eat farina during these last days of my life."

It was such unbearable suffering for him to eat even the farina! Every now and then he would throw it up through his nose.

The Master used to say: "I have been suffering for all of you. I have taken upon myself the miseries of the whole world."

The Master suffered because he had taken on himself the sins of Girish [Ghosh].

The Effect of Karma

Karma alone is responsible for our misery and happiness. Even the Master had to suffer from the effects of karma. Once his elder brother was drinking water while he was delirious with fever. The Master snatched the glass out of his hand after he had drunk just a little. The brother became angry and said: "You have stopped me from drinking water. You will also suffer likewise. You will also feel such pain in your throat."

The Master said: "Brother, I did not mean to injure you. You are ill. Water will harm you. That is why I have taken the glass away. Why have you, then, cursed me in this manner?"

His brother replied, weeping: "I do not know, Brother. Those words have come from my mouth. They cannot but bear fruit."

At the time of his illness the Master told me, "I have this ulcer in my throat because of that curse."

I said to him in reply, "How can a person possibly live if such a thing as this can happen to you?"

The Master remarked: "My brother was a righteous man. His words must come true. Can the words of anyone and everyone be thus fulfilled?"

The result of karma is inevitable, but you can lessen its intensity by repeating the name of God. If you were destined to have a wound as wide as a plowshare, you will get a pinprick at least. The effect of karma can be counteracted to a great extent by japa and austerities.

Body and Soul

Everything — husband, wife, even the body — is illusory. These are all shackles of illusion. Unless you can free yourself from these bonds you will never be able to go to the other shore of the world. Even this attachment to the body, the identification of the self with the body, must go. What is this body, my child? It is nothing but three pounds of ashes when it is cremated. Why is there so much vanity about it? However strong or beautiful this body may be, it ends in those three pounds of ashes. And still people are so attached to it. Glory to God!

The Master would say: "Musk forms in the navel of the deer. Fascinated by the smell, the deer run here and there. It does not know where the fragrance comes from. Likewise, God resides in the human body and people do not know it. Therefore they search everywhere for bliss, not knowing that it is already within. God alone is real. All else is false."

Practise, Practise, Practise!

Can one have the vision of God every day? The Master used to say: "Does an angler catch a big carp every day, the moment he sits with his rod? Arranging everything about him, he sits with the rod and concentrates. Once in a while a big carp swallows the hook, but many times he is disappointed. For that reason, don't relax your practices." Do more japa.

Why are you so restless, my child? Why don't you stick with what you have? Always remember, "I have at least a Mother, if none else." Do you remember those words of the Master? He said he would reveal himself to everyone who takes refuge in him. He will reveal himself at least on their last day. He will draw everyone to himself.

"In Every Age I Come Back"

The Master said he would return after 100 years. Meanwhile, for those 100 years, he would live in the hearts of those who love him. The Master said this as he stood on the semicircular veranda in Dakshineswar, pointing towards the northwest. I told him I could not come again. Lakshmi also said she would not come again, even if she were chopped into shreds like tobacco leaves! The Master laughed and said: "How can you avoid coming? Our roots are twined together like the *kalmi* plant [a vine that grows on the surface of a pond]. Pull one stem and the whole clump will come forward."[2]

8
Farewell
to Dakshineswar

Māyām samāshritya karoshi lilām
bhaktān samuddharttum ananta murtih;
He rāmakrishna tvayi bhakti-hine
kripā-katāksham kuru deva nityam.
— A hymn by Swami Abhedananda

O Infinite One, by embracing your divine maya, you play in various ways to redeem your devotees. O Ramakrishna, I am devoid of devotion to you. Lord, please bestow your grace upon me always.

In this transitory world nothing lasts forever. Holy Mother's joyful days in Dakshineswar came to an end in 1885. Ramakrishna's throat began hurting in April of that year. Despite his difficulty with eating and speaking, he continued to teach, though several physicians advised against talking and going into ecstasy. Holy Mother was concerned and began to prepare soft food for him, such as farina pudding.

Years before, Ramakrishna had predicted the time of his passing. Swami Saradananda wrote in *Sri Ramakrishna and His Divine Play*:

Four or five years before his throat disease appeared, he said to Holy Mother: "When you find me accepting food from anyone and everyone, spending nights in Calcutta, and feeding a portion of food first to someone else and afterwards eating what is left — then you will know that the day is near when I will leave this body." Such things began to happen sometime before the Master fell ill. He accepted invitations from various people in Calcutta to visit their homes, where he ate all sorts of food that anyone offered him, except cooked rice. The Master had also stayed some nights at Balaram's house in Calcutta. Before the Master's illness Narendra had been suffering from dyspepsia and did not visit Dakshineswar for many days, thinking that his special diet would not be available there. So early one morning the Master had Narendra brought to Dakshineswar, and he fed him some of the rice and soup that had been cooked for himself. He then ate what was left over. Holy Mother objected to this and wanted to

131

cook fresh food for him, but the Master said: "My mind did not hesitate when I offered the first portion of the food to Narendra. It will not do any harm. You do not need to cook again." Holy Mother later said, "Although the Master tried to reassure me, I was broken-hearted as I remembered his prediction."[1]

One day the Master said to Yogin-ma: "Look, my throat is paining me very much. You know a mantra to cure diseases. Please repeat it and pass your hand over the affected area."

Yogin-ma was at first struck dumb. But then she did just as the Master requested and passed her hand over his throat. Later she went to Holy Mother and asked: "How did the Master know that I received that mantra? I received it long ago from a woman of the Ghoshpara sect because I knew that it would be very useful to me in accomplishing some worldly goals. But eventually I realized that the goal of life is to call on God without any motive, so I renounced it. When I told the Master about myself I did not tell him that I had received a Kartabhaja mantra. I hid that from him because I thought he might not like it. How could he know about it?"

Smiling, Holy Mother replied: "Look, he knows everyone's thoughts and actions. He does not disapprove of anyone for doing something sincerely, with good intentions. Don't be afraid. I also was initiated into that mantra before I came here. When I told him about it, he said, 'There is no harm in your having that mantra, but now you must offer it to your Chosen Deity.'"[2]

The Festival at Panihati

For several years Ramakrishna had attended the famous Vaishnava Festival in Panihati, a few miles north of Dakshineswar. On 26 May 1885, not long after he fell ill, he again attended the festival with 25 devotees from Calcutta. The devotees rented two boats and anchored them at the ghat; another boat was hired for the Master. Holy Mother and the women devotees prepared an early lunch for everyone. When the Master had eaten, Holy Mother requested a woman devotee to ask the Master if she could accompany them. The Master said: "Well, you are all going. She may go if she wishes." When Holy Mother heard this, she said: "Many devotees are going with the Master. It will be very crowded and it will be difficult for me to get off the boat and visit the festival. I shall not go."[3]

Holy Mother fed two or three women devotees who were to accompany the Master and asked them to go in the same boat with him. The Master and the devotees left at ten o'clock in the morning and returned at eight-thirty that night. The Master had sung and danced in ecstasy at the festival, even though it had been raining. He was exhausted.

While having his supper that night, the Master told one of the women devotees about the Panihati festival: "What a crowd! Everyone was watching me because of my bhava samadhi. She [Holy Mother] did the right thing by not going with us. If people had seen her with me, they would have remarked, 'A pair of swans has come.'* She is extremely intelligent."[4] When the Master finished his supper, the women devotees returned to the nahabat and reported to Holy Mother what he had said. Holy Mother said: "From the way he gave me permission this morning, I immediately realized that he was not giving it wholeheartedly. If he were, he would have said, 'Yes, of course she may go.' Instead, he left the matter for me to decide by saying, 'She may go if she wishes.' I then decided that I had better give up the idea of going."[5]

This trip took a toll on the Master's health. The pain in his throat became worse, so the devotees brought several doctors to Dakshineswar. They diagnosed the disease as "clergyman's sore throat."

The Master and Gopal-ma

A couple of months later, in July 1885, Ramakrishna attended the Chariot Festival of Jagannath at Balaram Basu's house in Calcutta. He stayed for two days. On the third day he returned to Dakshineswar with Gopal-ma and other devotees. Balaram's family had given Gopal-ma some clothes, a ladle and other cooking utensils, and some other articles, knowing that she was poor and she needed them. When the Master saw the bundle of gifts in the boat, he became grave and talked about the glory of renunciation. He did not look at or talk to Gopal-ma at all, which broke her heart.

As soon as she reached Dakshineswar, Gopal-ma went to the nahabat to see Holy Mother and said anxiously: "O my child, Gopala [Ramakrishna] is annoyed with me because he has seen this bundle of things. What shall I do? Should I distribute them here instead of taking them home?"

Seeing her in such distress, the compassionate Holy Mother consoled her, saying: "Don't worry, Mother. Let the Master say what he wants. You have no one in the world to help you. You accepted these things because you need them."[6]

Nevertheless, Gopal-ma took a piece of cloth and a few other things

---

*Ramakrishna used the word *hamsa-hamsi*, which means male and female swans. Hamsa also means a soul. Sri Ramakrishna was known as *paramahamsa*, a great soul and an all-renouncing monk.

from the bundle and gave them away. Extremely anxious, she cooked two different curries for the Master and carried the food to him. The omniscient Master saw that she was repentant and said nothing about the matter. He smiled at Gopal-ma and began to talk with her and behave in his usual manner. She was greatly relieved. After feeding the Master, she returned to her home in Kamarhati that afternoon.

God endowed human beings with the power of speech: some people use that power to spread spiritual truths and some indulge in gossip. One day Rakhal's mother-in-law, Shyamasundari, came to Dakshineswar and said to Golap-ma: "The Master is a man of such great renunciation, whereas Holy Mother is adorned with so much jewellery! Does this look proper?"

Golap-ma was a very simple woman and could not keep secrets. She told Holy Mother what Shyamasundari had said about her jewellery. Holy Mother listened silently. When Golap-ma left, she took off all of her jewellery except two bangles. The Master knew nothing of this incident. The next morning Yogin-ma came to Dakshineswar and found Holy Mother wearing only one pair of bangles. Surprised, she asked, "What is the matter, Mother?" Holy Mother told her what Golap-ma had said. Yogin-ma persuaded her to put on earrings and one more piece of jewellery.[7] She never again wore the other jewellery, because just after this incident the Master fell ill.

A short time later, hearing about this commotion over the jewellery the Master said: "What is this? She did not adorn herself with jewellery. It is I who arranged for her to have that jewellery."[8]

The End Approaches

The Master was now preparing to end his divine play in Dakshineswar. One month after the Chariot Festival, he said to Holy Mother: "When you notice that many people accept me as God and show their love and respect for me, then you will know for certain that my time for departure from this world is imminent."[9]

In the last part of August the Master's throat pain grew worse and the devotees could find no remedy. One evening his throat began hemorrhaging. Narendra said to the devotees: "He who has made us all so happy may be leaving us. I have been reading medical books and questioning my doctor friends. They all say that this kind of throat ailment can develop into cancer. This bleeding makes me even more afraid that it is cancer. If so, there is no known cure for it." The next day a few senior devotees visited Dakshineswar to ask that the Master move to Calcutta so that he could be treated more easily by the doctors. He agreed.

There is a saying: "The water is pure that flows; and the monk is pure who moves and wanders." During the 50 years of his life, Ramakrishna lived over a period of 30 years at Dakshineswar, which was the stage for his divine play. He loved Dakshineswar dearly but he had no attachment to it. Ramakrishna left Dakshineswar on 26 September 1885. He stayed at Balaram's house in Baghbazar for seven days, and then on 2 October moved to a house that the devotees rented for him at 55 Shyampukur Street, not far from where Balaram lived. Golap-ma lived in her home, prepared the Master's food there, and the young disciples took responsibility for nursing him.

It was not an easy task to cook for Ramakrishna, who could not eat food touched by impure persons and had an extremely delicate system. The diet of a cancer patient is just as important as medicine. Because Holy Mother had been cooking for the Master a long time, she knew what kinds of food suited him, how much he could eat, and what he liked and disliked. In addition, Holy Mother would sit near the Master while he ate and talk to him so that his mind would remain on the normal plane. If she did not do this, he might go into samadhi and be unable to eat. It was not possible for any disciple or devotee to perform this important duty.

One can imagine the tempest that was blowing in Holy Mother's mind. She was alone in Dakshineswar; moreover, she was deprived of caring for her beloved husband, who was suffering from a fatal disease. Her body was in Dakshineswar but her mind was with the Master in Shyampukur, where she could not go because arrangements had not been made for her. She fortified her heart with hope, faith, and prayers as she patiently waited in her small room in the nahabat, crying to the Divine Mother for help so that she could serve her husband during that critical time.

While Holy Mother was thus passing anxious days at Dakshineswar, Golap-ma thoughtlessly made a cruel remark that hurt her deeply. One day in the course of conversation, Golap-ma said to Yogin-ma: "Yogin, it seems that the Master is annoyed with Mother, so he has gone to Calcutta." As soon as Holy Mother heard about that comment, she burst into tears. She immediately hired a carriage and went to the house in Shyampukur, accompanied by Ramlal. She tearfully asked the Master: "Is it true that you have come here because you are angry with me?"

Ramakrishna replied: "No, not at all. Who told you this?"

"Golap," she responded.

Ramakrishna replied angrily: "Ah, she made you cry with this falsehood! Does she not know who you are? Where is she? Let her come!"

Holy Mother returned to Dakshineswar with her peace of mind

restored. That evening Golap-ma went to see the Master. He scolded her severely and said: "Why did you make her cry with such a baseless story? Don't you know who she is? Go to her right now and beg for her forgiveness or I shall not accept your service anymore."

The next morning Golap-ma walked to Dakshineswar and fell at Holy Mother's feet, saying tearfully: "Mother, the Master is terribly angry with me. I made that statement without thinking. Either chop off my head with a kitchen knife or forgive me." Holy Mother, who could never harbour ill will against anyone, laughed and gently patted Golap-ma's back, saying, "Oh, dear Golap." Holy Mother asked Ramlal to write a note to the Master saying that she had forgiven Golap-ma.[10] Thus the misunderstanding was cleared up and Golap-ma returned to Calcutta to serve the Master.

Holy Mother was then 32 years old. She was an embodiment of patience and fortitude, and she spent her days in prayer and meditation. During her early days in Kamarpukur and Jayrambati, she learned the Bengali alphabet but she had not finished her studies. About this time, a girl from the Mukhopadhyay family came to bathe in the Ganges every day and stayed with Holy Mother at the nahabat for a while. She taught Holy Mother how to read, using the Ramayana and Mahabharata.

A few days after the Master moved to the Shyampukur house, his devotees called in Dr. Mahendralal Sarkar, whom the Master had met years earlier. When the doctor recognized Ramakrishna, he said to the devotees: "I shall treat him to the best of my ability, and to help you in your noble cause I won't accept any payment."[11] Now that the Master's medical care was settled, the devotees grew concerned about his diet, which was vital for restoring his health. They discussed bringing Holy Mother to the Shyampukur house because only she knew the Master's eating habits and what suited his system. They asked the Master to approve this plan. The Master reminded them of her shyness and said: "Can she live here? You had better ask her about it. If she is willing to come after knowing all the facts, let her do so." A messenger was sent to Holy Mother at Dakshineswar.

Holy Mother was waiting for this message. It is wonderful to compare these two incidents: While visiting the Panihati festival, the Master left Holy Mother to make the decision whether to go or not, and she did not go. Regarding Holy Mother moving to Shyampukur, the Master did not order her to go but instead left her to make the decision. Without a second thought, the Mother made the decision to go, and after bowing down to the Divine Mother, left her dear Dakshineswar for Shyampukur to care for her husband.

9

In Shyampukur
and Cossipore

Vidhritya rupam naravat tvayā vai
vijnāpito dharma ihāti guhyah;
He rāmakrishna tvayi bhakti-hine
kripā-katāksham kuru deva nityam.
— *A hymn by Swami Abhedananda*

Truly, O Lord, you have assumed a human form and proclaimed the greatest mystery of religion. O Ramakrishna, I am devoid of devotion to you. Lord, please bestow your grace upon me always.

Ramakrishna performed his divine play in three acts. The first, 1836 to 1852, covers his early life in Kamarpukur. The second, 1852 to 1885, comprises his adult life in Calcutta and nearby Dakshineswar. It was in Dakshineswar that he practised various sadhanas, attained illumination, and began to promulgate his divine mission. The third act, 1885 to 1886, encompasses the last months of his life at Shyampukur in Calcutta and nearby Cossipore, where he brought his divine drama to its close and laid the foundation for the future Ramakrishna Order.

It was probably in the second week of October 1885 that Holy Mother arrived at the house in Shyampukur to care for her ailing husband. She was beside her husband during the bad times as well as the good. Although she lived behind an impregnable veil of modesty, she had learned from the Master how to adapt to time, place, and person. Now she applied those teachings. Holy Mother took responsibility for preparing the Master's meals while she silently prayed for his recovery.

On 10 November 1885, the Master had another hemorrhage and his condition became critical. Holy Mother suggested through Sharat (later Saradananda) that someone should pour cold water on the Master's head and put a wet towel on his abdomen.

During her stay in Shyampukur, Holy Mother went out only once. One evening after cooking for the Master, she walked a mile with Yogin-ma and Golap-ma to see Balaram Basu's wife, who was ill.[1] Balaram's family

Above: House in Shyampukur, Calcutta, where Ramakrishna lived for three months during his cancer treatment in 1885.
Below: Attic room—now a shrine—where Sarada Devi cooked Ramakrishna's meals.

138

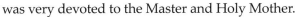

was very devoted to the Master and Holy Mother.

Swami Saradananda presents a vivid picture of the Shyampukur house where the Master stayed for nearly three months. The Master lived upstairs in a spacious room called the parlour:

> To the north and south of the parlour are two verandas, the northern one larger than the southern. To the west of the parlour are two small rooms — one used by devotees who stayed overnight, and the other by Holy Mother for sleeping. The visitors' room has a narrow veranda to the west. A staircase to the roof is at the eastern end of the corridor leading to the Master's room. At the top of those stairs, near the door to the roof, is a covered terrace about six feet by six feet in size. Holy Mother spent her days on that terrace, and there she cooked the special diet needed by the Master.
>
> It is really amazing how for three months she performed her duties, forgetting all personal inconveniences, while living in that single-family house surrounded by men whom she did not know. As there was only one bathroom for all, she would get up before 3:00 a.m., perform her bathroom activities, and then silently go to the terrace on the second floor, without anyone knowing. She would spend the whole day there. When the Master's meals were ready, at regular times she would send word downstairs through Swami Advaitananda or Swami Adbhutananda. At those times the people were asked to leave so she could bring the food and feed the Master, or we [the young disciples] would carry his meals to him if that was more convenient. At noon Holy Mother would eat and rest on the terrace. At 11:00 p.m., when everyone else was asleep, she would leave that room and sleep in her bedroom on the first floor until 2:00 a.m. Fortified by the expectation of the Master's recovery, she spent day after day in that way. She lived there so silently and invisibly that many of the regular visitors did not know that she was living there and carrying the responsibility for the most important service to the Master.[2]

Dr. Sarkar diagnosed the Master's condition as terminal cancer and continued to treat him with homeopathic medicine. The devotees consulted other doctors, but Ramakrishna's illness became worse. At last Dr. Sarkar suggested moving him to a suburb where he could escape the pollution of the congested city. The devotees quickly found a spacious garden house in Cossipore and arranged to move the Master there.

The Move to Cossipore

On 11 December 1885 Ramakrishna left for Cossipore by horse carriage with Holy Mother, Latu, Kali, and Senior Gopal. His other attendants took another carriage with the household belongings and necessities. At

Cossipore garden house, where Ramakrishna lived from 11 December 1885 to 16 August 1886.

the Cossipore garden house Holy Mother could move about more freely.

The two-storey house was in a quiet neighbourhood, and its garden comprised about five acres of land with trees, flowering plants, and two ponds. Ramakrishna occupied a large room on the upper floor, and Holy Mother stayed in a small room on the ground floor near the staircase. Narendra and some young disciples took up residence in two large rooms on the south side of the ground floor so they could attend to the Master around the clock.

Swami Saradananda wrote:

> As before, Holy Mother was in charge of preparing the Master's diet. If the doctor prescribed a special diet for the Master in addition to regular food, Brother Gopal or another devotee would learn how to prepare it, then teach Holy Mother how to do so. Holy Mother could converse freely only with Brother Gopal and one or two others. In addition to preparing the Master's meals, Holy Mother would carry the food tray to him a little before noon and shortly after sunset and wait until he had finished eating. The Master's niece Lakshmi was brought to Cossipore to help the Holy Mother cook and perform other household duties as well as to keep her company. In addition, some of the women devotees who had regularly visited the Master in Dakshineswar began to come to Cossipore and stay with the Holy Mother for a few hours, or sometimes for one or two days. After a week, the whole arrangement worked smoothly.[3]

The Master had a very restricted diet. Dr. Sarkar prescribed soft foods such as farina pudding, rice gruel, milk, barley, vermicelli, *palo* (a custard made from the zedoary root), and also meat and clam stew, so the Master could gain some weight and strength. When asked to prepare clam stew, Holy Mother objected, remarking that clams were living creatures. How could she kill them? Thereupon the Master said: "How is that? I must eat the stew and you can't prepare it?"[4] Holy Mother made up her mind to carry out his wish. While performing her duty, she had a revelation in which she saw that God alone is both the killer and the killed. However, that clam stew stopped oozing of saliva from the Master's mouth. Another day the Master said to her, "Look, I wish to eat potfuls of khichuri."[5]

Householder devotees paid the expenses for the Master and the household, and the Master's young disciples took responsibility for nursing, shopping, and other errands. Holy Mother had to do a great deal of cooking over a wood-burning stove. She also carried the Master's noon and evening meals to him. Later she recalled an accident that happened one day:

While living in the Cossipore garden, I was once climbing the steps, carrying a big bowl of milk. I felt dizzy and fell down, and the entire milk spilt on the ground. One of my ankles was badly sprained. Naren and Baburam ran there and took care of me. There was a great inflammation of the foot. The Master heard of the accident and said to Baburam: "Well, Baburam, it is a nice mess I am in now. Who will cook my food? Who will feed me now?" He was then ill with cancer of the throat and lived mainly on rice gruel and farina pudding. I used to make them and feed him in his room in the upper storey of the house. I had then a ring in my nose. The Master touched his nose and made a sign of the ring by making a circle with his finger, in order to indicate me. He then said, "Baburam, can you put her (*making the sign*) in a basket and carry her on your shoulder to this room?" Naren and Baburam were convulsed with side-splitting laughter. Thus he used to cut jokes with them. After three days the swelling subsided. Then they helped me go upstairs with his meals.[6]

The young disciples renounced their homes and surrendered themselves to Ramakrishna. Holy Mother was the only witness to the following incident, which reveals how the Master protected his disciples. One evening Niranjan and a few other disciples decided to get juice from a date palm near the southern boundary of the garden. The Master was told nothing about this. When it was dark, Niranjan and others walked towards the tree. A short time later, Holy Mother saw the Master running down the steps and through the door. She wondered: "How is this possible? How can one who needs help even to change his position in bed run like an arrow?" She could not believe her eyes, so she went to the Master's room to see if he was there. He was not. In great consternation she looked all around, but could not find him. With much apprehension, Holy Mother returned to her room.

After a while Holy Mother saw the Master running swiftly back to his room. She then went to him and asked about what she had seen. He replied: "Oh, you noticed that. You see, the boys who have come here are all young. They were proceeding merrily to drink the juice of a date palm in the garden. I saw a black cobra there. It is ferocious and it might have bitten them all. The boys did not know this. So I went there by a different route to drive it away. I told the snake, 'Don't come here again.'" The Master asked her not to tell the others about this.[7]

Holy Mother was frightened when she saw that people had begun worshipping the Master as God; she remembered that he had told her that when people regarded him as God, he would soon leave his body. She recalled:

The Master was then lying ill in Cossipore. Some devotees brought some offerings for Mother Kali at Dakshineswar, but instead of offering them to Her, they offered them to the Master's picture there, and then partook of the prasad. On hearing about this, the Master said: "Just see, the devotees did the wrong thing. All these things were brought for the Divine Mother, but they offered everything here [*meaning to himself*]." I was scared to death. I thought: "He is suffering from this dangerous disease. Who knows what will happen? What a calamity! Why did they do such a thing?" Late that night the Master told me: "You will see later that people will worship my picture in their homes. This is surely going to happen. I mean it. I swear it. Don't be worried." This was the only day I heard him using the first-person pronoun with reference to himself. Usually he would speak of himself not as "I" or "me" but would point to himself and say "this case" or "this place."[8]

At Cossipore, the Master distributed ochre cloths and rosaries to 12 disciples and thus laid the foundation for his monastic order. Another day the Master asked his disciples to go out and beg for food. It is an ancient Indian custom for monks to live on alms. Begging helps eradicate the ego and teaches one to depend solely on God. Narendra, Niranjan, Kali, and Hutko Gopal first went to Holy Mother and asked for alms, chanting this hymn to the goddess Annapurna:

> O Parvati, goddess of food, whose store is overflowing,
> O beloved of Shankara, give me alms so that I may attain knowledge and wisdom.

The merciful Holy Mother, taken by surprise, gave them a handful of cooked rice. They then went from door to door begging for food. Some people gave them rice, some gave vegetables or fruit. Some scolded them, saying: "You young fellows, are you not ashamed to dress yourselves as beggars and beg for food? Go away and find a job." Some remarked: "These young men are robbers. They have come to get information so that they can return at night and rob us." The young disciples endured all kinds of verbal abuse. When at last they returned to the Master with their alms, he was very pleased. Holy Mother cooked a portion of the food. After partaking of it, the Master remarked: "Food obtained by begging is pure. It is not defiled by anyone's selfish desire. I am very pleased to eat it today."[9]

Ramakrishna's physical condition deteriorated quickly. It soon became hard for him to swallow any food, and the medicine was ineffective. Holy Mother resolved to seek divine help. She left for the famous Tarakeswar

Shiva temple to get a remedy for her husband's illness. Lakshmi and a maidservant went with her. She later said:

> I went to Tarakeswar and lay down before Lord Shiva without food and drink for two days. I prayed and kept vigil, but got no response from the Lord. On the second night I was startled by a sound — a cracking sound as if someone were striking a heap of baked earthen pots with a heavy cudgel. I got up and this thought came to my mind: "Who is one's husband? Who are one's relatives? For whose sake am I about to commit suicide here?" All my attachments were completely cut asunder, and my mind was filled with renunciation. I groped my way through the darkness to the back of the temple, where the holy water offered to Shiva was accumulated in a basin. I splashed that water on my eyes and face and drank it. My throat was dry because I had been fasting. I felt a little refreshed. The next day I returned to Cossipore. The moment the Master saw me, he asked: "Well, did you get anything?" Then flexing his right thumb, he said: "Nothing is real. Isn't that so?"
>
> One day the Master told me that he had had a dream: An elephant was trying to get medicine for him. It was digging in the earth for his medicine when Gopal woke him up. Then he asked me whether I had any dream.
>
> Once I saw Mother Kali with her neck tilted to one side. I asked Her why She stood that way. She replied: "Because of his having that trouble [pointing to the Master's wound], I too am ill."[10]

Holy Mother described this vision in detail to Yogin-ma, who later related the story:

> When Sri Ramakrishna was gravely ill at the Cossipore garden house, Holy Mother was stricken with grief. One day she had a vision: A black girl with long hair appeared and sat near her. Realizing that it was Mother Kali, she exclaimed: "Oh, you have come!"
>
> "Yes, I have come from Dakshineswar."
>
> After further conversation, Holy Mother observed that the girl's neck was bent to one side. She asked: "What has happened to your neck?"
>
> Mother Kali: "Well, I have a sore throat."
>
> Holy Mother: "My goodness! The Master has a sore throat and you also have it?"
>
> Mother Kali: "That is true."
>
> Thus, Holy Mother was made to understand that the Divine Mother and Sri Ramakrishna were one and the same.[11]

Yogin-ma recalled another incident that took place in Cossipore:

> On another day in Cossipore Holy Mother carried the Master's food to his room, which was on the upper floor. The Master asked her, "Do you know

how to play *asta-kaste?*" [*This is a game similar to English ludo or American Parcheesi.*]

Holy Mother: "No."

Master: "If one can pair two checkers, the opponent cannot take them. Likewise, one should unite oneself with the Chosen Deity and thus be rid of fear. Otherwise, a ripe checker [*one that is near the goal*], if it is still single can be turned back. If a person can move in this world with his Chosen Deity, like a pair of checkers, he will be saved."

As Holy Mother listened she continued with a small household task in which she had been engaged. Suddenly the Master said jokingly, "Are you listening to me or not?" Holy Mother was embarrassed.[12]

In *The Gospel of Sri Ramakrishna*, M. records this for 24 April 1886:

M. came to the garden house accompanied by his wife and a son. The boy was seven years old. It was at the Master's request that he brought his wife, who was almost mad with grief owing to the death of one of her sons.

That day the Master several times allowed M.'s wife the privilege of waiting on him. Her welfare seemed to occupy his attention a great deal. In the evening the Holy Mother came to the Master's room to feed him. M.'s wife accompanied her with a lamp. The Master tenderly asked her many questions about her household. He requested her to come again to the garden house and spend a few days with Holy Mother, not forgetting to ask her to bring her baby daughter. When the Master had finished his meal M.'s wife removed the plates. He chatted with her a few minutes.

About nine o'clock in the evening Sri Ramakrishna was seated in his room with the devotees. He had a garland of flowers around his neck. He told M. that he had requested his wife to spend a few days at the garden house with Holy Mother. His kindness touched M.'s heart.[13]

Yogin-ma was a woman of strong determination. Whatever she undertook she carried through to perfection. After practising spiritual disciplines for some time according to the Master's instructions, she decided that Calcutta was not suitable for such practices. The sacred atmosphere of Vrindaban, she thought, would be better. Ramakrishna was then staying at the Cossipore garden house for his cancer treatment. When Yogin-ma asked his permission to go to Vrindaban, he readily agreed, but he asked her if she had talked to Holy Mother about it. Holy Mother was present and said: "You have said whatever there is to be said. What is there to add?" Nevertheless, the Master told Yogin-ma: "My dear child, go, after obtaining her consent. You will get everything."[14]

Just a few days before the Master passed away, Durgacharan Nag went to see him. As he entered the room he heard the Master ask for an amalaki fruit, which is soothing for the throat. A devotee replied that none were available because they were out of season. But Durgacharan thought that if the word *amalaki* came from the Master's lips, then the fruit must be available somewhere. Without saying anything, he left in search of it. For two days he checked different gardens in the suburbs of Calcutta. On the third day, he appeared before the Master with a few amalaki fruits. The Master was very pleased and said to Holy Mother: "Please prepare a mixed vegetable curry with hot chilis for him. He is from East Bengal, so he loves hot dishes."[15] When the food was served, however, Durgacharan would not touch it. It was his fasting day (*Ekadashi*, i.e., the eleventh day of the moon). So the Master himself touched the food and sanctified it, and Durgacharan took it as prasad. In his exuberant devotion, Durgacharan ate not only the food, but the leaf plate as well. From that time on the devotees were careful when serving Durgacharan prasad on a leaf plate. As soon as he finished his meal, they would snatch away the leaf plate. They even removed seeds and pits from fruits before offering them to him, lest he swallow them.[16]

One day while Holy Mother was cleaning the wound in the Master's throat with a cotton swab, he cried out in pain: "Uh! What are you doing?" Then he withdrew his mind from his body and said: "All right. You are cleaning with a swab. Go ahead."[17] He remained silent. Another day the Master said to Holy Mother: "All sufferings have gone through this body. None of you will have to suffer anymore. I have suffered for everyone in the world."[18]

Ramakrishna was slowly dropping the curtain on his divine play, so he started making arrangements for Holy Mother. One day when his nephew Ramlal came to see him at Cossipore, the Master said to him: "Serve the Divine Mother of Dakshineswar. Then you will not lack anything." He said to Holy Mother: "You will live in Kamarpukur and look after Lakshmi for a while. As the devotees lovingly serve me, they will do the same for you."

He then told Ramlal: "Look after your aunt so that she can live in Kamarpukur."

Ramlal replied in an unconcerned manner: "She can live wherever she wants."

The Master understood that Ramlal was trying to avoid his responsibility. The Master rebuked him, saying: "What is this? Why have you become a man?"[19] In fact, Ramlal never looked after Holy Mother.*

---

*Holy Mother later said: "Trailokya Biswas used to give me seven rupees every month [which Ramakrishna used to receive from the temple authorities]. (*continued*)

Ramakrishna was nearing the ocean of Satchidananda; he began to give his last instructions to Holy Mother:

"Let me tell you something. Do not stretch out your hand to anyone, even for a penny. You will not lack simple food and clothes. If you hold your hand out to anyone, remember, you will sell him your head also. If it is absolutely necessary, you may beg for your food, but never live in anyone else's house. Devotees may welcome you in their houses with great respect and affection, but never allow your own hut in Kamarpukur to fall into disrepair.[20]

"Please stay in Kamarpukur. Grow some spinach and eat that spinach with rice. Chant the name of God."[21]

One day shortly before his death, the Master was gazing intently at Holy Mother. She said: "Tell me what is on your mind."

He pointed to his body and replied in a tone of complaint: "Look here, won't you do anything? Must this do everything?"

"But what can I do?" she protested. "I am a mere woman."

"No, no," the Master insisted. "You will have to do many things."

Another day at Cossipore, Holy Mother carried the Master's food to his room and found him lying in bed with his eyes closed. She said aloud: "Please get up; it is your mealtime." When the Master opened his eyes, he appeared to have returned from a faraway realm. He said to her, in an abstracted mood: "Look at the people of Calcutta; they are like worms squirming in darkness. You must bring light to them. This is not my burden alone. You too shall have to share it."[22]

Ramakrishna promised Holy Mother: "Those who come and take refuge in you, I will come to them during their last moments. I will hold their hands and accompany them."[23]

A few days before the Master passed away, he sent for Holy Mother. He taught her eight mantras, and then said: "These are all siddha mantras [mantras for attaining illumination]. Please teach these mantras to those who come to you for initiation. Those who receive one of these mantras will have the vision of their Chosen Deities during their lifetime or at least at the time of death. Later many people will come to you for initiation. Initiate them with these mantras."[24]

Latu recalled:

I have never seen such an intelligent woman as the Mother. While serving the Master, if any of us were depressed or disappointed, she understood.

(*continued from previous page*) After the Master passed away, Dinu, the cashier, and others conspired to stop the pension. My relatives [Ramlal and others] treated me as an ordinary mortal and joined with them." (*Udbodhan*, 27:11-13)

She would send encouraging words through Jogin to that disciple: "Ask him not to be depressed. The Master's health is better today and the opening of the wound seems outwardly dry." This is how the Mother inspired us.

A day before the Master's passing away, there was a terrible thunderstorm at noon. The Mother and Lakshmi heard a loud crack of thunder and rushed to the Master's room upstairs. Lakshmi was very frightened. Seeing her fearful face, the Master said, "You see, I don't like to see a gloomy, grouchy face." Hearing these words, Lakshmi smiled.[25]

One day towards the end, the Master asked Shashi to call Holy Mother. When she arrived, the Master said: "You see, I do not know why my mind nowadays remains absorbed in Brahman." She understood what the Master meant. He was planning to merge into Brahman. She saw her husband's emaciated body and shed a few silent tears.

The Master's Passing

On 15 August 1886 Holy Mother saw some bad omens. She recalled: "On that day everything was topsy-turvy beginning in the morning. I was cooking khichuri (rice and lentils together) for the Master's disciples and it burnt at the bottom. I served the top portion to them and we ate the bottom portion. After my bath I hung my red-bordered sari outside to dry in the sun and someone stole it. I tried to lift the earthen water jar and it slipped from my hand and broke into pieces."[26]

At the end of the day the Master was seated on his bed reclining on a bolster. He was completely silent. The disciples and devotees were seated around him and their hearts were heavy with sorrow. They thought that the Master had lost his voice and would not speak anymore. Holy Mother and Lakshmi rushed upstairs. As soon as they arrived, the Master said in a feeble voice: "I am glad you are here. I feel as if I am going to a faraway country across water — very far away." Holy Mother burst into tears. The Master consoled her, saying: "Why should you feel troubled? You will live as you are living now. They [referring to Narendra and others] will do for you what they are doing for me. Look after Lakshmi and keep her with you."[27] These were the Master's last words to Holy Mother in his physical body.

That evening the Master was hungry, so Holy Mother made farina pudding. He relished it and ate a good quantity without any discomfort. His attendant washed his mouth and carefully laid him on the bed, stretching his legs and supporting them with pillows. Two attendants fanned him. Suddenly the Master went into samadhi.

It was 1:02 a.m., 16 August 1886. Suddenly a thrill passed through the Master's body, making his hair stand on end. His eyes became fixed on the tip of his nose. His face was lit up with a smile. In a clear voice the Master repeated the name of Kali, his beloved Deity, three times, and then entered into mahasamadhi. When Holy Mother heard the crying upstairs, she rushed up the steps and cried out: "O Mother Kali! What have I done that you have departed, leaving me alone in the world?"* Seeing her weeping, Baburam and Jogin went to her and Golap-ma took her to her room. Afterwards she remained silent.

Holy Mother Leaves Cossipore

The next day Ramakrishna's body was cremated at the Cossipore cremation ground and his ashes were brought to the garden house in a copper urn. The disciples put the urn on the Master's bed and began to consider what to do next. In the evening Holy Mother began to discard her jewellery, following the custom of Hindu widows. As she was about to take off her bangles, Ramakrishna appeared before her, looking as he did before he was stricken with cancer. He took her hand and said: "Am I dead that you are acting like a widow and removing your bangles? I have just moved from one room to another." Holy Mother wore the bangles as long as she lived.

Balaram brought Holy Mother a white borderless sari that is worn by orthodox widows. When he gave the cloth to Golap-ma to hand over to Holy Mother, Golap-ma shuddered at the very sight of it and said: "Good God! Who can give her this white cloth?" When Golap-ma went to Holy Mother, she saw that she had torn off the major part of the wide red borders of her sari. From that day on she always wore a sari with a narrow red border.

The following day Golap-ma told the disciples that the Master had appeared to Holy Mother and had forbidden her to remove her bracelets. The news of what he had said to her reassured them, gave them new strength, and consoled their sorrowful hearts. They cast away their doubts and resolved that they would continue serving the Master as before.

On 18 August 1886, Holy Mother, accompanied by Golap-ma, Lakshmi, and Latu, paid a visit to Dakshineswar. They returned to Cossipore the same evening.

Difficulties soon arose. How would the Cossipore garden house be maintained? What should be done with the Master's ashes? Narendra

---

*Many years later Holy Mother said to a disciple that she always looked upon the Master as Mother Kali.

and the other young disciples wanted to keep the house, but Ram Datta and some other householder disciples, who were bearing the expenses, disagreed. They decided that Holy Mother should move elsewhere, the young disciples should return to their respective homes, and the Master's ashes should be installed at Ram Datta's Kankurgachi garden house. The young disciples were helpless. Narendra tried to keep Holy Mother at Cossipore for a few days longer, so that she could recover somewhat from her grief, but he was unable to do so. As some of the monastic disciples did not want to give all of the Master's relics to Ram Datta, they put a large portion of them into another urn so that they could worship the Master on their own. As this squabble was going on between the young disciples and the householders, Holy Mother said to Golap-ma with a long sigh: "Such a golden person has left us, and now, Golap, they are quarrelling over his ashes!"[28]

The young disciples had no money to buy or rent a house for Holy Mother, so that she could live near the devotees of the Master. But Balaram's home was always open to Holy Mother and the disciples of Ramakrishna. He was truly a blessed soul and all the members of his family were great devotees of the Master. On Saturday, 21 August 1886, Balaram invited Holy Mother to stay in his Calcutta home. Holy Mother must have gone upstairs for one last time and bowed down to the Master's relics that were kept on his bed before she took her bundle of clothes and climbed into the carriage that Balaram* had sent for her that evening. As the carriage neared the garden gate, however, the gatekeeper stopped the driver and demanded the unpaid rent. Narendra was terribly embarrassed and somehow had her released.[29]

Holy Mother later described her mental condition at this time: "The Master's passing away was unbearable for me. I constantly asked myself: 'Such a golden man has left. Why then should I stay in this world?' Life became tasteless and meaningless for me, and I had no desire to talk to anyone.... The Master then appeared to me and said: 'No, you shouldn't leave the world. Please stay. You have many things to do.'"[30] Balaram decided to send Holy Mother on a pilgrimage to give her some peace.

---

*According to Latu, Balaram himself brought the carriage to pick up the Mother.

10
Pilgrimage
(August 1886-August 1887)

Rupam rupavivarjitasya bhavato dhyānena yatkalpitam,
Stutyā anirvachaniyatā akhilaguro durikritā yanmayā;
Vyāpitvancha nirākritam bhagavato yat tirthayātrādinā,
Kshntavyam jagadisha tadvikalatā doshatrayam matkritam.
— *Source unknown*

O Lord, in my meditation, I have attributed form to you who are formless.

O Teacher of the world, by chanting hymns, I have contradicted your indescribable nature.

O Lord, by going on pilgrimage, I have denied your omnipresence.

O Lord of the universe, pray, forgive me for these threefold faults.

I t is said that pilgrims make a place holy. Through their devotion and worship, japa and meditation, prayers and tears, fasting and austerity, vigils and longing, pilgrims sanctify the holy places of the world. The birthplaces of the divine incarnations — Ramachandra's Ayodhya, Krishna's Mathura, Buddha's Lumbini, Christ's Bethlehem, Muhammad's Mecca, Chaitanya's Navadwip, and Ramakrishna's Kamarpukur — have all been sanctified, as have been the places associated with their lives. Moreover, the places where saints and monks lived and practised austerities have become holy. That is why Varanasi and Vrindaban, Hardwar and Rishikesh, Puri and Dwaraka, Madurai and Rameswaram, and other holy places of India have attracted pilgrims throughout the ages.

Visiting holy places for even a short time cuts one's attachment to home and family and enhances one's longing for God. A pilgrim's experience of divine bliss depends upon forgetfulness of the world. Holy Mother wanted to forget her raw grief and the pain of separation from Ramakrishna. Towards the end of his life the Master had said to Holy Mother: "You should visit all those places that it was not possible for this [*meaning himself*] to visit."

Sarada Devi at Sister Nivedita Girls' School in Calcutta, 1905.

Two weeks after the Master's death, on 30 August 1886, Holy Mother left for pilgrimage, accompanied by Golap-ma, Lakshmi, Nikunja Devi (M.'s wife), Jogin, Latu, and Kali. The party travelled by train, first stopping at Vaidyanath Dham in Deoghar, Jharkhand.

In Vaidyanath Dham resides one of the 12 *jyotirlingams** of Shiva. In 1868 Ramakrishna visited this holy place. On her pilgrimage in August 1886, Holy Mother also worshipped the deity there, and then the next day the party left for Varanasi. They spent nearly 10 days in Varanasi, where they visited the temples to Vishwanath Shiva, Mother Annapurna, and other important deities. Holy Mother and her companions also climbed the high tower of Benimadhav to look upon the golden city of Varanasi.

One evening Holy Mother attended the vesper service of Lord Vishwanath and went into ecstasy inside the temple. She was hardly conscious of the world and had difficulty returning home. Later she said: "It was the Master who brought me home, holding me by the hand."

Latu recalled the incident: "One evening we attended the vesper service at the Vishwanath temple. On the way back to our residence, Mother was with a heavy step, yet walking rapidly — so rapidly, in fact, that it was difficult to keep up with her. As soon as we reached the house, she lay down on her cot and did not speak. Apparently she got up at midnight and sat to meditate. In the morning Golap-ma called her again and again, yet she could not be roused from meditation."[1]

Another day Holy Mother and others went to pay their respects to Swami Bhaskarananda, a well-known holy man who remained completely naked as part of his spiritual practices. When he met them, the swami said: "Don't feel nervous, mothers. You are all manifestations of the Divine Mother of the Universe. Why should you be embarrassed? Is it because of my genital organ? Why, it is like one of my fingers."

Holy Mother said later: "What a calm, great soul! He always remains naked, in winter and summer alike."[2]

When Holy Mother was in Varanasi, a nun from Nepal would sometimes visit her. This nun knew various rituals and spiritual practices.

---

*As per Shiva Mahapurana, once Brahma (the Hindu God of creation) and Vishnu (the Hindu God of Preservation) had an argument in terms of supremacy of creation. To test them, Shiva pierced the three worlds as a huge endless pillar of light, the *jyotirlinga*. Vishnu and Brahma went separately downwards and upwards respectively to find the end of the light in either direction. Brahma lied that he found the end, while Vishnu conceded his defeat. Shiva appeared as a second pillar of light and cursed Brahma that he would have no offerings in ceremonies while Vishnu would be worshipped till the end of eternity. The *jyotirlinga* is the supreme undivided reality, out of which Shiva appears in part.

Above: Sarada Devi's rooftop room at Kalababu's Kunja in Vrindaban.
Below: The walking trail for the pilgrims on the bank of the Jamuna near
Kalababu's Kunja.

154

She recognized Holy Mother's mental condition and suggested that she practise *panchatapa** to relieve her anguish. This nun also prayed to Holy Mother to send one of her disciples to her during her last moments. Holy Mother never saw the nun again, but that prayer was answered years later. (*See Chapter 33.*)

After visiting Varanasi, some of Holy Mother's companions suggested that the party go to Prayag and bathe in the confluence of the Ganges and the Jamuna. Holy Mother wanted to visit Ayodhya next, so instead they all took the train to the birthplace of Ramachandra. They stayed there for one day and visited the important temples and the Saraju River. After bathing in the Saraju River, the Mother cooked food and fed her companions. Jogin commented: "What great fortune! Today Mother Sita has fed us in this holy place of Ayodhya."[3]

The next day the party left for Vrindaban. In the train on the way Holy Mother had a vision of Ramakrishna. She was then wearing the Master's gold amulet on one of her arms. In the train she lay down with her arm on the window sill, leaving the amulet visible. The Master suddenly appeared and said to her through the window: "Hello, why are you wearing the amulet that way? A thief could easily snatch it."[4] Immediately she got up, removed the amulet from her arm, and put it in a small tin trunk where she kept the Master's photo. She realized that the Master was always with her, protecting her. She never wore that amulet again. Instead, she worshipped it every day, and later she gave it to Belur Math for the Master's shrine.

The train stopped at Mathura. From there the pilgrims went to Kalababu's Kunja, or grove, in Vrindaban. This estate belonged to Balaram's family. There was a gorgeous mansion with a Krishna shrine in the grove, which was situated on the bank of the Jamuna River.

Vrindaban is a holy place, the playground of Krishna's childhood. There Holy Mother met Yogin-ma, who had left Calcutta shortly before the Master's passing away. On seeing her, Holy Mother's grief welled up and she embraced her, saying, "Oh, Yogin!" Both wept profusely. At that time Holy Mother wept often. One night the Master appeared before her and said: "Why are you crying so much? Where have I gone? It is just a change from one room to another — isn't that so?"[5] Over time, repeated visions of the Master assuaged Holy Mother's intense grief.

---

* Panchatapa is an austerity involving five fires. The spiritual aspirant sits surrounded by four fires under the blazing sun (the fifth fire) and repeats a mantra from dawn to dusk. Some years later, in 1893, Holy Mother performed this sadhana at Nilambar Mukherjee's garden house in Belur. (*See details in Chapter 12.*)

Ramakrishna had visited Vrindaban in 1868 and experienced visions relating to various episodes of Krishna's life. At Vrindaban, Holy Mother was often in the mood of Radha and experienced spiritual ecstasy. Just as the gopis — the cowherd girls of Vrindaban — had searched for Krishna in the groves of Vrindaban, Holy Mother wandered alone to the bank of the Jamuna as if searching for her beloved Lord. Her companions would find her and bring her back to their residence. Later she said to a devotee: "I am Radha."

Orthodox Vaishnavas circumambulate Vrindaban in bare feet and visit the spots connected with Krishna's life. Holy Mother and her party followed this tradition. It took them 15 days. Holy Mother closely observed the banks of the Jamuna, the groves, trees, temples, mendicants, and the scenic views of Vraja. From time to time she stopped and could not go on. Yogin-ma guessed that Holy Mother was having divine visions. When she asked Holy Mother why she had stopped, Holy Mother kept quiet and only said, "Let us go."[6]

Swami Yogananda left a vivid account of Holy Mother's stay in Vrindaban:

> We saw how Holy Mother, even in the midst of her intense grief at the passing away of the Master, fully realized his divine grace and presence at all times. We thought of ourselves as helpless orphans, but Holy Mother's love became our anchor.
>
> At Vrindaban Holy Mother had many spiritual experiences. One day her women companions found her absorbed in deep samadhi. They uttered the name of the Lord in her ears and tried to bring her mind down. I repeated the name of Sri Ramakrishna with all my strength; at that, the Mother seemed to return to the ordinary sense plane. During such periods of ecstasy, her manner of speech, her voice, her way of taking food, her way of walking, and her general behaviour were exactly like those of the Master. We have heard that in deep meditation the worshipper and the worshipped become one. The scriptures mention a spiritual state known as *tadatmya-bhava* — being at one with God. We have read in the Bhagavata how the gopis, unable to bear separation from Krishna, became so deeply absorbed in the thought of him that for the moment they forgot their own individualities and behaved as though they were Krishna. In the same manner Holy Mother, too, forgot her own separate existence and acted just like the Master, feeling her oneness with him. When I asked her some complex questions about spiritual matters shortly after her states of samadhi, she replied from a god-intoxicated mood, very much like Sri Ramakrishna; that is, in the same manner characteristic of the Master, even using his same easy style of expression with metaphors and parables.

We all were surprised to see the spirit of Sri Ramakrishna united with hers. It was unique. We then realized that the Master and the Mother were one in essence, though appearing in separate forms. Is it not said in the scriptures: "Lord, thou art man, thou art woman"? The Master told me many times that there was no difference between him and the Mother.

On one occasion at Kalababu's grove, Holy Mother passed nearly two days in a superconscious state. A great transformation came over Holy Mother after that experience. Henceforward she was seen to remain always immersed in bliss. All her sorrow, grief, and feeling of separation from the Master vanished and a serene, blissful mood took their place. She sometimes behaved like a simple, innocent girl. Sometimes she expressed an eagerness to visit the various temples of Vrindaban for *darshan* [to see the deity] or to visit holy spots on the banks of the Jamuna associated with the divine sport of Krishna and the gopis. She was then in such a blissful state of mind that at times her yearning for Krishna's presence and her utterance of his name with intense love reminded us of Radha. I have heard from her women companions that the Mother at times spoke frankly of herself as Radha. She passed her time in constant meditation and japam and often went into ecstasy, remaining forgetful of herself for hours together.[7]

In contrast to her many years of confinement in Dakshineswar, Shyampukur, and Cossipore, Holy Mother moved freely around the temple city like a happy girl. She took long walks with Lakshmi, Jogin, or Latu on the sandy banks of the Jamuna. She often went from one temple to another and attended worship or vesper services. One day she saw a corpse decorated with flowers and garlands being carried to the cremation ground. Yogin-ma recalled: "When she saw that funeral procession, Holy Mother remarked: 'See, how blessed this person is to die in holy Vrindaban! I came here to die but haven't had even a trace of fever. And yet how old I am! I have seen my father and my husband's elder brother, both of whom died long ago.' We laughed and said: 'Indeed, you have seen your father! Tell us, who does not see one's father?' In those days she talked like a child."[8]

One day Holy Mother went to visit the Radharaman temple in Vrindaban, which is dedicated to Krishna. In a vision she saw Nistarini Devi, a devotee of the Master, fanning the deity with a *chamara* [a yak's tail]. After returning to her residence, she said to Yogin-ma: "Yogin, Navagopal's wife is very pure. I saw her fanning the deity."

Holy Mother later related the following incident concerning Golap-ma that occurred when they were in Vrindaban: "Our Golap's mind is perfectly pure. In Madhavji's [Krishna's] temple at Vrindaban somebody's baby had soiled the floor. Everyone remarked about it, but no one made a move to clean up the spot. When Golap noticed this, she tore a strip from her fine cloth and cleaned the spot with it. The other women said, 'Since she is cleaning it up, it must have been her baby.' I said to myself, 'Listen to what they say, O Madhavji!' Some others said: 'No, these are holy women. They are doing it for the sake of others.'"[9]

Holy Mother recalled: "In Vrindaban, Yogin and I used to repeat the mantra for long hours with great joy. Flies would sit on our eyes and lips and make sores, but we were not aware of it. One day I prayed to Radharaman: 'Lord, please take away my faultfinding nature. May I never see other people's blemishes.'"[10]

On another occasion the Mother said: "Formerly I too used to notice others' faults. Then I prayed to the Master and through his grace got rid of this habit. It is human nature to see defects. You should learn to appreciate virtues. Man is no doubt liable to err, but you must not take notice. If you constantly find fault with others, you will see fault alone."[11]

At Ramakrishna's command, Holy Mother began her spiritual ministry there in Vrindaban. One day the Master appeared and asked her to initiate Jogin. She was a little perplexed and embarrassed. She thought: "What is this? What will people think? Everyone will comment that Mother has started to make disciples." She ignored the vision, considering it to be a product of her imagination. But the Master appeared again over the next two days. On the third day the Master said: "I have not initiated him. You must initiate him." He even told her the mantra to give.

Holy Mother protested: "I do not even speak to Jogin. How can I initiate him?" The Master asked her to speak to him through Yogin-ma. Yogin-ma learned from Jogin that the Master had not given him a mantra. The Master had also appeared to Jogin and asked him to receive a mantra from Holy Mother, but he could not bring himself to approach her. When Holy Mother realized that the Master had instructed both of them in this manner, she decided to give initiation to Jogin.[12]

Yogin-ma recalled the initiation: "Holy Mother performed worship in front of the picture and the casket that contains the Master's relics. Afterwards she called Jogin and asked him to sit near her. While performing the worship, Holy Mother went into ecstasy and in that state she gave initiation. She repeated the mantra so loudly that I heard her from the adjacent room."[13] Thus Jogin became Holy Mother's first disciple. This was the beginning of a new chapter in her life.

Holy Mother loved the disciples of the Master as her own children. At

Vrindaban there were no fixed times for Latu's meals. He would come at odd hours to Holy Mother or her companions and ask for something to eat. Moreover, he would sometimes share his food with the monkeys, which annoyed the ladies. But Holy Mother knew his childlike nature and asked Lakshmi and Golap-ma not to scold him. She herself served him. She asked her companions to keep Latu's meals well covered in a certain place so that he might come at any time and take his meals when he liked. Once he vanished for three days and Holy Mother was terribly anxious. Then suddenly he reappeared. When Holy Mother asked him where he had been, he smiled and said, "On the bank of the Jamuna." Then like a child he said to Holy Mother: "I am extremely hungry. Please give me something to eat." She immediately brought some food. He ate it, and again disappeared. Holy Mother remarked: "Latu is strange indeed!"[14]

Latu recalled: "While staying at Vrindaban, Holy Mother would worship the picture of the Master with flowers and other items. She carried with her a tiny, round casket containing a bit of the Master's relics. After worshipping his photograph, she used to touch this casket to her forehead and then with great reverence put it back in its place. One day she touched it to our heads also.

"Holy Mother was very fond of hearing kirtan. Accompanied by Lakshmi and me, she would now and then go to Bhagavanji's Ashrama to hear the devotional songs to Krishna."[15]

After a month at Vrindaban, Nikunja Devi contracted malaria, so Holy Mother sent her back to Calcutta with Kali. In February 1887 Holy Mother heard that Ram Datta's daughter had died in a fire, so she sent Latu to him. (Latu had previously worked for him.) During her stay in Vrindaban, Holy Mother learned that the Dakshineswar temple authorities had discontinued her pension of seven rupees per month. She remarked: "They have stopped my pension. It is all right. Such a golden Master has gone. What would I do with money?"[16]

Towards the end of their stay in Vrindaban, Holy Mother, Lakshmi, Yogin-ma, Golap-ma, and Jogin went to Hardwar, where the Ganges descends from a high glacier in the Himalayas and enters the plains of India. In the train on the way, Jogin was suddenly stricken with a high fever. While he was unconscious, a terrible form of a deity appeared before him and said: "I would have put an end to your life, but I am helpless. On the order of your guru, Paramahamsa Deva, I am leaving you. However, you must offer some *rasagollas* [juicy cheese balls] to this woman." The figure pointed to a goddess wearing a red sari. The next morning Jogin's fever subsided.

The pilgrims stayed for a few days at Hardwar, where many mendicants practised austerities. Holy Mother bathed in the Brahma-kunda and consigned some of the Master's hair and nail clippings to the sacred river. She visited all the important holy temples, then climbed to the top of the Chandi Hill, where she worshipped the Divine Mother. After that, the party went to Jaipur in Rajasthan to visit the famous Govinda temple. While visiting the temples, Jogin saw a goddess with a red sari whom he recognized as the same deity he had seen during his fever. She was Shitala, the goddess of disease. Jogin bought a half-rupee worth of rasagollas from a nearby shop and offered them to the goddess.

From Jaipur, the party visited the Brahma temple in Pushkar, an ancient holy place in western India. Pilgrims bathe in Pushkar Lake, which is surrounded by hills on three sides. One of the hills is named after Savitri, the wife of Brahma. Holy Mother climbed up that 750-foot hill to worship Mother Savitri. Afterwards she and her party returned to Vrindaban.

Ordinary people torment themselves with grief when their dearest ones depart from this world, but the wise know that after union comes separation, and after life, death. Of course, in the beginning Holy Mother felt grief like other human beings, but she quickly got hold of her emotions and anchored her lifeboat to the eternal Godhead. Yet she badly needed this year-long pilgrimage and period of sadhana, which relieved her grief to a great extent. Repeated visions of and directions from the Master also reassured her, and she slowly began to fulfill his mission.

Finally, Holy Mother decided to return to Calcutta. On the way she and her companions stopped at Prayag in Allahabad, the confluence of the Ganges and the Jamuna Rivers. She bathed in that holy confluence and offered some of Ramakrishna's hair that she had been carrying with her. She later described the incident: "Is the Master's hair a mere trifle? After his passing away I carried his hair to Prayag to offer it at the confluence of the sacred rivers. The water was still. As I held the hair in my hand suddenly a wave rose and carried it away. The spot, already sacred, took the hair from my hand in order to increase its sanctity."[17]

The party returned to Calcutta in August 1887.

11
Ordeals
in Kamarpukur

Vipadah santu nah shashvat tatra tatra jagadguro;
Bhavato darshanam yatsyād apunarbhava-darshanam.
   —*Kunti's prayer to Krishna*

O Krishna, the supreme teacher of the world, let calamities always overtake us, because we will then have thy sight, which prevents rebirth.

Time has the power to heal many things. Holy Mother's grief subsided to a great extent during her year of pilgrimage and association with holy people. On 31 August 1887 she returned to Calcutta, where she stayed at Balaram's house for two weeks before leaving for Kamarpukur.

Holy Mother's biographers have struggled to follow the chronology of her life after her pilgrimage because there are not sufficient records for the years 1887 to 1920. She led a private life beyond the gaze of the public. We shall divide this period of 33 years into three periods: 1887-1898, for which no detailed information is available; 1898-1909, during which Holy Mother began her spiritual ministry; and 1909-1920, when she lived in Calcutta and Jayrambati and her ministry reached fruition.

During the first period (1887-1898), Holy Mother frequently travelled between Calcutta and Kamarpukur-Jayrambati; in addition she visited some holy places. Few details are available for this period partly because the monastic disciples of the Master were absorbed in austerities in various places, although they had a modest monastery in Baranagore.

Swami Vivekananda returned from the West in 1897 and established the Ramakrishna Math at Belur in 1898. Holy Mother began her spiritual ministry then in earnest. During the second period (1898-1909), she lived sometimes in Jayrambati with her brothers and sometimes in different rented places in Calcutta and other areas. She did not have any permanent dwelling place although she had inherited a small thatched hut in Kamarpukur. In 1909 Swami Saradananda built houses for Holy Mother

Above: Ramakrishna's family shrine room (at left) and his cottage (at right) in
Kamarpukur.
Below: Interior view of Ramakrishna's room, where Sarada Devi lived.

162

in Calcutta and Jayrambati so that she could live free from anxiety and devote herself to teaching her devotees.

During the third period (1909-1920), Holy Mother's spiritual ministry reached its culmination. She travelled to some important places of southern and northern India, and initiated many seekers of God. Most of her teachings and conversations were recorded in this period.

Return to Kamarpukur

Before leaving Balaram's house for Kamarpukur, Holy Mother visited Dakshineswar. She bowed down to Mother Kali, Krishna, and Shiva and prayed for their blessings. She also went to the nahabat, her old dwelling place, and to the Master's room. Sweet memories of the Master arose and she remembered his advice: "Look, don't extend your hand to anyone for a penny. You will never lack ordinary food and plain clothing. If you ask for money from anyone, your head will be sold to that person. It is better to get food from someone than to live with that person. Some devotees may lovingly offer their homes for you to live in, but never give up your cottage in Kamarpukur. Stay in Kamarpukur. Grow some spinach. Eat that spinach with rice and repeat Hari's name."[1]

In the middle of September 1887, Holy Mother left for Kamarpukur with Jogin and Golap-ma. They went by train to Burdwan and then began to walk the remaining 30 miles because they could not afford to hire a bullock cart. They crossed 16 miles and reached Uchalan. Holy Mother was exhausted and hungry, so they bought some rice and lentils from a roadside inn, and Golap-ma cooked khichuri for her. After eating, Mother exclaimed: "Golap, what nectar you have prepared!" They continued walking and finally reached Kamarpukur. Jogin stayed for three days and then joined his brother monks at the Baranagore Math. Golap-ma returned to Calcutta after spending a month with Holy Mother.

Ramakrishna's family home in Kamarpukur faces south and consists of three thatched huts with mud floors and mud walls, plus another small thatched hut that was the family shrine. (The shrine has since been replaced by a concrete structure.) The hut on the east was the parlour, the middle one belonged to Rameswar (who had passed away in 1873) and his family, and the hut on the west belonged to Ramakrishna. This hut has one door and one window; it is 12'10" by 8'10". To the south of the Master's hut there is the family shrine, where Kshudiram, Ramakrishna's father, installed the goddess Shitala, Raghuvir Ramachandra, and Rameswar Shiva. Holy Mother later mentioned that Mother Shitala was the original family deity in Kamarpukur and that her father-in-law had seen Mother Shitala in a vision, in the form of a little girl with a red sari sweeping away all evils with a broom, sprinkling water from the earthen pot with a mango-twig, and giving peace to all beings. Kshudiram used to offer khichuri to Raghuvir Ramachandra occasionally because Raghuvir belonged to the western part of India.[2] Holy Mother took shelter in her husband's hut.

Ramakrishna's closest surviving relatives were his brother Rameswar's children: Ramlal, Lakshmi, and Shivaram. Ramlal was the main priest of the Kali temple in Dakshineswar, and he and his brother Shivaram spent most of their time there. Lakshmi stayed in Dakshineswar with her brothers and did not go to Kamarpukur with Holy Mother. Lakshmi was outgoing and enjoyed singing and dancing to entertain devotees. But Holy Mother was shy and unassuming. At 34 years old, for the first time in her life, Holy Mother began to live alone.

Holy Mother was supposed to receive a monthly pension of seven rupees from the Dakshineswar temple authorities, but Ramlal and the temple cashier Dinu told Trailokya Nath Biswas, the owner, that Holy Mother was being taken care of by the Master's devotees. As a result, Trailokya stopped her monthly pension. However, the Master had left a small amount of money with Balaram. Balaram had invested this money and he gave the interest of five or six rupees to Holy Mother every month.

The Master's monastic disciples were themselves struggling to survive and were not aware of Holy Mother's difficult situation. In addition, her own mother and brothers were extremely poor and could not help her. Holy Mother had rice from the paddy fields, one of which had been bought by Ramakrishna in the name of Raghuvir, the family deity. She husked that paddy to make rice and grew some spinach and vegetables behind her hut. Sometimes she could not even afford to buy salt. Swami Saradananda later remarked: "We never dreamed that Mother did not even have the means to buy salt."[3] Whatever she cooked, she offered to Raghuvir and then ate the prasad. Generally, orthodox Hindu widows eat one vegetarian meal a day and at night have a light meal of whatever is available, such as sweets, fruits, or milk. Holy Mother had only a few saris, which gradually became worn out. Sometimes she patched the cloth, or else closed a hole by tying a knot in the fabric.

Holy Mother followed Ramakrishna's advice and lived alone in Kamarpukur. Because she was so shy, she knew only a few neighbours. Prasannamayi of the Laha family, a staunch devotee of the Master, and Dhani Kamarani, the Master's godmother, became Holy Mother's guardians. Either Prasannamayi's maidservant or Dhani's sister Shankari stayed

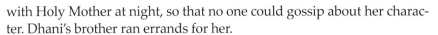

with Holy Mother at night, so that no one could gossip about her character. Dhani's brother ran errands for her.

Life was difficult for a young Hindu widow at that time. An orthodox Hindu widow was obliged to follow ruthless social rules that forbade her from remarrying. She was supposed to live like a nun. She had to wear a white sari and shave her head; she could not wear any jewellery. She could eat one vegetarian meal a day and was required to cook her food with sea salt, or rock salt. She was also expected to serve everyone in her husband's joint family, as if she were a maidservant. A widow was lucky if she had inherited some money, or if she had children who could take care of her.

Most of the villagers in Kamarpukur were not educated; in addition, they were conservative, narrow-minded, superstitious, unkind, and unsympathetic. In the name of religion, the village leaders followed their traditional caste and social rules and rigorously imposed them on helpless widows. Some leaders of society even used young widows to fulfill their carnal desires. Truly, it was a curse to become a widow in Hindu society in that era.

In Kamarpukur Holy Mother's initial problems were financial, but she soon started to face social difficulties as well. As long as Golap-ma stayed with her, no village woman dared say anything about Holy Mother's lifestyle. But when Golap-ma left for Calcutta, some narrow-minded, conservative village women and men began criticizing Holy Mother. They complained that she did not behave as a brahmin widow should: she did not shave her head, and she wore gold bracelets and a red-bordered sari. Holy Mother later said:

> When I left Vrindaban and went to Kamarpukur, the villagers began to gossip about me. I took off my bangles out of fear of public criticism. The Master appeared before me and said: "Don't take off the bangles. Don't you know the Vaishnava Tantra?" I replied: "No, I don't know anything about the Vaishnava Tantra." He said: "This afternoon Gaurdasi [Gauri-ma] will come and tell you about it." Gaurdasi arrived that afternoon and I told her everything. She began to quote from the scriptures and explained to me: "Mother, your husband is *chinmaya*, pure consciousness. The Master is ever-present and you are the goddess Lakshmi. It will bring the world bad luck if you wear a widow's clothing and do not wear jewellery. According to Vaishnava Tantra, a woman whose husband is Krishna is never a widow." I put my bangles back on.[4]

Holy Mother ignored the villagers' criticism and continued to wear her bangles and red-bordered sari. The village women went to Prasannamayi, whom everyone respected for her piety and mature judgement, and asked for her opinion of Holy Mother's unorthodox conduct. Prasanna-mayi, who had insight into Ramakrishna and Holy Mother, said: "Do not criticize either of them. They possess a divine nature." This silenced the villagers for a while.

Fortunately, Holy Mother's visions of the Master and his repeated reassurances sustained her and gave her glimpses of her future mission. Holy Mother later said: "At that time I was having visions of the Master off and on that removed my fear. One day he said: 'Make khichuri and feed me.'" Holy Mother understood that the Master and Raghuvir are the same, so she cooked khichuri and offered it to Raghuvir in the shrine while mentally feeding the Master. She described another vision: "I was alone in Kamarpukur. One day I said to myself: 'I have no children. There is no one in this world to call my own. What will happen to me?' Then the Master appeared to me and said: 'Well, you are thinking of children. I have left you so many of them, all jewels. In the course of time you will hear many, many people addressing you as Mother.'"[5]

For many years Holy Mother had lived in Dakshineswar a few yards away from the bank of the holy river Ganges. In Dakshineswar she had seen the scenic beauty of the Ganges day and night from the western veranda of her nahabat, heard the sweet murmur of the river, and breathed the unpolluted, fresh, and purifying air of Mother Ganges. She had bathed in the Ganges every day, drunk Ganges water, and cooked food with the water of the Ganges. Thus she had established a strong relationship with Mother Ganges. While living in Kamarpukur she felt nostalgic for the Ganges and she thought of travelling to Calcutta to bathe in the holy river. Around that time she had a wonderful vision, with her eyes open, as she explained: "I was very nostalgic for the Ganges all along. One day I saw the Master coming towards the house from the direction of Bhuti's Canal. He was followed by Naren, Rakhal, Baburam, and many other devotees. Further I saw that a stream of water, springing from his feet, was flowing in front of him in waves. I realized that the Master was everything. The Ganges had sprung from his feet. I hurriedly picked handfuls of hibiscus flowers from the tree next to the Raghuvir temple, and offered them again and again to that holy stream."[6]

Later, when Yogin-ma visited Kamarpukur, Holy Mother told her about the incident and took her to the place. She told Yogin-ma: "The Master was standing at the foot of this ashwatha tree. Then I saw the Master vanish into the body of Narendra. Eat a little dust from this holy spot and bow down."[7]

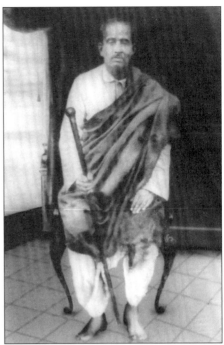

Ramakrishna's niece and nephews.
Above: Lakshmi and Shivaram Chattopadhyay. Below: Ramlal Chattopadhyay.

167

Holy Mother was the embodiment of patience and forbearance. She did not speak to anyone about her suffering, but the maid who stayed with her at night divulged her plight to some of the villagers. Shyamasundari eventually learned of her daughter's pitiful condition and she sent her second son, Kalikumar, to Kamarpukur to bring Holy Mother to Jayrambati. But Holy Mother refused to go. She knew that her mother's financial situation was difficult; moreover, she was trying to follow the Master's wishes and remain in Kamarpukur.

It was probably during the Jagaddhatri worship in the fall of 1887 that Holy Mother visited Jayrambati for three or four days. Shyamasundari burst into tears when she saw her daughter wearing a torn sari. After the worship, she insisted that Holy Mother stay with her in Jayrambati. Holy Mother declined, saying: "I am now going back to Kamarpukur. We shall see what the Lord ordains for me."[8]

Although Ramakrishna's nephews and niece lived in Dakshineswar, they occasionally visited Kamarpukur, especially during the harvest season so they could get their share of the crop. At this point Holy Mother was part of the joint family, and Ramlal, as the head of the family, was obligated to take care of her. Lakshmi mostly lived in Dakshineswar and she moved around with her disciples. When she visited Kamarpukur, she would entertain the villagers through her singing kirtan and dancing. The bashful Mother felt very uncomfortable in such situations. Shivaram was a simple, gentle, and unassertive person. He was fond of Holy Mother, who was a sort of godmother to him, and he maintained a good relationship with her. However, he had no power to make decisions about family matters. Ramlal was indifferent and even a little hostile to Holy Mother; he considered her a burden.

Once Holy Mother went to see her mother in Jayrambati. During her absence, Ramlal came to Kamarpukur and made drastic changes in the affairs of the family. He partitioned the family home and made arrangements for the worship of the family deity. He left the Master's cottage to Holy Mother and gave the Master's portion of the rice crop to her. Then Ramlal and his siblings abruptly left for Dakshineswar. Previously it was a joint family, but without consulting with Holy Mother, Ramlal took a unilateral action. Holy Mother was terribly hurt; she felt alone and helpless. Her husband's relatives had deserted her. She saw the ugly, selfish, cruel, unsympathetic, and ungrateful side of human nature. Ramlal had forgotten that he had been hired as a priest in the Dakshineswar Kali temple because of Ramakrishna.

It is painful for a mother to see her daughter in adverse circumstances.

Shyamasundari had to do something. She knew that the Master had many devotees in Calcutta who could help her daughter, so she contacted her eldest son, Prasannakumar, who was earning his livelihood in Calcutta as a priest. He went to Dakshineswar and remonstrated with Ramlal for abandoning his aunt. He also visited Golap-ma and told her that his sister was living in Kamarpukur in such poverty that she wore torn clothing and had no salt for her food. Golap-ma took the matter seriously and immediately informed Yogin-ma, who was her neighbour. That afternoon Golap-ma, Yogin-ma, and Krishnabhavini (Balaram's wife) met to discuss how to rescue Holy Mother from that terrible situation. Balaram informed the Master's monastic disciples at Baranagore. They were very upset, but helpless to assist her as they were then living on alms. Golap-ma then told Girish Ghosh, Kalipada Ghosh, Dr. Shashi Bhusan Ghosh, and M. about Holy Mother's situation. Everyone agreed to help and bring Holy Mother to Calcutta. On 5 March 1888 M. went to Kamarpukur and arranged for Holy Mother's needs according to his means.[9]

In the early part of 1888, Krishnabhavini went to Antpur to visit her mother, Matangini, who was a wealthy woman. Both women were very devoted to the Master and Holy Mother. As the distance between Antpur and Kamarpukur is only a few miles, they went to Kamarpukur with a brahmin girl and a trusted man to pay a surprise visit to Holy Mother. She was delighted to see them. As the wife of a wealthy man, Krishnabhavini was able to give sufficient money to Holy Mother for food and other necessities. After staying three days in Kamarpukur, they went with Holy Mother to Jayrambati, where they stayed for another three days. Holy Mother could not hide her condition from the eyes of the Master's loving devotees. After returning to Calcutta, Krishnabhavini and Matangini reported their observations to other women devotees. They all decided to bring Holy Mother to Calcutta. The Master's disciples wrote to Holy Mother, asking her to come to Calcutta. It was painful for the devotees to hear that Holy Mother was enduring poverty, loneliness, caste rules, and criticism.

In a small village, public opinion is more powerful than Providence. Society is bound by social rules and norms. If an individual's way of life is not approved of by the society's leaders, that person becomes an outcast. In Kamarpukur the Laha family was wealthy and influential, and Prasannamayi belonged to that family. When the village women learned that the young disciples of the Master had invited Holy Mother to live in Calcutta, some remarked: "How can she live with those young men?" Others said: "It is all right for her to move to Calcutta. Those boys are her disciples." Holy Mother wanted to know Prasannamayi's opinion, so she asked the maidservant who stayed with her at night to speak to Prasanna-mayi on her behalf.

Prasannamayi told the maid: "Gadai's [Ramakrishna's] disciples are the children of his wife. If they are eager to serve their mother in Calcutta, she should go."

"But some women of the village disapprove of this arrangement," the maid replied.

Prasannamayi responded: "What do they know about Gadai's wife? She is their mother. She must go. I will face those women."

After the maid told Holy Mother of Prasannamayi's opinion, Mother went to see her.

Prasannamayi told her: "Why are you hesitating? Of course you must go to Calcutta. Gadai's disciples are your own children. Do not listen to the village gossip. Surely you should go."[10]

Holy Mother then went to Jayrambati to get another opinion. The villagers of Jayrambati had already heard that Holy Mother was moving to Calcutta. Holy Mother told her mother: "The disciples of the Master want me to go to Calcutta. They will make all the arrangements as soon as they get my consent. Now I have come to Jayrambati for your opinion. Should I go or not?"

Shyamasundari said: "I am an ordinary woman. Let me consult with other villagers."[11] Holy Mother's brother Prasannakumar had told the villagers how some wealthy women in Calcutta loved and respected his sister and served her as they would their mother. The villagers of Jayrambati loved Holy Mother, so they did not create any problems for her. Moreover, they thought that Holy Mother's wealthy devotees might help to improve their village. They approved of the move, and in May 1888 Holy Mother went to stay in Balaram's house in Calcutta for a short time. She then moved to Belur, where the devotees had rented a house for her.

Holy Mother's Time in Kamarpukur

It is extremely difficult to ascertain how long Holy Mother stayed in Kamarpukur, given that she travelled frequently. According to M.'s diary and the biography by Swami Gambhirananda, Holy Mother lived in Kamarpukur from September 1887 to May 1888, and then from February 1889 to February 1890. While in Kamarpukur, from time to time she visited Jayrambati. Between May 1888 and February 1889, she went to Calcutta, Belur, and Puri.

The following incidents probably took place in Kamarpukur between

February 1889 and February 1890. Harish, a devotee of Ramakrishna, had stayed with the Master at Dakshineswar from time to time. His wife was greatly disturbed by his indifference to the family, so she gave him a strong drug to divert his mind to worldly life. This affected his brain. During this period Harish arrived at Kamarpukur in a deranged state of mind and began to act abnormally. Holy Mother was worried, so she wrote to the young disciples at the Baranagore Math. But before they could take any action, Harish lost control of himself. Holy Mother later described that incident: "Once Harish came to Kamarpukur and stayed for some days. One day as I entered the compound of our home after visiting a neighbour, Harish began to chase me. He was then insane. His wife had brought about this condition. There was no one in our house, and no place to escape. In a helpless state I began to walk fast around our granary. He pursued me. After going around seven times I stopped. I assumed my real form,* laid him on the ground, placed my knees on his chest, and then held his tongue and began slapping him hard. He began to gasp for breath. My fingers became red."[12]

As soon as Swamis Niranjanananda and Saradananda received Holy Mother's message, they rushed to Kamarpukur to protect her. She told them to take Harish to Calcutta. Harish knew that Niranjanananda was very strong and would not tolerate any kind of misbehaviour. When he saw Niranjanananda, he was so frightened that he left for Vrindaban without causing any further trouble. By God's grace he later recovered from his mental illness.

Holy Mother's financial condition improved during 1889 and 1890. The Master's women devotees and a couple of men devotees in Calcutta raised some money and began to support her. It was a common practice in villages for men to go to the market. Generally, high-caste women did not go. Holy Mother could now hire a maidservant to buy groceries for her and do other errands. The rice that she received from her share of the Master's family estate was more than sufficient for her needs, so she donated the surplus to the poor. She would cook some extra food during lunch to save for her maid, who ate in the afternoon. No guest or beggar left Holy Mother's door without receiving something. During the annual fall festival of Mother Shitala, Holy Mother cooked food to offer to the deity and served the prasad to the brahmins in the village.

During this period a monk from Orissa came to Kamarpukur. Prasan-namayi was a very pious woman, and she arranged for him to stay in a

*According to some, she assumed the form of Bagala, one of the ten forms of Mother Durga. Bagala is described as the destroyer of demons.

cottage near her house. Holy Mother and other villagers were very fond of that monk and took care of his needs. However, some undisciplined and rowdy young men in the village did not like him and tried to force him to leave. When the monk decided to leave, Holy Mother and some villagers came forward to help him. At Holy Mother's request, the villagers began building a cottage for the monk at the southwest corner of the Haldar-pukur. It was the beginning of the rainy season, and the thick clouds were about to pour rain. Holy Mother fervently prayed to the Master: "Master, please save the situation. Let this monk's thatched hut be completed and then it can rain as much as you like." By God's grace the hut was completed and the monk moved in. Despite her straitened circumstances, Holy Mother provided food for the monk and inquired about his condition. Unfortunately, that monk died there after a short time.

The Master's Wish Fulfilled

We are stricken with grief when we think of Holy Mother's ordeal in Kamarpukur, which lasted nearly a year. She did not want anyone to know about her suffering. If the Master's devotees had known of it, they would have handled the situation immediately. Despite her hardships, Holy Mother struggled to follow the Master's advice to live alone in Kamarpukur. But there must have been a special reason behind this divine plan. The scriptures say that the desires of illumined souls always come true. It seems that the Master had fulfilled his one unfinished wish through her. Swami Saradananda wrote:

> At the threshold of his youth a kind of fancy arose in the Master's mind, prompted by the influence of his inner feminine nature. Because they were born as women the gopis of Vrindaban attained Satchidananda Krishna through love. This led him to think that if he were born as a woman, he could worship and attain Krishna like the gopis. Thus, viewing the male body as an obstacle to attaining Krishna, he imagined that if he were to be born again he would be a beautiful young widow with long hair, born in a brahmin family, knowing none other than Krishna as husband. There would be provision for plain food and clothes and a small plot of land next to her hut, where she would grow a few kinds of vegetables. There would be an elderly woman with her who served as a guardian, a cow that she would milk herself, and a spinning wheel. His boyish imagination went further. After finishing the household work for the day, she would sing songs about Krishna while spinning the cotton. Then in the evening she would make sweets from the milk of that cow and cry piteously to feed the sweets to Krishna with her own hands. Pleased, Krishna would suddenly

appear as a cowherd boy and eat them; thus he would visit daily without anyone knowing.[13]

Holy Mother spent her time in Kamarpukur in much the same manner. She grew spinach and vegetables, cooked them with rice, offered them to Raghuvir, and partook of that prasad. She spent the remainder of her time chanting the Lord's name.

Blessed Kamarpukur

Later Holy Mother talked about leaving Kamarpukur: "At Kamarpukur I missed the Master very much. It was a painful experience. That is why I did not stay there....When I moved to Kamarpukur after the Master passed away, the Master's relatives were indifferent and the villagers tried to humiliate me. When my mother heard about it, she brought me to Jayrambati. Since then I have been living with my brothers amid their happiness and misery. Now those relatives say that I don't look after them. How strange is human nature!"[14]

Although Holy Mother did not remain in Kamarpukur, she kept an eye on her husband's cottage and paid for its maintenance. Today, nearly 200 years later, that thatched hut is still in excellent condition, bearing the memory of Ramakrishna and Holy Mother. Later Holy Mother reminded her devotees of the importance and sanctity of that cottage and asked them to stay there when they visited Kamarpukur. She also gave financial help to Ramlal when he added an upper floor to his cottage. She was always concerned about continuing the worship service of the family deity Raghuvir and bore her share of the expenses.

In 1950, a beautiful temple was erected on the spot where Ramakrishna was born, and the Ramakrishna Order has preserved that precious mud hut where the Master and the Mother lived. Now innumerable people from all over the world visit this holy site, the birthplace of an avatar — the Bengal Bethlehem.

12

In and Around
Calcutta

Vishayam kusumam parihritya sadā
charanāmbu-ruhāmrita shānti-sudhām;
Piba bhringa-mano bhavaroga-harām
pranamāmi parām jananim jagatām.
— *A hymn by Swami Abhedananda*

Renouncing the flower of sense objects, always drink, O my mind-bee, the nectar of immortal peace from the lotus feet of the Mother, which removes the disease of worldliness. I salute the Supreme Mother of the Universe.

Neither happiness nor misery is permanent. They rotate in cyclic order. A cyclone does not blow constantly, according to the law of nature. Misfortune could not reign long in Holy Mother's life. However, Holy Mother's stay in Kamarpukur is a great lesson to all of us. She demonstrated how to struggle against poverty and adversity; how to recognize true friends and loyal relatives; how to adapt to time, place, and person; and how to surrender oneself to God's will.

In May 1888, when Holy Mother was 35 years old, she arrived at Balaram's house in Calcutta. The Master's disciples and devotees were overjoyed by her presence. At first some householder devotees did not recognize Holy Mother's divinity, but Golap-ma and Yogin-ma convinced them of it by describing her exalted spiritual moods in Vrindaban. The Master's disciples and devotees now realized that the responsibility for looking after Holy Mother rested with them. Swami Yogananda, her first disciple, and Golap-ma were her primary caretakers.

Although Holy Mother appeared to be human, she sometimes ascended to the divine plane and remained absorbed in samadhi. One day she was meditating on the roof of Balaram's house when she merged into deep samadhi. Afterwards she described her experience to Yogin-ma: "I found that I had travelled to a far-away country. People there showed me warm tenderness. I looked exceedingly beautiful. The Master was there. Gently

Above: Nilambar Mukherjee's riverside garden house, Belur.
Below: Sarada Devi's room in Nilambar Mukherjee's house.

they made me sit by his side. I cannot express in words the joy I felt at that time. Regaining partial consciousness, I saw my body lying nearby like an ugly corpse. I began to worry about entering into it. I did not feel in the least inclined to do so. After a long while I persuaded myself to get into the body and again became conscious of the physical world."[1]

At Nilambar Mukherjee's Garden House in Belur

A few days after Holy Mother arrived in Calcutta, the devotees rented Nilambar Mukherjee's garden house at Belur, which is on the western bank of the Ganges, opposite the Cossipore cremation ground where the Master's body was cremated. Holy Mother moved there with Yogin-ma and Golap-ma; Swamis Yogananda and Adbhutananda became her attendants. During this period Holy Mother experienced samadhi quite often. Yogin-ma recalled: "One evening Holy Mother, Golap-ma, and I were meditating on the roof. When my meditation was over, I noticed that Mother was still absorbed in meditation — motionless in samadhi. After a long time she regained some outer consciousness and said: 'Oh Yogin! Where are my hands? Where are my feet?' I pressed her limbs and said: 'Here are your hands and feet.' It took Holy Mother a long time to regain consciousness of her body."[2]

This kind of experience has been described by the scriptures as *nirvikalpa samadhi*, in which one completely transcends body consciousness and the world, experiencing complete identity with Brahman. Regarding her spiritual ecstasies during that period she once said to a disciple: "At that time my mind became absorbed in lights — red, blue, and other colors. My body would not have survived long if these experiences had continued."[3]

Over time Holy Mother became the central figure of the Ramakrishna movement, and the disciples and devotees came to her for advice, blessings, and inspiration. One day Swami Abhedananda visited Holy Mother at Nilambar Babu's house in Belur and recited a hymn that he had composed about her. Here is the first verse:

Prakritim paramām abhyām varadām, nararupa-dharām janatāpa-harām;
Sharanāgata sevaka tosha-karim, pranamāmi parām jananim jagatām.
— O Divine Nature Supreme! Remover of all fears, giver of boons, who has taken a human form, who removes the miseries of humanity, who confers joy on those who take refuge in you, O Supreme Mother of the Universe! I bow down to you.

After listening to the entire 11-verse hymn, Holy Mother blessed him, saying, "May Saraswati, the goddess of learning, sit on your tongue."[4]

Years later, Lavanya Kumar Chakrabarty interviewed Swami Abhedananda about this hymn. After composing the hymn to the Mother, Abhedananda expressed his desire to recite it to her. She was startled and asked: "What kind of hymn? Whose hymn?" Abhedananda humbly replied, "Mother, I composed a hymn on you." Amazed, the Mother asked, "My son, what is the need for composing a hymn on me?" However, when Abhedananda sincerely repeated his request, the Mother calmly listened to the entire hymn. When the swami recited "*Ramakrishna-gata-pranām* — whose soul is absorbed in Ramakrishna," the Mother's whole body became motionless. When he recited "*Tannāma-shravana-priyām* — who loves to hear the Master's name," tears began to roll from her eyes. When he said "*Tadbhāva-ranjitā-kārām* — whose mental state is saturated with the Master," the swami saw that the Mother was no longer there: The Master was seated in place of the Mother.[5]

M. wrote *Sri Sri Ramakrishna Kathamrita* (*The Gospel of Sri Ramakrishna*) based on entries in his diary from 26 February 1882 to 24 April 1886. A couple of years after the Master's passing away, he began to develop his diary for publication, but he did not make all of the entries public. On 11 July 1888 M. read a chapter of the *Kathamrita* to Holy Mother. After she heard the manuscript read, Holy Mother praised M. and encouraged him to write more. Almost two years later, on 15 March 1890, M. read another chapter to Holy Mother and received her approval to publish it.

Just before Durga Puja in October 1888, the Master said to Holy Mother in a dream: "M. told me that he had a desire to perform Durga Puja. Now you arrange Durga Puja and install the ghat [the consecrated pitcher]."[6] Accordingly, on Saturday, 8 October 1888, Holy Mother installed and worshipped Sri Chandi Mangal-Ghat (the Durga Ghat) and Ramakrishna's photograph in M.'s shrine in Calcutta and arranged for their daily worship. The worship continues even today.

Pilgrimage to Puri

The lease on Nilambar Babu's house expired after six months, so in October Holy Mother returned to Balaram's house. After staying there for a few days, she left on a pilgrimage to Puri with Brahmananda, Yogananda, Saradananda, Golap-ma, Yogin-ma and her mother, and Lakshmi. At that time there was no train from Calcutta to Puri. On 7 November 1888 they took a big steamer from Calcutta to Chandvali and from there they took a canal motorboat to Cuttack. After lunch at Cuttack, they hired two bullock carts, one for Holy Mother and Lakshmi and another for the other women. The monks walked behind the carts.

After arriving in Puri they visited Lord Jagannath* in the famous temple in Orissa on the coast of the Bay of Bengal. From 9 November 1888 to 9 January 1889 Holy Mother and her women companions stayed at Kshetrabasi Math, which Balaram's family owned. The monks stayed in a place nearby.

Yogin-ma recalled:

> After leaving our luggage at Kshetrabasi Math, we went with Holy Mother to see Lord Jagannath without even washing our feet. The image of Govinda in Vrindaban is different from the image of Jagannath. Balaram's priest cordially received us and showed the deities. During the first month, Holy Mother and we visited Jagannath every morning and evening, and sometimes we all went to attend the *mangala arati,* the early morning service. After attending the vesper service, we used to meditate in the Lakshmi temple, which was in the same compound. Rakhal, Sharat, and Jogin also stayed with us in the temple. Balaram's brother Harivallabh Babu was highly respected there and the priests knew that we were staying at their house, so they made our visits to the deity comfortable. The Master had never come to Puri and seen Jagannath, so Holy Mother carried under her sari a picture of the Master and uncovered it before the deities on the altar.[7]

Holy Mother believed that a picture is the same as the person it depicts. Later she described a vision that she had at Puri: "I saw Jagannath, a Lion among men, as it were, seated on the sacred altar, and I was attending Him as His handmaiden."[8] She also saw Jagannath as Shiva.

In Puri, Holy Mother manifested the utmost humility. The main temple priest, Govinda, knew that Holy Mother was the wife of Balaram's guru, and he suggested that she take a palanquin to the temple from her residence. But Holy Mother said: "No, Govinda, you go ahead and show me the way. I shall follow you, walking behind like a helpless beggar." She and her companions visited all the important temples in Puri on foot.

Later, Holy Mother related one of her experiences in Puri: "Once I visited the image of Lord Jagannath in Puri at the time of the Chariot Festival. I wept in sheer joy to see so many people having a view of Lord Jagannath. 'Ah,' I said to myself, 'it is good. They will all be liberated.' But later on I realized that it was not so. Only one or two who were absolutely free from desires would attain their liberation. When I narrated the incident to Yogin, she corroborated this by saying, 'Yes, Mother, only those who are free from desires attain liberation.'"[9]

---

*Literally, Lord of the Universe, an epithet of Krishna. The images of Krishna, his brother Balaram, and his sister Subhadra are worshipped in the shrine.

Holy Mother returned to Calcutta on 12 January 1889 and stayed at M.'s house for nearly three weeks. On 22 January she visited the Divine Mother at Kalighat in South Calcutta, and then returned to Balaram's house for a few days. Yogin-ma and Golap-ma saw Holy Mother every day and meditated with her in the evenings. One day after meditation Golap-ma remarked: "Mother, the Master said, 'Only ishwarakotis [godlike souls] can have unconditional devotion, not jivakotis [ordinary souls].'"

Holy Mother replied: "Ishwarakotis have fulfilled all their desires. Because they are devoid of desire, they become recipients of unconditional devotion. Jivakotis have innumerable desires, so they cannot have unconditional devotion."

"It seems that I shall never achieve unconditional devotion," Golap-ma said.

"Why not, Golap? If you can give up desire, you will attain it."

"Can a jiva [individual soul] give up all desires?"

"Yes, one can give up desire. That is why one is supposed to practise japa, meditation, and other spiritual practices. The mantra purifies the body. A man becomes pure by repeating the mantra. When a man gets rid of desires by discriminating between the real and the unreal, then he does not remain a jiva anymore. He becomes eligible for liberation. Moreover, one can attain unconditional devotion by God's will."[10]

A Visit to Antpur

Matangini, Premananda's mother, asked Holy Mother if she would be interested in visiting her country home in Antpur. Holy Mother agreed. The devotees were excited to go with her to Antpur, and they planned to go to Kamarpukur with her as well. On 5 February 1889, Holy Mother left for Antpur with Matangini, Krishnabhavini, Yogin-ma, Golap-ma, Lakshmi, Yogananda, Saradananda, Nirmalananda, M., and Tulsiram Ghosh (Premananda's elder brother). Vivekananda, Premananda, and Vaikuntha Sanyal were already in Antpur. When Holy Mother's luggage arrived, Vivekananda carried it with great joy and playfully pretended to be a horse, making Holy Mother smile.[11] Matangini was a wealthy woman and also a devotee of the Master. She and her sons were delighted to be in the company of Holy Mother and the Master's disciples. It was a truly festive occasion.

After spending a week at Antpur, Holy Mother left for Kamarpukur with Lakshmi, M., Golap-ma, and Saradananda by bullock cart via Tarakeswar. After staying for three days in Kamarpukur, the party returned to Calcutta, leaving Holy Mother there.

Holy Mother Returns to Belur

In February 1890 Holy Mother returned to Calcutta and the devotees rented Raju Gomastha's house at Belur for her. The house was on the bank of the Ganges, which made Holy Mother very happy.

Holy Mother went to M.'s house at Kambuliatola in Calcutta on 4 March 1890. At that time she remembered that the Master had not been able to perform the funeral ritual for his departed mother because he was a monk, and he had asked her to offer a *pinda,* the traditional sacrificial cake, at the feet of Vishnu in Gaya. To fulfill his wish, on 25 March she and Swami Advaitananda went to Gaya. On the way they stopped at Deoghar and saw Vaidyanath Shiva. After performing the ritual to Vishnu in Gaya, she visited Bodh-Gaya, where the Buddha attained enlightenment.When Holy Mother saw the wealthy monastery in Bodh-Gaya, the pitiable condition of the Master's disciples came to her mind. She tearfully prayed: "Master, my children do not have a good place to stay, they do not have sufficient food to eat, and they roam from door to door begging. I wish they could have a monastery like this." Her prayer was answered in 1898 when Swamiji established Belur Math after returning from the West.

On 2 April 1890 Holy Mother returned to Calcutta. At that time Balaram was critically ill, so she stayed with his family to help them. The Master was very fond of Balaram and his wife, and their house was his Calcutta residence. Now and then he spent the night in their house and ate with them. After the Master's death, Balaram took care of Holy Mother and the Master's monastic disciples. Balaram passed away on 13 April 1890. Holy Mother consoled his family and stayed with them until the shraddha ceremony was performed on 13 May 1890.

Holy Mother at Ghusuri

Towards the end of May 1890 Holy Mother moved to a rented house in Ghusuri, which is situated between Salkia and Belur. The house was on the western bank of the Ganges and near a cremation ground. Yogin-ma, Golap-ma, Swami Yogananda, and Swami Trigunatitananda stayed with her. The house was very small and quiet and there were not many activities or visitors, so they spent their time practising japa and meditation and sharing stories about the Master.

One day Golap-ma talked about the Master's love for Balaram. She recalled how the Master had passed nights in Calcutta at Balaram's house, enjoyed his food, and danced in ecstasy in his parlour during kirtan. Then Holy Mother recalled a vision that Ramakrishna had: "The Master saw Balaram wearing a turban and standing by the image of Kali with folded hands. Balaram always remained with folded hands in front of the Master. He did not bow down to the Master and touch his feet. Knowing what was in his mind, the Master would ask: 'Balaram, this foot is itching. Could you rub it gently?' Immediately Balaram would send for Naren, Rakhal, or anyone nearby and ask him to massage the Master's foot."[12]

Then Golap-ma explained why Balaram would not touch the Master's feet: "The Master remained always in an ecstatic mood and sometimes in samadhi. At that time if any impure person entered his room, he would groan like a person groans in pain during a nightmare. Then Ramlal, Latu, Naren, Rakhal, Balaram, or whoever was there in his room, would say: 'Let us all go and sit outside. The Master is feeling discomfort.' When everyone was outside, the groaning sound would stop."[13] Although Balaram was a humble and pure Vaishnava devotee, he did not want to risk causing the Master discomfort by his touch.

One evening a Baul (a minstrel) was passing through the street singing this song: "Have you seen my Nimai going through this street? His body complexion is golden and he is walking with a monk." As they listened to that song, Yogin-ma asked Holy Mother: "Mother, what kind of complexion did the Master have in the early days?"

Holy Mother replied: "His complexion was like the colour of gold — like that of *harital* [a yellow mineral]. It blended with the colour of the gold amulet that he wore on his arm. When I rubbed him with oil I could clearly see a lustre emanating from his entire body. People were wonderstruck when they saw him walking with slow, steady steps to the Ganges to take his bath."[14]

Holy Mother's voice was soft and sweet. Her words were short and simple. Yogin-ma described Holy Mother's manner of speaking: "While talking about the Master or about japa and meditation, Holy Mother would stop from time to time, as if she were visualizing what she was going to say. At that time her look was vacant and her mind would merge into a mysterious realm."[15] Golap-ma and Yogin-ma were amazed by Holy Mother's ecstatic moods whenever she spoke about the Master.

One morning in July 1890 Swamis Vivekananda and Akhandananda came to receive Holy Mother's blessing before leaving for the Himalayas. After bowing down, Vivekananda said: "Mother, I shall see you again if I become a real man. Otherwise, I now say good-bye forever."

"What are you saying!" the Mother interrupted.

"No, no," Vivekananda assured her, "I shall soon return through your grace."

Holy Mother said to Akhandananda: "I am handing my treasure over to you. You know the conditions in the Himalayas. Please see that Naren does not suffer for want of food."

Golap-ma gave the monks some prasad and asked Vivekananda to sing for Holy Mother.

Vivekananda sang this song:

> I have made Thee, O Lord, the pole star of my life;
> No more shall I lose my way on the world's trackless sea.
> Wherever I wander here, Thy brilliance shines undimmed;
> With Thy serene and gracious light
> Thou drivest all the tears out of my troubled soul.[16]

Then he sang a song from a play by Girish Ghosh called *Vilwamangal*:

> He [Krishna] travels holding my hand.
> Wherever I go, He follows me,
> Even if I don't ask Him to.
> He wipes my face with great care,
> And intently looks at my face.
> When I smile, He smiles; and when I cry, He cries.
> How lovingly He takes care of me.[17]

Holy Mother blessed Vivekananda: "Wherever you go, the Master will be always with you. Mother Durga will protect you in the mountains and forests, in trials and tribulations."[18] She served lunch to Vivekananda and Akhandananda and then they returned to the Baranagore monastery. Vivekananda informed his brother disciples that Holy Mother was well taken care of by the Master's women devotees. This was a great relief to all of them.

Holy Mother stayed in Ghusuri from May to the middle of September 1890, when she contracted dysentery. Golap-ma and Yogin-ma realized that although it was a wonderful place to live, it would be difficult for doctors to come from Calcutta to treat her. Golap-ma wrote to her son-in-law, Raja Saurindra Mohan Thakur, and asked him to find a place in Calcutta for Holy Mother. He replied that he had a vacant rental property in Baranagore, and she and Holy Mother could live there rent-free for an indefinite period. In the third week of September, Holy Mother moved to Baranagore with Golap-ma, Yogin-ma, Yogananda, and Trigunatitananda. A doctor was engaged, and Holy Mother soon recovered. She then stayed with Balaram's family until Durga Puja.

Holy Mother in Jayrambati

Holy Mother left Balaram's home in October 1890 for Jayrambati, where she lived until July 1893. She was fond of Jayrambati because she could move about freely among her neighbours without wearing a veil. In Calcutta she wore a veil most of the time when she was with male devotees and disciples of the Master. She lived like a caged bird in the houses of her devotees, where she followed all the formalities and always had to be mindful of what she did and said. She did not have much freedom.

In Jayrambati, where she was born and brought up, she felt relaxed. When she was in Calcutta she always pined for the rural environment, fresh air, vast meadows, and the open-hearted conversations with her neighbours that she enjoyed in the village.

We have no detailed information of her life during this period, but we know that she must have helped her mother with housework and served the devotees.

A new chapter began in Holy Mother's life. She was no longer Sarada, the shy and timid village girl. She started to assume her role as Jagadamba, the Mother of the Universe. Her speech and demeanor changed. Her motherly love and compassion, her patience and forbearance, awakened to a greater extent. She had resolved to fulfill her mission to demonstrate the Motherhood of God. At that time it was not easy to reach Jayrambati, but devotees from far and near gradually began to visit Holy Mother there to receive her grace and spiritual instructions. She lived in a small mud hut that belonged to her brother Prasannakumar, and her visitors stayed in another mud hut, which was used as the parlour. (Holy Mother's cottage has been preserved by the Ramakrishna Order.)

In 1877 Shyamasundari had started to worship Mother Jagaddhatri every year, and Holy Mother tried to be present for the worship. During Jagaddhatri Puja on 10 November 1891, Swami Saradananda, Haramohan Mitra, Vaikuntha Nath Sanyal, Kalikrishna (later Swami Virajananda), Yogin-ma, and Golap-ma went to Jayrambati.

Virajananda left a wonderful account of Holy Mother's life there:

> How happy the Mother felt at our arrival! She seemed to be utterly at a loss as to how she could make us comfortable. All that she did ceaselessly for our entertainment from dawn to night did not appear to her sufficient! She herself cooked both morning and evening. What a variety of dishes and how delicious they were! There was something ethereal about that taste! She would be sitting close by as we took our meals and insisted that we must eat more. Sometimes she would prepare some curry that Sri Ramakrishna liked.

Four of us [Saradananda, Haramohan, Vaikuntha, and Virajananda] were accommodated in a small room in the outer apartment of the house. Just by the side of it, there was an open hall where the Jagaddhatri Puja was to be held. The back door of our room opened into the inner court- yard; at its other end was the thatched cottage of the Mother. Sometimes, when the door was kept open, I could see her on the veranda of her cottage dressing vegetables or doing some other household work. I saw Mother cleaning the dishes in the small pond and carrying cooking and drinking water in a pitcher from the Talpukur [Banerjee's pond] on her waist like other village women. I had voluntarily taken up the task of plucking flow- ers and bel leaves for the puja from the interior of the village and from the bushes and trees on the river. As I was very young, the Mother did not maintain her usual bashfulness in my presence. Hence it became my duty to run errands for Sharat Maharaj [Saradananda] and elderly devotees; in that connection I had to go to the inner apartments to bring this and that. This was for me a great blessing since I got the opportunity to see Holy Mother several times a day.

We used to call Holy Mother's mother "Didima" [grandmother]. She was a very simple and sweet-natured woman. She always kept herself busy with the many duties of her household, such as looking after the cat- tle, cleaning the cowshed, feeding the labourers in the field, husking rice, and so on. Yet one never missed the graceful smile on her face. She would tell us many stories of Sri Ramakrishna's youth — how he would sing and make women laugh with jokes and frivolous stories. When we called her Didima that elderly woman was beside herself with joy.

One day a Baul [Haridas Vairagi of Deshra] came to the door of the house and asked for alms. He was singing a song relating to Parvati, the consort of Shiva, to the accompaniment of a violin.

O Uma, my darling, what good tidings I hear!
People say you are adored in Varanasi as Annapurna. Is it true?
O Gauri, when I married you to Shiva,
He went as a beggar from door to door for a morsel of food.
But today how glad I am to hear
You are now Queen of the World, seated by His side.
And they called my naked Shiva a madman:
How much abuse I had to bear from everyone!
Now I hear that doorkeepers guard His palace
And gods like Indra, Chandra, and Yama can hardly see Him.
Shiva used to live in the Himalayas;
Many a day He got His food by begging;
Now He rules over Varanasi and is as rich as Kuvera.
Is it you who have brought Him all this good fortune?
No doubt He is very rich now,

Else why should Gauri be so proud?
She does not cast her eyes even upon her own children,
And turns her face away from Radhika*.

The song cast a spell on all of us who listened. Emotions rose high. Yogin-ma and Golap-ma asked him to sing that song again, and they gave him some money. Didn't the words bring a true picture of our own Holy Mother? Didima said: "Well, in those days people called my son-in-law a lunatic. They expressed their grief at Sarada's lot. How many abuses they hurled at me, too! There was no end to my silent agony. But today, see how many men and women from respectable families are looking upon Sarada as a goddess and worshipping her feet!"

During our stay at Jayrambati we visited Kamarpukur a number of times. While returning to Jayrambati we would bring jilipis and other sweets for Mother from Kamarpukur. Most of it, however, would be given to us during our refreshments, along with puffed rice mixed with ghee.

The Jagaddhatri Puja was performed with great éclat. The image of Mother Jagaddhatri was beautiful. One felt that She really had come in flesh and blood to accept the offerings of Her children. Holy Mother herself would be seen standing near the place of worship with folded hands during arati [vespers] and sometimes fanning the goddess with a chamara. All the days she was intensely occupied with other women in arrangements for the puja and cooking. The worship continued for three days, and many hundreds were sumptuously fed every day. There was a Yatra (theatrical performance) on two nights and many people of adjoining villages came to see the performance. After three days of worship, the immersion ceremony was a moving sight. Holy Mother and other women burst into tears.

Days passed in supreme happiness. A couple of days after the puja, all four of us were suddenly attacked by malaria. In that small room we lay in adjoining beds shivering with high temperatures. Holy Mother's worries knew no bounds. She would stand at the threshold of the door and look at us with love and compassion. One could hear her exclaim: "Oh, what a pity! My sons are suffering so much. What a wretched out-of-the-way village this is. It is hard to get any milk to prepare the sago." With a bowl in hand, Holy Mother would go to the villagers who had cows for a little milk. In those villages the farmers paid more attention to the bullocks that cultivated the land and fed them more. The milk cows were neglected so the output of milk was scanty. After collecting one or two cups of milk, Holy Mother would prepare our diet. However, we recovered after a few days and took our normal food. Because our long stay in Jayrambati might cause additional physical strain on Mother, we decided

---

*Radhika is the composer of the song.

to return to Calcutta. Although she insisted that we stay longer, we some-how convinced her that we should return to Calcutta. The bullock carts were ready and after lunch we boarded them. Didima and the neighbours were present and Holy Mother was standing in front of the back door of the house, silently watching the scene from a distance. Her face was puffy and reddish from the tears that rolled from her eyes. The carts moved on. Mother was following us. Repeatedly we implored her to return but she would not listen. At last the carts passed by Talpukur [the southern border of the village] and entered the extensive meadow outside the village. As long as I could see from inside the cart, I watched Mother standing by the side of the pond with her eyes fixed on us.[19]

Holy Mother Blesses Vivekananda

While in Madras in March and April of 1893, Vivekananda had a significant dream: He saw Ramakrishna walking into the ocean and beckoning him to follow. He also heard the command: "Go!" Although Swamiji was now certain of his journey to the West, he still felt it necessary to seek Holy Mother's permission. He wrote to Swami Saradananda: "I have had a vision in which the Master told me to go to the West. My mind is quite disturbed. Please tell Holy Mother everything and let me know her opinion." Saradananda went to Holy Mother and read Swamiji's letter to her. Holy Mother did not respond immediately, but asked Saradananda to wait. After a couple of days, Holy Mother had a similar dream. She saw Ramakrishna walking over the ocean waves and asking Narendra to follow him. Then Holy Mother told Saradananda: "Please write to Naren that he should go to the West." Swamiji was overjoyed when he received Holy Mother's approval.[20]

In his reminiscences of Swamiji, Kiran Chandra Datta included this story that Swami Turiyananda had shared with him:

> Swamiji was then in Madras and his devotees were arranging to send him to America. In a vision, Swamiji saw the Master motioning to him to go to the West, but he decided to get permission from Holy Mother before mak-ing his final decision. He did not know whether the Mother was in Jayram-bati or Calcutta at that time, so he wrote to Sharat Maharaj in Alambazar Math to forward his letter to Holy Mother. Sharat Maharaj forwarded the letter to Holy Mother who was then in Jayrambati.
>
> A few days later, Holy Mother said to her brother Kali: "Today Naren's letter will come. You go and pick it up from the mailman." Kali replied, "Today is not the mail delivery day." At that time the mail was delivered once or twice a week, and the mailman would wait at a particular place to give someone the letters for Jayrambati. [The post office was in Anur, 3 or

4 miles away.] As Holy Mother insisted, Kali went to the local mail station and found that the mailman was waiting with a single letter, which was addressed to Holy Mother. "URGENT" was written on the envelope. Amazed, he took the letter and returned to Jayrambati. He told the Mother, "Sister, you have a letter." She was cutting vegetables just then. She asked Kali, "Open the letter and read it to me." After listening to the letter, she said: "Bring some paper and a pen and write to Naren: 'Certainly you should go to the West. This is the Master's work. This will do good to humanity.'"

Shyamasundari was sitting nearby, repeating a mantra. She had heard everything and said: "Saru, where are you sending Naren? That country is beyond seven oceans and thirteen rivers." Holy Mother replied: "Last night the Master appeared to me and said, 'Tomorrow Naren's letter will come. This is the work of the Divine Mother. It will do good to humanity. Give him your permission to go.'"[21]

It seems Holy Mother's letter to Swamiji was mailed to Sharat Maharaj in Alambazar Math and he sent it to Swamiji in Madras.

Holy Mother Returns to Belur

Holy Mother returned to Calcutta in July 1893. She stayed with Balaram's family for a few days, and then her devotees rented Nilambar Mukherjee's garden house at Belur for her — the same house where she had stayed in 1888. Holy Mother moved there with Yogin-ma, Golapma, and Swami Trigunatitananda, who became her attendant and ran errands. It was a very quiet place. Holy Mother spent most of her time there in worship, japa, and meditation.

It is wonderful how the disciples of the Master sincerely and joyfully served Holy Mother. For example, Swami Trigunatitananda would pick flowers for Holy Mother to use in her morning worship. In the evening he would spread a white cloth under the *shefalika* [a fragrant white flower] tree so that its blooms would not fall into the dust. It was probably in July or August of 1893 that Holy Mother performed the panchatapa, or the austerity of five fires, on the roof of Nilambar's house. This severe austerity is observed by sitting for japa and meditation from dawn to dusk, surrounded by four fires and the blazing sun above. It may be remembered that when Holy Mother went to Varanasi after Ramakrishna passed away her mind was grief-stricken. A woman ascetic of Nepal, who was an adept in various kinds of sadhana, advised Holy Mother to perform the panchatapa to calm her mind. Holy Mother had also a couple of visions in Kamarpukur regarding the panchatapa ceremony. Accordingly, Holy Mother decided to perform it.

Above: Roof of Nilambar's house where Sarada Devi practised panchatapa.
Below: Bathing ghat on the Ganges in front of Nilambar's house.

A thick layer of earth was laid on the roof of Nilambar's house and four blazing fires of dried cow-dung cakes were lighted in a square, seven and a half feet apart from each other.

Holy Mother recalled:

> Sometime after the Master's passing away I often had a vision of a bearded sannyasin who asked me to perform the panchatapa ceremony. In the beginning I didn't pay any heed to it, and moreover I was unaware of what the panchatapa was. But when the sannyasin insisted, I asked Yogin [Yogin-ma] about it. She said: "Well, Mother, I shall perform it with you." Arrangements were made for the panchatapa ceremony at Nilambar Babu's house in Belur. Blazing fires of dried cow-dung were lighted on four sides and the scorching sun was overhead. After a morning bath in the Ganges, I approached the fire and found the flames up. I was seized with a great fear and I wondered how I could enter the area and remain seated there until sunset. After repeating the Master's name, I entered the area surrounded by fires. It felt as if they had lost their heat. Thus I practised this discipline for seven days. As a result my fair complexion became like black ashes. After that I never saw that sannyasin anymore.[22]

Holy Mother related another vision regarding the panchatapa practice: "While I was in Kamarpukur, I saw with my physical eyes a girl about 11 or 12 years old, like Radhu. She wore an ochre cloth and rudraksha beads around her neck, and her hair was dry and shaggy. She accompanied me wherever I went. After I performed the panchatapa ceremony at Nilambar Babu's house in Belur, that girl disappeared. I never saw her again."[23]

The external fire of the panchatapa relieved the burning anguish within that Holy Mother had felt since the Master's passing, and she felt an inner peace. Years later, when a devotee asked her about the panchatapa, she said: "Yes, it was necessary. Parvati, the Divine Mother, practised the austerity to obtain Shiva as Her husband." Then she added: "I performed this austerity to set an example for others. Otherwise people would say: 'What is extraordinary about her? She eats, sleeps, and moves about like ordinary people.'" When an intimate disciple wanted to know the real reason that she went through this ordeal, she said: "My child, I went through it for the sake of all of you. Can you practise austerities? This is why I had to do it."[24]

Holy Mother always felt the Master's presence wherever she lived. When she was in Nilambar's house in Belur, she had a vision. It was a moonlit night. She was seated on the steps leading to the Ganges, looking at the full moon reflected in the waves of the sacred river. Suddenly she saw Ramakrishna come from behind and proceed swiftly to the river. As soon as he touched the water his body dissolved in it. Later Holy Mother described this incident: "I looked at the phenomenon with my mouth wide open, in utter amazement. All of a sudden Naren also appeared, I don't know from where. Crying, 'Victory unto Ramakrishna!,' he took some water in his hands and began to sprinkle it upon innumerable men and women gathered around. Immediately they attained liberation."[25] This vision was imprinted on her mind so deeply that she could not bathe in the Ganges for some days. She said: "This Ganges is the body of the Master. How can I touch it with my feet?"[26] This experience finally convinced her that Ramakrishna's physical death did not mean he had ceased to exist. He had been incarnated to fulfill a cosmic purpose, and she must also contribute her share to accomplish it.

Holy Mother soon became the central figure for Ramakrishna's disciples and devotees. They came to her for solace and succour, and she treated them with great affection. Once Durgacharan Nag (known as "Nag Mahashay") came to visit Holy Mother at Nilambar's house. He considered Ramakrishna to be God and Holy Mother to be the Divine Mother. Holy Mother described Nag Mahashay's exuberant devotion and how the Master's devotees respected her:

> Ah, what shall I say about Durgacharan? He looked upon me as the Divine Mother Herself. He came to see me on Ekadashi.* In those days no men devotees were allowed in my presence. They used to bow down to me by touching their heads to the staircase. A maidservant used to announce the name of the visitor, saying, "So and so is saluting you, Mother," and I would send my blessings. On that day the maid said: "Mother, who is Nag Mahashay? He is bowing down to you and hitting his head so hard it might bleed. Yogananda Maharaj is trying to persuade him to stop, but he does not say a word. He seems to be unconscious. Is he mad, Mother?" I said: "Please ask Jogin to send him here." Jogin brought him to me. I saw that his forehead was swollen, tears were trickling from his eyes, and his steps were unsteady. He could not see me because he was blinded by tears. I made him sit down. He was uttering only "Mother, Mother," as if he were insane; otherwise he was calm, composed, and balanced. I wiped away his tears with the upper corner of my cloth. He came when I had just sat down for my meal — luchis, sweets, and fruits. I ate a little of the food and then tried to feed him with the prasad. But it was hard for him to swallow the food. He had no outer consciousness. He remained seated, touching my feet with his hands, repeating, "Mother, Mother." My women companions said, "Mother, your meal is spoiled. Let Yogananda Maharaj take him downstairs." I said: "Wait. Let him compose himself a

*The eleventh day after the new and full moon.

little." I stroked his head and body and repeated the Master's name, and after some time, he regained external consciousness. Then I began to eat my meal and also to feed him. After his meal, he was taken downstairs. While leaving he said to me, "Not I, Not I, but Thou, Thou." I told those who were near me, "Look, how wise he is." He would do anything for me.

On another occasion Nag Mahashay came to me wearing a dirty and tattered cloth and carrying on his head a basketful of delicious mangoes from his own trees. He intended to sit by my side and feed me, but he said nothing. He roamed around holding the basket on his head. Jogin sent word: "Please tell Mother that Nag Mahashay has brought mangoes. He will not say anything nor will he give the basket to anyone." I asked for him to be sent to me. He came with the basket on his head and a brahma-chari took it from him. I had not yet finished the daily worship of the Master. He bowed down to me and became unconscious as before. He was repeating the Master's name and also "Mother, Mother." Tears were streaming from his eyes. Those mangoes were of excellent quality. Some were cut and offered to the Master. Jogin brought some of that prasad on a leaf plate to me. I took a little and asked Golap to bring another leaf plate. I then put some pieces of mango from my plate onto the other plate and said to him, "Please eat." Who could eat? He had no body consciousness and his hands were numb. I took hold of his hand and tried to persuade him to eat, but he couldn't. Instead, he took a piece of mango and began to rub it on his forehead. I sent word to the attendants and they escorted him downstairs. He constantly bowed down on the floor and his forehead got swollen. He didn't eat his meal. I heard that after some time he regained normal consciousness and left.[27]

Once Nag Mahashay visited Holy Mother at her residence on Sarkarbari Lane in Calcutta. The Mother described his exuberant devotion: "What wonderful devotion he had! Look at this dry sal leaf-plate. Could anyone eat it? But out of overwhelming devotion, he swallowed even the leaf-plate because prasad had touched it. Ah, his eyes were full of devotion — slightly reddish and always moist with tears. His body was emaciated from severe austerities. When he came to see me, his body would tremble out of devotion and it was hard for him to climb up the stairs. His steps would falter. I have never seen such devotion in anyone."[28] Holy Mother once gave him a cloth, but Nag Mahashay never used it. On special occasions he would tie it around his head. Sometimes he would say, "Mother is more gracious than Father."[29]

Holy Mother Visits Bihar

Holy Mother stayed at Nilambar's house in Belur from July to October 1893 and then went to Jayrambati. Balaram's daughter Bhubanmohini died in December 1893 (5 Paush 1300) and her mother Krishnabhavini was sick with grief. The doctors suggested that she go to a health resort outside Calcutta. Accordingly, a house was rented at Kailwar on the bank of the Shone River in Bihar, eight miles east of Arrah. Krishnabhavini asked Holy Mother to accompany her and she agreed. In late January 1894 Holy Mother, now 41, went to Balaram's house in Calcutta and then in the early part of February left for Kailwar. The party consisted of Holy Mother, Krishnabhavini and her mother, Golap-ma, Yogin-ma, Swamis Yogananda, Saradananda, Trigunatitananda, and some cooks and servants.

Holy Mother later recalled her stay in Kailwar: "Once I spent a couple of months at Kailwar in the district of Arrah. It is a very healthy place. Golap, Baburam's mother, Balaram's wife, and others were with me. The country abounded in deer. A herd of them roamed about, forming a triangle. But no sooner had we seen them than they fled like birds. I had never before seen anything run so swiftly. The Master would say: 'Musk develops in the navel of the deer. Being fascinated with its smell, the deer run hither and thither. They do not know where the fragrance comes from.' Likewise God dwells in the human body, and human beings do not know it. Therefore they search for bliss everywhere, not knowing that it is already in them. God alone is real and everything else is false."[30]

After returning from Kailwar, Holy Mother left for Jayrambati in April 1894 and then returned to Calcutta in August 1894, again staying with Balaram's family. Every afternoon Yogin-ma, Golap-ma, Krishnabhavini, Matangini, and the women devotees would gather around Holy Mother to hear stories of her childhood and her time with the Master. Those were glorious days.

In 1894 Holy Mother attended the Janmashtami festival (the celebration of Krishna's birth) at Balaram's house. After that Matangini wanted to worship Mother Durga in her country home at Antpur. She invited Holy Mother to attend the festival and she agreed. On Janmashtami Day it was announced that Holy Mother would be going to Matangini's country home in Antpur to attend Durga Puja.

Shortly before Durga Puja in 1894, Matangini left for Antpur with Holy Mother, Yogin-ma, Golap-ma, and Swamiji's disciple Swami Sadananda. Matangini's daughter Krishnabhavini and son Shantiram also came. They went to Haripal by train and then by bullock cart to Antpur, but a palanquin was arranged for Holy Mother. In Antpur, Durga Puja was celebrated for four days with great éclat. Afterwards Holy Mother left for Kamarpukur with Yogin-ma, Golap-ma, and Sadananda. After staying a few days in Kamarpukur, they went to Jayrambati. Holy Mother stayed there and the others returned to Calcutta.

Holy Mother Returns to Calcutta

In February 1895 Holy Mother returned to Balaram's home after her visit to Jayrambati. Every evening Holy Mother would attend the vesper service of Balaram's family deity in the shrine and then meditate on the roof. One evening when Holy Mother was at vespers, Gauri-ma entered her room and hid under her cot. That evening there was torrential rain, so Holy Mother came back to her room for meditation. After an hour Holy Mother began to laugh and cry in an ecstatic mood, and finally she became motionless. After a couple of hours Gauri-ma touched her head to Holy Mother's feet. She opened her eyes and saw Gauri-ma.

Holy Mother asked, "Where have you been?"

"I was hiding under your cot," Gauri-ma said.

Smiling, Holy Mother exclaimed, "What a girl!"

"Mother, I was hiding under your cot for such a long time and you didn't see me," said Gauri-ma.

Holy Mother was late for supper, so Krishnabhavini entered the room to fetch her. Gauri-ma said to Krishnabhavini: "Baudi [sister-in-law], look, Mother says that she does not get ecstasy and samadhi. So I hid under her cot to see what she does during meditation." She then described everything to Krishnabhavini. Embarrassed, Holy Mother remained seated with her eyes cast down.[31]

Holy Mother Takes Her Mother on Pilgrimage

Every devout Hindu aspires to see Gaya, Varanasi, Vrindaban, Prayag, and other holy places at least once in his or her lifetime. Holy Mother wanted to fulfill this desire for her mother, who had gone through many ordeals throughout her life. She planned the pilgrimage for February 1895, and Yogin-ma, Golap-ma, and Yogananda decided to go with her. Accordingly, Holy Mother brought her mother and two brothers, Prasanna and Kali from Jayrambati to Calcutta. The party first went to Varanasi to worship Vishwanath Shiva and Mother Annapurna. One day Yogananda hired a boat and took the party to see where the Ganges flows in a half-crescent and to give them a panoramic view of Varanasi. They stayed in Varanasi for three days and then went to Vrindaban, where they stayed until the middle of April 1895. It was arranged for them to stay at Kalababu's Kunja, Balaram Basu's estate where Holy Mother had stayed during her last visit. They visited all the important temples in Vrindaban.

In April 1895 the party left for Prayag, the confluence of the Ganges and the Jamuna, where they bathed. On their way back they stopped at Gaya. As was the custom, Shyamasundari's eldest son, Prasanna, performed a ritual and offered *pinda* at the feet of Vishnu for their departed father, Ramchandra. Holy Mother was very pleased. On the fourth day they visited Bodh-Gaya and then returned to Calcutta. Holy Mother sent her mother and brothers to Jayrambati while she stayed with M.'s family at 51 Bhavani Datta Lane in Coolootola for a month.

On 13 May 1895 Holy Mother left for Jayrambati. She had with her a small brass image of Baby Krishna, or Bala-Gopala, that she had bought in Vrindaban. She kept the image on a shelf in her room. One day while she was lying on her bed, that image of little Gopala crawled to her and said: "You brought me here, but you don't care for me. You don't feed me or worship me. If you don't worship me, no one else will worship me." Immediately Holy Mother took the image in her hand and kissed it affectionately, touching its cheek with her finger-tips and then touched them with her lips. She offered flowers to the image and placed it next to the Master's picture, where she worshipped it daily.

Holy Mother's Travels 1895–1897

Although from 1895 to 1896, Holy Mother lived mostly in Jayrambati, she sometimes visited Kamarpukur. After attending Jagaddhatri Puja, Holy Mother and Golap-ma went to Kamarpukur. On 26 November 1895 she wrote to M.: "I received 10 rupees which you sent. I am now living in Kamarpukur. Golap had a fever but has now recuperated." In April 1896 Holy Mother returned to Calcutta and stayed for one month at Sharat Sarkar's house at 59/2 Ramkanta Basu Street. She could not stay at Balaram's home because his son Ramakrishna was soon to be married and the house was full of their relatives and guests.

In 1896 Vivekananda wrote a letter to his brother disciples at Alambazar Math encouraging them to serve human beings as God. Swami Trigunatitananda read that letter to Holy Mother, and she said: "Naren is an instrument in the hands of the Master. Naren will make his disciples and devotees fulfill his mission to do good to humanity. For that reason the Master is making Naren write those inspiring words."[32]

After Holy Mother had been at Sharat Sarkar's house for a month, a house was rented for her at Sarkarbari Lane in Baghbazar near the Ganges. The first floor of the house was a turmeric warehouse [according to M. a Jute warehouse] and the second and third floors were the living quarters. Holy Mother lived with Gopal-ma, Golap-ma, and other women devotees on the third floor. From there she could see the Ganges very clearly. Swamis Brahmananda and Yogananda, and a couple of brahmacharis, lived on the second floor so they could look after Holy Mother. Holy Mother stayed in this house for five or six months. After Kali Puja, she left for Jayrambati in November 1896.

Holy Mother returned to Calcutta in 1897, probably in the fourth week of April, and stayed in a rented house at 10/2 Bosepara Lane, Baghbazar. Swamiji went to see her there on 29 April. There was some discussion of Holy Mother visiting Kedarnath and Badrinath, but that plan did not work out.

Swami Vivekananda in Jaipur, 1891.

13
Holy Mother
and Vivekananda

Yā me buddhim suvidadhe satatam dharanyām;
Sāmbā sarvā mama gatih saphale aphale vā.
— *Ambāstotram by Swami Vivekananda*

She who is always guiding and inspiring my intellect in this world,
She is my all-auspicious Mother. She is my goal — whether I succeed
or fail.

Ramakrishna may have cast off his body, but his spirit began to flow in the veins of humanity. Swami Vivekananda, affectionately called Swamiji, carried the Master's ideal of a universal religion to both the West and the East. On 20 February 1897, three and a half years after his highly acclaimed achievement at the Parliament of Religions in Chicago, Vivekananda returned to Calcutta. He was totally exhausted from his constant lecturing and meeting people, so on 8 March, following his doctor's advice, he left for Darjeeling to rest and recover his health. He returned to Calcutta on 21 March to meet Raja Ajit Singh of Khetri and again left for Darjeeling on 23 March. Swamiji finally returned to Calcutta on 28 April 1897. The next day he visited Holy Mother at 10/2 Bosepara Lane in Baghbazar.

Kumudbandhu Sen left an eyewitness account of their meeting:

It was a memorable and historic occasion. All those who had the rare privilege to see this meeting between Holy Mother and the illustrious Swami Vivekananda, for the first time after the latter's return from the West with laurels of glory and fame, felt an exuberance of joy. Holy Mother stood silently at the door of her own room, wearing her usual veil-like covering. Swamiji prostrated himself before her. It was indeed a heavenly sight to see the world-famous Swami Vivekananda prostrating himself with deep reverence and humility before Holy Mother like a devoted son. Holy Mother, deeply moved at the sight of Swamiji after an interval of nearly seven years, stood speechless, as if in a trance. The whole atmosphere was surcharged with indescribable sublimity and divine bliss.

When he made pranams to Mother, Swamiji did not touch her feet, as is often customary. And when he stood up after prostrating to her, he turned to all of us who were standing behind and said in a soft voice: "Go and prostrate before the Mother, but don't touch her feet. She is so gracious, so tender and affectionate, that when one touches her feet she then readily draws unto and takes upon herself all the misery and suffering of the hapless soul, out of her infinite grace and unbounded love and compassion for one and all; thereby she has to suffer herself silently for others' sake. Go slowly one by one and prostrate before her. Pray to her and ask for her blessing from the bottom of your heart, with all sincerity, but without verbal expression. She is ever in a superconscious state and understands everybody's mind."

As directed by Swamiji, all of us, one by one, silently prostrated ourselves before the Mother. Swamiji quietly stood in a corner of the veranda. When we all had finished offering pranams to Mother, Golap-ma broke the silence and addressed Swamiji on behalf of the Mother, saying in a most affectionate tone: "Mother is eager to know how you have been keeping at Darjeeling. Is there much improvement?"

Swamiji: "Yes, I was much better there. Mahendra Banerjee and his accomplished wife very kindly looked after my comfort. I hope within a short time I will be all right."

Golap-ma: "Mother says that the Master is always with you. You have still many more things to do for the good of the world."

Swamiji: "I see directly, I feel, and I realize that I am a mere instrument of the Master. Sometimes I am myself surprised how such wonderfully great things are taking place and how in the West men and women are ready to devote their lives to this noble cause and to help me voluntarily in spreading the message of the Master. I went to America with the blessing of the Mother, and when I succeeded in moving the people there through my speeches and received tremendous ovations from them, I remembered at once the power of the Mother's blessings, which had worked such a miracle. When I rested in silence, I could clearly perceive that the same Divine Power, whom the Master called the 'Divine Mother,' was guiding me there."

Golap-ma conveyed the Mother's reply: "The Master is not separate or different from the Divine Mother. The Master is doing all these great things through you. You are his chosen disciple and son. He loved you intensely and predicted before all that you were one day destined to be a distinguished world teacher."

With great emotion, Swamiji said: "Mother, I want to spread the Master's message and establish a worthy and enduring organization for that purpose as soon as possible. But I feel distressed that I cannot do things as speedily as I wish."

Holy Mother herself spoke in a soft voice, with maternal affection: "Don't worry about that. What you have done, and what you will do, will endure forever. You are born for this world, for this mission. Thousands will look upon you as the enlightened teacher of the world. Rest assured that the Master will very soon fulfill your desire. You will before long find that your ideas are taking practical shape."

With prayerful reverence Swamiji said to Mother: "Bless me, Mother, that I may see my plan of work materialize as quickly as possible." With these words Swamiji took leave of Holy Mother and reverently prostrated before her again.[1]

Vivekananda was reassured and deeply moved by Holy Mother's blessings. In the course of this meeting he said to her: "Mother, I did not clear the ocean this time in one jump.* I went to America in a boat built by Westerners. I discovered there the great glories of our Master. Many good people listened to me, spellbound, about Sri Ramakrishna and accepted his ideas."[2]

At Pashupati Basu's house, on 20 February 1897, Swamiji said to M.: "Master Mahashay, whatever success you see in my life is the *lila* [play] of the Master. I am only an instrument. He sent me there. When the Master indicated that I should go to the West, I informed the Mother and asked for her permission and command. By the blessings of the Mother I easily overcame all difficulties there and became the most prominent figure amongst many famous learned pandits and scientists."[3]

Vivekananda's View of Holy Mother

One can know God only by His grace and not by means of austerity, or by japa and meditation. Grace dawns upon those who are endowed with purity and renunciation, humility and unselfishness, devotion and passionate yearning. Swami Vivekananda recognized Holy Mother's divinity long before he left for the West. From America he wrote to his brother disciples about Holy Mother:

You have not yet realized how precious Mother is. People will not understand her now, but they will, gradually. Brother, there will be no salvation of the world without the help of the Divine Power.... Why is it that our country is the weakest and most backward of all countries? Because Shakti is held in dishonour here. Without the grace of Shakti nothing will be accomplished. What do I find in America and Europe? The worship of Shakti, the worship of Power. Yet they worship Her ignorantly, through

*Swamiji was referring to the monkey Hanuman, a servant and devotee of Rama-chandra, who jumped from India to Sri Lanka in search of Sita.

sense gratification. Imagine then what a lot of good they will achieve when they worship Her with purity, looking upon Her as their Mother! I am coming to understand things every day, my insight is opening out more and more....Let Ramakrishna disappear, that does not frighten me. But it will be a calamity if people forget Mother....Don't be angry with me. None of you has understood Mother. Her grace upon me is one hundred thousand times greater than that of the Master....About Mother I am a little fanatic. I can do anything if she gives the order. I shall give a sigh of relief when you purchase a piece of land and install this living Durga there....Brother, when I think of Mother, I say to myself: "Who is this Ramakrishna?" I say this because of my fanaticism. Whether Ramakrishna was God or man — you may say whatever you like. But, Brother, shame upon him who is not devoted to Mother![4]

After receiving Holy Mother's blessings, Swamiji inaugurated the Ramakrishna Mission on 1 May 1897 at Balaram's house in Calcutta. Kumudbandhu Sen described the Mission's regular meetings: "The weekly meetings of the Ramakrishna Mission were usually held on Sunday evenings at Balaram Mandir, in Baghbazar. At several of these meetings, Holy Mother was present, accompanied by some of her women companions and devotees. Swamiji would often preside over these meetings and would sing many songs, especially when Holy Mother was present."[5]

On 6 May 1897 Swamiji left for Almora to recuperate his health, along with Swamis Yogananda, Adbhutananda, and Niranjanananda. Others joined him there later. One day in Almora, Swamiji talked with his brother disciples about the future Women's Math, which he wanted to centre on Holy Mother. In July Yogananda returned to Calcutta. One day he met Girish at Balaram Mandir and talked to him about Swamiji's plan. This conversation was recorded by Kumudbandhu Sen:

Swami Yogananda said: "Swamiji wants to establish a monastery for women sannyasinis under the direct guidance of the Mother. All the women disciples of the Master would be able to live together in the proposed Math for women, and other women, including even those from the West who desire to lead a life of renunciation and meditation may come and live there and derive immense benefit by coming into intimate contact with the living ideals and hallowed associations of the women disciples....The Mother's glowing personal example of purity and character, her spiritual talks and teachings based on her own realizations and her ennobling love and care will inspire and elevate the inmates of the proposed Math, at the same time instilling into them a new force that will awaken their dormant energy. They will be transformed entirely and endowed with a new vision and realization of their own shakti [potential] so that they too can work fearlessly for the highest good of humanity.

"Swamiji told me with great emotion: 'Our Mother is a vast reservoir of spiritual energy, though outwardly calm like the deep ocean. Her advent marks the beginning of a new era in the history of India. The ideals that she lives and teaches will not only spiritualize the efforts for the emancipation of women in India but will also penetrate into and influence the minds and hearts of women all the world over. Mother represents the highest expression of womanhood, especially in India. It [motherhood] is an innate instinct in every woman, the signs of which might be discovered even in a little girl. In the West the whole structure of society rests on the wifehood of women. But motherhood is the true expression of divine love — sublime, noble, and broad as the sky.'"

In reply, Girish Ghosh said: "It is an altogether new and bold idea of reforming our society and improving the lot of our women. Swamiji's will must be fulfilled, and I have not the least hesitation in fully supporting this proposal....But his failing health is making all of us anxious and the doctors have strongly advised him to take complete rest."

Swami Yogananda said: "Physical ill-health or any other impediment from any source is not going to daunt or dissuade him from his determination to carry out his plans, which he firmly believes will benefit society and contribute to the well-being of mankind. He only smiles at our anxiety for and worry over the condition of his health.

"After listening to all that he told me of his plan for starting a women's Math, I said to him: 'Do whatever you think will be conducive for the good of society at large, but please do not bring the Mother into public prominence now. Don't you remember the Master telling us that his body would not survive if we preached him before the public? The same may be said in respect to the Mother too. I do not allow all and sundry to meet the Mother or touch her feet while offering their salutations. I see that only sincere devotees of pure character have her darshan. Therefore, I humbly request you, brother, not to disturb the Mother at present. You may start the women's Math with the help and cooperation of women devotees of spotless character and spiritual realization, who also possess learning and skill in various branches of knowledge and work, and who are capable of taking charge of this organization without any direct association with men as such, not to speak of our sadhus.'

"As soon as I finished saying this, Swamiji heartily thanked me and smilingly said: 'Mantri*, you have given me a sound piece of advice and aptly reminded me of the Master's words in this respect. I shall not disturb the Mother. Let her fulfill her mission according to her own will and

*Literally, counsellor or minister.

in the manner she chooses. Who are we to dictate to her? Rather, we can accomplish everything with her blessings. I have personally seen and felt the power of her blessings, which can do miracles.'"

Girish replied: "Yogen Swami, you have done yeoman's service indeed. Now I see why you accompanied Swamiji to Almora."[6]

The Ramakrishna Math had been inaugurated in 1886 at Baranagore. In 1892 it was moved to Alambazar. But when Swamiji returned from the West he was desperately trying to build a permanent monastery on the bank of the Ganges. Finally on 3 February 1898 he succeeded in acquiring the present site of Belur Math, the permanent headquarters of the Ramakrishna Mission. The Math was then moved temporarily, on 13 February 1898, to Nilambar Babu's garden house in Belur, as it was very close to the property that had just been purchased. Holy Mother had previously stayed at this garden house. When the site was purchased, Holy Mother remarked: "I always saw the Master living in a cottage on the bank of the Ganges, where the Math now stands, surrounded by a banana grove. When the new land was purchased, Naren took me there one day. He showed me around and said, 'Mother, now you can move freely in your own place.'"[7]

It is said that the site of Belur Math had earlier been the timberyard of Captain Vishwanath Upadhyay of Nepal, and that Ramakrishna had once visited him there.

In April 1898 construction began on the monastery building. At the end of April, Holy Mother came from Calcutta by boat to visit the site with Golap-ma, Swami Yogananda, and Brahmachari Krishnalal.

As soon as she landed at the ghat of Nilambar Babu's house, the monks received her, blowing conches. They washed her feet, fanned her, and took her to the shrine. Holy Mother worshipped the Master that day and had prasad there. In the afternoon, at Swami Brahmananda's request, Holy Mother and her party went to the construction site. Sister Nivedita, Sara Bull, and Josephine MacLeod were then staying in an old house on the property. They had previously met Holy Mother in Calcutta and now cordially received her and showed her around. Holy Mother was happy to see how the work was proceeding. She remarked: "At long last the boys have a place to lay their heads. The Master finally has cast his grace on them." She then returned to Calcutta by boat.

In March 1898 there was an outbreak of plague in Calcutta. Swami Vivekananda immediately wanted to make plans for relief work, but there was no money. He told his brother disciples: "We shall sell, if necessary, the land that has just been purchased for the monastery. We are sannyasins; we must be ready to sleep under the trees and live on alms as we did before. Must we care for the monastery and possessions, when by disposing of them we could relieve thousands of helpless people suffering before our own eyes?"[8]

Swamiji had such a strong personality that it was not easy to dissuade him. Moreover, his brother disciples were very obedient. However, Swami Shivananda interjected: "Swamiji, you always consult with Holy Mother about important matters. Will you not consult with her before selling the Math property?"

Swamiji immediately replied: "You are right, Tarakda. It is my mistake. I shall go to Holy Mother right now."

Swamiji went to Holy Mother in Calcutta, accompanied by Brahmananda, Shivananda, and Saradananda. After bowing down, Swamiji said: "Mother, there is no money to serve the plague-stricken people. I am considering selling the Math property and using that money for relief work. We are monks; we can live under the trees. We need your permission."

Holy Mother had always supported Swamiji's projects, but she did not agree with him on this matter. She said: "My son, no, you cannot sell the Math property. This is not your Math. It belongs to the Master. You are my heroic sons; you can spend your lives under the trees. But those of my children who will come in the future will not be able to live under the trees. This Math is for them.... Will the purpose of Belur Math end after conducting only one relief work? The objectives of the Master's mission are many. The infinite ideas of the Master will spread all over the world in the future. His mission will continue through the ages."[9]

Swamiji immediately realized the truth of Holy Mother's statement. He told his brother disciples: "It is true; I have no right to sell the monastery land. What was my emotion leading me to do? It did not occur to me." Swamiji joyfully accepted Holy Mother's decision.

Holy Mother's words were final regarding any decisions of the Math. Once when a servant stole something from Belur Math, Swamiji asked him to leave. The poor man went to Holy Mother in Calcutta and confessed his guilt. He asked her to get his job back for him. She forgave him and sent him back to Belur with Premananda, saying: "This man is poor. He stole out of dire poverty. Naren threw him out. My son, there is so much suffering in this world. You are monks, so you don't understand worldly life. Please take him back."[10] Premananda accompanied the man to Belur and reported everything to Swamiji, who was happy to accept Holy Mother's decision.

Above: Belur Math from the Ganges, 1937.
Below: Leggett House at Belur Math, where Sarada Devi stayed.

In October 1898, Swami Vivekananda returned from a pilgrimage in Kashmir and visited Holy Mother at 10/2 Bosepara Lane, Calcutta. When Swamiji bowed down, the Mother blessed him touching his head with her right hand. He said to her in a rather piqued voice: "Mother, how slight is your Master's power! A Muslim fakir cursed me because one of his disciples came to me. He said that on account of stomach trouble I would have to leave the place in three days. And so it happened. Your Master could not protect me."

Holy Mother answered through Krishnalal: "This is the result of psychic powers that the fakir has acquired. You must accept the manifestation of such powers. The Master believed in them. He accepted all traditions."

Swamiji, still upset, replied: "Whatever you may say, Mother. I don't agree with you. The Master is powerless."

Holy Mother teased him: "My son, how can you deny the Master's power? Even the tuft of your hair is held in his hand."[11] When Holy Mother reminded Swamiji of the Master's love for him, he bowed down with tearful eyes and left after having prasad.

Holy Mother Blesses Belur Math

On 12 November 1898, the day before Kali Puja, Holy Mother, accompanied by several women devotees, again visited the site where the Ramakrishna Order was shortly to have its headquarters. Swami Vivekananda had invited his Western disciples also. All the monks were present, and elaborate arrangements had been made for worship. The picture of the Master that had been worshipped in the old monastery was installed in the new site, and the Holy Mother brought her own picture of the Master. She blessed the temple site with a special Puja.

That afternoon Holy Mother returned to Calcutta with her party, along with Vivekananda, Brahmananda, and Saradananda. Swamiji had requested them all to take part in the ceremonial opening of Sister Nivedita's girls' school at 16 Bosepara Lane in Baghbazar. Holy Mother and her companions attended the opening the next morning, on the day of Kali Puja.

Once Swamiji was carried away by a Vedantic experience, which he related to Holy Mother: "Mother, nowadays everything is disappearing from my mind."

Holy Mother said to him with a smile: "My son, please don't make me vanish."

"Mother, if I make you disappear," Swamiji replied, "where shall I stand? The knowledge that banishes the guru is ignorance. How can knowledge exist without the guru?"[12] Swamiji realized that Ramakrishna and Holy Mother were one and the same. He also pointed this out to his brother disciples.

Swami Vijnanananda, whom Swamiji called "Peshan," had great love and respect for Holy Mother, but he seldom visited her in Calcutta. One day he went with Swamiji to Balaram's house in Calcutta while Holy Mother was there. Swamiji asked, "Peshan, did you salute Holy Mother?"

"No, Swamiji, I did not."

"What! Go right now and bow down to the Mother," said Swamiji.

Accordingly, Swami Vijnanananda went to Holy Mother and bowed down to her from a distance, bending his head to the floor. As soon as Vijnanananda got up, he heard Swamiji, who was standing behind him, say: "What is this, Peshan? Does anybody salute the Mother in this way? Bow down to her by prostrating yourself on the floor. Holy Mother is the Mother of the Universe." Swamiji then prostrated himself to Holy Mother, and Vijnanananda did likewise. Later Vijnanananda remarked, "I did not imagine that Swamiji would follow me to the Mother."[13]

Ramakrishna had told Holy Mother that his disciples would look after her, and Holy Mother cared for them as her own children. Swamiji arranged for Holy Mother to be given 25 rupees per month for her expenses. On 20 June 1899, Swamiji left for his second visit to the West. Holy Mother arranged a feast for him that day. After having lunch at Holy Mother's place, Swamiji, Turiyananda, and Nivedita left for the Calcutta harbour, and other disciples also went to see them off.

When Swami Vivekananda returned a year and a half later, he visited Holy Mother. Surabala, Holy Mother's sister-in-law, was amazed when she saw a handsome prince-like man fall at the Mother's feet.

Sometime later Swamiji was not well, so Holy Mother went to see him at Belur Math with Golap-ma and other women devotees. When Holy Mother arrived, her boat was anchored at high tide. But when it was time for her to leave, low tide had mired the boat in the mud. Swami Vivekananda and the monks had come to the ghat to see Holy Mother off. When he saw that the boatmen were unable to push the boat into the water, Swamiji rushed to them and began to push. The monks joined him.[14] Holy Mother was moved by her heroic children's love for her.

In 1901 Swamiji wanted to perform Durga Puja at Belur Math and asked Holy Mother for her permission. She agreed: "Yes, my son, please worship Mother Durga at Belur Math. Nothing can be accomplished in this world without worshipping Shakti. But my son, do not sacrifice an animal [normally part of the ritual]. You are monks; you have taken the vow of offering fearlessness to all beings."[15] Swamiji had intended to perform the entire ritual, including the sacrifice, but he changed his plans as Holy Mother wished.

Holy Mother later described the event, which took place in 1901:

> Naren took me to Belur Math at the time of the first Durga Puja festival, and through me gave 25 rupees to the priest as dakshina [a donation]. They spent 1,400 rupees on that auspicious occasion. The place was crowded with people. The monks worked hard. Naren came to me and said, "Mother, please make me lie down with fever." No sooner had he said this than he was struck down with a severe attack of fever. I thought: "Goodness gracious! What is this? How will he be cured?" "Do not be anxious, Mother," said Naren, "I have myself begged for this fever. My reason is this: These boys are working hard. But if I see the slightest mistake, I shall fly into a rage and scold them. I may even slap them. It will be painful to them as well as to me. Therefore I thought it would be better to lie down with fever for some time." When the day's function was over, I came to him and said: "My son, the work is over now. Please get up." Naren said that he was all right and got up from his bed.
>
> Naren brought his own mother to the Math at the time of the Durga Puja. She roamed from one garden to another and picked chilies, eggplants, etc. She felt a little proud, thinking that it was all due to her son Naren. Naren came to her and said: "What are you doing here? Why do you not go and meet Holy Mother? You are simply picking these vegetables. Maybe you are thinking that your son has done all this work. No, Mother. You are mistaken. It is the Master who has done all this. Naren is nothing." Naren meant that the Math was founded through the grace of the Master. What great devotion![16]

It is natural for parents to be proud when their children are successful and talented. Conversely, parents become sad if their children are unlucky, unsuccessful, or dull-witted. If anyone mentioned Swamiji to Holy Mother, she would say: "Why do you drag Naren into everything? He is in a class by himself."[17]

Holy Mother never tired of describing the greatness and struggle of the Master's disciples and their dependence on him:

> The disciples of the Master accepted him only after thorough examination. What an austere life they led at the Baranagore monastery after his passing away! Niranjan and others often starved themselves. They spent all their time in meditation and prayer. One day these young monks were talking among themselves: "We have renounced everything in the name of Sri Ramakrishna. Let us see if he will supply us with food if we simply

depend upon him. We will not tell anybody about our wants. We will not go out for alms either." They covered their bodies with sheets of cloth and sat down for meditation. The whole day passed. It was late at night. They heard somebody knocking at the door. Naren left his seat and told one of his brother monks: "Please open the door and see who is there. First of all, see if he has anything in his hand." What a miracle! When the door was opened they saw a man standing there with delicious food from Lala Babu's temple of Gopala, on the bank of the Ganges. The disciples were exceedingly happy and felt convinced of the protecting hand of the Master. They offered that food to the Master at that late hour of the night and partook of the prasad. Such things happened many times. Another day Beni Pal of Sinthi sent luchis and other food to the monks. Now the monks do not experience any such difficulty. Alas! What hardships Naren and Baburam passed through! Even my Rakhal, who is now the president of the Mission, had to clean the pots and kettles, many days.

At one time Naren was travelling as an itinerant monk towards Gaya and Varanasi. He did not get any food for two days and was lying down under a tree when a man arrived with luchis, curry, sweets, and a jar of water in his hands. The man said: "Here is the prasad of Rama. Please accept it." Naren said: "You do not know me, my good friend. You have made a mistake. Perhaps you have brought these articles for someone else." The man said with the utmost humility: "No, Maharaj. I have brought this food solely for you. I was enjoying a little nap at noontime when I saw a man in a dream. He said: 'Get up quickly; a holy man is lying under yonder tree. Give him some food.' I dismissed the whole thing as a mere dream. Therefore I turned on my side and again fell asleep. Again I dreamt of the man, who said, giving me a push: 'I am asking you to get up and still you are sleeping! Carry out my order without any more delay.' Then I knew that it was not an illusory dream. It was the command of Rama. Therefore in obedience to His command I brought these articles for you." Naren realized that it was all due to the grace of the Master, and he cheerfully accepted the food.

A similar incident happened another day. Naren was travelling in the Himalayas for three days without any food. He was about to faint when a Muslim fakir gave him a cucumber. It saved his life. After his return from America, Naren was one day addressing a meeting at Almora. He saw that same Muslim fakir seated in a corner. Naren at once went to him, took him by the hand, and made him sit in the centre of the gathering. The audience was surprised. Naren said, "This gentleman saved my life once." He then narrated the whole incident. He also gave the fakir some money. At first, the fakir refused to accept the gift, saying, "What have I done that you are so anxious to make me a gift?" Naren did not yield and pressed some money into his pocket.[18]

Krishna gave divine sight to Arjuna so that he could see his cosmic form. It is not possible to recognize the divinity of an avatar with normal human understanding. By Holy Mother's grace, Swamiji realized her true nature. Once he remarked at Belur Math: "Mother is the incarnation of Bagala* in the guise of Saraswati. Outwardly she is all peace, but inwardly she is the destroyer of evil."[19]

Once Vivekananda and Turiyananda went to visit Holy Mother in Calcutta. In the boat from Belur Math, Turiyananda noticed that Vivekananda was drinking the muddy Ganges water. He warned him, "Swamiji, you will become sick."

Swamiji replied: "No, brother, I am afraid when I visit Holy Mother. Our minds are not pure enough, so I am purifying my mind by drinking Ganges water."[20] Swamiji was afraid that Holy Mother would absorb his impurities and suffer.

When Swami Vivekananda passed away on 4 July 1902, Holy Mother was in Jayrambati. When she got this heartbreaking news she remained silent for three days, weeping bitterly. She plaintively lamented, "Master, did you ask me to stay to see the death of my children?"[21] Later she would recall: "The Master would say, 'Naren is the crown of my head. He has two bad omens in his body: First, his breathing is long and rapid; and second, he eats a little more than a usual person. These signs indicate a short life.'"[22]

In 1909 at Koalpara, Keshavananda said to the Mother: "If Swamiji were alive today, how much he could have done for this country."

The Mother quickly answered: "Oh dear, if my Naren were here today, would the Company [the British Government] leave him in peace? They would have locked him up in jail. I could not see it and live. Naren was an unsheathed sword."[23]

One day towards the end Swamiji bowed down to Holy Mother and said: "Mother, I know for certain that with your blessing in the future many Narens will be born and hundreds of Vivekanandas will evolve. And I also know for certain that in this world there is only one Mother like you; there is no other."[24]

---

*Bagala represents one of the terrible aspects of the Divine Power, as the slayer of a fierce demon, and Saraswati represents wisdom.

14

Holy Mother
and Western Women

Lajjā-patāvrite nityam sārade jnāna-dāyike;
Pāpebhyo nah sadā raksha kripā-mayi namostu te.
— *A hymn by Swami Abhedananda*

O Sarada! O giver of spiritual knowledge! O you who always cover
yourself with the veil of modesty! Please always protect us from all
sins; salutations to you, O Compassionate One.

Everything in this world is subject to change. Science and technology
are rapidly changing the world, and human beings are adapting
to those changes. Nowadays people's education and upbringing,
culture and behaviour, way of life and style of living, food habits and
style of dress, values and goals in life are quite different from those of
people who lived in the nineteenth and early twentieth centuries. As we
study Holy Mother's life, we see that she lived according to the culture of
ancient India. When Vivekananda's Western women devotees met Holy
Mother, they were surprised to see how she lived. It was hard for them
to believe that a woman who wore only one cloth, walked barefoot, kept
herself veiled, and without formal education could conduct the spiritual
ministry of the Ramakrishna Order.

Holy Mother's life is a meeting point of the ancient and the modern.
She was born in a rural Indian village in the nineteenth century, and she
passed away in twentieth-century Calcutta. From her very birth she was
endowed with divine qualities, such as purity and modesty, love and
affection, devotion and humility, forgiveness and compassion, truthfulness
and simplicity, patience and perseverance, faith and forbearance,
renunciation and discrimination, service and self-control, courage and
fearlessness. During her maturity she conducted Ramakrishna's spiritual
ministry, advised his disciples and devotees, became a mother to the
Western women who came to Swami Vivekananda, asked her disciples to
learn English, and encouraged girls to have a modern education.

210

In Dakshineswar, Ramakrishna had a vision that he described to Holy Mother: "I was in the land of the white people. Their skin is white, their hearts are white, and they are simple and sincere. It is a very beautiful country. I think I shall go there."[1] Later when Vivekananda and other disciples went to the West to spread Vedanta and the universal message of Ramakrishna, some Western women helped them immensely. Swamiji observed that one of the causes of prosperity in the West was education for both men and women, whereas women were neglected in India. He remarked: "A bird cannot fly with one wing." He believed that both men and women were necessary to build a successful nation.

Swami Vivekananda wrote from America to his brother disciples: "We must first build a Math for the Mother." On 25 February 1897 he wrote to his devotee Sara Bull, the widow of Norwegian violinist Ole Bull: "My duty would not be complete if I die without starting two places — one for the sannyasins, the other for the women."[2] Vivekananda wanted to give Indian women an education centred on Holy Mother. For this purpose he received financial help from some Western women. Two Western initiated disciples, Margaret Elizabeth Noble (Sister Nivedita) and Christine Greenstidel (Sister Christine), dedicated their lives to educating Indian women.

On 17 March 1898 Mrs. Sara Bull, Miss Josephine MacLeod (another of Swamiji's devotees), and Sister Nivedita (then Margaret Elizabeth Noble) met Holy Mother at 10/2 Bosepara Lane in Calcutta. Although they did not know Holy Mother's language, they communicated through the language of the heart. Holy Mother received them affectionately and treated them as her daughters. When they were served refreshments, Miss MacLeod asked, through a translator, "Won't you eat with us?" Holy Mother readily agreed.

When Swamiji heard about this, he was overjoyed and wrote to Ramakrishnananda: "Mother is here, and the European and American ladies went the other day to see her. And what do you think? Mother even ate with them! Isn't that grand?" Swami Nikhilananda explained how unusual this was: "In general she was very punctilious about observing orthodox Hindu habits, especially in the matter of food, and avoided eating with people outside her own caste. This partaking of food with foreign ladies was, as it were, a sanction given by her to Hindu society to accept and absorb them into its fold."[3] After meeting these Western women, Holy Mother understood that the Master's vision in Dakshineswar of white people had been realized.

About this first meeting with Holy Mother, Mrs. Bull wrote:

We were the first foreigners to have received permission to see Sarada Devi, the widow of Sri Ramakrishna. She called us her children, and saying that our visit to her was of the Lord, she felt no strangeness in being with us.

When I asked her to define the obedience to a guru, who in her case was her husband, she replied to the effect that: when one had chosen a guru or teacher, one should listen to and obey all his directions for spiritual advancement. But in things temporal one could most truly serve a guru by using one's best discernment, even if at times it was not in agreement with suggestions given.[4]

It is interesting to note how these Western women regarded Holy Mother. On 22 May 1898 Sister Nivedita wrote to her friend Mrs. Eric Hammond in London:

I have often thought that I ought to tell you about the lady who was the wife of Sri Ramakrishna, Sarada as her name is. To begin with, she is dressed in a white cotton cloth like any other Hindu widow under fifty. This cloth goes round the waist and forms a skirt, then it passes round the body and over the head like a nun's veil. When a man speaks to her, he stands behind her, and she pulls this white veil very far forward over her face. Nor does she answer him directly. She speaks to another older woman in almost a whisper, and this woman repeats her words to the man. In this way it comes about that the Master [Vivekananda] has never seen the face of Sarada! Added to this, you must try to imagine her always seated on the floor, on a small piece of bamboo matting. All this does not sound very sensible perhaps, yet this woman, when you know her well, is said to be the very soul of practicality and common sense, as she certainly gives every token of being, to those who know her slightly. Sri Ramakrishna always consulted her before undertaking anything and her advice is always acted upon by his disciples. She is the very soul of sweetness — so gentle and loving and as merry as a girl. You should have heard her laugh the other day when I insisted that the Swami must come up and see us at once, or we would go home. The monk who had brought the message that the Master would delay seeing us was quite alarmed at my moving towards my shoes, and departed post-haste to bring him up, and then you should have heard Sarada's laughter! It just pealed out. And she is so tender — "my daughter" she calls me. She has always been terribly orthodox, but all this melted away the instant she saw the first two Westerners — Mrs. Bull and Miss MacLeod, and she tasted food with them! Fruit is always presented to us immediately, and this was naturally offered to her, and she to the surprise of everyone accepted. This gave us all a dignity and made my future work possible in a way nothing else could possibly have done.

Then you should see the chivalrous feeling that the monks have for her. They always call her "Mother" and speak of her as "The Holy Mother" — and she is literally their first thought in every emergency. There are always one or two in attendance on her, and whatever her wish is, it is their command. It is a wonderful relationship to watch. I should love to give her a message from you, if you care to send her one. A monk read the *Magnificat* in Bengali to her one day for me, and you should have seen how she enjoyed it. She really is, under the simplest, most unassuming guise, one of the strongest and greatest of women.[5]

Holy Mother and Josephine MacLeod

Miss MacLeod met Holy Mother many times. On one occasion she went to Calcutta to pay her respects to Holy Mother. She watched as the Indian women devotees bowed down to Holy Mother, touching her feet with their foreheads. Miss MacLeod stood there for a few moments unable to decide how she should pay her respects. Holy Mother caught her eye and with a slight movement of the hand indicated that Western devotees need not follow the Hindu custom. Miss MacLeod was impressed with the Mother's common sense, which she later spoke of as one of her most impressive characteristics.

Swami Vivekananda wanted his Western followers to see some other spiritual role models, so one day he sent Mrs. Bull, Miss MacLeod, and Nivedita to Kamarhati to meet Gopal-ma, who had the vision of Baby Krishna, or Gopala. She received them cordially and kissed them. As she had no other furniture in her room, they sat on her bed. She served them some puffed rice and sweet coconut balls and shared some of her spiritual experiences with them. When they returned to Calcutta, Swamiji said: "Ah! This is the *old* India that you have seen, the India of prayers and tears, of vigils and fasts that is passing away."[6]

In the middle of November 1898, Mrs. Bull and Miss MacLeod came to Calcutta and stayed with Nivedita in her house at 16 Bosepara Lane. Holy Mother was staying nearby at 10/2 Bosepara Lane. One day Mrs. Bull asked Holy Mother to consent to having her photo taken, but she declined. She was too shy to go to a studio and unveil her face in front of a photographer whom she did not know. Then Mrs. Bull said to her, "Mother, I wish to take the photo to America and worship it." Then Holy Mother consented, asking only that the photographer be a woman. When no female photographer could be found, an English photographer named Mr. Harrington was hired to come to Holy Mother's residence. Before he arrived, a black screen was set up as a backdrop on the wall of an attic room, and Holy Mother was seated on a fur asana (a small rug) over a cot. Two tubs containing a palm plant and a fern were at either side of her. Nivedita, Mrs. Bull, and Golap-ma arranged her cloth, hair, and veil. When the photographer came, Holy Mother cast her eyes down and went into an ecstatic mood. That was the first photo taken of Holy Mother. She regained her normal state after some time and the photographer took the second photo, which is now worshipped everywhere. A third photo was taken with Nivedita sitting facing her. Holy Mother was then 45 years old. Devotees of the Holy Mother should be grateful to these Western women for arranging to have these photos taken. (*See more details about the Mother's first three photographs in Appendix 1.*)

Years later when she saw her own photo, Holy Mother commented: "Yes, this is a good picture, but I was stouter before it was taken. Jogin [Swami Yogananda] was very ill at that time. I grew thin worrying about him. I was very unhappy. I would weep when Jogin's illness took a turn for the worse and I would be happy when he felt better. Mrs. Sara Bull arranged this photograph. At first I didn't agree to it; but she insisted and said, 'Mother, I shall take this picture to America and worship it.' At last the picture was taken."[7]

Nivedita wrote about this historic occasion: "That photograph was the first time she had ever looked at a grown-up man outside her own family, or been seen by one."[8] Miss MacLeod remarked of Holy Mother's picture: "That's Sarada Devi. She hadn't been seen by a man in her life.* Mrs. Bull and Nivedita wanted to have her picture. I asked her, 'Mother, will you be agreeable to sitting in front of the camera?' She agreed. Oh, what utter self-control! She was so calm! But she didn't care for this kind of pomp at all."[9]

Years later, Miss MacLeod had a wonderful experience regarding Holy Mother's divine presence. One day she went with Swami Nirbhayananda to pay her respects to Holy Mother at her Calcutta residence in Udbodhan, and returned to Belur Math at dusk. After attending the vesper service at the shrine of the Math and spending a little while in meditation, she was going back to her quarters at the guest house, accompanied by a brahmachari with a lantern. She was walking slowly, absorbed in thought, when the bramachari heard her say to herself: "I have seen her! I have seen her!" Then she whispered to him: "The Holy Mother! I have seen her." She walked all the way to her room muttering the word "Mother" and adding some other words that her companion did not understand.

---

*Meaning a man whom she did not know.

Holy Mother was fond of Miss MacLeod and called her "Jaya" and her sister, Betty, "Vijaya." On another occasion Miss MacLeod wrote in a letter: "I asked her [Holy Mother] about meditation and how to do it. She said to think of the Divinity in Swamiji, but I said that in ordinary life he was uppermost always in my mind, but in meditation I purposely excluded him. This did astonish her! But she said that Ramakrishna had said it had taken the power of seven sages to make Swamiji, and that in Ramakrishna the power of the sages had brought him down to earth!"[10]

Miss MacLeod loved to talk and was free with Holy Mother. Later she related to Romain Rolland a conversation she once had with Holy Mother regarding the difference between Ramakrishna and Vivekananda. As they had no common language, someone always acted as an interpreter. Through the interpreter, Miss MacLeod said to Holy Mother: "Your husband had the best part; he only had to speak sweet words in India among his fellow men; that is why it was a joy for him. Vivekananda's mission was more painful. He had to be the propagator of Indian thought abroad, among strange and hostile people. His role was the more heroic."

"Yes," the Mother answered. "Swamiji was the greatest. My husband used to say that he was the body and Vivekananda was the head."[11]

Miss MacLeod also told Romain Rolland about Holy Mother herself, saying: "The Holy Mother had a natural affinity with Western women, able to speak with them on any subject, and had a simplicity, a fineness, a delightful disposition. Just as pure as Ramakrishna or Vivekananda, she was all the while living a holy life and at the same time capable of being interested, with the joy of a child, in the attire of her European friends. Her great valour, however, was not recognized in her own village, where she did not show that she was any different from other women."[12]

Holy Mother and Sara Bull

Mrs. Bull was a wealthy and generous woman. She helped the Ramakrishna Mission and Nivedita's school financially, and in 1907 she began to send 60 rupees per month[13] to Holy Mother. In 1910 when Mrs. Bull was seriously ill in America, Holy Mother was concerned and dictated a letter to her. The letter was written by Nivedita and Holy Mother signed it with the Bengali word "Ma." It is noteworthy that Ramakrishna never wrote any letters, but Holy Mother dictated hundreds of letters to her Indian and Western devotees and disciples. (Many of those letters are presented in Chapter 27.) Here is an excerpt from the letter to Sara Bull written on 28 July 1910:

Mother,

Hearing that you are very ill, I am very anxious about you. I heard from your daughter Nivedita that you are a little better. I am praying to Thakur, the Lord, for your speedy recovery.

I have offered on your behalf, to the feet of the Master, a tulsi and a bel leaf, and three evenings sitting before him I have prayed for you. Please give her [Miss MacLeod] my warm blessings and do not forget Christine if you see her.

And now from our Lord I am sending you a flower and sandal dust which I offered to him, with worship. My deep love and blessing you will realize.

Your Ma (Mother)[14]

It seems that Nivedita left India in October 1910 for America to see Mrs. Bull during her illness, and also to raise funds for her school in Calcutta. Like the disciples of Ramakrishna, Nivedita was aware of Holy Mother's spiritual greatness. One day she went to a church in Boston where she saw the Madonna as Holy Mother. On her return home, she noted down in her diary: "Went to church. Saw Sarada Devi as Madonna. Her presence will sanctify," and she immediately wrote a letter to Holy Mother on 11 December 1910.

Beloved Mother:

This morning, early, I went to church — to pray for Sara. All the people there were thinking of Mary, the Mother of Jesus, and suddenly I thought of you. Your dear face, and your loving look, and your white Sari and your bracelets. It was all there. And it seemed to me that yours was the presence that was to soothe and bless poor S. Sara's sick-room. And — do you know? — I thought I had been very foolish to sit in your room, at the evening service to Sri Ramakrishna, trying to meditate. Why did I not understand that it was quite enough to be a little child at your dear feet? Dear Mother! You are full of love! And it is not a flushed and violent love, like ours, and like the world's but a gentle peace that brings good to everyone and wishes ill to none. It is a golden radiance, full of play. What a blessed Sunday that was, a few months ago, when I ran in to you, the last thing before I went on the Ganges, and ran back to you for a moment, as soon as I came back! I felt such a wonderful freedom in the blessing you gave me, and in your welcome home! Dearest Mother — I wish we could send you a wonderful hymn, or a prayer. But somehow even that would seem too loud, too full of noise! Surely you are the most wonderful thing of God — Sri Ramakrishna's own chalice of His Love for the world — a token left with His children, in these lonely days, and we should be very still and quiet before you — except indeed for a little fun! Surely the "wonderful things of God" are all quiet — stealing unnoticed into our lives — the air and the sunlight and the sweetness of gardens and of the Ganges, these are the silent things that are like you! Do send to poor S. Sara the mantle of your peace. Isn't your thought, now and then, of the high calm that neither loves nor hates? Isn't that the sweet benediction that trembles in God, like the dew-drop on the lotus-leaf, and touches not the world?

> Ever, my darling Mother, your foolish khooki*,
> Nivedita

Holy Mother and Sister Nivedita

Holy Mother's relationship with Nivedita was sweet and touching, yet awe inspiring. From the very beginning, Nivedita occupied a special place in Holy Mother's heart. During Nivedita's first visit to Holy Mother, Swamiji was a bit apprehensive: Holy Mother had been born and brought up in an orthodox brahmin family in a village. She was not familiar with Western etiquette, and she did not know English. How would she receive his Western disciples? Swamiji sent his disciple Swami Swarupananda as an interpreter. When Swarupananda brought Nivedita to Holy Mother, she asked her name. Nivedita replied, "My name is Miss Margaret Elizabeth Noble."

Swarupananda translated Holy Mother's Bengali: "My child, I shall not be able to utter such a long name. I will call you *Khooki* [baby]."

Nivedita said joyfully, "Yes, yes, I am Mother's baby."

She then went to Swamiji and said: "Mother blessed me touching my head, allowed me to bow down and touch her feet, offered prasad, and said she would call me 'Khooki.'"

Swamiji was overjoyed.

Nivedita began to learn Bengali from Swarupananda so that she could speak with Holy Mother directly.[15] In the beginning, despite Golap-ma's opposition, Holy Mother kept Nivedita in her residence at 10/2 Bosepara Lane so that she could teach Nivedita Hindu manners and customs. She ate her meals with Nivedita and encouraged her activities for women's education.[16]

At Swami Vivekananda's request, Nivedita moved to 16 Bosepara Lane and started a school for girls. On 13 November 1898 Holy Mother inaugurated the school, saying: "May the Divine Mother of the Universe bless this school. May the girls trained here be ideals for society."

Almost every day, Nivedita visited Holy Mother and took the dust of her feet. Every Sunday she cleaned Holy Mother's room, dusting the

---

* Khooki, literally, a little girl — an endearing term that Holy Mother used for Nivedita.

Sarada Devi and Sister Nivedita, Calcutta, November 1898.

bed, sweeping the floor, and polishing the glass panes in the doors and windows. Nivedita had taken on this work as her own duty. She was eager to provide even the smallest service and comfort to the Mother.[17]

Nivedita was financially supported by Mrs. Bull and Miss MacLeod. She did not have much money, but she loved to give gifts to Holy Mother.

On 24 February 1904, Nivedita wrote to Miss MacLeod, after Holy Mother had returned to Calcutta from a visit to Jayrambati: "The Holy Mother is here, so small, so thin, so dark, worn out physically I should say, with village hardship and village life. But the same clear mind — the same stateliness, the same womanhood, as before. Oh, how many comforts I would like to take her! She needs a soft pillow, a shelf, a rug, so many things. She is so crowded with people about her always. I would like to give her a beautiful picture, a piece of bright colour. But I suppose one must wait. Meanwhile, there is not a change in her."[18]

Sarala (later Pravrajika Bharatiprana) was a student at Nivedita's school. She recalled a memorable visit that Sister Nivedita paid to Holy Mother in Udbodhan House:

> After the Mother's return from Jayrambati, one afternoon Sister Sudhira and I went to see her in Udbodhan House. Sister Sudhira remarked: "Mother, you have become very dark and lean."
>
> "Our village is in open fields, you know," the Mother replied, "and so the complexion becomes dark. In addition, I had to work hard there." Meanwhile, Sister Nivedita came, bowed down to the Mother, and took her seat.
>
> Whenever Sister Nivedita visited the Mother, I watched her sit absorbed for a long time in front of the Mother. She would bow down to the Mother with full prostration and an indescribable wave of bliss would flow over her entire face. She seemed a joyful child closely looking at the face of her Mother. Once the Mother presented Sister with a palm-leaf fan that had woolen lace around the edges, which she had made herself. Receiving that fan from the Mother's hand, she was beside herself and exclaimed, "This fan has been made by Matadevi and she has given it to me." This she repeated again and again and touched that fan to her head and chest. And to those who were present there, Sister touched that fan to their heads, including myself. Observing her exuberant joy, the Mother remarked: "Do you see how Nivedita is thrilled having this trivial thing? Ah, how simple she is and what deep faith she has — as if she is a Goddess! How much devotion she has for Naren! Because he was born in this country, she has left her home and family and come to do his work with her heart and soul. What devotion to the guru! And what love for this country!"

One day Nivedita told us that Holy Mother would visit our school, and we should enjoy the festive occasion. She was anxiously running to and fro like a little girl. Holy Mother's carriage arrived in the afternoon instead of morning. Radhu, Golap-ma, and others were with her. As soon as she got down from the carriage, Nivedita prostrated to her and led her to the prayer hall. She gave us flowers to offer at Holy Mother's feet. The Mother asked the girls to sing a little. They did so and recited a poem composed by the poet Saralabala Sarkar. Holy Mother listened to it and appreciated the poem. Then she took a little sweet and asked Nivedita to distribute the prasad to us. Afterwards Nivedita took the Mother around and showed her the whole house, and the handicrafts of the girls. The Mother was very pleased and remarked: "The girls have learned well." Later Nivedita took the Mother to her own room for a rest.

It was due to her acquaintance with Holy Mother that Nivedita developed an exalted opinion of Indian womanhood. One day, by the bye, Sharat Maharaj said, "After all, our women are ignorant and unlettered." Nivedita interrupted him immediately, and forcefully contradicted him, saying: "The women of India are by no means ignorant. In that country [referring to the United Kingdom], has one ever heard such words of wisdom from women as one does here?"[19]

One day Nivedita and Sister Christine visited Holy Mother. Nivedita said in Bengali, "*Matridevi, apani han amadiger Kali* — Mother, you are our Kali." Christine repeated in English: "Oh, Holy Mother is our Kali." At this, Holy Mother said with a laugh: "No, my children, I can't be Kali or any such thing — I would have to stick out my tongue!"

When this was translated to them, they said: "No, you won't have to take that trouble. We shall regard you as our Mother Kali; Sri Ramakrishna is our Shiva."

Holy Mother said with a smile, "Well, that might be all right." Then they left after taking the dust of her feet.[20]

A disciple expressed his wonder to Holy Mother when he saw people coming from Western countries to see her. Holy Mother responded: "The Master once said in an ecstatic mood: 'In the course of time I will be worshipped in many homes. Innumerable indeed will be my devotees.' Nivedita once said to me: 'Mother, we were Hindus in our previous births. We are born in the West so that the Master's message may spread there.'"[21]

In 1900 when Nivedita went to America to collect funds for her school, Holy Mother dictated a letter to her that Saradananda translated into English. Here is an excerpt from that letter:

My dear, love to you, baby daughter Nivedita, I am so glad to learn you have prayed to the Lord for my eternal peace. You are a manifestation of the ever blissful Mother. I look at your photo, which is with me, every now and then and it seems as if you are present with me. I long for the day and the year when you shall return. May the prayers you have uttered for me from the heart of your pure virgin soul be answered! I am well and happy. I always pray to the Lord that He might help you in your noble efforts and keep you strong and happy. I pray too for your quick return. May He fulfill your desires about the women's home in India and may that would-be home fulfill its mission in teaching true dharma to all.

He, the Breath of the Universe, is singing His own praise and you are hearing that eternal song through things that will come to an end. The trees, the birds, the hills, and all are singing praises to the Lord. The Banyan of Dakshineswar sings of Kali to be sure, and blessed is he who has ears to hear it....

My dear, love to you and blessings and prayers for your spiritual growth. You are doing excellent work indeed. But do not forget your Bengali, else I will not be able to understand you when you come back. It gave me such a delight to learn that you are speaking of Dhruva, Savitri, Sita, Rama, and so on there. The accounts of their holy lives are better than all the vain talk of the world, I am sure. Oh! How beautiful are the Name and doings of the Lord!

Yours, Mother[22]

Holy Mother bestowed her grace on Nivedita and remarked: "Her outside is white [*meaning her skin*] and her inside is white [*meaning pure*]." Nivedita wrote about Holy Mother:

The Mother can read, and much of her time is passed with her Ramayana. But she does not write. Yet it is not to be supposed that she is an uneducated woman....It must be remembered that as the wife of Sri Ramakrishna she has had the highest opportunity of personal development that it is possible to enjoy. At every moment she bears unconscious witness to this association with the great. But in nothing perhaps does it speak more loudly than in her instant power to penetrate a new religious feeling or idea.

I first realized this gift in Holy Mother, on the occasion of a visit that she paid us in recent years, on the afternoon of a certain Easter Day. Before that, probably, I had always been too much absorbed, when with her, in striving to learn what she represented, to think of observing her in the contrary position. On this particular occasion, however, after going over our whole house, the Mother and her party expressed a desire to rest in the chapel, and hear something of the meaning of Christian festival. This was followed by Easter music and singing with our small French organ. And in the swiftness of her comprehension, and the depth of her sympathy with these resurrection hymns, unimpeded by any foreignness or unfamiliarity in them, we saw revealed for the first time, one of the most impressive aspects of the great religious culture of Sarada Devi. The same power is seen to a certain extent, in all the women about her, who were touched by the hand of Sri Ramakrishna. But in her, it has all the strength and certainty of some high and arduous form of scholarship.

The same trait came out again one evening, when in the midst of her little circle, Holy Mother asked Christine and myself to describe to her a European wedding. With much fun and laughter personating now the "Christian Brahmin," and again the bride and bridegroom, we complied. But we were neither of us prepared for the effect of the marriage vow.

"For better for worse, for richer for poorer, in sickness and in health — till death us do part," were words that drew exclamations of delight from all about us. But none appreciated them as did the Mother. Again and again she had them repeated to her. "Oh the *Dharmi* words! The righteous words!" she said.[23]

Holy Mother treasured anything that Nivedita gave her. Once Nivedita gave Holy Mother a small German silver box in which she kept locks of Ramakrishna's hair. She used to say, "Whenever I look at the box at the time of worship, I am reminded of Nivedita." In one of her trunks, Holy Mother kept an old tattered silk scarf that her attendant wanted to throw away. "No, child," she said. "Nivedita gave it to me with great love. Let us preserve it." She then took the scarf in her hand, scattered black cumin seeds in its folds as a preservative, and laid it carefully back in the trunk. She remarked: "The very sight of the scarf reminds me of Nivedita. What a wonderful girl she was! At first she could not speak to me directly, and the boys acted as interpreters. Later she picked up the Bengali language. She loved my mother very much."

One day Nivedita said to Shyamasundari: "Grandma, I shall go to your village and cook in your kitchen." The old lady replied at once: "No, my child, you must not do that. Our people will ostracize me if you enter my kitchen."[24]

Nivedita had penetrating eyes, a brilliant mind, indomitable energy, and deep spirituality. She observed that although Holy Mother had no formal education, her dealings with people and teachings were beautiful, catholic, practical, and appealing. Holy Mother's divine love and affection, strong common sense and sweet personality captivated her. Nivedita wrote:

To me it has always appeared that she is Sri Ramakrishna's final word as to the ideal of Indian womanhood. But is she the last of an old order, or the beginning of a new? In her one sees realized that wisdom and sweetness to which the simplest of women may attain. And yet, to myself the stateliness of her courtesy and her great open mind are almost as wonderful as her sainthood. I have never known her hesitate in giving utterance to large and generous judgement, however new or complex might be the question put before her. Her life is one long stillness of prayer. Her whole experience is of theocratic civilization. Yet she rises to the height of every situation. Is she tortured by the perversity of any about her? The only sign is a strange quiet and intensity that comes upon her. Does one carry to her some perplexity or mortification born of social developments beyond her ken? With unerring intuition she goes straight to the heart of the matter, and sets the questioner in the true attitude to the difficulty.[25]

When Nivedita died in Darjeeling on 13 October 1911, Holy Mother shed tears and said: "What sincere devotion Nivedita had! She never considered anything too much that she might do for me. She often came to me at night. Seeing that the light struck my eyes, she put a shade of paper around the lamp. She would prostrate herself before me with great tenderness and take the dust of my feet with her handkerchief. I felt that she hesitated even to touch my feet." As the women devotees expressed their sorrow at Nivedita's death, Holy Mother said: "All creatures weep for a great soul."[26]

A few days after Nivedita's death, Sister Christine and Sister Sudhira, a co-worker, came to see Holy Mother from Nivedita's school. Remembering the close relationship between Nivedita and Christine, Holy Mother said to Sudhira: "Ah, they lived together. Now it will be hard for her to live alone." She then consoled Christine: "Our hearts are crying for her, and undoubtedly your feeling will be more intense, my child. What a wonderful person she was! So many people are now crying for her."[27] Saying so, Holy Mother wept. Then she asked Christine about the activities of the school.

One day the Mother was resting on her bed and several women devotees were near her. Someone began to talk about Jesus Christ. The Mother got up and saluted Lord Jesus with folded hands. She then said:

I heard many things about Jesus Christ from Nivedita. She read many beautiful stories about him to me. Ah, Jesus came to deliver people in this world and how much suffering he had to undergo. He joyfully endured all. Despite all those persecutions, he loved people and forgave them unconditionally. His own disciple betrayed him. Ah, they killed him with nails in his hands, feet, and chest. In spite of that terrible torture and pain, he ungrudgingly forgave them. He prayed to God to not take offence at what they did. Is it possible for human beings to have such love, power of forbearance, and forgiveness? Who can endure this way other than God? God came as Jesus to teach divine love to the people of the world.

Look at Nivedita, a Western girl who came to our country and worked happily, forbearing insults and harassment; and also enduring so much discomfort. She tried to educate our children. When she visited some homes to register their children for her school, she was humiliated; some did not allow her to go inside their homes; and some allowed her to go inside but later purified the place by sprinkling Ganges water. She saw everything but did not mind. She left each place with a smiling face. There was no bounden necessity for her to educate the girls of our country by enduring such insults and ill-treatment and ruining her life little by little. You see, my daughter Nivedita had such a wonderful mind that she took on the responsibility of teaching our girls on her own shoulders because her guru Naren wanted it and asked her to do it. She did not care for physical suffering and discomfort, or for the insults and incivility of our people. Those for whom she dedicated her life, they treated her contemptuously. Under such circumstances, could the women of our country sacrifice to such a great extent for the sake of their guru? They would say, "We don't care!" So I say that except for the Master no one knows or understands how, when, what, or through whom he makes one work.[28]

Holy Mother and Sister Devamata

Laura F. Glenn heard Swami Vivekananda's lectures in New York and became a great devotee of Vedanta. She edited Swami Vivekananda's *Inspired Talks*, which Swamiji delivered at Thousand Island Park and Ellen Waldo recorded. Years later she became a nun and joined the Vedanta Centre of Boston, where she took vows from Swami Paramananda and became Sister Devamata. She visited India in 1909 and met Holy Mother in Calcutta many times. In her book, *Days in an Indian Monastery*, she wrote her memoirs of Holy Mother.

Holy Mother was very fond of Devamata and later dictated many letters to her. Devamata wrote: "We had no common language, but when there was none to interpret for us, she spoke that deeper wordless language and we never failed to understand each other."[29]

Devamata stayed with Nivedita and Christine but she visited Holy Mother every day. When Holy Mother blessed Devamata for the first time, Devamata recounted her experience: "A spring of new life seemed to bubble up from my innermost heart and flood my being." One day a desire flashed in her mind to render Holy Mother personal service by stroking her feet. Immediately Holy Mother motioned to Devamata to come near her and allowed her to massage her feet, because she had arthritis.

Devamata wrote: "Mother took me into her daily life at once and gave me the privilege of caring for her rooms. Every morning I came early to her, made her bed and put everything in order. In doing it I observed that the five large French windows opening on the front veranda were blurred with paint and putty. They always stood open and evidently no one had noticed it. One morning I brought with me some clean cloths and a cake of Monkey Brand soap, the Indian substitute for Bon Ami, and gave the panes of glass a good polishing. Mother was overjoyed when she saw them and that day whenever a visitor came she insisted on having a window closed to show how clear and shining the glass was."[30]

Here is an excerpt from Devamata's memoir:

Innumerable were the devotees who gathered at Holy Mother's feet to crave her blessings and learn of her. She herself told me that when she was in her village she would be awakened frequently at two or three in the morning by eager pilgrims, who not daring to cross the long stretch of unshaded fields under the scorching heat of the sun made the journey after nightfall, thus arriving very late. Most often they were personally unknown to her; but always it was her custom to rise, prepare food for them with her own hands and then send them to rest in the guest house, built by a village disciple for the use of her devotees.

Also in Calcutta nearly every day brought some group of devout pilgrims to pay her homage. It mattered not whence they came. Geographical boundaries, caste or creed did not exist for her. The same tender welcome awaited all who sought her whether from East or West. All alike were her children. Hers was an all-embracing mother-heart which wrapped itself in love about every child born of woman, and her family was the human race....

At the time when I came...Mother was living in a new dwelling given her by the devoted followers of Sri Ramakrishna. She occupied the upper floor with the few women disciples who were always with her.

She lived as they did, performing the same homely tasks, making no effort to differentiate herself from others save by greater modesty, greater gentleness and humility. I remember one day seeing her bow in deepest reverence before a rustic brahmin who had come to see her, because he chanced to be a village guru or spiritual teacher. By her outward manner she was the most obscure of the household, yet beneath the veil of simplicity which enveloped her, there was a lofty majesty of bearing which caught the heart and bowed it in prayerful homage at her feet. The human covering was too thin to hide the radiance of divine consciousness beneath. She never taught, seldom ever counselled. *She merely lived*. And who can tell how many lives were cleansed and exalted by that holy living?

A gentle cheerfulness there was about her always, and a lurking sense of humour which made it possible to talk to her of anything. The smallest concern was of interest to her and she could lose herself in childish play with as much zest as the little niece of eight, Radhu by name, who lived with her. I can still see her keen amusement over a jack-in-the-box which I brought for the little niece from an English shop. Each time it sprang out with the familiar squeak, she would repeat the sound, laughing heartily.

Another day when I came in, I found her engaged in stringing little glass beads and Radhu exclaimed, "My Baby Krishna had no jewels as the images in the temples have." There was no mockery of play in the Mother's manner. Even this little toy was a sacred symbol of Divinity, and she decked it with the same grave devotion as a devout nun might dress the Baby Jesus for a Christmas Crèche.

Those who had the rare blessing of living with the Holy Mother learned that religion was a sweet, natural, joyous thing; that purity and holiness were tangible realities; that the odour of sanctity was literally a sweet perfume overlaying and destroying the foulness of material selfishness. Compassion, devotion, God-union were her very nature; one scarcely knew that she possessed them. It was through the soothing benediction of a word or touch that one sensed their presence.

Such lives are like the lake or river. The sun may draw up its waters, but they fill again to refresh the earth. So these saintly ones in body may be lifted from our sight, but their holy influence falls back upon us to revive our fainting hearts and give us new spiritual life, new strength of purpose.[31]

Jyotirmayi Basu, a disciple of Holy Mother, recalled:

Devamata, an American woman, used to visit Holy Mother at Udbodhan House every morning at 7:00 a.m. We heard from the Mother that she had had a vision of the Master in America and later recognized him, in a photo shown her by Swamiji. She lived at 47 Bosepara Lane, Baghbazar. Devamata used to meditate in the Mother's room and tears would flow from her eyes out of devotion. It was hard to believe without seeing those wonderful tears.

The Mother often sat with us in her room and fed Radhu before she left for school. One day when Radhu's meal was finished, the Mother began to clean that place and we were watching it. But out of exuberant devotion, Devamata rushed to her, saying, "Matadevi, Matadevi," as she picked up Radhu's cup and plate and cleaned the floor. Seeing that Devamata's cloth had touched the defiled plate,* Nalini laughed loudly. Immediately the Mother signaled her with her eyes to keep quiet. When Devamata went to the wash room with those dirty dishes, the Mother said to Nalini: "That girl does not know our language and customs and you laughed out loud! She might think that she had done something wrong. Thinking of this, later she will get pain."[32]

Holy Mother and Betty Leggett

Towards the end of 1912 Betty Leggett visited Holy Mother. She was the sister of Miss MacLeod and a great admirer and helper of Swami Vivekananda's Vedanta work. She donated 10,000 rupees to Belur Math to construct a guest house for Westerners, which is now the president's quarters. She also donated 20,000 rupees to build Leggett House, to be used as monks' quarters.[33] Betty's daughter, Alberta, and son-in-law, the Earl of Sandwich, were also devoted to Swamiji, and they also met Holy Mother. On January 1913 Betty wrote to her sister:

Alberta had vast and intense experiences with Sarada Devi and I have my own....

I went to the little house [at Baghbazar] to see her, and stayed endlessly. She was quite free, with head and hands uncovered: calm and beneficent with the little women crawling to her feet and putting them aside gently in removed places and having a mat spread for me. She told me how she loved you and Alberta and how I was to tell you to come again with me to see her.

She related anecdotes of her early life, when at fifteen she sought her husband and from impulse set out alone and was lost in a forest and there overtaken by a notorious robber. She approached him and said, "Father, I have lost my way. Show me out of the forest." Whereupon he fell at her feet and then led her to his hut, where he and his wife both bowed and worshipped her....I have ordered one of the Holy Mother's photographs as it is both very excellent of her and of a beautiful woman. She took my face in her hands several times and kissed her hands** and we parted several times with much emotion.

I visited all her rooms, and objects, and images and pictures and thought of the similar simplicity and almost poverty of our Madonna who must have been so like her at fifty. When I had gone all over the house, I found her at the head of the stairs, fairly radiant, again taking my face in her

---

* Orthodox Hindus wash their clothes if they touch a dirty plate.
** Holy Mother showed her love and affection in this way: she would touch the chin of the dearest one with her right finger tips and then touch her fingers with her lips while making a kissing sound.

hands and blessing me. I had tears and I thought she had: but I couldn't see for my own.[34]

Holy Mother and Other Western Devotees

When flowers bloom, bees come of their own accord. As the spiritual consort of Ramakrishna, Holy Mother attracted many people who came to her for spiritual help or blessing. A lady from Poland came to India to learn Vedanta. She belonged to the Baha'i faith and was familiar with Ramakrishna's teachings about the harmony of religions. She heard about Holy Mother and visited her on 24 April 1912.[35]

During British rule many Westerners lived in Calcutta and some of them learned the Bengali language. Sarajubala Devi, a disciple of Holy Mother, recorded the following interview of a Western woman with Holy Mother.

It was four o'clock in the afternoon. After the worship in the shrine, Rasbihari Maharaj said, "A European lady has come to pay her respects to you. She has been waiting for a long time." The Mother asked him to bring the lady to her. As she bowed down before the Mother, the latter clasped the lady's hand as one does in shaking hands. The words of the Master, that one should behave according to time and circumstances, were verified in this instance. Then she kissed the lady by touching her chin. The latter knew Bengali and said: "I hope I have not inconvenienced you by this visit. I have been waiting for a long time downstairs to see you. I am in great difficulty. My only daughter, a very good girl, is dangerously ill; so I have come here to crave your favour and blessings. Please be gracious to her, so that she may be cured. She is such a nice girl. I praise her because one seldom finds, nowadays, a good woman among us. I can vouch that many of them are wicked and evil-minded; but my daughter is of quite a different nature. Please be kind to her."

Mother: "I shall pray for your daughter. She will be cured."

The European lady was much encouraged by this assurance from Holy Mother and said: "When you say that she will be cured, she shall be cured. There is no doubt about it." She spoke these words thrice with great faith and emphasis. The Mother with a kindly look, said to Golap-ma: "Please give her a flower from the altar. Bring a lotus." Golap-ma brought a lotus with a sacred bel leaf. The Mother took the lotus in her hand and closed her eyes for a few moments. Then she looked wistfully at the image of Sri Ramakrishna and gave the flower to the lady, saying, "Please touch your daughter's head with this." The woman accepted the flower with folded hands and bowed down before the Mother. "What shall I do with the flower after that?" she asked.

Golap-ma: When it is dried, throw it into the Ganges.

Lady: No, no! This belongs to God. I cannot throw it away. I shall make a bag out of a new piece of cloth and preserve the flower in it. I shall touch my daughter's head and body every day with it.

Mother: Very well, do that.

Lady: God is the supreme Reality. He exists. I want to tell you something. A few days ago, a baby was bedridden with fever in my house. With great fervor I prayed to God, "O Lord! I feel that you exist, but I want an actual demonstration." I wept and laid my handkerchief on the table. After a long time I was surprised to find three sticks in its folds. I gently touched the body of the baby thrice with the three sticks. Soon it was cured of the fever.

As she narrated the incident, teardrops trickled down her cheeks. She said, "I have taken much of your valuable time. Please forgive me." "No," said the Mother, "I am greatly pleased to talk to you. Come here again on Tuesday."

The following Tuesday, the Mother showed her special favour and initiated her. Her daughter, too, was cured of her illness.[36]

Although Holy Mother was a shy, orthodox village woman, her altruistic love bound these Western women to her. She did not know any Western language, or Western etiquette or culture, but her love and affection, simplicity and sincerity, compassion and spiritual power overwhelmed these devotees and removed all barriers. Love is reciprocal. It melts human hearts and then it unites them together.

Girish Chandra Ghosh, actor and playwright.

15
Holy Mother
and Girish Chandra Ghosh

Matsamah pātaki nāsti pāpaghni tvatsamā nahi;
Evam jnātvā mahādevi yathā yogyam tathā kuru.
   —*Devi-aparādha-kshmāpana Stotram by Shankaracharya*

Nowhere exists, in all the world, another sinner equal to me; nowhere, a power like thyself for overcoming sinfulness: O Goddess, keeping this in mind, do thou with me as it pleases thee.

During Ramakrishna's lifetime, the great Bengali playwright Girish Chandra Ghosh publicly declared him to be an avatar. As for Holy Mother, Girish also held her in high esteem as the wife of his guru and cherished great respect for her. One day Girish was pacing back and forth on the roof of his house with his wife Pramodini, when Holy Mother was on the roof of Balaram's house nearby. Girish's wife noticed her and said to him, "Look, there is the Mother walking on the roof." Girish at once turned his face away and replied: "No, no. My eyes are sinful. I won't look at her that way; I cannot be a sneak."[1] Immediately he went downstairs.

It is said that the exceptional good fortune of his second wife, Suratkumari, brought Girish fame, wealth, and the grace of the Master. Girish and she had three children — two girls and a boy. When his son was born, almost two years after the Master's passing, Suratkumari became very ill. Girish arranged for her treatment, which continued for a year. Nonetheless, she died on 26 December 1888. Grief-stricken, Girish tried to occupy himself by studying mathematics and caring for his little son. Girish had once asked the Master to be born as his son, so he believed that his boy was Ramakrishna reincarnated. He served the boy wholeheartedly. Girish bought new clothes, cups, glasses, and plates for him; he did not allow anyone else to use those things.

Girish's First Meeting with Holy Mother

In September 1890 Holy Mother was staying at Sourindra Thakur's house in Baranagore. Girish was still grieving for his wife, and Swami Niranjanananda knew this. He insisted that Girish visit Holy Mother. Girish paid his first visit to Holy Mother at Baranagore with his 3-year-old son. The little boy could not speak and expressed himself through sounds and gestures. As they entered the house, the little boy, who had seen Holy Mother before, anxiously pointed at the upper floor where Holy Mother lived and called out, "Ooh! Ooh!"

One of Holy Mother's attendants took him upstairs and he rolled on the ground before her. Presently he came down and began to pull at his father's hand. Girish burst out crying and said: "How can I go to the Mother? I am a great sinner." But the boy would not leave him alone. Finally he took his son in his arms and climbed the stairs, his body trembling and tears flowing from his eyes. He put the boy down, then fell flat at Holy Mother's feet and said: "It is through my son that I have seen your sacred feet."[2] Holy Mother always took the boy on her lap whenever she saw him. Unfortunately, the boy died not long afterwards.

Girish's Faith in Holy Mother

In his early life Girish had used alcohol in an attempt to relieve the grief he felt at the death of his first wife. Now he was determined to use divine intoxication to relieve the anguish of losing his second wife and his youngest son.

Kumudbandhu Sen wrote in his reminiscences:

Whenever Girish Ghosh referred to Sri Ramakrishna and the Holy Mother, his manner of expression was extraordinarily superb and different from that of the other devotees. His deep reverence for and strong faith in their divinity and unbounded grace were expressed in his utterances, and he inspired those who heard him. Once, Girish told me that at first he and other lay devotees of Sri Ramakrishna did not recognize the greatness of Holy Mother.

Girish said: "We used to pay our respectful tribute to her as the spiritual consort of our Master. We looked upon him alone as our guide, friend, father, and mother — all combined. It was Niranjan [later Swami Niranjanananda] who opened my eyes. In the midst of the grim tragedies of life, stricken with grief and sorrow, I felt for a time quite perplexed and could not console my disturbed mind. During my sad bereavement, Niranjan often came to me and tried to divert my mind with spiritual talk.

"One day I told him, 'Brother Niranjan, it is a pity that I cannot now see Sri Ramakrishna who is my shelter, my only refuge.' Niranjan interrupted me, saying: 'Why! Mother is there. Is there any difference between the Master and Mother? Can you imagine Narayana without Lakshmi, Shiva without Parvati, Rama without Sita, and Krishna without Radha or Ruk-mini?' I was taken aback. I told him, 'What do you say — the Master and Mother are one and the same?' Niranjan replied: 'Well, you believe that Sri Ramakrishna was an avatar, God incarnate in human form. Do you mean to say that he took an ordinary woman [*jiva*] as his spiritual partner in his divine life? You must remember the words of our Master, "Brahman and Shakti are one and the same — though in manifestation they appear to us as two." Mother is Shakti, the Shakti of Purna-Brahma Ramakrishna.'

"His words cleared my vision and I at once recognized the Divine Mother — the Mother of the Universe — incarnated as Holy Mother for the salvation of mankind. I felt a strong urge to go to Jayrambati and see our Holy Mother, who alone could wipe away my tears and remove my sor-row over my recent adversities. Niranjan approved of my suggestion and offered to accompany me there. But Balaram Basu vehemently opposed this proposal, as he did not like the idea that I should disturb Holy Mother with my worldly problems and miseries. At that time Swami Vivekananda was away from Calcutta and the matter was referred to him by Niranjan. Getting his approval we started for Jayrambati.

"I could hardly express my joy when I first went to Kamarpukur. To me the cottage where Sri Ramakrishna was born was like a Rishi's holy hermitage; the scenery and its surrounding environment were enchant-ing. Thence we proceeded to Jayrambati. There, during my stay, I directly asked the Mother, 'Well, Mother, are you my real mother or an adopted mother?' The Mother said, 'Yes, I am your real mother.'"

Further, Girish Ghosh told us in forceful language, pregnant with deep emotion: "Yes, Mother — the Divine Mother — has appeared as a poor vil-lage girl, living in a remote hamlet, away from the din and bustle of a town where life reflects only the formal and artificial ways of worldly-wise and sophisticated men and women. I did not ask for anything from Mother. As soon as I went to her all my sorrow and misery vanished completely, and I felt a supreme serenity of mind which I had never experienced before. Oh! Those days were spent in heavenly bliss and joy."

One day at the Mother's place at Jayrambati, a minstrel [Haridas Vairagi of Deshra] came and sang a Bengali song to the accompaniment of a bro-ken violin. A free English rendering of the song is given below:

O Uma, my darling, what good tidings I hear!
People say you are adored in Varanasi as Annapurna. Is it true?
O Gauri, when I married you to Shiva,
He went as a beggar from door to door for a morsel of food.
But today how glad I am to hear
You are now Queen of the World, seated by His side.
And they called my naked Shiva a madman:

How much abuse I had to bear from everyone!
Now I hear that doorkeepers guard His palace
And gods like Indra, Chandra, and Yama hardly can see Him.
Shiva used to live in the Himalayas;
Many a day He got His food by begging;
Now He rules over Varanasi and is as rich as Kuvera.
Is it you who have brought Him all this good fortune?
No doubt He is very rich now,
Else why should Gauri be so proud?
She does not cast her eyes even upon her own children,
And turns her face away from Radhika*.

When the minstrel finished singing the song, Girish Ghosh, Swami Niranjanananda, and others who heard it could not restrain their tears.** The Mother too shed tears, as did all her women companions. The song reminded them of Holy Mother's early life when Sri Ramakrishna was often referred to as the "mad son-in-law" by the people of Jayrambati, when her own parents repented giving her in marriage to Sri Ramakrishna, and her neighbours pitied her and expressed sorrow at her "miserable" fate. She did not and could not then protest, and she humbly suffered all those humiliating remarks in silence, though she knew in her innermost heart that her husband was a god-intoxicated man far above ordinary people. She tasted divine bliss whenever she came into contact with her husband. She did not go to anybody's house or attend social functions in Jayrambati lest people make humiliating remarks about her husband and blame her for her ill luck. Now that Sri Ramakrishna is revered as a prophet and an avatar and is worshipped in many places, people come to her for her *darshan* even in that village, which is situated in an out-of-the-way place. The Holy Mother is now regarded by many devotees as the Mother of the Universe.

The song drew tears from the eyes of the listeners as it aptly applied to and conjured up a vision of the early life of Sri Ramakrishna and Sri Saradamani. I heard from Girish Ghosh that for over an hour all remained spellbound and their eyes glistened with tears. But those happy days came to an end.

Holy Mother used to travel back and forth between her Calcutta and Jayrambati residences. One day we heard that Mother was leaving for Jayrambati after Kali Puja [1896]. On the day of her departure, Girish

---

*Radhika is the composer of the song.
**Swami Parameswarananda recalled: "Listening to this song, Girish Babu gave Shyamasundari ten rupees and bowed down to her. He also gave ten rupees to the singer. Delighted, Shyamasundari said, 'My Saru, may I have a daughter like you birth after birth.' Holy Mother replied: 'What? You are asking for me again? I shall never come back to you again.'" (*Sri Srima O Jayrambati*, 107)

Ghosh came to bid her farewell. He did not utter a word, and with a serious countenance he called for Yogananda and went directly to Holy Mother [who was then living at Sarkarbari Lane]. We all followed him. Full of emotion and deep reverence, he prostrated at the feet of Holy Mother and with folded hands said: "Mother, when I come to you I feel that I am a little child coming to its own mother. Had I been a grown-up son, I would have served my mother. But it is quite the opposite. You serve us and we do not serve you. You are going to Jayrambati to serve the people, even by cooking food for others in that village kitchen. How can I serve you, and what do I know about service of the Divine Mother?"

Girish's voice was choked and his whole face was red with emotion. He said: "Mother, you know our minds, which we ourselves do not know. We cannot go to you. It is through your grace and kindness that you come here to see your children. Whenever you wish to come here, please do not hesitate for a moment. We, your children, will always be happy to see our Mother and shall deem it a privilege to render you whatever service you will graciously allow us to offer."

Girish then addressed us who were standing behind him: "It is difficult for human beings to believe that God may incarnate in a human form like any of us. Do you realize that you are standing before the Mother of the Universe in the form of a village woman? Can you imagine the Divine Mother doing all kinds of domestic work and fulfilling social duties like any ordinary woman? Yet she is the Mother of the Universe — *maha-maya*, *maha-shakti* — appearing on earth for the salvation of all creatures and at the same time exemplifying the ideal of true motherhood."

His words made a deep impression on all present, and the whole atmosphere was charged with serene sublimity and calmness. Yes, it was then a veritable paradise, pervaded with spiritual bliss and benediction. We accompanied the Mother to the railway station. She blessed us all as we touched her feet in salutation.[3]

Swami Bodhananda left a vivid account of Girish's visit to Jayrambati in the early part of 1891, which is presented here in an abridged form:

Our party consisted of Swami Niranjanananda, Swami Subodhananda, Girish, Kanai [later Swami Nirbhayananda], Kalikrishna [later Swami Virajananda], and myself. Girish also took a cook and a servant with him. After breakfast at Girish's house we left for the Howrah railway station and reached the Burdwan station at noon. We had our lunch there and bought luchis, fried potatoes, halwa, and sweets for our supper and some special sweets to offer to the Master in Kamarpukur. Five bullock carts were hired and we started our journey just before evening. We crossed the Damodar River, which was almost dry. After crossing the river by bullock cart, we finished our supper. At 10:00 p.m. we resumed our journey, but shortly after, the jerking motion of the cart upset Girish's stomach. We were then in the middle of a vast meadow. Swami Niranjanananda stopped all the carts and asked the drivers to unfasten the bullocks from the carts. Within an hour, Girish fell asleep and in the morning he felt normal.

We resumed our journey and reached Uchalan (16 miles from Burdwan) at 10:00 a.m. We went to an inn and had lunch. After resting we had tea. We again bought luchis, fried potatoes, and halwa for supper. The drivers drove the whole night, covering 14 miles from Uchalan to Kamarpukur. We arrived there at 9:00 a.m. and met Brother Ramlal and Sister Lakshmi, the Master's nephew and niece. We took a bath in the Haldarpukur, had the prasad of Raghuvir, and spent the night at Kamarpukur. The next morning we left for Jayrambati, which is four miles from Kamarpukur. Girish went by palanquin, and the rest of us walked along the mud road. We arrived in Jayrambati at 11:00 a.m. Girish took a bath in the Talpukur and went to visit Holy Mother wearing his wet cloth and carrying a mango in his hand. He fell flat on the courtyard and bowed down to the Mother. This scene is still vivid in my memory.

I had a great opportunity to associate closely with Girish in Jayrambati. We stayed in the same room; we ate together, walked together, and talked freely. When he was in the mood, he would sing some devotional songs in praise of the Divine Mother.

Because of the many guests in Jayrambati, Holy Mother was extremely busy from morning till 11:00 p.m. taking care of our food, sleeping arrangements, and so on. Although Girish's cook and servant worked, the Mother had to supervise everything. It was not easy to get milk early in the morning in Jayrambati, but the Mother would go to the villagers and collect some milk so that we could have tea. We had breakfast with puffed rice, sandesh, and tea; and then after a bath we had some prasad. Mother served lunch with eight or nine kinds of preparations, as well as curd and sweets. In the afternoon we had tea and snacks, and at supper luchi, rice, vegetables, and sweets.

Girish would listen to the dialect of the illiterate farmers and imitate their language. He considered hiring a farmer and bringing him to Calcutta to act in one of his plays. After staying for two weeks in Jayrambati, everyone returned to Calcutta except for Swami Niranjanananda and Girish. The Mother looked after us as her own children. I still remember that I rolled chapatis a few times and the Mother baked them. It was her grace that I could be near her. Those are unforgettable memories![4]

Swami Nikhilananda, author of *Holy Mother*, supplied some more information about Girish and Holy Mother:

After arriving at Jayrambati, Girish took his bath and bowed down to Holy Mother. His body was shaking with emotion. Casting his eyes upon her, he exclaimed with surprise: "Ah, you are that Mother!" He suddenly recalled a vivid dream of many years before, when he had been bedridden from cholera. A luminous goddess wearing a red-bordered sari appeared to him and offered him some sacred prasad, which soon cured him. He now recognized Holy Mother as that deity and felt that she had always been looking after him as his guardian angel. To verify this, Girish asked her: "What kind of Mother are you?" Immediately Holy Mother replied: "Your real Mother, not just the wife of your guru, not a foster mother, not a vague sort of mother. Your real Mother."[5]

Girish spent a happy and carefree time in Jayrambati, wandering about freely with the villagers in the meadows and drinking in the beauty of the sunset in the open fields. Soon his fame spread throughout the area, and he would sing now and then to entertain the villagers. One day, Holy Mother heard Girish singing this song for the villagers; later, she sang the song herself in a soft voice:

Gopala crawls away from the queen
Lest she should catch hold of him.
He casts at her a furtive glance.
As she eagerly cries, "Stop, stop!"
Gopala crawls farther away.[6]

One day at Jayrambati, Girish had a heated discussion with Holy Mother's brother Kalikumar regarding whether Holy Mother was an ordinary human being or a goddess. Kalikumar naturally regarded her as his sister and said: "It is you who call her the Divine Mother or the Mother of the Universe. But we were born from the same womb. I do not understand what you say."

"What are you talking about?" replied Girish firmly. "You are the son of an ordinary brahmin, born and reared in a village. You have forgotten the duties of your caste, such as worship and study, and are now living as a farmer. If a man promises you a bullock for your plough, you will run after him for at least six months. Is it not possible for Mahamaya, who can make the impossible possible, to appear as your sister and hoodwink you for the rest of your life? Listen to me. If you want liberation in this life or afterwards, go immediately to the Mother and take refuge at her feet. I urge you to go at once."

Such was the power conveyed in Girish's words that Kalikumar immediately went to Holy Mother and clutched her feet, begging for her grace. She said: "Kali, what are you doing? I am your sister. What are you saying?" Kalikumar returned to Girish the same person he was before. Girish asked him to go back, but he would not. Girish once remarked that Holy Mother's brothers must have performed bone-breaking austerities in a previous life to have obtained her as their sister.[7]

Girish's Relationship with Holy Mother

Holy Mother usually wore a veil when she was with the monastic disciples and male devotees of the Master, except for Swamis Adbhutananda and Advaitananda and a few others. When Girish ate his lunch at Jayrambati, Holy Mother would say to him from behind her veil: "My son, please have a little more rice. You will feel hungry if you eat such a small amount of food." Girish was overwhelmed by Holy Mother's affection. Observing her shyness and unwillingness to talk to her male devotees, Girish once told her: "Mother, the Master has become a *chhabi* [a picture] and you have become a *bauma* [a bashful bride who wears a long veil]."[8] Girish meant that people now see the Master only in a photograph, so Holy Mother should not maintain such a distance from and formality with her children.

Girish later recalled his days in Jayrambati: "What infinite affection did I see in the Mother! She was my real mother. She kept her vigilant eyes on every minute detail. One day in Jayrambati I saw the Mother going to the pond with a piece of soap, a bed sheet, and a pillow cover. When I went to bed that night I found that my pillow cover and bed sheet had been beautifully washed. Tears trickle from my eyes when I think of her affection."[9]

Because of the bereavement he had suffered, Girish realized the emptiness of family life. During his visit to Jayrambati he approached Holy Mother several times for her permission to embrace the monastic life. She would not give her consent, instead suggesting that he continue his literary and acting careers. Girish at last gave up the idea of becoming a monk. Shortly after this, Girish took the opportunity to spend a few days in Kamarpukur, and Holy Mother joined his group. His long association with Holy Mother and his visits to the sacred places of Jayrambati and Kamarpukur finally brought solace to Girish's broken heart. He returned to Calcutta and resumed his acting career with fresh vigour and a clearer spiritual outlook.

Girish often visited Holy Mother when she was in Calcutta. Once Holy Mother was returning from a long stay in Jayrambati. Swamis Brahmananda and Premananda went to Howrah Station to receive her.

Though the train was three hours late, the swamis and her devotees waited. When the train finally arrived, Yogin-ma and Golap-ma helped Mother out of the train and the swamis rushed to take the dust of her feet. Golap-ma was Holy Mother's guard and caretaker. In her high-pitched voice and brusque manner she scolded Swami Brahmananda: "Maharaj, have you no sense whatsoever? The Mother has just gotten off the train, tired and exhausted from the heat. If you make such a fuss about prostrating, how can I restrain the others?" The venerable swamis were embarrassed and stepped back. Holy Mother was then driven to Udbodhan House in a carriage, and she went upstairs to rest.

A little later, Brahmananda and Premananda decided to go to Udbodhan House to confirm that proper arrangements had been made. Girish arrived soon after and asked them about Holy Mother. When Golap-ma heard Girish's voice, she came downstairs and said to him: "My words beat a retreat, Girish Babu, before your grotesque devotion. You have come to see Mother! She is exhausted. She is supposed to have some rest now, but you have come to disturb her."

Girish retorted: "You are a boisterous woman! I had thought that the Mother's heart would be soothed by seeing her children's faces after such a long time. Yet this woman is teaching me devotion to the Mother! Phew!" Girish and Brahmananda and Premananda went upstairs to pay their respects to Holy Mother. As they bowed down to her, she blessed them. Girish's love and devotion overruled Golap-ma's decrees. After Girish had left full of joy, Golap-ma complained to Holy Mother about his rudeness. Holy Mother replied: "I have warned you many times about criticizing my children."[10]

In 1907 Girish decided to perform Durga Puja at his home. He and his sister Dakshina wanted Holy Mother to be present for the occasion. However, Holy Mother was then at Jayrambati and had been suffering intermittently from malarial fever. Swami Saradananda wrote to Holy Mother about Girish's wish that she attend Durga Puja, and the gracious Mother agreed to come to Calcutta. At that time there were riots in Calcutta and there was a blackout at night in the city. M. (Mahendra Nath Gupta) and Lalit Chattopadhyay left Calcutta and went to the Vishnupur railway station where they waited for Holy Mother who had travelled there by bullock cart. When she arrived, they accompanied her by train to Howrah Station, arriving after dark. Holy Mother, accompanied by Radhu and her mother, got into Lalit's waiting carriage. M., Lalit, and some devotees escorted them, sitting on the top of the carriage or standing on the footboard. Holy Mother stayed with Balaram's family, close to Girish's house.

Durga Puja began a few days after they arrived, and it continued for four days. Holy Mother attended the puja at Girish's house from beginning to end. In addition, many devotees came to Balaram's house to pay their respects to her. Despite her poor health, she sat for hours to fulfill her devotees' wishes. Thus two days passed. It was decided that Holy Mother should rest and not attend the sandhi puja, which takes place between the ashtami and navami pujas (the second and third days of the worship). The time for this special ceremony happened to fall at midnight that year. Girish was upset when he heard this, and he decided to stay in his room while the worship was going on. However, when the time for the sandhi puja came, Holy Mother changed her mind. She covered herself with a chadar, walked through the narrow lane, and knocked at the back door of Girish's house, saying: "I have come." Girish's maidservant opened the door, and news of Holy Mother's arrival quickly spread. Girish hurriedly went to the worship hall, bowed down to Holy Mother, and joyfully remarked: "I thought that my worship of the Divine Mother would be incomplete. Meanwhile the Mother has tapped on the door and announced, 'Here, I have come.'"

Thus after four days of worship and Holy Mother's presence, Girish felt that Mother Durga had graciously accepted his worship. On that auspicious occasion, Girish invited his friends and relatives, as well as the actors and actresses of his theatre, who all received Holy Mother's blessings.[11]

Holy Mother and the Theater

Aparesh Mukhopadhyay, an actor and playwright, wrote: "A man sees the outer form of a man, but God sees inside him, and I witnessed this truth: Holy Mother, the spiritual consort of Sri Ramakrishna, came to a theatre in Calcutta and embraced an actress who was a courtesan. Thus she demonstrated that God's grace does not discriminate between good and thorny plants, between good and bad human beings, and does not care for the injunctions and prohibitions of the empirical world. That divine grace only purifies all — irrespective of caste and creed."[12]

The ever-pure Holy Mother accepted all of the actresses in Girish's theatre and blessed some of them. In those days actresses were generally recruited from red light districts. As Ramakrishna gave respectability to the Bengali stage by watching various plays, such as *Chaitanya Lila*, so also Holy Mother saw several of Girish's plays and saw him act as well.

It was probably in the last part of the nineteenth century that Holy Mother went to see *Daksha Yajna* performed at the Minerva Theatre at 6

Beadon Street in Calcutta. This was the first of Girish's plays the Mother saw. Ramakrishna had also seen this play. Girish acted in the role of Daksha, the father of Sati, Shiva's consort. Brahmachari Akshaychaitanya wrote, "Holy Mother went into ecstasy seeing the play *Daksha Yajna*."[13]

Several years later, Girish invited Holy Mother to see *Vilwamangal Thakur*, a popular devotional play. Holy Mother went to see it at the Minerva Theatre on Wednesday, 25 January 1905. Girish arranged a royal box seat for Holy Mother and engaged an attendant to fan her with a large palm-leaf fan. Girish performed the role of a hypocritical monk who was trying to teach Thakmani, a female confidante of the courtesan Chintamani, how to love Krishna. As she watched Girish's performance, Holy Mother commented with a smile, "Why are you behaving like this in your old age?" Later, observing the one-pointed love of Vilwamangal, Holy Mother said, "Ah! Ah! What wonderful love!"[14]

Holy Mother went to the Minerva Theatre again on 1 March 1905 to see a performance of *Jana*.* Girish based this play loosely on the Mahabharata. In it he introduced the role of a court jester, taking the role himself. He portrayed his own character in that role, criticizing and using abusive words against Krishna — but at the same time showing deep devotion to him. He had once treated his guru, Ramakrishna, in the same way. Holy Mother laughed as she watched Girish's performance. Swami Saradananda asked, "Mother, why are you laughing?" Mother replied: "I see Girish's own character reflected in that role. I know he is endowed with deep faith and he believes that one can have liberation by calling on God — and again he abuses God."[15]

Holy Mother's next visit to the Minerva Theatre was on 22 April 1906. She saw the play *Chaitanya Lila*, which the Master had seen on 21 September 1884.

Ashutosh Mitra wrote:

> Last night Holy Mother went to see *Chaitanya Lila*. Girish arranged for this play to be performed for one night after a long time and offered a royal box

---

* Jana, a highly powerful and spiritual soul, was the wife of Niladhvaja, the virtuous king of Mahishmati. This royal couple had a son named Prabir. Prince Prabir was a great hero and had been made invincible by Shiva's grace. In the play King Yudhishthira performs the horse sacrifice, in which his horse roams through all of the kingdoms, and their rulers pledge their allegiance to him. Arjuna was protecting the horse. Instead of paying obeisance to Yudhishthira, the heroic Prince Prabir captured the horse and kept it for himself. War between Arjuna and Prabir was inevitable. Prabir won the first battle. To protect Arjuna, Krishna schemed to tempt Prabir with Rati, the goddess of lust. She took away Prabir's power, and the next day he was killed. Krishna later blessed Niladhvaja and Jana.

seat to the Mother. The roles of two villains — Jagai and Madhai — were enacted by Ardhendu Shekhar and Girish. Bhushan Kumari, a famous actress, had retired from the stage, but she acted in the role of Chaitanya without any remuneration because of Holy Mother. Sushilabala acted in the role of Nitai, a disciple of Chaitanya. Both actresses came and bowed down to the Mother before the play started. Holy Mother later commented: "That girl [Bhushan] was full of devotion; otherwise one cannot act in that role. She looked and dressed like the real Chaitanya. Who could tell that she was a woman?" About Jagai and Madhai, the Mother remarked: "Where will you find devotees like them? Likewise, where can one find devotees like Ravana and Hiranyakashipu? Girish used to scold the Master, and at the same time he had so much devotion for him. They came to this world like that. Is it easy to become a devotee? Does devotion come automatically?"[16]

On Sunday, 12 September 1909, Holy Mother again went to the Minerva Theatre, this time to see *Pandav Gaurav*, "The Glory of the Pandavas." Girish based this drama on the story of Dandi, the king of Avanti, and Urvasi, a celestial nymph.* In this drama, Girish performed the role of Kanchuki, an old brahmin minister in King Dandi's court.

Swami Shantananda recorded in his reminiscences:

I was then serving Holy Mother at Udbodhan House in Calcutta. One day Girish came to see her and invited her to see him act. Holy Mother agreed. She, Radhu, Maku, and other women devotees went in one carriage; Lalit Chattopadhyay, Dr. Kanjilal, and I went in another carriage. Girish was extremely happy that the Mother had come to see his performance and was busy trying to make the play perfect. He arranged a special box seat for the Mother and we sat next to her. The Mother silently watched the play. When Kanchuki appeared on the stage, the Mother commented: "Oh, that is Girish. He has dressed very well with wonderful makeup. It is hard to recognize him."

---

*Urvasi was disrespectful to the sage Durvasa, so he cursed her, saying that she would be a beautiful woman at night and a mare during the day. She would be released from the curse when the eight divine powers came together. One night Dandi went out to hunt and met Urvasi. He fell in love with her, although she told him her whole story. Girish connected this legend with Krishna and other characters of the Mahabharata. Just before the war described in the Mahabharata, Krishna wants Dandi to give him the mare, who is really Urvasi. Dandi leaves his kingdom and runs away with the horse. At last he takes refuge with the Pandavas, who are devoted to Krishna. Bhishma says: "The pole star of this world of maya is dharma, and the essence of dharma is to protect a person who has sought refuge." A conflict arises between the Pandavas and Krishna that is averted only when the gods and the Divine Mother appear, manifesting all of the eight divine powers. Urvasi is thus freed from the curse and returns to heaven.

The companions of the goddess sang this closing song:

> Look, look, at the charming Divine Mother;
> Who says that She is a black woman?
> Open your eyes and see how Her beauty makes the world luminous.

The Mother calmly watched the play. I observed that when the song was sung, she became absorbed in deep meditation, and she remained in that ecstatic state for some time. The Mother saw the entire play, and when we returned to Udbodhan it was 1:30 a.m.[17]

There was a benefit performance for the Ramakrishna Mission in Varanasi at the Minerva Theatre on 12 July 1910. On that occasion Holy Mother saw two of Girish's plays: *Vilwamangal Thakur* and *Jana*.

According to Akshaychaitanya, Holy Mother went to see *Kalapahar*, another play by Girish, at the Manomohan Theatre at 68 Beadon Street on 1 September 1915, a few years after Girish passed away.* Girish had based *Kalapahar* on a historical incident, but embedded in it devotional elements and Ramakrishna's teachings.

In September 1918 Holy Mother went to see *Ramanuja* performed at the Minerva Theatre. This play, about a saint and philosopher of the eleventh century, was written by Aparesh Chandra Mukhopadhyay, a close associate of Girish who was an actor and playwright. Pravrajika Bharatiprana, an attendant and disciple of Holy Mother, wrote:

> Holy Mother, Golap-ma, Yogin-ma, I, and many others went to see the play *Ramanuja* at the Minerva Theatre. Aparesh arranged special seats for us. Holy Mother was happy to see the play. There was a scene in which the guru tells Ramanuja during initiation: "Never tell this mantra to others. He who hears this mantra will be liberated. But if you share this mantra with others, you will go to hell." For the benefit of humanity, the great soul Ramanuja disobeys his guru and loudly utters that mantra to others. Seeing that scene, Holy Mother went into samadhi. The famous actress Tarasundari acted in the role of Ramanuja. After that scene she came to bow down to Holy Mother, but found that she had no outer consciousness. After Golap-ma's repeated calls, Holy Mother regained partial consciousness. Then Tara bowed down to her. The Mother hugged Tara, considering her to be Ramanuja. When the play was over, all of the actresses came and bowed down to Mother and she blessed them. Later Tara would come to Udbodhan House to pay her respects to Holy Mother.[18]

Kshirod Prasad Vidyavinod, a famous playwright and a devotee of Holy Mother, wanted her to see *Kinnari*, a musical. On Sunday, 18

*Girish passed away on 8 February 1912.

September 1918, Holy Mother went to see it with Swami Saradananda.[19]

As a mother never discriminates between her good and bad children, so Holy Mother loved the stage actresses although they came from questionable backgrounds. Holy Mother appreciated their talents in acting and music, as well as their sincere devotion for her. She had been born and brought up in a conservative and orthodox brahmin family, but she understood the importance of the theatre: It carries art and culture, religion and philosophy, history and tradition to the masses. The puritans of society gradually became silent when Ramakrishna, Holy Mother, and Swami Vivekananda visited theatres and gave recognition to the actors and actresses, who, in those days, were treated like outcastes by society.

Girish's Passing

Girish's talent and magnetic personality attracted many people, whom he brought to the Master and Holy Mother. He was also extremely generous in his financial support of the Master, Holy Mother, and the disciples of Ramakrishna. Later, Holy Mother recalled some incidents regarding Girish: "It was Suresh [Surendranath] Mitra who gave money regularly to support the monastery. Girish also gave something. He bore all my expenses for a year and a half while I was at Nilambar Babu's house at Belur. Earlier he was a wretch and moved in bad company, running a theatre. But he was a man of great faith, so he received the Master's unbounded grace. The Master gave him liberation. Once the Master said: 'Girish was born as a part of Shiva.'"[20]

On another occasion Holy Mother said: "The Master's disease was due to accepting the sins of others. He said: 'I have this cancer because I took on Girish's sins. Girish would not have been able to bear the suffering of his sinful actions.' The Master had the power to die at will. He could have easily given up the body in samadhi. But he endured all that pain in order to 'unite his young disciples.'"[21]

On 11 February 1912 Holy Mother said to a devotee: "Alas, Girish is dead. Today is the fourth day. His relatives came here to invite me to their house to attend the ritual. He is no more; so I did not feel the need to go there. Ah! A veritable Indra [the king of the gods] has fallen! Oh, what tremendous faith and devotion he had for the Master!"[22]

16
Holy Mother
and Mahendra Nath Gupta (M.)

Tava kathāmritam tapta jivanam
  kavibhir-iditam kalmashāpaham;
Shravana-mangalam shrimad-ātatam
  bhuvi grinanti ye bhuridā janāh.
  —*Bhagavata, 10:31:9*

O Lord, your nectar-like words relieve the burning misery of afflicted souls. Your words, which poets have sung in verses, destroy the sins of worldly people forever. Blessed are those who hear of your vast glory. Blessed indeed are those who speak of you. How unparalleled is their bounty!

Providence chose Mahendra Nath Gupta — known by his pen-name, M. — to record *The Gospel of Sri Ramakrishna*. Although M. was a householder devotee, he often lived with his guru Rama-krishna and served him with heart and soul. When the Master passed away on 16 August 1886, M. became devoted to Holy Mother and served her according to his means for the rest of her life. The Mother was very comfortable with M. and his wife, Nikunja Devi, because she was aware of M.'s steadfast love, unflinching devotion, unselfish service, and com-plete obedience to the Master. In the early days, she did not hesitate to stay with M.'s family in Calcutta when she had no place of her own.

M.'s mother died when he was a young man, and he felt a terrible emptiness inside. His departed mother consoled him in a dream: "I shall always be with you, but you will not see me." Shortly after his mother's death, M. began to have difficulties with his extended family. Distraught, M. thought of committing suicide. One night he and his wife left the family home and went to his sister's house at Baranagore. A few days later, on 26 February 1882, M. met his guru, Ramakrishna, in Dakshineswar and eventually found his lost mother in Holy Mother.

Above: Sarada Devi in Calcutta, 1905.
Below: Money order for ten rupees signed with Sarada Devi's thumbprint.

246

M. said: "We visited the Master over a period of five years but never saw Holy Mother. From time to time the Master would refer to 'Ramlal's aunt.' One day I asked, 'Who is Ramlal's aunt?' The Master replied, 'Oh, she lives in the nahabat.' She was the guide and polestar of my life, but I never saw her face during that time. When she became elderly, she lifted the veil a little from her face."[1]

M. brought his wife to meet the Master on a number of occasions, two of which were described in *The Gospel of Sri Ramakrishna*. On 7 March 1885 M. wrote:

Holy Mother, Sri Ramakrishna's wife, was living in the nahabat. Occasionally she would come to Sri Ramakrishna's room to attend to his needs. Mohinimohan [M.] had brought his wife and Nabin's mother with him to the temple garden from Calcutta. The ladies were with Holy Mother; they were waiting for an opportunity to visit the Master when the men devotees would leave the room.

Sri Ramakrishna was sitting on the small couch talking to Mohini. Mohini's wife was almost mad with grief on account of her son's death. Sometimes she laughed and sometimes she wept. But she felt peaceful in Sri Ramakrishna's presence.

Master: "How is your wife now?"

Mohini: "She becomes quiet whenever she is here; but sometimes at home she becomes very wild. The other day she was going to kill herself."

When Sri Ramakrishna heard this he appeared worried. Mohini said to him humbly, "Please give her a few words of advice."

Master: "Don't allow her to cook. That will heat her brain all the more. And keep her in the company of others so that they may watch her."

Mohini's wife entered the room and sat at one side.

The Master suddenly addressed Mohini's wife and said: "By unnatural death one becomes an evil spirit. Beware. Make it clear to your mind. Is this what you have come to after hearing and seeing so much?"

Mohini was about to take his leave. He saluted Sri Ramakrishna. His wife also saluted the Master, who stood near the north door of the room. Mohini's wife spoke to him in a whisper.

Master: "Do you want to stay here?"

Mohini's wife: "Yes, I want to spend a few days with Holy Mother at the nahabat. May I?"

Master: "That will be all right. But you talk of dying. That frightens me. And the Ganges is so near!"[2]

On 24 April 1886 M. recorded another such story in the *Gospel*:

M. came to the Cossipore garden house accompanied by his wife and a son. The boy was seven years old. It was at the Master's request that he brought his wife, who was almost mad with grief owing to the death of one of her sons.

That day the Master several times allowed M.'s wife the privilege of waiting on him. Her welfare seemed to occupy his attention a great deal. In the evening Holy Mother came to the Master's room to feed him. M.'s wife accompanied her with a lamp. The Master tenderly asked her many questions about her household. He requested her to come again to the garden house and spend a few days with Holy Mother, not forgetting to ask her to bring her baby daughter. When the Master had finished his meal M.'s wife removed the plates. He chatted with her a few minutes.

About nine o'clock in the evening Sri Ramakrishna was seated in his room with the devotees. He had a garland of flowers around his neck. He told M. that he had requested his wife to spend a few days at the garden house with Holy Mother. His kindness touched M.'s heart.[3]

In the beginning, Nikunja Devi had disapproved of her husband's close relationship with Ramakrishna. When M. reported this to the Master, he told M. that one should give up a wife who was an obstacle on one's spiritual path. But he assured M. that if he had sincere faith in the Divine Mother, She would change his wife's mind. Soon Nikunja Devi became an ardent devotee of Ramakrishna and Holy Mother, and it was through his wife that M. learned more about Holy Mother.

On 6 April 1886, when the Master was ill in Cossipore, M. confided to the Master: "My wife is having temper tantrums from time to time. She has no feeling for our children. She feels good if she comes to you. She says that sometimes she sees you. She was lamenting the other day that you had bestowed grace on Balaram's wife and not on her. She has no peace. She becomes upset if I don't come here and also if I do come here. The other night she had a dream that your disease had become worse and she began to cry, saying, 'O Master, I became rid of all my pain by visiting you.' I share your teachings with her, but she does not listen to me. She acts according to her whims."[4]

Nikunja Devi stayed with Holy Mother both in Dakshineswar and Cossipore. It was through Nikunja that M. learned of Holy Mother's patience, perseverance, forgiveness, renunciation, service, and motherly affection for all. Thus M. became convinced that the Master and Holy Mother were manifestations of the same divine power.

M.'s Attitude towards Holy Mother

At Belur Math on 18 December 1924, Josephine MacLeod asked M.: "Mr. M., today is Holy Mother's birthday. What was she to you?"

M. replied:

The same as Sri Ramakrishna, God-incarnate on earth. He and Holy Mother are one in the same way that Christ said, 'I and my Father are one.' The Master said that Brahman and Shakti are one. He illustrated this with the example of a serpent. When the serpent is coiled, it is like Brahman in the undifferentiated Absolute state. When the serpent moves on in a zigzag manner, that is when Brahman as Shakti creates, preserves, and destroys the world; Holy Mother is the embodiment of Shakti or the Primordial Energy.

This Ultimate Energy, Brahma-shakti, incarnates in a human body at times for the good of the world. It is this Ultimate Energy that incarnated in dual forms as Sri Ramakrishna and Holy Mother. So these dual forms — Thakur [the Master] and Ma — are one and the same in essence.[5]

On 30 August 1886, after the Master's passing away, M. sent Nikunja Devi on pilgrimage with Holy Mother. They visited Vaidyanath, Varanasi, Ayodhya, and Vrindaban. But within a month Nikunja contracted malaria and returned to Calcutta with Kali (later Swami Abhedananda).

In August 1887 Holy Mother returned to Calcutta and then in September left for Kamarpukur. She returned to Calcutta in May 1888. At that time Holy Mother did not have her own residence in Calcutta; she lived either in Balaram's house or M.'s house, or she sometimes stayed in rented homes.

M. mentioned some of the places where Holy Mother lived from 1888 to 1909: "First, Holy Mother stayed at Raju Gomastha's house; second, near the cremation ground; and third, at Nilambar Mukherjee's house. These three places are in Belur. Fourth, she stayed on the second floor of a warehouse in Baghbazar. It was a jute warehouse and her entrance was through the warehouse. Fifth, she stayed in a house in front of Girish's house; sixth, near Nivedita's house [Bosepara Lane]; and seventh at her own house in Udbodhan*."[6]

---

*M.'s description is not complete. Apart from living in Balaram's house and M.'s house, Holy Mother lived in different rented places in and around Calcutta. It is difficult to ascertain the period of her stay in those places due to lack of records.
1. Nilambar Mukherjee's garden house at Belur: May to October 1888
2. Raju Gomastha's house at Belur: February 1890, for a month
3. A house near the cremation ground of Ghusuri, near Belur: May to September 1890
4. Nilambar Mukherjee's garden house at Belur: July to October 1893
5. Sharat Sarkar's house, 59/2 Ramkanta Bose Street, Baghbazar: April 1896, for a month
6. Sarkarbari Lane (second floor of the warehouse), Baghbazar: May to October 1896
7. 10/2 Bosepara Lane, Baghbazar: April 1897 to August 1899 *(continued next page)*

M. recalled: "Once Holy Mother lived with us for a month. Before leaving our home, she presented to our brahmin cook two dhotis [cloths] and money, and she bowed down to him. She also asked blessings from him with folded hands. We were all amazed observing her humility. Thus she taught us how to pay respect to others."[7]

When Holy Mother was staying at M.'s house, his sister-in-law Krishnamayi said to Holy Mother: "M. says, 'I have forgotten my previous father and mother; now Paramahamsadeva is my father and Holy Mother is my mother.'"

Holy Mother replied: "He is right. He is providing food for us. I can talk to him, but I feel shy." This was because Holy Mother seldom spoke to any of the Master's male devotees or disciples directly. Sometimes she communicated to them through Golap-ma or some other woman attendant. Nikunja Devi was the medium of communication between Holy Mother and M. Gradually, M. realized that Holy Mother and Ramakrishna were the same spiritual entity; there was no separation between them.

Swami Prabhananda probably quoted the following conversation from M.'s record of 23 April 1890. M., Narendra, Jogin, and others were at Balaram's house. Narendra said, "The Master said so many things but rarely spoke about Holy Mother."

Jogin replied: "What are you saying? If the Master is *Ishwara* [God], the Mother is *Ishwari* [Goddess]."[8]

Later Narendra wrote of Holy Mother that she was the "Living Durga." Her divinity and greatness touched the hearts of the devotees and disciples.

Holy Mother Gives Initiation to M. and Nikunja Devi

M. and Nikunja Devi were fortunate to have received the grace of both the Master and Holy Mother. When the Master was alive, he wrote a seed mantra on M.'s tongue; and then on 15 May 1887 M. received a mantra from the Master through a dream. On 30 October 1888, Nikunja Devi received initiation from Holy Mother, who was then staying at Nilambar Mukherjee's house in Belur.

From May to June of 1891, M. and Nikunja Devi stayed in Jayrambati with Holy Mother. Holy Mother and the women devotees lived in the

(*continued from previous page*)
8. 16 Bosepara Lane, Baghbazar: October 1900, for a year
9. Nilmani Shantidham, 2/1 Baghbazar Street, Calcutta: 14 February 1904
10. Udbodhan House, Baghbazar, Calcutta: 23 May 1909

house of Holy Mother's brother Prasanna. The male devotees stayed in a separate cottage that Prasanna used as his parlour.

One night after dinner, Holy Mother had a vision. She saw M. as a 5-year-old boy running naked in the streets of Jayrambati. The Master appeared and pointed to the young M., saying, "Initiate him." Holy Mother wondered: Didn't the Master already initiate him? Nonetheless, she immediately summoned M. and gave him initiation.[9]

M. served Holy Mother as he would have served his own mother. On her part, Holy Mother felt free while living with M.'s family. When the Master was in Cossipore, M. wanted to perform Durga Puja at his home. The Master said that his desire would be fulfilled. In October 1888 Holy Mother was staying at M.'s house. Just before Durga Puja, the Master said to her in a dream: "M. told me that he had a desire to perform Durga Puja. Now you arrange Durga Puja and install the ghat [the consecrated pitcher]."[10] Accordingly, on Saturday, 8 October 1888, Holy Mother installed and worshipped Sri Chandi Mangal-Ghat, the Durga Ghat, and Ramakrishna's photograph in M.'s shrine and arranged for their daily worship, which continues even today. From then on M. called his house "Thakur Bari," meaning "the Master's House." This historic event inspired M. to record *The Gospel of Sri Ramakrishna.*

Holy Mother initiated many devotees in this holy shrine. Swami Vivekananda and other direct disciples meditated there. Once Shyama-sundari, Holy Mother's mother, visited M.'s shrine. When she saw the Master's shoes in a glass case, she remarked: "When Saru was married, could I have known that my son-in-law was God and his shoes would be worshipped in this way?"[11] M.'s house is now like a museum where devotees can see an original print of the Master's photo, his shirt, his shoes, Holy Mother's footprints, and many other precious relics.

M. Supports Holy Mother

After Ramakrishna passed away, the monastic disciples practised austerities and travelled throughout India. They had no means with which to support Holy Mother. Both Balaram and Surendra, who had financially supported the Master, died in 1890, and Holy Mother suffered as a result. Other householder devotees were not aware of Holy Mother's financial condition. At that time, M. took three jobs and distributed his salaries to Holy Mother, the Baranagore monastery, and his own family. In 1894 he purchased a rice field of more than one acre in Jayrambati for Holy Mother; he also provided 1,000 rupees to build a new house for her in Jayrambati and to dig a well nearby. In addition to this support, M.

gave Holy Mother 10 rupees every month without fail. M. and his wife accompanied Holy Mother when she went on pilgrimage to Puri in 1904 and to Varanasi in 1912.

Holy Mother was very fond of M. and his family, as Ramakrishna had been. She praised M.'s loving service and steadfast devotion. Holy Mother said to Nikunja Devi: "I know that Master Mahashay [M.] has many noble qualities." On another occasion she said, "The way Master Mahashay walks reminds me of the Master, who would walk the same way." One day, as she heard M. read the *Gospel,* she remarked, "It seems that the Master is saying those words."

During Kali Puja in 1904, Holy Mother was staying at a rented house in Bosepara Lane, Calcutta. M. had informed her earlier that he would visit her that day. It was getting late at night. When someone said that perhaps M. would not come, Holy Mother replied: "Is he an unreliable, ordinary man? He has deep passion for truth. You will see, he will definitely come." M. arrived shortly thereafter.

On another occasion Holy Mother said to Nikunja Devi: "Master Mahashay's love and devotion are phenomenal. His letter forced me to come to Calcutta from Kamarpukur. He is a rare devotee. He is endowed with knowledge and devotion. His mind is pure and the blood, bones, and flesh of his body are pure." Once a devotee bowed down to Holy Mother at Udbodhan. She told that devotee: "Master Mahashay is downstairs. Please go and bow down to him. Know for certain, he is a great soul."[12]

Holy Mother once remarked of M.: "Is he an ordinary man? He has recorded so many of the Master's teachings. Is there any other avatar whose picture and conversations have been taken or recorded in such detail? It is as if the Master is talking in M.'s book."[13]

A Dialogue between Nikunja Devi and Holy Mother

Nikunja Devi was a close companion of Holy Mother, so on many occasions the Mother shared with her stories of her life with the Master. Nikunja Devi related those stories to M., and he recorded them in his diary.

Nikunja: "Mother, in family life there is only suffering and no peace. When I come to you, I get a little peace in my arid heart. It calms my soul when I address you as 'Mother.'"

Holy Mother: "My daughter, you have seen the Master, so you have nothing to worry about. He was very fond of you. He said to me: 'M.'s wife is simple and open-hearted. She looks at me with wonder.' Let me tell you, child — happiness and misery, good and bad — both exist in this world. They come in the course of time and people reap the results of their karma.

One should make the mind strong and keep it on God. It is not good to always harp on 'suffering, suffering.'"

Nikunja: "Mother, when I talk to you I feel strong and my mind becomes peaceful. That is why when I feel restless, I long to come to you."

Holy Mother: "Child, when I was 18 or 19 years old [at Dakshineswar in 1872], I used to sleep in the Master's room. One day he asked me, 'Who are you?' I replied, 'I have come to serve you.' One day there was no salt during lunch, so I said, 'There is no salt.' He scolded me, saying: 'What is this? Never say negative words. Try to collect everything.'

"When I was at Kamarpukur [in 1867], Ramlal's father asked me to go to the Master's room to sleep at night. The Master would laugh. At that time we shared a bed but spent the night talking about God. He taught me how to perform household work, how to behave with people, and how to know that God is your own and the only reality.

"When my mother visited Kamarpukur, the Master treated her with love and care, and asked her, 'Please make some pickles for us.'

"When I was at Jayrambati, the Master came there. He asked me to wash his feet with fuller's earth [a type of clay]. At this, the other women commented about my loving service to husband.

"When my mother-in-law was grief-stricken at the demise of her son [Rameswar], the Master would spend most of his time with his mother and console her. One day he prayed to the Divine Mother: 'Mother, I want to chant your name, but if my mother always grieves and cries, how is it possible to call on you? Please change my mother's mind.' Actually this prayer was answered; and my mother-in-law remained most of the time in an ecstatic mood.

"Shambhu Mallick made a cottage for me, but I was reluctant to live there. When I told the Master, he said to Hriday, 'Hride, bring your wife here [from Sihar].' Hriday replied, 'Did Shambhu Mallick build that cottage for my wife?'

"At that time there was a brahmachari [Tantric sadhak] in Dakshineswar. I was scared of him, thinking that he might do some harm to the Master; so I offered 10 rupees to him. Learning about it, the Master came to the nahabat and said: 'Don't worry. I have the Divine Mother. Who can do any harm to me?'

"One day the Master said to Ram Datta and others: 'You see, she talks about children. You all go to the nahabat and tell her, "Mother, we are your children."'

"Once we went together to Kamarpukur by boat via Bali-Deoanganj [in 1877]. We ate wonderful prasad and he sang so many songs on the way. Ah, what a great mood he was in! And he said to me: 'I know who you are, but I will not tell you now. (*Pointing to himself*) He said, 'Everything is inside this place.'

"When my mother-in-law was dying [13 February 1877], he said: 'O Mother, who are you that you carried me in your womb? Mother, you have looked after me in this form; henceforth please do the same.'

"One day, after his mother's passing away, he told me before lunch, 'Please wait. Let me go to the Panchavati and cry for my mother.'

"About his monthly salary of 7 rupees, he said to the manager: 'If you wish, give that money to her [meaning Holy Mother]; otherwise throw it into the Ganges, or spend it for the guests. Do whatever you like.'

"When I was living in the nahabat, once I spent the whole day making a beautiful garland. I requested him to put the garland on. He put the garland around his neck and then sang a song: 'Is there anything left for my decoration? I put on the necklace of universal jewels.'

"When I was about to leave for Jayrambati, I went to see him [in his room] several times, which he did not like. He said to Hriday, 'Why is she coming so many times? Ask her to go.'

"One day he said to Golap-ma about me: 'What power of forbearance she has! I salute her.'

"One day he said: 'I know who you are and who Lakshmi is, but I won't tell you. To pay my debt to you, I shall be born as a Baul [minstrel] and take you as my companion.'

"Hearing that Lakshmi was fasting on Ekadashi Day, he said, 'I am beyond the injunctions of the scriptures. Please eat well.' He did not care to see women wearing a cloth without a border. He commented, 'It is a dress that an ogress would wear.'"

"During his sadhana, he saw Sita with diamond-cut bangles in the Panchavati. Observing the pattern on the bangle, he had a set made for me. However, he could not touch money.

"One day I said to him, 'I have not had any spiritual ecstasy.' To this, he remarked: 'What do you expect? Does ecstasy mean that one will dance, letting the cloth fall? Who will then manage to keep the cloth in its proper place?'"

"A few days before his passing away, the Master said, 'It is better to be miserly than to be an extravagant wretch.'"[14]

M.'s Stories of Holy Mother

On different occasions M. recounted stories about Holy Mother to the devotees. These stories were recorded by Swami Nityatmananda and are excerpted here:

When the Master passed away, Holy Mother said, "His gross body is gone, but his spiritual body exists eternally." Once Hriday teased Holy Mother, saying, "Aunt, if you call uncle 'father,' I shall give you five seers of sandesh [sweets]." Holy Mother replied: "You will not have to give me sandesh. I tell you on my own that he is my father, mother, guru, friend, and husband — he is everything to me." She found the Master in every type of relationship. What faith she had!

Sometimes the Master talked to Holy Mother in front of the nahabat. Golap-ma, Yogin-ma, and Gauri-ma occasionally stayed with her. Brinda helped her do the household work.

The Master said to Holy Mother: "This mud hut of Kamarpukur is yours. Live on spinach and rice, and chant God's name the entire day." He gave Holy Mother his cottage in Kamarpukur and 400 rupees. Mathur gave some jewellery to the Master when he was practising sadhana as a confidante of Radha. That jewellery was sold for 400 rupees* and the money was invested in Balaram's estate. It earned an annual interest of 30 rupees. The Master sometimes asked us: "Well, are 2 rupees a month enough for a brahmin widow? What do you think?" Nonetheless, he was oblivious of day and night, even to his wearing cloth. He was so concerned about Holy Mother. He set the example, so that others would follow.

One day Holy Mother was meditating and someone loudly called to her. Her meditation broke and she cried out. When he heard this, the Master rushed to the nahabat, and gradually Holy Mother became calm. The Master said to others: "During meditation, one should neither call nor make any noise near that person."

The Master arranged for Holy Mother to sleep on the small cot in his room for eight months in Dakshineswar. Why? To teach devotees. They slept close to one another but had no physical relationship. His action was meant to bring strength and encouragement to the householder devotees so that they also could live like brother and sister. His marriage was an example for others. He demonstrated how to lead a married life.

The Master suffered in Dakshineswar after Mathur's passing away. There was no one to look after him. He would eat cold spicy food at 1:00 p.m. His mat was torn, and his pillowcase and bedsheet were dirty; but his mind was on God. Gradually his health broke down. [When Hriday left], he wrote to Holy Mother: "There is no one to look after me here. I shall appreciate it if you come here." Holy Mother returned to Dakshineswar and began to cook for him.

*   *   *

Once Holy Mother said to a woman devotee: "I have seen many holy people, but none can be compared with the Master." The woman devotee replied: "What do you say, Mother? Other holy men come to be liberated and the Master came to liberate others." Holy Mother said with a smile, "You are right." Holy Mother said this to test that devotee.

*Actually 600 rupees were invested and Holy Mother received 6 rupees per month from the interest.

Those who search for genuine monks get confused. They do not see their own imperfections. The Master said, "Both good and bad qualities exist in human beings; only God — the avatar — is free from blemishes." Holy Mother said, "Even in the moon there is a stain, but there is no stain in the Ramakrishna-moon."

*   *   *

Sometimes we sent some food and other things to Holy Mother [in Udbodhan] through our servant. She would feed the Master's special prasad to our servant with great care. She did not discriminate like other people, who make one kind of food for themselves and another kind for the servants. All were equal to her.

Once it was proposed that a cow be brought from Belur Math to Udbodhan so that Holy Mother could have fresh milk. But she immediately protested: "No, no. Those cows are freely grazing in the holy atmosphere of the monastery compound where they can see the Ganges. Here the cow would be tied with a rope and kept in a room! I couldn't bear it. I couldn't drink that milk."

Holy Mother said to a young man: "My son, never marry. If you are not married, you will be able to sleep peacefully at night. My child, never enter this burning fireplace." As she initiated a young man into brahmacharya, she said, "My child, now you will be able to sleep happily."

Ah, how Holy Mother tied the devotees with her love and affection! Once at Jayrambati five male devotees went to get initiation from Holy Mother. One of them belonged to a low caste. He was asked by the others to sit outside because his presence might pollute the shrine. He began to cry. When Holy Mother entered the shrine, she found four men and inquired about the other person. They replied, "He belongs to the washerman's caste; he is outside." She rushed to that devotee and escorted him into the shrine. He was reluctant to enter, but Holy Mother took him inside and initiated him with the others.

*   *   *

Holy Mother said four things:

1. "The devotion of those who are desireless is unconditional. They are Ishwarakotis [god-like souls]."

2. "Those who have money, give charity; and those who have nothing, repeat the mantra." Charity means worshipping and serving others as God with money. Otherwise, spend your time repeating the mantra.

3. "Grace is flowing all around, but human nature does not change." This means people are listening to the words of God, but nothing is happening. Why? Because maya is pulling those people back.

4. Someone asked Holy Mother, "What happens if a person dies after losing outer consciousness?" Holy Mother replied: "There is nothing wrong

with losing consciousness while dying. It is enough if a person remembers God just before becoming unconscious. That brings good results."

*   *   *

One should serve others when one visits an ashrama. The monks are busy taking care of the devotees, while the devotees are practising japa and meditation — this is not right. Once several women devotees visited Holy Mother in Jayrambati. They were meditating with closed eyes while Holy Mother was mopping the mud floor. A woman devotee [M.'s wife] got up from her meditation and went to help Holy Mother. Holy Mother said, "The others are meditating, so why have you come?" The woman replied: "Shame! I don't care for that kind of meditation. You are mopping the floor and I shall close my eyes and meditate? I can't do that." That devotee understood the right thing to do.

Some fortunate devotees saw Holy Mother in samadhi. Her body remained motionless and her eyes did not blink....Ah, what a rare scene!

The Master was sometimes criticized. Once someone offered a small amount of money to Holy Mother as a gift. Trailokya commented, "The young priest brought his wife here to earn money." The Master went to the Kali temple and cried to the Divine Mother, saying, "Mother, the authorities of the temple say such things."

*   *   *

Holy Mother said to a monk: "During your last moments, the Master will come and take you with him. You belong to him, so you will go to him. But if you want peace while living, practise austerities and meditate on him. Grace dawns on one who practises austerities. The Master's grace is not subject to any conditions."

Holy Mother said:

1. To those who have taken refuge in the Master, he will appear at the time of death.

2. Misery is inevitable for an embodied being; even the creator has no power to stop it. If you want peace, practise spiritual disciplines.

3. There is no certainty about when death will come, so it is better to visit holy places soon without discriminating between auspicious or inauspicious times.

4. Someone asked, "Why is my karma not ending?" Mother replied: "There is plenty of string in the spool of a kite; the spool will be empty when all of the string has played out."

5. The Master never caused me pain, even for a day.

The Master promised: "I swear that those who think of me will attain my spiritual wealth, just as children inherit their parents' wealth." He said this with such emphasis, yet people still do not believe it. Holy Mother had so much love for the devotees! Once when a devotee was leaving Jayrambati after receiving initiation, she came out from her room to see him off, with tears in her eyes. She watched that devotee walk away, as far as she could see him. Although she had known him for only a couple of days, her love surpassed even that of a biological mother.

*   *   *

Holy Mother had strong common sense. On one hand, she said, "You will not have to practise japa and meditation"; and on the other, she said, "If you want peace in this life, you will have to practise sadhana." How nicely she reconciled two opposite things!

These two aspects we learn from Holy Mother's life: (1) brahmacharya and absorption in God, (2) self-control and service. She did not know anything other than God. Seeing God in every being, she served Him day and night. All her teachings are mantras. Many highly-educated women, including Nivedita, sat at her feet with folded hands. Modern ideas and education were subordinate to her towering personality.

One day we were in the Baranagore monastery talking about Holy Mother, who was in Vrindaban at the time. Swami Vivekananda related this incident: One day at the Cossipore garden house the devotees mentioned Holy Mother's affection for them to the Master. She was there to serve the Master. The devotees said, "We have never seen such a noble heart." I asked Swamiji, "What did the Master say about it?" Swamiji replied: "The Master laughed and then remarked: 'She is my Shakti. That is why she is noble.'"[15]

17
Holy Mother's
Caretakers

Mridunā dārunam hanti mridunā hanti adārunam;
Nāsevyam mridunā kinchit tasmāt tikshnataram mriduh.
  —*Mahabharata, 3:28:31*

Gentleness conquers the hearts of the cruel as well as the kind. There is nothing in this world that gentleness cannot conquer. So gentleness is a powerful virtue.

Holy Mother was the embodiment of modesty and gentleness, love and compassion, simplicity and humility, unselfishness and forgiveness. As a divine being, she was endowed with a preponderance of sattva, so she did not behave like other women of her time. As an ideal Indian woman of the early twentieth century, she was not demanding or aggressive; she found joy through love and unselfish service. She was extremely modest, but that does not mean she was meek or docile when challenged by injustice or wickedness. She represented the Motherhood of God in this age and conducted Ramakrishna's spiritual ministry through her divine power, which overwhelmed everyone who approached her. Nonetheless, as a sweet and compassionate mother, it was not possible for her to say a harsh word to anyone, so she sometimes endured the ill behaviour of strangers and unbalanced disciples. She forgave them as a loving mother does her children.

When she came in contact with people of the wider world and began to act as a guru, she needed people to protect her. Ramakrishna had foreseen her future role as a guru, so he selected two strong and wise companions for her: Golap-ma and Yogin-ma. At Cossipore, just before the Master passed away, Holy Mother felt helpless and burst into tears. The Master consoled her, saying: "Why should you feel troubled? You will live as you are living now. They [the disciples] will do for you what they are doing for me."

Sarada Devi in Calcutta, 1905.

All of the Master's monastic disciples loved and respected Holy Mother and offered their services when needed, but Swamis Yogananda and Saradananda especially became her devoted attendants and served her with heart and soul. These two disciples became her trusted caretakers.

Swami Brahmananda

Although Swami Brahmananda, as the head of the Order, was busy travelling to various places, initiating people and training monks, he always kept an eye on Holy Mother. Once Holy Mother described her caretakers: "Jogin [Yogananda] and Sharat [Saradananda] are my real caretakers. Rakhal [Brahmananda] is not of that temperament. He can't put up with difficulties.* He can look after me mentally or through someone else. He is cast in a different mould."[1]

Swami Brahmananda's reverence for Holy Mother was too deep for words. At the very sight of her, he was overwhelmed with spiritual emotion. As a spiritual son of Ramakrishna, he was often absorbed in an ecstatic mood that made him practically unapproachable. But in the presence of Holy Mother, he acted like a child. Whenever he visited her, he prostrated before her with great love and respect. Holy Mother affectionately caressed him, touching his chin, and gently stroked his head and chest. Once he received her blessing, he left the room quickly. The Mother would send him a tray of sweets, which he enjoyed immensely.

Brahmananda truly worshipped Holy Mother as a goddess. Once he remarked: "It is very difficult to understand Mother. She moves about, veiling her face like an ordinary woman, but in reality she is the Mother of the Universe. Could we have recognized her if the Master himself had not revealed to us who she was?"[2]

On another occasion Brahmananda said:

> Is it possible for an ordinary being to accept the worship of an Incarnation like Sri Ramakrishna?** From this one may understand what a great fountain of power Mother is. We have seen with our own eyes that Mother takes the sins and afflictions of many people upon herself and gives them liberation. Can anyone but the Divine Mother have this power?…Inside, the great ocean of realization; outside, absolute calm. How ordinary and simple she appears! Even the Incarnations cannot keep divine moods under control. Sri Ramakrishna manifested them outwardly. But it is extremely difficult to understand Mother. She has kept us all deluded with her motherly love![3]

---

*Holy Mother was referring to difficulties among the women around her and between the members of her family.
**He was referring to the Master's worship of Sarada Devi as Shodashi in Dakshineswar.

Swami Yogananda

When Swami Yogananda was a young man, then known as Jogin, he was suspicious about the Master's relationship with Holy Mother. One evening in Dakshineswar, Jogin decided to spend the night with the Master, with the intention of serving him if needed. Ramakrishna was pleased. After dinner the Master went to bed, and Jogin made his own bed on the floor and slept.

Throughout his life Jogin was a light sleeper. At midnight he woke up and found that the Master was not in his bed. He looked for the water pot that the Master used for washing and found it in its proper place. He thought that the Master might be walking outside but could not find him there. Suddenly a terrible suspicion gripped his mind: "Has the Master gone to the nahabat to be with his wife? Can it be possible that his actions are contrary to his teachings?"

Determined to find out the truth without delay, Jogin stationed himself near the nahabat. But while he waited there and watched the door of the nahabat, he heard the clattering of the Master's sandals coming from the direction of the Panchavati. Within a few moments Ramakrishna appeared in front of Jogin and asked, "Hello, why are you standing here?" Embarrassed, Jogin hung his head in shame for having doubted the Master. He could not utter a single word. The Master understood everything from the expression on his face. Instead of taking offence, Ramakrishna reassured Jogin: "Well, you are quite right — you must examine a holy man by day and by night before believing in him." Though forgiven, Jogin could not sleep that night.

After his passing away, the Master uprooted Jogin's doubt and relieved his feelings of guilt. When Holy Mother was in Vrindaban, the Master appeared to her and asked her to initiate Jogin and to make him her first disciple and caretaker.

Later Kumudbandhu Sen recalled: "As Swami Yogananda began describing this event [of initiation], his voice became choked with deep emotion. In conclusion he remarked: 'The image of the Master and the Mother will never fade from my memory. I realized that both of them were of divine origin and that they had incarnated in human form out of compassion for the devoted millions.'"[4]

Swami Saradananda wrote: "Swami Yogananda completely atoned for his offence, first by surrendering himself completely to his guru and serving him, and then when the Master passed away, by devoting his life to the service of the Holy Mother."[5]

Above: Swami Yogananda; Swami Trigunatitananda.
Below: Swami Saradananda.

In August 1886, after the Master's passing away, Yogananda went on pilgrimage with Holy Mother. Then in September 1887, he accompanied her to Kamarpukur and stayed there for three days. In November 1888 Yogananda went to Puri with Holy Mother and stayed with her there for three months. In February 1889 he again went to Kamarpukur with the Mother, who stayed there for a year. After leaving Holy Mother in Kamarpukur, Yogananda left for his own pilgrimage and to practise severe austerities. He spent most of his time in meditation. Once a day he would go out to beg for food; sometimes he ate only dry bread soaked in water for two or three days at a time. This practice ruined his digestive system.

In 1898 when Holy Mother lived at 10/2 Bosepara Lane, a rented house in Baghbazar, Calcutta, Yogananda and Brahmachari Krishnalal took care of her and ran all her errands. Yogananda posted himself at the entrance as a gatekeeper, receiving gifts for Holy Mother and regulating the devotees' visits.

Sister Nivedita described the place in *The Master as I Saw Him*: "It was a strange household, of which I now found myself a part. Downstairs, in one of the guard-rooms beside the front door, lived a monk [Yogananda], whose severe austerities, from his youth up, had brought him to the threshold of death, from consumption, in the prime of manhood. To his room I used to go for Bengali lessons. In the kitchen behind, worked a disciple [Krishnalal] of his [actually of Holy Mother's], and a brahmin cook; while to us women-folk belonged all above stairs, with roof terraces, and the sight of the Ganges hard by."[6]

Holy Mother later commented: "Jogin and Sharat belong to my inner circle. No one loved me as Jogin did. If anybody gave him money, he would save it, saying, 'Mother will use it for her pilgrimage.' The other monks teased him for living in this household full of women. He asked me to address him as 'Yoga.'"

Yogananda was so respectful towards Holy Mother that he would not touch her feet when he bowed down, but instead waited until she left the room and then touched his head to the spot where she had been. When asked about this strange behaviour, Yogananda replied: "What? I don't have the audacity to keep the Mother standing and waiting for me so that I can bow down to her."[7]

Love is demonstrated by emotion and thoughtfulness. Regarding Yogananda's concern for her, Holy Mother recalled: "Every year since that time [after the vision of the goddess Jagaddhatri] I have gone home for Jagaddhatri Puja as often as possible. I used to help by polishing the puja utensils and looking after other things. Formerly there were not many people in the family, so I went home to clean the pots and pans. Later Jogin got a set of wooden utensils for me. He said, 'Mother, you do not have to scour pots and pans anymore.' He also secured a piece of land to provide for the expenses of the puja."[8]

Yogananda's loving service and devotion left a deep impression on Holy Mother's heart. He once presented her with a quilt. When it eventually became worn out from constant use, Holy Mother considered changing the cover and having it stuffed with fresh cotton, but then she gave up the idea since, she thought, it would change the look of the gift from her beloved disciple.

Swami Yogananda passed away in samadhi at 3:10 p.m. on 28 March 1899 at the age of 38. Towards the end, he said to Holy Mother, "Mother, Brahma, Vishnu, Shiva, and Sri Ramakrishna have come to take me." That morning, while performing worship, Holy Mother saw that the Master had come to take Yogananda. When Yogananda breathed his last, Brahmachari Krishnalal cried out. Holy Mother was upstairs and realized what had happened. She burst into tears and said, "My Jogin has left me — who will now look after me?" Because Yogananda was the first of the Master's disciples to die, Mother remarked with a deep sigh: "A brick has slipped from the structure; now the whole thing will come down."[9]

Even a divine being like Holy Mother was grief-stricken by Yogananda's passing. The Mahabharata says: "At the end of prosperity, there is decline; after union, there is separation; after life, there is death."

Swami Trigunatitananda

After Swami Yogananda's passing, Swami Trigunatitananda took charge of Holy Mother's physical needs in addition to editing the *Udbodhan* journal. He served her from 1899 until he left for America in 1902. His zeal in serving her sometimes appeared almost obsessive. In October 1899 Holy Mother was going to Jayrambati in a bullock cart via Burdwan. It was past midnight. Trigunatitananda was walking in front of the cart as her bodyguard, with a heavy stick on his shoulder. Suddenly he saw a wide breach in the road made by a flood. At once he realized that the cart would either be overturned or receive a terrific jolt, not only disturbing the Mother's sleep but possibly injuring her. Immediately he laid his large body in the breach and asked the driver to continue over him. Fortunately, Holy Mother awoke before this happened. She took in the situation and rebuked her disciple for his rashness.

Trigunatita's love for and faith in Holy Mother was phenomenal. Once Yogin-ma asked the swami to buy some hot chilies for Holy Mother. In his

eagerness to get the hottest chilis possible, he walked through many markets from Baghbazar to Barabazar, a distance of four miles, tasting all the
hot chilies until his tongue became red and swollen. At last he found the
hottest ones at Barabazar and brought them to the Mother. When Holy
Mother heard about this, she said, "What devotion to the guru!" Later
when Trigunatita went to America, he sent money regularly for Holy
Mother's personal service.

Swami Saradananda

Once when the Master's disciples were young, Sharat (later Saradananda) said to Jogin (Yogananda): "I do not always understand what
Naren [later Vivekananda] means. He talks about many things. Whenever he speaks about something he does it with such emphasis that all his
other statements become practically meaningless."

Jogin replied: "Let me tell you something, Sharat. You stick to Mother.
Whatever she says is right."[10]

When Swami Trigunatitananda left for America on 27 September 1902,
Saradananda took over responsibility for Holy Mother and continued
serving her until she passed away in 1920.

Many years earlier at Dakshineswar, Ramakrishna one day sat upon
Saradananda's lap in an ecstatic mood. He later explained to the curious devotees, "I was testing to see how much weight he could bear." The
young disciple passed his guru's test. In later years, despite his heavy
responsibilities as general secretary of the Ramakrishna Order, he took
charge of Holy Mother's day-to-day affairs. Saradananda often referred
to himself as the gatekeeper of her Calcutta home. He took responsibility
for the Mother's food and lodging, looked after her health, managed her
household, cared for her relatives, handled her financial needs, directed
her visitors and devotees, and arranged for her travels. He also built a
home for her in Calcutta. While Holy Mother was in Jayrambati, he sometimes travelled there to manage her finances or care for her when she
was ill. He also settled the complicated problems of her family members,
and had a home built for her in Jayrambati where she could move about
freely. Like a dutiful and dependable son, Saradananda tried his utmost
to make Holy Mother happy and comfortable. To him, the Mother came
first, before everything else in this world. In fact, his life is a glowing
example of complete dedication to service.

Holy Mother once said: "I shall be able to live in Calcutta as long as
Sharat is there. I do not see anyone who can be responsible for me after
that. Sharat can, in every respect. He is the man to bear my burden."

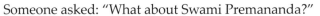

Someone asked: "What about Swami Premananda?"

"No, he can't do it."

"But he runs Belur Math!"

"That may be, but looking after women is a bother. He can only keep an eye on me from a distance."[11]

From 1902 to 1920 Saradananda's life was intertwined with Holy Mother's. This period is recorded in detail in this book, but here we shall record some significant events that affected Saradananda directly.

When Saradananda began looking after Holy Mother, he was upset that she had no place of her own in Calcutta or in Jayrambati. In Calcutta she lived either in a rented house or, when the disciples could not find a suitable house for her, in a devotee's home. She was very shy, so it was difficult to be a guest in a householder devotee's house and witness their family quarrels and frivolous activities, or join them in sickness and grief. Moreover, she suffered from malaria from time to time and could not bear the thought of becoming a burden to others. Regardless of whether she stayed with a devotee's family or in a rented house, it was inconvenient for her to be frequently changing lodgings. Realizing Holy Mother's uncomfortable situation, Saradananda was determined to build a permanent home for her in Calcutta.

In July 1906 Kedar Chandra Das donated a small piece of land on Gopal Neogi Lane, Baghbazar, for building a publication house for *Udbodhan*, the official Bengali journal of the Ramakrishna Order. Previously the publication house was located in Girindralal Basak's house, but that devotee died in 1906. It was suggested that they build a tiled shed on the donated plot, but Saradananda decided to build a brick house instead. His plan was to use the first floor for the publication office with a shrine to the Master, and the second floor as living quarters for Holy Mother and her companions. Towards the end of 1907, depending on the Master's grace, Saradananda undertook responsibility for the building project. The publication fund had 2,700 rupees, which was consumed by the construction of the building's foundation. Saradananda borrowed a total of 5,700 rupees from different devotees, but this was still not enough. Finally, some distinguished devotees came forward to fund the project. The building, known as Udbodhan House, had 10 rooms — six on the first floor, three on the second floor, and one on the third floor. By the end of 1908, the Udbodhan Office had moved into its new house. (*See Chapter 29 for more details on Udbodhan House.*)

Holy Mother was not in Baghbazar for the opening ceremony of Udbodhan House. In 1908, she went to Kamarpukur to attend the festival celebrating the anniversary of Ramakrishna's birth, arranged by Swami Yogavinod of Kankurgachi, a disciple of Ramchandra Datta. Following the festival, she went to Jayrambati, where she lived with her brothers' joint family. Their mother, Shyamasundari, had died in 1906 and Holy Mother had become her brothers' guardian. By late 1908 her brothers were grown and married, and they had begun to quarrel over their share of the family property. They had tremendous respect for Saradananda, so Holy Mother asked him to help divide up their inheritance.

On 23 March 1909 Saradananda left for Jayrambati with Yogin-ma, Golap-ma, and Brahmachari Jnanananda (later Swami Bhumananda) to fulfill Holy Mother's request. The train reached Vishnupur in the afternoon. They left for Jayrambati that evening in two bullock carts, arriving the next day before noon. Saradananda bowed down to the Mother, and she blessed him by touching his head and chin.

Holy Mother was extremely busy in Jayrambati. Apart from her daily duties, she cooked a couple of dishes for Saradananda and the others. In the evening Saradananda talked to the villagers about the Master and spiritual life. He knew that arbitration takes time, so he carried Swami Vivekananda's *Jnana Yoga* with him to edit.

Three arbitrators — Swami Saradananda, Sarada Prasad Chattopadhyay of Tajpur, and Shambhu Chandra Roy of Jibta — were selected with the approval of Holy Mother's brothers. Kedarnath Datta of Koalpara (later Swami Keshavananda) came to measure the family homestead and farmland.

Swami Bhumananda recalled:

It took several days to measure the dwelling places and the farmlands. All documents were in Uncle Kali's possession. Uncle Prasanna* wanted to see those documents but Uncle Kali would not share them. One day Sharat Maharaj went to Kali's house to hand out the documents according to the distribution of the property. He secretly told me to guard the documents because he knew the nature of the Mother's brothers. Sharat Maharaj sat on a mat on Kali's veranda and I stood behind Prasanna. Kali opened the iron safe and brought out all of the documents, placing them in front of Maharaj. He began to scrutinize the documents. Meanwhile Yogin-ma said, "Sharat, the Mother wants to talk to you." Immediately Maharaj got up and told Prasanna, "Uncle, don't touch these documents. I shall check them when I come back." Maharaj gave me a look and I understood what he meant. As soon as Maharaj left, Prasanna began to quarrel with Kali. Prasanna jumped up and grabbed the documents. I stopped him from

---

*Bhumananda is referring to Holy Mother's brothers Kalikumar and Prasanna.

leaving, but the brothers began to pull at the documents. Sharat Maharaj heard the noise and returned. Prasanna placed the documents in front of him. Finally, Sharat Maharaj distributed the documents.

Later Sharat Maharaj told us: "Look at us — some are monks of 25 years and some of 30 years — we become extremely angry for a little offence. Now look at the Mother! How she is forbearing all these things! Faced by her brothers' erratic behaviour, the Mother remains calm, serene, and unperturbed."[12]

The arbitrators discussed the whole affair for many days and finally settled the matter. It was decided that the property and the legal documents would be divided among the brothers. According to the local law of the time, sons inherit their fathers' property, but daughters inherit their husbands' property. As she lived with her parents and brothers in Jayrambati even after her marriage, Holy Mother had her own cottage. So Sarada Babu asked her which of her brothers' households she would prefer to live in. He wanted to be sure that her cottage was allotted to the brother whom she preferred. Holy Mother had intense renunciation and she said that she would live in another person's household like "a snake lives in a rat's hole." When Sarada Babu insisted on a decision, she replied: "Some days I shall live in Prasanna's house and some days in Kali's." Sarada Babu was prudent and he knew the nature of her brothers. He put Holy Mother's cottage in Prasanna's share of the family estate. The documents were executed and duly registered in the court at Kotalpur. When the brothers took possession of their respective shares, Holy Mother was greatly relieved. Years later, when the number of Holy Mother's devotees began to grow, Saradananda had another house built in 1916 for Holy Mother in Jayrambati.

On Friday, 21 May 1909, Holy Mother left Jayrambati for Calcutta via Vishnupur. She was then 56 years old. Four bullock carts were hired — one for Holy Mother and her two nieces, Radhu and Maku; one for Yogin-ma and Golap-ma; one for Saradananda; and one for Brahmachari Jnanananda and a devotee from Jayrambati named Ashutosh. The party stopped briefly at Koalpara in the afternoon and then resumed their journey in the evening. At ten o'clock they bought some food from a shop in Kotalpur for supper and ate it on the veranda of a Shiva temple. The party reached an inn at Jaipur in the morning. They had an early lunch, rested, and then continued to the Vishnupur railway station that evening. Holy Mother and her women companions boarded an inter class* car; Saradananda and the others travelled third class. They reached Calcutta the next morning.

*At that time there were four classes on the train: first class, second class, inter class, and third class.

On Sunday, 23 May 1909, Holy Mother entered her new living quarters in Udbodhan House (which is now called Mayer Bari, or "Mother's House"). Saradananda's joy knew no bounds when he saw that Holy Mother had entered her own home. Although it was not a fancy house, it was very convenient for her to bathe in the Ganges. At that time there were no huts in front of the house but only an open field. From the rooftop Holy Mother could see the domestic cattle grazing in the field, and she could see the Ganges to the west, bordered by tall deodar trees. From one particular spot she could even see the pinnacles of the Dakshineswar temple, which brought back many sweet memories to her.

A few weeks after arriving at Udbodhan House, Holy Mother contracted chicken pox. The brahmin priest of the Shitala temple in Baghbazar treated her with naturopathy every day, and she always bowed down to him. One day an attendant told her not to bow down to such an ordinary priest, who might not have a good character. Holy Mother replied: "My child, he is a brahmin after all. One should have respect for his brahminical garb. The Master did not destroy any rules or customs."

When Holy Mother had recuperated from her illness, Saradananda arranged for her sightseeing and she visited the Parswanath Jaina temple and Kankurgachi Yogodyana in Calcutta, and Ramrajatala and Navagopal's house in Howrah. Lalit Chattopadhyay, one of the Mother's disciples, provided his horse carriage. Yogin-ma and Golap-ma accompanied her.

On 12 September 1909, Holy Mother went to see Girish's play *Pandav Gaurav* at the Minerva Theatre. While watching the play and listening to the song, "Hera Hara-manamohini" she went into samadhi. On that day Girish Ghosh performed the role of Kanchuki, an elderly minister of a king. On another occasion Holy Mother went to hear kirtan at Kiran Datta's house at Baghbazar. The theme of the kirtan was Radha's separation from Krishna. At the end of the kirtan, Holy Mother went into ecstasy and lost body consciousness. Golap-ma cautiously held her up and took her to the carriage. After arriving at Udbodhan, an attendant began to repeat "Ma, Ma." Gradually she regained normal consciousness and replied, "Yes, my son."

Golap-ma began to live with Holy Mother in Udbodhan and became her full-time attendant. She and Radhu's mother shared a room adjacent to Holy Mother's room. Yogin-ma came twice a day to give the cook rice, lentils and other cooking supplies from the pantry and also to help him chop the vegetables. After vespers in the evenings, Holy Mother sometimes asked Saradananda to sing some songs. The swami had a tanpura and drums in his office, which was a small room next to the building's entrance. He played the drums and someone else played the tanpura. He sang some devotional songs, especially on the Divine Mother, to entertain the Mother.

Providence sometimes provides difficulties to facilitate its own designs, and Saradananda experienced this situation. He had borrowed money from devotees to complete Udbodhan House in Calcutta but could not pay the interest on the loan. He was embarrassed because he could not keep his word. He had few alternatives, so he decided to write the life of the Master to pay off the loan. With the permission and blessing of Holy Mother, Saradananda began to write *Sri Sri Ramakrishna Lilaprasanga*, which has been translated into English as *Sri Ramakrishna and His Divine Play*. He later described the adverse conditions under which he wrote the *Lilaprasanga*:

> Holy Mother was living upstairs along with Radhu; I was surrounded by devotees, and I had to keep the accounts also; the burden of the loan for the house was on me. I used to write the *Lilaprasanga* sitting in the small room downstairs. Then nobody dared to talk to me, as I had no time to chat for a long time. If anybody would ask anything, I would say, "Be quick," and finish the talk briefly. People would think that I was egotistic. I could not write much about the devotees [except Gopal-ma and Vivekananda], because there was so much material to write about the Master. When the mind was ready, only then could I write.[13]

Saradananda's service to Holy Mother is legendary in the Ramakrishna Order. Although Holy Mother now had her own place in Calcutta, she was always surrounded by devotees and their problems, and she could not move freely. Sometimes she felt suffocated in Udbodhan House. Every now and then she would visit Jayrambati for a change. When Holy Mother was in Jayrambati, Saradananda would visit other centres of the Ramakrishna Mission.

Swami Nikhilananda wrote: "To attend Holy Mother, with her eccentric relatives, was a delicate and difficult task. As she herself put it: 'I shall have no difficulty as long as Sharat lives. I do not see anybody else who can shoulder my burden.' If anyone spoke of her going to Calcutta when the swami was not there, she would say: 'I simply cannot think of going to Calcutta when Sharat is not there. While I am in Calcutta, if he says that he wants to go elsewhere for a few days, I tell him: "Wait awhile, my child. First let me leave and then you may go."'"[14]

Another occasion illustrates Saradananda's tender care for Holy Mother, and her concern for him. It was quite cold in November of 1910 and the devotees wanted Holy Mother to have some warm clothing. Accordingly, Saradananda provided 10 rupees for a warm cotton sweater to be bought from a foreign shop. Delighted, the Mother wore it for three days. On the fourth day she took it off and said to her attendant: "My child, it is not proper for a woman to wear this kind of sweater. I used it for three days just to please you all."[15] Although the Mother did not wear a blouse under her sari, like other women, she covered her whole body with her sari by tying it under her arm. During winter she used a thick cotton chadar. She maintained her rural way of living and did not care for urban luxury. People were impressed by her inner beauty.

On 16 November 1909 Holy Mother left for Jayrambati. On 14 December 1909 Saradananda bought a small plot of land adjacent to Udbodhan House for 1,800 rupees with money that devotees had donated. A few rooms were added to the main house in 1915.

In 1918 a devotee from Ranchi went to Jayrambati and said to Holy Mother: "Mother, I have come to take you to Ranchi for some days. We have rented a house and made all the arrangements."

Holy Mother asked, "Does Sharat know?"

"No," the devotee replied.

Holy Mother said: "Then I can't go. Sharat came here to take me to Calcutta, but I refused. Let me go to Calcutta first and then I shall consider it if Sharat approves."

The devotee insisted, saying, "Mother, we have arranged everything."

Holy Mother responded: "Who asked you to arrange this without my consent?"

When the devotee left, Holy Mother told Sarala: "Look, my child, they think it is easy to take me here and there. They love to create excitement. One time in Dhaka the devotees printed pamphlets announcing that I would be going there; I knew nothing about it. Anyone can serve me for two or three days. Is it so easy to carry responsibility for me for a long time? I can't find anyone capable of this except Sharat. He is like my Vasuki [a thousand-hooded mythical snake] engaged in thousands of activities. Whenever rain falls, he spreads his umbrella to protect me."[16]

Saradananda was proud of his position as the Mother's doorkeeper. From his small room to the left of the entrance to Holy Mother's residence in Calcutta he kept an eye on the devotees who went upstairs to pay their respects. It was not an easy task. Surendranath Roy, a young medical student, used to visit Holy Mother every week. One day he walked several miles under the scorching sun to see the Mother in Udbodhan. He arrived at about three o'clock in the afternoon. It was very hot. Holy Mother had just returned from a devotee's house and was resting. When Saradananda saw Surendra going upstairs, he stopped him near the steps and said: "I won't allow you to go up now; Mother is tired." Surendra answered, "Is she only your mother?" Practically pushing Saradananda aside, he continued up the stairs. Very soon, Surendra felt repentant for his rash act and prayed that he might avoid the swami on his way out. He told the Mother about his bad behaviour, and she reassured him. Sheepishly he came down the stairs and found Saradananda seated in the same place. Surendra bowed down before the swami and asked for his forgiveness. Saradananda embraced him and said: "Why do you talk about offending me? Can one see Mother without such yearning?"[17]

It was not an easy job to be Holy Mother's doorkeeper. Saradananda was sometimes humiliated for protecting Holy Mother, yet he endured everything calmly. On 2 January 1917 Swami Premananda asked Dhirananda to accompany Dhirendra Kumar Guhathakurta, a young man from Barisal (now in Bangladesh), to Holy Mother to be initiated. Dhirendra recalled: "I was about to climb the steps of the Mother's house to see the Mother. Revered Sharat Maharaj was writing at his desk in the entrance room. As soon as I neared the steps, he loudly said: 'Who is going upstairs? The Mother's health is not good. Don't go.' He came forward to stop me, but I was so obstinate that I went upstairs, pushing him aside. The Mother was then performing worship. Looking at me, she realized that I wanted initiation. She told me with a smile, 'Come tomorrow.'"[18] The next day the Mother initiated him.

On another occasion, when Holy Mother was ill, a prominent devotee came to her and asked for his brother to be initiated. She asked him to come a few days later when she was feeling better. However, the man insisted. She asked him to speak to Saradananda about it. "I do not know anybody else," he insisted again. "I have come to you. Please initiate my brother."

"What do you mean?" the Mother replied. "Sharat is the jewel of my head. What he says will be done." The devotee went to Saradananda and reported to him what the Mother had said. The swami then fixed a date for the initiation.[19]

Despite Holy Mother's affection for him and confidence in him, Saradananda was extremely humble. Once he was in his office about to begin work on the *Lilaprasanga* when a disciple of the Mother prostrated fully and took the dust of the swami's feet. The swami humorously asked: "Why such a big salutation? What is the idea?"

"Maharaj, why do you say that?" the disciple replied. "Whom else should I salute but you?" The swami said: "I am seated here awaiting her grace by whom you have been blessed. If she wishes, she can this very moment seat you in my place."[20]

When Saradananda prostrated himself before the Mother, as a witness observed, it was an unusual sight. It was as if he melted on the ground before her. He showed with his salutation that he offered his body, his soul, and everything at her feet.

Saradananda poured his heart and soul into serving Holy Mother in addition to performing his duties as the general secretary of the Ramakrishna Order, which was a heavy responsibility. Furthermore, he lovingly looked after the welfare of the Mother's relatives, nursed her younger brother when he was dying, and made provisions for her niece Radhu's financial security.

For more than fifteen years, Saradananda had the unique privilege of being close to Holy Mother and looking after her needs. How small he felt in her presence! Once he remarked: "What can we understand of Mother? This, however, I can say: I have never seen such a great mind; and I do not hope to see one. It is not within our capacity to comprehend the extent of Mother's glory and power. I have never seen in anyone else such attachment; nor have I seen such detachment. She was so deeply attached to Radhu. But before her death she said: 'Please send her away.' Radhu lost all attraction for her."[21]

Blessed are the Master's and the Mother's disciples who had the opportunity to serve Holy Mother personally. They must have accumulated great virtues in their previous lives to have been blessed by living near the Divine Mother in human form and watching her divine play.

Towards the end, when the Mother's treatment was going on in Udbodhan House, an unknown gentleman came to visit her. He met Saradananda at the entrance room and asked, "What do you do here?" Saradananda humbly replied: "I am the doorkeeper of the Mother's house." The gentleman went to the office and asked another monk the name of the person in the entrance room. The monk said: "He is Swami Saradananda, the general secretary of the Ramakrishna Math and Mission." Surprised and embarrassed, the gentleman exclaimed: "My goodness! He introduced himself as the doorkeeper of this house." The monk said with a smile: "Yes, he introduced himself truly: he is the doorkeeper and an attendant of Holy Mother." Overwhelmed by the swami's humility, the gentleman left.[22]

18
Mahamaya's Maya

Yā devi sarva bhuteshu vishnu māyeti shabditā;
Namastasyai namastasyai namastasyai namo namah.
  —*Chandi, 5:14*

Salutations to the Divine Mother, the Lord's own maya, the inscrutable power pervading all things. Salutations to Her again and again.

What is Mahamaya's maya? According to Vedanta, Brahman is Existence-Knowledge-Bliss Absolute, without name and form, free from the three gunas — sattva, rajas, and tamas. It is the unchanging Reality beyond space, time, and causation. The infinite Brahman becomes manifest as the finite universe and individual beings through Its inscrutable power of maya. Thus the One becomes many. When Brahman is associated with Its cosmic power of maya, It is called Ishwara (God), or Mahamaya (the Divine Mother). In reality Brahman and the Divine Mother are the same as fire and its power to burn. It is Mahamaya who creates, preserves, and destroys. She releases a soul through Her *vidya maya*, the maya of knowledge, and binds souls to the world through *avidya maya*, the maya of ignorance.

When religion falls into decline and irreligion prevails, God becomes incarnate, controlling His own maya to preserve the eternal religion. God cannot take a form without maya, but He is the ruler of maya. When God takes a human form as an avatar, he or she does not come alone. If the avatar is male, he is accompanied by his Shakti, or female counterpart, as well as a group of disciples who will carry out his mission. As Ramachandra came with Sita, Krishna with Radha, Buddha with Yashodhara, Chaitanya with Vishnupriya, so Ramakrishna came with Sarada. Ramakrishna was an incarnation of God and Holy Mother was an incarnation of the Divine Mother. Holy Mother said on many occasions: "The Master and I are one."

Maya makes it possible to function in this world. When the mind is free from maya, free from attachment to the world, it merges into samadhi. This happened to Holy Mother. After the Master passed away in 1886,

Sarada Devi, Calcutta, 1905.

she lost her attachment to the world and felt no reason to remain. She regained some peace of mind during her pilgrimage and by practising the *panchatapa*. (*See Chapter 12.*) She then followed the Master's advice to stay in Kamarpukur and practise austerities there. Afterwards she stayed with her mother and brothers' families in Jayrambati. Over the years she travelled back and forth between Jayrambati and Calcutta and initiated many people.

From 1887 to 1899, her mind remained detached. She said: "At that time I did not care for anything in this world. My mind was full of renunciation and was soaring high. I did not feel any point in living longer, so I was praying to depart from this world."[1] During this period the Mother had very little body consciousness and was in an ecstatic mood most of the time. Golap-ma and Yogin-ma would make her sit when the devotees came to pay their respects to her.[2] She was indifferent to household activities and her mind was focussed on her real nature. The Master appeared before her on many occasions and told her: "You stay. You have many things to do. I have helped only a few people; you will have to help many more. They will come to you." Holy Mother said, "After that, I resolved to keep my body." But Providence also planned to tie her mind with a strong attachment, so that she could continue her divine mission.

Mother Embraces Her Own Maya

Holy Mother was very fond of her youngest brother, Abhay. For some time he lived with M.'s family and went to school in Calcutta. After graduating from school he entered Campbell Medical School (now Nil-ratan Sarkar Hospital) and became friendly with the monastic disciples of Ramakrishna. Swami Brahmananda helped him buy medical books. Swami Vivekananda remarked: "I didn't know that Mother had such an intelligent brother. Her other brothers are mere priests, practically illiterate, and always asking for their priestly fees."[3] Two of Holy Mother's other brothers, Prasanna and Barada, lived at this time in a rented house in Chorebagan, Calcutta, performing rituals in private homes to support their families. Soon after obtaining his medical degree, Abhay contracted cholera. Swamis Saradananda and Prakashananda cared for him in his brothers' residence. When Holy Mother went to see him, she sat at Abhay's side, held his head on her lap, and began to caress his hair. Abhay kept his eyes on his sister's face and said plaintively: "Sister, I am going. They are left behind. Please keep an eye on them."[4] Abhay passed away on 2 August 1899.

Abhay's wife, Surabala, was pregnant at the time and living in her father's house. She was an unfortunate woman, having lost her mother when she was very young. Now she lost her husband — and shortly thereafter she lost her grandmother and aunt, who had raised her. Her mind broke under the strain of so much grief. In October 1899, Holy Mother left Calcutta for Jayrambati and brought Surabala to stay with her. On 26 January 1900, Surabala gave birth to a baby girl who was named Radharani and called Radhu or Radhi. Responsibility for caring for this baby fell on Holy Mother, since Surabala was mentally incompetent. In February 1900 Swami Achalananda and a woman devotee named Kusum came from Varanasi to visit Holy Mother. Kusum volunteered to care for the infant and stayed in Jayrambati for five months. This was a great relief to Holy Mother.

Although Holy Mother mainly lived in Jayrambati during this period, she visited Kamarpukur from time to time. Once in Kamarpukur she had an attack of cholera and became bedridden. Her maid, Sagar-ma, cared for her devotedly. Pleased with her loving service, Holy Mother blessed her, saying: "You will never suffer from lack of food or clothing."[*5] The news of her cholera was sent to Belur Math and Jayrambati. When the Mother was a little better, her brother Kalikumar took her to Jayrambati by bullock cart. Within three or four days, Swami Trigunatitananda and another monk from Belur Math arrived at Jayrambati hoping to take her to Calcutta, but the Mother would not go, as she had recuperated from that illness.

In October 1900, Holy Mother returned to Calcutta with her Uncle Nilmadhav, Surabala, Radhu, and Aunt Bhanu, a neighbour and longtime friend. At that time Nivedita's school was moved from number 16 Bosepara Lane to number 17, and Holy Mother's devotees rented the house at 16 Bosepara Lane for her household. Kusum continued to care for Radhu there. Holy Mother's uncle became the guardian of the household and Golap-ma lived with the Mother whenever she was in Calcutta. Holy Mother practised japa and meditation with her women devotees, and Swamis Trigunatitananda and Saradananda looked after her needs.

According to the diary of Belur Math, on 24 February 1901 Holy Mother attended Sri Ramakrishna's birth anniversary at Belur Math.[6] In October 1901, Swamiji invited Holy Mother to attend the first Durga Puja held at Belur Math and for her convenience arranged for her to stay at

---

*Later in her old age when Sagar-ma was asked about the Mother's blessing, she confirmed that she had never had any difficulty with food and clothing.

Nilambar Babu's house, which was close to the monastery grounds. The Mother and her companions attended the worship festival from 18 to 22 October 1901.

One day Holy Mother said to Surabala: "Look, one should always do something. Work keeps the body strong and the mind pure." She said to Aunt Bhanu, "You remember previously when I was in Jayrambati, I was engaged in household work day and night." Holy Mother took Surabala's hand and said: "Look, Golap is busy all the time. One can cut the bond of attachment by performing action, and then comes nonattachment. One should not live without performing action even for a moment."[7] So Surabala began to do some housework. Thus the Mother's household ran smoothly for a year.

Once late at night Surabala went to the bathroom downstairs with a lamp in her hand and saw a thief break a window and enter the kitchen. She screamed, and then fainted as the thief ran away. Members of the household rushed to the kitchen and revived Surabala, but this incident made her mental condition worse. Holy Mother decided to return to Jayrambati with Surabala and Radhu. Yogin-ma then suggested that Radhu and her mother should be sent to Jayrambati and a nurse should be engaged to look after Radhu. The Calcutta devotees would bear their expenses, but Holy Mother should stay in Calcutta.

Holy Mother listened to Yogin-ma's suggestion but did not respond. She had had a vision of Radhu in Jayrambati being treated carelessly by her insane mother and saw that the baby's life was in danger. She later described her vision: "While I was performing my morning worship [in Calcutta], I saw various scenes in which Radhu was in horrible situations, as one sees the change of drop scenes in a theatre. I saw Radhu's mother in a pitiful condition. She threw a little puffed rice to Radhu, who ate the rice dirtied by the dust and straw in the courtyard. Surabala tied red and blue threads around her arms like a crazy woman. The other children of the family were eating puffed rice with sweets. Having these visions one after another, I felt as if I were drowning, as if someone were forcibly holding me underwater. I realized Radhu's condition would be like that if I left her with her mother."[8] This vision so upset the Mother that she left her asana and went to Yogin-ma, told her what she had seen, and said that it was not possible for her to stay in Calcutta without Radhu. Holy Mother, Surabala, Radhu, and Nilmadhav returned to Jayrambati in April 1901.

Later, one day in Jayrambati Holy Mother narrated the following vision that she had of Yogamaya to Kedar Datta (later Swami Keshavananda):

Calcutta, 1905.
Standing left to right: Brahmachari Ganen and Ashutosh Mitra.
Sitting left to right: Nalini, Sarada Devi, Radhu and Lakshmi.

After the Master's passing away I felt that my life was empty. I was praying to the Master, asking why I should keep my body. Suddenly in a vision I saw a girl of 10 or 12 years old, dressed in a red cloth, moving about in front of me. Immediately the Master appeared, pointed to the girl, and said: "Take her as a support and live. Many spiritual seekers will come to you." The next moment both he and the girl disappeared. Another time, I was seated on the same spot facing west and I saw Surabala, who was then totally insane, dragging some cotton shawls and saris under her arms to the other side of the courtyard. Crawling behind her was Radhu, crying. As I watched this scene I shuddered and my heart was pierced with agonizing pain. I ran to Radhu and held her in my arms. I thought: "Ah! Who will look after the poor thing if I do not? Her father is dead and her mother insane." Immediately the Master appeared and said: "This is the girl you saw before. Take her as a support. She is Yogamaya.*"[9]

As soon as Holy Mother took Radhu in her arms, maya entered her divine body, meaning that her mind became drawn to worldly affairs. She told a monk: "There was no maya in my body before Radhu's birth. The very moment I took Radhu in my arms, maya entered me."[10]

Holy Mother's life became inextricably entwined with Radhu's. They were almost inseparable. The Mother fed her little niece, dressed her, entertained her, and put her to bed. To outsiders she appeared to be inordinately attached to Radhu. One day Swami Vishweswarananda, a disciple, said to her: "Mother, why are you so obsessed with Radhu? Day and night you talk of nothing but Radhu. You seem to be terribly entangled in the world. Many devotees come to you and you pay no heed to them. Is such attachment good for you?" Holy Mother had heard similar complaints before and had always said with her usual humility: "We are women, and I follow my womanly nature." But this time she replied in a rather animated voice: "Where will you find another like me? Try and see. Let me tell you something. Those who constantly contemplate the Supreme Reality develop a subtle and pure mind. Whatever object such a mind takes hold of, it clings to with tenacity; people regard this as attachment. When lightning strikes a building, the flash is seen in the glass panes** and not in the wooden shutters."[11]

On another occasion she remarked: "This constant doting of mine on Radhu is a form of attachment. But I can sever it this very moment by my mere wish. I do not do so only out of compassion. How can maya bind

---

* Yogamaya is the Divine Power that fulfills the wishes of God.
** Holy Mother compared the pure mind with the glass pane.

me?"[12] Holy Mother's visions concerning Radhu gave her a reason to live and allowed her to resume her active life.

Life in Jayrambati and Calcutta

Holy Mother made Jayrambati her country residence from 1897 until she passed away in 1920. Although it was a remote place, hard to reach, ravaged by malaria, completely lacking city comforts with no markets nearby, still many devotees from far and near visited her there. This gave the villagers an opportunity to supplement their meager income by selling fruits, vegetables, fish, milk, and other articles to the devotees. In this manner Holy Mother helped her poor village neighbours. She often felt suffocated by her restricted life in Calcutta, so she would go to Jayrambati to relax. There she could happily move about freely among the simple villagers whom she had known from her childhood, and who loved her. Moreover, she felt that she needed to look after her brothers' families.

Swami Nikhilananda wrote: "Perhaps there was a deeper reason for her choosing her parental home as a place of residence. She thus taught the world how one could be burdened day and night with worldly responsibilities and at the same time lead a saintly life. Here she demonstrated that even the most humdrum duties of the world can be performed as spiritual acts."[13]

Holy Mother was brought up in an extended family and she was the eldest child. Among her three uncles, little is known about two of them. The youngest uncle, Nilmadhav, was a bachelor and worked as a cook for a wealthy family in Paikpara, Calcutta. After his retirement he settled in Jayrambati. Since no other relative came forward to look after him in his old age, Holy Mother took responsibility for him and personally served him.

On 14 February 1904 Holy Mother came to Calcutta with Radhu, Surabala, and Nilmadhav, residing in a rented house at 2/1 Baghbazar Street. Saradananda made special efforts to make the Mother's life comfortable in Calcutta. A horse carriage owned by Nivedita's school was always ready for her use. Holy Mother used the carriage to go to the Ganges every day for her bath, and on holidays she visited the Maidan, the zoo, the museum, Kalighat, or some other place of interest. The main purpose of these outings was to make her walk, as she had a slight limp due to rheumatism, which she had developed in Dakshineswar.

At the time of the chariot festival of Lord Jagannath, Holy Mother went to the Archanalay ashrama of Deven Majumdar, a devotee of the Master, and enjoyed hearing the ashrama children sing. On Janmashtami,

Krishna's birthday, she went with Lakshmi, Golap-ma, Nalini, and Radhu to Kankurgachi Yogodyan, where Ramakrishna's relics had been installed. At Swami Yogavinod's request, Holy Mother sat there till six o'clock in the evening and received devotees. She was very uncomfortable seated for such a long time in the hot weather, covered with a thick chadar, or shawl. After returning to her residence, she mentioned this to Golap-ma, who generally guarded her under such circumstances.

The saintly woman Gopal-ma lived in one of the rooms at Nivedita's school. She was then very old and ill, and Nivedita and a disciple named Kusum looked after her. As Gopal-ma considered Ramakrishna to be her son, Holy Mother respected her like a mother-in-law. Sometimes she visited this remarkable old woman. The Mother also sent her food from her kitchen. In this last part of her life, Gopal-ma was not very aware of the outside world, but she was conscientious about performing japa with her rosary. She did not recognize most people, but when Holy Mother came to visit, she would feebly say: "Who is this? Is it *Bauma* [daughter-in-law]? Please come and sit near me."

In 1904 Holy Mother did not go to Jayrambati to attend the Jagaddhatri Puja. Though she was reluctant to miss it, her household had grown so large that it was expensive to travel back and forth. Moreover, she had had several attacks of malaria in Jayrambati. Her health was improving in Calcutta, so her devotees asked her to not make the trip. However, she sent everything needed for the worship through her brother Barada and a devotee. Holy Mother was delighted to hear their description of the worship when they returned.

Pilgrimage to Puri

In November 1904 Holy Mother and some companions went on pilgrimage to Puri by train. Her party included her Uncle Nilmadhav, Surabala, Radhu, Lakshmi, Golap-ma, M.'s wife, Chunilal's wife, Kusum, Swami Premananda, her attendant Ashu (Trigunatitananda's brother), and a servant. A second-class car was reserved for the Mother and her female companions; the three men went by an inter class car. The distance from Calcutta to Puri is 300 miles. Holy Mother and her companions boarded the train in the evening and reached Puri the next morning. Most of the party stayed in Kshetravasi's Math, a guesthouse owned by Balaram's family that was near the Jagannath temple. Premananda stayed in Shashi Niketan, near the sea. When Holy Mother arrived in Puri, she went straight to see Lord Jagannath in His inner sanctuary, as arranged by Balaram's family. They were wealthy and influential people in Orissa.

Every morning Holy Mother and her party visited the deity, and they also attended the evening vesper services regularly. As she wished to hear of the glory and history of Lord Jagannath, a priest came one day to read to her from an ancient scripture. On this occasion the *mahaprasad,* cooked food that had been offered to Jagannath, was purchased from the temple stall and 50 priests were fed. The Mother ate Jagannath's mahaprasad every day in Puri.

In Puri the Mother developed an abscess on her foot. She suffered terribly but would not consent to surgery. One day in the temple someone pressed against her abscess and she cried out in pain. When Premananda learned of this, he brought a doctor the next day. The devotees bowed down to her that day as usual, and she sat with her face veiled as was her custom. The doctor also bowed down to her, holding his lancet ready. When he touched her foot, he quickly pierced the abscess with the lancet and left, saying, "Mother, please forgive me for my offense." Premananda was waiting outside. Holy Mother was very upset and scolded Ashu when he pressed the abscess to clear it out. However, this relieved the Mother's pain immensely. Ashu washed the wound with a solution of margosa leaf and bandaged it. After a few days of care, she was fully cured. She then heartily blessed her sons.

Holy Mother wanted to show her mother and her brother Kalikumar the holy city of Puri, so one day she secretly sent Ashu to Jayrambati to bring them. She did not want Surabala to know of this because she was very possessive and quarrelsome. It upset her when Holy Mother paid attention to her brothers and their wives. Ashu travelled to Jayrambati via Vishnupur and conveyed the Mother's wishes to Shyamasundari and Kalikumar. Both were elated and prepared to start the following day. Kalikumar hired two bullock carts to bring his wife, two sons, and father-in-law. Sitaram, a villager, asked Shyamasundari if he could go with her on this pilgrimage and she agreed. The group reached Puri the following day. When Surabala saw all these people she was angry at Holy Mother, but the Mother said: "Shall I live with you alone? Are they not my own relatives? I have brought you here and shall I not bring my elderly mother?"

Kalikumar and his group visited Lord Jagannath and other important temples and returned to Jayrambati after a few days. Shyamasundari stayed with Holy Mother. After Holy Mother recuperated from the abscess, her health improved. She bathed twice in the sea, regularly circumambulated the Jagannath temple, and visited the important places of Puri — the vast kitchen of Lord Jagannath, the Gundicha

House of Jagannath, the Lakshmijala paddy field, Narendra Lake, the Govardhan Monastery of Shankara, Swargadwar on the sea, and so on. Holy Mother was in a wonderful mood and she related many stories of the old days to her companions. She and her party returned to Calcutta in late January 1905, and after a few days there, Shyamasundari returned to Jayrambati.

With the Relatives

Holy Mother was very fond of her Uncle Nilmadhav and treated him as she would her own father. When devotees offered her expensive, out-of-season fruits, she gave them to her uncle. If her attendant protested against this excessive kindness, she would say: "Uncle has only a little while to live. Let him fulfill all his desires. We shall live a long time and will have many opportunities to enjoy these things."[14]

Nilmadhav suffered from asthma from time to time, and in March 1905, after returning from Puri, he became bedridden. Despite treatment by several doctors and Holy Mother's devoted care, Nilmadhav's illness became critical. Ashu and a woman devotee nursed him on his last day. On that day Holy Mother finished her worship and rushed to her uncle's sickbed. She wanted to stay by his side and refused to eat her midday meal. Ashu told her that death was not imminent and persuaded her to have her meal. Holy Mother hurriedly finished her meal and returned to her uncle, but there she saw sadness on the attendants' faces. Startled, she asked, "Is he then no more?" They remained silent. In a voice shaking with grief and anger she said: "Why did you send me away to eat that trash? I could not see him in his last moments." She wept loudly, as if she had lost her own father. She then went to the shrine to get two flowers that had been offered to the Master. She placed those flowers on her uncle's head and chest and repeated a mantra to pray for the peace of his soul. Nilmadhav's body was carried to Kashi Mitra's ghat on the bank of the Ganges to be cremated. Prasanna performed the last rites, and, according to custom, on the fourth day after his death, Holy Mother fed those who carried her uncle's body and gave a cloth to each of them.

Holy Mother's brother Prasanna lived in a cheap rented house with a tiled roof on Simla Street in Central Calcutta. Shortly after Radhu's birth in January 1900, he married his elder daughter Nalini to Pramatha Nath Bhattacharya of Goghat, Hooghly. Prasanna then brought his wife, Ramapriya, his new son-in-law, and his two daughters — Nalini and Maku — to his Calcutta residence. Soon after their arrival, Pramatha became very ill with a fever and cough. Holy Mother was concerned and sent Ashu to look after him. She also visited Pramatha frequently. Ashu knew a young doctor and brought him to examine the patient. He diagnosed the disease as double pneumonia and provided medicine that cured Pramatha within a few days.

It so happened that this young doctor had been betrayed by his wife; as a result, he used alcohol and drugs heavily. He confided his problem to his friend Ashu and said that he was planning to kill himself. Soon after this, M. invited Holy Mother and some other devotees to his Jhamapukur house for a festival. Holy Mother performed the worship in M.'s shrine. Meanwhile Ashu visited his doctor friend who lived nearby and said to him, "Please come with me." Without knowing where he was going, the doctor followed Ashu, wearing casual clothing. On the way Ashu told him, "I told you previously if you received initiation from Holy Mother, your mental agony would go away." "But I have already eaten my food," said the doctor.

Ashu said, "The Mother will decide about it." Ashu took his friend to M.'s house and asked him to wait downstairs. He went to Holy Mother, who was still in the shrine, and requested her to give his friend initiation. The Mother agreed and said that the doctor should immediately come to the shrine. After receiving initiation, the doctor felt tremendous peace and his face beamed with joy. Thus Holy Mother changed this young doctor's life. Later in 1906 or 1907, this doctor helped with the relief work of the Ramakrishna Mission in East Bengal and treated many devotees without charge.

When Holy Mother was living at 2/1 Baghbazar Street, she was taken by horse carriage to various places for sightseeing. One day in April 1905, Ashu took her to the studio of B. Datta on Chitpore Road and arranged to have some photographs taken. A group picture was taken with Holy Mother, Lakshmi, Nalini, Radhu, and others. Sometime during the next month Swami Virajananda arranged to have a picture of Holy Mother taken at the studio of Van Dyke Company on Chowringhee Road (now Jawaharlal Nehru Road).[15]

Lalitmohan Chattopadhyay: The Mother's Heroic Devotee

During this period, Lalitmohan Chattopadhyay, a wealthy man who held an important position at the Dickinson Company, became a devotee of Holy Mother. One day he arranged a festival in his house on Chhutarpara Lane and invited M., Dr. Kanjilal, and some devotees of the Master and Mother. On that occasion Holy Mother initiated him and his wife, Prasadi Devi, in his shrine. Lalit had his own carriage, which he placed at Holy

Mother's disposal. The Mother used his carriage whenever she needed it. When gramophones first became available in Calcutta, Lalit bought one and played it for Holy Mother. She and her companions enjoyed hearing kirtan and other songs played on the machine.

Lalit was a heroic devotee and a great benefactor of the Ramakrishna Mission. He had a moustache like the German Kaiser, so Swami Brahmananda used to call him "Kaiser." Whenever Holy Mother had any problem, Lalit was there to take care of it, and whenever she was ill, Dr. Kanjilal would rush to look after her. When these two visited Jayrambati, the Mother cooked for them and tried to make their lives comfortable there.

Once Lalit was seriously ill and several famous doctors were treating him. Every day Holy Mother sent Ashu for news of Lalit's condition. When his condition became critical, Prasadi rushed to Holy Mother and asked her to bless her dying husband. Holy Mother told Ashu: "Take this offered flower and put it on his head. Tell him that he will be cured soon. Ask him to have ayurvedic treatment. I am offering *tulsi* [holy basil] every day to the Master for him."[16] Lalit came around after taking the ayurvedic treatment, but the Mother said: "It is due to Prasadi's virtue that Lalit got back his life this time. I can't bear to hear Prasadi's pitiful cries."[17]

On 19 December 1909 Holy Mother told Arupananda: "Lalit has given me much financial help. He takes me out in his carriage. He regularly sends money for worship services in Dakshineswar and Kamarpukur. My Lalit has a heart worth a million rupees! There are many who are miserly despite their wealth."[18]

A Story of Padmabinod

Binod Bihari Som was a student at M.'s school. He had visited Ramakrishna a few times and received the Master's blessings. His home was on Ramkanta Bose Street in Baghbazar close to Holy Mother's residence. He is known to the devotees as "Padmabinod." In his youth, he joined the theatre and became a famous actor. Over time, however, he became an alcoholic and had financial difficulties. Sometimes he visited Swami Saradananda, whom he called *dosta,* or friend.

On his way home late one night after a performance, the drunk Padmabinod knocked at Saradananda's window calling out "dosta, dosta." The swami did not respond, and he asked others to keep quiet. Holy Mother lived upstairs, and Saradananda did not want her sleep to be disturbed. After calling a few times, Padmabinod said, "Dosta, I came and called you and you did not respond." He then left.

Another night Padmabinod, drunk, came again. When no one answered his call, he started to sing to Holy Mother in a plaintive voice:

Waken, Mother! Throw open your door.
I cannot find my way through the dark;
My heart is afraid.
How often I have called out your name,
Yet, kind Mother,
How strangely you are acting today!
Soundly you are sleeping in your room,
Leaving your poor child alone outside.
I am all skin and bones from crying,
"Mother, O Mother!"
With proper tone, pitch, and mode, using
All the three gamuts,
I call so loud, and still you sleep on.
Is it because I was lost in play
That you shun me now?
Look on me kindly, and I shall not
Go playing again.
To whom can I run, leaving your side?
Who but my Mother will bear the load
Of this wretched child?[19]

As Padmabinod sang in the street with all his soul, Holy Mother opened one of her windows. When Saradananda heard the shutters open, he said, "Ah, he broke the Mother's sleep!" Holy Mother looked down at Padmabinod. He said: "Mother, so you have gotten up. You have finally heard your child's call. Now please accept my salutation." Saying so, he rolled on the street and put the dust on his head. Saradananda and Ashu watched him through a shutter. As he walked away Padmabinod began to sing another song:

Cherish my precious Mother Shyama tenderly within, O mind;
May you and I alone behold Her, letting no one else intrude.

With emphasis, he improvised a new line, "And surely not my dosta," referring to Saradananda. The next day Holy Mother asked about him and was told his story. "Did you notice his firm conviction?" she remarked.

Padmabinod came again another night. When Holy Mother heard him call out, she opened her window. Seeing her from the street, Padmabinod sang the following song:

O Mother Shyama, you love cremation grounds, so I made my heart

A cremation ground and you dance there.
The blazing fire of a funeral pyre is burning day and night,
And all my desires of the heart are burnt to ashes.
Now do thou reveal yourself unto me.
Mother, you have put Lord Shiva under your feet,
I want to see your rhythmic dance.

The next morning Ashu told Holy Mother, "He is disturbing your sleep."

She replied: "It is all right, my son. I cannot contain myself when he calls on me in that way."

Padmabinod stopped coming soon after. Some days later his young son came to tell Saradananda that Padmabinod was seriously ill. The swami arranged for his treatment. Padmabinod was suffering from dropsy, so Dr. Pranadhan Basu tapped and removed some water from his belly. This treatment was not helpful, so Padmabinod was sent to Shambhunath Pandit Hospital, in South Calcutta where an English doctor performed surgery. The doctor lost hope when he found that Padmabinod's intestines had become septic as a result of his alcoholism. Padmabinod asked Ashu, who was attending him, to read *The Gospel of Sri Ramakrishna* to him. Ashu opened the book at random and began to read where Padmabinod's name was mentioned. As Padmabinod listened, tears trickled from his eyes. Just after 1:00 a.m., repeating the name of the Master, he breathed his last. His friends and relatives carried his body to the Keoratala cremation ground in South Calcutta.

At noon Ashu returned to Holy Mother's residence and reported everything to her. The Mother remarked: "Why should it not be like that? Surely he was a child of the Master. No doubt he covered himself with mud, but now he has gone back to the Master's arms where he belongs."[20]

Holy Mother in Jayrambati

In May 1905, Holy Mother decided to visit Jayrambati. Before her departure she called for Swami Premananda to come from Belur Math. She then handed the Master's amulet to him and asked him to worship it every day. She had carried it with her for many years, and now she wanted it kept in a safe place. She did not want to risk taking it to Jayrambati because someone might steal it if she became ill.

This was the first time Holy Mother took the train to Jayrambati. Krishnalal (Swami Dhirananda) and Brahmachari Ganen accompanied her to Vishnupur, arriving at 1:30 p.m. Ashu had gone to Vishnupur on the previous day to make arrangements for the Mother to rest and eat in an inn. The Mother was very pleased with the arrangements. Krishnalal and Ganen returned to Calcutta by the night train. She and all her companions left Vishnupur for Jayrambati in the evening, taking four bullock carts. In the morning they arrived at Kotalpur and had their noon meal in an inn. A palanquin was hired for Holy Mother and Radhu, while the others travelled in bullock carts.[21]

The previous year Holy Mother had not attended the Jagaddhatri Puja in Jayrambati, so this year it was done on a grand scale. Swami Saradananda sent all the necessary articles from Calcutta.

Holy Mother was highly respected in her community, because the villagers observed how many famous and distinguished people would come to Jayrambati for spiritual instruction from her. But she was extremely humble. Once Ganesh Ghosal of Kamarpukur, one of the Master's schoolmates, came to visit the Mother. When she was about to bow down to him, he protested and said, "Mother, it is inauspicious if a mother bows down to her son." He bowed down to the Mother instead and received her blessing.

In the later part of 1905, Brahmachari Girija went to Jayrambati for initiation, accompanied by his friend Batu Babu. As soon as they arrived, Holy Mother told them: "My eldest sister-in-law, Ramapriya [Prasanna's wife], has contracted cholera. She cooked lunch, fed the servants, and then all of a sudden began vomiting." There was no doctor or medicine available in Jayrambati, and Ramapriya died within 12 hours. Her two daughters — Nalini and Maku — were very young. Prasanna was then working in Calcutta, and there was no one to look after them, so Holy Mother took responsibility for them, as she had done for Radhu.

Girija reconsidered asking for initiation under the sad circumstances, so instead he asked for her permission to visit Vishalakshi in Anur. Holy Mother said: "Well, you have come from such a distance and with a great expectation. You had better go and have your bath, and I shall give you a mantra."[22] The ever-gracious Mother initiated Girija as well as Batu Babu even though he was not a candidate.

Shyamasundari's Passing

In January 1906, on a cold winter day, Holy Mother, Shyamasundari, and some other women were sitting on the veranda enjoying the early morning sun. At that time a village woman came who made her living by buying vegetables from the Shiromanipur market and then selling them to the villagers in Jayrambati. Holy Mother used to buy vegetables from her, and Shyamasundari would give her rice and mustard seeds in exchange. On that day Shyamasundari was feeling well, and she even helped husk the paddy. She left to answer the call of nature. When she came back, she lay down on Kalikumar's veranda. Shyamasundari told Ashu: "My child, I feel dizzy; perhaps this is the end." Holy Mother and other family members rushed to Shyamasundari's side. She expressed a desire to eat pumpkin curry, and Holy Mother assured her she would cook it for her when she got well. Shyamasundari then realized her last moment had arrived. She asked to drink some water, and Holy Mother poured Ganges water in her mouth three times. With her fingers on her mother's head and chest, she repeated a mantra. At nine o'clock that morning Shyamasundari breathed her last. Holy Mother wept loudly.

Holy Mother's brothers Barada and Kalikumar carried their mother's body to the bank of the Amodar and cremated it there. The next day Holy Mother asked her brothers to arrange their mother's shraddha ceremony, and a list of necessary items was prepared. Ashu left for Calcutta with the list. Swami Saradananda arranged to get the articles and sent Ashu back to Jayrambati within three days.* The shraddha ceremony was performed on a grand scale: many people were fed with various dishes, including pumpkin curry to fulfill Shyamasundari's last wish. Moreover, various things were donated to needy people.

Holy Mother was exhausted by grief and the hard work required to manage this ceremony. It took her a month to recover. She was worn down physically, and she felt empty. Her mother had been her support, her friend, and her guide. Shyamasundari was a strong woman who endured many difficulties. She calmly faced poverty after her husband's death and brought up her children heroically. When she married Sarada to Ramakrishna, she suffered for a few years. Along with the other villagers, she initially thought Ramakrishna was insane. Later, of course, her joy knew no bounds when she saw people coming to Jayrambati from all over the country to worship her daughter as a goddess. She also witnessed the Master's prediction being fulfilled: "Mother, your daughter will have so many children that her ears will burn from constantly being called 'Mother.'"

Shyamasundari was a simple, sweet village woman. She was extremely fond of the Master's disciples and she was overjoyed when Holy Mother's disciples and devotees addressed her as Didima, or grandmother. Deeply religious, Shyamasundari considered her household to consist of "God

*Brahmachari Akshaychaitanya quoted from Swami Saradananda's diary on 25 January 1906: "Ashu went to Jayrambati this morning with purchases for Didima's [grandma's] Shraddha."

and godly people." Occasionally she had a glimpse of Holy Mother's divine personality. She once said: "Child, who are you? Do I really know your true nature?" Holy Mother replied with a show of annoyance: "Who do you think I am? Do you see me with four arms?* If I were not a human being, why should I have been born of your womb?"[23]

Another day Shyamasundari said to her: "May I have a daughter like you in my next birth, and may my husband have plenty of money. It is so painful to bring up children in dire poverty."

"Why do you drag me in?" Holy Mother replied. "Do you mean to say that I should bring up your children again?"[24]

Holy Mother was extremely devoted to her godly parents and served them with her heart and soul. She later said about them: "My father was a great devotee of Ramachandra and was extremely benevolent. My mother was also very loving and compassionate. That is why I was born in this family.... My mother was like the goddess Lakshmi. She would collect and keep everything neatly ready for Jagaddhatri Puja. She would say, 'Mine is a family of devotees and gods. Perhaps during the festival my Sarada [Swami Trigunatitananda] will come, and Jogin [Swami Yogananda] may come.' So she would preserve good rice and other things for the festival. She further said: 'As long as I am here, Brahma is here, so is Vishnu, Shiva, and Jagadamba. When I go, they also will accompany me. Is it possible for you to take care of those deities and devotees? My home is the abode of gods and devotees.'"[25]

Gopal-Ma's Passing

After losing her mother, Holy Mother returned to Calcutta in April 1906 and lived in the same rented house at 2/1 Baghbazar Street. Among the women devotees of Ramakrishna, Yogin-ma, Golap-ma, and Gopal-ma were Holy Mother's trusted companions. Towards the end of her life, Gopal-ma was staying with Nivedita in her school, and Holy Mother regularly went to see her. One day Gopal-ma said to her: "Gopala, you have come. Look, you have sat on my lap all these days; now you take me on your lap." The Mother took Gopal-ma's head on her lap and caressed her affectionately.[26] Shortly before Gopal-ma's death, Holy Mother went to her bedside. The saintly lady said feebly: "Is it you, Gopala, who have come?" and stretched out her hand. Holy Mother did not understand what she meant, but an attendant explained to her that Gopal-ma was looking upon her as Gopala and wanted to take the dust of her feet. Holy Mother was hesitant, but the attendant took the dust of the Mother's feet

* Some goddesses in Hinduism have four arms.

with the corner of her cloth and put it on Gopal-ma's head. Holy Mother returned to her residence with a heavy heart.

The end came at dawn on 8 July 1906. Gopal-ma was carried to the Ganges, where she breathed her last, touching the holy water. A monk bent over her and whispered in her ear the words that a Hindu loves to hear at the last hour: "Om Ganga Narayana! Om Ganga Narayana Brahma!"[27]

Laughter and tears are part of human life. All human beings encounter happiness and misery. Holy Mother experienced the pain of separation from her dearest ones — her husband, father, uncle, mother, brother Abhay, disciple Yogananda, companion Gopal-ma, and others. But she continued her journey to fulfill her mission, holding her Yogamaya, Radhu, in her arms.

Sarada Devi and Radhu in Jayrambati, 1918.

19
Radhu

Yā devi sarva bhuteshu dayā rupena samasthitā;
Namastasyai namastasyai namastasyai namo namah.
  —*Chandi, 5:65*

Salutations to the Divine Mother, who exists in all beings in the form
of mercy. Salutations to Her again and again.

As explained in Chapter 18, Radhu was an incarnation of Yogamaya.
Yogamaya is a special Divine Power that helps to fulfill the
wishes of God. We find in the Bhagavata that Krishna called
upon Yogamaya for his own birth. He asked Yogamaya to be born as a
daughter of Yashoda and he himself entered the womb of Devaki; then
Vasudeva exchanged the children. Krishna used Yogamaya again during
the Raslila when he multiplied himself to dance with the gopis. Ramakrishna also used Yogamaya to fulfill his mission.

One day at Dakshineswar, Ramakrishna stood on the semi-circular
veranda and called out, "O maya, please come." Gauri-ma was with him.
Astonished, she asked the Master why he was summoning maya. The
Master explained that the natural tendency of his mind was to soar to
a very high realm, and it was hard to bring it down. He was calling for
maya so that his mind would stay in a lower plane, making it possible for
him to help his disciples.[1]

Once when Holy Mother was asked what the Master's main characteristic was, she replied, "renunciation." Ramakrishna practised and
demonstrated fully the monastic ideal, but it was not possible for him to
demonstrate the life of an ideal householder. Of course he taught householders their duties, as M. recorded in *The Gospel of Sri Ramakrishna*, but
his devotees always saw him as a god-intoxicated Paramahamsa rather
than a regular householder. To complete his mission, he used Yogamaya
in the form of Radhu in Holy Mother's life, so that Holy Mother could be
an example to householders — otherwise, people would say that Ramakrishna came only for monastics.

Even though Ramakrishna and Sarada Devi appeared in two different
human forms, in essence they were the same entity. As on many occasions

the Master said, "Sarada is my Shakti," so also Holy Mother said, "Remember that the Master and I are the same." The scriptures say that Shakti and the upholder of Shakti are identical, just as fire and its power to burn.

Radhu's Important Role as Yogamaya

When we observe the unending suffering that Radhu caused Holy Mother, we feel pained. Yet we are indebted to her. Radhu helped Holy Mother keep her mind on the earthly plane for 20 years so that she could carry out her divine play in this world. It is a sight to see the Divine Mother behaving like a regular village woman, involved with her brothers' families and their children and at the same time initiating spiritual aspirants, giving sannyasa to young disciples, and guiding the monks of the Ramakrishna Order. During the last 30 years of her life, she initiated and instructed hundreds of monastics and householders and also demonstrated to them their respective ideals. Regarding Holy Mother, Saradananda once remarked: "I have never seen in anyone else such attachment, nor have I seen such detachment."[2]

There may be another mystery behind Holy Mother's attachment for Radhu. Just as some seekers of worldly prosperity abandoned Ramakrishna when they found that he was suffering from cancer, so also some people stopped visiting Holy Mother when they saw that she was entangled with Radhu and her family. Thus the Master protected her from insincere worldly people. He used to say: "Let the boat be in the water, but not water be in the boat. Let a spiritual aspirant live in the world, but let not worldliness enter him." Holy Mother is a living example of the Master's teaching.

In her childhood, Radhu was a charming girl, and her simple, innocent nature attracted people. Holy Mother poured her love and affection upon her little niece. Radhu called her aunt "Ma," or "Mother," and she addressed Surabala, her biological mother, as "Nedi-ma" or "Bald Mother," since she shaved her head, as was the custom for Hindu widows. Radhu herself was not greedy or demanding, but her mother was terribly jealous when Holy Mother gave presents to her brothers and other nieces. She wanted the Mother to give everything to Radhu and told the girl: "My sister-in-law is generous to others. She is keeping nothing for you. Why should you live with her? Come away to my house." Annoyed, Radhu would scold her mother, and she avoided her. Holy Mother fulfilled all of Radhu's wants and Radhu was happy.

Holy Mother raised Radhu as her own daughter. She braided her hair, dressed her, fed her, and sent her to school. A woman devotee recorded in her reminiscences how Holy Mother made plans for Radhu's future:

> It was late in the morning. Radhu was ready to go to the Christian Missionary School of the neighbourhood. Golap-ma said to the Mother: "Radhu is now a grown-up girl. Why should she go to school anymore?" She asked Radhu not to go to school. Radhu began to cry. The Mother said: "She is not quite grown-up. Let her go to school. She can do immense good to others if she gets an education and learns some useful arts at the school....Through education she will not only improve herself but will be able to help others." So Radhu was allowed to continue her schooling.[3]

In the evening Holy Mother practised japa in the shrine and asked Radhu and her cousin Maku to sit with her. The Mother ate a little of Mother Simhavahini's holy earth and gave some to Radhu. She also disciplined Radhu when she behaved improperly. One day Radhu's sari was above her knees. Immediately the Mother said: "What is this? A woman should maintain modesty. Her sari should not be above the knees."[4] Another day Radhu was running down the steps of the Udobodhan House and her anklets were making a jingling sound. Holy Mother stopped her and said: "Radhu, are you not ashamed? My monastic children are staying downstairs and you are running down the steps with your anklets on. Tell me, what will they think of you? Take off the anklets right now. My children are not living here for fun; they have come here to practise spiritual disciplines. Do you know the consequences if their practices are disturbed?"[5] At this, Radhu took off the anklets and angrily threw them at Holy Mother.

Radhu was a sickly girl and mentally stunted. Despite her shortcomings, Holy Mother loved her. One day in Udbodhan, something got into Radhu's eye. She ran to the Mother and lay down, putting her head on the Mother's lap. She said: "Look, there is something in my eye and it is burning. Please pass your hand over my eye, then it will be all right." Smiling, the Mother pulled Radhu's head close to her and gently passed her hand over Radhu's eye. Radhu said: "My eye is all right now. I don't feel any pain."[6]

As Radhu grew older, she became a difficult person — eccentric, petulant, and stubborn. She not only disobeyed Holy Mother, but also abused her, cursed her, and treated her badly. In fact, her behaviour towards Holy Mother became intolerable.

Radhu's Marriage

Before Holy Mother left for a pilgrimage in South India in December 1910, she and her brothers arranged Radhu's betrothal to Manmatha

Chattopadhyay, a son of a wealthy man in the nearby Tajpur village. Radhu was then 12 and Manmatha was 15.

On 11 April 1911, Holy Mother returned to Calcutta, and left for Jayrambati on 17 May. She stopped at Koalpara Ashrama briefly and asked the residents to help her with the wedding. A few days later, Swami Saradananda, Yogin-ma, Golap-ma, and two brahmacharins came to Jayrambati to attend Radhu's wedding, which was set for 10 June 1911. Although Radhu's family was poor compared to Manmatha's, Swami Saradananda spent money without stint for the wedding to make Holy Mother happy. The devotees presented Radhu with jewellery, including a gold crown. Holy Mother was happy seeing Radhu bedecked with gold and silver from head to foot.

Manmatha's family demanded a larger dowry from Saradananda, and Kedar Datta (later Swami Keshavananda) protested. Holy Mother called him aside privately and said that it was not auspicious to quarrel before the marriage ceremony. The village priest officiated at the ceremony, and Prasanna gave his niece Radhu away. The next day the bridegroom's party and the people of Jayrambati were entertained with a sumptuous feast, and they blessed the newly married couple.

Radhu left for Tajpur with her husband the following day, as was customary. However, Radhu did not want to live at her husband's house; so both she and Manmatha came to stay with Holy Mother.

Before the wedding, an astrologer had examined Radhu's horoscope. He predicted that she would become a widow. After Manmatha had been married to Radhu for some time, he asked Holy Mother for initiation. She was not eager to initiate a relative, but finally she initiated him. She remarked: "One should not interfere with divine dispensation, but Radhu might escape her widowhood* by the force of this initiation."[7]

After her wedding, Radhu began to have physical problems and became even more moody and irritable. Holy Mother lamented to her disciple Kedar Datta: "My son, Radhu was rather pleasant when she was younger. Now she is married and suffers from various ailments. I am afraid this daughter of an insane mother may herself become insane. Alas, am I bringing up a mad person?"[8] At the Master's command, Holy

---

*By Holy Mother's grace Radhu did not become a widow, but she lived like one later in life. In April 1921, nine months after Holy Mother's passing away, Manmatha took a second wife. Deprived of conjugal love, Radhu lived in Jayrambati with her son and her mother. When Radhu was very young, Swami Saradananda had made arrangements for an allowance for her. Later Manmatha began to have financial problems and he often went to Jayrambati to claim a share of Radhu's allowance. She did not refuse to help him.

Mother had embraced this girl as Yogamaya, and as a result she now had to endure Radhu's verbal abuse. One day Holy Mother cautioned a woman who wanted to adopt a son: "Never do such a thing. Do your duties to all. But love you must not bestow upon anybody except God. If you love human beings, there will be no end of suffering for you. Look at how much I suffer on account of Radhu!"[9]

Manmatha was a carefree person. One day at Udbodhan House, Manmatha went out and Radhu was restless for him. Holy Mother expressed her agony to a woman disciple: "Look at the Master's *lila* [play]. My mother's family was so noble, but look at my present companions: This one [Surabala] is totally mad; that one [Nalini] is on the verge of insanity. And now look at that one [Radhu], my child. I wonder at this person I raised. She is completely silly. She is standing on the porch, holding on to the railing, eagerly waiting for her husband to return. There you hear some music in a house [of ill repute]. Radhu is afraid that Manmatha may enter the place. Day and night she watches him. What attachment! I never dreamt she would be so attached."[10]

Another day in Udbodhan House, Radhu angrily said to the Mother: "What do you know? Can you comprehend the importance of a husband?" At this, the Mother replied with a laugh: "You are right. My husband was a naked sannyasi."[11]

Holy Mother told Radhu on another occasion: "You have been nursed by a lioness, and you are acting like a vixen. I have brought you up with such care, and you have not imbibed any part of my virtues. You have gotten everything from your mother." Radhu became angry, pulled down her veil, and turned her head away. Holy Mother laughed and said: "You cannot get along without me, and now you are hiding your face from me."[12]

Sushila Majumdar recorded Radhu's misbehaviour in her reminiscences:

Radhu returned from school at four o'clock. When she finished her refreshment, the Mother told her: "Radhu, come here. I shall braid your hair." "No, I shall do it myself," replied Radhu. As the Mother took a comb to braid her hair, Radhu took the comb and began to hit the Mother with it. The Mother remarked: "Mad girl. What shall I do with her?" Meanwhile Yogin-ma came in, and seeing Radhu hitting the Mother, she said: "What is this? Why should Radhu hit our Mother? I'll punish her." Still Radhu continued to hit the Mother. Then the Mother said: "Now I shall call Sharat. I can't bear the pain anymore." When Yogin-ma informed Saradananda, he immediately came out from his room and shouted from downstairs, "Radhu, don't hit the Mother." Hearing his voice, Radhu stopped and moved away from her. Kusum then braided Radhu's hair.[13]

Between 1911 and 1917 Radhu developed neurasthenia and from time to time suffered from fits of hysteria. One evening in Udbodhan House, Holy Mother placed a poultice on Radhu's abdomen. When a devotee asked, "What happened to Radhu?" Mother replied: "Radhu has been attacked by the same pain. I wonder where this horrible pain came from. So many doctors are attending her and I am promising offerings to so many deities, but all to no avail."[14]

In spite of her illness, in 1910-11 Radhu went on pilgrimage with the Mother to South India and in 1912 to Varanasi. (*See Chapters 21 and 22.*)

On 8 May 1913 Holy Mother was in Jayrambati. Radhu was indisposed, laid up with pain and fever. Surabala began to scold Holy Mother, saying, "You are about to kill my daughter with medicines." When she continued her verbal abuse, Holy Mother called her brother Barada, who chased Surabala out of the house. Holy Mother could bear it no longer and lamented: "I was married to one who never addressed me as *tui**....And look at Radhu's mother. How she abuses me day and night! I do not know what sin I committed to deserve all this. Perhaps I worshipped Shiva with a thorny bel leaf and that thorn has now become Radhu's mother."[15]

Holy Mother was passing through a hard time with Radhu. On 12 May 1913 she said: "My mind now does not dwell upon Radhu even in the slightest degree. I am sick of her illness. I force my mind upon her. I pray to the Master, saying: 'O Lord, please divert my mind a little to Radhu. Otherwise who will look after her?' I have never seen such an illness. Perhaps in her former birth she died of an illness for which she had not performed any penance [to redeem the effects of bad karma]. I have in mind to do these two things — one, to engage a *Chanda* [a medium] to find the cause of Radhu's illness, and the other, to undertake the *Chandrayana* [a penance] for her."[16]

In January 1918 Holy Mother was in Jayrambati when she became very ill. Swami Saradananda travelled with Dr. Kanjilal, Dr. Satish Chakrabarty, Yogin-ma, Golap-ma, and Sarala (later Bharatiprana) to Jayrambati to look after her. In a short time she felt better, and Saradananda and the doctors returned to Calcutta. Holy Mother then went to Koalpara. There her fever relapsed and her condition became critical. At that time Radhu suddenly left for her husband's house. She said to the Mother, "You have many devotees to look after you, but who else do I have except my husband?" Holy Mother told her disciples about this incident and said: "The way Radhu cut the bond of my attachment yesterday and left for her husband's house

*Bengalis typically use this familiar form of "you" when they are speaking to inferiors.

worried me. I thought perhaps that the Master does not want me to live any longer. My doting on Radhu is nothing but a form of maya, which I am holding in order to function."[17]

Human beings judge others according to their own understanding. They do not have the insight to evaluate the behaviour of divine beings. Now and then Holy Mother's disciples and devotees complained to her about her attachment to Radhu. Sarala recalled:

> One afternoon the Mother was talking on various topics. She said: "People think I worry about Radhu and am strongly attached to her. But they do not know that without this attachment my body would not have been preserved after the Master's death. He himself kept the body alive through Radhu, for the sake of his work. When my mind withdraws from her I shall give up the body."
>
> In 1918 the Mother was in bed with a high fever in Koalpara Ashrama. Yogin-ma and Sharat Maharaj were attending her. Even seeing her serious condition, Radhu left for her husband's home. The Mother did not want her to go. Then the Mother lamented to Yogin-ma, "Look Yogin, Radhu has left, abandoning me." Yogin-ma replied: "Why shouldn't she go, Mother? Don't you remember that you walked all the way to Dakshineswar to be with the Master?" The Mother smiled a little and then said, "You are right, Yogin."[18]

On 10 April Saradananda received a cable saying that the Mother was ill again, and on that very night he sent Dr. Kanjilal to Koalpara. On 17 April Saradananda brought Dr. Chakrabarty and Yogin-ma to Holy Mother. She slowly recovered under their care. By May 1918 she had gained some strength, and Saradananda wanted her to go with him to Calcutta. She agreed, but wanted to visit Jayrambati for a week to see her relatives and the villagers before going to Calcutta. She sent Brahmachari Barada (later Swami Ishanananda) to Tajpur to bring Radhu to Jayrambati. As soon as Radhu got down from the palanquin, the Mother embraced her, saying, "Come, my child Radhu." The Mother realized that Radhu had become independent. Holy Mother asked Radhu to go with her to Calcutta, but Radhu declined. The Mother accepted her decision.* With tearful eyes, Radhu bowed down to Holy Mother. Unperturbed, the Mother blessed her and calmly said good-bye. This was the first time Holy Mother had gone to Calcutta without Radhu since Radhu's birth.[19] On her way back the Mother stopped at Koalpara for a day,

---

*Saradananda's diary, 18 Vaishakh 1325 (May 1918): "Radharani came from Tajpur. Decided that Radhu will come to Calcutta with her husband in the month of Jaishtha [June] and not with H.M. at present."

and as her body was weak, a horse carriage was hired for her while the others went by bullock carts.

Sarala wrote:

> One day in Udbodhan Holy Mother said: "Look, when Radhu left me, cutting my attachment to her, I thought perhaps this time my body would not last. But I see still there is more of the Master's work to be done."

> Even Yogin-ma, one of the Mother's intimate companions, once felt some doubt about the Mother and said to herself: "Sri Ramakrishna was the embodiment of renunciation, and the Mother is engrossed in the world, preoccupied day and night with the thought of her brothers, sisters-in-law, and nephews and nieces. I can't understand this." One day soon after this she was seated on the bank of the Ganges, meditating, when Sri Ramakrishna appeared in a vision before her. The Master said: "Do you see what is being carried by the water of the Ganges?" Yogin-ma saw the corpse of a newborn baby, smeared with blood, with the placenta still attached to it. She also saw that thousands of people were offering worship to the holy water of the river. The Master said to Yogin-ma: "Can anything make the Ganges impure? Regard her [meaning Holy Mother] in the same way. Never have any doubt about her. Remember she is not different from this [meaning himself]."

> Returning from the Ganges, Yogin-ma bowed down to Holy Mother and said, "Mother, please forgive me." "Why, Yogin? What happened?" the Mother inquired. Yogin-ma then narrated the incident and said: "I harboured doubt about you, but today the Master has revealed the truth to me." Smiling, the Mother said: "Don't feel bad. Doubt is natural for the human mind. Doubt will arise and again faith will come. One develops faith in this way. Thus finally one attains firm faith."[20]

In the middle of June 1918 Radhu wrote a letter to Holy Mother. She wanted to come to Calcutta because she had an abscess on one of her fingers. Holy Mother wrote to Kedar in Koalpara: "Radhu is not well. She wants to come to Calcutta with her husband and mother. If Radhu thinks it is necessary, then send Brahmachari Barada to accompany them."[21] Accordingly Radhu and her companions went to Koalpara, and from there, the brahmachari accompanied them to the Mother's residence in Calcutta. Dr. Kanjilal began to treat Radhu and within a couple of weeks she recovered. Radhu and her husband had a room upstairs in Udbodhan House.

Radhu became pregnant in August 1918, and towards the end of the year her neurasthenia became worse. She became very weak and could not bear any noise. It was difficult for Holy Mother to care for Radhu in Udbodhan House. It was a noisy place — there was a shrine upstairs, a publication department downstairs, and many visiting devotees. On the morning of 31 December 1918, Saradananda sent a message to Swami Shivananda at Belur Math telling him that Holy Mother and Radhu would go to Leggett House, located north of the old Belur shrine. Immediately the monks made that place ready, but at three o'clock another message came saying that Holy Mother and Radhu had moved to the boarding house of Nivedita's School, which was on a secluded lane. They had moved there because Radhu would not have been able to bear the sound of the bells and conch of the Belur monastery shrine and the whistles of the steamers plying the Ganges.

The next morning Swami Shivananda sent Brahmachari Barada to the Mother with some vegetables and flowers from Belur Math. When Barada arrived at the boarding house, Holy Mother said to him: "I am now here with this turbulent ocean [meaning Radhu]. What will happen, Barada? Now, wait and see how many days Radhu will stay here. She is always lying down and cannot stand any noise. I don't know, my son. What kind of disease is this? Only the Master knows how she will be free from this illness."[22]

Brahmachari Barada visited the Mother regularly every two or three days. One day the Mother said to him: "Radhu does not like this place anymore. She is asking me to take her to Jayrambati. But look at her condition! There are no doctors or medical facilities there. It would be easier to get them here. Radhu is very stubborn and does not stop until her wish is fulfilled. Let us wait and see what happens next."[23]

On Swami Vivekananda's birthday (26 January 1919) Saradananda sent a devotee to Belur Math to ask Brahmachari Barada to return to Calcutta immediately. The Mother had decided to go to Jayrambati the next day. In the evening Barada arrived at Udbodhan House and met Swami Saradananda, who sent him to the Mother. He went upstairs and saw her seated in the middle of the room with some coconut ropes for binding the bedding and trunks. When she saw Barada, she said: "I am going to Jayrambati tomorrow with this turbulent ocean. Will you go with me? You boys are my only support there."

Barada replied: "Whatever you command will be done. Of course I will go with you." Relieved, the Mother said: "My son, take these ropes, pack everything, and tie the bundles up. I was just waiting for you." Barada and Holy Mother packed the baggage of Radhu, Maku, and others until 11 o'clock at night.

When Barada came downstairs, Saradananda told him: "I want you to stay with the Mother and help her as long as she wants you." Barada joyfully agreed. He remained with Holy Mother and served her until her last day.

Early in the morning of 27 January 1919 Holy Mother left by horse carriage for the train with Radhu, Surabala, Maku and her son Neda, Nalini, and Mandakini Roy (a widow disciple and attendant of the Mother), as well as Brahmachari Ganen, Dwijen (later Swami Gangeshananda), and Brahmachari Barada. The Mother and her women companions travelled in a reserved second-class compartment, and the men went in an inter class coach. The Mother sat on a blanket on the floor of the coach and extended her legs to relieve her rheumatism. After arriving in Vishnupur, the party went to Sureshwar Sen's house, which was kept ready for Holy Mother. They stayed there for two days. One morning Sureshwar brought an astrologer, who read the palms of Radhu and Maku. He predicted that Radhu would not have an easy delivery and that Maku would have several children but they would not see each other. This made Maku very upset. She reported this to the Mother, crying. Holy Mother was concerned as Neda was then 2 1/2 years old and Maku was pregnant. She called the astrologer privately and asked how she could counteract Maku's destiny. He suggested Maku should listen to the Chandi attentively for three Tuesdays, and perform a fire ceremony and a ritualistic worship. Later, Holy Mother arranged for this.

On the morning of 29 January the party left for Jayrambati in six bullock carts. Brahmachari Barada recorded a marvellous story concerning the Mother's presence of mind, strong common sense, and ability to adapt to time and situation:

> It was the winter of 1919. Holy Mother and her party went from Calcutta to Vishnupur by train and then by six bullock carts to Koalpara. On the way we stopped at Jaipur [8 miles from Vishnupur] where the cook began to prepare dal near a roadside inn. The Mother was happy to see the arrangements for cooking. She washed her hands and feet in the nearby pond and then helped by cutting vegetables. The cooking was nearly done when the cook accidentally broke the earthen rice pot while removing the extra foamy water. The cooked rice was scattered on the ground. What to do? We were in a dilemma. We thought that if we bought another pot and cooked more rice, it would be too late to reach Koalpara, and moreover the road was not safe. We still had to go another 14 miles.
>
> The Mother was not upset at all. She slowly removed the foam from the rice with a straw ladle and collected the rice that had not touched the ground. She then washed her hands, took out the Master's picture from her tin box and placed it on the corner of the box. On a sal leaf, she put some rice, dal, and vegetables, and placed this in front of the Master. With

rada Devi and Radhu in a bullock cart near Kumbhasthal Inn, on the way to yrambati, 1913. (*This photo has been digitally enhanced; inset shows original.*)

folded hands she prayed: "Master, you have arranged this food for us today. Please eat it now quickly while it is warm."

Observing the Mother's unconventional behaviour, we began to laugh. The Mother then told us: "Look, one should act and adapt according to circumstances. Now all of you sit down and I shall serve the food." The Mother's women companions and the rest of us sat on the ground. She scooped rice with a wooden ladle from the top of the heap and put it on our leaf plates one after another, and then added other dishes. She also took food in the same way and began to eat, extending her legs. She commented: "The food is delicious." We hurriedly finished our lunch, packed the luggage, and resumed our journey. We reached Koalpara Ashrama at 11:00 p.m.[24]

On this occasion Holy Mother and Radhu shared a bullock cart. When the cart approached Kotalpur, Radhu began to push Holy Mother with her feet and said: "Get away from here, get away! Get out of the cart." Holy Mother moved to the back as far as possible and said, "If I move away, how then shall I practise all these austerities through you?" When Radhu kicked her again, the Mother said hastily: "What is it you have done, Radhi? What have you done?" Quickly she took the dust of her own feet and touched it to Radhu's head.[25]

With Holy Mother in Koalpara

It was decided that the party would rest in Koalpara for a couple of days before continuing to Jayrambati. However, Radhu slept well for two nights, and she wanted to stay in that quiet village. The Mother consulted with Kalikumar and others, and they suggested that it would be good for Radhu to stay in Koalpara rather than continue to Jayrambati. Radhu remained in Koalpara for six months (29 January to 22 July 1919).

Koalpara Ashrama stands on the main road from Kotalpur to Desra on the way to Jayrambati. It has a shrine, a kitchen, a dining room, rooms for the monks and devotees, and a well. On 14 November 1911 the Mother had installed photos of the Master and herself on the altar of the ashrama shrine. Holy Mother and Radhu stayed at Jagadamba Ashrama, which was at the farthest end of the village, about two furlongs east of the monastery. It had been built in 1915. This compound was in a solitary place, surrounded by high walls. The Mother's cottage was spacious and had a cement floor. Near it was the kitchen. A big cottage at the southeast corner could accommodate seven or eight women devotees. Another cottage at the southwest corner served as a visitors' room for the men devotees who visited the Mother from time to time. Monks and men devotees

bove: Jagadamba Ashrama in Koalpara, where Sarada Devi lived with Radhu in
)19. Below: Shrine at Koalpara Ashrama where Sarada Devi installed pictures of
amakrishna and herself on 14 November 1911.

ate at Koalpara Ashrama while the women ate at Jagadamba Ashrama. Nearly 40 people lived in the two ashramas and Saradananda bore most of the expenses. During this period many devotees came to Koalpara and received initiation from Holy Mother.

After spending a few days in Koalpara, the Mother said to Brahmachari Barada: "Something has happened lately — whatever thought arises in my mind comes true, be it good or bad. Radhu likes this wild jungle because it is quiet. You are gone the whole day doing all sorts of errands. You come here before dusk to eat and you stay in the visitors' room at night. I am a little scared because Radhu and Maku have jewellery here. I have asked Brahmachari Rajen also to come here at 10 or 11 at night after finishing his work in the ashrama."[26]

After supper the Mother used to talk to Brahmachari Barada about the Master and about her problems. They would sit under a tree in the courtyard and speak in low voices so that Radhu could not hear. One evening the Mother said: "Look Barada, this jungle is so dense that I wonder if one day a bear may appear here."

"Mother, we have never seen any bear in this area."

"Well, my son, this jungle is so dark that it frightens me."

A couple of days later, news came that the mother-in-law of Ambika, the village watchman, was mauled in the Desra field by a big bear. The villagers shot and killed the bear.

Holy Mother engaged a brahmin pandit to read the Chandi and perform the rituals suggested by the astrologer to ward off Maku's evil portent. Now Holy Mother hoped for Radhu's safe delivery. Radhu's heart palpitated with even the slightest noise, so she remained lying down, clutching some blankets to her chest. Swami Saradananda sent a doctor and a midwife to Koalpara for Radhu.

Late one evening while the Mother, Mandakini, and Brahmachari Barada were talking under the courtyard tree, Mandakini said to Barada: "Brother, the Mother and I were seated under the shade of this tree at noon. The Mother said, 'For some days two crows would come at noon and caw, and this would disturb Radhu; but I haven't seen them the last few days. Where have they gone?' Immediately those two crows came and began to caw from the tree." The Mother smiled and corroborated the story.

It was the middle of June 1919. It had been raining for a few days. One night at ten o'clock the Mother, Mandakini, and Brahmachari Barada were seated under the tree. Suddenly the Mother said: "That madman from Sihar has not shown up for some days. He is totally mad, but he sings well. I am afraid lest he should come and create a row here." Mandakini said: "Mother, why did you mention his name? He may appear here right now." Barada said that it would be impossible for him to come there at night, crossing the overflowing river. Just then that madman appeared with a palm-leaf hat on his head and some spinach under his arm. He said to the Mother, "I have brought this spinach for you."

The Mother told him in a low voice: "Please go now. Don't make any noise."

The man replied: "How can I go now? The river is overflowing."

Barada asked, "Then how did you come?"

"I swam," he replied.

The Mother said in a sweet tone, "My child, please don't make any noise." The man then left without saying a word.[27]

The Mother had been deeply concerned about Radhu for months, and she followed any suggested remedy with all sincerity and full faith. Regarding difficult and complicated matters, she depended on the Master's will and remained calm. In March 1919 Nalini suggested: "Aunt, when Radhu's mother became mad, you made her wear the bangle from the Wild Kali of Tirol, and that improved her condition. I think Radhu will recover if she wears the Wild Kali's bangle." Accordingly, the next day the Mother sent Brahmachari Barada to Tirol, which is 20 miles from Koalpara. Barada walked to Arambagh where he spent the night at a devotee's house. The next morning, he went to Tirol. He offered five rupees for the Kali worship, two rupees to the priest, and seven rupees for an iron bangle. He returned to Koalpara in the evening and kept the bangle hanging on a tree branch so it would not touch the ground. The next morning Radhu took her bath and put it on. She fasted for the rest of the day. Holy Mother prayed to Mother Kali and promised to offer a special worship after Radhu's recovery.[28]

There was no change in Radhu, but Surabala became even more unstable and angry because Holy Mother was following Nalini's suggestions. Surabala said to the Mother: "Why did you bring Radhu here? She would have been better off in Calcutta, where everything was available. Here the weather is hot. If you can arrange to put an ice pack on Radhu's head, she will get well." To pacify Surabala, the Mother sent Barada to get ice from Bankura. The next day Barada rode his bicycle to Vishnupur and then took a train to Bankura. He bought 20 pounds of ice and packed it in sawdust so that it would not melt. He returned to Vishnupur by train and to Koalpara by bicycle. The Mother and Surabala began to put ice on Radhu's head.

Meanwhile Kalikumar came from Jayrambati and said to the Mother: "Sister, you are putting ice on the head of a pregnant woman on the advice of a madwoman. I hope nothing bad happens to her because of the ice." The Mother then stopped putting the ice on Radhu's head. Now Kalikumar suggested: "Sister, you don't understand. This is not a disease; if it were, the Calcutta doctors would have cured it. I think she is possessed by a demigod or a ghost. Why don't you bring the famous tantric sadhu from Sushnegere and get his opinion." Holy Mother agreed. The next day she sent Brahmachari Barada to Jayrambati, and Kalikumar accompanied him to Sushnegere. Kalikumar told the tantric sadhu everything and offered a special worship to his deity. The tantric sadhu threw some mustard seeds on the altar and said that he had received the command to go to Koalpara the next day.

When the tantric sadhu arrived, the Mother bowed down to him, described Radhu's condition, and fervently begged for his help. He considered the case to be a ghostly affair and he prescribed a remedy: sesame oil from two and a half pounds of black sesame seed, fish oil from a carp weighing 40 pounds, and various kinds of herbs and plants boiled in an iron cauldron over a fire of dry ox dung fuel. The substance produced was to be rubbed on the patient's body, who must also wear an iron amulet. The tantric sadhu took five rupees from the Mother and left. Holy Mother was unable to attempt this remedy, however, because those ingredients were impossible to obtain.[29]

One day Holy Mother engaged a Chanda (medium) who also prescribed various kinds of medicines. They were applied to Radhu, with no effect. Frustrated, Mother said: "I am praying to all the gods and goddesses, but no one is answering my prayers. It will happen according to Providence. The Master is the only protector."[30]

Nalini became jealous that her aunt was spending so much money on Radhu, and she was always quarreling with Surabala. This family squabble was ruining the Mother's mental peace. Finally, Nalini took her sister Maku, who was also pregnant, and left for Jayrambati by palanquin. In the evening the Mother lamented: "Nalini did not bring Neda to me for my blessing before she left. Nalini's mind is full of jealousy and getting more impure day by day."[31] She sent Brahmachari Barada to Jayrambati every day for news of them.

In April news reached Holy Mother that Mandakini's mother was seriously ill in Nabasan and there was no one to look after her. Holy Mother brought her to Koalpara and engaged a doctor for treatment, but the old lady passed away within a couple of days. Meanwhile Neda, Maku's son, had become sick with fever and a sore throat. The Mother asked Brahmachari Barada and Dr. Vaikuntha (later Swami Maheswarananda) to go to Jayrambati the next day. Vaikuntha diagnosed Neda's illness as diphtheria, a serious disease. They returned to Koalpara and reported to the Mother that the boy needed an injection that was available only in Calcutta. The Mother sent Barada to the nearest telegraph office in Arambagh, a distance of 14 miles, to send a cable to Saradananda. The swami immediately bought the injection and sent it through Bhupeswar Sen, who reached Jayrambati at nine o'clock in the morning. When he arrived, however, it was too late and the injection did no good: Neda died at five o'clock on 20 April 1919. That night the Mother cried and lamented for Neda.

The next morning the Mother made a remark about Neda: "This boy was a fallen yogi in his previous birth, or a great soul. A little karma was left that he had to finish in this life. This was his last birth. Seldom does one see such good tendencies in such a little boy. He would collect some plumerias every day and worship me by putting them on my feet." The Mother talked about Neda for a few days and sometimes shed tears for him.[32]

One day Dr. Prabhakar Mukhopadhyay said to her: "Mother, this world is full of suffering. There is no escape since I am already in it. Could you tell me how I can have peace? I am disgusted with this worldly life."

The Mother consoled him: "You are right, my son. There is no peace in worldly life. The Master exists and he will surely protect you. It is extremely troublesome to live in this world with relatives. Look, I made a big mistake arranging Radhu's marriage and now I am suffering."[33]

In Koalpara sometimes the Mother would feed Radhu, but Radhu spat the food out at her. One day the Mother was irritated and said to Sarala: "Look, my child, know this body [*pointing to her own*] to be a divine body. How much abuse can this body tolerate? Can any human being bear so much torture? Only a divine being can bear it. These relatives are tormenting me. This time if the Master somehow cures Radhu, I will withdraw myself. Look, my child, as long as I am alive, they will not know my real nature; they will understand it later."[34]

Radhu's prolonged neurasthenia led doctors to believe that an operation might be necessary at the time of her delivery. Saradananda arranged for Dr. Vaikuntha and Sarala, who had studied nursing, to be present during the delivery of Radhu's child. Someone suggested the need for a specialist at Radhu's delivery, but the Mother said: "Dogs and jackals live in the jungle. Do they not give birth to young ones there?" On 9 May 1919

Radhu gave birth to a son in a natural way without much difficulty. It was a great relief to Holy Mother. The boy was named Banabihari* on account of being born in the jungle (*vana*) of Koalpara; his pet name was Banu.

On 23 July 1919, Holy Mother moved with her household to Jayrambati. Radhu was very weak. She could not stand, but crawled about; sometimes she had to be forced into bed. Now her eccentricity reached its height. According to custom, when Banabihari was six months old, Holy Mother arranged Banabihari's rice feeding ceremony (*annaprashan*) and fed many people. At dawn Holy Mother sang to Banu just as Mother Kaushalya of the Ramayana did while rousing her son, Prince Rama, from sleep:

> It is morning. Awake, my child, Thou who art merciful to the gods, men, and sages.
> Bathe now and offer the gods cattle, elephants, gold, and betel-nuts.[35]

Brahmachari Barada wrote in his diary about Holy Mother's ordeal with Radhu during this period:

> Radhu's baby was now six months old, but still Radhu could not stand up because of weakness. To make things worse, she became addicted to opium for her stomach trouble. Holy Mother, too, of late had not been well. She was having occasional attacks of fever. She tried to wean Radhu from her opium habit, but Radhu was adamant. One morning Holy Mother was cutting vegetables when Radhu came for opium. Holy Mother understood her intention and said to her: "Radhi, you have had enough of this. Why don't you stand up? It is impossible for me to take care of you anymore. For your sake I have given up my devotion and everything else. Can you tell me how I can possibly meet all your expenses?"
>
> At these words, Radhu lost her temper, picked up a big eggplant from the vegetable basket, and threw it at Holy Mother's back with great force. It struck her hard and she arched her back in pain. Her back became red and swollen. Looking at a photograph of the Master, Holy Mother prayed with folded hands: "Lord, please forgive her misdemeanor. She is not sane." Then she took the dust of her own feet, put it on Radhu's head, and said: 'Radhi, the Master never hurt me, not even with a rude word, and you torture me so much. How can you understand where I really belong? Simply because I live with you all, you do not think anything of me." Radhu burst into tears. Holy Mother continued: "Radhi, if I get angry with you, there will be no one in the three worlds to give you shelter." Addressing Sri Ramakrishna, she said, "O Master, please do not be offended with her."

*Banabihari is an epithet of Krishna.

A few months earlier, Narayan Iyenger, a devotee from Bangalore, had spent some time with Holy Mother at Koalpara. He gave her 100 rupees per month for Radhu's expenses. As he was leaving Koalpara, he said: "Mother, whenever you need money, please let me know without the slightest hesitation." At Jayrambati her expenses increased a great deal. Swami Saradananda had written to her that since he had to collect money from here and there, he found it difficult to send her monthly expenses on time. Holy Mother said to a disciple: "I think Sharat does not have much money to spare, or he would not have written that way. The other day the devotee from Bangalore promised to send me money. But how can I write to him about it? Shall I disobey the Master's last injunction about not asking for money from others?" To Radhu she said: 'Look here, Radhu, I am going to lose everything for your sake! The Master asked me not to stretch out my hand to anybody even for a pice. He assured me that I shall never lack simple food and clothing. He admonished me, saying that if I begged even a pice from any person, I would sell my head to that person in return."[36]

The Mother knew that her life was coming to an end, so she began to work quickly to finish her mission. She had taken responsibility for Radhu after her birth and now she decided to complete her duty towards her niece. Despite all of Radhu's shortcomings, the all-forgiving Mother tried to protect her spiritual life by giving her initiation. Later Radhu told Kamala Ghosh, wife of Bibhuti Ghosh of Bankura: "I never said anything about initiation to the Mother. One day during worship the Mother was seated on the asana and suddenly she called me, 'Radhi, come here.' When I went, she said: 'Sprinkle Ganges water on your body. Take an asana and sit near me.' Then she gave me a mantra. She then bowed down and said addressing the Master: 'I have done enough. Now you please look after her.' Sister, I could not understand what the Mother was talking about. But after that initiation, my health greatly improved."[37]

Afterwards Radhu said to Brahmachari Akshaychaitanya: "I knew the Mother as my aunt. Did I know that she was not human but a goddess?" — saying this Radhu fell down unconscious.[38]

Mother Returns to Udbodhan

On 13 December 1919 the Mother's devotees observed her 66th birthday in Jayrambati. Holy Mother had been suffering off and on from malaria, and as a result her body became weak and emaciated. When local treatment failed, Saradananda sent Swamis Atmaprakashananda and Bhumananda, and Boshiswar Sen to bring Holy Mother back to Calcutta. It was decided to also bring Radhu and her mother, Nalini, Maku,

Mandakini, and Brahmachari Barada. The Mother left Jayrambati on 24 February and arrived at Udbodhan House on 27 February 1920.

Several doctors were engaged to treat Holy Mother. Although weak and fragile, she continued to accept a limited number of visitors. Slowly she was withdrawing her mind from Radhu, though Banu had his full share of her love. Since Radhu could hardly look after her baby, Sarala took responsibility for the baby's care. Dr. Kanjilal gave notice that he would not treat the baby unless the child was kept away from his mother. One day Holy Mother remarked: "She cannot even take care of herself. Why did God give her a child?"[39]

In Holy Mother's divine drama, Radhu played her part very well. The Mother explained again and again the role of Radhu in her life. We should be indebted to Radhu in that she was responsible for keeping the Mother on earth for such a long period. During the 20 years that Holy Mother's life was intertwined with hers, the Master fulfilled his unfinished mission through Holy Mother. She exemplified the ideal of a householder, the ideal of womanhood, and the Motherhood of God. In her relationship with Radhu, Holy Mother also showed how to maintain equanimity of mind in spite of ill-treatment and abuse. Holy Mother was the embodiment of patience and perseverance, love and affection, compassion and dispassion, forgiveness and forbearance. She set an example for how one should live in this world under untoward circumstances. Through Radhu, Holy Mother also demonstrated the ideal of a karma yogi as described in the Bhagavad Gita.

20
Holy Mother
in the Midst of Her Family

Twam vaishnavi shaktih ananta-viryā
vishvasya bijam paramāsi māyā;
Sanmohitam devi samastam-etat
tvam vai prasannā bhuvi muktihetuh.
—*Chandi, 11:5*

O Mother, You are the great primal energy, the source of infinite strength. You are the seed of the world, and illusion divine. You have enchanted the whole universe, O goddess supreme, with Your deluding charms. In Your benevolence You bestow liberation upon human beings.

Once Ramakrishna asked Jogin, "What do you think of me?" Jogin replied, "You are neither a householder nor a sannyasin." He meant that the Master was God — beyond attributes. Ramakrishna was greatly pleased and exclaimed, "What an extraordinary statement!" Similarly, one cannot put any designation — nun or householder — on Holy Mother. She was the Divine Mother. By himself, Ramakrishna could not demonstrate how to lead an ideal householder's life. His householder devotees were in awe of his incredible renunciation and frequent experiences of samadhi. They felt helpless because they knew it was impossible to follow such an uncompromising and lofty ideal. For that reason, Ramakrishna put Holy Mother in the role of an ideal householder so that people could see how to live in a family yet remain detached from the world.

As a swan swims in the water but becomes dry the moment it shakes its wings on dry land, Holy Mother lived in the midst of her family circle yet remained free, like a Paramahamsa, a Supreme Swan. Of course, like regular householders she cried and smiled, and she suffered from worries and anxieties, grief and pain, and financial and physical problems. In addition, she faced abuse and was beset by demands from close relatives. Still, she maintained her calm and serenity, forbearance and forgiveness,

Sarada Devi, Jayrambati, 1913. Swami Gauriswarananda told Swami
Abjajananda that the photos on these two pages were taken at Satish Biswas's
house. (*The background of the photos tallies with Swami Saradeshananda's
description in* Sri Sri Mayer Smritikatha, *p. 125.*)

rada Devi, Jayrambati, 1913.

love and compassion. As an actor performs two roles — one on the stage and the other at home — so the Mother acted in two roles simultaneously. She performed her duty towards her brothers, sisters-in-law, nieces and nephews, and yet she also acted as a spiritual teacher, initiating and awakening God-consciousness in her devotees' minds.

Sometimes in family life we find much selfishness, cruelty, hatred, jealousy, quarrelling, and ill-feelings — no peace or joy. Many worldly minded people turn their homes into hell. Ramakrishna and Holy Mother demonstrated how to transform that hell into heaven. Ramakrishna graphically described the worldly minded:

> The worldly minded never come to their senses, even though they suffer and have terrible experiences. Camels are very fond of thorny shrubs. The more they eat of them, the more do their mouths bleed, yet they do not refrain from making them their food.[1]
>
> The worldly man is like a snake trying to swallow a mole. The snake can neither swallow the mole nor give it up. The bound soul may have realized that there is no substance to the world — that the world is like a hog plum, only stone and skin — but still he cannot give it up and turn his mind to God.[2]
>
> There is another characteristic of the bound soul. If you remove him from his worldly surroundings to a spiritual environment, he will pine away. The worm that grows in filth feels very happy there. It thrives in filth. It will die if you put it in a pot of rice.[3]

Before Ramakrishna passed away, he asked Holy Mother to look after the people of Calcutta, most of whom were worldly minded and materialistic. Later the Mother remarked that the Master had concentrated on a selected few and left the masses for her.

How can we harmonize the world and God, the active life and contemplative life? Spiritual aspirants all over the world ask this question. Ramakrishna answered it with the following illustration:

> In Kamarpukur I have seen the women of carpenter families making flattened rice with a husking machine. One woman kicks the end of the wooden beam, and another woman, while nursing her baby, turns the paddy in the mortar dug in the earth. The second woman is always alert lest the pestle of the machine should fall on her hand. With the other hand she fries the soaked paddy in a pan. Besides, she is talking with the customers; she says: "You owe us so much money. Please pay it before you go." Likewise, do your different duties in the world, fixing your mind on God. But practice is necessary, and one should also be alert. Only in this way can one safeguard both — God and world.[4]

Holy Mother demonstrated this teaching in her own life and in her relationship with her family.

Worldly but Blessed Brothers

Holy Mother's father died in 1874 and her mother in 1906. Although Holy Mother had been blessed with godly parents, she was truly unfortunate regarding her other relatives. Her brothers Prasanna, Kalikumar, and Barada were greedy, selfish, and quarrelsome; her sisters-in-law were opportunists and jealous of one another; and her nieces were demanding, annoying, jealous, and eccentric. Holy Mother was the eldest among five brothers and one sister. Her sister, Kadambini, died soon after she was married, leaving no offspring. Her brother Umesh died at the age of eighteen or nineteen, unmarried. Abhaycharan, the youngest, died from cholera after finishing medical school, leaving his insane wife, Surabala, who was pregnant with their daughter Radhu. The remaining three brothers — Prasanna, Kalikumar, and Barada — lived to old age.

Prasanna and Barada spent most of their time in Calcutta and supported their families by performing rituals in different homes. Prasanna married Ramapriya and had two daughters — Nalini and Sushila (also known as Maku). When Ramapriya died in 1905, Prasanna married Subasini, who bore him three children — Kamala, Bimala, and Ganapati. Nalini and Maku were later married but had unhappy lives. They were tossed between irresponsible husbands and their stepmother, who disliked them, so they lived mostly with Holy Mother.

Barada married Indumati, and they had two sons — Kshudiram and Vijaykrishna.

Kalikumar lived in Jayrambati and made his living through priestly duties and farming. Kalikumar was short-tempered and never got along with his brothers. He loved power and wanted to control the family affairs, and he always pestered Holy Mother for money. Kalikumar married Subodhbala and had two boys — Bhudeb and Radharaman.

The members of Holy Mother's immediate family were all associated with her life in various ways. Her sisters-in-law were much younger than she, and she taught them their household duties, including how to cook.

Only a jeweller knows the value of a jewel; an eggplant seller knows only eggplants. Neither Ramakrishna's nor Holy Mother's relatives recognized the divinity of the two. Ramlal, Lakshmi, and Shivaram considered the Master to be merely their uncle. Prasanna, Kalikumar, and Barada thought of Holy Mother simply as their sister, and to their children she was merely an aunt. Divine beings cannot play the role of humans if people recognize

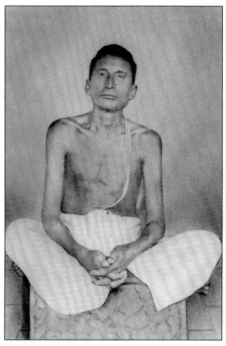

Above: Sarada Devi's brothers Prasannakumar and Kalikumar.
Below: Indumati, wife of Sarada Devi's brother Baradaprasad.

their true nature. One can know God only through His grace. The Upanishad says: "The Atman is attained by that person whom It chooses."[5]

Girish Ghosh once remarked that Holy Mother's brothers must have performed bone-breaking austerities in a previous life to have obtained her as their sister.

Kalikumar always took advantage of Holy Mother's goodness with a view to getting some money from her and also to show his power. In 1917 he proposed that the family observe Sri Ramakrishna's birthday festival in a grand way in Jayrambati.

Holy Mother responded: "Look, Kali, I do not have the devotion and energy that you have, so I cannot observe the Master's birth anniversary on such a large scale myself. You make a feast for the entire household as well as some villagers with whatever vegetables are available in this village. As you see, my health is failing day by day."[6] Kalikumar took money from her and arranged the feast.

Before Durga Puja in 1918, Prasanna went to Calcutta to perform his duties there. Before he left, he said to Mother: "Sister, you have just come to Jayrambati and I am leaving for Calcutta. Please look after my wife and children. Now Kali will have a nice time. He has sufficient land to live well here with his family — but I must leave my family to earn money." Kalikumar overheard the conversation and remarked: "Now you are whining before our sister to get money from her."

Prasanna replied: "Look, Kali, it doesn't matter if you respect me. We both know that I was born after our sister, and you after me. Do you have any love and devotion for our sister? I know our sister's greatness more than you do. You only know about her money."

Kalikumar replied: "I served Paramahamsadeva [Ramakrishna] and he used to love me. You never tried to be close to him. Moreover, I take care of our sister and her devotees here."

"You don't understand how much devotion I have for our sister," Prasanna responded. "You can't respect her as I do. Only our sister knows and I know."

Holy Mother listened to her two brothers' arguments and smiled. She later remarked: "My brothers are all truly jewels! They practised severe austerities in their previous births so that I now live with their families. I have never seen such attachments as they have."[7]

When Prasanna lived in Calcutta, he made good money. However, he was very miserly and calculating. Once when Holy Mother was in Jayrambati, his 2-year-old daughter Kamala fell ill with a fever. The local doctor could not bring the fever down, and more money was needed to hire a better doctor. News was sent to Prasanna but he refused to come and would not send any money. He thought that his sister would take care of everything. This time Holy Mother did not tolerate his demands. She gravely remarked: "He has a child every year. Why will he not pay for his children's medical expenses?" Fortunately, Kamala got well under the local doctor's care.

One day in December 1918, Holy Mother was seated on the veranda of her house in Jayrambati. Suddenly Kalikumar and Barada began to quarrel about a fence that Kalikumar had put up. That extended fence created an obstruction for carrying paddy to Barada's farmyard. They were about to come to blows when Holy Mother jumped between them and grabbed each one by the hand, blaming both for the quarrel. During the commotion her veil fell aside, and she did not notice. When some monks rushed to the spot, the brothers walked away to their homes cursing each other. The Mother returned to her veranda and suddenly burst into laughter. "What an illusion Mahamaya — the Great Enchantress — has conjured up!" she exclaimed. "Here is this infinite world, and what one claims as his possession will be left behind at death. Still men cannot understand this simple truth."[8] After she uttered these words, she was convulsed with laughter for some time.

When Holy Mother was not in Jayrambati, her brothers would write to her about their woes and wants. Her disciples read those letters to her and she dictated answers. Once a disciple said to her: "Mother, please give them plenty of money and pray to the Master about it. Let them have their enjoyment to their hearts' content. Afterward they will develop dispassion."

Holy Mother replied: "Will they ever have dispassion? They will never be satisfied. Do worldly people ever feel satisfied? My brothers only tell me their woes. Kali always demands money. Prasanna is now imitating him. Only Barada hardly makes any demands. He says, 'Where will sister get money?'"

On another occasion she remarked about her brothers: "Their sole thought is money. They only demand, 'Give us money, give us money.' Not even absent-mindedly have they ever asked for knowledge and devotion. All right, let them have what they want."[9]

A Compassionate and Forgiving Sister

Despite their greediness, once in a while Prasanna and Kalikumar had glimpses of their sister's divine nature. Once Holy Mother wrote to her brothers that she was returning to Jayrambati on a certain date. She asked them to send someone to help her cross the Amodar River. When Holy Mother and her companions reached the bank of the Amodar, no one was there to help. Somehow she and the others strode through the shallow river and reached Jayrambati in the evening. While eating supper, Holy Mother asked Prasanna for an explanation: "I informed you but you did not send anyone to help me cross the river. Fortunately, these boys were with me."

Prasanna replied: "Sister, my fear of Kali kept me from sending any-one. You see, Kali would say that I was trying to win you over. Do I not know how precious you are? I see it all, but I am helpless. I cannot be nice to you for fear of arousing Kali's jealousy. Please bless me so that I may also have you as my sister in future births. As for me, I want nothing else."

"Catch me coming to your family again!" exclaimed Holy Mother. "I have had enough of it this time. To come again to you? The idea!"[10]

Another day Prasanna said to her: "Sister, I have heard that you appeared to a devotee in a dream, gave him initiation, and also assured him of his liberation. You have cared for us from birth and have brought us up. Shall we remain like this forever?"

The Mother replied: "Things will happen as the Master ordains. Let me tell you something. Sri Krishna played with the cowherd boys, laughed with them, walked with them, and even ate the leavings from their plates. Did they know who he was?"

Another time Prasanna asked: "Sister, we all were born in the womb of the same mother. Shall we not achieve anything?"

"True," she assured her brother. "What should you be afraid of?"[11]

Narayan Iyenger, a wealthy devotee of Holy Mother, expressed a desire to dig a well for her on the family's land, so that she could have good drinking water. Kalikumar appreciated Iyenger's intention but demanded 700 rupees for the small piece of land on which the well was to be dug — which was worth only 15 rupees. However, the deal did not go through at that time for various reasons. Kalikumar said to Brahma-chari Barada: "You see, if Sister saved the money that she receives from her devotees, she would be wealthy. But she spends lavishly for Radhu and gives money away to her other brothers. I am sorry that our sister is not saving anything. Could you tell me who gets the most from her?"

Kalikumar was very calculating, but sometimes he understood the greatness of Holy Mother. Kalikumar continued: "You see, Barada, our sister is so respected because she has not the slightest attachment to money. Had she been different, people would not care for her. She is not a human being but a veritable goddess. You are blessed indeed. You have renounced the world so young and are devoting yourself day and night to her service."[12] Kalikumar was an interesting character: he was both a troublemaker and a troubleshooter. He was selfish and greedy, and he took every opportunity to exploit his sister, yet he always came forward to help her when needed. He was grave and serious. Nalini, Maku, Radhu, and her mother were afraid of him. Whenever they got out of control, Holy Mother would say, "Call for Kali right now," and everyone would become quiet. One day Kalikumar said to the Mother: "Sister, you have now so many members in your household, and your elderly woman cook cannot handle it. You need a male cook. Moreover, your birthday is coming. Many people will come, so a lot of shopping will need to be done. These young boys will not be able to handle it."

Holy Mother replied: "Look, Kali, I am surrounded by several women, so how I can engage a male cook? The boys who are helping me, remember, they are like my daughters. But you are right: we need a lot of groceries for this large household." In the evening she said to Brahmachari Barada: "Look, we shall have to give Kali the responsibility for shopping at the Kotalpur market; otherwise he will be angry and create a disturbance."[13]

Holy Mother gave Kalikumar complete responsibility for her birthday celebration. With great enthusiasm he did most of the shopping, and he assigned Brahmachari Barada to buy firewood and spices from the market at Haldigram. Holy Mother performed the worship, and the relatives and villagers enjoyed a grand feast. Kalikumar supervised everything, yet he refused to eat: his feelings had been hurt sometime during the festivities. Piqued, he went to his farmyard and began to arrange his hay; he intended to teach his sister a lesson. Despite her ill-health, the Mother could not rest until she had fed Kalikumar, and she waited on the veranda with his food. When Holy Mother told Brahmachari Gopesh (later Swami Saradeshananda) about the situation, he rushed to Kalikumar's farm and began to help him. He said nothing as he worked. Slowly Kalikumar's anger melted, and he said, "My boy, why have you come here to help?"

Gopesh replied: "Uncle, the Mother is waiting for you with your food."

"What? I didn't know that sister is waiting with my food. Let us go right now," said Kalikumar.[14]

Holy Mother was pleased to feed her brother, and then went to rest. It is sad how she had to endure this kind of petty behaviour from her family.

Kalikumar was very shrewd and took every opportunity to extract money from his sister. Once he took money from Holy Mother and built a big parlour on his property. He allowed Holy Mother to perform the annual Jagaddhatri worship in the parlour and also allowed her out-of-town devotees to stay there when they visited.[15]

Holy Mother was extremely careful about Kalikumar, as he was very touchy. The caste system was followed rigidly in her village. According to that system, a brahmin does not eat food cooked by a nonbrahmin. An elderly brahmin lady cooked for the Mother's household, but sometimes Brahmacharis Barada and Hari (later Swami Haripremananda) helped her in the kitchen, even though they were not brahmins. Holy Mother was apprehensive lest Kalikumar stir up trouble with relatives and villagers because nonbrahmins worked in her kitchen. She tactfully invited Kalikumar to have dinner with her from time to time, so that he would not raise his voice against her household. However, one day her brother Barada raised this issue and solved it with this remark: "Sister, these brahmacharins are your disciples and pure souls. If they cook rice, that is also pure. It is repugnant to eat in a hotel or a restaurant in Calcutta, and that food does not give me any satisfaction either.[16]"* Prasanna and Barada were very liberal and never opposed their sister's wishes.

Land for the Mother's Temple

One day in the winter of 1919, Kalikumar was seated on Holy Mother's veranda in a joyful mood — the harvest had been very good that year. Sometime previously devotees from Ranchi had brought two marble stones to be placed on the spot of Holy Mother's birth, but Kalikumar objected. That plot of land was the joint property of all three brothers, so nothing could be done. Kalikumar pointed to the stones, which were lying nearby, and said to Brahmachari Barada: "You see, those stones are lying there all these days and they have not yet been installed on sister's birthplace. If that land is transferred to my sister's name during our lifetime and a temple is built there, then everybody will be happy. It would be a joy to feed people who came to the temple. We should inform Sharat Maharaj [Saradananda]."

Then Kalikumar said to Holy Mother: "Sister, I am ready to transfer my share to you; now you need the consent of our two other brothers. Sharat Maharaj will pay me as he thinks best. It is my sincere and heartfelt desire that this should be done immediately." Holy Mother listened and gave mild approval to her brother's decision but did not show any eagerness. That evening, Holy Mother said to Brahmachari Barada: "My son, please write to Sharat and tell him what Kali said this

* The cooks or chefs in Calcutta hotels and restaurants are not all brahmins, so the issue of the caste system does not arise there.

morning. Since Kali is in favour of this project, I think it is not wise to delay. Kali creates obstacles. Because he himself has raised this issue, it seems it should be done soon. Moreover, Prasanna and Barada are now in Calcutta and they will not object to this proposal. You remember when Narayan Iyenger wanted to dig a well so that everyone could have good drinking water, Kali would not give his consent." The bramachari wrote to Swami Saradananda. The next morning, Holy Mother said to Kaliku-mar: "Look, Kali, Brahmachari Barada has written to Sharat and told him what you said yesterday."

Kalikumar replied: "Sister, you will have to arrange to give me some extra money apart from the estimated price of the land. My family is large and my income small."

Holy Mother said: "Well, if our other brothers know this, they may also demand extra money." In fact all three brothers demanded and received something in addition to their individual share of the sale (300 rupees each). Saradananda did not miss this opportunity. He had the document registered immediately without concern for the cost.[17]

Holy Mother's Nieces

Holy Mother's household in Jayrambati consisted of her three nieces — Radhu, Nalini, and Maku, and her sister-in-law Surabala, a woman cook, and some disciples. Radhu and Maku had children, but Nalini was child-less. Radhu's husband (Manmatha) and Nalini's husband (Pramatha) also lived with her from time to time. One evening Pramatha came to Jayram-bati from Goghat by bullock cart to take Nalini to his home, but as soon as she saw her husband, Nalini closed her door. She threatened to commit suicide if she was forced to go with him. She was ill-treated there, and her husband had financial problems and was dependant on his family. Holy Mother waited outside Nalini's door with a lantern for most of the night. Nalini opened her door only when promised that she would not be sent. Later the Mother remarked: "Nalini does not want to go to her father-in-law's house. Perhaps she has a trace of her aunt's [*referring to herself*] dispassion."[18]

Nalini had a morbid mania for cleanliness and purity. One day in Udbodhan House, Nalini cleaned the toilet and then went to bathe in the Ganges. This surprised Holy Mother because Nalini was not well. Holy Mother told her that she could easily have sanctified herself by sprinkling a little Ganges water on her head. She said: "In Jayrambati I sometimes walked over dry excreta and then repeated 'Govinda, Govinda,' a couple of times. Immediately I felt myself to be pure. Purity and impurity are

arada Devi with her niece Maku at Jayrambati, 1918. Maku is holding her son,
eda.

both in the mind."[19] Another day Golap-ma cleaned the toilet, washed her hands, changed her cloth, and then began to cut fruit for the offering to the Master. Nalini said to her: "Sister Golap, what is this? You better go to the Ganges and have a bath to purify yourself."

Golap-ma replied, "If you wish, you go and have a bath in the Ganges."

Holy Mother said to Nalini: "How pure and high is Golap's mind. That is why she does not discriminate so much about purity and impurity, nor does she bother about external sanctity. This is her last birth."[20]

Nalini and her aunt Surabala were terribly jealous of each other and never got along. They hissed at each other like cobras and often quarrelled about petty matters. This situation is common in a large extended family. Holy Mother always maintained her equanimity and worked to pacify the members of her family. Sometimes she consulted Nalini about household matters to make her feel important. During Durga Puja Holy Mother would send presents to Radhu's husband's family. One year she suggested some items to Nalini and asked for her opinion. Excited, Nalini said: "Aunt, these articles are not enough. Radhu is abnormal and the behaviour of her husband's family may be strange, but you have dignity. You should give generously according to your position."[21] When Nalini added a few items to the list, Holy Mother smiled. If she had not consulted Nalini and sent the presents secretly, Nalini would have been very upset. The Mother was very discreet and tactful when dealing with these sensitive women. The Mother said of her nieces: "I show these girls due respect for their views. Remaining detached, I watch their movements so that they do not go to extremes. One should be humble and give some amount of freedom to all."[22]

Nalini was very sentimental. One day she became very angry for some reason and refused to eat in order to get her aunt's attention. Holy Mother attempted to coax her to eat, but Nalini continued to fast. Finally she told Nalini: "Don't consider me to be merely your aunt. If I wish, I can give up this body right now."[23]

Nalini's sister Maku was very unhappy and restless. She was married at a young age, and her husband was poor. His meager income was not adequate to support his wife and their son. Maku and the boy lived with Holy Mother most of the time, and the Mother took responsibility for them. She sent Maku to school and looked after her son, Neda. Holy Mother always maintained a good relationship with Maku's in-laws and sent presents to them.

In Chapter 19 we described how Maku's son, Neda, died from diphtheria. Holy Mother cried profusely at his death, and realized how much people suffer when their children or other loved ones pass away. When Narayan Iyenger saw Holy Mother weeping, he asked, "Mother, why do you weep like an ordinary person at the death of that child?"

She replied: "I live as a householder. I must taste the fruit of the tree of the world. That is why I weep. The Master once remarked: 'When God is incarnated in a human body, he acts exactly like a man. He feels the same hunger, thirst, sickness, grief, and fear as others do. Even Brahman weeps when caught in the trap of the five elements.'"[24]

Holy Mother's In-Laws

Holy Mother acted as a mother figure in her extended family. Two of her sisters-in-law, Subasini and Indumati, addressed her as "mother." She loved all four of her brothers' wives and helped them physically, spiritually, and financially.

Indumati, Barada's wife, recalled:

I was married when I was 10 or 11 years old. I used to help the Mother in her household. One day she told me: "Look, you are young. Work here carefully. My Master is a living God. It will not be auspicious if you serve Him carelessly." In the beginning the Mother used to cook every day. Nalini and I were young and did not know much about cooking. The Mother told us: "Come to me and learn how to cook. Shall I cook in your household all the year round?" Later, I used to cook fig curry, *amrul* chutney, and *gime* spinach for the Mother, and she praised my cooking. The Mother was fond of my two sons — Kshudiram and Vijaykrishna. I was seriously ill after giving birth to Vijay. The Mother was very concerned and brought three doctors to treat me. She finally blessed me so that I would not have any more children.[25]

Subasini, Prasanna's wife, gave her reminiscences:

One day I was cleaning the Mother's room and found a bundle of notes (50 or 60 rupees) with some old papers. When I handed them over to her, she caressed me by touching my chin with her fingers. She was reluctant to initiate me, but when Gauri-ma insisted she blessed me with initiation.

Once the Mother went to Kamarpukur for a couple of weeks. I sent some lotuses and sweets for her. She said: "No one in my family sends any presents to me except this girl." When the Mother was in Calcutta, I sent a container of tooth powder for her, which I made from roasted tobacco leaf and coconut leaf. Later my husband told me that the Mother praised my thoughtful gift. One day I said to her: "Mother, you have given me a mantra but I do not know sadhana and I cannot concentrate on japa either." She replied: "You are practising sadhana by performing your household duties and serving me — that is enough sadhana for you. Pray to the Master for devotion."

The day before Jagaddhatri Puja, my daughter Bimala's foot became swollen. Soon after, she developed a high fever and lost consciousness. Dr. Vaikuntha Maharaj gave up hope. I grasped the Mother's feet and cried for her blessing. I took a little water, touched it to the Mother's toe, and put it in my daughter's mouth. Holy Mother caressed Bimala's body and then stood in front of the image of Jagaddhatri, praying with tearful eyes: "Mother, you will be worshipped here tomorrow. Is it your wish that my sister-in-law will cry for her daughter?" The next day Bimala regained consciousness. The Mother taught me: "Have the company of holy people and that will protect you from obstacles. Serve all with loving care. Even a wild animal comes under control through love."[26]

Once Holy Mother admonished Kalikumar's wife, Subodhbala: "Look, you are worn out and disheveled raising one or two children and cannot take care of them properly. I, however, without giving birth am raising thousands of children. Some of them are monks, some are wicked or crazy. They all come to me for guidance. How will you understand this? You do not have wisdom or common sense. You only know about money, rice, the paddy bin, your house, and your belongings. As you have come to this world, in the same way you will depart. It is said: 'It is a great fortune to have a human birth.' What have you achieved with this precious human life?"[27]

Sometimes we try to visualize how Holy Mother, a divine being, participated in the birth, marriage, and death ceremonies of her family. While she was in Dakshineswar, Ramakrishna sent her to Kamarpukur to attend the wedding of his nephew Ramlal. She was also present at the marriage ceremony of Ramlal's youngest daughter, Radha. The Mother was very fond of her nephew Bhudeb, a son of Kalikumar. During Bhudeb's wedding on 7 May 1913, she worked so hard that her feet swelled. Bhudeb was 13 years old when he was married, and his wife Elokeshi was about 10. One day Subodhbala was admonishing her daughter-in-law, and Holy Mother intervened: "Keep quiet — keep quiet! Elo [Elokeshi] is an innocent girl. You have brought her home and so much music was played during her marriage ceremony! Don't scold her. She is a sweet girl!"[28]

Holy Mother made everyone her own through love, and she taught others to do the same. The Mother initiated six members of her family: Subasini; Maku; Radhu and her husband, Manmatha; and Bhudeb and his wife, Elokeshi.[29]

Radhu's husband was not an easy person to live with. He came from a wealthy family, but he was lazy, foppish, undisciplined, and extravagant. He was not well suited to living in the household of Holy Mother, who was always surrounded by monastics and devotees. However, the Mother absorbed Manmatha into her family and accommodated his way of life for Radhu's sake. In Udbodhan House, Manmatha had a harmonium that he played while he sang, and devotees would bring meat curry for him. When the Mother was in Koalpara with Radhu, Manmatha sometimes came to stay. Although he was living in a monastery, he did not care for the routine. Once during the vesper service, Manmatha was chatting and singing with his friends. The abbot mildly reproached him, and he angrily left Koalpara that night. When the Mother heard about this, she sent someone to him the next day to bring him back.[30]

Once in Jayrambati, Manmatha asked Holy Mother to give him 200 rupees to pay his property tax or his estate would be auctioned. The Mother did not have that much money; she lived on donations from devotees. Nalini saw how anxious Holy Mother was, so she suggested that some of Radhu's jewellery be pawned to raise the money. The Mother followed Nalini's advice and took two pieces of Radhu's jewellery to Jogindra Biswas, the village mailman, who also made loans. He was very surprised that Holy Mother had come to him to borrow 200 rupees. However, he loaned her the money, which she gave to Manmatha. When Manmatha left, the Mother lamented: "Radhu's marriage went wrong. Kalikumar arranged this marriage because Manmatha came from a wealthy landlord's family. But now Manmatha pesters me for money." Then she dictated a letter to Saradananda asking for 200 rupees from the interest of her investment in Balaram's estate to retrieve Radhu's jewellery.[31]

Happiness and misery, disease and death, union and separation, affluence and poverty, misunderstanding and quarrelling, selfishness and unselfishness, dharma and adharma are all parts of family life. As soon as human beings enter this world, they taste the sweet and bitter fruits of the tree of samsara, or relative existence. Holy Mother experienced both in her human birth. She tried to create a peaceful and joyful atmosphere in her family, but did not always succeed. Although she was endowed with supreme divine power, she did not want to change Providence. Regarding her dealings with Surabala, Radhu's mother, we observe the Mother's infinite patience, perseverance, compassion, and forgiveness.

In early February 1907, Surabala went to visit her father at Majte in Midnapore District. She carried her jewellery and Radhu's jewellery with her in a small box because she did not trust anyone in Jayrambati. Her greedy father, however, cleverly took the jewellery box from his insane daughter and kept it. This aggravated Surabala's madness, and when she returned to Jayrambati she went to the Simhavahini temple and began to cry, saying, "Mother, give me my jewellery; give me my jewellery." It was evening and Holy Mother was talking with Rasbihari (Swami Arupananda). Suddenly she said: "My son, Surabala is crying to Mother Simhavahini for her jewellery. She has no one except me. I must go." Holy Mother brought Surabala home. Then Surabala accused Holy Mother, saying, "Sister-in-law, you have taken all my jewellery for yourself."

Holy Mother replied: "If I had that jewellery, I would throw it away this moment, as I would the filth of a crow." She then told Rasbihari, "Girish used to say that Surabala was born as my mad companion."

Soon afterwards Holy Mother sent Rasbihari with a servant to Surabala's father and asked him to return the jewellery or to come and see her. He came to see Holy Mother, but did not bring the jewellery. Holy Mother fell at his feet and begged him, "Please save me from this terrible situation." But the old brahmin did not relent. Finding no alternative, Holy Mother wrote a letter to Saradananda informing him of the matter. The swami consulted with M. and Lalit Chattopadhyay, and both agreed to help. Before leaving Calcutta, Lalit obtained a letter from a high-ranking police officer. Lalit and M. first went to Jayrambati. Dressed in a Western suit, Lalit went to the Badanganj police station by palanquin and showed the letter to the officer in charge. Accompanied by a few constables, he then went to Surabala's father, acting as if he were a high-ranking police officer. Holy Mother was very concerned lest Lalit humiliate the old brahmin, so she made certain that M. followed him. Before evening, M. and Lalit returned to Jayrambati with Surabala's father and the jewellery box, which he handed over to Holy Mother. Although the episode ended there, Holy Mother became very sick that night with terrible dizziness. When asked about the cause of her illness, she replied: "When they left to collect the jewellery, I had severe anxiety lest that old brahmin be humiliated, and that caused this dizziness."[32]

On 11 February 1913 Holy Mother was at Udbodhan House and Surabala's abuse reached its limit. Surabala complained that the Mother had used drugs to hold her daughter captive, and that she spent money on her other relatives without saving anything for her daughter. Holy Mother said to her: "Do not regard me as an ordinary human being. You do not abuse me alone, but my father and mother also. I do not take offense. I say to myself that these are mere words. If I were really offended, then who would protect you? As long as I am alive, things will be well with you. Your daughter will remain yours. I shall look after her as long as she cannot stand on her own feet. Do you think I have any maya? This very moment I could cut all attachments. Someday I shall vanish like camphor in the air, and you will not even know it."

Surabala then changed her tone and said: "When did I show disrespect to your father? I never did. All I meant was that if you want to give something to a person, you give him everything." Surabala wanted the Mother to leave everything to Radhu. Holy Mother told her: "I have a childlike nature. I don't have a calculating mind. I give to any person who wants my help."[33]

After her bath, the Mother would pray: "O Divine Mother, please do good to all beings." Surabala used to scold and say all sorts of things to the Mother, but the Mother ignored them. One day Surabala said to the Mother, "You are a *sarvanashi*, a destroyer of all." Immediately the Mother cautioned her: "You can say whatever you wish, but never call me sarvanashi. My children are all over the world and such a curse will be harmful to them."[34]

Surabala could occasionally be humorous. One day in Udbodhan House Holy Mother was decorating the Master's picture with flowers and sandal paste before beginning the worship. With a twinkle in her eye Surabala said to a woman devotee: "Look, what is the Mother doing? She is decorating her husband with her own hands." She would even, on rare occasions, show respect to Holy Mother. Once in Jayrambati, Radhu was ill and the Mother was feeding her milk. Surabala came to see Radhu and inadvertently the Mother's hand touched her feet. Surabala immediately cried out: "What will happen to me? Why did you touch my feet?"* Holy Mother laughed aloud at this show of respect and said to a disciple: "Ravana knew fully well that Rama was Narayana Himself, the Supreme Brahman, and that Sita was the Primordial Power, the Mother of the Universe. Still he did not refrain from ill-treating Sita. Surabala also knows who I am. She is fully aware of it. Yet she must play her part."[35]

One day in Jayrambati, Subasini and Surabala were quarrelling. Prasanna came to Holy Mother and said: "Sister, this is unbearable. Please settle their fight." Meanwhile both sisters-in-law came to the Mother and Surabala began to abuse her. The Mother calmly said to her: "Look, as long as I am in this family, Brahma, Vishnu, and Shiva will dwell in this household. As soon as I leave, there will be no end to your misery."[36]

Tormented by her insane sister-in-law, Holy Mother once remarked: "My mind is eager to soar high into a spiritual plane. I feel compassion

---

*According to the Hindu tradition if a holy person touches an ordinary person's feet, it is very inauspicious. The ordinary person at once asks forgiveness.

for them and keep it down. And what do I get in return? Only abuse and insults."[37]

Once Holy Mother said to Surabala: "You are so proud of a daughter who is whining, whimpering, and sniffling all the time. Look at them," she continued, pointing to her devotees, "my wonderful jewel-like children. I am the Mother without giving birth to any child."[38]

Radhu and Manmatha were Surabala's mainstay. She felt insecure if she was not with them. Unfortunately, her mental disorder sometimes caused her to have delusions concerning the pair. One day while she was cooking in Jayrambati, the thought of Manmatha suddenly came to her mind. She searched for Manmatha in the house but could not find him. Then she thought perhaps he had gone to bathe in the Banerjee's pond. She went there and began to search in the water. When she could not find him, she concluded that he must have drowned. She returned to the house, fell at Holy Mother's feet, and burst into tears, crying: "Sister-in-law, my son-in-law has drowned in the Banerjee's pond. What will happen now?" Startled, the Mother called loudly for her disciples and told them what Surabala had said. Hari responded, "Just now I saw Manmatha playing cards in a shop." Holy Mother asked her disciples to bring him home right then. They went to the shop and escorted him to the Mother. Surabala was ashamed and embarrassed when she saw Manmatha and immediately went to her room. Holy Mother was greatly relieved.

One afternoon a few days later, Holy Mother was cutting vegetables on the veranda of her house. Brahmachari Barada was writing letters in the front room. Suddenly Surabala appeared in the courtyard and said to Holy Mother: "You are feeding my daughter opium. You have made her a cripple in order to exercise control over her. You do not allow my daughter and grandson to come near me."

Holy Mother replied with utter detachment: "There is your daughter. Take her away. Have I hidden her?" But Surabala was determined to pick a quarrel and became flushed with anger. She picked up a piece of firewood from the kitchen veranda and was about to strike the Mother with it. The Mother cried out aloud: "Who is there? O Barada, come quickly. This insane woman is going to kill me." Barada rushed to the spot and found Surabala about to hit the Mother's head. He hurriedly snatched the firewood from her hand, and then drove her from the house and forbade her to enter it again. Agitated, the Mother forgot herself momentarily and said: "You mad woman, what were you about to do? Your hand will wither away." The next moment she regretted her slip and bit her tongue. She folded her hands and prayed to the Master: "Oh Master, what have

I done? My lips have never uttered any curses. At long last, that too has happened. Why live anymore?"* Barada saw the Mother weeping and was astonished by her compassion. Shortly after Holy Mother passed away, Surabala was attacked with leprosy. She began to lose her fingers, and before long she died.

Bhavini, a Cousin of Holy Mother

Bhavini lived with her mother next to Holy Mother's house in Jayrambati. Holy Mother's attendants looked after Bhavini's mother, who was not well, and Holy Mother regularly gave them vegetables, fruit, and other necessities. One day she gave two pomegranates to Bhavini for her mother. While Bhavini was there a big parcel of fruit arrived from Ranchi. Bhavini heaved a sigh and commented: "Ah, at first it was proposed that I marry Paramahamsadeva [Sri Ramakrishna], but my father did not give me in marriage to him, considering him to be mad. If I had been married to him, then all these things would have come to me. I would not have to depend on anybody; rather I would distribute these things to others."

At this, Holy Mother and the other people in the household laughed. She said to Bhavini: "It does not matter that you were not married to the Paramahamsa. Please take whatever you need." She then said to Brahmachari Barada: "Keep a few fruits for the Master, and give some papayas, pomegranates, and other fruits to Bhavini."[39]

Mother's Detachment

Swami Satyaswarupananda, a disciple of the Mother, related this incident:

Holy Mother was in Udbodhan preparing to leave for Jayrambati. Swami Saradananda asked Ashok and Rasbihari to help the Mother pack. Saradananda bought a beautiful and expensive mosquito curtain for the Mother's use in Jayrambati, which Rasbihari put in the Mother's trunk. In the evening, the Mother left for Howrah Station with her companions and those two attendants. The train arrived at Vishnupur Station very early in the morning. They travelled by bullock carts for the rest of their journey, reaching Jayrambati before evening. Ashok and Rasbihari carried the Mother's luggage to her room and then went to their cottage. When the Mother was unpacking, Uncle Kali came to inquire about his sister. When he saw the mosquito curtain, he grabbed it and said, "Sister, you will have to give this one to me." As he said this, he put it under his arm and left. The Mother stood there like a speechless spectator.

*This happened during Holy Mother's last visit to Jayrambati, and a few months later she passed away.

After supper, Ashok and Rasbihari came to make the Mother's bed and set up the mosquito curtain. They could not find it even after searching through all the clothes in the trunk. They asked the Mother about it, but she remained silent. Finally, she said, "My sons, Kali wanted so I gave to him." Rasbihari said: "Mother, Sharat Maharaj gave it to you for your use and you did not use it even for a day. What will he think?"

Mother replied "My son, what can I do? You set up the old mosquito curtain for me."

Helpless, they followed the Mother's order and left the room. While walking to their cottage, they met Uncle Kali in the courtyard as he was returning to the Mother's cottage. Both of them grabbed Kali's arms and insisted, "Uncle, where is the mosquito curtain? Please return it to the Mother."

Uncle Kali replied, "Sister gave it to me."

"No, she didn't give it to you; you have taken it."

Then Uncle Kali shouted, "Sister, your attendants are going to kill me!"

The Mother rushed to the courtyard when she heard the cry. Meanwhile, Uncle Kali broke out of their grip, ran to his room, and closed the door.

The Mother mildly reprimanded her attendants: "You are monks. You should have detachment. It is not proper to quarrel over a petty mosquito curtain."

Observing the Mother's nonattachment and forbearance, they went to their room.[40]

The Divine Drama

After reading this chapter, the reader might wonder why Holy Mother endured all these trials. Why was this divine being surrounded by selfish, jealous, quarrelsome, and greedy relatives? She could easily have had a joyful and comfortable life in Calcutta with her wonderful devotees and disciples. The reader should remember that Holy Mother was acting in her divine drama: she needed both good and bad characters in her play. A drama cannot be interesting if there is no friction between good and evil. The more the hero or heroine of the play is opposed, persecuted, and ill-treated, the more that character shines and arouses affection in the audience. For example, when in a performance, Sita is abducted by Ravana, or Dushashan publicly humiliates Draupadi, the viewers' love and sympathy wells up for Sita and Draupadi, and at the same time, they are filled with anger and abhorrence towards the villains. In her own drama, Holy Mother selected bad and worldly roles for some of her relatives and good and spiritual roles for her devotees — just as Ramakrishna had done before her.

21
Pilgrimage
in South India

Bhavad-vidhā bhāgavatāh tirthabhutāh svayam vibho;
Tirthi kurvanti tirthāni svāntah-sthena gadābhritā.
— *Bhagavata, 1:13:10*

Yudhishthira to Vidura: O great one, lovers of God like you, having yourselves risen to the height of holiness, sanctify the holy places by your visit, bringing the presence of Narayana, who resides in you.

Travel breaks the monotony of daily life, drawing people to explore new places, new people, new cultures, and new languages.

Spiritual pilgrims are a special type of traveller: they seek to breathe the freshness of the eternal. Pilgrims travel to broaden their outlook and education, destroy their self-centredness and narrowness, eradicate their physical lethargy and mental laziness, and enhance their love and hunger for God. They get inspiration from the saints and sages who have resided in the holy places they visit, and they also come in contact with many other seekers of God. The ancient sages remind us that all people are pilgrims, and this world is but a temporary place for pilgrimage. We must live here as pilgrims without worldly attachments and must always go onward towards the goal. Pilgrims understand this: The world is a bridge. Pass over it, but build no house upon it.

The longest journey is the journey to the inmost Self. Holy Mother had completed her inward journey when she was young, but after the Master's passing away she began to travel in India to distribute her spiritual treasures. It had not been possible for Ramakrishna to travel far because he was in an ecstatic state most of the time.

Generally people go on a pilgrimage to purify themselves and attain virtue, but spiritual giants like Holy Mother and the Master went to purify those places of pilgrimage and make them holy. When sinners bathe in the Ganges, the goddess Ganges absorbs their sins and makes them pure. However, when holy people bathe, She gains virtue and gives

Sarada Devi in Calcutta, 1905.

back peace and bliss. Holy Mother was so pure that the redeeming power of the Ganges, Jamuna, Saraju, Lake Pushkar, and Godavari increased a hundredfold when she bathed in those holy waters.

Holy Mother travelled from Hardwar in the north at the foothills of the Himalayas to Rameswaram in the south on the coast of the Indian Ocean, and from Rajasthan's Lake Pushkar in the west to Puri in the east on the Bay of Bengal. She travelled throughout India, covering Andhra Pradesh, Bihar, Karnataka, Orissa, Rajasthan, Tamil Nadu, Uttar Pradesh, and West Bengal.

In June 1909, shortly after Holy Mother moved to Udbodhan House, her new Calcutta residence, she was laid up with chicken pox. After her recovery she stayed in Calcutta a few months and then on 16 November she went back to Jayrambati. Over a year later, in July 1910, she was still feeling unwell. Krishnabhavini, Balaram's wife, asked Holy Mother to visit Kothar in Orissa where her family owned an estate. She hoped that the change of climate would restore Holy Mother's health. Holy Mother agreed and left Calcutta on 5 December 1910, accompanied by Golap-ma, Radhu, Surabala, Swami Atmananda, Swami Dhirananda, Ashu, and Krishnabhavini and her sister-in-law (Nitai's mother). Shantiram (Premananda's brother) reserved a second class compartment for the women and bought inter-class tickets for Holy Mother's attendants.

The train arrived at the Bhadrak station close to midnight, and Balaram's son, Ram, along with Premananda's brother, Tulsiram, received Holy Mother and her party and took them to their Bhadrak residence. They rested there that night, and in the morning the women left for Kothar by palanquin. They reached there by noon after covering nearly 16 miles. Later the monks and devotees came with the luggage by bullock cart.

At Kothar in Orissa

Balaram's family was wealthy and they owned a lot of property and farmland in Orissa. Their Kothar estate had a large house at the back of the property and an office compound in the front. The Mother and her women companions lived in the house, and the men lived in the office quarters. The house has 17 rooms and a garden behind it. Near the house there is a big pond, named Krishna Sagar, surrounded by trees. Holy Mother bathed in this pond during her stay in Kothar.

Balaram's family members were Vaishnavas, and they had a Radha-Shyam temple in Kothar. Apart from the daily worship, they observed various festivals and held yatra performances in the front hall of the temple, which neighbours and people from other villages attended. Holy

Mother attended the Saraswati Puja. As part of the festivities, two young boys acted in the roles of Krishna and Radha. They sang and performed a folk dance called *Guti ponach,* which Holy Mother and her companions enjoyed so much that another performance was given the next evening. The following day the image of Saraswati was immersed in the family pond. On the day of Saraswati Puja, Holy Mother initiated Ramakrishna Basu (Balaram's son) and his wife.

Devendra Nath Chattopadhyay, the local postmaster, had in his youth converted to Christianity in order to marry a Christian girl. The marriage did not last, however, and the girl soon left him. Repentant, Devendra desperately wanted to return to his Hindu religion, but none gave him any hope.* When Holy Mother arrived at Kothar, Devendra talked to Ashu and other monks about his situation. When Ashu and Ram placed the matter before Holy Mother, she agreed to initiate Devendra on the day of Saraswati Puja. According to the Mother's suggestion, on the previous day the priest of the Radha-Shyam temple performed an expiatory ritual for Devendra, who shaved his head, drank *charanamrita* (sanctified water from the temple), and received the sacred thread and the Gayatri mantra from Swami Dhirananda. The next day Holy Mother initiated him and presented him with a cloth. Thus blessed by the Mother, Devendra was accepted by the Hindu community and he shared prasad with the assembled devotees.

Kothar is a rural place with a scenic and quiet ambience. Holy Mother lived there for 66 days and her health improved significantly. She felt relaxed and moved around the village freely, as if she were in Jayrambati. She initiated quite a few people in Kothar. During the Christmas season she initiated three devotees who had travelled to Kothar from Shillong.[1] One of her disciples noticed that Holy Mother was a vegetarian, so he also gave up eating fish and meat. When she encouraged him to resume his old habits, the disciple referred to her own vegetarianism. The Mother replied: "Do you think that I eat only through one mouth? Don't be foolish. I am asking you to eat fish and meat."[2] The disciple obeyed her.

A young man from Cuttack named Vaikuntha visited Holy Mother at Kothar at the behest of his elder brother, who worked for Ramkrishna Basu's estate. Although his brother was a devotee, Vaikuntha did not know much about Ramakrishna and Holy Mother. When Ram introduced Vaikuntha to the Mother, he simply bowed down to her and left

*At that time orthodox Hindu society was very strict about accepting people from other faiths into the Hindu religion.

for home after lunch. However, divine grace dawns on pure souls: Vai-kuntha soon felt a deep longing to see the Mother again, so he returned to Kothar and stayed for a few days. When he went to Holy Mother to take leave, she asked him to stay another day. After a while the Mother's attendant told him that she wished to bestow grace on him. The atten-dant asked him to bathe in the morning and to keep himself ready. Radhu called Vaikuntha the next morning. When he went to the Mother's room, she asked him to sit down and asked, "Will you accept initiation?" Vai-kuntha replied: "If you are pleased, kindly give it to me. I know nothing about it." Holy Mother selected a suitable mantra and gave him initia-tion.[3] Vaikuntha asked, "Mother, can one accept another guru to learn yoga?" She replied, "Yes, you may have teachers to learn other things, but you should not have another mantra-guru." The Mother poured her love and affection on this young man. When he was leaving, the Mother gave him some sweets to eat on the way and asked him not to eat food from the market.

At Kothar the Mother experienced various spiritual moods. One day Ashu found her seated alone. Her eyes were open but she was completely oblivious to her surroundings. After some time her eyes fell on Ashu, who had been waiting there for 15 minutes. Holy Mother remarked: "I don't like to be confined to my room all the time, so when everyone else rests after lunch, I sit in this solitary place." (In Calcutta also, she sometimes sat alone on the roof.) The Mother was in an exalted mood. She began to speak:

> Is there no end of this coming to the world again and again? Where there is Shiva, there is Shakti. Shiva and Shakti incarnate again and again to deliver human beings from the bondage of maya. As the same moon rises again and again, so the same God incarnates to look after His own creation and beings. The Master practised austerities and suffered for others. It is all his play. The Master was a Kalpataru, a wish-fulfilling tree. Those who sincerely seek him, find him.
>
> Sometimes I see the Master has become everything. I see the Master in whatever direction I look. I see him in the blind and in the lame. He has become every being. The beings are not suffering; it is he who is suffering. So whenever people cry to me, I rush to deliver them. Here people ask me to sleep. How can I sleep? I think the time I shall spend in sleeping is better spent doing japa that will benefit human beings.
>
> The other day I saw that Radhu was about to kill an ant. I stopped her. I saw the Master in that ant. At any rate, how many people can I see? The Master left the responsibility for all on me. It would be nice if I could look after everyone.[4]

Soon, the sounds of the vesper bell and conch reverberated in the temple, and the Mother left to attend the service.

Another afternoon Ashu went to Holy Mother to help her answer the devotees' letters. In the course of conversation she inquired about the distance to Rameswaram: "How far is Rameswaram? How many days does it take to reach there?" Ashu understood that the Mother wanted to visit, so he said: "Mother, let us go to Rameswaram. One can go there by this rail route. Shashi Maharaj [Swami Ramakrishnananda] is in Madras and he will arrange everything." Holy Mother was as excited as a little girl, and said: "You have given the right suggestion. My father-in-law went there and brought back the Shiva linga that is worshipped in Kamarpukur. I shall go."[5]

It seems that the Mother had been thinking of this pilgrimage for some time. Probably she was drawn to see a place that had been important in her past incarnation as Sita. When letters were sent to Swamis Brahmananda, Saradananda, and Ramakrishnananda informing them of the Mother's wish to go on pilgrimage, they immediately approved it. Of course, they were also concerned about her health as she had gone to Kothar to recuperate, but in fact she now felt well.

Swami Saradananda sent sufficient money to Kothar through Kishori Roy, so that the Mother could travel with her party. Swami Ramakrishnananda, who was in charge of the Madras Math, made elaborate arrangements for the Mother's journey and reception. He had always cherished a desire to sanctify South India by bringing Holy Mother and Swami Brahmananda there, because Ramakrishna had never been there himself.

Holy Mother asked Dhirananda to write to Ramakrishnananda and tell him that as the distance between Kothar and Madras is long, it would be better if she could break her journey somewhere en route. As justification for Holy Mother's request, Dhirananda wrote: "First, she performs daily worship to the Master; second, she might get rheumatic pain if she sits long hours on the train, and moreover Radhu might be restless. We feel it would be better if the Mother could break her journey at Berhampore in Ganjam, a border town between Orissa and Andhra Pradesh. It would be wonderful if you could find someone there who could host the Mother and her party for a day. The Mother further advised me to inform you that it is not necessary for you to come here to accompany her as we are all going with her." Accordingly, Ramakrishnananda arranged for Holy Mother and her party to spend a night at the home of a Bengali devotee who was the manager of the Kelner Company, the caterer for the railways.

Finally, the date of departure from Kothar was fixed: Wednesday, 8 February 1911. Surabala had earlier returned to Jayrambati because of her mental illness, but the Mother sent Ashu to bring her and also Kedar Datta's mother to go with her to Rameswaram. The party left at two o'clock in the afternoon and arrived at Bhadrak in the evening. Ramlal was waiting there to join them. The party consisted of 13 members — Holy Mother, Radhu, Surabala, Golap-ma, Krishnabhavini and her sister-in-law (Nitai's mother), Kedar's mother, Swamis Atmananda and Dhirananda, Ashu, Ramlal, a brahmin cook named Gadadhar, and a woman attendant.

After eating supper at Bhadrak, the Mother boarded a second-class compartment on the Madras Mail at two-thirty in the morning. At dawn, when the train was passing near the Chilka Lake, Holy Mother was delighted to see flock after flock of white cranes flying, then landing on islands in the lake to search for food. With the sunrise, a mist taking various forms arose from the water. The Mother enjoyed the natural scenery and pointed it out to others. When she saw a flock of Nilkantha birds, she saluted them with folded hands.

The train arrived at Berhampore at eight o'clock in the morning. The Bengali devotee received Holy Mother and her party and took them to his house, where Holy Mother and her party ate lunch and rested. In the afternoon several local devotees visited her, bringing bananas and coconuts as was their custom. The party stayed the night and then took another Madras Mail in the morning. In the afternoon, when the train was passing through Waltair, a health resort, Holy Mother saw the beautiful cottages on the slopes of the mountain. She joyfully exclaimed, "Just see, it looks like a picture." At night the Mother slept on the upper bunk of the compartment.

At Madras

The train reached Madras at noon the next day, Saturday, 11 February 1911. Ramakrishnananda and some local devotees were at the station with three automobiles, and they received the Mother and her party with great enthusiasm. Holy Mother rode in an automobile for the first time. As her seat was hot because of the sun, Ramakrishnananda wiped the seat repeatedly with a wet chadar. A two-storey building named Sundar Vilas (now 221 Ramakrishna Math Road), which was opposite the Madras Math, had been rented for her. Special food arrangements had been made for the Mother and her companions. Ramakrishnananda collected various kinds of vegetables, fruit, *papadam,* and other things from

Madras, Bangalore, and Trivandrum. It is natural that we love to feed and serve a person whom we love. At Holy Mother's request Ramakrishna-nanda took his lunch and dinner at the Mother's place while she was there.

Ramakrishnananda was then not well at all. Since March 1910 he had been suffering from severe complications of diabetes, and towards the end of that year his feet were aching because of a minor accident. More-over, in the beginning of 1911 he developed tuberculosis and was suffer-ing from cough and fever, but the disease was diagnosed only after Holy Mother returned to Calcutta from her South Indian pilgrimage. Rama-krishnananda, however, forgot his body and served the Mother along with his assistants and her devotees, including Ramaswami, Ramanuja, Rangaswami, Gopalan, and others. The Mother and her party stayed in Madras for nearly a month. During the day, the swami stayed at the Mother's residence like a gatekeeper. He would ask her: "Mother, please let me know if you need anything or have any difficulties."

Although the Madras Math was suffering financial difficulties at that time, Ramakrishnananda lavishly spent money for the Mother's pilgrim-age in South India. He was able to do this by collecting funds from devo-tees to make the Mother's stay and pilgrimage in the South comfortable. Before the Mother arrived, Ramakrishnananda wrote to Dr. P. Venkata-rangam of Bangalore on 2 February 1911:

> My dear doctor,
> A very happy news for you. Our most Holy Mother is on her way to Rameswaram. She is coming here to bless all of you. You should not lose this very rare and unexpected opportunity to worship the Motherhood of God in her. She is your real Mother. Come and be blessed by her. She is expected here on the 11th of this month. Please collect as much money as you can from your friends and admirers of our Mission. We shall have to meet the expenses of a large party consisting of ten souls. See that our Holy Mother does not lack for anything. Feel within your being that the whole responsibility is on you and you alone. It is so fortunate that you are to have the Mother of the Universe at your very door! Come to worship her as soon as she places her holy feet on this soil. With my best love and blessings.
>
> Yours affectionately,
> Ramakrishnananda[6]

Holy Mother's visit created a festive atmosphere in Madras, and many people came to see her from different places. She initiated many devotees including Brahmachari Amritananda, an American. Neither the Mother nor her new disciples understood one another's language, and yet they were able to follow her instructions regarding japa and meditation without the help of an interpreter. In general conversation, however, her attendants helped her communicate. Several of the new disciples had seen the Master and Holy Mother in dreams. Holy Mother said later: "When asking for initiation they all just repeated the word 'dream.'"[7]

About her Madras trip, she later recalled: "Many people visited me there. The women of those parts are very educated. They asked me to deliver a lecture. I said to them: 'I do not know how to deliver lectures. If Gaurdasi [Gauri-ma] had come, she would have been able to do so.'"[8]

Almost every afternoon, Swami Ramakrishnananda arranged visits for Holy Mother to places of interest in Madras by horse carriage. Holy Mother visited the famous Parthasarathi temple in Triplicane and the Kapalishwara Shiva temple in Mylapore. One day she walked on the beach and saw the Madras Aquarium. Another day she visited the British fort in Madras by rickshaw, which had been recently introduced in the city. One day women teachers of the girls' school sang some Tamil devotional songs to her while the girls played violins. On 2 March 1911, the Mother attended Ramakrishna's birth anniversary celebration; on Sunday, 5 March 1911, she attended the public festival. The Mother was moved by the devotion of the South Indian devotees.

In Madras, Nitai's mother was stricken with typhoid fever, so Holy Mother's pilgrimage to Rameswaram was temporarily postponed. When it was understood that it would take a long time for the patient to recover and because Ramlal's vacation was limited, it was decided that the Mother's pilgrimage should not be delayed. A nurse was engaged to look after Nitai's mother, who stayed in Madras. Holy Mother and her party, including Ramakrishnananda, left Madras on 11 March 1911 by night train and reached Madurai in the morning. Rao Sahib K.V. Ramachari, the chairman of the local municipality, hosted Holy Mother and the group.

At Madurai and Rameswaram

Holy Mother and her party went to visit the famous Meenakshi-Sundareswarar Temple located in the holy city of Madurai. The temple is dedicated to the Divine Mother Parvati and Lord Shiva, and it is the heart and lifeline of the 2,500-year-old city of Madurai. The temple complex contains 14 magnificent towers, including two golden towers for the main deities that are elaborately sculpted and painted. The temple, which has five entrances, covers an area 847 feet (254.1 meters) long by 792 feet (237.6 meters) wide in the north-south direction. The tallest temple tower is 170

Above: Meenakshi temple in Madurai.
Below: Rameswara Shiva temple in Rameswaram.

feet (51.9 metres) high. The four-foot-high image of Mother Meenakshi, decorated with clothes, ornaments, and garlands, is gorgeous.

Holy Mother and her companions bathed in the Shivaganga, a pond adjacent to the temple and then visited the deities. Afterwards, following the local custom, everyone in the party lighted lamps on the bank of the Shivaganga in their respective names.

During Holy Mother's stay at Madurai, she and her party saw the huge palace of Tirumal Nayaka, which is supported by 125 stone pillars, and also Teppakulam Lake, which is 1,000 by 950 feet. In the centre of that large lake there is a beautiful temple on a small island. Seeing all these vast and magnificent temples and sights, the Mother remarked: "How wonderful is the Master's lila!"[9]

The party left Madurai at noon by train and reached Mandapam Station. They crossed the Pamban Strait by a steamer and boarded another train at Pamban, reaching Rameswaram at 11 o'clock that night. (Nowadays pilgrims can go to Rameswaram directly, by train or by car.) Holy Mother was quite exhausted during this segment of the journey. By previous arrangement, the priest Gangaram Pitambar had rented a house in Rameswaram for the Mother and her companions. They rested that night, and the next day they bathed in the Indian Ocean and then went to worship Lord Rameswar Shiva in the temple.

According to the *Rameswaram Sthala Purana*, Ramachandra incurred a sin by killing the demon king Ravana, a great devotee of Shiva who was born to the great brahmin sage Vishravas. Some rishis advised Rama to worship Lord Shiva within an auspicious time to expiate the sin of killing a brahmin. Rama asked his devotee Hanuman to bring a Shiva linga from Varanasi. But Hanuman did not arrive within the stipulated time, so Sita hurriedly made an image of Shiva with sand. Rama worshipped this image. The name of the image is Rama-lingam, or Rameswara (the Lord of Rama). When Hanuman brought his image, Rama installed it next to the first one, and it is called Vishwa-lingam. To reward Hanuman for his devotion, Rama told him that rituals would be performed first to the image he had brought. This made Hanuman happy.

The Rameswaram temple is spread over an area of 15 acres and has lofty towers (gopurams), massive walls, and a colossal statue of Nandi, Shiva's bull, measuring 12 feet long and 9 feet high. The Rameswaram Jyotirlinga also boasts a 4,000-foot long pillared corridor with more than 4,000 pillars, supposedly the longest such corridor in the world. The carved granite pillars are mounted on raised platforms. The eastern tower rises to a height of 126 feet and has nine levels. The western tower is also quite impressive though not as tall as the eastern one. The temple has several halls (mandapams) with small shrines to other deities. High walls enclose the temple forming a rectangle with huge towers providing entrances on each side.

After crossing two corridors from the main entrance, one can reach the sandstone image of Lord Rameswara, which is placed in a basin (kunda). It is about nine inches high and is covered with a gold crown and gold decorations. One can see the uncovered image only during the early morning service. Priests use only Ganges water for bathing Lord Rameswara and cooking His food. No pilgrim is allowed to enter the inner sanctum.

At the time of Holy Mother's visit, the island where the Rameswara temple complex is located was under the jurisdiction of the Raja of Ramnad, Rajeswar Setupati. His father, Bhaskar Setupati, had been a disciple of Swami Vivekananda.* Rajeswar Setupati sent a special message to the temple authorities in advance saying that the guru of his father's guru would be visiting the temple. As a result, all restrictions were withdrawn for Holy Mother and her companions. Holy Mother was allowed to enter the inner sanctuary and worship Lord Rameswara with Ganges water and 108 gold bel leaves, which had been procured by Ramakrishnananda in Madras.

Holy Mother and her party stayed at Rameswaram for three nights, and Holy Mother worshipped the Lord every day. She also attended the vesper service and watched the lighted festival image sitting in a palanquin and being worshipped with music and dance. On the third day of her visit, she performed a special worship following ancient traditions and listened to a recital of the glory of Rameswara from the old scriptures. She also fed the priests and presented a water pot to each of them.

The Raja of Ramnad had given orders to his officers to open the royal treasury for Holy Mother and offer her anything she asked for. The Mother later recalled:

Ah, Shashi [Ramakrishnananda] arranged my worship of Lord Rameswara by supplying 108 gold bel leaves. When the Raja of Ramnad heard that I had come to Rameswaram, he ordered his minister to show me the treasury of the temple, and if I liked to have anything, that it should be immediately presented to me. I could not think of anything. At last I said: 'I don't need anything. Shashi is supplying everything we need.' Again thinking they might be hurt, I said: 'Well, if Radhu needs anything, she may have it.' Then I told Radhu that she could have anything she wanted. My heart

---

*Rajeswar Setupati ruled from 1903 to 1928, while his father Bhaskar Setupati, a disciple of Swami Vivekananda, ruled from 1873 to 1902.

began to palpitate seeing those precious diamonds and jewels. I fervently prayed to the Master that Radhu might not ask for any of these. Radhu looked at those treasures and said: 'What shall I take from here? I don't require these things. I have lost my pencil. You may buy one for me.' At this, I heaved a sigh of relief. After the tour, I bought a two-pice pencil for her from a roadside shop.[10]

When people go on a pilgrimage, they buy various gifts and mementos for their loved ones at home. Holy Mother was not an exception. We would love to have seen the Mother shopping in the gift shops of Rameswaram. She bought a pencil for Radhu and photos of each of the two Shiva lingams that are in the main shrine of the Rameswara temple. Because Holy Mother's father-in-law, Kshudiram, had bought a Rameswara Shiva lingam for his shrine in Kamarpukur, Holy Mother herself bought two pictures for the shrine of Koalpara Ashrama.

Dhanushkoti, or Dhanush-tirtha, is situated at the end of the island and is about 14 or 15 miles from the temple complex. According to the Ramayana, monkeys built a bridge from Rameswaram to Sri Lanka so that Rama could conquer Ravana. After the war, Rama rescued Sita and brought her back to the mainland. At that time the god of the ocean prayed to Rama to destroy the bridge so that ordinary people could not walk over it. Rama took his bow and arrow and destroyed the bridge, and since then the spot where that bridge once stood has become a holy place. Holy Mother could not visit it, so she sent Dhirananda and Ashu on her behalf to perform worship according to the custom with a silver bow and an arrow. After three days in Rameswaram, Holy Mother and her party stopped for a day in Madurai and then returned to Madras.

At Bangalore

While Holy Mother was in South India, some devotees from Bangalore asked Ramakrishnananda to arrange for Holy Mother to come there. Although it was not certain that Holy Mother would go, Swami Nirmalananda, the president of Bangalore Ashrama, came to Madras and assumed responsibility for her visit. Holy Mother and her party left for Bangalore by train on Friday, 24 March 1911.

She later described her reception: "What a huge crowd there was in Bangalore! As soon as I got down from the train, there was an incessant shower of flowers all the way to the ashrama. Ultimately, the road became full of flowers."[11] When her car reached the ashrama, hundreds of people were waiting to see her, holding flowers and fruit. Nirmalananda carried the box containing the Mother's puja articles on his head to her room. Holy

Above: Shrine on Sarada Devi's Rock behind the Bangalore Ashrama.
Below: Sarada Devi's room in the Ashrama. The shrine is to the right.

Mother stayed in a room at the south end of the monastery building (now known as the Mother's room) and her female companions occupied other rooms. The monks and devotees lived in tents on the ashrama grounds, as it was a new centre and did not have sufficient accommodations.

Swami Vishuddhananda, a disciple of the Mother, recalled:

Holy Mother came to visit South India with her entourage. We gave the whole monastery building of the Bangalore centre to her for her stay, and we moved to a tent in front of the monastery. Holy Mother did not want any publicity about her in the newspaper, so nothing was published. Still many people came to see her with fruits and presents and Balaram Basu's wife took care of them. She was overwhelmed when she saw the heaps of fruit. She asked me, "Can you tell me, what I shall do with them?"

I replied: "Please put them in the storeroom next to the shrine. These were given to the Mother; she will decide what to do."

Holy Mother's room was adjacent to the Master's shrine. I was the worshipper. When Mother arrived, I asked her to worship in the ashrama's shrine with the Master's picture that she kept with her. The Mother said: "My child, I shall worship the Master with a couple of flowers in the corner of my room. You continue your worship as usual." What humility!

I said: "What do you say, Mother? How is that possible? You will have to perform worship in the main shrine. I will not do the worship as long as you are here."

Holy Mother had rheumatic pain in her legs and she limped a little. One day in the early afternoon when there was not much of a crowd, I accompanied the Mother on a visit to the nearby temples of Ganesha and Shiva [the cave temple of Govipura]. She acted like any other pilgrim. She bowed down to the deities and then took dust from the floor and rubbed it on the painful spot on her leg for recovery. She also took some dust and put it on Radhu's head. At this, I smiled.

When I was returning with the Mother, I saw in the distance a large crowd waiting to see her. I told her, "Mother, you are attracting so many people!" She just smiled a little. When the horse carriage arrived at the gate of the ashrama, she said: "Let me get down from the carriage. I shall walk among these devotees slowly. So many people have come to see me."

I said: "No, Mother. It is not possible. Rather, let the driver drive the carriage slowly from here." She agreed.

The Bangalore Ashrama had been inaugurated a couple of years before these events. There were no big trees on the monastery grounds then but some small plants had just been planted. The devotees were seated, and they all stood up when they saw the Mother. They then prostrated themselves before her. At this, Mother went into an ecstatic mood. She remained in the carriage, making the gestures of offering boons and showing fearlessness. Five minutes passed. I was overwhelmed, but I controlled myself and then slowly helped her get down from the carriage and to sit in front of the devotees. They were all overjoyed.

Another day the Mother sat in our big hall. Nearly 40 devotees came to see her. The Mother sat there watching those devotees; they were looking at her intently. The Mother sometimes closed her eyes and then opened them again to look at the devotees. There was no conversation. Fifteen minutes passed in this manner. I stood there as a spectator, looking at the Mother and again at the devotees. Another fifteen minutes passed and the Mother went into deep meditation. After another fifteen minutes the Mother said to me softly: "My child, what a pity I do not know their language! They would feel peace of mind if I could say a few words. Please tell them." I translated the Mother's words to them. The devotees were so joyful that one of them said: "No, no. This is very nice! Our hearts are filled with joy at seeing you, Mother! There is no need for spoken words." I translated those words into Bengali for her. Upon hearing this, her face beamed with an Elysian smile. How did she learn to smile in such a beautiful way?[12]

This scene reminds us of a verse from the Dakshinamurti-stotram by Shankara: "A wonderful picture! Beneath the banyan tree, the disciples are old and the preceptor is young. The instruction given by the preceptor is in silence, and the doubts of the disciples are dispelled."

In those days the surroundings of the Bangalore Ashrama were quiet and charming. There was a small hillock inside the compound behind the ashrama building. During her short stay, Holy Mother was surrounded by people most of the time. Late one afternoon, despite her difficulty in walking, she wanted to climb to the top of the hillock. With two or three companions, the Mother went there to watch the beautiful sunset through the scattered clouds. The twilight offered a heavenly scene and the Mother was in an exalted mood. As soon as Ramakrishnananda heard of this, he exclaimed in exultation, "Indeed, the Mother has become *parvata-vashini**!" He hurried to the hillock, prostrated himself before Holy Mother, and recited a hymn from the Chandi:

> O auspicious One, Thou art the source of all auspiciousness. Thou art the accomplisher of all cherished desires. Thou art the giver of refuge. Thou possessest the eye of wisdom and a beautiful form. O Narayani, salutations to Thee.

> O eternal One, Thou art the energy of creation, maintenance, and destruction. Thou art the abode of different modes of energy, and art beyond them. O Narayani, salutations to Thee.

*The dweller on the mountain, an epithet of Mother Durga.

O Mother, Thou art the saviour of the distressed and of the care-worn who take refuge in Thee. Thou art the remover of the misery of all. O Narayani, salutations to Thee.

Overwhelmed, Ramakrishnananda uttered with deep devotion, "Kripa, kripa — grace, grace." The compassionate Mother blessed the swami by passing her palm over his head. It is wonderful to reflect on how the Master's disciples loved and respected Holy Mother. The swami slowly calmed down and left the place in great joy. At Nirmalananda's request, the Mother repeated a mantra as she sat on that hillock. Since that day, the place has been considered sanctified. Later, a monument was erected on that spot. Now many people visit this holy place every day, and some practise japa and meditation there. Devotees remember this episode and try to feel the Mother's presence.

Holy Mother liked the calmness and climate of the Bangalore Ashrama. Referring to the people of Bangalore, the Mother later remarked, "They have great devotion." Although the Mother's visit was not publicized, people heard of her through word of mouth, and many began coming — from the Dewan, or minister, of Mysore down to the poor and downtrodden. Observing their enthusiasm and spiritual hunger, and listening to their prayers for *mantram* (initiation) and *upadesham* (instruction), the Mother's heart melted and she initiated some of the devotees, including Narayan Iyengar, Raja Gopal Naidu, Narasimha Rao Naidu, and Adimulam.

Adimulam's story is very interesting. One day the Mother was in her room and saw a little boy looking through her window from outside. On enquiry, she learned that the boy was a Harijan — that is, a member of the untouchable community. She asked him to come inside the room. His cloth was torn and his hair uncombed, so the Mother applied oil to his hair and combed it. According to her instruction, he was given a new cloth and the Mother then initiated him with a mantra. Adimulam became a great devotee and later gave much service to the Bangalore Ashrama.[13]

One day Holy Mother was seated in the hall of the Bangalore Ashrama to receive the devotees. A wealthy woman wearing a fancy sari and much jewellery entered the hall to pay her respects. She sat down close to Holy Mother. Soon after, a group of women came to the hall and mistook her for the Mother. When they tried to bow down to the rich lady, she protested in their language but could not stop them. Embarrassed, the lady hurriedly made her way out of the hall, pushing her way through the crowd. The Mother could not follow their conversation but understood what was going on. She smiled.[14]

On 25 January 1959 Swami Vishuddhananda described a similar incident: "Golap-ma went to South India with Holy Mother. Golap-ma's appearance was like that of the goddess Dhumavati — gray hair with a bright complexion. The devotees were bowing down to Golap-ma while the Mother was seated calmly nearby. Her body was then lean because she had recently been ill. Golap-ma became angry and told the devotees: 'Shame on you! I am not the Mother. She is there. Look at her face. Does any human have that kind of face?'"[15]

Holy Mother's visit to Bangalore was brief. Ashu Mitra wrote that the Mother spent three nights in the Bangalore Ashrama and first saw electric lights in that city. The room where she stayed is now used as the Master's bedroom.* She travelled to Bangalore by train in a first-class compartment, and Nirmalananda made her comfortable at the ashrama. Narayan Iyengar gave silver glasses to Lord Raghuvir of Kamarpukur, Holy Mother, and Radhu; he gave silk cloths for Golap-ma and Surabala; and he gave money for Ramlal's travelling expenses. Ramakrishnananda wrote to Narayan Iyengar from Madras, "Mother is highly pleased with your offerings." Before she left Bangalore on 27 March 1911, the devotees wanted to have her footprints. She allowed them to make impressions of her feet on a few pieces of cloth. One of them still exists in the Mother's room at the Bangalore Math.[16]

Return from South India

Holy Mother and her companions returned to Madras on 28 March and then left for Puri on 1 April 1911 by train. Ramakrishnananda's health broke down due to the excessive strain from this trip, so Nirmalananda took responsibility for travelling with the Mother. He arrived in Madras from Bangalore in the morning and left with the Mother that evening. On the way they stopped at Rajahmundry in Andhra Pradesh, where they were the guests of Dewan Bahadur M.O. Parthasarathi Iyengar, the judge of the Godavari district. Ramakrishnananda had arranged for Holy Mother and her party to rest there for a day. Mr. Iyengar was a scholar and spoke with Nirmalananda in Sanskrit about the scriptures. His home was on the bank of the Godavari River, so the Mother and her companions got a chance to bathe there.**

The party left Rajahmundry on 3 April and reached Khurda Road station at one-thirty the next morning. There they changed trains and

---

*According to Indian tradition, each deity has a room for rest adjacent to the shrine.
** In 1991 the devotees of Andhra installed a large statue of Holy Mother on the ghat where she bathed.

arrived at Puri on the same day. Holy Mother stayed at Sashi Niketan for nearly a week and visited Lord Jagannath every day. On 10 April the Mother and her party* left Puri by the Fast Passenger train at six o'clock in the evening, reaching Calcutta on Tuesday morning, 11 April 1911. On 17 April Holy Mother wrote to Ramakrishnananda that she had reached Calcutta safely and was well. She sent her blessings to him.

One day in the course of conversation about her pilgrimage to South India, Holy Mother remarked: "Shashi spent about one thousand rupees." Another day she said: "Finally, the Master's words have come true. I have seen so many places, such as Madras, Rameswaram, and Bangalore, where he did not go."[17] Perhaps she meant that the Master visited those places through her.

We shall conclude the Mother's South Indian pilgrimage by telling of an incident that took place at Rameswaram. As soon as Holy Mother saw the uncovered image of Lord Rameswar, she exclaimed: "I see it is just the same as when I placed it here." When asked by the devotees what she meant, she controlled herself and then said with a smile: "Never mind, I was absent-minded. It was a slip of the tongue."[18] As already mentioned, according to the *Rameswaram Sthala Purana*, it was Sita who installed the image of Rameswar.** On several occasions Holy Mother spoke of her identity with Sita. Although she behaved like a human being, Holy Mother could not always hide her divine nature.

Kedar (later Swami Keshavananda) and Brahmachari Barada came from Koalpara Ashrama when they heard that Holy Mother had returned to Calcutta. When Kedar asked Holy Mother about the pilgrimage, she said: "I brought two pictures of Lord Rameswara for Koalpara Ashrama. Please frame them nicely and worship them."

Kedar replied: "Mother, you have already installed the Master on the altar and asked us to worship him as the embodiment of all gods and goddesses. Now you are giving us these pictures of Lord Shiva. How many deities shall we worship? It is better that we should not worship other deities."

"All right," she responded. "But frame these pictures and hang them on the wall of the shrine." (Those two pictures were later hung on either side of the altar at Koalpara Ashrama.)

---

*Radhu and her mother, Golap-ma, Krishnabhavini and her sister-in-law, Kedar's mother, Dr. Bipin Ghosh and his wife, Ramlal, Nirmalananda, Atmananda, Dhirananda, and Ashu.

**The story of Sita installing the Shiva linga at Rameswaram is not given in the popular Ramayana, but is related in the *Rameswaram Sthala Purana*.

Kedar then asked: "Mother, tell us about everything that you saw at Rameswaram."

The Mother replied: "The image exists there intact just as I placed it."

Golap-ma was passing through the veranda and overheard Holy Mother's words. She asked, "Mother, what did you say?" Embarrassed, the Mother said, "Never mind. What have I said? I just said that I was overjoyed seeing the image I had heard about from you all."

Smiling, Golap-ma said: "It is not so, Mother. I heard everything clearly. Now you can't retract your words. What do you say, Kedar?" Golap-ma reported this to Yogin-ma and others.[19]

Holy Mother once said to one of her disciples: "The Master could not touch money. He had a vision of Sita in the Panchavati wearing diamond-cut bangles, and he had two bangles made for me in that same design."[20] With his divine eyes, Ramakrishna saw that in one of her previous incarnations, Sarada Devi had been Sita.

22
Last Visit
to Varanasi

Na hi ammayāni tirthāni na devā mrit-shilā-mayāh;
Te punanti urukālena darshanādeva sādhavah.
  —*Bhagavata, 10:48:31*

Krishna to Akrura: The waters of holy rivers, or images made with clay and stone from a holy place, do not form a tirtha (a holy place); these things take a long time to purify people. But, by virtue of God residing in their hearts, saints purify by their mere sight.

Everyone encounters grief or misery at some point in their lives. One should not grieve over the unavoidable. When someone dies or a serious mishap occurs, an ignorant person remains depressed for a long time. A wise person suffers briefly and then turns the grief-stricken mind to a higher plane of consciousness where the pairs of opposites cannot cause suffering. This can be done through discrimination, devotion to God, studying the scriptures, observing how great teachers dealt with similar situations, seeking out holy company, and going on pilgrimage. Holy company and pilgrimages quickly uplift a depressed mind.

Holy Mother experienced great joy during her pilgrimage to South India, but sadness was soon to follow. She suffered as do all human beings, and she taught us: "There is no wealth equal to contentment and no quality equal to forbearance."[1]

Holy Mother returned to Calcutta on 11 April 1911, and on 12 May Nivedita came to see her before leaving for Darjeeling. This was the last time that she and Nivedita met. Holy Mother was grief-stricken when Nivedita passed away five months later.*

Five days after Nivedita left Calcutta, Holy Mother went to Jayrambati to be present at Radhu's wedding, which took place on 10 June 1911.

---

*Sister Nivedita died of blood dysentery in Darjeeling on 13 October 1911.

Group photo taken in Calcutta, 1909. Left to right: Gauri-ma, Durga, Radhu, Sarada Devi, Maku, Kusum, and Hari's mother. (*Previously the left half of Gauri-ma's figure was cropped from available copies of this photo. It is digitally replaced here.*)

At the time Swami Ramakrishnananda was seriously ill in Madras, so Swamis Brahmananda and Saradananda asked him to come to Calcutta for treatment. He arrived at Udbodhan House on 10 June, and several physicians began to treat him. He urgently desired to see Holy Mother, but she could not leave Jayrambati.* However, the Mother appeared to him before his death in her subtle body, and Ramakrishnananda saw her and exclaimed, "Ah, the Mother has come."[2] On 21 August 1911 Ramakrishnananda passed away. When the Mother heard the sad news, she remarked: "Alas, Shashi is gone. My back is broken."[3]

On 24 November 1911 Holy Mother returned to Calcutta from Jayrambati. A few months later, on 8 February 1912, Holy Mother grieved when Girish Ghosh passed away. After enduring the loss of her dearest ones, the Mother expressed a desire to make a pilgrimage to Varanasi.

It was a great privilege to go on a pilgrimage with Holy Mother, so when her relatives and devotees heard that she was going to Varanasi, many of them wished to join her party. Ultimately Holy Mother's companions included Radhu, Surabala, Maku and Bhudeb, Aunt Bhanu, Kedar's mother, Golap-ma, M.'s wife, Mahamaya Mitra, Bibhuti Ghosh, Dr. Kanjilal's wife and mother-in-law, and several attendants. On 4 November 1912 the Mother and her companions left Calcutta by train. They arrived at Moghulsarai the next day and continued by another train to Varanasi. As the train passed over the bridge on the Ganges, the Mother was delighted with the view of golden Varanasi. At the Varanasi station the party disembarked. The thoughtful Brahmananda arranged a palanquin for Holy Mother so she would not have to cross the bridge over the rail lines, which entailed climbing many steps.

Holy Mother and her party arrived at Ramakrishna Advaita Ashrama at one o'clock in the afternoon. The ashrama was beautifully decorated. Swamis Brahmananda, Shivananda, Turiyananda, Vijnanananda, and others received the Mother. Swami Shantananda wrote: "When the Mother got down from the palanquin, Brahmananda told an attendant, 'Hold the Mother so that she will not fall.' It was a wonderful scene to see."[4] The Mother sat on a chair, wearing her veil as usual, and the disciples and devotees bowed down to her. After a brief rest in the ashrama, she went to Lakshmi Nivas, which was her residence while in Varanasi.

*Holy Mother later explained why she did not go to Calcutta: "If I went there, Shashi would have to move somewhere else because there was not sufficient accommodation in Udbodhan House. One should not move such a patient [who was in an advanced stage of tuberculosis]. His treatment would have been disrupted. Moreover, it would have been unbearable for me to be there if anything worse had happened." — *Shatarupe Sarada*, 103

Above: Ramakrishna Mission Home of Service in Varanasi.
Below: A ten-rupee note donated to the Home of Service by Sarada Devi.

This house belonged to Kiran Datta's family. It was a new house with many rooms and was close to the ashrama. When she saw the wide veranda, the Mother remarked: "We are rather fortunate that we have got this residence. A narrow place narrows the mind, while a commodious place expands it."[5] Holy Mother and her women companions lived upstairs, and the monks and men devotees stayed downstairs.

On 6 November 1912 Holy Mother went to visit Lord Vishwanath and Annapurna in the morning by palanquin; her women companions accompanied her in a horse carriage. Swami Arupananda and some attendants also came. The Vishwanath temple is always crowded, so the priest and the Mother's attendants escorted Holy Mother so that she and her companions could freely worship the Lord. She visited Mother Annapurna afterwards and then returned to her residence.

Kali Puja was held at Ramakrishna Advaita Ashrama on Saturday, 9 November. Holy Mother was invited but she could not attend. However, at ten o'clock in the morning the next day she went to Advaita Ashrama and sat in front of the deity for some time. On 25 November 1912 Swami Shivananda wrote to a devotee: "This year Kali Puja and Jagaddhatri Puja were held in this ashrama with great éclat. Holy Mother was staying in a house near our ashrama and she came to attend the worship. The deities came to life when she offered flowers. She brought a current of ecstasy, bliss, and purity into the devotees' hearts."[6]

There are two Ramakrishna centres in Varanasi adjacent to each other: the Ramakrishna Advaita Ashrama, where monks devote themselves mainly to scriptural study and meditation, and the Ramakrishna Mission Home of Service, where monks conduct a free hospital and dispensary for the poor. On 10 November Holy Mother was taken around the hospital in a palanquin, as it was difficult for her to walk through the large hospital compound. Swami Achalananda gave her a guided tour of the different hospital wards. She also saw the flower and kitchen gardens and the living quarters of the monastic workers. She then sat on the southern veranda of the hospital with Brahmananda, Shivananda, Turiyananda, and several other monks and devotees. Greatly pleased with the visit, she remarked: "Sri Ramakrishna is ever present in this place, and Mother Lakshmi always casts her benign glance upon it."[7]

Holy Mother was told how the work had originally been started by a few young men who were inspired by Swami Vivekananda's exhortation to dedicate their lives to the service of the sick and the needy. They began with only a few pennies. Brahmananda described how Swami Achalananda, Swami Satchidananda, Charu (later Swami Shubhananda), and others had built this institution through their sincere efforts, enthusiasm, and dedication. Moved, the Mother said, "The place is so beautiful that I feel like living here." After returning to her residence, she sent a small donation of ten rupees to the hospital. That ten-rupee note has been preserved permanently in a frame in the Home of Service as the Mother's blessing.

After a while when M. arrived, the members of the Home of Service talked about how much Holy Mother appreciated the institution. M. often said that the Master did not approve of a person performing social service before realizing God. One of the monks said to M.: "Mother has just told us that the activities of the Home of Service are service to the Master himself and that he is tangibly present here. Now what do you say?" Swami Brahmananda interjected: "Master Mahashay, have you heard what the Mother said? The Mother has seen the Master in the Home of Service. And she mentioned that the activities of the hospital are the Master's work. Now you cannot deny it." M. replied with a smile: "How can I deny it anymore?"[8]

Every morning during his walk, Brahmananda visited Holy Mother's residence and called for the Mother's nephew, Bhudeb, from downstairs. He inquired about the Mother's health from Golap-ma. He did not go upstairs to see the Mother for fear of being overwhelmed with emotion. One morning he stood in the courtyard to pay his respects to the Mother. Golap-ma said, "Rakhal [Brahmananda], the Mother asks why a devotee propitiates Shakti, the Divine Mother, at the beginning of worship."

Brahmananda replied: "It is because the key to the knowledge of Brahman is in the Divine Mother's custody. There is no way to commune with Brahman unless the Mother graciously unlocks the door."

Then he sang this song:

O mind, remain immersed in meditation on Shankari's feet,
Remain immersed and escape the suffering of life.
All these three worlds are unreal — in vain you roam about them.
Meditate on the Divine Mother in your heart.
Kamalakanta says: Sing the Mother's glory
And the world will become a river of bliss; paddle slowly in it.

While singing, he danced in ecstasy and finally he rushed out of the house, joyfully roaring, "Ho, ho, ho!"[9] The Mother, who was watching from the veranda of the second floor, was delighted to see his fervour and his dancing. M. and a couple of devotees also witnessed this event.

Visit to Saranath

One day Radhu expressed a desire to see Saranath, where Buddha preached his first sermon after attaining nirvana. Situated about seven miles from Varanasi, it is an important holy place of the Buddhist tradition. At that time Alberta Montagu and her husband, George (later the Earl of Sandwich), were staying in a hotel in Varanasi. Alberta was the daughter of Betty Leggett and the niece of Josephine MacLeod. Alberta and her husband visited Holy Mother, who inquired about Alberta's mother and aunt.[10] They offered a phaeton for the Mother's visit to Saranath, but it did not arrive on time, so the Mother left with Radhu, Bhudeb, and others in a hired carriage. When Alberta's phaeton arrived, Swami Brahmananda followed the Mother's carriage with two attendants and a devotee.

Holy Mother toured the holy site and saw the various ruins of ancient monasteries associated with Buddha and his disciples. Holy Mother noticed that several European visitors were also visiting the holy site. Referring to them, the Mother remarked: "They built all this in a previous birth, and now they have come back again to see what they did centuries ago. They are speechless with wonder, admiring these amazing relics."[11]

Before they returned to Varanasi, Brahmananda asked the Mother to travel in the phaeton, but she said that the hired carriage was quite comfortable for her. The swami insisted, however, so Holy Mother and her party rode in the phaeton while Swami Brahmananda and his companions took the hired carriage. On the road back to Varanasi the swami's driver had problems controlling his horse. The horse became agitated while taking a sharp turn after crossing a bridge and it pulled the carriage down into a shallow ditch. Fortunately, no one was seriously hurt although they were badly jolted. Brahmananda joyfully remarked: "It is fortunate that the Mother did not go by this carriage." When the Mother heard about Brahmananda's accident, she said: "I was fated for this mishap, but Rakhal, by force as it were, took it on his own shoulders. I had several children with me; who knows what would have happened to them?"[12]

Days in Varanasi

One day Brahmananda asked his attendant Sankarananda to prepare some vegetable chops (fried vegetable patties) for the Mother. Accordingly Sankarananda went to the market and bought fresh *mocha* (banana flowers) and potatoes. He boiled them, added roasted farina and some spices, and shaped them into round patties. After that, he fried the chops, arranged them on a plate, and carried them to the shrine. Holy Mother offered them to the Master and ate the prasad during her lunch. The Mother and her companions greatly enjoyed the crispy and tasty vegetable chops. When Golap-ma praised the dish, Brahmananda said to her: "Golap-ma, you think that only women know how to cook. Now you see our boys know cooking better than you."[13]

Swami Shantananda, an attendant of the Mother, recorded the following incidents in his diary:

When the Mother was at Varanasi, she would perform rituals in her residence. I would pick flowers from Advaita Ashrama and carry fruits and sweets for offering to the Master. One day as I was close to her residence, a kite swooped down and took away some jilipis from my hand. I was depressed and told the Mother what had happened. She did not offer the remaining jilipis to the Master, nor did she give us any to eat. She said, "It is not good for you to eat this sweet because the kite's claws might carry some impurity." It is amazing how she loved her children.

Sunday, 7 December 1912: In the morning the Mother went by horse carriage to the Dashaswamedha Ghat. After having a bath in the Ganges, she visited Vishwanath, Annapurna, and Dhundi Ganesha, and then returned to her residence.

Tuesday, 9 December 1912: The Mother had a bath at the confluence of the Asi and the Ganges and visited the Jagannath temple. Then she went to the Sankatmochan temple. Seeing the large banyan tree nearby, she commented, "This tree is similar to the one in our Panchavati of Dakshineswar." She touched the tree. She then bowed down to Ramachandra and Mahavir Hanuman. She also visited the Durga Bari and Swami Bhaskarananda's temple.

Friday, 12 December 1912: The Mother and Radhu went to visit Kalbhairav Shiva by palanquin, and a monk [Swami Shantananda] went as her guide. Golap-ma and others went by carriage. Brahmananda arranged for the palanquin so that the Mother would not have to walk much. The Mother sat at the northwest corner of the temple and repeated a mantra for some time. Then she visited Trailanga Swami's temple and the Benimadhav temple. With the Mother's permission, Radhu and Bhudeb went to the top of the Benimadhav tower and the Mother and her disciple waited below. By and by the Mother said: "You see, now I am old so I cannot go to the top. When I came to Varanasi after the Master's passing away, I climbed up to the top of this temple. I also climbed up to the top of Savitri Hill at Pushkar and Chandi Hill at Hardwar." Afterwards the Mother visited the Divine Mother at Sankata, Vireswar Shiva, and the Manikarnika cremation ground. She returned to her residence in the evening.

Wednesday, 30 December 1912: It was Holy Mother's birthday. She attended a special worship and homa fire at Advaita Ashrama and many devotees paid their respects to her. She then took some prasad and returned to her residence.

During her stay at Varanasi, the Mother would go for a bath in the Ganges almost every other day and she visited various temples and places, such as Batuk Bhairav, Kamakhya, Vaidyanath, Shankar Math, Ramkunda and so on. A Raslila party came from Vrindaban to give a performance on Krishna's life at the Sankatmochan temple. Dr. Nripen Mukhopadhyay arranged a performance at Advaita Ashrama so the Mother could see it. She watched the Raslila for three evenings and was very pleased. She remarked: "I found the representation the same as the real." She then gave a few rupees to those actors to show her appreciation.

One day Holy Mother decided to feed the disciples of the Master at Lakshmi Nivas, her residence. A sumptuous feast was arranged and Swamis Brahmananda, Shivananda, Turiyananda, Vijnanananda, and other monks enjoyed the food. They all sat on the ground-floor veranda. When the Mother was asked to eat her lunch, she replied, "Let my children eat first; then I shall eat." She stood near the monks as they ate and supervised the serving of food. Each monk received a cotton cloth except Swami Brahmananda, who got a silk cloth. When Holy Mother was asked why she had given a silk cloth to Maharaj and to others an ordinary cloth, she replied, "Because he is the Master's spiritual son." After the meal, the monks washed their hands and mouths, tied their cloths around their heads, and danced joyfully in front of the Mother.

Then the Mother decided to present cloths to all monks of both Advaita Ashrama and Sevashrama and asked me to buy cloths from the market. When the cloths were distributed, it happened that one cloth was short for a monk from the Sevashrama. When I suggested that it would be all right not to buy him a new cloth, Holy Mother replied: "If you do not have one, it does not matter. But those monks are nursing the patients and working so hard. I will give cloths to those monks first. Go to the market and buy another piece of cloth." I obeyed. Another day the Mother arranged a feast at Advaita Ashrama and fed the monks of Shankara's order.[14]

Varanasi is a temple city and a citadel of India's spiritual tradition. A devotee put his carriage at the Mother's disposal so that she could visit any place in Varanasi whenever she wished. One day the Mother and her companions went to see Tilabhandeswar Shiva. Upon seeing the deity, she remarked: "This is a Swayambhu Linga* — self-manifested image." Another evening she went to attend the vesper service of Kedarnath

---

*The image which is not man-made, but found in natural surroundings, springing from the earth.

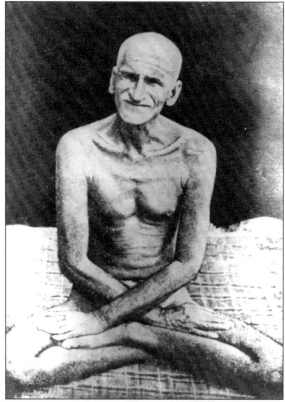

Above: Chameli Puri. Below: Swami Bhaskarananda.

Shiva on the bank of the Ganges. After the service, she said: "This Kedar and the Kedar of the Himalayas are identical — they are connected. If you see this image, it is as good as seeing that one. This deity is truly living."[15]

One day when the Mother visited the Sankatmochan temple, the priest asked, "Mother, where have you come from?"

"She is from here," replied the monk who was with her.

The Mother told the monk: "No, no. Please tell him that I have come from Jayrambati."[16] The Mother did not refer to Kamarpukur or Calcutta, as she had a deep love for her native village.

One day in Varanasi the Mother met a monk of the Nanak sect on the bank of the Ganges. She offered him a rupee and bowed down to him. Holy Mother also met the old monk Chameli Puri. Golap-ma asked him who provided him with his food. "Mother Durga," the holy man answered in a strong voice, "Who else, do you think?" Holy Mother was impressed. That evening she said: "Ah, the face of that old monk is appearing in my mind. He is just like a child." The next day the Mother sent him some oranges, sweets, and a blanket. After seeing Chameli Puri, Holy Mother did not desire to visit any other holy man.

One day several women called on Holy Mother and found her busy with her nephew and niece. She asked Golap-ma to mend her torn cloth. One of the visitors said: "Mother, we see you are terribly entangled in maya."

"What can I do?" she replied. "I myself am Maya." It is doubtful whether the visitor understood the meaning of the Mother's words.

Another day Holy Mother was seated with Golap-ma and several other companions when a woman whom she had never met came in wanting to show her respect. Her eyes first fell upon the dignified figure of Golap-ma. As she moved towards her to take the dust of her feet, Golap-ma pointed to Holy Mother. Now she approached the Mother, but Holy Mother, in fun, pointed to Golap-ma. Golap-ma again directed the woman's attention to Holy Mother, but the Mother again pointed to Golap-ma. This teasing game continued for some time. Then Golap-ma said to the stranger, rather sharply: "Don't you have any sense? Can't you distinguish a divine face from a human one? Does any human being look like that?" The woman at last recognized the elusive grace and charm of the Mother's face.[17]

As a magnet attracts iron, so divine beings draw spiritually inclined people. Holy Mother's visit to Varanasi was not publicized, but people came to see her in large numbers. Betty Leggett, her daughter Alberta, and her son-in-law George Montagu knew Swami Turiyananda, who had lived with them in America. After having a guided tour of the Sevash-rama, they went to pay their respects to the Mother, whom they had pre-viously met in Calcutta. A large crowd gathered on the street in front of the ashrama. The Indian devotees were amazed to see American and English people paying respects to the Mother.

One day the Mother was resting after her noonday meal when sud-denly her sleep was broken. She went to the veranda and found a beggar woman singing in a plaintive voice:

> Where have you gone, my Mother?
> I haven't seen you all this time.
> Please take me on your lap.
> What kind of Mother are you, so stony-hearted towards the child!
> Reveal yourself to me, Mother, and don't let me cry anymore.

The beggar approached her, bowed down to her, and said: "My long-cherished desire has been fulfilled at last. I cannot tell you, Mother, how happy I am." Holy Mother learned where this woman lived and that she supported herself on alms. The woman did not ask for anything from the Mother except devotion for God. She further told the Mother that she had been hoping for a long time to see her, but was afraid that she, a mere beggar, would not be allowed in her presence. At the Mother's request, she sang again. The Mother told her to visit her whenever she wished. The woman took some prasad and left.

A few days later, the beggar woman arrived again holding a guava that she had received as alms. With great hesitancy, she offered that ordinary fruit to the Mother. Holy Mother very graciously took the fruit, touched it to her head, and said: "Food obtained by begging is very pure: the Master loved it. I will eat your fruit."[18] Tears trickled from the beggar woman's eyes when Holy Mother accepted the fruit. The Mother asked her to sing, and she sang a song on Baby Krishna. Impressed, the Mother asked her attendant to give some prasad to the woman and told her to come back again.

Another day Holy Mother went to visit an ashrama for old women. The women offered flowers at her feet. She told the caretaker: "You are doing wonderful work. You are serving these helpless and hapless women, which is akin to serving God."[19]

Once a poor woman whose husband had renounced his family came with her young daughter to the Mother for help. She asked her to tell the monks of the ashrama to help her financially. Holy Mother did not prom-ise but gave her a sari, a rupee, and fed her and her daughter.

Swamis Prajnananda and Chinmayananda had once been freedom fighters against the British. They later took initiation from Holy Mother and became monks of the Ramakrishna Order. Although they had renounced political life, they were constantly under surveillance by the British government. In 1912 the Viceroy of India, Lord Hardinge, was the target of assassination attempts by Indian nationalists. A bomb was hurled at him, but he was unhurt. News came to the ashrama that the police were looking for suspects, and they were targeting former revolutionaries who had been connected with earlier bomb cases. Prajnananda was connected with one of those earlier cases. Holy Mother heard of this, but she was unperturbed. She said firmly: "What is the matter? He is no longer involved in politics. There is nothing to fear." Nonetheless, Swami Brahmananda asked Prajnananda to leave Varanasi temporarily. Not wanting to create any inconvenience, he left for Simla to visit his brother. His friend Swami Chinmayananda accompanied him.[20] Holy Mother felt bad that they had gone so suddenly. She felt a little relief when she heard from Sudhira, Prajnananda's sister, that she had fed them before their departure.[21]

Although many people in Varanasi asked Holy Mother for initiation, she refused, explaining that in Varanasi, Shiva is the guru. She advised them to come to her in Calcutta or Jayrambati for initiation.

Spiritual life becomes inspiring if one practises japa and meditation, studies the scriptures and the lives of illumined souls, and performs worship. Although Holy Mother did not study, she often attended the Bhagavata class in the Advaita Ashrama. One evening Sudhira and Sarala went with the Mother to hear the class. Sarala recalled: "The talk lasted two hours. After the talk was over, Holy Mother bowed down to the pandit and offered him one rupee. Then in the course of conversation the Mother said: 'Ah, what a wonderful exposition! The pandit explained it nicely.'

"Another evening Sister Sudhira and I were seated near the Mother. She said: 'He who has really prayed to the Master, even once, has nothing to fear. By praying to him constantly, one gets ecstatic love [prema bhakti] through his grace. This prema, my child, is the innermost thing of spiritual life. The gopis of Vrindaban attained to it. They were not aware of anything in the world except Krishna.'"[22]

She also expressed a desire to listen to the *Kashi Khanda*, which is part of the *Skanda Purana* that describes the glory of Lord Vishwanath and the Shaiva tradition of Varanasi. One of the Mother's disciples, Swami Girijananda, began to read the *Kashi Khanda* to her every afternoon. One day Arupananda asked Holy Mother a controversial question: "It is men-tioned in the *Kashi Khanda* that a person who dies in Varanasi attains lib-eration. Is this true?"

The Mother replied: "Well, it is mentioned in the scriptures, and many people come here with this faith, so it must be true. Moreover, those who take refuge in God will definitely be liberated. Varanasi is pervaded with pure consciousness. All living beings in this place are filled with divine consciousness. This is the glory of this holy place."[23]

On 11 December 1912 Swami Shantananda asked Holy Mother: "The Master had many visions in Varanasi. Did you have any?"

Mother: "Last night I lay awake on my bed when I suddenly saw the image of Narayana of the Seth's temple of Vrindaban standing by my side. The garland of flowers around the neck of the deity hung to the feet. The Master stood with folded hands in front of the image. I thought, 'How could the Master come here?' I said, 'Rasbihari does not want to believe that one dying in Varanasi attains liberation.' The Master said: 'He must. This is all true.' That Narayana image said to me two things. One was: can one ever get the knowledge of reality unless one knows the truth about God? The other thing I do not recall."[24]

Another day Girijananda tried to argue with the Mother by quoting Shankara, who said, "Liberation is not possible without the knowledge of Brahman."

Holy Mother told him: "My son, you have read much; you will go in a roundabout way. The Master said that one would be liberated by dying in Varanasi." Later the swami found that the Mother's statement was sup-ported by the Jabala Upanishad.*

Girijananda recalled another such story:

In 1912 the Mother came to Varanasi and stayed nearly three months. I was then studying Panini's Sanskrit grammar along with the Upanishads with Shankara's commentary. I was so absorbed in my study of grammar that during meditation all those rules of grammar would flash through my mind. The grammar possessed me and I could not concentrate on God. I decided to place my problem before the Mother. One day I found her alone and asked: "Mother, nowadays my mind is very restless. I can't prac-tise japa and meditation." She asked, "What do you study?" I replied: "I

---

*According to Hindu tradition, Varanasi and Kurukshetra are called *Avimukta*, which means "Shiva never leaves that place." According to the Jabala Upanishad, verse 1: "When the prana departs from the body of a jiva, Rudra gives a saving mantra. As a result, the individual soul becomes immortal and attains liberation. So one should always live in Varanasi, the abode of liberation. Never leave Avimukta."

study Sanskrit grammar and the Upanishads in the Hindu College, and at noon I study grammar and literature from a pandit."

As soon as I said this, Radhu blurted out: "So I see, being a monk, why does he go to college every day with books?" Then the Mother said emphatically: "Don't think that a little girl is saying this to you. Know for certain that the Divine Mother is telling you this through Radhu's mouth." I said, "Then should I give up my studies?" The Mother replied: "You have only one mind. Now in what direction do you want to focus — study or God? Give up your study." I obediently accepted my guru's order, but it hurt me immensely. However, I stopped going to the college and discontinued the study of grammar and literature forever.[25]

It is amazing how Holy Mother would sometimes answer highly philosophical questions in one or two sentences. One day in Varanasi, Arupananda said to the Mother: "Mother, I don't want nirvana. If I have nirvana, then I shall not have you." The Mother replied: "My foolish boy, the true nature of God is nirvana.*"[26]

In October 1912, after Durga Puja, Swami Adbhutananda left Calcutta and moved to Varanasi. When he arrived, he stayed at Advaita Ashrama for a few days and Swami Nirbharananda took care of him with great joy. At that time Swamis Brahmananda, Shivananda, and Turiyananda were there. Adbhutananda found there were not sufficient rooms for himself and his attendants. Moreover, he was a mystic and ascetic, so it was hard for him to adjust to the Ashrama routine as his eating, sleeping, and meditation times were extremely unpredictable. He accordingly moved to Mr. Kundu's house in Godhulia, which was nearby.

Bibhuti Maitra, an attendant of Adbhutananda, recorded the swami's last meeting with Holy Mother at Varanasi: "Sometimes we were surprised when Latu Maharaj would say, 'I don't venerate your Holy Mother.' We were truly astounded because he had served the Mother for such a long period. How could he say that he does not adore Mother? Later we realized that he intentionally kept his devotion for the Mother a secret. One day he told us that he would go to worship the Lord Vishwanath. We then collected flowers, bel leaves, fruits and so on. Accompanying us, he left the house. When we reached the main street, he suddenly said to me, 'Well, let us first go to the Mother.' We walked to Kiran Datta's house (Lakshmi Nivas, the Mother's residence]. Latu Maharaj went straight upstairs. He became overwhelmed with emotion in front of the Mother's room. His body began to tremble and he fell down at the

---

*The Mother meant that God is nityamukta (ever-free), so one cannot separate God from nirvana, or liberation.

Mother's feet. He wept and wept, saying, 'Ma, Ma.' With tearful eyes, he then offered flowers at the Mother's feet. During that time Holy Mother passed her hand on his head continuously. She showed her affection to him by touching his chin with three fingers and then serving him prasad. It was a wonderful sight to see. After saying goodbye to the Mother he visited the Vishwanath temple."[27]

Holy Mother visited Advaita Ashrama in Varanasi many times. Whenever she arrived, she always went to the shrine to bow down to the Master, and then she sat for a while. Swami Apurvananda left this account, which he heard from Shivananda, Shantananda, and others.

> Two or three days before leaving for Calcutta, Holy Mother came to Advaita Ashrama at ten o'clock in the morning. Swami Shantananda accompanied her. She went alone straight inside the shrine and closed the door. Later it was known that she carried a small picture of her own under her cloth along with some flowers and bel leaves. She bowed down to the Master, placed her picture in the empty niche of the eastern wall of the shrine, and worshipped it with those flowers and bel leaves. After a while, she came out and called Chandra [Swami Nirbharananda], the abbot of Advaita Ashrama, and said: "My son Chandra, please offer a couple of flowers to this picture every day." The swami bowed down to the Mother and accepted her command joyfully. Meanwhile, the monks of both ashramas got the news that the Mother had come to Advaita Ashrama, and they all came and bowed down to her. She blessed them and then returned to her residence.
>
> When the Mother left, Nirbharananda went to the niche in the shrine and found that the Mother had worshipped her own picture. He immediately reported this to Shivananda, who also went to the shrine and saw the Mother's picture in the niche. He bowed down to the Master and then the Mother. He then went to the Sevashrama and described the incident to Brahmananda. The swami became grave and said sadly: "Tarak-da, this is not a good sign. It seems that the Mother is planning to leave the world." Shivananda then told Turiyananda, who remarked with a heavy heart: "The wish of the Mahamaya will be fulfilled."[28]

After staying in Varanasi for nearly two and a half months, Holy Mother left for Calcutta on 15 January 1913 and arrived the next day. It was her last pilgrimage. She left for Jayrambati on 23 February 1913, and for the remaining years of her life she travelled only between Jayrambati and Calcutta.

23

At Belur Math
and with Disciples

Rāmakrishna-gata prānām tannāma-shravana-priyām;
Tadbhāva-ranjitā-kārām pranamāmi muhurmuhuh.
 —*A hymn by Swami Abhedananda*

She whose life-energy is merged in Ramakrishna, who delights in hearing his name, whose personality has been coloured with his spirit—to her I bow down again and again.

The Chandogya Upanishad tells us that the life of a knower of Brahman is established in Truth, and so his "desires come true" and his "thoughts come true": "Whatever country he longs for, whatever objects he desires, by his mere thought, all these come to him. Having obtained them, he is happy."[1] If this is true in the case of an ordinary knower of Brahman, then what to speak of Holy Mother, who was the Divine Mother herself? She intensely prayed for a place where the Master's disciples could live, instead of roaming around. As a result of her prayer, Belur Math came into existence. It is unbearable for a mother to see her children homeless and hungry. Holy Mother was relieved when the disciples bought the land for Belur Math, the future headquarters of the Ramakrishna Order.

Ramakrishna Math and Mission

Some historical background is helpful in understanding the Mother's role in the Ramakrishna Math and Mission. The Ramakrishna Order was founded by Ramakrishna in the Cossipore garden house when he gave ochre cloths to his disciples. He then asked the disciples to beg for their food following the ancient custom. They first went to Holy Mother and asked for alms, chanting this hymn to the goddess Annapurna:

O Parvati, the goddess of food, whose store is overflowing.
O beloved of Shankara, give me alms so that I may attain knowledge and wisdom.

Sixteen Monastic Disciples of Sri Ramakrishna. Left to right, standing: Adbhutananda, Yogananda, Abhedananda, Trigunatitananda, Turiyananda, Vijnanananda, Ramakrishnananda, Niranjanananda. Seated in center: Brahmananda, Vivekananda. Seated on ground: Shivananda, Saradananda, Subodhananda, Akhandananda, Premananda, Advaitananda.

Photo illustration by Diane Marshall, adding seven direct disciples to the group photo taken at Alambazar Monastery, 1896.

The merciful Mother, taken by surprise, gave them a handful of rice.

Ramakrishna passed away on 16 August 1886. Some of his young disciples had to return to their homes against their wishes, while others had no place to go. They were like orphans. One evening, early in September, while Surendranath Mitra was meditating in his shrine, the Master appeared to him and said: "What are you doing here? My boys are roaming about without a place to live. Attend to that before anything else." Immediately Surendra rushed to Swami Vivekananda's house and said to some of the disciples who were assembled there: "Brothers, where will you go? Let us rent a house. You will live there and make it our Master's shrine, and we householders shall come there for consolation. How can we pass all our days and nights with our wives and children in the world? I used to spend a sum of money for the Master at Cossipore. I shall gladly give it now for your expenses."[2] Accordingly, a house was rented at Baranagore, near the Ganges, at 11 rupees per month. Surendra paid the rent and provided food and other necessities for the Master's monastic disciples. Afterwards the monastery was moved to Alambazar, then to Nilambar Mukherjee's house at Belur, and finally it was established at Belur Math.

Holy Mother's Reception

In Chapter 13, we briefly mentioned that the disciples invited Holy Mother to Belur Math on Saturday, 12 November 1898. They wanted Holy Mother to consecrate the headquarters of the Order. The Mother left Calcutta by boat and landed at the Belur Math ghat with her women companions and attendants. According to Swami Adbhutananda: "All members of the monastery took the dust of her feet, and that dust is still worshipped in the Math.* The Mother was overjoyed by seeing the monastery building."[3] The Mother first went to the shrine, and then the monks bowed down to her. An elaborate arrangement was made for worship in the new monastery. At that time the construction of Belur Math was not complete and the monks were living at Nilambar Babu's garden house. The Mother went to the second floor of the Math house. When she saw Dakshineswar on the other side of the Ganges, she remarked: "This is a wonderful place. From here one will be able to think of Dakshineswar."[4]

The monastery diary includes this entry: "Holy Mother came to see the new Math with her Thakur.** Our Thakur was taken to the new house and

* The disciples collected the dirt where Holy Mother first stepped onto the monastery ground. The dirt is kept in a casket and worshipped every day even now.
** Meaning Holy Mother's photo of Ramakrishna.

Mother performed the worship there. [Thereafter] she came to the Math [at Nilambar Mukherjee's house], offered bhoga [cooked food for the Master] and took her meal. She was much pleased to see the new house."[5]

Ashutosh Mitra left this eyewitness account:

> Today is Kali Puja [12 November 1898]. The monks of Belur Math were overjoyed because Holy Mother was coming. Swami Brahmananda arranged to set the *mangal-ghat* [a consecrated pitcher of water] and banana tree at the gate of the Math house. Brahmachari Nandalal was busy with puja preparations. Swami Saradananda was supervising the cleaning of the shrine, courtyard, and all around. Swamiji was in his room.
>
> Meanwhile the Mother's boat arrived and the disciples bowed down to her. The Mother entered the shrine and began to worship the relics of the Master. Tears flowed from her eyes and she was in bhava samadhi. When that news spread, the monks began to sing: "Let us call 'Victory to the Mother,' and she will take us on her lap. We have our mother and we are her sons." They danced with drums and cymbals in the courtyard under the tree. Listening to the song, Swamiji came out of his room and joined the group. He also played a drum and danced. It was a wonderful sight to see."[6]

Festivals at Belur Math

After Holy Mother consecrated the monastery, Swami Vivekananda performed the public dedication ceremony on 9 December 1898. He carried Ramakrishna's relics to Belur and installed them in the monastery. He said: "The Master once told me, 'I will go and live wherever it will be your pleasure to take me, carrying me on your shoulders — be it under a tree or in the humblest cottage.'"[7]

The Ramakrishna monastery was finally moved from Nilambar's house to Belur Math on 2 January 1899. Holy Mother was relieved that the Master's children now had a permanent home and was happy that her prayer had been answered.

The local orthodox Hindu people of Belur and neighbouring Bali were not as pleased. They began to gossip that Swami Vivekananda had established Belur Math according to a Western method, and they complained that traditional Hindu customs and dietary restrictions were not being observed there. Swamiji did not pay any attention to the criticism, nor did he allow others to protest. He only remarked: "It is a natural law that when a new idea enters society, the old orthodox group goes against it. All pioneers of world religions had to pass through this test. Without persecution no great ideas can penetrate society. Work without any motive. One day you will reap the result."[8]

A few days before Durga Puja in 1901, Swamiji was coming from Calcutta to Belur Math by boat when he had a vision of a luminous form of Mother Durga in the Math. When the boat landed, he told Brahmananda about his vision and asked him to arrange the worship with an image. Brahmananda told Swamiji of a similar vision. "I was seated on this bench watching the Ganges," he said. "I saw Mother Durga come from Dakshineswar over the Ganges and reach that bel tree." Swamiji was excited. Fortunately an image was available in Kumartuli and it was brought to Belur Math on 17 October 1901.

On 18 October Holy Mother and her attendants came to attend Durga Puja and stayed at Nilambar's house. Brahmachari Krishnalal was the worshipper, and Ishwar Chandra Chakrabarty was the prompter of the mantras. According to Swamiji's direction the worship was performed in the name of Holy Mother, who offered 25 rupees to Ishwar Chakrabarty as dakshina, a gift for performing the worship. Swamiji also invited brahmin pandits from neighbouring Belur, Bali, and Uttarpara to attend the worship. They came and partook of the prasad and cleared up their misunderstandings about Belur Math.

On 21 October after the vesper service Swamiji sang some devotional songs that the Master used to sing, thus entertaining Holy Mother and others gathered there. When the immersion ceremony was held on 22 October, Swami Brahmananda danced on the boat in ecstasy. Holy Mother and her party returned to her Calcutta residence on 23 October.

Ten years later, in April 1911, when Holy Mother returned from her South Indian pilgrimage, Swami Brahmananda wanted to give her a grand reception at Belur Math. The long pilgrimage and rest in Orissa had restored her health. For her arrival, the entrance of Belur Math was decorated with banana trees. *Mangal-ghats* (auspicious pitchers) filled with water and mango leaves were placed at the gate. Hundreds of devotees and monks stood in two rows to receive the Mother. Brahmananda ordered that no one should break the line and rush to take the dust of her feet. As soon as the Mother's carriage reached the gate, nine firecrackers exploded loudly. Holy Mother got down from the carriage. As she walked slowly between the rows of devotees, they chanted with folded hands:

O auspicious One, Thou art the source of all auspiciousness.
Thou art the accomplisher of all cherished desires.
Thou art the giver of refuge.
Thou possessest the eye of wisdom and a beautiful form.
O Narayani, salutations to Thee.

Suddenly, Subodhananda came running from behind the line, took the dust of the Mother's feet, and quickly disappeared into the crowd. Amused, Brahmananda cried out: "Who is he? Catch him!"[9] Everyone laughed at Subodhananda's childlike nature.

Her face fully covered with a veil, Holy Mother sat on a chair in a room on the second floor of the Math building as the monks and devotees bowed down to her. A special worship service and feast were arranged. The men devotees sat on a carpet in the courtyard, and Brahmananda asked a kirtan party to sing devotional songs. Brahmananda smoked his hubble-bubble while listening to the songs. Suddenly he lost outer consciousness and the pipe fell from his hand. He was in samadhi for a long time. When news reached the Mother, she asked her attendant to repeat a mantra in the swami's ear. It worked like a miracle. The swami regained normal consciousness and encouraged the singers, saying, "Continue, continue to sing," as if nothing had happened.

A plate of prasad was placed before the Mother. She took a little, and the remainder was distributed among the devotees by Girish Ghosh and Sharat Chakrabarty. After lunch Holy Mother took a short rest and then left for Udbodhan that afternoon. In her honour nine firecrackers were set off during her departure, and thus the festival ended.[10]

In October 1912 Swami Premananda arranged Durga Puja in Belur Math and invited Holy Mother to attend. On 16 October, the day of *Bodhan* (the awakening ceremony before Durga Puja) Premananda was running around, supervising the arrangements. In late afternoon, when he saw that the auspicious pitchers [*mangal-ghats*] and the banana trees were not yet set at the gate, the swami told the monks: "You have not yet completed the Mother's reception, so she has not arrived yet." Just after the awakening ceremony, the Mother arrived in a carriage along with Golap-ma, Radhu, and some other companions. The horses were unharnessed at the gate to allow Premananda and other monks and devotees to pull the carriage up to the courtyard with great joy and excitement. On the way they shouted: "Victory to Guru Maharaj! Victory to the Divine Mother!" Golap-ma cautiously held the Mother's hand and helped her out of the carriage. Observing the reception and decorations, the Mother remarked with a smile: "See, everything is clean and neat. We, too, have come here dressed like Mother Durga."[11]

The little house at Sonar Bagan (now the Leggett House) on the north side of the monastery was prepared for the Mother's stay. Holy Mother and Radhu stayed in the southernmost room, and Yogin-ma, Golap-ma, Lakshmi, and Aunt Bhanu stayed in other rooms.

On the day of the *ashtami* puja (18 October 1912) Holy Mother sat on her cot facing west, and 300 devotees bowed down to her one after another as she blessed them. On that day she initiated three or four people. That night, from the second-floor veranda of the Math building, she watched Girish's play *Jana,* based on a story from the Mahabharata. At noon on the day of the *navami* puja, Golap-ma said to Swami Saradananda, "The Mother is highly pleased with your loving care and sends you all her blessings."

"Is that so?" replied the swami in a serious voice and said to Premananda, "Brother, did you hear that?" The two swamis embraced each other joyously.[12] After the dashami puja, the image of Durga was taken in a boat to be immersed in the Ganges. Dr. Kanjilal danced, gesticulated, and made faces at the image like a child, evoking roars of laughter. However, a brahmachari protested this behaviour. The Mother and her companions were watching the immersion ceremony from their cottage. When a monk drew the Mother's attention to the brahmachari's objections, she replied: "No, no, this is fine and proper. The goddess should be entertained with song and music, fun and frolic."[13]

At night there was another musical performance, *Ramashwamedh-Yajna* ("The Horse Sacrifice by Ramachandra," based on a story in the Ramayana) by Ahibhusan Bhattacharya. The Mother and her companions watched it. The next day (22 October 1912) Holy Mother returned to her Calcutta residence.

During Durga Puja in 1916, Holy Mother came again to Belur Math and stayed in the same cottage at Sonar Bagan. She arrived on 3 October for the saptami puja and stayed till 6 October. After attending the first day of the worship, news came that Radhu was sick. Swami Dhirananda gave this news to Premananda and asked him to request Holy Mother to stay till the last day of the worship. Premananda replied: "My goodness! Who is going to stop the Divine Mother? Whatever she wishes, that will happen. We are helpless to do anything against her will."[14] However, Radhu soon felt better and the Mother decided not to return to Calcutta.

On the day of the ashtami puja, the Mother attended the worship in the pandal. On her way she saw the monks and brahmacharins preparing vegetables to feed people. She said with a smile: "The children know how to cut vegetables very well." The Mother's disciple Swami Jagadananda replied: "Our aim is to please the Divine Mother of the Universe, whether through spiritual practices or cutting vegetables or turning spices into paste." The Mother replied with a smile, "You are right, my son."[15]

On that day many people bowed down to the Mother, touching her feet. She later washed her feet with Ganges water several times. Yogin-ma noticed this and asked: "What are you doing Mother? You will get a cold."

The Mother replied: "What shall I say, Yogin? I feel a soothing sensation when one person touches my feet, but another person's touch produces a burning sensation all over my body. It is hard for me to get any relief without washing my feet."[16]

After the sandhi puja, a special worship between the ashtami and navami pujas, Saradananda gave a gold coin to a brahmachari and asked him to offer it at the Mother's feet. The brahmachari thought that the offering was meant for Mother Durga, so he asked about it. The swami replied: "You will find the Mother in the house of the garden next door. It is she who has received our worship through the image of Durga."[17]

In a letter dated 9 October 1916, Swami Shivananda described Durga Puja at Belur Math: "The presence of Holy Mother made the worship come alive. Though it rained constantly during the three days of the worship, everything went off smoothly through her grace. The rain stopped whenever the devotees sat for their meals. We were all surprised. We learnt later from Yogin-ma that just at the time of meals Holy Mother prayed: 'O Mother, how will the devotees eat their meals in this rain? The leaf plates will be washed away. O Mother, please save the situation.' Really, her prayers were answered on all the three days."[18]

Holy Mother's disciple Swami Girijananda recalled:

> The Mother, Golap-ma, Radhu, and other women devotees were staying at the Sonar Bagan house. I had a desire to worship the Mother's feet all three days of Durga Puja with flowers and bel leaves. After bathing I would go to the Mother's room and offer flowers at her feet. One morning the Mother came to bow down to Mother Durga in the pandal. She was seated on the upper southern veranda of the shrine building and Golap-ma was with her. As I was offering flowers and bel leaves at the Mother's feet, Golap-ma said in a loud voice, "Don't put bel leaves at the Mother's feet." I said, "The Master worshipped the Mother with flowers and bel leaves, so why shouldn't I?" The Mother smiled. I joyfully worshipped the Mother.[19]

Holy Mother's disciple Brahmachari Haripada (later Swami Pranavananda) was the worshipper for Durga Puja in 1916. He reminisced:

> On the morning of the saptami puja, the Mother's carriage entered the monastery. Yogin-ma, Golap-ma, Sudhira, and others were with her. The entrance gate and worship pandal were well decorated with flowers and leaves. Swami Premananda welcomed the Mother, and the sound of the conch, bell, drum, and flute reverberated throughout the monastery along with the shouts, "Victory to the Mother." When the Mother arrived near

the steps of the shrine, Swami Atmananda waved a lamp with five wicks in front of her and Premananda waved a fan. The Mother went upstairs to the shrine and then came down after a short while. She entered the puja pandal and sat on a carpet reserved for her. I offered flowers at her feet three times and she blessed me, touching my head. When the saptami puja was over, the Mother asked me to repeat the flower offering mantra for her and her women companions. I distinctly remember she uttered this verse of the Chandi in her melodious voice: "Om Jayanti mangalā kāli bhadrakāli kapālini, Durgā shivā kshamā dhātri swahā swadhā namostute. — O goddess, you are always victorious, all-auspicious, the destroyer of evil, the embodiment of gentleness, and adorned with skulls (letters of the alphabet). O Mother Durga, you are the consort of Shiva, all-forgiving, the supporter of the universe, and the nourisher of gods and human beings. We bow down to you."[20]

One year during Durga Puja the Mother went to Belur Math but stayed at Nilambar Mukherjee's garden house. On Maha-ashtami Day the devotees went to pay their respects to the Mother. Holy Mother was seated on a wooden stool; Golap-ma stood near her and was fanning her. There was a long line of devotees entering through one door and going out through the other. Swami Saradananda was seated near the entrance. A devotee offered flowers at the Mother's feet and began to recite hymns to her. After a long while Golap-ma said to him: "Hello, please get up. Enough! How many devotees are waiting in the line? Don't you realize that the Mother is suffering from the heat in this crowd? Why are you taking so long?"

When he heard Golap-ma, Saradananda remarked: "Golap-ma, he has many wishes. Will you not allow him to submit the list of his desires — '*Rupam dehi, jayam dehi, bhāryām manoramām dehi* — Mother, give me beauty, give me victory, give me a beautiful bride after my own heart'?* Please don't pressure him to hurry." All the devotees burst into laughter. The Mother also smiled a little. Without saying another word, that devotee hurriedly left the place.[21]

The Master's disciples did not look upon Holy Mother as their guru's wife; by the Master's grace they knew that she was the Divine Mother in human form. One year during Durga Puja in Belur Math, Brahmananda worshipped the Mother with 108 lotuses.[22]

During the Master's birthday celebration one year, Holy Mother came to Belur Math. Brahmananda and the devotees received her, shouting "Victory to the Mother!" The Mother first went to the shrine and then came down to the courtyard and stood on her asana facing south.

*Saradananda was quoting a prayer from the Chandi.

Brahmananda waved a lamp with five wicks in front of her and asked all of the assembled monks and devotees to kneel down before the Mother and chant the salutation mantra (*Sarva-mangala mangalye...*) of the Divine Mother. The swami was on his knees facing the east and tears trickled from his eyes.[23] Whenever the Mother attended Durga Puja or the Master's birthday at Belur Math, the joy of the monks and devotees knew no bounds.

In 1911, Holy Mother came to Belur Math for a festival celebrating the Master's birthday. The entrance gate was decorated with flowers and leaves, and on the top there was a banner inscribed "Welcome." The Mother's carriage reached the courtyard, which was a little muddy, so Brahmananda had asked the monks to spread a red cloth for her. When Holy Mother got down from the carriage, Swami Brahmananda prostrated fully at her feet and Swami Atmananda waved a camphor flame before her. The Mother went upstairs to the shrine, bowed down to the Master, and meditated for a while. She then walked over the roof and went to the western upper room of the Math building, which was reserved for her. The Mother and her companions watched the Master's festival through the window and listened to Kali kirtan sung by devotees from Andul. The group sang: "O mind, why are you in this world anymore? Let us go to that divine city."

Swami Brahmananda danced during the kirtan and lost outer consciousness in ecstasy. Swami Saradananda directed that he be taken to the lower southwest room of the Math building. There, he sat motionless on a cot for a long time. He was offered refreshments and tobacco but his samadhi continued unbroken. Premananda and Saradananda were extremely concerned. Finally Holy Mother was informed. She came downstairs, touched Brahmananda's arm, and said: "Rakhal, here is prasad. Please eat." Immediately the swami regained his consciousness and became normal. He bowed down to the Mother and joyfully ate the prasad that she offered him.[24]

Holy Mother's disciple Swami Mukteswarananda mentioned the following incident, which probably took place in 1915 during the Master's birthday celebration at Belur Math. When the Master's worship and food offering were over, Swami Arupananda called Brahmachari Ishwar (Swami Mukteswarananda) to serve food to the Mother and her women companions. They sat facing east on the eastern upper veranda of the Math building. Ishwar carried the plate of food that had been offered to the Master and placed it in front of Holy Mother. She took some food from it and began to eat, then asked Ishwar to distribute what remained to the others. After the meal, Ishwar poured water on the Mother's hands for washing, and when he was about to wash her feet with Ganges water, she stopped him and asked him to sprinkle the Ganges water on her head first. At that time there was no filtered tap water in Belur Math. Ishwar told her that in the monastery, everyone used the Ganges water for everything, even in the bathroom for washing. The Mother said: "My child, it is holy Ganges water. One should pay respect to it by sprinkling it on the head first and then using it for other purposes."

After lunch the Mother and her companions sat in Swami Shivananda's room facing the western courtyard and listened to Kali kirtan through the window. Ishwar carried a plate of betel rolls for her. She took one without saying a single word. Observing the Mother's stern look, Ishwar realized that the Mother disapproved of his coming into a room where there were so many women. She was very strict with the young monks about their association with women. She listened to the kirtan for some time and then returned to Udbodhan House in the afternoon.[25]

Belur Math through the Eyes of Holy Mother

Although the Mother spent most of her time in Calcutta and Jayrambati, she kept a vigilant eye on Belur Math and the welfare of the monks. In 1919 some women from Jayrambati came to visit the Mother in Calcutta. She arranged for them to visit Kalighat, Pareshnath (a Jain temple), Dakshineswar, and Belur Math. When they returned from Belur Math, the Mother inquired, "What did you see in Belur Math?"

One lady replied: "Mother, we saw many big cows there. We do not have cows like that in our village."

The Mother asked: "Did you not visit the Master's shrine? Did you not see how the monks have nicely displayed the Master's articles? Did you not meet the disciples of the Master?"

Another lady responded: "Yes, we met them and they took care of us very well because we had come from your village. They served food with loving care."

"Those monks are doing wonderful work," Holy Mother said. "One can attain virtue just by seeing them. Have you seen Dakshineswar from the Ganges ghat in Belur?"

Another woman responded: "Yes, we saw everything, but we have never seen cows like that before."[26]

Once a devotee asked: "Mother, how can those who are poor and cannot afford to go to Varanasi and other holy places achieve the merit of such pilgrimage?"

She replied: "Why, they can achieve the same merit by visiting Dakshineswar or Belur Math, provided they have genuine faith. He [the Lord]
for whom one visits Varanasi is present in Dakshineswar and Belur."[27]

A woman disciple of the Mother recalled: "One day an old woman
devotee told me, 'Nowadays there is no spirituality in the Math and other
places.' I reported this to the Mother. Startled, she said: 'If there is any true
religion, it can be found only here [in Udbodhan House] and in [Belur]
Math.'"[28]

Holy Mother and Some Disciples of the Master

In previous chapters we have written about Swamis Adbhutananda,
Advaitananda, Yogananda, Trigunatitananda, and Saradananda, who
were Holy Mother's attendants. We also wrote a chapter on Swami
Vivekananda and Holy Mother. It is wonderful to see how the disciples
loved, respected, looked after, and interacted with the Mother. Every one
of the Master's disciples considered Holy Mother's decision on any crucial matter to be final, and they obeyed it implicitly. By the grace of their
guru they realized that the Master and the Mother were the same divine
being in two different forms. They realized that the Mother's power was
working behind them and the Ramakrishna Order. The following quotes
indicate how some of disciples understood Holy Mother.

Swami Brahmananda said:

Who can understand our Mother? Even great yogis cannot understand
her, what to speak of others? Is it possible for an ordinary human being to
digest the worship of an incarnation like Sri Ramakrishna? From this one
may understand what a great fountain of power the Mother is. We have
seen with our own eyes that the Mother has been taking the sins and afflictions of many people upon herself and giving them liberation. Can anyone
but the Divine Mother have this power?[29]

It is extremely difficult to understand the Mother. She moves around
with her face veiled like an ordinary woman, but in reality she is the
Mother of the Universe. Could we have recognized her if the Master himself had not revealed to us who she was?[30]

Our Mother is Mahamaya Herself. But such is her maya that none can
understand her. Inside, the great ocean of realization; outside, absolute
calm. How ordinary and simple she appears! Even the Incarnations cannot keep divine moods under control. Sri Ramakrishna manifested them
outwardly. But it is extremely difficult to understand the Mother. How she
has kept us all deluded by her motherly love!...If you want the grace of
Sri Ramakrishna, first propitiate the Mother. The Mother is the supreme
Primordial Power Herself. She holds the key to the knowledge of Brahman

in her hand. Liberation, bliss, and all that are in Mother's keeping. There is no difference between Sri Ramakrishna and the Mother. Through Mother's grace, the attainment of liberation becomes easy.[31]

Swami Saradeshananda wrote in his reminiscences that Swami Brahmananda once visited Jayrambati and stayed with Prasanna, one of Holy Mother's brothers. Out of joy he sang and danced there.[32] When Brahmananda visited Calcutta, he stayed at Balaram's house. Occasionally he came to visit Holy Mother when she was in Calcutta. Swami Premeshananda said: "Maharaj [Swami Brahmananda] would go to bow down to the Mother, but could not stay long near her. His body trembled when he bowed down to her and when he returned from her. It seemed Maharaj could see that the Mother was all-inclusive — the whole universe was contained within her. We could not understand this mysterious phenomenon."[33]

Swami Ishanananda recalled:

One morning at nine o'clock Maharaj came to see the Mother at Udbodhan from Balaram's house. She sat on her cot veiling herself with a chadar and dangling her feet. She asked me to call Maharaj, who was in Sharat Maharaj's room downstairs. Maharaj walked up the steps and I followed him. I noticed his legs were trembling. Maharaj prostrated before the Mother, took the dust of her feet, and asked: "Mother, how is Radhu? O Radhu, where are you?" The Mother touched Maharaj's chin with her fingers and touched them with her lips and blessed him, placing her hand on his head. The Mother then told him of Radhu's illness and inquired about Maharaj's health. Maharaj briefly answered the questions and left the room quickly, then returned to Sharat Maharaj's room. I noticed he was perspiring.

The Mother asked me to arrange a plate with biscuits, oranges, and sweets. She took it from my hand, showed it to the Master, took a little with her tongue, and then asked me to carry the plate to Maharaj. He joyfully received the plate. Sharat Maharaj said, "Will you eat all of the Mother's prasad alone?" Maharaj replied: "Sharat, you are having the Mother's prasad every day and now you want to take a share from my plate? All right, please have some. You are the doorkeeper of the Mother's house. None can go to her without pleasing you." Sharat Maharaj immediately replied: "Maharaj, it is you who have appointed me." Then both of them enjoyed the Mother's prasad and I served two glasses of water."[34]

Swami Shivananda said:

Holy Mother is the ideal of womanhood for this age all over the world. Her life is wonderful. She accepted a human body and lived like any ordinary housewife, though in reality she was none other than the Mother

of the Universe, the primal divine Energy. She was one of those ten
Mahavidyas — Kali, Tara, Shodashi, and others. She came down to earth
as the counterpart of the Master to complete his spiritual mission in this
age. How can ordinary mortals understand her? Even we could not understand her in the beginning. She hid her divinity so completely that it was
not possible to recognize her real nature. The Master alone knew who she
really was, and Swamiji knew a little.[35]

Our Mother's name is Sarada. She is the goddess Saraswati Herself. Out
of her grace, she bestows knowledge of God. Without this knowledge one
cannot have devotion. Pure knowledge and pure devotion are the same,
and one can attain both by her grace alone.[36]

In March 1892, Swamis Shivananda, Ramakrishnananda, and Subodhananda went to visit Holy Mother at Jayrambati. At that time it was a
difficult journey. They informed the Mother before they left and got her
permission to visit. When they arrived, the Mother was very happy. She
had arranged milk, fish, and various vegetables for them.

Swami Shivananda recalled:

At night, as we were going to bed after dinner, I planned with Swami Ramakrishnananda that we should cook for Holy Mother on the following day.

The next morning, when we broached the subject before her after
breakfast, she at first laughed at the idea, and said: "How can that be, my
sons? I am your mother; it is my duty to cook for you. And here you want
to cook for me instead! You will hardly be able to bear the smoke in the
kitchen." With such words, she tried to dissuade us. But we did not mind
her objections and were firm in our resolve. As a last argument, I said:
"We come from brahmin families, so why should you have any objection
to taking food from us? Even the Master ate my cooking." Ultimately, she
had to agree. Swami Ramakrishnananda and I cooked, and the Mother
was highly pleased with the food.

We stayed with Holy Mother for three days that time in great joy. Her
affection was boundless. She was extremely busy from morning till night
so that we might not have the slightest discomfort. After a few days, one
night, I had a fever accompanied by shivering, and it increased as the
night advanced. I had been feeling feverish since evening. Added to that
I had my supper too, for I could not help taking food in the presence of
the Mother. All night I passed in an almost unconscious state. In the early
hours of the morning, I told Shashi Maharaj: "Brother, no more of this
here. If I stay here with my fever, I shall only be burdening the Mother
with great worries. We shall bid farewell to the Mother in the morning and
leave this place. After that, I do not care what happens." He too agreed to
the proposal. As soon as the day dawned, we three saluted the Mother and

left Jayrambati. At first the Mother would not agree to our departure so soon. But when she found that we were insistent, she kept silent.[37]

On another occasion Swami Shivananda said: "Sri Ramakrishna incarnated himself in human form for establishing the *yuga-dharma* [the religion of this age]. The Mother incarnated herself for fulfilling his mission. How can ordinary mortals understand her? In the beginning even we [meaning the disciples] did not understand her in the least. She used to keep her divinity such a close secret that one could not understand anything about her. Mother assumed this human body in order to awaken the entire womanhood of the world."[38]

Swami Premananda wrote:

Who has understood the greatness of Holy Mother? You have heard about Sita, Savitri, Vishnupriya, and Radharani, but the Mother occupies a higher place than them. Not an iota of supernatural power is noticeable in her. The Master was endowed with the power of knowledge and we witnessed many times his ecstasy and samadhi. And what about the Mother? She holds these powers suppressed within herself. What a great superhuman power she has! Victory to the Mother! Don't you see how many people are coming to her to receive her grace? The poison that we cannot digest, we pass on to the Mother.* The Mother is giving refuge to all. She is the embodiment of infinite power and boundless grace. Victory to the Mother! Even the Master would accept people only after a lot of testing and screening. And what do we see in the Mother's life? It is indeed amazing that she gives refuge to all indiscriminately.

Being the Empress of the Universe, she has assumed the mask of a poor woman. She sweeps the floor, washes dishes and vessels, husks paddy, and even removes the leavings of devotees after eating. She has been undergoing this hardship at Jayrambati in order to teach householders their household duties. She has infinite patience, boundless compassion, and above all complete absence of ego.[39]

Premananda was one of the few disciples of the Master who had free access to Holy Mother. She was very fond of him, and Premananda was also very devoted to her. Whenever any monk went to visit Holy Mother at Udbodhan House, Premananda sent flowers, vegetables, and milk for her from Belur Math, asking the monk to convey his salutations. Because he never initiated anyone, he would send devotees to Holy Mother or Brahmananda for initiation. Premananda's face actually glowed when he spoke about Holy Mother. He once said that those who differentiated

---

*By this the swami means that Holy Mother absorbed the worst sins of sinners by giving them initiation.

between her and the Master would never make any spiritual progress: she and the Master were like the two sides of one coin. In the course of a talk at Belur Math, he said to the devotees: "We have seen that she has a much greater capacity than the Master. She is the embodiment of Power, and how well she controls it! Sri Ramakrishna could not do so, though he tried. His power became manifest through his frequent ecstasies, which were seen by all. The Mother repeatedly experiences samadhi, but others do not know of it. What wonderful self-control she exercises! She covers herself with a veil, like a young bride in her husband's home. The people of Jayrambati think that she is busy day and night looking after her nephews and nieces."[40]

When Holy Mother was in Calcutta, Premananda always asked her permission before going anywhere to lecture. In 1914 Premananda was invited to speak during the Ramakrishna festival in Malda, in North Bengal. He came with the devotees to Udbodhan to receive the Mother's permission, but she refused it because Premananda had been sick only a fortnight before. When the devotees again importuned Holy Mother about the trip, she asked Premananda if he wanted to go. He replied with great emotion: "What do I know, Mother? I shall carry out your order. If you ask me to jump into fire, I will jump; if you ask me to plunge into water, I will plunge; if you ask me to enter into hell, I will enter. What do I know? Your word is final." At last Holy Mother gave her permission, but she asked him to return soon. To the devotees she said: "You see, they are all great souls. Their bodies are channels for doing good in the world. Look after their physical comfort and well-being."[41]

Swami Abhedananda said: "She who was Sita and Radha has incarnated in this age in the form of Sri Sarada Devi. The Mother is Saraswati, the goddess of wisdom. She bestows knowledge and liberation. The Master and Mother are identical, as Shiva and Shakti."[42]

The disciples of the Master consulted with Holy Mother even in personal matters when they could not come to a decision themselves. Swami Abhedananda left for America in 1897 where he lived on strict vegetarian food. From time to time he suffered illnesses. His doctor suggested that he take non-vegetarian food for health reasons. About this, he wrote a letter to Holy Mother seeking her advice. She replied:

8/1 Baghbazar Street, Calcutta
March 1899

Dear Son,
I am delighted to receive your letter yesterday with the news that your

activities are going on well. You are glorifying the face of the Master. I always pray to him, and I will bless you so that you may be crowned with success. There is no doubt that the Master will always help you in your noble activities. Do not be so strict about food. In that country you should take fish and meat instead of purely vegetarian food. It will not do any harm to you. I am giving you permission to eat non-vegetarian food without any hesitation. Always take care of your health. Take rest in solitude from time to time and write to me occasionally about your health.

My blessings to you,
Your Mother[43]

Swami Turiyananda said: "The Mother is the great divine power. She exists in this world to do good to humanity. We try our utmost to raise our minds to the throat centre, while she uses Radhu to force her mind down to that place. Try to understand this mystery! Victory to the Mother, the Primordial Power!"[44]

Swami Subodhananda said:

The Master and the Mother are one, as the obverse and reverse of the same coin. As fire and its power to burn are identical, so are they. They are complementary to each other. The Mother is Mahamaya — the Primordial Power. When God incarnates, She also comes with Him; otherwise the play of an avatar remains incomplete. She came with Ramachandra as Sita, with Krishna as Radha, with Buddha as Yashodhara, with Chaitanya as Vishnupriya, and now with Ramakrishna as Sarada.[45]

Know for certain that when Holy Mother has blessed you, from that very moment your fate has changed. Many people even now deeply regret that they did not have *darshan** of the Mother. Only he can understand Sri Ramakrishna or Holy Mother to whom they reveal themselves. The sun can be seen only with sunlight. It is by their grace and compassion that people can know them and have their darshan. If you can make the Mother your own, through her grace you will attain everything.[46]

Swami Vijnanananda said:

I repeat the Mother's name as "Ma Anandamayi." There is a special effect of chanting the Mother's name: She protects spiritual aspirants from lust. I experienced this. One can attain devotion, faith, sincerity, intelligence, wealth, and opulence by the power of her name. I derive more strength from the Mother's name than from the Master's.[47]

You must look upon the Master and the Mother with an eye of non-differentiation. Remember, one cannot realize the Master without the grace of the Mother, and vice versa. The Master is, as it were, Lord Narayana,

*Being in the presence of a deity or a holy person.

and the Mother, Goddess Lakshmi. One should ask for strength from the Mother. Without strength nothing can be achieved.[48]

Swami Akhandananda said:

Holy Mother is the goddess Annapurna, the Mother of the Universe, and Lakshmi of Vaikuntha (heaven). This time God himself incarnated as Sri Ramakrishna, and the Goddess as our Holy Mother. God and Goddess both are necessary to perform the avatar-lila, or the divine play on the earth. As many times God has incarnated as an avatar from Ramachandra to Chaitanya, so many times His consort has come. So our Mother became Sita, Radha, Yashodhara, and Vishnupriya. The Master disclosed the true nature of the Mother to some of us. He said to Swami Trigunatitananda: "Radha's infinite power of maya is beyond description. Millions of Krishnas and Ramas evolve, abide, and dissolve in it."[49]

When a devotee said that he had met Holy Mother, Swami Akhandananda remarked: "When you have seen the Mother, the same result of having the darshan of Sri Ramakrishna will accrue to you. To have had the darshan of the Mother or the Master is the same thing."[50]

The disciples considered an order from Holy Mother to be their guru's order. In 1897 Swami Akhandananda was the first monk to start famine relief in Murshidabad, and Swamiji encouraged him to work even unto death. Forgetting food and rest, he served human beings as God, which is one of the principles of the Ramakrishna Mission. Eventually his health broke down and he suffered from malarial fever and a lack of proper food and rest. The brother disciples asked him to take care of himself, but he disregarded their advice. Finally the Mother called for him to come to her Calcutta residence. He immediately came from Sargachi and bowed down to her. Holy Mother told him: "Now you should stay in Balaram's house, and an ayurvedic doctor will treat you. Please follow his instructions implicitly. And don't go away from that place without my permission." The swami obeyed the Mother like a little boy. When he was under the ayurvedic treatment, Premananda visited him and asked him to come to Belur Math for a day. Akhandananda replied: "Brother, the Mother asked me to stay here and have the treatment. I can't go any-place without her permission; otherwise she will scold me." Premananda then went to Udbodhan, got the Mother's permission, and brought him to Belur Math.[51]

Nowadays some people do not look after their elderly parents, who brought them into this world and raised them. They do not realize how much suffering and trouble a mother undertakes to bring up a child. In one of the hymns on the Divine Mother, Shankara says, "O Mother, a bad son may sometimes be born, but never has there been a bad mother." An ocean has its bottom and its limits, but a mother's affection is bottomless and limitless. The difference between an ordinary mother and Holy Mother is this: An ordinary mother thinks that her children came from her body, so they belong only to her; Holy Mother knew that all human beings originated from her and all are her children. She demonstrated pure and unselfish love to humanity. Ramakrishna left a group of wonderful children who looked after Holy Mother more than they did their own biological mothers. The relationship between the Master's disciples and Holy Mother was so loving and sweet that it should be the paradigm of mother-child relationships all over the world.

Swami Nirlepananda described how the Master's disciples respected Holy Mother:

We noticed that when the Master's disciples came to bow down to the Mother, she became established in her real Self. And when these great ones left, it would take some time before she came down from the higher plane to the normal state. Swamiji saw that the Mother was *Adya-shakti* (the Primordial Power). He recognized that a jiva attains the knowledge of Brahman by her grace only. After initiating Sudhir (later Swami Shuddhananda), Swamiji asked Holy Mother, "Mother, please bestow your best blessings on this boy." Swami Brahmananda said to Shuddhananda: "Sudhir, I can give you the experience of samadhi, but the Mother can do it better and more easily."

In 1906 Swami Saradananda said to a young man: "Today you have received the Mother as a guru. If you practise spiritual disciplines according to her instruction, you will realize that the Mother is the Divine Mother Herself. But you will have to work hard. Some say, 'I have seen the Mother and received the mantra from her, so I don't need to practise any more sadhana.' In one sense they are right, but truly those who say that are deceitful. The Mother opens the door for liberation. Now you will have to go and reach that door."

In 1913 Swami Vijnanananda came to Udbodhan House to see Holy Mother. He said: "I was seated in Sharat Maharaj's room downstairs. I got a call from upstairs to bow down to the Mother. While I was walking up each step, I could feel the lotus of each centre of Kundalini opening up. My whole body and mind were flooded with bliss."

In 1918 at Balaram Mandir, Swami Turiyananda said to Dr. Durgapada Ghosh, a disciple of the Mother: "Doctor, what are you seeing? What do you think about the Mother? Is it enough to receive a mantra in the ear if there is no practice of sadhana? It is sure and certain that you will get liberation at the end and it is registered. But if you sincerely practise sad-hana by repeating the mantra, you will be blessed by tasting the bliss of jivanmukti [liberation-in-life]. Then only will you realize who the Mother is and leave this world happily.[52]

Swami Adbhutananda said: "Mother knows my past and future. She knows everything. What is the point in writing to her just for the sake of appearance? What is the necessity of writing to one who knows every-thing about my past, present, and future?...Will the Mother become a stranger to me just because I do not go to see her? You ask how I look upon the Mother. She is Mother Lakshmi, yet she is sometimes Sita."[53]

In 1907 Holy Mother came to Calcutta from Jayrambati to attend Durga Puja at Girish's house, and she stayed at Balaram's house for a month. Latu (Swami Adbhutananda) lived in a room to the right of the main entrance. While entering the house, the Mother saw her dear Latu. She inquired: "Hello, my son, Latu! How are you?" Latu replied in his unpolished rustic language: "Go away, Mother! You are a dignified lady. Why have you come to the outer apartment to speak to me? Please go upstairs right away. I will not speak to you here. You could have sent for me, and I would have come up to see you. Mother, I am your servant, you know." Laughing, Holy Mother went upstairs to her room.

As long as Holy Mother stayed at Balaram's house, she sent prasad to Latu every day. Other devotees would go to see Holy Mother, but Latu stayed in his room. Some devotees misunderstood him because he did not go to pay his respects to the Mother. One day he told them: "Look, is it so easy to understand the Mother? Just imagine — she accepted the Master's worship! Only the Master knew the real nature of the Mother, and Swamiji understood a little. She is Mother Lakshmi Herself. It needs a lot of austerity to understand her grace."

The day arrived when Holy Mother was leaving for Jayrambati. All the devotees went to bow down to the Mother upstairs, but Latu did not go. He was pacing in his room and muttering to himself: "Who is a mother or father to a monk? He is free from all maya." When the Mother was coming down the steps, she overheard what Latu was saying. When she reached his door, she said, "Dear Latu, you will not have to accept me, my son." Immediately Latu sprang from his room and fell at the Mother's feet and began to sob. Seeing her child Latu cry, tears came from the Mother's eyes. Latu took the corner of his chadar and began to wipe the Mother's tears. He said to her with a choked voice: "Mother, you are going to your father's house. You should not cry. Sharat will bring you back soon. Don't cry, Mother, don't. Is it proper for one to cry when one departs?"[54] This touching departure reminds us of Latu's childlike simplicity and deep love for the Mother. He was the first disciple whom the Master introduced to the Mother in Dakshineswar, and he remained devoted to her throughout his life.

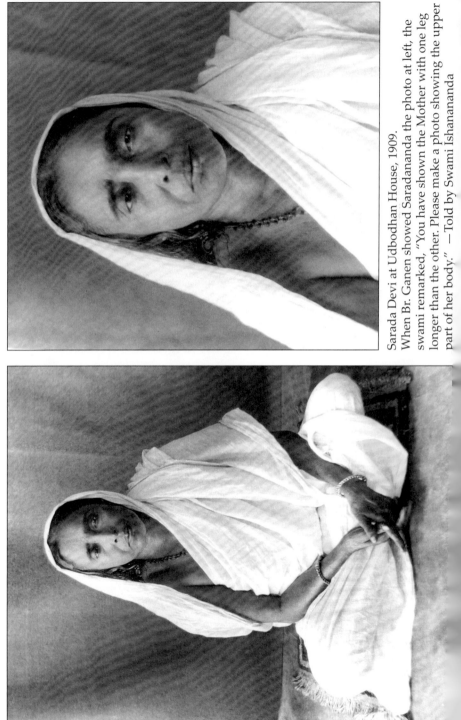

Sarada Devi at Udbodhan House, 1909. When Br. Ganen showed Saradananda the photo at left, the swami remarked, "You have shown the Mother with one leg longer than the other. Please make a photo showing the upper part of her body." —Told by Swami Ishanananda

24
Mother
of the Ramakrishna Order

Yathā agner-dāhikā shakti rāmakrishne sthitā hi yā;
Sarva-vidyā-svarupam tām sāradām pranamāmi-aham.
— *A hymn by Swami Saradananda*

As the power to burn dwells in fire, so Sarada dwells in Ramakrishna as his Shakti, the Cosmic Power. I bow down to that Mother, who is the embodiment of knowledge.

One day in 1884 Ramakrishna was seated in his room at Dakshineswar, talking about the three salient disciplines of the Vaishnava religion. Chaitanya taught his disciple Sanatan:

Jive dayā nāme ruchi vaishnav sevan, Ihā vinā dharma nāi shunu Sanātan.
Listen, O Sanatan, there is no other dharma than practising compassion for all living beings, having love for God's name, and serving the devotees.

Reflecting upon these three teachings, the Master repeated the word "compassion" and then went into samadhi. After a while he returned to normal consciousness and said to the devotees: "How foolish to speak of compassion! Man is an insignificant worm crawling on the earth — and he is to show compassion to others? This is absurd. It must not be compassion, but service to all. Recognize all people as God's manifestations and serve them." Only Narendra (later Swami Vivekananda) understood the implication of these words and resolved to implement this practical Vedanta — serving human beings as God.

After returning from the West, Swami Vivekananda officially inaugurated the Ramakrishna Math and Mission* on 1 May 1897 in Calcutta. As of December 2013, it has 179 centres all over the world. Swamiji

---

*The Ramakrishna Order includes two organizations: the Ramakrishna Math and the Ramakrishna Mission. The members of the former devote themselves mainly to worship, contemplation, study, and preaching, and those of the latter to such philanthropic activities as are necessary in times of famine, flood, epidemics, or other calamities. Further, the Mission maintains hospitals, dispensaries, and various educational institutions. Householders can be members of the Ramakrishna Mission.

understood the difficulty of organizing, but at the same time he realized that no religion can function or spread without an organization. The only things that can keep organized work from becoming corrupt, he felt, are purity of life and renunciation.

In 1890, Holy Mother visited Bodh-Gaya. There she noticed how comfortably the members of a local monastery lived with all their physical needs supplied. She later recalled:

> Ah, how much I wept, how often I prayed to the Master! That is why you see all these monasteries established by his grace. Immediately after his passing away, the children renounced the world and sought out a temporary shelter. But soon after, they began to wander about independently. I felt very sad and prayed to the Master: "Oh Master, you came down to earth, had fun with a few companions, and then departed in a happy mood. Was that the end of everything? If so, what was the need of assuming a human body and going through all this suffering? I have seen many sadhus at Varanasi and Vrindaban who live on alms and seek shelter under trees. There is no dearth of sadhus like them. I cannot bear the sight of my children, who have renounced everything in your name, going from door to door for a morsel of food. I fervently pray to you that those who give up the world in your name may not lack simple food and clothing. Let them live together with you and your teachings as their centre. Those who are afflicted with the sorrows of the world will come to them and obtain peace by listening to your teachings. That is the purpose of your advent, isn't it so? I cannot control myself when I see them drifting about helplessly." Afterwards Naren slowly organized all this.[1]

The Role of the Mother

Who manages a household? Swami Vivekananda replied: "In the Western home, the wife rules. In an Indian home, the mother rules."[2] In many religions God is worshipped as the male principle, but in India God is worshipped not only as Father but also as Mother. The Taittiriya Upanishad says: *Matri devo bhava* — Worship the mother as God. Why? Vivekananda replied: "Because she made herself pure. She underwent harsh penances sometimes to keep herself as pure as purity can be."[3] It is the mother's love and affection, compassion and selflessness, patience and forbearance that hold the family members together. When the Master's young disciples wanted to be monks and form the Ramakrishna Order, they had to go through insurmountable difficulties. Holy Mother stood behind them.

In his lecture, *My Life and Mission* (given in America on 27 January 1900), Vivekananda acknowledged the role of Holy Mother after the

Master's passing away: "Then came a terrible time — for me personally and for all the other boys as well....That one's sympathy brought blessing and hope. She was a woman, my Master's wife. We all have great respect for her."[4]

Holy Mother was Ramakrishna's first disciple and he transmitted the results of his sadhana to her. Later he left his spiritual power and legacy to his disciples. Gradually, the disciples realized that the Master's power was working through Holy Mother; they were identical. During her lifetime, Holy Mother was the Shakti, or Power, behind the Order. That power is still working invisibly.

Although Holy Mother was not involved in the administration of the Order, Swami Brahmananda, Swami Saradananda, and the other leaders always consulted with her on crucial issues. She watched over the monks' physical, mental, and spiritual welfare. Her practical knowledge and common sense guided them in adjusting to community life in the monastery, and she gave shelter in Udbodhan House to those who could not get along with others.

Her spiritual power, unselfish love, and maternal affection transformed the lives of many undisciplined monks. However, she disciplined without compromise those who deviated from the ideal of the Ramakrishna Order. She also lifted their minds to a higher realm through her spiritual power and compassion. Her loving service and sweet behaviour, forgiveness and gentleness overwhelmed those monks, and they obeyed her implicitly.

Regarding the monastic ideal, she said that those who could not uphold this ideal should marry rather than pollute the purity of the Order. She initiated and recruited many monks and gave ochre cloths to some of them who later spread Ramakrishna's message in India as well as abroad. She foresaw that there would be temples and monasteries at Kamarpukur and Jayrambati, and she made arrangements for them during her lifetime. She was behind the establishment of the Udbodhan, Jayrambati, Koalpara, and Kamarpukur centres. She also encouraged the monks to do relief work during natural calamities.

As a mother bird protects her fledglings from the storm by spreading her wings, so the Mother protected the Master's disciples from various vicissitudes. In 1889 Swami Brahmananda had a desire to practise austerities in the western part of India. The Mother was then at Jayrambati. When she came to know of his intention, she wrote to Balaram Basu: "I hear that Rakhal wants to go to the western part of India to practise austerities. The last time he did this in Puri he suffered from the cold. It will be better if he goes in February after the winter. But if his desire is strong, then I have nothing to say."[5] This approval was enough for Brahmananda, and he left for tapasya in December.

Holy Mother was not a selfish or possessive mother, overly attached to her children or keeping them too close to herself. She gave sannyasa to some disciples, and then sent them away to the Himalayas for tapasya. She even gave them permission to go to foreign countries to spread Ramakrishna's message. Holy Mother said to Swami Girijananda: "My mother was very fond of Sharat. He came to me for permission to go to America. I blessed him and said: 'Don't be afraid. The Master is always protecting you.' When Sharat left, my mother said to me: 'Look Saru, being a mother, why did you give permission to Sharat to go far away beyond the seven seas and thirteen rivers? Your heart is as hard as stone!'"[6]

Holy Mother tied the monks to her with unfathomable love and affection. She watched over their physical needs as well as their spiritual welfare. Swami Virajananda recalled:

> Towards the end of the summer of 1893, Holy Mother was staying at Nilambar's garden house in Belur. She lived on the second floor with Golap-ma and Yogin-ma. Swamis Yogananda and Trigunatitananda lived downstairs as her attendants and they did all her errands. The Ramakrishna Math was then at Alambazar. I joined there and went to visit the Mother, which was my second meeting with her.* I prostrated at her feet and she asked me to stay there that night. The next morning when I was about to take leave, she said to me affectionately: "My son, this time I am very much pained to see you. What a nice plump body you had previously. Repeated attacks of malarial fever have now brought your health to such an emaciated condition. Well, you have joined the monastery, but you know those people there are penniless fakirs. How can they procure the requisite nutritious food for you? What necessary care for your health is possible there? So I suggest that you go back to your home and stay there till you regain your health with proper diet and medicine."
>
> I was least prepared for these words of the Mother. Astounded, I couldn't utter anything for some time. After a while I said: "Mother, you are asking me to go home. What shall I do there?" She replied: "You spend your time practising meditation, japa, worship, and studying the scriptures."
>
> Coming downstairs I could not hold back my tears. I went to a secluded corner of the garden and wept bitterly. Swami Yogananda heard the whole story from Golap-ma about me. He consoled me and asked, "Have you received any initiation?" "No, I have not," I replied. "Then why did you

---

*Swami Virajananda met Holy Mother for the first time in Jayrambati in the autumn of 1892.

not ask the Mother what meditation and japa you were to do at home?" said Yogananda. "Well, ask her tomorrow after your bath."

Those words of the swami were to me a revelation. I did not know till then that the Mother gave initiation to anybody. However, as per the instructions of Yogananda, I went to the Mother the next morning after she had finished her worship and put to her the tutored question. The Mother then initiated me formally. The mantra that she gave me for japa and meditation was not in tune with the particular aspect of sadhana I had been following. So I was a little confused and asked her openly, "Mother, I have been meditating on God in such and such a manner and that gives me great satisfaction." "No, my son, what you have received from me is better for you," was her short reply. How strange! I felt within myself an instantaneous transformation of my outlook on sadhana.

I spent the whole day at the Mother's place before my evening departure for the Alambazar Math. It was July — right in the middle of the rains in Bengal. The Ganges was full to the brim. A thick mist had enveloped the atmosphere and the evening darkness was to follow soon. It was drizzling. Suddenly I felt a sob deep in my heart. The gloomy inclement weather outside represented my state of mind. With a heavy heart I went to the Mother and said, "Mother, I will take leave of you now." "Yes, my son," she said, "it is time. Well, come here now and then. See that the body gets strong." She then touched my chin by way of motherly blessing. I went out of the house and got on the boat at the ferry ghat close by. The boat plying northwards passed in front of the garden house. In that background of twilight I looked at the Mother's room on the terrace. She was standing on the open terrace with her gaze fixed towards the Ganges on the boat. As long as the house was visible from the boat I saw her in the same position. My heart surged with emotion and tears came in profusion. Later I learned that Golap-ma had protested her standing that way in the drizzling rain, but she said with tearful eyes: "Oh, I am thinking how very sad the boy must be feeling. So I am looking at him."[7]

Swami Nikhilananda wrote:

Holy Mother was a source of unfailing inspiration to the members of the Ramakrishna Math and Mission and showered her blessings upon all who renounced the world, inspired by the Master's teachings. She had felt the need of a religious organization for the purpose of preaching the Master's teachings and giving them practical shape, and also of affording shelter to the monks where they could be assured of food, clothes, and other simple necessities of life. After the establishment of the Math and Mission she became its spiritual centre. During her lifetime she kept her eyes on the monks to see that they faithfully discharged their duties. Like Swami Vivekananda, she looked on the organization as the visible body of Sri Ramakrishna, and its every part as one of his own limbs. She gave freedom to the monks to develop their inner potentialities in their own way, but did not shrink from severity when such an attitude was found necessary."[8]

Once Yogin-ma told Swami Saradeshananda: "Whatever Math and Ashrama centres you see around are the outcome of Holy Mother's grace. Wherever she visited any deities, she prayed with tearful eyes: 'Master, please create a shelter for my children to live in and arrange a little food for them to eat.' The Mother's prayers have been fulfilled."[9]

At Koalpara Ashrama

Koalpara Village is located four miles north of Jayrambati on the route between Vishnupur and Jayrambati. When Holy Mother began to travel by train from Calcutta, she would stop at the Vishnupur station and then take a bullock cart to Jayrambati. She would break her journey at Koalpara Ashrama, which she called her "parlour," her resting place.

Kedarnath Datta, a local schoolteacher, started Koalpara Ashrama with a few young men. They practised meditation and read the Bhagavad Gita, the Bhagavata, and the Ramakrishna-Vivekananda literature. They became drawn to Holy Mother and eventually took initiation from her. When the Mother was in Jayrambati, many Calcutta devotees visited her. The young men from Koalpara carried groceries, vegetables, and other necessities to her. In addition to their spiritual practices, these young men were involved in the freedom movement against the British, and the police had an eye on this ashrama. The ashrama also had a weaving school, a primary school, a charitable dispensary, and a small orphanage. While Holy Mother and Swami Saradananda encouraged their philanthropic activities, they did not approve of any revolutionary activities.

When Kedar approached Holy Mother for sannyasa, she was reluctant to confer it because he was his mother's only son. Moreover his health was not good: he suffered from asthma from time to time. However, his mother gave him permission for sannyasa and asked a boon from the Mother that she might die before her son. (Her desire was later fulfilled.) Holy Mother gave the ochre cloth to Kedar, Rajen, Amulya, and Kishori. They later took formal sannyasa at Belur Math and became Swamis Keshavananda, Vidyananda, Dhruvananda, and Parameswarananda, respectively. Afterwards Barada, Gagan, and Rammay took initiation from the Mother and became monks. They were later known as Swamis Ishanananda, Ritananda, and Gauriswarananda, respectively. Thus Holy Mother began to recruit monks into the Ramakrishna Order.

Monks of Koalpara and Jayrambati.
Top: Keshavananda and Parameswarananda.
Middle: Ishanananda and Gauriswarananda.
Bottom: Maheswarananda and Saradeshananda.

Keshavananda donated his parental home near Koalpara Ashrama to build Jagadamba Ashrama where Holy Mother stayed on several occasions for long periods at a time. In 1911 Holy Mother installed pictures of Ramakrishna and herself in Koalpara Ashrama and worshipped both pictures with flowers and sandal paste. She asked Kishori to perform a *homa*, or fire ceremony, on that occasion. In 1918, Koalpara Ashrama became affiliated with the Ramakrishna Math and Mission.

Although Holy Mother hid herself behind a veil, she had a dynamic personality. Her divine personality and inspiration produced wonderful monks for the Ramakrishna Order. The monks came from various parts of India, and from different castes, social positions, and backgrounds. Holy Mother always emphasized friendship and brotherly love as the cement necessary to strengthen the organization. She reminded the monks that mutual love and respect, purity and renunciation, humility and obedience are essential for the monastic organization. Although she knew that it was necessary to maintain discipline in a monastery, Holy Mother disapproved of any unnecessary harshness or excessive exercise of authority. Swami Keshavananda, the head of Koalpara Ashrama, was a hard taskmaster and demanded strenuous labour from the monastic workers, some of whom were his students. He often acted like a dictator over the centre and was negligent in giving the monks proper food and care. As a result of this ill treatment, some of the ashrama members left to take shelter under Holy Mother or Swami Saradananda.

Keshavananda lodged a complaint to the Mother, saying: "Mother, my workers formerly always obeyed me. Now it seems they have become smart. They don't always carry out my orders. They know they can find shelter with you or Swami Saradananda. You give them affection and good food, too. If you and the swami do not keep them with you but return them to me, I shall be able to keep them under control." Stunned by these words, the Mother said: "What is the matter with you? What do you mean? Love alone is the essential thing. The Master's organization is growing only through love. I am their mother. How impudent you are to make such a caustic comment to me about their food!"[10] Keshavananda was quite austere and frugal. He did not want to spend money on healthy food even when the monks were suffering from malarial fever. In Koalpara Ashrama they would offer to the Master rice and a vegetarian dish with spinach, which the monks afterwards partook of as prasad.

Generally the monks of Koalpara brought vegetables and groceries to Jayrambati, but once they did not show up for a couple of weeks. Concerned, Holy Mother sent her maid to investigate and learned that they were all suffering from malaria. She dictated a letter to Radhu for Kesha-vananda and sent it through her maid Nibu: "Dear Kedar, I have installed the Master at Koalpara. The Master used to eat rice and fish also. So I tell you, please offer rice and fish at least on Saturdays and Tuesdays and not on Sundays, and a minimum of three kinds of vegetables. If they practise severe austerity without good food, how will the monks fight malaria?"[11]

She was extremely practical. If monks are physically weak, how will they serve the Order? The Mother later indignantly told Keshavananda: "What is this? How can you run the ashrama through shrewd manip-ulation? Those boys may be your students, but if you scold your own children too much, they will leave you."[12]

The Mother was fond of Keshavananda for his dedication, and he also was very devoted to her. But the Mother did not indulge any inappropri-ate requests from her disciples. Once at Koalpara when Holy Mother was staying with Radhu, Keshavananda reported to her that his workers were not obeying him and wanted to go elsewhere. He wanted her to persuade them to stay in Koalpara and asked her to see that they did not find shel-ter in any other ashrama. Angrily the Mother replied: "How dare you ask me to speak to the monks that way? Do you mean to say they should not be allowed to find accommodation anywhere else? They are my children and have taken shelter with the Master. Wherever they go, the Master will look after them. And you want to extract a promise from me that they will not find shelter at any other place! I can never utter any such a promise."[13] Everyone was frightened by her loud voice and reddened face. Keshava-nanda at once fell at the Mother's feet and begged her forgiveness.

Although Holy Mother admonished the head of the Koalpara cen-tre, she also advised monastic workers to adjust to community life. One day in Jayrambati she told a brahmachari: "Look, monks in the ashrama should live together, adjusting to each other. The Master used to say, 'sha, sha, sa — forbear, forbear, forbear.' Have patience and forbearance in all situations. The Master is looking after you."[14] Despite various difficulties in ashrama life, Holy Mother always encouraged monks to live together harmoniously and work sincerely for the Master.

Because the Ramakrishna Order is an international organization, Holy Mother always inspired the monks to learn English well so that they could communicate with foreigners. One day Keshavananda said to the Mother: "Mother, all of your children are highly educated except a few like us. Swami Saradananda wrote the biography of the Master [Sri Rama-krishna Lilaprasanga] and is spreading his message. Your other children are also giving lectures and doing so many things."

The Mother replied: "What are you saying? The Master did not have much education. The main thing is to keep the mind on God. A great deal of work will be done through you in this part of the country. All these boys do so many errands for me. This time the Master has come to liberate all — the rich and the poor, the literate and the illiterate. The Malaya breeze is blowing. Those who unfurl the sail reach the destination, and those who take refuge in him will be blessed. Don't worry. You are my own people. However, learned monks are like ivory covered with gold."[15]

When the monks faced a dilemma, they sought Holy Mother's advice. Koalpara Ashrama had a charitable dispensary. Some people took advantage of the ashrama by accepting free medicine though they had the means to pay for it. The head swami did not like this, so he sought the Mother's permission to discontinue giving medicine to those people for free. With a charitable outlook, the Mother replied: "All seekers of help are considered to be needy, so keep the door of the dispensary open to all."[16]

Holy Mother encouraged the monks to work and at the same time she cautioned them not to be egotistic and narrow-minded while managing the centre. She warned them against inordinate attachment to the monastery or entanglement in activities that might interfere with their spiritual practices. One day she scolded Swami Tanmayananda because of his undue involvement in the ashrama activities. She said: "You have renounced the world to repeat God's name. Now you are involved with too many activities. The ashrama has become your second world. People come to the monastery having given up their families, but they become so attached to the monastery that they do not want to give it up." Quoting a Bengali proverb, she added: "A man eager to keep away from acidic food builds a home under a tamarind tree!"[17]

The blessing of a divine being never fails. Holy Mother always thought about the monks' welfare. Once in Jayrambati during Durga Puja, the monks and devotees offered flowers at her feet. When they were finished, she said to Brahmachari Barada: "Bring some more flowers and offer them while mentioning the names of Rakhal, Tarak, Sharat, Khoka, Yogin, and Golap. And offer flowers on behalf of all my known and unknown children in the world." Afterwards she remained silent for a while with folded hands looking at the picture of the Master. Then she prayed: "Master, bestow welfare on everyone in this life and the next. Please look after them."[18]

In 1918 during her birthday celebration, the Mother accepted flower offerings from monks and devotees in Udbodhan House. When everyone had left she said to Brahmachari Barada: "Today is an auspicious day. Please offer flowers on behalf of the monks and devotees of Koalpara and Jayrambati." Then she prayed to the Master to bless them all.

Holy Mother and her Disciples

Holy Mother's love was so deep and so rare that those who lived with her felt it even in her actions. Once in Jayrambati, Brahmachari Jnana (later Swami Jnanananda) had such a severe case of eczema that he could not feed himself. While he was sick the Mother fed him and then removed his leaf plate for him.

Brahmachari Rasbihari (later Swami Arupananda) was busy with the construction of Holy Mother's new house in Jayrambati. One day he went to a neighbouring village to do some errands but did not return before lunch. It was a short winter day. He returned a few hours before evening and heard that the Mother had not had her meal but was instead waiting for his return. He rushed to her and remonstrated: "Mother, your health is not good. Why have you been fasting all this time?" The Mother replied: "My son, how can I eat when you have not yet eaten?"[19] Rasbihari immediately sat for his meal so the Mother and other women devotees could take their food. How many mothers in this world would treat their children this way?

In Jayrambati and Koalpara, the Mother lived a normal life among the villagers, free from the routines and restrictions of Calcutta. In 1911 Saradananda sent a young monk named Prakash to escort Holy Mother from Jayrambati to Calcutta. On the way to Calcutta the Mother stopped at Koalpara. She wanted to walk with Keshavananda's mother to her house, but Prakash wanted her to go by palanquin. This upset Holy Mother and she scolded him: "Look, this is a village and I regard the ashrama as a part of my home. These boys are my own people. I want to lead a free life in Koalpara. I give a sigh of relief here to be free from my cage in Calcutta. There you keep me confined, and I am always cautious about my movements. I simply will not be controlled here at every step. If you like you may write to Sharat about it."[20] The monk immediately begged forgiveness.

That evening, Prakash hurried the local monks to prepare Mother's supper so they could resume their journey quickly. The Mother said to him sternly: "Why are you losing your temper and yelling at these monks? This is a village. Here everything does not move according to the clock like in Calcutta. Don't you see how these boys have been working tirelessly since morning? Whatever you may say, we shall not start before eating."[21] The Mother had so much feeling for the monks! Finally, she left for Vishnupur by bullock cart at eight o'clock.

On 31 January 1917, the Mother left for Jayrambati from Calcutta. On her way she stayed at Jagadamba Ashrama for a couple of days and then continued her journey. A few days before Ramakrishna's birthday, Brahmachari Barada brought some groceries for the Mother by bicycle from Koalpara. The Mother gave him some prasad and asked him to stay at Jayrambati that day as there was a thunderstorm imminent. But Barada did not listen to Holy Mother because he had some duties in Koalpara. On his way back to Koalpara, he was caught in a hailstorm and suffered terribly. He walked the rest of the way back to Koalpara with his bicycle along the muddy path. That night he had a fever. The next day Holy Mother sent her maid with a letter to Koalpara to get news of Barada. When he visited Holy Mother in Jayrambati a few days later, she said: "You were stubborn and did not listen to me. I was worried about you when you left. I suffer when someone does not listen to me and gets into trouble. My son, you should listen when someone advises you from the heart."[22]

Holy Mother as Guru

In 1907 Jiten, Khagen, and Tarun — three young disciples of Holy Mother — visited her at Jayrambati. Filled with the spirit of renunciation, they sought her blessing to spend the rest of their lives as wandering monks practising austerities. They also wanted to take sannyasa vows from her.

Holy Mother told them that the Master's monastic disciples generally initiate aspirants into sannyasa, but they insisted that she herself give them the ochre cloths. She told them that she would think about it and let them know the next day. The next day she said: "Today you must shave your heads and dye your cloths ochre; tomorrow I shall initiate you into sannyasa."

On 29 July 1907 the Mother finished her worship in the morning and then handed over the ochre cloths and loin cloths to her disciples. She prayed to the Master: "O Master, please see that they keep their monastic vows. Please also see that wherever they may be — in hills, jungles, or wildernesses — they may get something to eat." Jiten wanted to go to Rameswaram on foot; the other two wanted to go to the Himalayas as wandering monks. Holy Mother did not approve of their plans, and she told them: "You have now come under the shelter of the Master, so you don't need to practise too much austerity. As you have a desire to be itinerant monks, walk to Varanasi. Stay in the ashrama there and practise spiritual disciplines under the guidance of Tarak [Swami Shivananda]. Take your monastic names from him. Carry my letter to him."[23]

Holy Mother shed tears as they took leave of her, and she walked with them up to Talpukur, a pond located at the border of the village. Following Holy Mother's instructions, Shivananda gave monastic names to Jiten, Khagen, and Tarun, who became Vishuddhananda, Shantananda, and Girijananda, respectively.

Ordinary parents may encourage their children to get married and lead a regular householder's life, but all children are not meant for family life. Some have finished their desires for a family in a previous incarnation, and in the present life they are born with the spirit of renunciation and love for God. They are the unsmelt flowers of the earth. When young men came to the Master and Holy Mother, they encouraged some to be monastics and others to be householders. They could see the inner tendencies of those who came to them and they advised them accordingly. When Sharat and Shashi brought their friends to the Master in Dakshineswar, he talked to them about renunciation.

"Then, sir, is it wrong to marry? Is it against the will of God?" asked one of the boys. The Master asked him to take a certain book down from the shelf and directed him to read a particular passage that quoted Christ's opinion of marriage: "For there are eunuchs who were born that way, and there are eunuchs who have been made eunuchs by others — and there are those who choose to live like eunuchs for the sake of the kingdom of heaven. The one who can accept this should accept it." (Matthew 19:12) The Master then asked him to read Saint Paul: "I say therefore to the unmarried and widows, it is good for them if they abide even as I. But if they cannot contain, let them marry: for it is better to marry than to burn." (1 Corinthians 7:9)

Someone interrupted the Master, saying: "Do you mean to say, sir, that marriage is against the will of God? And how can His creation go on if people cease to marry?" Ramakrishna smiled and said: "Don't worry about that. Those who wish to marry are at perfect liberty to do so. What I said just now was between ourselves. I speak on what I have got to say; you take as much of it as you like and no more."[24]

Holy Mother did not indiscriminately advise young men to renounce the world. She saw their past, present, and future through her divine sight and told them what course was right for them. Regarding marriage, she advised one person: "The householder's life is very painful and full of problems. If you don't marry, you will be able to sleep happily without any disturbance." Yet she said to another: "I can't give my opinion about your marriage. If you have any trouble after marriage, you will say, 'Mother, you gave me permission to be married.'" Another time a devotee said, "Mother, I shall not marry." The Mother said with a smile: "Why not? In this world everything goes in pairs, such as two eyes, two ears, two hands, two feet, and so also Purusha and Prakriti — the male and the female." That devotee later married.

A young devotee wrote: "Mother, I have no desire for marriage, but my parents are forcing me to get married." The Mother commented: "Look, what torture!"[25]

Once another devotee said to her: "Mother, I tried my utmost all these years to remain a bachelor, but now I see I shall not be able to make it." The Mother assured him, saying: "My son, don't be afraid. The Master also had many householder devotees. Don't worry. It will be fine if you marry."[26]

These two paths — the path of enjoyment and the path of renunciation — have continued from the beginning of creation, so great teachers advise human beings accordingly. One day the Mother's attendant Mandakini said to her: "Mother, all of your children are equal to you. Yet you are giving permission to marry to those who seek your opinion about marriage, and again you encourage those who want to renounce. You are supposed to inspire and guide everyone along the path of good."

Holy Mother replied: "You see, those who have a strong desire for worldly enjoyment — will they listen if I forbid them? And shall I not help those who have understood this play of the deluding power of maya and have made God their only goal from the meritorious deeds of many past lives? My child, is there any end to suffering in this world?"[27]

Once a young man had passed his M.A. degree examination and wanted to be a monk. M. suggested that he wait because his mother might be hurt, but Shivananda encouraged him to join the monastery quickly. Soon after, that young man came to the Mother and asked for her blessing. She said: "My son, may your wish be fulfilled. Tarak [Shivananda] gave you the right advice."

Rammay was a young disciple of the Mother in Jayrambati. He was studying for his B.A. and wanted to become a monk, which was known to everyone in his household. One day the Mother was cleaning her teeth and Rammay was standing nearby. Nalini said to the Mother: "Aunt, look, he is such a good boy! He has passed two examinations and is now studying for his B.A. His parents raised him with great effort and are paying his educational expenses. And now he wants to be a monk! He should earn money and support his parents. What do you think?"

Holy Mother replied: "How can you understand this? They [meaning future monks] are not fledglings of a crow but of a cuckoo. When they are grown up, they recognize their real mother and return to her, leaving the mother who nursed them.*" Rammay later took monastic vows and became Swami Gauriswarananda.

During her last days in Jayrambati, Holy Mother gave the ochre cloth to a young man named Manasa. Overjoyed, that evening in Kalikumar's parlour he sang devotional songs on Mother Kali, accompanied by a harmonium. He sang:

There is nothing essential in this world except the Divine Mother Shyama. O Mother, I shall cast your form in my mind and save it there.

The Mother was happily listening to his songs along with Radhu, Maku, and a couple of her sisters-in-law. Moved with sympathy, one sister-in-law commented: "Sister made this young boy a monk!"

Maku added: "This boy's parents raised him with great expectation and now everything has fallen apart. Marriage is also a part of dharma in this world. Aunt, if you continue to make monks like this, Mahamaya will be mad at you. Those who want to be monks, let them be of their own accord. Why should you be an instrument in this respect?"

Holy Mother listened to their comments and then replied: "Maku, they are divine children. They will remain in this world as pure as untouched flowers. Tell me, is there anything happier than that? How much happiness are you experiencing in this world? Can't you develop a little purity in your heart? You people live like animals. Can't you live with your husband like brother and sister? Your troublesome, miserable family life torments me; it is as if my bones are burning."[28]

Although Holy Mother was willing to initiate youths into sannyasa, before she did so she always checked whether their families would suffer without their financial support. During the summer of 1913, Brahmachari Devendra travelled from Varanasi to Jayrambati to ask the Mother for sannyasa. She inquired about his family's financial condition and also about his parents before asking him to bring a new ochre cloth from Koalpara Ashrama. She initiated him into sannyasa the next day.

In some cases, however, Holy Mother refused to give the vows of sannyasa. Once two young men came to her during Durga Puja and asked her to initiate them into monastic life. They worshipped the Mother's feet

---

*It is said that cuckoos lay their eggs in crows' nests. The crows hatch the eggs and feed the young cuckoos till they can fly.

with lotuses. Observing their behaviour and overflowing emotion, she said with a smile, "My children, you will have to wait."[29]

Another young man wanted to be a monk and told his wife: "Go to your parents with the children. I shall not stay at home anymore. I will be a monk." This helpless wife, who was the Mother's disciple, wrote to the Mother about her pitiable condition. Irritated, the Mother said: "Look, this is a horrible injustice! Where will this unfortunate girl go with her children? If he wanted to be a monk, then why did he marry and have children? If you want to be a monk, you should first arrange for their food and shelter."[30]

In 1911, Holy Mother returned to Jayrambati after her pilgrimage to South India. One of her young attendants (Ashu) went with her on the pilgrimage and later told another monk that he missed the Mother's company. On 26 May 1911 when Holy Mother heard about this comment from the other monk, she said: "How strange! A sannyasin must sever all the bondage of maya. A golden chain is as good a shackle as an iron one. A sannyasin must not entangle himself in any form of maya. Why should he constantly say, 'Oh Mother's love! Mother's love! I am deprived of it!' What ideas! I do not like a man constantly hanging on me. At least he has the form of a man; I am not talking of God. And I am to move about with women. Ashu also used to come to me frequently in Udbodhan to make sandal paste or on some other pretext. One day I warned him."[31]

Receiving the vision of God depends on divine grace. One monk was practising austerities in Rishikesh. He wrote a letter to Holy Mother: "Mother, you told me that I would see the Master in time. But nothing has happened so far." The Mother dictated a reply to her attendant: "The Lord is not under any obligation to go forward to meet you just because you have gone to Rishikesh in the Himalayas. You have become a monk. What else will you do other than call on God? God will reveal Himself when it pleases Him."[32]

Holy Mother always emphasized that monks must observe their monastic rules and precepts. In 1906 when her brother Prasanna asked if a young brahmachari could join the wedding party for his second marriage, the Mother said: "No, he cannot go. He is a monk."[33] The next day Holy Mother would not even allow her monastic attendants to eat the sweet curd from the ceremony. Although surrounded by householders, she protected her monastic disciples from the influence of worldly life.

The scripture says: "The difference between the lives of monks and householders is like the difference between Mount Meru and a grain of mustard seed, the sun and a firefly, the ocean and a river." Holy Mother always asked monks to keep the banner of renunciation high and to maintain the dignity of their glorious lives. Once a distinguished householder devotee of the Master wanted Swami Shantananda to accompany him to Varanasi, and he offered to pay the monk's travelling expenses. When the Mother heard about it, she told the swami: "You are a monk. Can you not procure your own train fare? Why will you go with those householders? If you travel in the same compartment, they may tell you, 'Do this, do that.' You are a monk. Why would you take orders from householders?"[34]

Holy Mother showed tremendous respect for her monastic disciples. Brahmacharis Barada and Hari were two of the Mother's young disciples who did all kinds of errands for her and Radhu, and also rendered her personal service. She initiated them into brahmacharya but did not give them the ochre cloth. She said to them, "If you wear the ochre cloth, could I order you to do all these things? I would feel hesitant even if you touched my feet." As their monastic vows were delayed, she consoled them, saying: "Don't worry. Later Sharat [Saradananda] will arrange your sannyasa." After the Mother passed away, the two received sannyasa from Swami Brahmananda (in 1921) and became Ishanananda and Haripremananda, respectively.

When Holy Mother was in Jayrambati in January 1920, she was not well. Nonetheless, she still got up at three o'clock in the morning to sit on her bed for meditation. Then she would lie down again. Some of her young disciples would go to her room and meditate with her. Sometimes the Mother gave them some specific instructions. Once one of the monks of the Order was ill and was staying at a householder's house. She remarked:

"Why should that monk live with a householder just because he is ill? One can stay in the monastery or at an ashrama. It is not right for that sick monk to stay in that devotee's house for such a long time. A monk must not lower the ideal of renunciation. If a wooden image of a woman lies upside down on the road, a monk must not turn it over, even with his foot, to look at its face. It is extremely bad for a monk to possess money. There is nothing the round pieces [silver rupees] cannot do — even to the extent of endangering one's life."

After saying this, the Mother told a story: "A monk used to live on the seashore at Puri. He had some money. Two of his disciples came to know about it. They could not resist the temptation — they stole the money and killed the monk."[35]

Holy Mother insisted that her devotees pay respect to the monks. In 1919 when she was staying with Radhu at Koalpara Ashrama,

Brahmachari Barada was preparing the shopping list according to Holy Mother's instructions. At that time a woman devotee happened to pass that way, and her cloth inadvertently touched Barada's back. Although he did not notice it, the Mother did. Irritated, she said to the woman devotee: "Hello, don't you see this young boy is sitting in front of me and writing? Are you not aware that your cloth has brushed over his back? He is a brahmachari and you are a woman. You should pay respect to the monks. Touch the upper corner of your cloth on the ground and bow down to him." The Mother spoke in such a serious tone that it became a lesson for the other women.[36]

Krishna says in the Gita that four kinds of people worship God: the afflicted, the inquiring, the solicitors of wealth, and the jnani. All are noble souls indeed, but the jnani worships God without any selfish motive, so he is the best. One day Swami Kaivalyananda asked Holy Mother: "Mother, those who have taken refuge in the Master are equal, whether they are monks or householders, and will be freed in the end."

The Mother replied: "What do you mean? How can a monk and a householder be equal? Householders possess so many worldly desires, whereas monks have renounced everything for God. Who else belongs to them other than God? Can householders be compared with monks?"[37]

Sometimes spiritual egotism is an obstacle to seekers of God. Swami Vrajeswarananda served the old monks of Belur Math and was loved and appreciated by them. But he thought: Instead of gratifying my self-importance in this way by gaining the affection of the old monks, I would do better to leave here and practise austerities. He knew that the Math authorities would not give him permission to leave, so he went to the Mother in Udbodhan and opened his heart to her. She asked him where he was going and inquired whether he had any money. He replied that he had no money; he was planning to walk to Varanasi and practise austerities there. The Mother tenderly told him: "My son, this is the month of Kartik [October-November]. People say that all four doors of Yama [the God of death] are open in this month. Being a mother, how can I let you go? You say that you have no money; then what will you eat when you are hungry, my son?" Vrajeswarananda abandoned his plan.[38]

Sometimes monks can also develop a superiority complex, getting upset if people do not show proper respect to them. The Mother once cautioned Swami Arupananda, saying: "This spiritual egotism is terrible. Some monks have inflated egos and seek praise and honour." She gestured to her white sari and continued, "It is better to wear a white cloth and cultivate inner renunciation than to wear an ochre robe."[39] Holy

Mother asked the monks not to follow too many external formalities but instead to develop intense faith and steadfast devotion.

When a devotee (later Swami Jagadananda) asked the Mother for sannyasa, she took the ochre cloth, touched it to the Master's feet in his picture and then touched it to her head and gave it to him. She said, "I have given you the ochre cloth. Now you must go to Belur Math and take formal vows through the *viraja homa* [a special fire sacrifice] from Rakhal and he will give you a monastic name."[40]

As Holy Mother encouraged some young men to follow the path of renunciation, she also encouraged some young women. When Narayan Iyenger's daughter wanted the vow of brahmacharya, Holy Mother asked Saradananda to write to the girl's father for permission. Another time a devotee's daughter refused to marry. The girl's mother requested Holy Mother to ask her daughter to marry. The Mother replied: "What misery to be a slave to a man all through life and to please him always!" Then she explained that there might be some difficulties for a girl in leading an unmarried life, but it would be unfair to force any girl into wedlock against her will.[41]

Whenever any monk had a problem, he would rush to Holy Mother for help. After Premananda passed away, Shivananda was made manager of Belur Math. The younger Nagen (Brahmachari Aksharchaitanya) did something foolish. The other monks told him that Swami Shivananda would throw him out of the monastery. Scared, he left the monastery without informing anyone and walked barefoot to Jayrambati without even a spare cloth. When he reached there with dirty clothes and a haggard look, no one recognized him as a brahmachari of Belur Math. Seeing how exhausted he was, the Mother gave him a fresh cloth, asked him to bathe, and fed him. After listening to his story, she dictated a letter to Shivananda: "My dear son Tarak, what offence has the younger Nagen committed? Being afraid that you will turn him out of the monastery, he has come to me all the way on foot. My son, can a mother take heed of her child's offence? Please don't take any action against him."

She kept Nagen with her till the reply came. Shivananda responded: "Mother, we are relieved knowing that Nagen went to you. We have been searching for him. Kindly send him back here. There is a shortage of workers to perform the worship here. I will not take any action against him." After receiving the letter, the Mother gave the brahmachari permission to return.

Meanwhile Prabodh, a disciple of the Mother's from Badanganj, came to see her in Jayrambati. According to his guru's instruction, Prabodh accompanied Nagen to his house in Badanganj, bought him a couple of shirts, and gave him train fare back to Belur Math. When Nagen arrived, Shivananda embraced him and said: "My boy, you went to the High Court to complain against me!"[42]

Sometimes Holy Mother disapproved of some monks' improper behaviour. Once a monk in Belur Math slapped a servant for insubordination. When the Mother heard about it, she said: "They are monks. A tree is their proper shelter. Now they have monasteries, houses, and servants to boot. They even go to the length of beating the servants!"[43]

The disciples believed that Ramakrishna dwells in his Order. It was at the Master's behest that Swamiji established the Ramakrishna Order, where people would come to attain perfection. No one becomes a monk after having attained perfection. On 19 August 1929 Swami Shivananda said to the monks:

> The Supreme Brahman Itself has now come down as Sri Ramakrishna. We have seen with our own eyes how infinite was his forgiveness, how wonderful was his mercy. As for Holy Mother, there can be no comparison with her — she is none other than the Mother of the Universe. I have even heard that when someone came and reported to her that somebody had committed the most despicable sinful act, the Mother heard the whole report gravely. Then the reporter requested the Mother, "If you summon him and take him to task a little, it will be good." The Mother replied: "My son, it is all very well for you to talk like that, but I am his mother. To you he may be an offender and so detestable, but to his mother he is not so. Being his mother, can I hate my son?" So wonderful was her forgiveness! All these things have happened before our eyes.[44]

The monks consulted Holy Mother whenever any question arose regarding the ideal of the Ramakrishna Order, and they accepted her answer without hesitation. They knew the Master was working through her.

In January 1901 Vivekananda went to Advaita Ashrama at Mayavati in the Himalayas and stayed there for a couple of weeks. He dedicated this ashrama to Advaita and to Advaita alone and decreed that no ritual should ever be performed there, and no shrine set up. He established this centre for people who cherish the monistic ideal, especially Westerners, so that they could practise the nondualistic philosophy of Vedanta.

One morning Swamiji happened to enter a room in the ashrama building and found a shrine with a picture of Ramakrishna. A monk was performing worship with flowers, sandal paste, and other offerings. Swamiji said nothing at the time, but that evening when all the members were gathered around the fireplace, he vehemently expressed his disapproval of ritualistic worship in Advaita Ashrama. He asked the ashrama members to pay attention only to the subjective side of religion — practising meditation, studying the scriptures, and absorbing the monistic ideal — free from dualistic weakness or dependence. He did not order them to close the shrine or hurt the feelings of those who were in favour of the ritual. He wanted them to see their mistake and rectify it. They closed the shrine on 18 March 1902. After returning to Belur Math, Swamiji remarked: "I thought of having one centre at least from which the external worship of Sri Ramakrishna would be excluded. But I found that the Old Man had already established himself even there! Well! Well!"[45]

Later, soon after Vivekananda's passing away, his disciple Swami Vimalananda, who favoured the dualistic ideal, wrote to Holy Mother and asked her to clarify the matter. She answered his letter from Jayrambati on 31 August 1902: "He who is our guru [Ramakrishna] is an Advaitin [nondualist]. Since you are all his disciples, you too are Advaitins. I can emphatically say that you are all definitely nondualists."[46] This letter settled the issue for the members of Advaita Ashrama and ritualistic worship was never performed there again.

When Swami Vivekananda established the Ramakrishna Order, he also envisioned a monastic order for women. When Sharat Chakrabarty doubted that there would be enough suitable women to start an Order, Swamiji replied: "Even now there are some women devotees of Sri Ramakrishna. I shall start this monastery with their help. Holy Mother will be their central figure and the wives and daughters of the Master's devotees will be its first inmates. They will easily appreciate the usefulness of such a Math. Then following their example, many householders will help this noble work.... With Holy Mother as the centre of inspiration, a Math is to be established on the eastern bank of the Ganges. As Brahmacharins and Sadhus will be trained in this Math [Belur Math], so in the other Math also, Brahmacharinis and Sadhvis will be trained."[47]

Swamiji's wish was fulfilled in 1954 during events celebrating Holy Mother's birth centenary, when a small piece of land with a few buildings was procured at Dakshineswar and Sarada Math was established.

It was Swamiji who named Holy Mother "Sangha-janani," the Mother of the Order. She always nurtured and protected the Order, especially during critical times. In December 1916 Lord Carmichael, the governor of Bengal, accused the Ramakrishna Mission of giving shelter to political revolutionaries under the umbrella of its philanthropic activities, saying: "[They] often seize the opportunity which membership in a charitable society like the Ramakrishna Mission or participation in the relief of the distressed gives them to meet and to influence the boys who have noble ideas, but who have not enough experience to judge where a particular course must lead."[48]

The government discovered that some revolutionaries had been inspired by Vivekananda's books, so they surmised that the monks of the Ramakrishna Order were behind the freedom movement. The governor's remark created great apprehension among the monastics as well as the general public. Some well-wishers of the Mission suggested that Saradananda remove those monks who had a revolutionary background* from the Order. But Swami Saradananda was deeply concerned about the future of those dedicated, pure, and noble souls.

Saradananda recalled: "I went to Holy Mother and informed her of the whole situation. She listened to me calmly and then said firmly: 'My goodness! What is the matter? The Master was the embodiment of truth. These boys have taken shelter in the Master, embraced his ideal, and become monks renouncing their families. They have shunned personal worldly enjoyment and dedicated their lives to serve the country and suffering people. My son, why would they pretend? You had better go to the governor and meet him. He is the representative of the king. If you explain to him the activities of the Ramakrishna Mission, he will definitely listen.'"[49]

Another eyewitness recorded that after listening to everything, Holy Mother firmly said: "The Ramakrishna Math and Mission have come into existence by the will of the Master. To break the rules of the monastic order due to the pressure and rage of the government is *adharma* [unrighteous]. Those who have taken the monastic vows and surrendered to the Master will stay in the monastery; otherwise no one should stay here. My children will take shelter under a tree, and nonetheless will not deviate from the truth."[50] The Mother's resolute statement reassured everyone in the Order. Swami Premananda joyfully remarked: "Now there is a satisfactory solution on this matter."

Saradananda followed Holy Mother's advice. He consulted with the attorney Dasharathi Sannyal, one of Swamiji's former classmates, and they prepared a memorandum on behalf of the governing body of the Ramakrishna Math and Mission. On 23 January 1917 Saradananda met with Mr. Gourley, the governor's chief secretary, and handed the memorandum to him. On 2 March Mr. Gourley and Mr. Denham, a high-ranking police official, came to Belur Math to meet with Saradananda. They arranged for him to speak with the governor on 10 March. On that day the

*Swamis Prajnananda, Chinmayananda, Atmaprakashananda, and Satyananda.

swami talked to the governor for nearly an hour. He was able to remove the governor's misgivings regarding the activities of the Ramakrishna Mission. Following the meeting, Lord Carmichael wrote Saradananda on 26 March 1917:

Dear Sir,

I thank you for having come to see me and for the trouble you have taken to tell me about the origin of the Ramakrishna Mission, and its aims and objects.

I read with great interest the memorial which the Mission authorities submitted to me some time ago. I regret very much to hear that words used by me at the Durbar in December last regarding the Mission should have led in any way to the curtailment of the good Religious, Social, and Educational work the Mission has done and is doing. As you, I know, realize, my object was not to condemn the Ramakrishna Mission and its members. I know the character of the Mission's work is entirely non-political, and I have heard nothing but good of its work of social service for the people....

Yours very sincerely,
Carmichael[51]

It was very unusual for a British governor to apologize for a statement and withdraw it in writing. This removed the cloud of doubt that hung over the Ramakrishna Mission.

It is natural for every organization to go through ups and downs. However, the Mother guided the Ramakrishna Order in the right direction and thus the journey of the Ramakrishna Mission continued triumphantly with her blessings.

The Ramakrishna Mission is well known for its philanthropic activities including relief work when there is any natural disaster. Holy Mother always encouraged the monks to help suffering people when needed. In the last part of 1918 there was a famine in Orissa. Swami Saradananda went to Puri to supervise the Mission's relief work. He wrote a long letter to the Mother describing the suffering of the people and requested her to pray to the Master. Prabodh Chattopadhyay, a disciple of the Mother, read the letter to her. She listened to the letter and cried, saying: "Master, I can't see or hear of any more suffering. Please stop the people's pain and misery."

Then she said to Prabodh: "Do you notice the gigantic heart of Sharat? He is like Vasuki.* Wherever there is rain, Sharat spreads an umbrella.

*A mythological thousand-hooded snake, who carries the whole universe on his head.

Sharat is a large-hearted person and his heart cries out on behalf of suffering beings. He is serving and feeding all like a protector." Then she prayed, "Master, supply Sharat with everything. Give him plenty so that he can provide enough for all."[52]

At Udbodhan House

Holy Mother always reminded the monks of the Master's great teaching: "Adapt according to person, place, and time." This is especially important in community life because selfishness and egotism disrupt peace and harmony in a monastery or in a family. In 1911, a monk living in Udbodhan House made a serious mistake. Swami Brahmananda asked him to move to Belur Math, but the monk was reluctant to do so. Saradananda reported this to the Mother and told her that the monk was disobedient. Holy Mother also asked the monk to go to Belur Math, but he would not listen to her either. She then remarked about that monk: "It is not right that he does not listen to the disciples of the Master. He does not like to do any work. Can anyone improve one's mind without work? Can anyone practise japa and meditation 24 hours a day? It is better to have some work; it keeps the mind in good condition."[53]

In 1912 a disciple told Holy Mother: "Some say that hospital work, selling books, and accounting are not proper work for monks because the Master did not do such work. A monk is supposed to perform worship, japa, meditation, and kirtan, which turn the mind to God. Other mundane activities turn the mind to the world."

Holy Mother listened and then said firmly: "How will you pass the whole day without work? Can anybody practise japa and meditation all 24 hours of the day? You are referring to the Master's life. His life was different. Mathur provided nourishing food for him. You have regular meals because you give some service here; otherwise you will have to beg for your food from door to door. That is why my Naren started all these centres for work. Our organization will function this way. Those who cannot adjust must leave."[54]

Once a monk was leaving the Order and he came to receive the Mother's blessings. It was heartbreaking for the Mother to see a monk leave. Both she and the monk wept. After a while, the Mother wiped her tears with a corner of her sari and asked the monk to wash his face. She affectionately told him: "My son, don't forget me. I know you won't, but still I say so."

The monk said, "Mother, will you forget me?"

Holy Mother replied: "Can a mother forget her son? Know for certain, I will always be with you. Don't be afraid." When the monk left

Udobodhan House, the Mother watched him through her window till he was no longer visible.[55]

Swami Sadananda, a former station master in Hathras, was the first monastic disciple of Swami Vivekananda. He served his guru and the Ramakrishna Order so intensely that he died on 18 February 1911 at the age of 46. Holy Mother came to him during his last illness:

> On 25 November 1910, during Sadananda's last illness, Holy Mother, along with Yogin-ma and Golap-ma, came to see him. Sadananda prostrated himself at her feet, and said with tears in his eyes: "Mother, please bless me in the same way that you blessed me twenty-two years ago. With that blessing I have been able to lead a monastic life. Now the time has come to depart. I do not know what awaits me on the other shore." Holy Mother blessed him and said: "What fear have you, my son? The Master himself is waiting there with open arms to embrace you." But Sadananda was not satisfied. In a voice choked with emotion, he said, "Please bless me once again, the way you blessed me twenty-two years ago." Holy Mother remained quiet. Seeing this, Sadananda grew all the more restless and said, "Mother, if you do not bless me the way you did before, then sitting at your feet, I shall put an end to my life right now."
>
> The compassionate Holy Mother then blessed Sadananda by touching his head with her feet. No one knows how Holy Mother had blessed him twenty-two years earlier, nor does anyone know what blessings she bestowed upon him that day. Sadananda's devotion to Holy Mother was truly unique. Earlier, Sadananda would often visit the house at Baghbazar where Holy Mother lived, yet he would rarely go upstairs to see Holy Mother and pay his obeisance. When asked why, he said, "Everything in spiritual life is attained if one sees Holy Mother but once!" These words, which emerged from the innermost depths of his soul, reveal Sadananda's deep devotion for Holy Mother.[56]

One afternoon in 1920 at Udbodhan House, Holy Mother was lying in bed. She was not well, but she was talking with her women devotees. In the course of conversation, they spoke of the monks of the monastery. Maku said about a monk: "He is a dandy monk. He is neat and clean and wears expensive clothes." Nalin commented that he was the son of a wealthy man, so that was why he was a little fastidious. Holy Mother remarked: "Look, it is renunciation and only renunciation that is needful in monastic life. Why is he so much inclined to external paraphernalia? Renunciation is the main ornament of a monk. He who collects all ingredients of a curry, will he not gather a little salt?*"[57]

*She meant that if a person gathers all necessary items for enjoyment, he will definitely get the object itself.

In March of the same year Holy Mother was under ayurvedic treatment. One afternoon Lakshmi and Ramlal and his daughter, Krishnamayi, came to visit the Mother on their way to attend a festival at Archanalay in Entally. Ramlal bowed down to the Mother and then went downstairs to meet Saradananda. Lakshmi entertained Holy Mother and her companions with her singing and acting as she used to do for the Master in Dakshineswar. By and by Lakshmi raised the issue of the future temple in Kamarpukur. Lakshmi asked: "When the temple of the Master is built, will it be under our management? Will the children of our family be worshippers there?"

Holy Mother replied: "How can that be possible? As the devotees have no caste, so the monks of the Ramakrishna Order do not observe caste distinctions. People of various countries, including Westerners, will come and stay there, and they will also partake of prasad. We are connected with all sorts of devotees, whereas you are householders. You have your society and will have to follow social customs regarding marriages of your children and other things.* How can you live with monastics?"

The Mother continued: "The monks will build a separate house for you as you have now."

Lakshmi asked: "Will Raghuvir and Shitala be installed inside the Master's temple?"

"How is that possible?" asked Holy Mother. "Those are your household deities, and the womenfolk of your family will worship them during festivals. The monks will build a separate small brick building for Raghuvir and Shitala. When you, Ramlal, or Shibu visit Kamarpukur, you will stay and eat with them."[58]

Lakshmi then went downstairs and reported everything that the Mother had said to Ramlal and Saradananda. They wholeheartedly accepted the Mother's proposal. Thus during her lifetime, Holy Mother settled the management of the future Ramakrishna temple at the Master's birthplace.**

From the very inception of the Ramakrishna Order, Holy Mother nourished the monks and devotees with her love and affection. She

---

*Ramakrishna's family was brahmin, so its members are supposed to follow strict caste rules.

**In accordance with this settlement, the Master's birthplace was handed over to Belur Math by a document that was signed by Holy Mother and others on 27 July 1918. Prior to this, a small piece of land contiguous to the birthplace was purchased by Belur Math on 14 December 1917. Construction of the present temple started after acquisition of the Master's house on 16 July 1946, and it was dedicated on 11 May 1951.

demonstrated the ideal of the Order through her own life. She always pointed out the goal of monastic life — purity and renunciation, unselfishness and truthfulness, mutual love and respect, selfless service and dependence on God. To the householders, she also set the example of an ideal householder's life. In times of difficulty or crisis, she protected the Order with her wise counsel and spiritual power. She was the Order's source of inspiration and spiritual power. That is why she is called the Mother of the Order.

Sarada Devi at Udbodhan House, 1909.

25
Mother of All

Yā devi sarva bhuteshu mātri rupena samasthitā;
Namastasyai namastasyai namastasyai namo namah.
— *Chandi, 5:71*

Salutations to the Divine Mother, who exists in all beings as the
Mother. Salutations to Her again and again.

O
rdinary people think of a mother as a woman who gives birth to
children, raises them, takes care of the household, and holds the
family together. She might not be as physically strong as a man,
but she is more patient and has more perseverance and endurance than
most men. Her love and affection, selfless service and care, compassion
and forgiveness make her great. In fact, a mother or wife is the anchor
of a house, and without her, the house seems a desert. The Hindu scripture says, *grihini griham uchyate*: "A housewife makes the house." There is
another old saying: "Men make houses, and women make homes."

The Hindu scripture says that all women in the world are parts of the
Divine Mother, but they cannot be considered the mother of all because
they have a limitation: they do not feel and care for the children of others
as they do for their own. But Holy Mother was truly the mother of all
because she was an incarnation of the Divine Mother. She knew that she
exists in all beings as the Mother and that all living beings — men and
women, birds and beasts, trees and plants — emerged from her cosmic
body.

There is a prayer in the Chandi: "O Mother, you are the infinite power
of God and the supreme maya, which is the source of the universe. O Devi,
you have enchanted the whole world with your divine enchantment.
When you are gracious, you bestow liberation upon human beings."[1]

Mother of the Universe

In the Vedanta tradition, a person's spiritual experience is ascertained
in two ways: *sva-samvedya*, which means those thoughts and spiritual
visions that are seen within one's own self and which are known only to

423

oneself; and *para-samvedya*, which means a person's thoughts and experiences that are visible to others. Holy Mother herself declared that she was the Mother of the Universe — and her life, speech, actions, and dealings with people convinced others that her statement was true.

Rasbihari (later Swami Arupananda), a young man from East Bengal, went to meet Holy Mother at Jayrambati on 1 February 1907. She was very fond of him because of his simplicity and guilelessness, and she made him one of her attendants. He was also very free with the Mother. The following dialogue between the two reveals Holy Mother's true nature. He wrote:

> I used to visit the Mother almost daily in her room. She would lie down on her bed and talk to me, with Radhu lying asleep by her side. An oil lamp cast a dim light in the room. On some days a maidservant rubbed her feet with medicated oil for rheumatism.
>
> One day she said to me in the course of conversation: "Whenever the thought of a disciple comes to my mind and I yearn to see him, then he either comes here or writes a letter to me. You must have come here prompted by a certain feeling. Perhaps you have in your mind the thought of the Divine Mother of the Universe."
>
> "Are you the Mother of all?" I asked.
>
> Mother replied, "Yes."
>
> "Even of the subhuman beings — birds and animals?"
>
> "Yes, of these also."
>
> "Then why should they suffer so much?"
>
> "In this birth they must have these experiences."[2]

According to Vedanta, Brahman is Existence-Consciousness-Bliss Absolute. Brahman is neither he nor she. But when that power of Brahman takes a form, it can be either Purusha or Prakriti — he or she. Moreover, the Personal God can be *both* father and mother. A devotee once questioned Holy Mother's active role in the Master's spiritual ministry, saying that the spiritual consorts of other avatars did not take such roles. The devotee asked why she was different. She replied: "My son, you are aware that the Master saw the Divine Mother in all beings. This time, he left me behind to demonstrate that Motherhood in this universe."[3]

Holy Mother as Protector

Prabodh Chandra Chattopadhyay and his wife were disciples of Holy Mother. They lived in Shyambazar Village, which is 12 miles from Jayrambati. Inspired by the Mother, Prabodh started a high school in Badanganj and became the first headmaster of that school. Rammay (later Swami Gauriswarananda) was one of its first students. Prabodh was also

arada Devi at Udbodhan House, 1909.

president of the village Union Board. But because of his popularity, he had some enemies. His son, Shivaprasad Chattopadhyay, wrote:

> I heard this incident from my father: Once he was visiting Jayrambati. A man came there and gave him a letter with this message: "Please return to your home this evening." My father got ready to return home and went to bow down to the Mother. At that time a few villagers had some enmity against my father for various reasons. It came to light later that there was a plot to murder my father that evening near a secluded canal on his way home.
>
> Upon hearing of the letter, the Mother asked my father, "Do you recognize the handwriting of the person who has written this letter?" "Yes, I do, Mother." "Do you know the person who has come with the letter?" "No, Mother. I don't know him." Then the Mother said: "My son, do not go home tonight. Tomorrow morning, go home through a different route via Maragere with the watchman Ambika and Rammay." My father bowed down to the Mother and said: "All right, Mother, I shall not go tonight. I shall go tomorrow according to your instruction."
>
> The next morning he returned home with Ambika and Rammay via Maragere. My father later said, "I never disobeyed the Mother's order whatever it might be." My father did not know about the murder plot, but the omniscient Mother knew it. Later I heard from my father that a case was concocted so that he should return home that night. Long after my father's passing away, I verified this incident, which took place in 1917, through Swami Gauriswarananda.[4]

The story of a Muslim bandit named Amzad also shows how Holy Mother protected those who took refuge in her. It is a fascinating tale of a Muslim robber who became a devotee of the Mother and played a wonderful role in her divine drama.

Human beings are not born with friends or enemies. They make friends and enemies through their actions and their words. There is a saying: "A small-minded person discriminates between a relative and a stranger, but all are considered relatives to a great soul." The life and teachings of an avatar or an illumined soul are not the exclusive property of a particular clan, or a country, or a religion; they belong to the whole of humanity. Their universal outlook breaks all barriers between human beings and religions. Holy Mother made Muslims and Christians her own through her maternal love and affection.

The Story of Amzad

Shiromanipur is a predominantly Muslim village located three miles from Jayrambati. Its inhabitants were forced by the English to make their living by cultivating silkworms. But the local silk industry could not compete with imported silk industries, so the villagers lost their jobs. Growing silk had kept them from cultivating rice and crops, so they had no food. To survive, they were forced to become bandits. The neighbouring villagers were afraid and kept a vigilant eye on them. People refused to give them jobs thinking that they might return at night to steal.

As the saying goes, bad times do not come alone. In 1915-16 there was a drought and famine in the Bankura district. The poor had no food, so they became desperate. During this time, a Muslim villager named Amzad was caught in a robbery and sent to jail. Amzad's mother, Fatema, and his wife, Matijan, came to Holy Mother for help. She fed them puffed rice and molasses, and then gave them rice, oil, cloths, and a rupee. When news of her assistance spread, other Muslim families came to the Mother and she helped them also. Eventually, the Ramakrishna Mission opened a relief centre in Koalpara for the destitute.[5] The rich and middle-class people of Sihar, Jibta, Phului, and Shyambazar remained indifferent.

All these years the Mother was living in her old cottage and using her two brothers' cottages for her disciples and out-of-town guests. As the number of disciples was increasing, Swami Saradananda felt that the Mother needed a house of her own. Construction began on her new house in April 1915 and it formally opened on 15 May 1916. Bibhuti Ghosh, the Mother's disciple, hired Amzad and other Muslim workers to construct the house, which had a thatched roof, a mud floor and mud walls. Swami Arupananda was in charge of the construction. Some narrow-minded, fearful villagers tried to discourage Holy Mother from hiring convicted thieves, but she did not listen to them. She treated the Muslim workers with kindness and talked to them in her soft, sweet voice. Those Muslim workers, many of whom were formerly bandits, called her "Mother." Observing their good behaviour, the villagers later said: "By Mother's grace even these robbers have become devotees of God."[6]

One day the Mother invited Amzad for lunch and served him on the porch of her house. Owing to caste prejudices, Nalini, the Mother's niece, threw the food at Amzad's leaf plate from a distance. Holy Mother noticed this and said: "How can one enjoy food when it is served with such scorn? Let me wait on him properly." After Amzad had finished his meal, Holy Mother cleaned the place where he had sat with her own hands. Nalini shrieked: "Aunt, you have lost your caste!"

"Keep quiet," the Mother scolded her. Then she added: "As Sharat is my son, exactly so is Amzad." Sharat was a direct disciple of Ramakrishna, the secretary of the Ramakrishna Mission, and a monk endowed with saintly virtues; Amzad was a Muslim and a convicted robber. Thus Holy Mother demonstrated that she is the Mother of the good and the bad. She also showed that kind treatment can enkindle faith in the heart of a weak, lowly man and prove to him that he is a son of the Divine Mother. Her example brought to life the words of Krishna: "I am the same towards all beings; to Me there is none hateful or dear. But those who worship Me with devotion — they are in Me, and I too am in them."[7]

About two years later Holy Mother was in Jayrambati, bedridden with malarial fever. Devotees from various places came to see her. One morning a brahmachari attending her noticed that an emaciated man of dark complexion, clad in rags and leaning on a stick, had entered the house. As he approached the Mother's room, her eyes fell upon him. "Who is there?" she said in a feeble voice. "Is it my child Amzad? Come in." Amzad stepped onto the veranda, sat at the threshold of the room, and began to converse with the Mother about his painful life.

Observing that the Mother was freely talking to him, the brahmachari left the room. He later returned to pick up the jar of Ganges water that was in the Mother's room. Generally when the Mother was well, she offered food to the Master after sprinkling Ganges water in the kitchen. That day the brahmachari was supposed to offer the food. Now he was in a dilemma: He could not ask Amzad to leave without offending the Mother, yet his caste prejudice was pricking his conscience: He would have to pass close by a Muslim to get to the jar of water. However, he decided to carry out his duty, thinking that if it was wrong, the Mother would stop him. After offering food, he came back and put the holy water in the Mother's room. She watched everything but said nothing.

At Holy Mother's request, Amzad was given oil to rub on his body, allowed to bathe in the pond, given a new cloth, and fed with good food until his stomach was full. That afternoon as Amzad was returning home, chewing a betel roll, he seemed to be a completely different person. He carried in his bundle many gifts, including a bottle of ayurvedic oil from the Mother.

Later Holy Mother told the brahmachari: "Amzad was unable to sleep because he had taken some kind of strong drug that overheated his brain. I had kept a bottle of Narayan oil with me for a long time and I gave it to him. It will cool his brain if he uses it. That oil is very effective."

Amzad soon recovered his health. Whenever he was informed that something needed be done in the Mother's house, he came immediately and performed the task faithfully. Once the Mother lost her appetite due to a prolonged illness, and the doctor suggested that she eat pineapples.

That fruit was not in season in Jayrambati. However, word was sent to Amzad, who searched in different villages until he found some pineapples for the Mother.[8]

Despite the Mother's affection, Amzad did not abandon his life of crime. The people of Jayrambati were afraid of him, but due to his devotion to the Mother, her village was free from robbery. Once, after being released from jail, Amzad returned home and found some pumpkins growing on his vine. He picked them and went straight to the Mother in Jayrambati. "I have been thinking of you for a long time," Holy Mother said. "Where have you been all these days?" He frankly replied that he had been in jail because he had stolen a cow. The Mother paid no heed to his crime and said with great kindness, "I was worried by your long absence."[9]

Amzad was the leader of a gang of thieves. Bibhuti Ghosh recalled the following story, which Holy Mother told him with a smile: "O Bibhuti, have you heard of Amzad's wit and intelligence? An immoral girl from an oil-caste family of Sihar had a paramour. She offered money to Amzad to kill her husband. She told him to knock at her door gently at night, and she would open the door. He should murder her husband and leave immediately. According to the plan, Amzad knocked on the door at night and the girl opened it. But instead of killing her husband, Amzad snatched her earrings and ran away."[10] As a result, Amzad was sent to jail.

Swami Ishanananda wrote: "When the Mother was in Calcutta during her last illness, a letter arrived from Jayrambati with the news that Amzad had committed a robbery in the neighbouring village of Chandipur, and had been severely injured. After hiding for a few days, he was arrested. When she heard this news, the Mother remarked: 'My goodness! O Barada, I knew his robbing instinct was dormant. Do you think I took care of him for no reason? I kept him under my control by feeding him and giving him various gifts. He always obeyed me like a servant bending his head in humility. I lived with all my nieces and they have so much jewellery. You boys were not always around me and moreover you were very young.'"[11]

It is said that after Holy Mother passed away, Amzad suffered a sword wound during a robbery. That wound became septic and ultimately caused his death. Thus he reaped the result of his karma. It is not known what was in Amzad's mind after the Mother's passing away. He must have missed a mother who showed him such love, compassion, and forgiveness. The Mother demonstrated through Amzad how the power of love can counteract the power of evil, and as a result her family was never attacked by those Muslim robbers.

Mother of the Muslims

No human being is perfect, yet everyone struggles to attain perfection. Christ said: "Be ye therefore perfect even as the Father in Heaven is perfect." Only God is perfect, and the goal of religion is to attain that perfection which is within all beings. People make mistakes — small or big — and those mistakes are our teachers. They uplift human souls and help people make progress on their journeys. But one does not make any progress by brooding over mistakes or lamenting one's sins. Ramakrishna said: "If you do 99 good deeds for a person and one bad, he will remember the bad one and won't care for you anymore. However, if you commit 99 sins but do one thing to God's satisfaction, He will forgive all your wrongdoing. This is the difference between the love of man and the love of God."[12]

One day a Muslim man offered Holy Mother some bananas and said: "Mother, I have brought them for the Master. Will you accept them?"

"Of course, I will," replied the Mother. Extending her hands, she said: "Give them to me. You have brought them for the Master. I shall certainly take them."

A woman attendant of the Mother was present and immediately protested: "Mother, we know he is a thief. How can you offer his things to the Master?" Without acknowledging her protest, the Mother gave puffed rice and sweets to the man. After he left, the Mother scolded her attendant and said sternly: "I know who is good and who is bad."[13]

Rasan Ali Khan of Paramanandapur (a village adjacent to Shiromanipur) met the Mother when he was 14 years old and later told some incidents about her that he had heard from his uncles Mapheti Sheikh and Hamedi Sheikh. They made their living by farming lands owned by Hindus, and they also had a bullock cart business. Holy Mother hired their carts when she travelled from Jayrambati to Koalpara or Vishnupur and from Koalpara to Jayrambati. The Mother's devotees also hired their carts so that the Muslim family could make some money. The wives of those bullock cart drivers sometimes visited the Mother. She called them "*Bibi bau* — daughters-in-law." She fed them and listened to stories of their families.

There was no market in Jayrambati. Badanganj and Kotalpur had big markets, and Shiromanipur had a small one. Almost every inhabitant of those Muslim villages grew vegetables. As Holy Mother had many visitors, Mapheti quite often brought various kinds of vegetables to her, such as pumpkins, gourds, *kachu* (an edible root), and *sajina* (also called "drumstick bean"). During the winter season, some Muslims brought date palm juice and molasses to the Mother. They were reluctant to accept money from her, but she insisted, saying: "My sons, you must accept a fair price for goods that you have produced with hard labour." The Mother gave them money, fed them the Master's prasad, and gave them puffed rice and sweets.

Sabina Bibi, an elderly Muslim woman, purchased mangoes and jack-fruits in Kotalpur and sold them in Jayrambati. Holy Mother often bought fruit from her. Holy Mother called her "aunt." During Muslim festivals, the Mother would send offerings to the *darga* (a tomb of a Muslim saint) in Shiromanipur. One day Mapheti asked: "Mother, you are a Hindu. Why do you send sweets and other offerings during Muslim festivals?"

She replied: "My son, is God different? All are one. You see, the Master practised Islam sadhana and prayed like the Muslims. Names of God are many but He is one."

Mapheti once had a divine vision of the Mother. From then on he believed that Holy Mother was a *pir*, or saint.[14]

Mother of the Christians

Chapter 14 details Holy Mother's relationship with Western women. Without knowing their language, she communicated with Sara Bull, Josephine MacLeod, Betty Leggett, Laura Glenn (Sister Devamata), Margaret Noble (Sister Nivedita), Christine Greenstidel, Alberta Sturges Montagu (Countess of Sandwich), and others. Her maternal love and affection broke all barriers of religion and culture, language and upbringing, and made these women her own.

Holy Mother initiated a few Westerners, including men, two of whom later became monks. In 1911 at Madras, the Mother initiated Charles Johnston of New York, who later received the vows of brahmacharya from Saradananda and became Brahmachari Amritananda. The same year Holy Mother gave initiation to Cornelius J. Heijblom, known as Gurudas. During his initiation, the Mother told him that he could repeat the mantra at all times, but if he really wanted to get results, he should meditate at set times and concentrate on the meaning of the mantra. Later Gurudas was asked how he had felt at the time of his initiation — since he did not understand Bengali, and Holy Mother did not speak English. He explained: "When a child sits on its mother's lap, in which language do they converse? Similarly, I felt at that time as though the whole world dissolved, and I was a small baby sitting on the lap of my mother. I felt inebriated, and I had no doubts."[15] In 1923 Gurudas received his monastic vows from Swami Abhedananda in Belur Math and became Swami Atulananda.

The Mother also initiated Dr. Hallock of New York and his wife, Gray Hallock. Sindhunath Panda wrote an eyewitness account: "One evening the Mother was seated in her room in Udbodhan. Dr. and Mrs. Hallock sat in front of her. Dr. Kanjilal and I were present and Girish Ghosh sat at the threshold of the door and acted as an interpreter. Mrs. Hallock said, 'Mother, I am your daughter.' 'Yes, you are my daughter,' replied the Mother. Dr. Hallock: 'Mother, how shall I know that you are the Mother of the Universe?' The Mother replied: 'As you have come here, you will understand in the course of time.' I was moved listening to their conversation and seeing her in that domestic setting."[16]

One day a Western woman came to see the Mother at Udbodhan House. When she was talking, the Mother was smiling and communicating by nodding her head. When that woman left, the Mother told the devotees: "With a view to talking to me she bought a copy of *Balya-shiksha* [a Bengali primary book] and learned Bengali. She heard that I get up at four o'clock in the morning, so she also started to get up at that time."[17] Blessed are those souls who came in contact with the Mother and received her blessings.

Some of the Mother's Indian disciples were very patriotic and did not care for English people. The Mother told one of them, "My son, you and your other brothers [the English people] may quarrel among yourselves, but they are also my children."[18]

The Mother's Thoughts on British Rule

India was under British rule during Holy Mother's lifetime. As a universal Mother, she loved her English children, but she raised her voice against the government's injustices when necessary. As some of Holy Mother's disciples had previously been connected with the Indian revolutionary movement, the police kept an eye on the Mother's place, which displeased her. In 1917 the Mother was in her new house in Jayrambati. Her brother Kali, Brahmachari Barada, and others were on the veranda of the parlour when they heard some bad news. A villager by the name of Deben Ghosh had a wife and sister; both women were named Sindhubala. One of them was a political suspect. Deben's sister was in an advanced stage of pregnancy.

The police of Bankura arrested both women and forced them to walk to the police station from their village of Juthbehar. The police were told they had made a mistake and a suitable conveyance was suggested to transport the women to the police station, but the police paid no heed. The request for bail was refused and the women were subjected to various humiliations. Kali rushed to Holy Mother and reported everything.

Holy Mother shuddered and her face turned red. She said in an extremely angry voice: "What does all this mean? Has it been done by the order of the government or is it a clever act by the police officer concerned? We never heard of such cruelty to innocent women during the reign of Queen Victoria. If the government is responsible for the matter, then it will not last long. Was there no young man nearby who could slap the policemen and snatch away the girls? Where were Deben's brothers?"[19]

Kali and the monks discussed the matter, but news came that evening that the women had been released. When Kali gave the news to Holy Mother, she said: "If I had not heard of their release, I could not have slept tonight." A couple of days later the Mother said to Prabhakar of Arambagh: "This British rule will not last long. It will continue only as long as Queen Victoria's merit lasts."[20]

Holy Mother was very thoughtful and farsighted. She sensed that in the near future many Westerners would come to India, attracted by the ideals of Ramakrishna and Vivekananda. Swami Ritananda recalled: "Krishnaprasanna, a learned devotee, stayed at Koalpara Ashrama for some days. One day the Mother told us: 'Look, in the course of time many devotees will come from Western countries. You should learn English well from Krishnaprasanna.' Accordingly we started to take English lessons. But it was discontinued some days later when Krishnaprasanna left."[21]

Holy Mother's Patriotism

Swami Ishanananda recalled:

Once during Durga Puja, the Mother gave me the responsibility of buying clothes for her nephews and nieces. I bought clothes made of coarse native cloth, but the girls did not like them. They wanted fine English stuff. Irritated, I told them: "Those clothes are made in England. Do you think I will buy those foreign goods?" The Mother was seated there and she listened to the discussion. Then she said with a smile: "My son, the English people too are my children. I must live with all. I cannot be exclusive. Please buy clothes according to their choice." Later I noticed that whenever any foreign articles had to be purchased, the Mother would ask someone else to buy it instead of me. It was against her nature to hurt anyone's feelings.[22]

During World War I there was a tremendous scarcity of cloth in India because all of the mills were in England. The British took cotton from

India and produced cloth in their country, and then exported that cloth to India at high prices.

One day Bibhuti Ghosh, a devotee of Holy Mother, went to visit his fellow devotee Sureshwar Sen in Vishnupur. A young girl of the Sen family said to him, "Uncle, I can't leave my room, so I must pay my respects to you from here." Bibhuti threw his chadar [cotton shawl] into the girl's room; she covered herself with it and came out. When Bibhuti told this story to Holy Mother, she cried.

A few days later, someone read Holy Mother some heartbreaking news from the newspaper: Some women had committed suicide because they had no clothing and could not leave their rooms. This made Holy Mother very sad. She cried loudly, and then said: "What will the women do if they have no cloth to cover themselves? Is there any other way to protect their modesty except suicide?"[23]

Swami Nikhilananda described the Mother's patriotic feeling at this time:

> Holy Mother was patriotic in her own way and cherished the welfare of the country. During the First World War people suffered intensely, especially the women from scarcity of clothes. Many of them could hardly go out in public, and the newspapers often reported the news of their suicides. One day, after hearing several reports of these heart-rending episodes, Holy Mother could not control herself. Weeping bitterly she said: "When will the English go? When will they leave our country? Formerly we had spinning wheels in every house. People used to make yarn and weave their clothes. There was no scarcity of wearing apparel. The British have ruined the whole thing. They tricked us and said: 'You will get four pieces of English cloth for a rupee, and one piece extra.' All our people took to an easy life, and the spinning wheel disappeared. Now, what has happened to these fops? There is no end to their misery. She asked a disciple to give her a spinning wheel.[24]

One afternoon the Mother asked a devotee: "Hello, there was such a great war going on. Why did it stop all of a sudden?" The devotee replied: "Mother, President Woodrow Wilson of America submitted to the Peace Conference 14 points that brought a truce. Each party agreed and thus peace was established." The Mother asked what those conditions were.

The devotee explained: "Not to invade another's country, give mutual respect, give compensation for destruction, and so on."

Holy Mother commented: "These are admirable words. But what they say comes from their lips. It would be wonderful if the words came from their hearts."[25]

Mother of the Birds and the Beasts

In the tenth chapter of the Gita, Krishna described his divine manifestations: "I am the Self, O Arjuna, seated in the hearts of all creatures. I am the beginning, the middle, and the end of all beings."[26] He further said that among trees, he is the *asvattha*; among horses, Uchchaisravas; among elephants, Airavata; among cows, Kamadhuk; among animals, the lion; among birds, Garuda; and so on. The entire creation, preservation, and dissolution of the universe are in the domain of Shakti, who is the Divine Mother. She exists in all beings as consciousness and the Mother.

In the Chandi, Brahma prayed: "O Mother of the universe, you are the power behind the creation, preservation, and dissolution of this universe."[27] All these scriptures say that both immobile objects and mobile beings originated from the Divine Mother, so they are all parts of God, or the Divine Mother.

Ramakrishna was fond of dogs and cats. Ramlal recalled: "There was a dog in the temple garden that the Master called Captain. Captain quite often sat on the front terrace of the Mother's temple. Whenever the Master would call him, the dog would come and roll at his feet. Then the Master would feed him *luchis* and *sandesh*. The Master once said: 'Look, there are so many dogs here but none of them sits in front of the Mother except Captain. I have not seen any other dog that sits on the steps near the Ganges and drinks Ganges water. Captain was born as a dog as the result of a curse. He had some good *samskaras* [tendencies] in his previous life, so he is here. He is a blessed soul.'"[28]

Nistarini Ghosh reminisced: "Once a cat took refuge in Sri Ramakrishna's room at Dakshineswar with her little kittens. The mother cat would sometimes sleep on his bed near his feet and if he reached down and touched her with his hand, at once she would get up and seem almost to make a *pranam* [bow before him]. It troubled the Master much to know what to do with the cat and her kittens, for he felt that they did not get proper food at the temple. One day when I came to see him, he asked me, 'Will you do something for me?' I clasped my hands before him and said, 'Whatever it is, that I must do.' But again he asked and I replied as before. Then he told me of the cats and asked me to take them. 'Remember,' he said, 'that they have taken refuge with me, so see that they get the best of care.'"[29] Nistarini obeyed the Master's instruction implicitly.

Holy Mother took care of cows, cats, and birds. During Durga Puja, a goat sacrifice is part of the ritual. But when the monks performed Durga worship at Belur Math, Holy Mother forbade them to perform the goat sacrifice.

A monk is not supposed to perform any cruel action. When the Mother was living at Udbodhan House, good milk was not available, so the monks told her that they would send a cow to Calcutta. But Holy Mother protested. The cows in Belur Math move freely about the monastery compound on the bank of the Ganges, but in Calcutta they would be confined to a dark room in the city, and the Mother could not bear that.

Holy Mother also did not approve of her disciples doing things that would inconvenience others. When Brahmachari Jnan wanted to buy pure milk in Jayrambati from milkmen, he paid them double the asking price so the milk would not be watered down. The Mother forbade him to continue this practice. She said that it would increase the price of milk, and the poor villagers would not be able to buy it for their children.

When Girish Ghosh visited Jayrambati, Holy Mother went from door to door to get a little milk in the morning so that she could make morning tea for Girish and other devotees. Once a disciple wanted to write a letter to a wealthy devotee to ask him to buy a cow for the Mother. When he sought her consent, she scolded him and forbade him to write any such letter. Despite the shortage of milk, the Mother was reluctant to buy cows and create more work for her attendants. She reluctantly gave her consent when Surendranath Gupta (later Swami Satsangananda) offered two cows, and her attendant Jnanananda was eager to look after them. Later Jnanananda became very sick and needed to move temporarily to Katihar. Before he left, with Surendranath's help, he built a cowshed and engaged a boy named Govinda to take care of the cows.

Govinda was an orphan boy, 10 years old, well-behaved, and cheerful. The Mother was fond of him. After some time he developed eczema all over his body and suffered from excruciating pain. Once he passed a sleepless night, crying. The next morning Holy Mother ground some margosa leaves and raw turmeric into a paste and taught Govinda how to rub it all over his body. This antiseptic herbal treatment eventually cured him.[30]

Swami Ishanananda mentioned in his reminiscences that there was another boy who took care of the Mother's cows. Ramendra was 14 years old. Surendranath paid his salary and bore all the expenses with regard to the cows. One morning in August, Ramendra was cutting grass at the northeast corner of the Punyapukur when he was bitten by a water snake on his left index finger. He ran to Holy Mother's house, where Dr. Rampada immediately cut the spot so that the poison would come out with the blood. Ramendra's wrist was tied tightly with ropes in two or three places to keep the poison from spreading throughout his body.

Holy Mother was performing worship when this occurred. When she heard the commotion, she left the shrine and went to see what had happened. She asked Dr. Rampada to remove the ties and said: "Take him to the temple of Mother Simhavahini right now. Nothing else needs to be done. Ramendra will be cured by the grace of Simhavahini." Two persons escorted Ramendra to the temple, which was located in the southeast corner of the Jayrambati village. The Mother followed them.

According to Holy Mother's instruction, Ramendra prostrated before the deity and then lay down on his back with his head towards the north. The Mother put a little earth and an offered flower into his mouth and put a little earth on the wound. She asked her attendants to mix the earth of Simhavahini with a little water to make mud and smear that all over his body.

Soon the left side of Ramendra's body began to swell. Holy Mother sat there with her attendants till two o'clock in the afternoon. When the worship of the deity was over, she took a little buttermilk and sanctified water and fed Ramendra with it. She then went home for lunch, returning to the temple at three o'clock. That evening Ramendra's body swelled so much that it seemed his skin would crack. His eyes were closed and he could not speak. The clay had dried on his body, so a new layer was smeared over it. A message was sent to Ramendra's widowed mother in Nakunda Village, who came that night and began to cry for her son. The Mother consoled her, saying: "Don't worry. By the grace of the living Goddess Simhavahini, your son will be cured. Don't cry near your son." Holy Mother returned to her home at eleven o'clock.

Early the next morning, Holy Mother visited the temple and found that Ramendra had opened his eyes. His swelling was reduced and some fluid oozed from his wound. Holy Mother asked her attendant to put another layer of mud on his body, but as he was doing so, some flesh around the wound fell off. When Holy Mother saw that, she said: "Well, now the danger is over. There is nothing to fear, by the grace of Mother Simhavahini. The Mother has saved his life. As a result of the doctor's surgery that poisonous part fell off and his life is spared."

Ramendra gradually came around in the afternoon and began to talk normally. The Mother fed him buttermilk and sanctified water again and kept him lying there. The next day Ramendra offered worship to the deity and came to the Mother's house for lunch. He recuperated quickly and returned home with his mother.[31]

Later, in order to solve the milk problem in Holy Mother's household, four cows were purchased and a boy named Dinu was appointed to look after them. A neighbour, Gopal Mandal, recalled: "Aunt [Holy Mother] had four cows — Mahanta, Maharaj, Lakshmikanta, and Indraraj. In between her household work, Aunt would feed the cows with water from boiled rice and then caress their foreheads, dewlaps, and backs. Sometimes she would rub oil on their horns. Dinu used to take the cows to graze. Aunt was very fond of him. After his breakfast, Dinu would take the cows to the field and come back at one o'clock. Aunt would wait to eat until Dinu had his lunch."[32]

Surendranath Sarkar also wrote an eyewitness account: "Very early one morning in Jayrambati, a calf was piteously crying in the outer courtyard of the Mother's house. The calf was kept separate from its mother at night for the purpose of milking the cow. Hearing its cries, the Mother rushed out, saying: 'I am coming, my child, I am coming. I will release you right now.' She immediately freed the calf from its tether. Amazed, I witnessed the Divine Mother's compassion for all beings."[33]

In Holy Mother's house there was a pet parrot named Gangaram. Every day the Mother gave it a bath, cleaned its cage, and gave it food and water. Every morning and evening, the Mother said to the bird: "My child, Gangaram, now repeat your mantra." The parrot would then call out, "Hare Krishna, Hare Rama; Krishna, Krishna, Rama, Rama." The Mother had taught it to chant God's names. It also learned from the Mother the names of the brahmacharins and could utter them clearly. Sometimes it called, "Ma, O Ma!" and Mother responded, "Coming, my child, I am coming." She would carry some gram and water for the bird, as she knew that the bird's call meant that it was hungry.[34]

Radhu had a pet cat and the Mother arranged a daily ration of milk for it. It would lie down near Holy Mother's feet peacefully and fearlessly. When it was a little naughty, Holy Mother would pretend that she was going to punish it with a stick, but this only made the cat creep nearer her feet. Laughing, she would throw away the stick and everyone would laugh seeing the Mother's playful mood. Cats are given to stealing food, but this did not bother the Mother at all. She remarked: "To steal food is its dharma. Who is always there to feed it lovingly?" One day two cats fought over some food and the leg of one of them was sprained. Concerned, the Mother said: "One leg of this cat is injured; now how will it hunt for food? Please call Dr. Nalin." The doctor came and put a bandage on the cat's leg with a small piece of wood and cloth. The cat got well within a few days.[35]

At one time Brahmachari Jnan declared war on Radhu's cat. One day he treated the cat roughly, throwing it to the ground. The Mother's face turned pale with pain. Despite Jnan's ill treatment, the cat found a safe haven in the Mother and Radhu, and eventually it gave birth to a few kittens. When the time came for Holy Mother to leave for Calcutta, she said to Jnan: "My son, please cook some extra rice for these cats, so that they will not go to the neighbours' houses for food. Otherwise the neighbors will revile us." She knew that this common sense advice might not be heeded, so she continued: "Look, Jnan, don't beat these cats. Know for certain that I dwell in them." That was enough. Jnan could no longer lift his hand or a stick against those cats. Although he himself was a vegetarian, he bought some small fish every day, fried them, mixed them with rice, and fed this food to the cats.[36]

In Udbodhan House a cat gave birth to her kittens on Brahmachari Ganendranath's bed. Holy Mother and Golap-ma hurriedly cleaned Ganen's bed and changed the sheet. Holy Mother was apprehensive that Ganen might throw the cat out of the house, so she said to him affectionately: "That cat lives here and eats here. Where could it have gone for delivery? My son, don't hurt that cat."[37]

Pravrajika Bharatiprana recalled:

> In Udbodhan House, Radhu had two cats — Ranga and Ramani. They were good-natured and never tried to get food from others' plates. They ate only when Radhu or Golap-ma fed them. The Mother was also fond of them. One day Ranga soiled a bed, so Rasbihari banished it to a distant place. The Mother lamented: "My goodness! What is this? What has Rasbihari done this morning? He is a monk; he does not have any maya [that is, feelings]." Radhu and Golap-ma felt very bad for that cat. However, that cat returned to Udbodhan House after four months. It was emaciated and died on the street after a few days. Golap-ma immersed it in the Ganges and got the Mother's permission to perform a ceremony for it. The Mother commented: "You see, that cat was a devotee who had been cursed." Golap-ma collected some funds and arranged a festival on the 13th day after its demise. Some monks from Belur Math came and sang Kali-kirtan and all enjoyed a nice feast. They remarked: "This cat is definitely fortunate, so its memorial festival has been held in the Mother's house."[38]

Once in Jayrambati, Radhu's pet cat was lying in the courtyard. A woman was caressing it with her foot and she touched her foot to its head. Observing this, Holy Mother said: "My goodness! What are you doing? The head is the seat of the guru. Should one place one's foot there? Salute the cat." The lady replied: "I never knew that, Mother. Just now I have learned this from you."[39]

The Mother's maid, Basanabala, reminisced: "One day in Jayrambati the Mother sat for her lunch but had not yet started eating. I also made my plate ready. Suddenly a cat began to eat from my plate. The Mother did not say anything, nor did she take any action against the cat. She simply said: 'Basana, let me share my food with you.' She then gave half of her food to me and we ate together."[40]

It was 28 March 1913 at Jayrambati. Swami Arupananda wrote in his reminiscences:

> The crazy aunt [Radhu's mother] was arranging lunch for a relative by placing a leaf plate and a glass of water on her veranda. Radhu's cat sipped water from that glass, so she replaced it with another glass of water. This time also the cat sipped the water. The crazy aunt chased the cat, shouting, "I shall kill you." The Mother was nearby. She said: "No, one should not prevent a thirsty animal from drinking. Moreover, the cat has already touched that water." Immediately the crazy aunt flared up, saying: "You will not have to show your overflowing compassion to that cat. You have shown enough compassion to people. Why not reserve your kindness for human beings?" The Mother gravely said: "That person is really unfortunate who is deprived of my compassion. I don't know anyone, even an insect, who is not a recipient of my compassion."[41]

Once in Jayrambati a Naga monk came into the village riding on a small elephant. The Mother carried some rice and fed the elephant. She then put a vermilion mark on the elephant's forehead. She also gave some money to the monk to buy his food.[42]

"I Am the Mother of the Virtuous and the Wicked"

In this world there is no glory in making a good person good, but it is praiseworthy if one can make a bad person good. One cannot help a weak person or a sinner by reminding him of his weakness or sin. No one in this world is absolutely good or absolutely bad. The Mother knew her children's bad and good qualities. She said: "People, by nature, often do evil things. How few know how to make them good."

Probably in 1901 Holy Mother was staying in a rented house at 10/2 Bosepara Lane, Baghbazar. Swamiji had sent an Orissan servant away from Belur Math for stealing. He was a poor man and his family depended on his income. The helpless man went to the Mother, confessed his crime, and begged her forgiveness. The Mother gave him shelter and fed him. In the afternoon, when Premananda came to pay his respects to her, the

Mother said to him: "Look, Baburam, this man is very poor. Impelled by poverty, he committed a mistake. For that reason Naren reprimanded him and drove him out. You see, this world is full of misery. You are monks, so you understand very little of it. Take him back to Belur Math." Premananda tried to convince the Mother that this might displease Swamiji. Agitated, the Mother said: "I say, take him back." When Premananda returned to the Math with that servant, Swamiji remarked: "Look at Baburam's senseless act. He has brought back that fellow." When Premananda told Swamiji the whole story, he did not utter another word.[43]

Holy Mother had all sorts of devotees. Some were pure and virtuous, some impure and sinful, and some strange and crazy. As the five fingers of a person are not all of equal length, so all of a mother's children are not the same. Generally a mother is more compassionate to her weak children than to her strong ones.

A young disciple of the Mother talked privately to her on the northern veranda of her room in Udbodhan House. He lamented: "Mother, I have suffered a lot because of my bad karma. You are my guru, Chosen Deity, and all in all. In fact, I have committed so many sins that I am ashamed to tell them to you. Your grace is holding me." The Mother caressed his head with her hand and said, "Despite everything, a son remains a son to his mother." Touched by the Mother's affection, the young man said: "Mother, you are right. I have received so much grace from you, but may I never think that your grace is easily available."[44]

An educated young man from a wealthy family in a village close to Jayrambati received initiation from Holy Mother. He established an ashrama in his village and did a lot of social work. Unfortunately he fell in love with a young widow who was his close relative. Gossip spreads fast from mouth to mouth. The people of Jayrambati heard about it and the devotees asked Holy Mother to forbid him from visiting. The Mother was sad when she learned of her disciple's fall, but she said: "I am a mother. How can I forbid him from seeing me? Such words will never pass through my lips." That young man continued to visit the Mother and one day he brought the woman to her. The Mother considered it to be Providence and forgave them.[45]

There was a young widow in Jayrambati who was very poor and earned her livelihood by hard manual labour. She did not remember when she had been married or even who her husband had been. It was only when she grew up that she learned she was a widow, and at that time a Hindu widow could not marry again. Such girls generally lived with their parents or husband's family like maidservants. She used to be called to the Mother's house to carry the devotees' luggage. The Mother had great affection for this young widow. When the girl attained womanhood, she fell in love with a young man — and when their love affair became known, there was a big commotion in that conservative society. Hard-hearted social leaders wanted to punish her. For most of her life no one had thought to help her or give her any education, and now they began to verbally abuse her.

Holy Mother heard the whole story and was worried about the young woman's future. She wholeheartedly prayed to God for the young woman's welfare. God answered Holy Mother's prayer. A wealthy landlord of a neighbouring village, who was a disciple of the Mother, intervened and reminded the leaders to have a compassionate outlook towards that girl. Peace returned to the village. The Mother heaved a sigh of relief. When that landlord came to bow down to the Mother, she joyfully blessed him, saying: "My son, you have saved that poor girl from misery. I am extremely pleased and relieved. May the Lord bless you for this intervention."[46]

Swami Keshavananda related an important incident that took place in Koalpara in 1919:

> One day I said to the Mother, "Mother, your health is not good and you are suffering from illness off and on. The person who is cooking for you, you know her questionable character. If you allow me, I can find another cook for you." Hearing my words, the Mother became very grave and then said: "If you wish, you can get rid of her; but if I forsake her, where will she go?" I immediately fell at the Mother's feet and begged forgiveness: "Mother, I made a big mistake. Please be gracious to me and forgive me." Who else can give this kind of reassurance: "If I forsake her, where will she go?" Whatever we may be, we are none other than the Mother's children. She herself said: "If my children are covered with dirt, I will have to take them on my lap after cleaning and washing them. I am their real mother and not a foster mother."[47]

Holy Mother was all-knowing, and a saviour of the fallen. Swami Bhumananda wrote this eyewitness account of a famous actress who had led a sinful life and came to the Mother for succour:

> One morning at eight o'clock a woman came to Udbodhan House by car. She walked straight to the steps as if the house were known to her. Later I learned that it was her first visit. The Mother was in her room with Yogin-ma, Golap-ma, and the wife of Dr. Aghorenath Ghosh. The Mother was talking when all of a sudden, she said to her companions: "Please wait a little. I will return soon." She walked from her room towards the steps.

The woman on the steps was a well-known actress. She was sobbing with her head on the railing of the steps. The Mother came down, touched her head, and then hugged her affectionately. Then the Mother said to her, "When you come to the Master, you will not have to cry anymore." This assurance made the woman cry even harder. The Mother led her upstairs and wiped her eyes with the corner of her cloth. She said: "Now go to the Master and bow down to him with a smiling face."

On the upper veranda, the actress first bowed down to the Mother who blessed her by touching her head. The Mother also touched her chin with her fingers and kissed them, which was her way of showing love and affection. She took the actress to the shrine. Pointing to the Master's picture on the altar, she said, "Now bow down to the Master." That noon the actress had her prasad sitting next to the Mother, who shared some of her food with her.[48]

Another time the Mother was staying at Jagadamba Ashrama in Koalpara. A young woman from a low-caste family came to her with a broken heart and complained that her paramour had suddenly deserted her. She wept bitterly as she related her sad tale to the Mother. She had given up her friends and family to live with him, and now she was completely helpless. Touched by her sad plight, the Mother sent for the man and rebuked him gently: "This girl has given up everything and everyone for you, and you have taken her service for a long time. Now if you leave her, you will incur a great sin. You won't find a place even in hell." The Mother's words penetrated his heart; he had a change of heart and accompanied that girl home.[49]

It was not possible for Holy Mother to see faults in others, and she did not like others seeing faults either. Once in Jayrambati some devotees complained to Holy Mother that someone who had been her attendant now lived in Rishikesh and was quarreling with the monks there. They added: "How could he have such bad tendencies after having lived with you and served you so long?" When they left, Holy Mother said to Brahmachari Barada:

My son, I can no longer see or hear of anyone's faults. One will have to reap the results of one's own past karma. If one were destined to have a deep cut, at the very least, one would get the prick of a needle. They talked about A.'s faults to me, but where were they in those days? He served me so well. In those days I lived with my brother's family and I would boil the paddy and then husk it. I used to do all the household work because my sisters-in-law were quite young. Without caring for cold or rain, and covered with soot, A. would help me by taking the big vessels of boiled paddy down from the wooden stove. Now many devotees come, but who was helping me then? Should I forget it all? Well, people should not be blamed. Previously I noticed people's shortcomings. Later I prayed to the Master with tears, "Master, may I never see faults in others." Thus after long prayers, I got rid of that bad habit.[50]

Holy Mother always saw the good qualities in her children. Ramakrishna accepted disciples only after testing them, but the Mother accepted everyone who came to her without discrimination. It is not possible for a real mother to reject her bad children and welcome only the good ones.

Once M. was so offended by the conduct of a certain devotee that he requested the Mother not to allow him to be anywhere near her. She replied: "If my son is besmeared with dust and dirt, I will have to clean him and take him on my lap."[51]

Girish Ghosh, the bohemian devotee of Ramakrishna, said: "The Master gave shelter to a horrible sinner like me. If I had known that there was such a large dustbin to dump all my sins in, I would have enjoyed more pleasures in my life."[52] Like the Master, the Mother also gave shelter to many people with questionable character. Although her whole body burnt with their sins, she endured it silently without a murmur.

One afternoon when the visitors had left, Brahmachari Rasbihari saw Holy Mother washing her feet up to the knees again and again. When she was asked why, she replied: "Don't allow anyone to salute me by touching his head to my feet. Thus all sins enter through my body, and my feet burn. So I have to wash my feet. For this reason I suffer from illness. Tell people to bow down from a distance." Then she immediately changed her mind and said: "Please don't tell these things to Sharat [Saradananda]. He will stop salutations altogether."[53]

The great teachers of the world do not compromise truth. Even an avatar cannot satisfy everyone since each person is different. Sometimes a great teacher's actions are misunderstood because people judge according to their own viewpoints. Once a fallen woman came to Udbodhan House and fell at the Mother's feet. Holy Mother embraced her and said: "Come to me, my daughter. Now you have realized what sin is. You are repentant. I shall initiate you with a mantra. Offer yourself at the feet of the Master. Don't be afraid." Some aristocratic women from Baghbazar, including Krishnabhavini, Balaram's wife, heard that the Mother had given shelter to a woman of questionable character, so they decided to stay away. Krishnabhavini told this to Golap-ma, and she reported it to Holy Mother. She remarked: "Those who have taken refuge in me will come here. What can I do if someone's coming to me stops others' coming?"[54] Later Krishnabhavini came to the Mother and apologized for her wrong judgement.

Swami Shyamananda came to Calcutta regularly from Belur Math to shop. If the tide was high, he would return straightaway to Belur Math by boat with the groceries. Otherwise, he would come to Udbodhan House, bathe, and then have lunch. Once he arrived at two o'clock when everyone had finished lunch. Irritated, Golap-ma said: "He does not inform us in advance that he will come for lunch. It would be more convenient for us and for him if he would let us know in the morning." The Mother overheard Golap-ma's remark and came out of her room. She said: "You see, our family is growing day by day. Every day we will have to make food for a couple of extra people. What to do?"

Golap-ma said, "Kshudu [Shyamananda] comes often, but he does not tell us when he will stay for lunch."

"Let it be," Holy Mother responded. "Please serve him lunch soon. Already it is late. My son has come after doing many errands."

"You have too much affection for him. It seems he is your father-in-law*."

"Yes, you are right," Holy Mother agreed. "These boys are like my venerable father-in-law. They are my own."[55]

Swami Mahadevananda recalled:

It was July and raining continuously. I carried some vegetables from Koalpara Ashrama to Jayrambati. When the Mother saw me, she said: "You have come — very good! No one has come here for some days. There is a shortage of groceries. You stay here today and do some shopping for us." In the afternoon I went to the Haldipukur market to buy kerosene, flour, sugar, ghee, rock-candy, and some other things. The weight of all the items was about a maund [82 pounds]. The shopkeeper told me: "It will be difficult for you to carry such a heavy load. Let me call a porter for you." I was thinking that the Mother did not ask me to engage a porter, so I said: "I don't need a porter. I shall be able to carry it. Please lift the basket onto my head." After carrying that basket for a while, I felt the weight of it and had an ache in my head. It was raining. I held the umbrella over the basket with one hand and the basket with the other. The road was slippery and I was walking carefully. I was determined to walk the entire path. Along the way there was a slope for crossing the bullock cart, and when I crossed it, I felt that the entire load became light. I could not figure out what had happened and I stopped for a minute. Then without any difficulty I reached

*Holy Mother's father-in-law's name was Kshudiram and Shyamananda's pre–monastic name was also Kshudiram.

the Mother's house. When I entered the house I saw the Mother pacing back and forth on her veranda. Her face was red, and eyes were bulging. She was asking herself: "Why did I not ask him to hire a porter?" When I put down the basket, she said: "Why did you not hire a porter? You should not carry such a heavy load."[56]

Mahadevananda realized that during his journey Holy Mother had relieved him by carrying the weight herself.

Holy Mother's Care for her Children

During World War I people suffered from a terrible financial crisis and scarcity of goods. Poor villagers had no money even to buy clothes. One morning Haridas Vairagi, an old minstrel from Deshra, came to Jayrambati. He used to make his living by playing his violin and singing devotional songs from door to door. He had sung the Agamani songs when Girish visited Holy Mother. The Mother was very fond of this old minstrel. Now, when she saw his pitiful condition, she gave him some oil to rub on his rough skin. The Mother heard his sad stories while preparing a betel roll for him, and she then fed him prasad. In the course of conversation, Haridas told the Mother that he had no spare cloth. That morning after her bath, the Mother had spread a wet cloth in the sun that she had used only a couple of times. After hearing his story, she picked up that cloth and gave it to Haridas. Overwhelmed, the old man wept as he touched the Mother's gift to his head and left.

Akshay Sen, a householder devotee of the Master and author of *Sri Ramakrishna Punthi*, used to live in Maynapur, which is some miles from Jayrambati. Because of his old age, he could not visit the Mother, but from time to time he sent some buffalo ghee and other things for her personal use. Once a middle-aged woman brought Akshay's gifts to Holy Mother. She arrived before noon and had her bath and lunch at the Mother's house. Seeing that she was exhausted, the Mother asked her to rest and stay overnight. A bed was made for her on the veranda outside the Mother's room. The woman was a little feverish and achy, so she fell fast asleep. During the night she unconsciously soiled her bed. The Mother got up very early in the morning, as usual. When she saw the situation, she realized that the woman might be abused if others in the household found out about it, so the Mother gently woke her up. She handed her a package of puffed rice and molasses, and then tenderly told her: "My child, start your journey now so that you can reach home before the sun gets hot." The woman bowed down to the Mother and left. The Mother quickly took the soiled mat to the pond, washed it, and laid it on the grass to dry. She also cleaned the veranda and mopped the mud floor with cow-dung paste. No one at the time knew what had happened.[57]

At the time of our story, Jayrambati was truly a remote village, accessible only by foot or bullock cart. In the autumn, the road was soft and muddy from the monsoon rains, so bullock carts could not reach the village. A couple from Garbeta, nearly 20 miles from Jayrambati, had heard about Holy Mother and wanted to receive her grace. One afternoon they started their journey by bullock cart with their four children. The next morning they reached Jibta, a couple of miles south of Jayrambati, and then walked to the Mother's house. Everyone was exhausted, especially the baby, who was suffering from malaria. The place and people were completely unknown to them. Utterly puzzled, they just stood at the Mother's door. As soon as the Mother heard of their arrival, she called them inside the house and received them cordially. They all bowed down to her and the magic of her affection greatly reassured them. The Mother arranged for milk and medicine for the baby. The couple bathed in Banerjee's Pond, and the Mother initiated them after performing her daily worship.

After lunch they wanted to resume their journey to Burdwan, 34 miles from Jayrambati. With tearful eyes they bowed down to the Mother. She reluctantly bade them farewell and gazed at them as long as they were visible. She was so sad at their departure that she did not go to take her noon rest, but instead remained seated on her veranda, deeply thinking of this family. Meanwhile a woman devotee found a towel that belonged to them lying in the sun and took it to the Mother, which increased her sadness. Observing the Mother lamenting, Brahmachari Gopesh (later Swami Saradeshananda) took the towel and ran to catch up with the couple. They were then near Banerjee's Pond at the border of the village. Naturally they were embarrassed. They expressed their gratitude to him and continued their walk to Deshra where their bullock cart was waiting for them. Having the news from Gopesh, Holy Mother was pleased.

But soon after the woman's wet sari was found hanging in the sun near Punyapukur. The Mother loudly lamented: "Ah, my child will not find her sari tomorrow. She will remember that she left it in the Mother's house." Another woman made a rude comment: "How can she manage herself with such a regiment of children?" The Mother said in a choked voice: "It is natural to make mistakes. It was hard for my child to leave this place. She could not stay here even for a night, nor did she get a chance to talk to me fully." Gopesh was ready to go, but Nalini said: "Enough! You will not have to go again; they have gone quite a distance now." But Gopesh took the sari and said to the Mother: "They have not gone too far. I shall be back soon." Pleased, the Mother said: "My son, the sun is hot. You had better take an umbrella." In fact, the family had almost reached their bullock cart on the main road. Seeing Gopesh running towards them with the sari in hand, the devotees were ashamed and apologized to him. They said: "Truly there was no necessity for your taking so much trouble to bring the sari to us." But Gopesh explained that the Mother was worried and was sorry for their plight, and to make the Mother happy he carried the sari. This brief meeting with Holy Mother left a deep impression in their minds. They had experienced the genuine affection of a real mother.[58]

Rajen (later Swami Vidyananda) was the full-time cook for Koalpara Ashrama and did all sorts of other tasks for the centre. He was simple, austere, and very devoted to the Mother. At one time he was not getting along with the head swami, and moreover his health was failing due to his heavy workload and the lack of nourishing food at the ashrama. He came to the Mother at Jayrambati and told her his problem. He asked permission to move to Varanasi. The Mother asked him to stay with her at Jayrambati instead. Rajen agreed and joined Gopesh in looking after the activities of Holy Mother's household.

Holy Mother always offered a glass of rock-candy syrup to the Master during the worship and then drank it as prasad. Thus she broke her fast and distributed the other prasad to the monks and devotees. Now, every day after worship, the Mother called Rajen to her room. She would sip a little of the rock-candy syrup and then hand the glass to Rajen to drink. One day the Mother privately told Gopesh: "My son, Rajen's head has become overheated from cooking over the fire in the ashrama. Despite his ill health, he has worked hard. Moreover, he had a difficult time adjusting in Koalpara and wanted to go to Varanasi. I asked him to stay with me to give his brain some rest. Later when his health improves, he should return to Koalpara Ashrama and resume his work there. To that end, every morning I share with him that offered syrup so that his system will calm down." Gopesh was moved by the Mother's love and affection towards her monastic disciple.

A couple of months later, Rajen regained his health and returned to Koalpara. After Holy Mother's passing away, Rajen worked very hard to build the Mother's temple in Jayrambati. He was the first caretaker of the temple, but he passed away a year after it was established.[59]

Sometime in January 1917, four of Holy Mother's disciples came to visit her in Jayrambati from Mymensingh (now in Bangladesh). As she had not been well for some time, they intended to stay for only a couple of days.

The Mother was happy to see them. During their stay in Jayrambati, they visited Kamarpukur and on their way back, they were caught in a rainstorm. The group's leader became ill with malarial fever. The Mother was very anxious. The guest room was small and several people were staying there. Furthermore, there was no bathroom facility for the patient. The Mother arranged a special diet and quinine medicine for the sick man. When the fever did not abate after three days, the devotees discussed the matter and decided to move the patient to Koalpara Ashrama where there was sufficient room and also a government hospital nearby. The Mother remained silent. Vidyananda hired a palanquin that afternoon and escorted the patient and his companions to Koalpara. The Mother repeated "Durga, Durga" and bade them farewell. Exhausted, she went to bed with a heavy heart. Her attendant Gopesh sat on the veranda so no one would disturb her rest.

Suddenly a thick cloud covered the sky and created darkness all around. A thunderstorm began to blow with a terrible roar. Holy Mother awoke and came out of her room, crying out loudly, "What will happen to my son?" Her veil dropped on the ground and her hair was dishevelled. She was completely oblivious of her surroundings. She rushed to the edge of the veranda. Looking up at the sky, she prayed with folded hands: "O Master, please save my son. Save my son by all means, O Lord." Observing her tearful eyes, Gopesh was dumbfounded. He consoled her, saying: "Mother, don't worry. By this time they have reached Deshra. Vidyananda is intelligent. He and the other three devotees are with him. Moreover, the palanquin carriers are known to be obedient and faithful." Gopesh escorted the Mother to her room. When Holy Mother entered, she stood in front of the Master's picture, cried, and prayed again and again: "O Master, please be gracious to me and save my child." Gopesh was speechless and overwhelmed by the Mother's love for her devotees. Gradually the sky became a little clearer. The rain stopped at midnight. The Mother passed a restless night. The next morning Vidyananda returned and informed the Mother that the group had taken shelter in a home in Deshra during the thunderstorm. When the rain stopped, they took a lantern and continued to Koalpara. They had supper there and slept well. The patient and his companions were doing fine. Holy Mother was greatly relieved.[60]

Shaurjendranath Majumdar of Mymensingh belonged to an aristocratic family and worked for the royal family of Coochbehar. He was a disciple of the Mother, and many of his family members followed his lead and also took initiation from her. From his early life, he was accustomed to taking tea when he awoke in the morning. After initiation he said to Holy Mother, "Mother, I have a habit of taking tea as soon as I get up in the morning. It will not be possible for me to practise my sadhana without taking tea. What shall I do?" The Mother answered with a smile: "My son, it is not a problem. You may take your tea or anything else before you practise japa and meditation."[61]

In Jayrambati Holy Mother served fruits, sweets, and puffed rice to the devotees for breakfast; she would eat puffed rice with green chili, and drink a glass of rock-candy syrup. Once when Shaurjendra was visiting the Mother, she served puffed rice and molasses to him for breakfast. Shaurjendra said to her: "Mother, what have you given me? I don't eat this kind of food." The Mother told him: "My son, these are the things available here. Please eat. It will not do any harm to you. When I go to Calcutta, I shall feed you nice things."[62]

The monks in Koalpara worshipped in the shrine at ten o'clock in the morning on empty stomachs. One day the Mother told Vidyananda: "You boys perform worship before eating anything. It makes the mind restless. If the stomach is calm, the mind remains calm. Please have your breakfast and then do the worship."[63] Her advice was very practical.

People normally walked barefoot in Jayrambati, including Holy Mother's devotees from Calcutta, who considered it holy ground. Sometimes the village children carelessly scattered broken brick chips and small broken pieces of earthen vessels in Holy Mother's courtyard. Swami Saradeshananda told this touching story:

> I remember this insignificant incident: The Mother was at Jayrambati. She was over 60 and not well. It was the dead of the night, about one-thirty. My sleep broke and I saw a light in the courtyard from my room. Out of curiosity I came out and saw someone doing something with the help of a kerosene lantern. I went down and saw the Mother digging with a spud [spade] and picking up broken pieces of earthen vessels and bricks and putting them in a basket. Dumbfounded, I asked, "Mother, what are you doing?" Embarrassed, she replied, "I am cleaning this courtyard by picking up these broken chips." "Why are you doing this?" "My son, speak softly; otherwise others' sleep will be broken." Then she said in low voice: "You see, my son, some children have come from Calcutta. They live in the city and don't have the habit of walking barefoot. Here people walk barefoot. Today someone's foot was cut. So I am cleaning up these broken chips so that they will not get hurt." I said: "Mother, we can do this work. Why are you doing such a thing and giving up your sleep?" "Yes, my son, I know you can do it. But you are tired from doing so much work in the household the whole day, so you need sleep. I have no work. So when you went to

sleep, I came to clean the courtyard." I said: "All right, now you give me the spud [spade] and I shall clean the courtyard. You go to your room and sleep." Mother said with a gentle tone: "My son, I shall do it because I am the Mother. A mother does many things for her children. I do very little for you all. My son, you go and sleep. I have almost finished — only a little is left." I could not say anything more. Tears trickled from my eyes. I thought: This is why she is the Mother of all. Without sleep she is not only cleaning the courtyard, she is also clearing the obstacles of her children from the path of their journey and she will continue doing so.[64]

Mother of the Outcast and the Wretched

It is hard for a Westerner or a modern Indian to understand the caste system in nineteenth- and early twentieth-century India. For example, brahmins, the highest caste, would not eat food or even drink water that had been touched by anyone from the other three castes — khsatriya, vaishya, and shudra — or from non-Hindus. Society was extremely rigid regarding these caste rules, especially in the villages. Anyone who broke caste rules was considered an outcast and his or her family would be shunned. Even some wealthy and famous families were victims of those merciless social restrictions. For example, the Dakshineswar Kali temple's founder, Rani Rasmani, was from a low caste and was told not to offer cooked food to Mother Kali. Fortunately, Ramakrishna's brother Ramkumar found a way around that problem. Even Rabindranath Tagore's family was looked down upon by high-caste brahmins because of their close association with Muslims.

Holy Mother followed the Master's teaching that devotees have no caste. How can there be caste distinction among the children of God? She did not deviate from her ideal. She had disciples and devotees from all castes, and she served them in Calcutta as well as in Jayrambati.

Once Mother initiated a devotee who was a *yugi,* which was a low weaver caste. He was hesitant to associate freely with other devotees in Jayrambati. Holy Mother reassured him, saying: "My son, why do you feel insecure because you are a yugi? You belong to the Master's fold — you belong to his family." When she had initiated him, she had not asked him about his caste. She accepted him as her disciple, so, she felt, no one in her village should question him about his social position, nor was it necessary for him to talk about it with others.

Once during Durga Puja many devotees were offering flowers at her feet. A man from Tajpur was standing outside. He was afraid to come inside and offer a flower to her because he was a *bagdi,* which was a low caste. But Holy Mother herself asked him to come into her room and offer his flower, which he did. He then left for home, overwhelmed with joy. These incidents might seem insignificant nowadays, but at that time caste was an important issue in Indian society.

Once a group of snake charmers came to Jayrambati and began to play their *dugdugi* (small tabors) on the street. When they came near the Mother's house, she became curious to see their snakes. She called them into her courtyard and asked them to perform their show. She offered to pay them. Listening to the sound of the snake charmers' dugdugi, many villagers and their children assembled at the Mother's house. The snake charmers opened the boxes of snakes, and when they played their flutes the snakes raised their hoods and began to move their heads rhythmically. When the show was over, Holy Mother gave them two rupees and a cloth, and fed them puffed rice and molasses. The leader took the dust of the Mother's feet and she blessed him by touching his head. One of her sisters-in-law remarked: "It is enough that you have given them money, a cloth, and refreshments. Why did you touch that snake charmer? Day and night they touch snakes; there must be poison on their hands. You are not supposed to touch them."

Holy Mother humbly replied: "Well, what can I do? That man saluted me by touching my feet. And how could I forbid him? If a person salutes me, shall I not bless him by touching his head?"[65]

It was August 1917. Holy Mother went to visit the sick widow of Rajendra Bandyopadhyay, who had a little boy and no one to care for her. She had an abscess in her ear and it was infected. Worms grew in the sore and it smelled so bad that no one would go near her. The Mother made a solution from margosa leaves and, with the help of a brahmachari, cleaned her wound with a syringe. She then said to Barada: "You sometimes take helpless patients in Koalpara Ashrama and care for them. It would be nice if you would take this helpless widow and serve her. Please consult with Kedar [Swami Keshavananda]. This woman does not have anyone to look after her. No one goes near her because of the bad odour. I am pained when I see how her little boy is suffering."

Immediately Barada left for Koalpara and reported everything to Keshavananda, who agreed to take in the widow. Barada could not find a palanquin, so they hired a bullock cart and travelled to Jayrambati via Shiromanipur and Sihar. Holy Mother was pleased to see them. She served refreshments of puffed rice and sweets, and asked them to pick up that woman right away or it would be too late to reach Koalpara. Holy Mother fed the patient a little warm milk and consoled her. The monks collected a wooden plank and used it as a stretcher to get the patient on the bullock cart. They reached Koalpara in the evening after going seven or eight miles. Puss and blood were oozing from both of the woman's ears and the smell was horrible.

The doctor treated her, and the monks cared for her day and night, but unfortunately she died after a few days. The monks cremated her body and went to Jayrambati to give Holy Mother the news. She said: "My son, you all worked like her own children. If she had stayed here, she would have died without any care and even without a little water."[66]

Mother of the Eccentrics and the Crazy

Mental balance is extremely important in spiritual life. Holy Mother advised her disciples to maintain calmness in the brain and stomach, which is indispensable for practising japa and meditation. Those who suffer from headaches and stomachaches cannot concentrate their minds on God. Krishna says in the Gita: "Equanimity of the mind is called yoga." The Mother attracted all types of people — some were sane and some insane. The difference between the sane and the insane is that a sane person has control over his or her emotions whereas an insane person does not. It is amazing how the Mother endured the eccentricity and craziness of her disciples, devotees, and relatives by her herculean patience and perseverance, love and forgiveness. The following stories will inspire us to develop interpersonal relationships and the ability to adjust to circumstances with compassion and a charitable outlook.

One day a woman bit Holy Mother's big toe while taking leave of her. The Mother cried aloud: "Goodness gracious! What kind of devotion is this? If you want to touch my feet, why not do so? Why bite the toe?"

The woman said: "I want you to remember me."

"Indeed!" the Mother replied. "I have never before seen such a novel way of making me remember a devotee."[67]

Another time a male devotee, while saluting her, struck her little toe with his forehead with such force that the Mother cried out in pain. When those present asked the devotee the reason for his shameful conduct, he replied: "I purposely gave her pain while saluting her so that she would remember me as long as the pain lasts."[68]

In 1909 Saradananda went to Jayrambati to partition the family property among the brothers of Holy Mother, who was also there. A young man wanted to see the Mother, so Swami Saradananda asked his attendant Brahmachari Jnanananda (later Swami Bhumananda) to take him to her. He bowed down to the Mother, who was then standing on her veranda, and then he began to pull her feet, so that they would touch his chest. Luckily the Mother was holding a pole in her cottage; otherwise she would have fallen down. Instantly Jnanananda grabbed that crazy fellow's hand and took him out. When Saradananda learned of this bizarre incident, he remarked: "Swami Yogananda never bowed down to the Mother while she was standing. When she left a place he would take the dust from that spot and put it on his head."[69]

There was no end to the bizarre demands placed upon Holy Mother, yet she unflinchingly fulfilled her devotees' wishes. A man came to her in Jayrambati and said that he would not drink water until he had worshipped her feet. Holy Mother was working in the kitchen. She left her work and stood on a low wooden seat on the veranda, so the devotee could offer flowers at her feet. Then she rushed back to the kitchen to finish preparing food for the devotees.[70]

A devotee named Umesh Datta wanted the Mother's rice prasad, which he had planned to dry in the sun and carry home with him after three days. The Mother gave him a plate of her prasad and asked him to watch it, so that it would not be eaten by crows. The devotee put the plate of rice in the sun in front of the Mother's room and said that he would be back soon. He went to the guest room for a smoke and then fell asleep, forgetting the rice. At three o'clock after his nap, he remembered the rice, went to the house, and found the Mother seated there. She told him: "My son, I am seated here lest the crows eat this rice." Ashamed, he apologized: "Mother, I am sorry that you did not get any rest today."[71]

One day a devotee grabbed Holy Mother's feet and said: "Mother, promise that you will appear before me at the time of my death."

The Mother replied: "I shall pray to the Master so that you can have his vision." When the devotee was persistent, with no other alternative, she said: "All right, my son, let it be so."[72]

One afternoon in Jayrambati the Mother was lying on a mat on the veranda. When Brahmachari Barada came, she indignantly said: "You boys went out on errands and no one was here to look after me. An old man came with X. When I saw him, I went inside the room and sat on my cot. He was anxious to take the dust of my feet and I forbade him. He forcefully took the dust of my feet. Since then, I have had a burning sensation in my feet as well as a terrible stomachache. I have washed my feet four times, and still that burning is there. If you had been here, I would have signaled you to stop him. In Calcutta, they are strict about my visitors. All sorts of people come to me. You boys are young, so you do not understand the nature of those people."[73]

Often devotees made unreasonable demands upon Holy Mother. Some would demand a vision of God or liberation. She always succeeded in soothing their restless minds. Once in Udbodhan House the Mother had just finished her daily worship when an unknown devotee appeared with some flowers, evidently to worship her feet. At the sight of a stranger, she sat on the bed with her feet hanging and wrapped herself with a cotton shawl, as was her habit. The man made an elaborate genuflection, offered flowers at her feet, and began to perform breathing exercises and other rituals, as one does before an image. Everyone was busy with their duties and no one was near the Mother. This went on for a long time and Holy Mother began to perspire heavily under the shawl. Golap-ma saw the devotee offering the flowers at Holy Mother's feet and then left to do some work. When Golap-ma returned quite a while later, she saw that the devotee was still seated in front of the Mother. Realizing the Mother's predicament, she rushed to rescue her. Pulling the man up by the hand, she said in her usual loud voice: "Do you think she is a wooden image that you would awaken her spirit by pranayama and other rituals? You have no common sense. Don't you see the Mother is getting hot and is very uncomfortable?"[74]

The greater the number of disciples and devotees, the more Holy Mother's troubles increased. But the compassionate Mother was the embodiment of forbearance and forgiveness. She took the pain and suffering of her children upon herself. Sometimes she lamented: "Master, I can't bear any more burdens." But she did forbear more. Satyendranath, Shaurjendra Majumdar's brother, left this eyewitness account:

Some afternoons I was entrusted with the task of lining up the devotees who wanted to visit the Mother in Udbodhan House. Some eccentrics pestered the Mother. I saw an elderly man crying loudly and bumping his head in front of the Mother. I noticed another person begin to tell his life story to her without caring that other people were waiting in line. Again, someone put his head on the feet of the Mother and remained there motionless. Another day a man lay down in front of her and requested her to place her foot on his chest and awaken his consciousness right then. It was extremely difficult to make them understand or to stop their importunate demands. Sometimes I was irritated, observing their childish emotions, and other times I could not control my laughter, watching their immature behaviour. One day when I joked about those people in front of the Mother, she said to me: "My son, when you grow up, you will understand how much pain these distressed people carry in their hearts. You are not a mother."

On another occasion I was in Jayrambati and met a young man on the street there. He had walked the whole night from Vishnupur (28 miles). His figure was strong and stout. He had bushy hair and his eyes were red like a hibiscus. He asked me, "Can you tell me where the Mother's house is?" I told him: "Please come with me. I am also staying there." When I asked his name and dwelling place, he laughed and replied: "I have no name, no lineage, and no home. I am the sacrifice in the Mother's worship, and I am waiting for the offering." I was dumbfounded observing the nature of this strange devotee. He was not mad. He bowed down to the Mother and she asked him to take a bath in the pond. Immediately he dipped in the pond, and then the Mother served him puffed rice and jilipis. Sitting near the Mother he began to eat like a child. The Mother caressed his body with her hand and then said, "My son, now drink some water." She escorted him to her shrine and I left. I don't know what transpired there, but I understood the Mother initiated him. After having lunch prasad, that devotee fell into a deep sleep. Later the Mother told me: "This is his last birth. Such a person becomes desperate like this."

The man and I went for a walk in the afternoon and became close friends. His nature was then gentle and his voice, calm. He said: "Today is my new birth — my last birth too. I could not sacrifice my life for the motherland doing some heroic deed, so I offered myself to the Mother of the Universe. I have no more distress or agony." Afterwards I met him a few times in Udbodhan House. Once that young man and I went to do plague relief in Monghyr [Bihar] with the monks of the Ramakrishna Order. Seldom have I seen such a dutiful, humble, and untiring worker. While serving others, that terrible disease infected him. Just before his death, he opened his eyes and said: "The Mother has come. Let me go." After returning to Calcutta, I gave this news to the Mother and she remained motionless for some time with her eyes cast down.[75]

Holy Mother could see inside human beings and knew their potential. Jnan (later Swami Jnanananda) was a daredevil vagabond boy of East Bengal who came to Calcutta. He knew Arupananda and through him went to bow down to the Mother in Udbodhan House. After some months he went to Jayrambati and met her there. She received this youth and asked him to stay at her place. Jnan recalled:

One afternoon the Mother asked me, "Jnan, do you go to bathe in the Amodar River?" "Yes, I do," I replied. The Mother then said: "Tomorrow you go a little early in the morning for your bath. There is a yellow flowering tree on the bank of the river. Collect a basket of flowers from that tree for the Master's worship." Saying, "All right, Mother," I went back to my room with the basket. The next morning when I went to the Mother with the flowers, she sat for worship in front of the Master's picture. She sig-naled to me to sit on an asana next to her. I sat there quietly. After finishing her worship, she asked me to come a little closer and she gave me a mantra and a few spiritual instructions. Pointing to the Master's picture, she said, "Bow down to him."

As I was obstinate by nature, I argued: "Why should I bow down to him? I don't know him." The Mother looked at me and commanded sternly: "I say, bow down to him. You don't know him? He is all in all. He is the teacher of the universe — the guru of all beings." Again I protested: "How can he be my guru? You have given me the mantra, so you are my guru." Interrupting me, the Mother said: "I am no one's guru. I am the Mother of all. He is the only guru." Again I said: "How can you be my mother? My mother is at home and she is still alive." "I am that mother," she said. "Look at me closely. See whether I am that mother of yours or not." Stupefied, I saw that my biological mother was seated in front of me. My body was thrilled with awe. I fell at her feet, saying, "Mother, Mother!" All my arguments ceased and I surrendered at her feet forever. She gave me this knowledge: that she was not only the mantra-guru, she was my own mother, the Mother of All Beings, and the Mother of the Universe.[76]

Mother of All

One day in Jayrambati, Nalini saw the Mother clearing away a dev-otee's dirty plate. She remarked: "My goodness! Aunt, you are clearing away the defiled food of people of all castes!" The Mother calmly replied: "People of all castes are my children."[77] Her love unified the high and low, the rich and poor, regardless of caste.

Swami Vishweswarananda recalled: "One day at Jayrambati after my meal I was about to carry away my dirty plate, but the Mother took my hand and stopped me. She then took the plate herself. I said: 'Why should you do this, Mother? I can wash it.' The Mother replied: 'How little I am doing for you. A child, as you know, soils the lap of the mother and shows its temper tantrums, but the mother calmly does her duty. You are highly cherished even by the gods.'"[78]

Once in Udbodhan House a woman came to see the Mother with her baby daughter. The baby lay down next to the Mother on her blanket and soiled it. Embarrassed, the baby's mother took the blanket and wanted to wash it; but the Mother took the blanket from her and washed it herself. When the baby's mother objected, the Mother said: "Why should I not wash it? Is she not my own?"[79]

Gradually the number of devotees began to increase and sometimes they came to Udbodhan House at odd hours. They would unburden their problems to the Mother and she would guide them. She had very little rest. Observing her inconvenience, one day Golap-ma lovingly reproached her: "Mother, what is the matter with you? You are too lenient. You extend your feet to whomever approaches you and calls you 'Mother.'"

The Mother replied: "What can I do, Golap? As a mother, I cannot withhold myself if someone seeks my help."[80]

Although the Mother was a divine being, she acted exactly like a human mother. She could not utter the monastic names of the Master's and her disciples; rather, she would call them by their premonastic names — Naren, Rakhal, Jogin, Sharat, Baburam, Krishnalal, Rasbihari, and so on. When she was asked why, she replied: "You see, I am a mother. It hurts me to call them by their monastic names."[81] It is true, a son may be a president or a judge or a monk, but to the mother he remains a son.

One day Vishweswarananda asked: "Mother, how do you look upon us?"

"I look upon all of you as Narayana," Holy Mother replied. The swami said: "Mother, we are your sons. If you consider us to be Narayana, you can no longer think of us as your sons."

The Mother calmly replied: "I look upon you as Narayana as well as my sons."[82] This indicates how her divine and human aspects merged in her life.

In 1918 Suhasini went to see Holy Mother at Udbodhan House with her friend Sarala (later Bharatiprana). She lived in Baghbazar, so she visited the Mother quite often with her little daughter Shanti. One day Suhasini went to Udbodhan House without Shanti because the little girl was restless and would disturb others. When the Mother heard this, she said: "Well, I never feel that she disturbs me. Moreover, it is the nature of small children to be a little naughty. Look at Radhu! How much she disturbs me! Her mother is mad. I have to face all her problems and demands. Her demands are endless and some are meaningless. There is a Bengali saying: 'I shall make the wet sugar dry and the dry sugar wet, and then eat it.' This is the kind of demand that Radhu has. If her demands are not fulfilled, she will shout and cry. I cannot tell you how many slaps and blows I have received from Radhu. Radhu's ill treatment of me greatly upset my mother. Sometimes she would grumble and say: 'You did not have a child of your own. I don't understand how you maintain your smiling face while taking on the troubles of others.' I would then console my mother with some pleasing words." Then Holy Mother kept quiet.

Another woman devotee said with a smile: "Mother, if Grandma were alive today, she might have been irritated. Now so many men and women are calling you 'Mother, Mother' and disturbing you. Though we are not born from your womb, that does not mean we are not your children."

Immediately the Mother stood up and said firmly: "What did you say — that you were not born from my womb? Then from whose womb were you born? Are you not my children? Then whose children are you? Is there any mother other than me? I exist in all women and in all mothers. Those who come to me from any place are all my children. Know it for sure and certain. Those who come to me, calling me 'Mother,' they are all my children. My mother understood this towards the end of her life when she saw Naren, Rakhal, Sharat, Sarada, Jogin, Niranjan, Girish, and Nivedita. My mother was so happy when she heard them calling me 'Mother.' She used to say: 'Ah, finally Mother Durga has fulfilled my wish. My Sarada has now so many children! When they call me "Grandma," my heart is satisfied. I can't express my joy when they ask me for something to eat, or when they talk and tell me their stories!' My mother gave them puffed rice and sweet balls, and they ate with great relish. She watched them and laughed. At that time I saw great joy and satisfaction on her face. Then there were not too many women devotees and very few could go to Jayrambati. By the time women devotees began to visit Jayrambati, my mother had passed away. But she left with great joy, seeing me as Mother."[83]

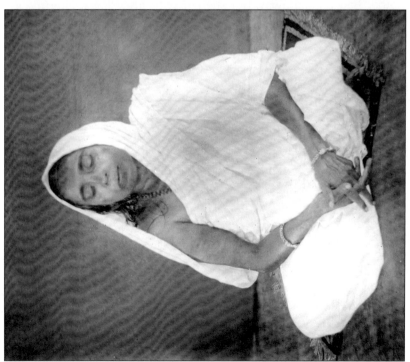

Sarada Devi at Udbodhan House, 1913. "As Holy Mother was meditating in the shrine, Br. Ganen set up a tripod for his camera. He made some noise. When she opened her eyes, Ganen apologetically said, 'Mother, I am taking your photo.'"

26
Holy Mother
as a Guru

Aneka-janma-samprāpta karma-bandha-vidāhine;
Atma-jnāna-pradānena tasmay srigurave namah.
— *Vishwasara-tantra*

I bow to the Divine Guru who imparts to the disciple the fire of Self-knowledge and burns away the bonds of karma accumulated through many births.

I t is extremely important to understand the concept of the guru and his or her role in awakening spiritual consciousness. According to the Vishwasara Tantra, *gu* means "darkness" or "ignorance," and *ru* means "remover" or "destroyer." In other words, the person who removes ignorance, or the veil of maya, from the minds of the disciples is a guru. Human beings suffer because of ignorance, and this ignorance can be banished only by the knowledge of God. Vedanta says that people are hypnotized by maya. They must learn to dehypnotize themselves with Self-knowledge, which leads to liberation. Ramakrishna described the role of a guru with this parable:

Once a tigress attacked a flock of goats. As she sprang on her prey, she gave birth to a cub and died. The cub grew up in the company of the goats. The goats ate grass and the cub followed their example. They bleated; the cub bleated too. Gradually it grew to be a big tiger. One day another tiger attacked the same flock. It was amazed to see the grass-eating tiger. Running after it, the wild tiger at last seized it, whereupon the grass-eating tiger began to bleat. The wild tiger dragged it to the water and said: "Look at your face in the water. It is just like mine. Here is a little meat. Eat it." Saying this, it thrust some meat into its mouth. But the grass-eating tiger would not swallow it and began to bleat again. Gradually, however, it got the taste for blood and came to relish the meat. Then the wild tiger said: "Now you see there is no difference between you and me. Come along and follow me into the forest."

So there can be no fear if the guru's grace descends on one. He will let

you know who you are and what your real nature is. If the devotee practises spiritual discipline a little, the guru explains everything to him. Then
the disciple understands for himself what is real and what is unreal. God
alone is real and the world is illusory.[1]

A human guru, who is a knower of God and an illumined soul, plays
a vital role in spiritual life. Of course the real guru is Satchidananda, or
God, and the spiritual light or power comes from Him alone. But when
this Divine Power manifests through some extraordinary illumined souls,
they become gurus and have the power to illumine others just as a lighted
candle can light other candles.

However, there are false prophets and self-styled gurus in this world.
The Katha Upanishad warns us about them: "Fools dwelling in darkness,
but thinking themselves wise and erudite, go round and round by various tortuous paths, like the blind led by the blind."[2]

The Hindu scriptures testify that the Divine Power does not become
fully manifest in the guru till his or her raw ego is completely wiped out.
When this limited I-ness is annihilated, that person becomes an instrument of the Cosmic I, or the Divine Mother. So the power of the guru
is not human: It is the Divine Mother's special power that possesses the
guru's body and mind. Regarding the identity of guru-consciousness with
God-consciousness, the Guru-Gita proclaims: "The guru is Brahma; the
guru is Vishnu; the guru is Shiva. I bow down to the guru who removes
the darkness of ignorance from the eyes with the collyrium stick of knowledge." The compassionate Lord removes ignorance and delusion from
human minds through the divine power of the guru. This is why devotion
to the guru and devotion to God are the same. The Svetasvatara Upanishad says: "He is truly a great soul who has the highest devotion for God
and as much devotion for his guru as for God. The truths explained to such
a person will surely reveal their meaning to him."[3] The mystery of God or
the Atman is unfathomable because it is beyond thought and speech. That
is why one needs an illumined guru who can show the way. The Katha
Upanishad says: "Wonderful is the expounder and rare the hearer; rare
indeed is the experiencer of the Atman taught by an able preceptor."[4]

There are many gurus or spiritual teachers in the world, but as manifestations of God's power, all gurus are the same. At the outset of the
spiritual journey one should have love, faith, and steadfast devotion for
one's own guru and follow his or her instructions implicitly. Later, in the
advanced stage, one will realize this truth: "*Mannatha sri jagannatha mad-
guru sri jagatguru* — My Lord is the Lord of the universe and my guru is the
Guru of the world." Despite this sublime teaching, some narrow-minded

fanatics develop guru cults and think their guru is the greatest. Without understanding the main purpose of the guru, they create various factions and fight to prove the supremacy of their respective gurus.

Once Swami Satprakashananda said to Swami Shivananda: "Some receive initiation from Holy Mother and some from Maharaj [Swami Brahmananda]. Is there any difference?"

Swami Shivananda replied: "I don't see any difference. The same Ganges water is coming through two faucets. The same grace of the Master is coming through Holy Mother and Maharaj."

According to Swami Shivananda, this "Ganges water" is Ramakrishna, who is purifying and awakening the God-consciousness of people who receive initiation from the gurus of the Ramakrishna Order. As an incarnation of God, the Master always reminded his devotees: "Satchidananda, or God, is the only guru, father, and master." He could not bear anyone calling him "guru," "baba" (father), or "karta" (master). To avoid developing a narrow guru cult, all gurus of the Ramakrishna Order — from Holy Mother and the direct disciples down to the present swamis — have pointed out that Ramakrishna is the Ishta, or Chosen Deity, as well as the guru. He is "the goal, the support, the Lord, the witness, the abode, the refuge, and the friend."[5]

The Kularnava Tantra says that a person will go to hell if he or she thinks of the guru as a human being, the mantra as a word, and the image of God as a piece of stone. Swami Bhuteshananda said: "If one thinks that the body of the guru is the guru, then the doctrine of the guru will end with the doctrine of the body (*dehātmavād*). But if one considers the guru as the Ishta, or the Chosen Deity, then when the guru dies, one will not miss the guru. That guru is the eternal guru."

Swami Saradananda wrote:

The Master used to say: "The guru is like a female companion of Radha. As there is no end to her love-errands until her friend Radha is united with Krishna, so there is no rest for the guru until the spiritual aspirant is united with God. Thus the great guru accompanies the sincere devotee to higher and higher realms of spirituality and finally presents the devotee to the Chosen Deity, saying, 'My child, look there!' and then immediately the guru disappears."

One day when a devotee heard the Master saying this, he realized that someday separation from the guru would be inevitable. So with a sorrowful heart, he asked, "Sir, where does the guru go then?" The Master replied: "The guru merges into the Chosen Deity, or Ishta. The guru, Krishna, and the devotee — these three are one, and the One is manifest as three."[6]

The guru transmits spiritual power during the initiation ceremony and connects the disciple with God through a mantra. This is called *diksha*, or initiation. According to the Tantra, *di* means *diyate jnanam, or* "gives knowledge"; *ksha* means *kshiyate pashu vasana, or* "destroys animal, or worldly, desires." According to the *Agama* scriptures, the Supreme Lord Shiva established three kinds of initiation: Shambhavi, Shakti, and Mantri. When a disciple attains knowledge instantly by merely seeing, touching, or paying obeisance to the guru, it is called *Shambhavi* initiation. When an illumined guru transmits his or her divine power into the disciple's heart and awakens spirituality, it is called *Shakti* initiation. In the Mantri initiation, the guru draws a diagram, installs a *ghat* or sacred pitcher, performs worship of the deity, and then utters a mantra into the ear of the disciple.

When the disciple repeats the mantra while fixing the mind on the Ishta, his or her worldly desires subside and the mind becomes pure. At that time the mind becomes the guru or acts like the guru. Actually the word *mantra* is connected with the mind: *Mananat trayate iti mantrah* — that word is the mantra upon which one reflects to attain salvation. It is amazing how the infinite God remains hidden in the seed mantra.

On 11 February 1913, Swami Arupananda carried a tiny banyan seed to Holy Mother in Koalpara Ashrama and said: "Look, Mother, this seed is smaller than the seed of red spinach. And yet from this comes such a huge tree! What a wonder!"

She replied: "Why not? Just see, how small the *Bija* [seed mantra] of the Lord's Name is. Yet from that springs forth in due time spiritual consciousness, ecstasy, devotion, and love!"[7]

Ramakrishna said: "There is great power in the seed of God's name. It destroys ignorance. A seed is tender and the sprout soft; still it pierces the hard ground. The ground breaks and makes way for the sprout."[8]

Mother — Guru — Goddess

Ramakrishna said about Holy Mother: "Sarada is an incarnation of Saraswati [the Goddess of Learning]. She was born to bestow knowledge upon others."[9] He transferred the results of his spiritual experiences to her and taught her various mantras relating to particular deities so that she could continue his spiritual ministry after his passing away. In Holy Mother's life, we find the goddess acting as a guru and also as a mother.

Swami Gambhirananda described how these three aspects — goddess, guru, and mother — blended harmoniously in Holy Mother's life: "Whenever she appears to us as the Mother, we get a glimpse of her inherent power of imparting that true knowledge that dispels all ignorance; when we approach her as a guru, she draws us to her lap as a mother; and when we recognize the mother and guru in her, we find her seated transcendentally in her own divine effulgence. In fact, we cannot discern where any of these mutually dependent aspects ends and another begins."[10]

Although Holy Mother appeared to be an affectionate and loving mother, it would be a great mistake if we were to consider her an ordinary human being. Truly the Divine Mother incarnated as Sarada Devi and acted as a human mother and guru. Endowed with divine power, wisdom, glory, purity, renunciation, love, and compassion, she awakened spirituality in the hearts of her disciples and granted liberation to them.

The human guru imparts the mantra in the ear, and the divine guru transmits the mantra to the soul. A true guru is an awakener and redeemer of souls and takes upon himself or herself the burden of sin from the disciples and suffers on that account. Holy Mother did not seek disciples. She once said: "Those who care to come to me will do so of themselves after severing the shackles of the world. I shall not send for them."[11]

Holy Mother lived a secluded life. Very few knew of her existence. During her lifetime, her photographs were not shown in public and nothing was written about her except for brief mentions in *The Gospel of Sri Ramakrishna* and *Sri Ramakrishna and His Divine Play*. How, then, did people come to know about her?

As a magnet's attraction is irresistible to iron, so was the attraction of Holy Mother as a guru. Tormented by worldly afflictions, many weary souls took refuge in her, seeking release from maya. Some aspirants approached her for initiation upon recommendation from the Master's disciples and other swamis of the Ramakrishna Order. Some heard about her from friends and relatives who had already been initiated. Some came to know of her through dreams or visions. Holy Mother looked into their hearts and accepted them without considering their race or social position. Ramakrishna chose disciples after testing them, but the Mother initiated all who asked her for it.

Once in a women's gathering in Udbodhan House, Yogin-ma commented with a smile: "The Mother undoubtedly loves us all but not as intensely as the Master did. What concern and love he had towards his disciples! We saw it with our own eyes. Words cannot describe it."

Holy Mother said: "Is that to be wondered at? He accepted only a few select disciples, and that too after various kinds of testing. Towards me, he has pushed a whole row of ants."[12]

After Ramakrishna's passing away in 1886, Holy Mother spent a year on pilgrimage, staying mostly in Vrindaban. Her spiritual ministry started at the Master's bidding when she gave her first formal initiation in Vrindaban to Swami Yogananda. She lived for another 33 years after that. During the first 11 years (1887-1898), she led a secluded life in Kamarpukur, Jayrambati, and Calcutta. During the second 11 years (1898-1909), the public began to hear about her and she initiated a few disciples. During the third 11 years (1909-1920), she initiated innumerable men and women who came to her from various stations and stages of life. Among them there were rich and poor, young and old, students and teachers, lawyers and physicians, noble souls and sinners, revolutionaries and eccentrics. She even initiated a few monastic and householder disciples of the Master, and also some aspirants who came to her from other parts of India and the West, whose languages were unknown to her.

Swami Nikhilananda wrote:

A silent yearning constantly welled up from her heart: "Come, all of you, I am here for your sake. I shall soothe my heart showing you the way to liberation." She did not publicly summon devotees. She did not write books, issue statements, or mount a public platform. The disciples of Sri Ramakrishna were extremely reticent about her. Perhaps they were afraid that ordinary people would take her lightly or not show her proper respect. But drawn by her irresistible attraction they all came. She seemed to be waiting for them. "Let them all come," her motherly heart said. "None will be rejected. Suppose they have lived sinful lives. Will they be deprived of my blessings on that account?" She initiated them in the shrine room and from her sick-bed, on roads and railway platforms, in meadows and under trees. All felt, when with her, that they were in the presence of an affectionate mother and made all kinds of demands upon her — reasonable and unreasonable. To the best of her power she tried to satisfy them. She had hardly any respite even when she badly needed it. If no devotee came to her on a particular day, she would say: "No one has come. This day seems to be passing in vain." Very shortly a seeker would arrive. This went on till nearly the end of her life. One day Holy Mother said seriously to a disciple: "He is unfortunate indeed who does not feel my compassion. I do not know anyone, not even an insect, for whom I do not feel compassion."[13]

While giving initiation, Holy Mother selected the disciple's Ishta, or Chosen Ideal, and a mantra connected to that deity. Sometimes she asked about the disciple's family tradition. But regardless of whether the disciple was Vaishnava or Shakta, she initiated him or her according to what she considered best for the disciple. When the disciple could not decide on an Ishta, Holy Mother herself chose the particular form and name of the Godhead. Sometimes just before initiation, she would meditate to discover the mantra suitable for the aspirant. It would be revealed to her pure mind.

The mantra has an intrinsic power. Holy Mother said: "The mantra purifies the body. One becomes pure by repeating the name of God given by the guru." Once a disciple asked Holy Mother if the mere repetition of the mantra as taught by an adept guru really helped the aspirant if he or she did not possess intense devotion. Holy Mother answered: "Whether you jump into water or are pushed into it, your cloth will be soaked, will it not?"[14]

Holy Mother was not an ordinary guru who initiates with elaborate rituals and follows traditional methods. Her initiation was simple and short. She selected the Chosen Deity and gave the mantra accordingly, and showed the disciple how to count repetitions of the mantra on the fingers or a rosary.

Swami Aseshananda was initiated by Holy Mother; after she passed away, he became Swami Saradananda's private secretary. When he observed Saradananda's elaborate method of giving initiation, he said to the swami: "Maharaj, Holy Mother instructed me in a very simple way. She did not ask me to repeat the mantra for a fixed number of times in the morning or evening, or for special days and all that. She did not give me any fixed method. Maharaj, I want a step-by-step procedure. Could you please add something?"

Swami Saradananda responded: "You are the greatest fool. Holy Mother is the Divine Mother herself. All these methods and procedures are given by other teachers, but not Holy Mother. Whatever Holy Mother has given you is the last word in spiritual life. You cling to the mantra, repeat it, meditate, and think of your Chosen Ideal; and when longing for the vision of God comes, you will find that your mind will know it, that your mind will be fixed on the Divine Spirit, and that all your desires will be fulfilled. Do you mean to say that I should add something to what Holy Mother has given? It is due to her grace that I am even here."[15]

One day Sarala (later Bharatiprana) asked Swami Saradananda: "Maharaj, why does it take so much time for you to give initiation? I saw the Mother initiate disciples very quickly." After a long silence, the swami replied: "You see, the Mother's very touch is enough for her disciple to achieve everything, but that is not possible for me. I have to pray and meditate for a long time. I have no relief until I see that the Master has accepted and taken responsibility for the disciple."[16]

Remover of Sin and Bad Karma

Being a guru is not easy. It is beyond the capacity of an ordinary guru to take responsibility for another's bad karma or to absorb a disciple's sin and its consequences. Only a divine being has the power of redemption. The Christian tradition speaks of vicarious atonement: Jesus took upon himself the punishment for the sins of others. We find that Ramakrishna took Jagadamba's (Mathur's wife) illness on himself and suffered from dysentery for several months. He also took on Girish's sins and suffered from cancer.

Towards the end of Holy Mother's life, when she was bedridden in Udbodhan House, Brahmachari Ashok was dejected, thinking that he would be helpless without her. To encourage him, she said:

Do you think that even if this body passes away, I can have any release unless every one of those whose responsibility I have taken on myself is out of bondage? I must constantly live with them. I have taken complete charge of everything, good and bad, regarding them. Is it a trifle to give initiation? It is a tremendous responsibility. How much anxiety I suffer for them. Just see, your father has died, and that at once made me feel worried about you. I thought, 'How is it that the Master is again putting him to the test?' That you may come out of this ordeal is my constant prayer. For this reason I gave you all this advice. Can you understand everything I say? If you could do so, that would lighten my worries to a great extent. The Master is playing with his different children in diverse ways, but I have to bear the brunt of it. I cannot simply set aside those whom I have accepted as my own.[17]

The relationship between the guru and the disciple is eternal.

Holy Mother demonstrated how to lead a spiritual life by continually practising japa. Even when she was sick in bed, she repeated her mantra mentally. She slept very little. One night Brahmachari Barada asked, "Mother, don't you get any sleep?" She replied: "What can I do, my child? All these children come to me with great longing for initiation, but most of them do not repeat the mantra regularly. Why regularly? Many do not repeat it at all. But since I have taken responsibility for them, should I not see to their welfare? Therefore I do japa for their sake. I constantly pray to the Master, saying: 'O Master, awaken their spiritual consciousness. Give them liberation. There is a great deal of suffering in this world. May they not be born here again!'"[18]

In spiritual life when clouds of doubt and depression hover in the mind, we need someone to reassure us. Holy Mother told Indubhusan Sengupta: "Why do you worry, my child? You have occupied a place in my heart. You will not have to do any spiritual discipline. I am doing it for you."

Indu asked, "Mother, do you do the same for all who have received initiation from you?"

"Yes, I do," replied the Mother.

"You have so many disciples. Do you remember them all?"

"I don't recollect them all, but I repeat the mantra for those whose names I can recall. And for those I cannot remember, I pray to the Master, saying: 'Master, I have many children in various places. Please look after those whose names I can't recall and take care of their well-being.'"[19]

Swami Vishweswarananda was a disciple of the Mother and lived in Udbodhan House. One day he candidly said to her: "Mother, you initiate so many people, but you never enquire about them. You don't even give a thought about what is happening to them. A guru keeps a keen eye on his disciples, seeing whether they are developing spiritually. It would be better if you did not give initiation to so many people. You should initiate only as many as you can keep in touch with."

Holy Mother replied: "But the Master never forbade me to do so. He instructed me about so many things; would he not have told me something about what you have said? I give the responsibility for my disciples to the Master. Every day I pray to him: 'Please look after the disciples, wherever they may be.' Further, I received these mantras from the Master himself. These are *siddha mantras* — very potent. One is sure to attain liberation through them."[20]

Once in Jayrambati, Vishweswarananda asked: "Mother, how does one realize God? Worship, japa, meditation — do these help?"

"None of these helps," replied the Mother.

"Then how does one get the vision of God?"

"It is only through God's grace. But one must practise meditation and japa. They remove the impurities of the mind. One must practise spiritual disciplines, such as worship, japa, and meditation. As one gets the fragrance of a flower by handling it, or as one gets the smell of sandalwood by rubbing it against a stone, in the same way one gets spiritual awakening by constantly thinking of God. But you can realize God right now if you become desireless."[21]

On 11 February 1913, at Udbodhan House Holy Mother told Arupananda the mystery of the mantra and its power: "Power passes through the mantra. The guru's power enters into the disciple and the disciple's power enters into the guru. That is why, when I initiate and accept the disciple's sins, I fall sick. It is extremely difficult to be a guru because the guru assimilates the disciple's sin. If the disciple commits any sin, that affects the guru. On the other hand, by leading a virtuous life, the disciple does good to the teacher."[22]

It is hard for ordinary people to comprehend how one can absorb the result of another person's karma. Although Holy Mother was without sin, she suffered terribly from taking on the sins of others. She knew the cause of her suffering, yet she continued to give initiation and look after the devotees. One day when several devotees came for initiation, she told her attendant: "My son, I feel as if I am wrestling all day. The devotees are coming without any break. This body cannot bear any more. I am praying to the Master and keeping my mind in this world by holding onto Radhu."

This feeling was momentary. It disappeared when anybody approached her for initiation. Arupananda said, "Mother, don't you initiate those whom you wish to initiate?"

Holy Mother replied: "No, I initiate people purely out of compassion. They do not leave me alone. They weep. That moves my heart and I give initiation out of kindness. Otherwise, what do I gain? When I initiate devotees, I have to accept their sins."[23]

Her motherly heart bled when she saw the pain and agony of her children. Then she forgot her rheumatic pain and malarial fever. She said: "This body will one day surely perish. Let it go now, if it must, but let them realize the Truth through initiation."[24] On another occasion she remarked: "Now and then I think if this body, instead of being such a small frame of bones and flesh, were a big one, how many more people I could help."[25]

At Koalpara, Narayan Iyenger, a disciple of the Mother, hesitated to touch her feet because he thought this would cause her pain. Holy Mother said: "No, my child, we are born for this purpose. If we do not accept others' sins and sorrows and do not digest them, who else will? Who will bear the responsibilities of the wicked and the afflicted?"[26]

Sarajubala Sen, a disciple of the Mother, recorded in her memoirs the purpose of the advent of Ramakrishna and Holy Mother: "One day I went to Udbodhan to see the Mother and heard the monks telling her: 'Mother, after your recovery this time, we will not allow anyone to receive initiation from you. You suffer terribly by absorbing the sins of your disciples.' The Mother smiled softly and said: 'Why do you say so, my children? Did the Master come this time only to eat rasagollas [juicy cheese balls]?' This compassionate statement silenced everyone."[27]

One day the Mother was in excruciating pain from her rheumatism.

Her attendant said: "I hear that you have this horrible disease because you take on the sins of your devotees. I have a humble request: Please do not suffer for my sake. Allow me to suffer the consequences of my own sins." Immediately the compassionate Mother replied: "What do you mean, my son? You keep well. Let me suffer."[28]

Another disciple realized his shortcomings and lamented: "Mother, in spite of having a mother like you, I have achieved nothing." The Mother consoled him, saying: "Don't be afraid, my son. Always remember that the Master is always behind you. I am also with you. What should frighten you as long as I, your Mother, exist? The Master said to me, 'At the end, I will appear to those who come to you, and lift them up, holding them by the hand.' The Master must reveal himself to you at the hour of death, no matter what you do or how you live. God has given you hands, feet, and organs, and they will play their part."[29]

Swami Gaurishananda recalled: "One day in Jayrambati the Mother was in terrible pain from her rheumatism. Despite her suffering, she addressed Ramakrishna, looking at his picture: "Master, today is gone in vain. No one came for initiation. You said that I would have to help people."[30] After saying this she left her room as if waiting for someone.

The next morning, three devotees arrived and Holy Mother was happy to see them. They brought a letter from Swami Brahmananda requesting her to initiate them. Later when her attendant read the letter to her, she called the devotees to see her. When they bowed down to her, she realized that they had much bad karma and had committed many sins, so she refused to initiate them and asked them to go to Belur Math for initiation. The devotees left her for the time being and went to the outer apartment. The Mother lamented: 'Alas, Rakhal has sent me this stuff. A son generally sends his mother good things." But the devotees were brokenhearted. They again requested the Mother for initiation and again she refused.

Addressing the Master, she lamented: "O Lord, yesterday I prayed to you that I might not spend a day in vain. And now you have brought this to me. All right. As long as the body lasts I shall continue to do your work." She knew that absorbing the sins of these people would take a heavy toll on her body. Finally she relented, and the devotees received initiation.

Some days later the news of what the Mother had said reached Belur Math, and Swamis Brahmananda, Shivananda, Premananda, and Saradananda listened to the report attentively. Brahmananda became grave and remained speechless. Premananda said, with a deep sigh: "Grace! Grace!

By this unique grace, the Mother has been protecting us. I cannot describe in words the poison that she swallows. If we had done so, that very suffering would have burnt us to ashes."[31]

Once in Jayrambati, Holy Mother had been suffering from malaria for a long time. She was bedridden and her body was emaciated and weak. Swami Parameswarananda recalled:

> Swami Saradananda wrote to me: "Please always watch the Mother's physical condition. Be strict with the visitors and don't allow the devotees to see her when she is not well. And there will be no initiation for the time being." Accordingly, I became the gatekeeper of the Mother's house. A young man from Barisal [now in Bangladesh] came one day and insisted on seeing the Mother. I told him that the Mother was bedridden and not well, and that I would tell her that he was there. The devotee was adamant and said, "I have come from such a long distance, and I will not be able to see the Mother." Eventually there was a heated exchange between us. Holy Mother overheard it and sent her woman attendant to see what was going on. The attendant reported to her that I was not allowing a devotee to see her. The Mother immediately came out of her room with dishevelled hair and said to me, "Why are you not allowing him to see me?" I replied: "Mother, you have a fever and are not well. Sharat Maharaj wrote to me that I should not allow any visitors at present." Agitated, the Mother said: "Who is Sharat to prohibit my giving initiation? I am born for this purpose. Send him to me." The young man bowed down to the Mother and begged for initiation from her. The Mother initiated him the next day.[32]

On Doubt and Restlessness of the Mind

Many aspirants suffer from doubt and confusion in spiritual life. Swami Basudevananda had this problem. He recalled:

> Once I returned to Udbodhan from Noakhali [now in Bangladesh} after conducting a relief mission. I said to the Mother: "Sometimes I get confused and cannot find anyone to speak with about my doubt. What shall I do then?"
>
> The Mother replied: "Always keep a picture of the Master with you. Remember that he is with you and looking after you. If you have any question, pray to him; you will find that he will deliver the solution to your mind. He is always within you. Because the mind is extroverted, people do not search within; rather, they search for God outside. When you pray for something, if it is absolutely necessary for you, you will find that the answer arises within all in a flash. If any person prays to the Master wholeheartedly, the Master listens and arranges things accordingly. Is it necessary to say something 20 times to a gentleman?"[33]

Once Nalin Bihari Sarkar asked Holy Mother about the weaknesses of the mind. She replied: "My son, that is the law of nature, like the new moon and the full moon. Similarly, the mind harbours sometimes good and sometimes bad thoughts."

Nalin asked: "Mother, I have visited you so often and have received your grace, yet I still don't make any progress. I feel that I am as I was before."

Mother replied: "My son, suppose you are asleep on a cot and someone carries the cot, with you on it, to another place. Would you immediately realize that you have been moved to another place? Not at all. Only when your drowsiness clears up completely will you see that you have come to a new place."[34]

In 1911, Vaikuntha of Cuttack received initiation from Holy Mother when she was at Kothar in Orissa. Some years later he found it impossible to control his mind and said to the Mother with great anguish: "Mother, I have no inclination to repeat the mantra anymore because it did not remove the impurities of my mind. I have the same lust, anger, and delusion as before."

Holy Mother assured him: "My son, all impurities will go away by repeating the mantra. Pray to the Master."

"I am helpless," Vaikuntha replied. "Either remove my inner restlessness or take back your mantra. I have no intention of giving you suffering, for I have heard that the guru suffers if the disciple does not repeat the mantra."

Holy Mother's eyes became filled with tears at her disciple's suffering and she said fervently: "All right, you will not have to repeat the mantra anymore."

These words frightened Vaikuntha and he thought that his relationship with the Mother was severed once and for all. Distraught, Vaikuntha said: "Mother, you have taken everything away from me! What shall I do now? Does this mean that I am going to hell?"

The Mother said in an animated voice: "What do you mean? You are my child. How can you go to hell? Those who are my children are already free. Not even Providence has the power to send my children to hell. Be at rest, entrusting your responsibility to me. And always remember that someone stands behind you and will come at the last moment to lead you to the eternal abode."[35]

On a different occasion she reassured another depressed disciple: "You may not be able to practise japa regularly, but the Master will have to come to receive you at the final moment. He himself promised this to me.

Can his words be otherwise? Do whatever you like and enjoy your life."[36]

Swami Mukteswarananda, a disciple of the Mother, was passing through a dry spell, which is also called the "dark night of the soul." He even stopped visiting the Mother although he was living at Balaram Mandir, only a few blocks from Udbodhan House. Finally, he wrote a letter to Holy Mother asking her to take back the mantra. The Mother sent for him. When he came she said: "Look here, my child, the sun dwells high in the sky and water remains on the earth. Does the water have to shout at the sun and ask: 'O Sun, please take me up?' It is the very nature of the sun to take up the water in the form of vapour. Let me assure you that you will not have to practise any discipline."[37] What reassurance! This is similar to Ramakrishna assuming "the power of attorney" for Girish.

Christ told his disciples that as long as they were with the bridegroom (meaning himself) they should enjoy festivities. He encouraged them, saying: "In the world ye shall have tribulation: but be of good cheer." Similarly, Holy Mother also gave joy and rest to her disciples who were overwhelmed by various responsibilities in this world. In 1914, Mahendra Nath Gupta of Barisal received initiation from Holy Mother in Udbodhan House. In 1915 he went to Jayrambati to see her again. He thought that he would attain merit by practising japa and meditation in the Mother's house. After the first day when he went to bow down to the Mother, she said to him: "You have come to the Mother. What is the necessity of practising so much japa and meditation? I am doing everything for you. Now enjoy food and rejoice without worry and anxiety."[38]

A disciple is supposed to be blessed and uplifted by the company of the guru. In 1907 at Jayrambati, the Mother advised Brahmachari Girija: "My son, it is not necessary to practise japa in the guru's house." However, a little earlier she had said: "You must repeat the mantra 108 times, according to the instruction of your guru. Moreover, you are a monk; you are supposed to repeat the mantra most of the time as you have plenty of time." Girija asked: "Shall I not repeat the mantra 108 times, as you asked me to do during initiation?" The Mother replied: "Yes, it will be enough if you repeat the mantra 108 times in the place of your guru and not more."[39]

One should not conclude that the Mother did not encourage her disciples to practise japa and meditation. When her disciples visited her, she poured her love and affection upon them, served them food, and made sure that they were comfortable. Association with the guru is extremely precious in spiritual life because those sweet memories become stronger after the guru passes away. For that reason, Holy Mother told Mahendra and Girija not to spend too much time practising japa while they were with her. She herself practised japa long hours for her disciples' benefit.

After his initiation, Naresh Chakrabarty asked: "Mother, will you command that I eat vegetarian food?"

Holy Mother replied: "What do you mean? Why should you become a vegetarian? My children are free to eat nonvegetarian food. Enjoy a variety of food and live happily. I shall take care of you."

"What if I cannot repeat my mantra?" Naresh asked.

Holy Mother replied heatedly: "What do you mean? You don't want to repeat your Ishta-mantra? Then why did you take initiation? If you don't repeat your Ishta-mantra, you will lose your spiritual life — I will not be the loser."[40]

At Jayrambati in 1907, Brahmachari Rasbihari asked: "Mother, why is it necessary to receive a mantra from a guru?"

Holy Mother replied:

The mantra purifies the body. Human beings become pure by repeating God's name. Listen to a story: One day Narada went to Vaikuntha [heaven] and had a long conversation with Vishnu. When Narada left, Vishnu asked Lakshmi to sprinkle a solution made from cow dung to sanctify the spot where Narada had sat. Lakshmi said: "Why, Lord? Narada is your great devotee. Why, then, do you say this?" Vishnu said: "Narada has not yet received initiation. One's body does not become pure without initiation." After giving the mantra, the Vaishnava guru says to his disciple, "Now the *man tor**— the mind is yours." The human guru imparts the mantra to the ear, but the divine guru transmits the mantra into the soul. Everything depends upon one's mind. Nothing can be achieved without purity of mind. It is said: "One may have the grace of the guru, of God, and of the Vaishnava [the devotees], but one comes to grief without the grace of one." That "one" is the mind. One needs the grace of one's own mind.[41]

In spiritual life these are the universal and eternal questions: How do I control the restless mind? How do I overcome lust and anger? How do I attain peace and joy? How do I practise spiritual disciplines? How can I see God? What will happen after death? Holy Mother answered all these questions. Even though today we do not have the good fortune to have Holy Mother as our guru, we have inherited the spiritual instructions that she gave to her disciples. Her teachings solve our spiritual

*In Bengali, the sounds of *mantra* and *man tor* are very close, but the latter has an indicative meaning.

problems, remove our doubts, and create love and longing for God. Of course some of the Mother's teachings are universal and some were given to specific individuals. It is extremely harmful if a person takes medicines indiscriminately without consulting a doctor; similarly it is dangerous to practise spiritual disciplines without the advice of a guru. Holy Mother taught monks as well as householders according to their tendencies, so one should follow only those teachings that are suitable for one's circumstances and temperament.

In March 1904 Swami Virajananda went to visit the Mother at Jayrambati. He had not seen her for a couple of years, and his health had broken down from practising too much austerity. When Holy Mother saw his sickly body she shuddered, realizing that it was not a physical illness. She asked: "Where do you meditate — in the heart or in the *sahasrara**?"

Virajananda responded: "In the sahasrara, because I love to meditate on that chakra and I get immense joy."

"My son, what have you done?" exclaimed Holy Mother. "One meditates on that spot in the final stage. Only the mind of a paramahamsa dwells there. Is it possible to keep the mind in such a high realm in the initial stages? One should begin by concentrating the mind on the crown chakra, but then bring it down to the heart chakra and meditate there on the Ishta."

Virajananda had previously gone through various kinds of treatment and received a special diet; he had followed disciplines meant to relieve his mental fatigue and illness. Nothing had worked. Now he began to follow Holy Mother's simple instructions and slowly he got well. Towards the end of his life, referring to this event, he said: "For this reason one needs a *siddha guru* [an illumined teacher]. If I had not received that advice from the Mother, perhaps my life would have been destroyed. Probably I would have been a permanent invalid or ended up insane."[42]

All gurus, without exception, have to listen to their disciples' complaints. Once a devotee came to Swami Vijnanananda, a disciple of Ramakrishna, for initiation. The swami told him he would initiate him on one condition: that the devotee would not write any letter of complaint to him.

A monk came to the Mother and complained: "Mother, why does my mind become restless every now and then? Why can't I constantly meditate on you? Many worthless thoughts disturb my mind. Tell me, how can I get peace? Shall I never receive your grace? Nowadays I seldom have visions. It is better to die than to lead such a worthless life."

* The highest centre of consciousness, or chakra, located at the crown of the head.

"What are you talking about, my son?" Holy Mother responded. "Don't think such horrible things. Can one have a vision every day? The Master used to say: 'Does an angler catch a big carp every day the moment he sits with a rod? He throws the line with spiced bait and then waits with deep concentration. Some days a carp might swallow the hook and other days it might not.' So never give up your habit of spiritual practices. Increase your japa."

The monk said: "Please tell me how many times I should repeat the mantra, so that I may have good concentration."

Holy Mother replied, "Well, you may repeat it 10,000, or even 20,000 times, or as many times as you can."[43]

On another occasion Holy Mother said to Swami Dhirananda: "The mind will be steadied if one repeats the name of God 15,000 or 20,000 times a day. It is truly so. Oh Krishnalal [Swami Dhirananda], I myself have experienced it. Let them practise it first; if they fail, let them complain. One should practise japa with some devotion, but this is not done. They will not do anything. They only complain, saying: Why do I not succeed?"[44]

A true guru, like parents, carries the responsibility of his or her disciples. Sometimes Holy Mother had to face problems. But she had much regard for Yogin-ma's judgment and consulted her not only about domestic matters but also about spiritual affairs and even mantras. Once an elderly gentleman asked the Holy Mother to bless him with initiation. She agreed out of compassion, but when he came for the ceremony, she asked him a few questions and learned that he was skeptical about Ramakrishna's divinity. Holy Mother was disturbed. She anxiously called Yogin-ma, who hurried to the shrine. "Yogin, what shall I do?" asked the Mother. "This person does not accept the Master." Yogin-ma immediately replied: "Well, Mother, it does not matter. The mantra you will give him has the power and will change him in time. Don't worry. Initiate him." Holy Mother followed Yogin-ma's advice, and Yogin-ma's prediction came true. After a short time the man became devoted to Ramakrishna.[45]

Swami Tanmayananda once said to Holy Mother, "Mother, so many bad thoughts come when I sit for meditation."

Holy Mother replied: "It is natural. Does anyone want to leave one's place easily? Those thoughts try to drag the mind down."

"Mother, please do something so that I may forget all those things," Tanmayananda implored.

Touching his head, the Mother said: "From now on all those thoughts will not come to your mind."

Swami Tanmayananda: "Mother, I can't meditate on a form."

"It does not matter," said Holy Mother. She pointed to the Master's picture and said: "Think of him and repeat your mantra. Read one chapter of the Gita every day. The day you don't have much time, read at least a few verses of the Gita. Make your asana comfortable so that you can sit a couple of hours at a stretch. Thus you will be able to sit for a long time. If your leg goes to sleep or gives you pain, move your leg. Later you will not find any difficulty. You can practise japa and meditation simultaneously or alternately."[46]

Efficacy of Japa and Meditation

Some people think it is a waste of time to sit in the shrine and practise japa and meditation. One could use that time and energy to make money or do something substantial. They believe that one can achieve peace and joy from money, friends, family, and worldly possessions. This is the materialistic attitude. All great teachers say that abiding peace and bliss come only through spiritual practices and God's grace. On different occasions, the Mother described the efficacy of japa and spiritual practices:

Do you know the significance of japa and other spiritual practices? These disciplines cut asunder the bonds of past karma and subdue the outgoing tendencies of the sense organs. But one cannot realize God without ecstatic love.[47]

One should practise japa and meditation at regular times, giving up idleness. While living at Dakshineswar, I used to get up at three o'clock in the morning to practise japa and meditation. One day I felt a little indisposed and left my bed rather late. The next day I again woke up late through laziness. Gradually I found that I did not feel inclined to get up early at all. Then I said to myself: "Ah, at last I have fallen a victim to laziness." Thereupon I began to force myself to get up early. Gradually I got back my former habit. In such matters, one should keep up the practice with unyielding resolution.[48]

Routine is very important in spiritual life. Meditation becomes very effective if it is practised at a fixed time on a regular basis. Patanjali says in the Yoga Sutra (3:53): "By samyama* on the indivisible moments and their succession, one obtains discriminative knowledge."

Time is a great mystery. It begins when we begin to think. "Time is the continuous and homogeneous ocean of Pure Existence, which passes through moments and successions. Seconds, minutes, hours, days, weeks, months, and years, as well as past, present, and future, are practical

---

*When concentration, meditation, and samadhi operate simultaneously, it is called samyama.

divisions of the mental processes. In essence, there is no division in time. The whole division is a mental concept without which the operation of the psychic mechanism seems to be impossible."[49]

It is a great discipline for the mind to sit for meditation every day at the same time. For example, we have our breakfast, lunch, and dinner at set times, and our stomachs feel hungry at those times. Similarly, if we set aside time for meditation in the morning and evening, our minds will seek spiritual food at those fixed times. Holy Mother told Nalin Bihari Sarkar: "One should maintain a regular time for the practice of japa and meditation. No one knows when the auspicious moment will come. It comes suddenly without any advance warning. Therefore, one should be consistent in one's spiritual practices, no matter how busy one may be in worldly matters."

Nalin said, "Worldly duties and illness prevent me from being regular in my sadhana."

"Illness is not under man's control," Holy Mother replied. "And if you are really tied down with work, then simply remember God and make salutations to Him."

"What is the best time for spiritual practice?" Nalin asked.

"The junction of day and night and the junction of night and day are very auspicious for calling on God. The mind remains calm and pure at those times."[50]

One night at Jayrambati Holy Mother talked about the active and the contemplative life. Brahmachari Barada said: "Mother, Swami Keshavananda says, 'Labour hard to fulfill your duties, and then you will achieve everything as ordained by God.'"

Holy Mother replied: "No doubt, you must do your duty. It keeps one's mind in good condition. But it is also necessary to practise japa, meditation, and prayer. One must practise these disciplines at least in the morning and the evening. Such practice is like the rudder of a boat. When a person sits for prayer in the evening, he can reflect on the good and bad things he did during the course of the day. Then he should compare his mental state on that day with that of the previous day. Next, while performing japa, he should meditate on his Chosen Ideal. In meditation, he should first think of the face of his Chosen Deity, and then meditate on the entire body of the Deity from the feet upward. Unless you practise meditation in the morning and evening side by side with your work, how can you know whether what you are doing is desirable or undesirable?"

Barada said: "Some say that one achieves nothing through work. One can succeed in spiritual life only through japa and meditation."

Holy Mother responded: "How do they know what will give success and what will not? Does one achieve everything by practising japa and meditation for a few days? Nothing whatsoever is achieved unless Mahamaya clears the path. Didn't you notice the other day that one person's brain became deranged because he forced himself to do excessive prayer and meditation? If one's brain is deranged, one's life is useless. The intelligence of a human being is very precarious. It is like the thread of a screw. If one thread is loosened, one becomes crazy. Or one becomes entangled in the trap of Mahamaya and thinks oneself to be very intelligent. One feels quite all right. But if the screw is tightened in a different direction, one follows the right path and enjoys peace and happiness. One should always remember God and pray to Him for right understanding. How many are there who can meditate and practise japa all the time? At first they earnestly practise these disciplines, but like N., their brains become heated in the long run by constantly sitting on their prayer rugs. They become very vain. They also suffer from mental worries by reflecting on things other than God. It is much better to work than to allow the mind to roam at large. When the mind has free scope to wander, confusion comes. My Naren [Swami Vivekananda] thought of these things and wisely established institutions where people would do work without concern for the results."[51]

In April 1919 at Koalpara, a devotee received initiation from the Mother. Before returning home he asked, "Mother, what is the secret of spiritual life?" In reply, Holy Mother pointed to a small clock and said: "As that timepiece is ticking, so you go on repeating God's name. That is the way you will find fulfillment. You will not have to do anything else."

Holy Mother emphasized japa and meditation to her disciples, but she also reminded them that devotion and self-surrender are the keys to attaining God's grace. She said: "We have practised so much japa; we have observed so many spiritual disciplines; but nothing whatsoever is of any avail. How can anyone get liberation unless Mahamaya clears the path? O Man, take refuge in God. Take refuge in Him! Then alone will Mahamaya be gracious and pave the way for liberation."[52]

Once Surendranath Sarkar asked Holy Mother whether *prarabdha karma** could be counteracted by repeating the name of God.

The Mother replied: "One must experience the result of prarabdha karma. No one can escape it. But japa, or repetition of God's holy name, minimizes its intensity. It is like the case of a man who was destined to lose his leg but instead suffered only from a thorn in his foot."[53]

*Actions performed in the past that bear results in the present.

Holy Mother Answers Questions

As we make progress in spiritual life, we encounter various problems and become confused. At that time we need a guru to answer our questions. We are indebted to the Mother's disciples who asked questions on our behalf and left those answers for us — answers that are simple, direct, practical, convincing, and inspiring. Swami Shantananda asked these vital questions to Holy Mother:

Swami Shantananda: "What should be our mode of life?"

Holy Mother: "Spend your life in the same way as you are doing now. Pray to the Master earnestly. Think of him always."

Shantananda: "Mother, I am overtaken by fear when I see how even highly spiritual persons meet with a fall."

Mother: "If you are constantly in touch with objects of enjoyment, you are likely to succumb to their influence. My son, don't look at a woman, even if it be only a figure made of wood. Avoid the company of women.... The Master said: 'Monk, beware!' A monk should always be alert. A monk's path is very slippery. One should tiptoe on the slippery path. Is it a small thing to become a monk? A monk must not even glance at a woman. While walking he should keep his eyes fixed on his toes. The ochre cloth of a monk protects him as does the collar on a dog. No one hurts such a dog, for they know it has a master."

Shantananda: "Mother, is it good to practise asanas and pranayamas [yogic postures and breathing exercises]?"

Mother: "These practices lead to supernatural powers, which deflect a person from the spiritual path."

Shantananda: "Is it good to be going about from one place of pilgrimage to another?"

Mother: "If the mind feels at rest in a particular place, there is no need for pilgrimage."

Shantananda: "I find it impossible to meditate. Please awaken my kundalini."

Mother: "It will awaken in the course of time. Do japa and meditation. It does not rise of itself. Continuous meditation will make the mind so steady that you will not feel inclined to give it up. When the mind is not in a mood to meditate, do not force it to do so. In such conditions, get up from the seat of meditation after making prostrations. Real meditation is of a spontaneous nature."

Shantananda: "Mother, why is it that the mind does not become steady? When I try to think of God, I find that the mind is drawn towards other objects."

Mother: "It is wrong if the mind is drawn towards worldly objects. By 'worldly objects' is meant money, family, and so on. But it is natural for it to think of the work in which one is engaged. If meditation is not possible, do japa. *Japāt siddhi* — Realization comes through japa. If a meditative mood comes, well and good, but by no means do it by force."

Shantananda: "Is it better to do spiritual practices staying at the monastery in Varanasi than in a solitary place?"

Mother: "If you undergo spiritual practices for some time in a solitary place like Rishikesh, you will find that your mind has become strong, and then you can live in any place or society without being affected by it in the least."

Shantananda: "I have been practising asanas for some days to keep my health in good condition. These postures help one in digesting food and in practising continence."

Mother: "Be a little careful about it. If you continue such exercises for a long time, the mind may be diverted to the body. Again, if you give them up, it may affect your health. Therefore, you should exercise discretion."

Shantananda: "Mother, I only practise them for five or ten minutes for good digestion."

Mother: "That's all right. I warned you because if you practise any exercise and then give it up, it may ultimately impair your health. I bless you, my child, that you may have God-consciousness."

Shantananda: "I am practising pranayama. Shall I continue it?"

Mother: "Yes, you may do a little. But don't go to excess and heat your brain and nervous system. If the mind becomes quiet of itself, then what is the need of pranayama?"

Shantananda: "Nothing is gained, Mother, without the awakening of the kundalini."

Mother: "Quite so, my child. The kundalini will gradually be awakened. You will realize everything by the repetition of God's name. Before the awakening of the kundalini, one hears the *anahata* sound [OM], but nothing can be achieved without the grace of the Divine Mother."

Shantananda: "Mother, the stone image does not satisfy us any longer."

Mother: "Why do you say so, my child? How many hopeless sinners come to Varanasi and attain liberation by touching the image of Lord Shiva? And He, the Great God, carries on his shoulder the iniquities of all without any murmur."

Shantananda: "Mother, so many days have passed away, but I have realized nothing."

Mother: "God has been gracious in withdrawing your mind from the noise and turmoil of the world and keeping it steady at his feet. Is this a trifle? Jogin [Swami Yogananda] used to say, 'We may not be able to practise meditation and prayer to our heart's content, but we are free from the anxieties of the world.' Look at me. I am suffering a great deal on account of Radhu."[54]

Holy Mother could see the sincerity in the hearts of devotees, so she taught each one differently. One day, finding the Mother alone, Sarajubala asked her: "Is it permissible to perform worship to the Master during a woman's monthly cycle?"

Holy Mother told her what the Master had suggested: 'If your mind is distraught if you do not perform the worship, then do it; there will be no transgression in it. But if you have any compunction, then don't do it.' If you are at all hesitant, don't perform worship."

However, some days later she answered the same question differently from another woman: "How is it possible to serve the deities under such a condition? Don't perform any ritual at that time."[55]

Come Unto Me

Language was not a barrier in Holy Mother's spiritual ministry. When she went to South India, she understood two of their words, *mantram* and *upadesham,* meaning "mantra" and "advice." Knowing only these words, she could understand the intention of people and initiate them. Although the initiates did not know Bengali, they understood the Mother's words through her divine expressions and gestures.

Once Holy Mother returned to Calcutta from Jayrambati after suffering from malaria for a long time. She was very weak and the devotees were not allowed to see her. At that time a young Parsi man named Sorab Modi* came from Bombay. He had read a book by Vivekananda and felt drawn to Vedanta. Impressed by his sincerity, Saradananda gave him permission to bow down to Holy Mother. Arupananda escorted him to her. After bowing down, Sorab prayed in Hindi: "Mother, please give me a mantra so that I can realize God."

Holy Mother asked Arupananda: "Shall I initiate him? Let me do so."

Arupananda replied: "How is it possible? You just recovered from a fever. Moreover, no one is even allowed to see you now. What will Sharat Maharaj think? You had better initiate him later."

Holy Mother said: "You go and ask Sharat." Arupananda rushed to Saradananda and informed him of the matter.

Saradananda replied: "What can I say? If the Mother wants to initiate that young Parsi man, let her do it."

When Arupananda returned to Holy Mother, he found that she had already spread two asanas and was ready with the Ganges water. After initiation, she said to Arupananda: "This boy is good. He understood

*Sorab Modi later became a famous actor and director of Hindi films in Bombay.

whatever I said."[56] Amazed, Arupananda realized that this was the Mother's play.

Later Sorab Modi related his reminiscences to Swami Niramayananda:

It was 1918. I was then a young man. My elder brother was a devotee of Sri Ramakrishna and from him I first heard about Sri Sarada Devi. My brother sent me from Bombay to Calcutta to meet Holy Mother. After arriving in Calcutta, I went to Baghbazar to see the Mother, who was then very ill. I had heard that no devotees were allowed to see her. I bowed down to Swami Saradananda and said: "I have come from Bombay to see the Mother and I want initiation from her." Observing my passionate appeal, his mind softened. He asked a monk to escort me to the Mother and asked me to seek blessings from her. After bowing down to the Mother, I expressed my desire for initiation. Out of compassion she immediately initiated me. Although she did not understand my language and I also did not know Bengali, we communicated well without any difficulty. The Mother spoke in Bengali and I answered in Hindi. While taking leave from her, I said, "Mother, I am going." The Mother said: "My son, don't say 'I am going,' rather say, 'I am coming.'" When the Mother's attendant translated her words to me into English, I was amazed. I was unaware of the Bengali custom that one should speak that way while leaving. However, I returned to Bombay with a sweet memory of the Mother. She was wonderful and beautiful.

Thus many years have passed and now I am an old man. I almost forgot the Mother all these years (as I was busy with the movie industry). Now I am waiting for the call from above and that call can come at any time. I have no attraction for this world anymore. Now the forgotten Mother is coming to my mind again and again. Now those words of hers – "My son, don't say 'I am going,' rather say, 'I am coming.'" — are ringing in my ears. Now I realize what was then inscrutable to me: I wanted to go away from the Mother but could not succeed. No one can go away from the Mother. Everyone will have to return to the Mother. This is the last realization of my life: I am coming to my Mother.[57]

Once Holy Mother was waiting at the Vishnupur railway station to catch a train for Calcutta. A poor porter saw her at the platform and approached her. He was not Bengali, so he addressed her in Hindi: "You are my Mother Janaki.* How long I have been searching for you! Where have you been all this time?" With these words he began to weep profusely. The Mother consoled him and asked him to bring a flower from near the railway platform. When he offered that flower at the Mother's feet, she initiated him then and there.

*A name of Sita, the consort of Ramachandra.

Surendranath Sen, a young man from East Bengal, was a great follower of Swami Vivekananda. He went to Belur Math and requested initiation from Swamiji. On an auspicious day, Swamiji initiated three persons in the shrine, one after another, and then finally called Surendra. He meditated for a while and then said to Surendra: "The Master has told me that I am not your guru. He has shown me that the person who will initiate you is greater than I. Don't be discouraged. You will be initiated at the right time." Broken-hearted, Surendra thought: "Who could be greater than Swamiji? Considering me unfit, he did not initiate me but rather got rid of me."

Sometime after this event, Surendra had a dream in which he saw himself seated on the lap of Ramakrishna. The luminous form of a goddess appeared and said, "Take this mantra."

"Who are you?" Surendra asked.

"I am Saraswati," replied the goddess. She then uttered the mantra and asked Surendra to repeat it at least 108 times a day. But Surendra never repeated that mantra.

Seven years later, in 1906, Surendra and his friend Dr. Lalbihari Sen went to Belur Math to attend Durga Puja. Sharat Chakrabarty, a disciple of Swamiji, asked them to go to Jayrambati to meet the Mother. After Durga Puja, Surendra and Lalbihari went to Kamarpukur and then to Jayrambati. On the second day, Holy Mother called Surendra, asked him to take initiation, and suggested that he bring some flowers the next day, which was Lakshmi Puja — an auspicious day.

Surendra recalled: "During the initiation the Mother put her right hand on my head and left hand on my chin and then imparted the mantra. As soon as I heard the mantra, the whole episode of my dream initiation flashed through my mind and I felt dizzy. Momentarily I lost outer consciousness, but I felt inner bliss. Regaining normal consciousness, I saw that the Mother's form and the form of the goddess in my dream were the same. As soon as I said, 'Mother, I received this mantra long ago in a dream,' she said: 'Well, my son, does it not tally? You received the right mantra. Don't you see the Master now and then?'"[58]

Most people pay no heed to dreams because they seem unreal. But we find that some devotees had dreams about Ramakrishna and Holy Mother that turned out to be real. The Mother also mentioned that divine dreams are real, especially dreams connected with the Master.[59]

Premananda Dasgupta of Barisal dreamed that a luminous female form said to him: "You are still sitting here idly. You are getting old. Come with me." Premananda had heard about Ramakrishna and Holy Mother, but had never seen Holy Mother or her picture. His brother was Swami Bhumananda, who lived in Udbodhan and served the Mother. Shortly after his dream, Premananda went to Jayrambati. When he arrived at the Mother's door, she was leaving to take her bath in the pond. He was amazed that the female form in his dream and the Mother were the same. When she saw him, Holy Mother said: "My son, you have come. I was waiting for you. Please go and have your bath. When I return, I shall call you for initiation."[60] Thus Premananda's dream was fulfilled.

In spiritual life reason and faith are like two friends; both guide the aspirants. We verify the truth through reasoning and then proceed as far as the intellect can take us. Afterwards, faith takes over and leads the soul to its destination. Holy Mother said to Swami Asitananda, who prayed for faith: "My son, it is not easy to attain real faith. It comes at the last stage. If you have faith, you will achieve everything."[61]

In December 1913, a woman's faith and longing took her from Raipur in Madhya Pradesh to Calcutta to see Holy Mother. She privately narrated her dream to the Mother: "Mother, I saw Sri Ramakrishna and you in my dream and you were giving me a mantra. But before you completed the mantra, my dream broke. Since then I have been anxious to have initiation from you."

Holy Mother said with a smile: "Very well, I shall initiate you today. But do you have your husband's consent?"

"I told my husband about my dream," the devotee replied. "He told me: 'I have no objection to your having initiation, but I shall not take initiation now.'"

Holy Mother pointed to the bathroom and said: "Please wash your hands and feet there and come to me."

The devotee responded: "Mother, I have not taken my bath yet."

"That's all right," Holy Mother said, "You need not take a bath."

Holy Mother spread two asanas in the shrine and sprinkled Ganges water on herself and the devotee, and then asked: "Which deity are you devoted to?" After listening to the reply, the Mother gave her the mantra and showed how to repeat it while counting on her fingers. When Holy Mother asked for dakshina,* the devotee said that she was unaware of the custom and had not brought any money. The Mother got up, picked up some flowers and fruits, put them in the woman's hands, and said: "Please say: 'I offer to you whatever good and bad deeds I have done

---

*According to custom, after initiation the disciple is supposed to give dakshina (a gift) to the guru as a token of love and gratitude. The dakshina may be money or fruits.

in my past and present life, knowingly and unknowingly.'" The devotee repeated this and the Mother accepted her offering.[62]

The Mother did not worry about the time and place for initiation if she considered the aspirant to be sincere. A devotee of Shillong wanted to test the divinity of the Mother, so he resolved not to go to see the Mother unless he saw her seven times in his dreams. By her grace, this came to pass and he went to Jayrambati to see her. Holy Mother asked him to take initiation before he left for Calcutta. The devotee said that he preferred to have it in Calcutta. But the Mother insisted: "No, my son, let it be finished. I shall initiate you today."

The devotee still objected: "Mother, I have eaten prasad."

But Holy Mother did not consider that a hindrance to initiation and she imparted the mantra. Truly, a guru's grace is unconditional.[63]

In 1919 Holy Mother was in Koalpara. Suresh Chaudhury, a young revolutionary, had just been released from police custody in Sunderban. He came straight to the Mother for initiation that evening. Koalpara Ashrama was under surveillance at that time and the police checked every evening to see if any revolutionaries were hiding there. Keshavananda told Suresh that he could not stay in the ashrama and would have to leave after bowing down to the Mother. Holy Mother heard everything. She said to Brahmachari Barada: "Ah, Barada, this boy has walked all day from Vishnupur to see me. Could you arrange for his stay in someone's home or living room for one night? I will initiate him tomorrow morning and send him away."

Barada fed Suresh the leftovers from lunch and arranged for him to stay at the Chandimandap, an open hall that Nafar Koley maintained for festivals. Holy Mother was very pleased. Early the next morning the Mother and Barada were going from the Jagadamba Ashrama to Radhu's cottage. On the way they saw Suresh waiting for them, having finished his bath. Holy Mother asked Barada to bring a little water from a pond nearby. Guessing that the Mother would need an asana in order to sit on that dusty path, Barada asked, "Shall I bring an asana?"

Holy Mother replied: "No, you will not have to go back to the house. Fetch two bundles of hay and we shall sit on them." Barada watched from a distance as the Mother initiated Suresh on the path. Afterwards, she called to Barada to bring some rock candy that she had offered to the Master. She ate a little herself and gave the prasad to Suresh. When he had finished, Holy Mother sent Suresh to Jayrambati for lunch and asked him to return to his home after visiting Kamarpukur in the afternoon.[64]

Once a young married woman took initiation from the Mother and then returned to her husband's home. She practised japa regularly there, but she had a doubt as to whether she was repeating the mantra properly. After three years she had an opportunity to visit the Mother and wanted to resolve her doubt. Listening to her problem, the Mother said: "Well, my child, it happened long ago. Do I have the mantra in mind still? Don't tell me anything. Please wait a little. Let me ask the Master." Holy Mother went to the shrine and returned shortly. She said, "Yes, my child, I gave you this mantra." The woman admitted that that was her mantra. Then the Mother said: "Repeat it as you have been doing. There is no error in the mantra."[65]

The scripture says: *Vāsanā pushyati vapuh,* desires preserve the body. Human beings have innumerable desires and they force people to move forward. Most people are satisfied when they have fulfilled their worldly desires, and only a rare one among millions seeks God. Chandra Mohan Datta, a young man from Dhaka, came to Calcutta for a job. He heard about the Ramakrishna Mission and came to Udbodhan House, where he met Holy Mother. She listened to him describe his family background and appointed him to do marketing for her household. Saradananda also engaged him to pack books in the publication department. The Mother was very fond of him, because of his simplicity, honesty, and guileless-ness. He lived with the monks on the ground floor of the house. He was very fond of eating, and the Mother loved to feed him. Whenever he came to her, he got something to eat.

Sometimes we wonder: if God were to appear to us this moment and offer us a single boon, what would we ask for? Undoubtedly, most people would ask for money, considering that money can fulfill all of their needs. Among millions, perhaps, one would ask for liberation. Chandra Datta once faced this test. He recalled:

Once I was about to go for a bath in the Ganges from Udbodhan House. Swamis Shuddhananda and Prajnananda were with me. Suddenly Swami Shuddhananda said to me: "Chandra, you have free access to Holy Mother and she is also very fond of you. Could you go to the Mother and ask something that I tell you?"

"Of course, I can. Tell me what I have to ask from her."

"Nothing much. It is a trivial thing. Just tell her, 'Mother, I want liberation.'"

"I shall tell her right now."

Immediately I ran to the Mother's room upstairs and found her wor-shipping the Master. I had come to her room so many times before, but on that day I was a little scared to see her performing worship. My body began to tremble. I was thinking I should leave the room but I did not have that strength. My legs were shaking, my throat became parched, and my body began to perspire. Suddenly the Mother turned towards me and asked, "Do you want to say something?" My voice choked. Again she asked with a sign, "Did you come to say something?" Quite involuntarily I blurted out one word, "prasad." The Mother pointed to the prasad kept on a plate under the bed. Then she resumed the worship. Shivering and perspiring profusely, I ran downstairs with the prasad and found that both swamis were waiting for me anxiously. Swami Shuddhananda asked: "Well, Chandra, could you ask for liberation? What did the Mother say?" I told them what happened. I could not go to the Ganges that day and it took many hours to calm down.[66]

On 3 August 1911, Sarajubala Sen recalled:

This morning I went early to Baghbazar. I had the desire to be initiated by Holy Mother today, so I took a few articles with me for the purpose. Gauri-ma had given the list of articles, and she also accompanied me to the Mother's place. When I arrived there, I found her absorbed in worship. She asked me by signs to take a seat. After the worship was over, Gauri-ma broached the subject of my initiation. I had also spoken about it to her on another day. I had brought some good bananas with me. She was very pleased to see the fruit and said, "Ah, I see you have brought many bananas. One of the monks expressed a desire for a banana." Then she added: "Take a carpet and sit on my left." I replied: "I have not yet taken my bath in the Ganges." The Mother said: "That does not matter. It is enough if you have changed your clothes."

I sat by her side. I felt my heart palpitating. The Mother asked others to leave the room and then said to me, "Now tell me what mantra was revealed to you in your dream." I said, "Shall I utter those words or write them down?" "You may tell them to me," replied the Mother.

At the time of initiation the Mother explained to me the meaning of the mantra that I had received in my dream. She at first asked me to repeat that mantra and then communicated to me a new one. I was instructed to repeat the first mantra a few times every day, and then repeat the second one and meditate.

I saw the Mother absorbed in meditation for a few minutes before she explained the meaning of the mantra to me. At the time of initiation my whole body began to tremble. I began to weep, for which I could not divine any cause. The Mother put a big mark of red sandal paste on my forehead. I gave her a few rupees for offering at the shrine. She handed over the money to Golap-ma.

I noticed the Mother was severely grave at the time of initiation. Then she left the seat of worship. She asked me to repeat the mantra for some time and to meditate and pray. I did as I was asked to do. As I bowed at her feet she blessed me with these words, "May you attain devotion to God!" Even now I remember those words and pray to her: "Please remember your blessing. May I not be deprived of its result."[67]

The Mother and Some Young Disciples

Spiritual advancement does not depend upon age. Sometimes young boys or girls are more spiritual than mature men and women. Holy Mother once commented that some people have practised spiritual disciplines in their previous lives and are born endowed with those experiences.

One day a 12-year-old boy came to Udbodhan House and began to cry out to the Mother for initiation. Everyone considered this a childish whim and attached no importance to his emotional demand. The next day Holy Mother's attendant saw the boy seated on the outer porch of the Mother's house. He paid no attention to the boy and left for the market. When he returned he noticed the boy walking away with a smiling face. The attendant learned from the boy that he had been initiated and he was going to buy fruit and sweets for Holy Mother. While the attendant was at the market, Holy Mother had asked Radhu to bring the boy to her. Then the Mother initiated him. The attendant went to Holy Mother and objected: "Mother, how strange that you have initiated such a young boy! What does he understand?"

Holy Mother replied: "Well, my son, he is a guileless boy. Yesterday he held my feet and cried for initiation. Tell me, how many people weep for God? How many have such strong spiritual inclination?"[68]

In 1912 when the Mother returned to Calcutta from a pilgrimage, a young devotee of Koalpara Ashrama named Barada asked for initiation. Barada was then only 13 years old at the time. Golap-ma heard of this and objected in her usual loud voice: "This little boy will forget the mantra within a couple of days, and he now wants initiation! Kedar [Keshavananda] sent this boy for initiation — he has no sense." She told Barada: "Look, Mother belongs to your part of the country. When she goes there, ask for initiation from her after more deliberation."

When Golap-ma left, Holy Mother remarked: "See how Golap talks! Does she forget that one learns well in boyhood? Let him start now and do as much as he can. Later I shall give him more guidance." On the day of Janmashtami Holy Mother initiated Barada and taught him how to repeat the mantra. She said: "Very well, you will definitely remember the mantra. In the future, I shall show you everything over again, if necessary." She then blessed Barada by touching his head and chest and prayed to the Master, "Please look after him in this life and the next." She got up from her asana and gave him two sweets as prasad. When Barada hesitated to eat in front of her, she said: "My son, don't be shy. One should partake of prasad after initiation."[69]

Swami Parameswarananda wrote about how the Mother sometimes initiated people on her own initiative. One day she asked a young boy, "Do you want initiation?"

"I don't know what it is," replied the boy.

"Have initiation," the Mother said to him.

The boy again said, "I don't have money."

"You will not have to pay anything," said the Mother. She asked her attendant to give a myrobalan (a small fruit) to the boy, which he offered to her at the time of initiation.

Another time some boys came from Chapadanga and begged for initiation from the Mother. She immediately agreed. They bathed in the Punyapukur and the Mother initiated them all.[70]

In the late nineteenth and early twentieth centuries, the life of a young Hindu widow was painful. She could not marry again and she spent her life as a burden on her husband's or father's family. Social rules and customs of the time restricted her activities and forced her to lead a life like a nun. Some widows dedicated their lives to spiritual pursuits and social services. One such young widow came to the Mother. She left the following reminiscences:

> After initiation, Holy Mother said to me: "Look here, my daughter, I do not usually initiate a young woman who has just lost her husband, but I have made an exception in your case, as you have a spiritual temperament. See that I do not have to repent of it. The guru suffers from the sin committed by the disciple. Always repeat the mantra of your Chosen Deity like the ever-moving hand of a clock."
>
> Once when I was going to my father-in-law's house, the Mother gave me the following advice: "Don't be familiar with anybody. Don't take much part in the social functions of the family. Say, 'O mind, always keep to yourself. Don't be inquisitive about others.' When you go back home, please prepare coconut balls and offer them to the Master. He was fond of coconut balls. Gradually increase the period of japa and meditation, and read the teachings of the Master."
>
> Another day I was alone with the Mother. She said to me: "Look, my child, never be intimate with any man — not even with your own father and brother — and what to speak of other men? Let me again repeat, don't be intimate with a man, even if God comes to you in that form."

The Mother forbade me to frequent the monastery and other places where the monks lived. She would say: "You may have no bad intention in your mind. You might be visiting them with deep devotion. But if your presence brings any impure ideas to their minds, then you will also be partly responsible for it."

She also forbade me from going on pilgrimages without choosing carefully the time and company. She told me: "Whenever you have some money in hand, feed some holy men." Pointing to a woman devotee who was present, she said: "Look at her. She has learned a great lesson while visiting a holy place." The Mother then quoted from a song: 'Pilgrimages and excursions are causes of misery. O my mind, don't be restless for them.' You can attain more in your house if you are really earnest."

One day some women devotees were criticizing a particular person. At that time the Mother said to me: "Do not lose your respect for her. It was she who first brought you here."

Once I asked the Mother's permission to adopt a child. In reply, the Mother pointed out her own difficulties with Radhu. She said: "Never take such a step. Always do your duty to others. But love you must give to God alone. Worldly love always brings in its wake untold misery."

Learning that I had received initiation from Holy Mother, our family guru cursed me. I informed the Mother about this through a letter. She wrote me back: "Even the curse of Brahma can do no harm to one who has taken refuge in the Master. Be free from all fear."[71]

Obstinate Disciples

It is very difficult to be a guru. All disciples are not obedient, respectful, loving, and considerate. Some are obstinate, selfish, complaining, and demanding. Sarajubala described in her reminiscences what the compassionate Mother had to go through with an inconsiderate woman devotee:

I visited the Mother one afternoon and found a woman kneeling near her feet, begging with tears for initiation. The Mother was seated on her bedstead. She refused to comply, saying: "I have already told you that I will not be able to initiate you now. I am not well." The woman was insistent. The Mother was annoyed and said: "You think only of yourself. You are perfectly satisfied if you get the sacred mantra. But you never think of the consequences." But the woman was inexorable. All of us felt disgusted. Holy Mother at last asked her to come another day. Then the woman requested the Mother to ask one of the monks to give her initiation.

Mother: "Suppose they refuse."

Woman: "What do you mean, Mother? They must obey you."

Mother: "In this matter they may refuse to comply with my request."

Finding the woman unrelenting, the Mother said, "Well, I shall ask

Khoka [Swami Subodhananda]. He will initiate you."

But the woman started insisting again and said: "I shall be happy to be initiated by you. You can certainly fulfill my desire if you like." The woman brought out ten rupees and said: "Here is some money. You may purchase the necessary articles for initiation." We all felt mortified at her impudence. At last the Mother was angry and said severely: "What? Do you mean to tempt me with money? You cannot coax me with these coins. Take them back." Holy Mother immediately left the room. Being hard pressed by the woman, the Mother at last agreed to initiate her on the sacred Mahashtami day. That woman soon took leave of us.[72]

It is easy to raise good and well-behaved children, but it is extremely painful for the mother if the children are disobedient, disrespectful, demanding, and difficult. Every mother in this world should take a lesson from Holy Mother on how to handle ill-behaved children. Swami Arupananda recalled:

One morning a disciple, an eccentric young man, came to Holy Mother at Jayrambati and demanded monastic initiation. He urged her to make him "mad" and give him a vision of the Master immediately. Somehow she pacified him for the time being and sent him home. But his eccentricity increased and he returned to Jayrambati. He felt that the Mother had the power to give him a vision of Sri Ramakrishna but was refusing to do so. He said: "Mother, won't you let me see the Master?"

Mother: "Yes, you will see him. Don't be so restless."

Disciple (angrily): "You are only deceiving me. Here is your rosary. Take it back. I don't care for it anymore."

He flung the rosary at her. "All right," said the Mother. "Remain forever the child of the Master." He left the place at once. Now he really became insane and began to write abusive letters to the swamis of the Ramakrishna Mission not sparing even Holy Mother. One day I asked the Mother: "Did he return the mantra with the rosary? Can anyone ever return the mantra?" The Mother replied: "Can that ever be possible? The mantra is a living thing. Can anyone who has received it give it back? Can he, once having felt attraction for the guru, give him up? Some day in the future this man will come around and fall at the feet of those whom he now abuses. He once said to me: 'Mother, make me mad.' 'Why?' said I. 'Why should you be mad? Can anyone, without committing many sins, ever be mad?'"

This devotee again began to visit Udbodhan House but was rebuffed by the swamis. He lived on the bank of the Ganges and sometimes took his meal on the outer porch of Udbodhan. One day he was taken to Holy Mother with her permission. Trying to pacify him in various ways, she said: "The Master used to say: 'At the time of death I shall have to stand by those who pray to me.' These are his words. You are my child. What should you be afraid of? Why should you behave like a madman? That will disgrace the Master. People will say that one of his devotees has become mad. Should you conduct yourself in a way that discredits the Master? Go home and live as others do. Eat and lead a normal life. At the time of your death, the Master will reveal himself to you and take you to him." The devotee was consoled by the Mother's words and gradually regained his normal state of mind.[73]

Holy Mother's Omniscience

Mukunda Bihari Saha was a student of Scottish Church College in Calcutta. He became very close to M., the recorder of *The Gospel of Sri Ramakrishna,* and he heard about the Mother from him. One day Mukunda approached Holy Mother, asking for initiation. Smiling, she said, "Very well, my son, come tomorrow morning." He asked, "What should I bring?" She answered, "Nothing, just a few flowers." Mukunda recalled:

The next morning I went to the Mother's house with only a few flowers. When the initiation was over the attendant monk asked me, "Haven't you brought any sweets?" I was deeply embarrassed. The next day after classes, I hastened to pay homage to the Mother. Mindful of my embarrassment on the previous day, I brought some sweets. The attendant monk who had mentioned the sweets on the previous day asked me, "From where are you coming?" I replied, "Straight from college." Showing him the packet of sweets, I said, "I've brought this for the Mother." He exclaimed: "Silly boy, to have brought sweets for the Mother without changing your clothes! I doubt whether the Mother will eat any of them." I was very sad. I went upstairs, intending only to offer *pranam* and then go away. As soon as I rose after touching her feet, the Mother said, "My son, won't you give me the sweets you have brought for me?" The all-knowing Mother! I stood silently. The Mother repeated, "Well, my son, give me the sweets." When she stretched out her hand, I handed over the small packet to her with great hesitation. Tears trickled from my eyes. I told her that I had come straight from the college without changing my clothes. "It does not matter," she replied. She opened the packet, took a little sweet, and then returned the whole packet to me, saying, "Please eat." It tasted like ambrosia.[74]

Annada Charan Sengupta, a disciple of the Mother, recalled:

During Christmas vacation I went to visit the Mother at Udbodhan from Barisal. I had read the story of Girish giving the power of attorney over his life to Sri Ramakrishna and that thought penetrated my mind. I decided that I would offer the power of attorney to the Mother mentally without making it known to anyone. After bathing in the Ganges, I went to Udbodhan House, and Swami Saradananda asked a brahmachari to escort me to the Mother. I saw that the Mother was seated on her bed dangling her feet with a long veil over her face. Disappointed, I waited a while. When the brahmachari asked me to finish *pranam* quickly, I bowed down, putting an apple at her feet and mentally said, "Mother, please accept the power of attorney over my life." When I raised my head, I saw her veil on the top of her head and she was looking at me graciously. There was an affectionate smile on her face. I received the answer to my prayer in the Mother's smile. After some time I wondered whether the Mother still remembered me. Then I heard from one of my relatives in Calcutta that the Mother had inquired about me.[75]

Holy Mother's Advice to Disciples

Krishna says in the Gita (4:34): "Learn it [wisdom] by prostration, by inquiry, and by service. The wise, who have seen the Truth, will teach you that wisdom." True seekers of God encounter various obstacles and doubts on their spiritual journey. It is always wise to have those doubts cleared by the guru. On different occasions Holy Mother gave the following advice on spiritual life to some of her disciples.

To Kailash Kamini Roy: "One should transform this gross body into a spiritual body through sadhana, so one should take care of the body."

To Swami Avyaktananda: "Disease and austerity are the same thing. One can destroy the results of past actions through austerity and also through disease."

Swami Kaivalyananda asked: "Mother, there are so many bad and good thoughts arising in my mind. What will happen to me?"

Holy Mother replied: "Don't worry about it. In this Kaliyuga, mental sin is not considered a sin unless that sinful thought is executed. In other ages virtue and vice would take place through the resolution of the mind. In this Kaliyuga, good thoughts will definitely bear good results."

Nalin Sarkar said: "Mother, my mind does not always like to practise japa and meditation. Sometimes I like it, and sometimes it is distasteful."

Holy Mother responded: "As there is a dark fortnight and a bright fortnight, so is the condition of the mind — sometimes good and sometimes bad. This is the law of nature. Whatever be the condition of the mind, never give up your habit of sitting [for meditation] in the morning and evening. Sometimes the mind does not like to sit for meditation even when the mind is in good condition; again sometimes it becomes absorbed despite a restless condition. It is hard to say when the mind will get absorbed in God."

After initiating Gopalkinkar Sen, the Mother said to him: "For all these years you have been a man, and now you are an awakened man. Repeat the mantra as much as you can, but always pray to the Master."

Swami Pranatmananda asked: "I have a desire to go on a pilgrimage. Is it good?"

Holy Mother replied: "Visiting holy places is very good; it purifies the mind. But it is better to have initiation before going on a pilgrimage."

In a letter to Taraknath Roy Chaudhury, Holy Mother advised: "The meaning of giving the power of attorney is to surrender one's entire responsibility to God. Even after giving the power of attorney, one should repeat one's Ishta-mantra and remember God at least at the end of the day."

Once when Radhu was sick, Holy Mother asked Nandarani to perform the Master's worship. Nandarani replied that she did not know the mantra. The Mother instructed her: "First wipe the Master's picture with a moist cloth, then offer a flower and tulsi leaves with sandal paste at his feet. Afterwards offer to him food that you have prepared, saying, 'Master, please eat this food.' Finally, repeat your Ishta-mantra."

Swami Varadananda came from Kalighat with a vermilion mark on his forehead. He looked very handsome with his fair complexion, ochre cloth, and the vermilion mark. After Varadananda bowed down to Holy Mother, she looked at his face and remarked: "The Master used to say, 'One should not exhibit the mark of one's religion outside.'"[76]

True religion is realization of God. It is not in external religious marks or in scriptural scholarship. Swami Nikhilananda, one of Holy Mother's disciples, wrote: "Holy Mother did not care much for book-learning if it did not lead to faith in God and love for Him. 'Does one get faith,' she asked, 'by the mere study of books? Too much reading creates confusion.' She did not argue or reason, though she stressed the value of discrimination between the real and unreal, between God and the world. Whatever she taught came from her heart and her inner experience. Once, asked for a proof of God's existence, she said: 'Why argue about something which you clearly see to exist?' She said to a devotee: 'Give up dry discussion, this hotchpotch of philosophy. Who has been able to know God by reasoning?'"[77]

Ramakrishna and Holy Mother were very much against a guru cult, which develops narrowness, bigotry, quarrelling, fanaticism, and fights. Once Swami Arupananda said to Holy Mother: "Those who are obtaining your blessings are fortunate indeed. What will happen to people in the future?"

"What do you mean?" the Mother asked with great surprise. "Why will they too not succeed? God exists everywhere and at all times. Are people not realizing God in other countries?" On another occasion she said: "Holy men are born on earth to show people the way to God. They teach differently. There are many paths leading to the same goal. Therefore the teachings of all the saints are true."[78]

There are innumerable stories and eyewitness accounts of the Mother as a guru. However, only some important ones are recorded in this chapter. Holy Mother was an incarnation of the Divine Mother, so she could liberate souls by cutting the cord of maya. Blessed are they who received initiation from her. Fortunately, Holy Mother's grace was not limited to those few who went to her: her grace and unconditional love continue to flow through millions of people all over the world who come in contact with her through her divine life story and teachings.

Sarada Devi at Jayrambati, 1913.

27
Ministry
through Correspondence

Medhe saraswati vare bhuti bābhravi tāmasi;
Niyate tvam prasideshe nārāyani namostu te.
 —*Chandi, 11:23*

O Mother Narayani, you are Saraswati, our intelligence. You are the supreme goddess endowed with sattva, rajas, and tamas. Be propitious unto us, O Mother. We bow to you.

As the human face is reflected on a mirror, so the human mind is manifested through letters. When we read someone's letter, we get some glimpses of that person's mind. Goethe said: "Letters are among the most significant memorial a person can leave behind them." In the old days when there was no telephone or internet, people who lived some distance away from each other communicated through letters. St. Paul conducted part of his spiritual ministry through correspondence. His letters to the Romans, Corinthians, Galatians, Ephesians, Philippians, Colossians, Thessalonians, and others carried the message of Christ, and still inspire millions of Christians. Swami Vivekananda also inspired people through his immortal letters.

Although Ramakrishna and Holy Mother did not have much formal education, they were endowed with communication skills, which are indispensable for disseminating ideas. Ramakrishna went to the Lahas' primary school in Kamarpukur for a brief period and learned to read and write. He could sign his name, and he also copied some scriptures, which are now preserved in the archives of Belur Math. On 9 March 1883 he said to M.: "During my childhood I could paint well; but arithmetic made my head spin. I couldn't learn simple arithmetic."[1] The Master did not care for a bread-earning education, so he eventually became a dropout.

There is no record that Ramakrishna wrote any letters to anyone or dictated letters, but on 29 August 1885, the Master received a letter from Purna Chandra Ghosh in which Purna had written: "I am feeling extremely happy. Now and then I cannot sleep at night for joy." After hearing this letter, the Master said: "I feel thrilled to hear this. Even later on he will be able to keep this bliss. Let me see the letter." He pressed the letter in the palm of his hand and said: "Generally I cannot touch letters. But this is a good letter."[2] Is it not a great fortune for a devotee that an avatar was thinking of his welfare?

Holy Mother learned how to read and write, but according to Yogin-ma, she did not know how to count money. Holy Mother now and then received some money, which the devotees sent to her through a money order or gave to her as a gift. She would touch the money to her forehead (as money represents the Divine Mother Lakshmi) and then put it in a box. Later she would give it to her disciples to buy groceries.

One day in Udbodhan House, Swami Arupananda said to Holy Mother: "Mother, I sometimes see you reading the Ramayana. When did you learn to read?" The Mother replied that she had learned the alphabet when she was a little girl from her brother Prasanna and cousin Ramnath. She and Ramakrishna's niece Lakshmi later learned *Barna Parichay – Part 1* (the Bengali primer) at Kamarpukur, but Hriday took the Mother's book away because he did not believe girls should be educated. Later, at Dakshineswar, the Master engaged a boy named Sharat Samanta to teach her *Barna Parichay – Part 2*. Then in 1885, when the Master left for Shyampukur to be treated for cancer, a girl from Bhava Mukherjee's family in Dakshineswar taught Holy Mother to read fluently the Ramayana and other holy books. (*See Chapter 2 for more details on Holy Mother's education.*)

Ramakrishna once said about Holy Mother: "She is Sarada — Saraswati. She has come to give knowledge." Saraswati is the goddess of learning. By Her will, the Mother received whatever education she needed to conduct her spiritual ministry. As she had many disciples and devotees in various parts of India and abroad, she often received letters from them asking for help with their problems or asking questions about spiritual practices. All these she answered.

When the disciples' letters were read to her, she would dictate her answers, which were written down by some of her disciples, including Swami Arupananda, Swami Parameswarananda, Brahmachari Gopesh, Brahmachari Barada, Brahmachari Jnanananda, Brahmachari Hemendra, and Sarajubala Sen. Shivaram (Ramakrishna's nephew), her nieces Radhu, Maku, and Nalini also sometimes took dictation from her. Even her mailman, Yogendra, wrote down letters for her.

In the early days, there were not many educated people in Jayrambati. When Yogendra the mailman brought a letter to her, she asked him to read it to her. She then dictated an answer to him, and he mailed it for her. Of course, she gave him refreshments in appreciation.

In May 2006, the Ramakrishna Mission Institute of Culture published a Bengali book entitled *Mayer Chithi* (Holy Mother's Letters), which contains 361 letters. This book includes 108 letters that were originally published in *Sri Sri Mayer Padaprante, Part 3,* by the Udbodhan Office in Calcutta.

As the present book is a biography of Holy Mother and not a collection of her letters, we will only look at some letters that illustrate various facets of her life. In this chapter, we shall first reproduce the available letters of the Mother that were written in English. Then we shall include translations of some important letters originally written in Bengali. (The translations are my own, except as indicated.) Finally, we shall translate a few letters written by the Mother's disciples. For uniformity and style, we have taken some liberty regarding the spelling and punctuation in these letters.

These letters are replete with spiritual instructions, historical facts, and incidents concerning the Ramakrishna Order. Above all, they shed light on Holy Mother's life. During her lifetime, she travelled between Calcutta and Jayrambati many times, she went on pilgrimages in various parts of India, and she was extremely busy serving and initiating disciples in Jayrambati and Calcutta. Sometimes she suffered from malaria and rheumatism. It is amazing how she maintained contact with the disciples of the Master and also with her own disciples. Despite her lack of a modern education and her rural upbringing, she was always dignified in her manners. Whenever anybody sent money or a gift to her, she always acknowledged it and sent her blessings.

Letters to Western Devotees

Holy Mother's letters to her Western devotees* demonstrate her affection for them and her deep interest in the Vedanta work in the West.

Written on 4 April 1900 in Jayrambati to Sister Nivedita in the West:

May this letter carry all blessings! My dear love to you, Baby Daughter Nivedita! I am so glad to learn that you have prayed to the Lord for my eternal peace. You are a manifestation of the ever-blissful Mother. I look at your photograph which is with me, every now and then. And it seems as if you are present with me. I long for the day and the year when you shall return. May the prayers you have uttered for me from the heart of your

---

*Letters dictated by her in Bengali, but translated into English, mostly by monks.

pure virgin soul be answered! I am well and happy. I always pray to the Lord to help you in your efforts and to keep you strong and happy. I pray too for your quick return. May He fulfill your desires about the women's home in India, and may the would-be home fulfill its mission in teaching true dharma to all.

He, the Breath of the Universe, is singing His own praise, and you are hearing that Eternal song through things that will come to an end. The trees, the birds, the hills, and all are singing praises to the Lord. The Banyan of Dakshineswar sings of Kali to be sure, and blessed is he who has ears to hear it.

I was so glad to hear of the faith of Mrs. Waterman. She who thinks she has not lost her beloved, even after the fall of the body, has really attained to light; for the soul can never die, even when the body falls. I am glad to hear that it has strengthened her to hear of me. May she be a help to your work. My love and blessings to Mrs. May Wright Sewell.

My dear, love to you and blessings and prayers for your spiritual growth. You are indeed doing good work — but do not forget your Bengali! Or I shall not be able to understand you when you come back. It gave me such delight to know that you are speaking of Dhruva, Savitri, Sita-Ram, and so on there.

The accounts of their holy lives are better than all the vain talks of the world. I am sure. Oh how beautiful are the Name and the doings of the Lord!

Your Mother[3]

Written on 28 July 1910 in Baghbazar, Calcutta, to Sara Bull, United States
Mother,

Hearing that you are very ill, I am very anxious about you! I heard from your daughter Nivedita that you are a little better. I am praying to Thakur, the Lord, for your speedy recovery. Your recovery will cause me great joy.

I have come here [to Calcutta], and all my children here are well, except Yogin, who is not quite well, about which I am a little anxious, and very, very sorry.

I have offered on your behalf, to the feet of Ramakrishna, a tulsi and a bel leaf, and three evenings sitting before him I have prayed for you. Also I want to know if Jaya [Josephine MacLeod] is going to you. Please give her my warm blessings, and do not forget Christine if you see her. I am so sorry to hear that your daughter is not at present with you, in this time of illness.

And now from our Lord I am sending you a flower and sandal dust, which I offered to him with worship. My deep love and blessing you will realize. I love you very much and bless you from my heart. We are far away from you, but I always feel as if you were quite near.

Your Ma [Mother]*⁴

Holy Mother wrote to Sister Devamata, an American disciple of Swami Para-mananda, a few days after Devamata's arrival in Madras from the United States. This letter was written in Bengali and translated by Swami Ramakrishnananda.

Date and location unknown

My dear Devamata,

I am very glad to hear of your great devotion to my Lord. You are my daughter. May infinite devotion rise up in your heart — this is my blessing to you. For this I pray to my Lord. May you live long and along with all my other children. May you remain merged in bliss eternal.

I am doing well,

Your affectionate Mother⁵

Devamata visited Holy Mother in Calcutta and then returned to Madras and finally to the United States. She published the following extracts from Holy Mother's letters in her book *Days in an Indian Monastery.*

Date and location unknown

My sweet daughter,

Your loving letters are duly at hand. Excuse me please not to answer you in time. I always remember you. Whenever I see the place you used to sit and meditate your loving form comes to my mind. All the inmates of this house always speak of you. I am glad to learn in your last letter that Swami Ramakrishnananda is feeling better. All well here.

With my blessings,

Your most affectionate Mother⁶

Date and location unknown

My sweet daughter,

Your letter of the 1ˢᵗ of November, I received. I cannot tell you the joy I felt on receiving it. I have come here [to Puri] for a change and will stay here for a month or two more. I hope you will write to me every now and then. I am feeling better now. I am glad to learn of the removal of the

---

*She signed this letter herself, in Bengali.

quarters of the Boston work and the spreading of the Lord's doctrine progressively day by day. I always think of you, my sweet daughter. Hope you are quite well now. With my loving blessings,

Your loving Mother[7]

Date unknown; Baghbazar, Calcutta, India

My beloved daughter,

Your letter of August 16th received. I was thinking of you when the letter came to me. So you can easily guess how much joy it has given me.

I am glad to go through the part which gives the report of the work there. Please convey my love and blessings to Paramananda and to all the devotees there, both in Washington and Boston. I am more glad to find you well again and doing Thakur's work with earnest zeal. I am indeed very happy to receive this news. I am feeling myself somewhat better now.

Saradananda, Yogin-ma, Golap-ma, Satyakama, Kusum Devi, Ganen, Nivedita, and Sudhira are all right. They often speak of you.

With my love and blessings to you,

My beloved daughter,

Your affectionate Mother[8]

Date unknown; Sundaravilas, Madras, India

My sweet daughter,

I am glad to receive your letters dated Jan. 17 and Feb. 9. The report of the work of both Washington and Boston is interesting to me and I would like to hear more in future....

I was at Kothar for nearly two months and have come over here. Now I am residing in the same house in which you lived. I have been here for a month and a half. Meanwhile I went to visit Rameswaram and stayed there for four days. The family of Balaram Babu is here with me. All are doing well here except a lady of the same family who is suffering from enteric fever. As soon as she gets cured we will start for Calcutta. Tomorrow I will have to go to Bangalore and will spend there a day or two. Thence I will come back here.

Swami Ramakrishnananda is somewhat better now. All the other swamis are well....

My blessings to you and to Swami Paramananda and to all the devotees both in Washington and Boston.

Your affectionate Mother[9]

Devamata writes regarding the following letter, "A short time before her going came this last letter from her."

Date and location unknown

My sweet daughter,

My blessings be on your head. After a long time I have received a letter from you. Sriman Basanta (Swami Paramananda) and you are keeping well; hearing this I am very happy. You are my daughter; you are also my mother because you have prayed for my welfare to the Lord. Give my blessings to Sriman Basanta, and for you also my blessings — my blessings to all. What grief I have suffered due to the passing away of Baburam (Swami Premananda) I cannot convey in a letter. I am happy to know that Basanta's [Paramananda] work is going on so well. I am sorry to hear that because of much pressure of work he cannot come here. I hope he will try to come when it is again possible. Convey my blessings to all the people living at the Math [monastery]. May the Lord make you all His true children is my prayer. Write to me about your own welfare. Write me.

From the one who blesses you,
Mata Thakurani[10]

Letters to Swamis, Indian Disciples, and Devotees

Written in English on June 4, 1917 in Jayrambati, Anur, and Hooghly to Prabhu (later Swami Vireswarananda)

My dear Prabhu,

Your letter is at hand. I remember you, my darling, very well. I am very glad to hear that you have become a sadhu and taken brahmacharya from Rakhal, my favourite son. You should not come to me now. Carry out the order of Rakhal. I hope that you shall be able to overcome all such difficulties by His [Thakur's] grace. Pray to Him, and He will favour you. Try to meditate yourself every day regularly, and you will progress gradually. Don't be downcast, my boy. I am very glad to hear that the new Math [at Madras] has been opened. I hope that it will be completed well in time.

I am well. I bless you affectionately. You should write to me whenever you want. Do not be sorry because you do not know Bengali.

With blessing to you and all my sons of the Math.

Your Holy Mother

P.S. You may write in English, but write clearly.[11]

Written on 7 May 1913 in Jayrambati to Nishi Kumar Ganguli of Ibrahimpur, Tripura

My dear son,

I am very pleased to receive your letter. At present I am doing fine. Pray to the Master. By his grace your mind will gradually become pure. Does the mind become calm suddenly? Many sages and rishis practise severe sadhana and austerities their whole lives; still sometimes they fall from the spiritual path. So one should practise sadhana. The mind becomes pure and calm by crying to God with a longing heart. Are the devotees of the Master equal even though all of them received his grace? One needs to practise sadhana.

Please accept my blessings.
Your Mother[12]

Written on 18 December 1913 in the Udbodhan Office, Baghbazar, Calcutta to Nishikanta Majumdar

My dear son,

I have received your letter. You have mentioned that the condition of your mind is bad. The mind is like a mad elephant. Control the restless mind by discrimination. Pray to the Master. Everyone experiences such condition of the mind.

Please accept my blessings,
Your Mother[13]

Written on 2 October 1916 in Calcutta to Kamala Bala Devi in Sadarpur

My dear daughter,

I learned from your letter everything about your present condition. When one assumes a human body, one has to undergo various kinds of sufferings. What can you do? This is the natural law of this world. The more a person lifts his mind from these worldly affairs and puts it in God, the more he attains peace. Real peace dawns when one becomes absorbed in chanting God's name. Surrender to the Master and tell him all of your difficulties. He will do everything favourable for you.

Please accept my blessings,
Your Mother[14]

Written on 11 November 1916 in Calcutta to a now-unknown recipient

My dear son,

I am pleased to receive your letter. I have no opinion about your investiture of the sacred thread ceremony. It is good. It is a social affair. You decide what is good for you in this respect. If you are initiated into this ritual, you must repeat the Gayatri mantra. And if you think you would not be able to follow it properly, then don't get involved just because you wish to. First repeat your Ishta-mantra and then, if you wish, repeat any other mantra. There is no fixed time for repeating japa, but the morning and evening are the best times. Every day at any time repeat your mantra. It is not good to skip daily sadhana.

Please accept my blessings,
Your Mother[15]

Written on 19 March 1917 in Jayrambati to Manada Sankar Das Gupta

My dear son,

I learned everything about you from your letter and recognized you also. I am greatly concerned about your illness. If you wish you can consult Dr. Durgaprasad Sen and use his medicine. His medicine cured Radhu. Try not to always think about your illness. Reduce your japa and meditation for some days. As you have mentioned the number of japa, please repeat a minimum 108 times and if you can do more, that is well and good. If you have a keen desire to meditate on my form, do it, because there is no difference between me and the Master. The only difference exists between the two forms. The Master dwells inside my body.

I bless you so that you may have unflinching devotion and faith at the feet of the Master,

Your Mother[16]

Written on 17 August 1917 in Jayrambati to Indradayal Bhattacharya (later Swami Premeshananda)

My dear son,

I learned everything from your letter. The Master will bestow grace on you. I bless you so you may have unwavering devotion to the Master. Those who are coming to you will surely attain the Master's grace. The Master himself said that he who sincerely calls on him even for a day, he will bestow grace on that person.

I bless you with a long life,
Your Mother[17]

Written on 20 May 1918 in Baghbazar to Mrinalini Ghosh, an initiated disciple of the Mother and the wife of Aurobindo Ghosh.

My dear daughter,

I am delighted to receive your letter and the fruit. I was doing well after arriving in Calcutta, but I have had a fever again for the last two days.

Today I am better. I hope I will not get a temperature again. I received the news of Sudhira from Bhubaneswar.

Please accept my blessings,
Your Mother[18]

Written in May 1918 in Calcutta to Kamala Bala Sengupta in Sadarpur
My dear daughter,

I am pleased to receive your letter. Always try to lose yourself in the name of the Master. Make an effort to see him in everything and every being in this world. Try to know that both good and bad are the results of your karma, which come from God. When you understand this, you will attain happiness and peace. I hope you are doing well.

Please accept my blessings,
Your Mother[19]

Written on 31 August 1902 in Jayrambati to Swami Vimalananda, Mayavati (See Chapter 24 for the background to this letter.)
My dear son,

I have received your letter. I cannot express in words how much pain I have been experiencing after the passing away of Vivekananda. He who is our guru [Sri Ramakrishna] is an Advaitin [nondualist]. Since you are all his disciples, you too are Advaitins. I can emphatically say that you are definitely nondualists. Please convey my love and blessings to Mrs. Sevier. I learned from Matilal's letter that Kalikrishna [Virajananda] will go to Mayavati. Be careful, as women live in the monastery. The power of Swamiji is now absent there. We are doing well. Write to me with all news [of Mayavati].

All of you accept my blessings,
Your Mother[20]

Written in April 1909 in Jayrambati to Mahendra Nath Gupta (M.)
My dear son,

I just received your letter. I am concerned about Charu's [M.'s youngest son] illness. I pray to the Master for his quick recovery. I am a little relieved that you have arranged for good treatment for him and sent him to Puri for a change. May the Lord make him well.

Sri Sri Kathamrita [*The Gospel of Sri Ramakrishna*] consists of the words of the Master. You did a great service to humanity by publishing that book. Your plan for the future publication arrangement of the book is very good. May the Master fulfill your noble intention. All are well here.

Please accept my blessings,
Your Mother[21]

Written in Jayrambati to Swami Virajananda, Mayavati [undated]

My dear son,

I received all news from your letter. You have mentioned various kinds of sadhana, which you are doing on your own. If you wholeheartedly call on God, the Master will graciously fulfill the result of your sadhana. I assure you definitely there will be no mistake in it. I am physically well. Please convey my love and blessings to Mrs. Sevier and Christine Greenstidel. I am glad to hear that Mrs. Sevier is transferring the deed of Mayavati Ashrama to the name of the Master.

Please accept my blessings and convey it to others.

Your Mother[22]

Written in Kamarpukur to Mahendra Nath Gupta (M.) [undated]

My dear son,

I received all news from your letter. As you have seen the Master, then what are you afraid of? This world is the playground of lust and gold. As a cow eats grass, extending her neck through a fence, so one should enjoy this world keeping oneself on the safe side. Regarding financial affairs, first protect your family and then give in charity. You are not alone. There are seven people who depend on you. You give in charity according to your means. Don't be worried about these unimportant things. This is the way of the world. One should live in this world holding the essential thing, as one takes the fish and discards the head and tail. I am well.

Your well-wisher,
Your Mother[23]

Written in the Udbodhan Office, Calcutta, to Nishikanta Majumdar [undated]

My dear son,

I learned everything from your letter. Call on the Master. By his grace you will gradually achieve everything. The ancient sages practised austerities over the ages to attain renunciation. Still they faced so many obstacles. Even now the Master's presence is living. So people are quickly imbibing the spirit of renunciation. Can everything be achieved in a moment?

Please accept my blessings,
Your Mother[24]

Written in February [year?] in Jayrambati, recipient now unknown

Dear X,

I learned everything from your letter. I have heard what you have written about meditation. It is not so easy to have meditation. When all the thought waves of the mind stop, then one's mind becomes calm and then one can have meditation. Now repeat the name of God, which you have received during initiation. Gradually your mind will be still and you will get meditation. Have full faith in God. My health is fine.

Please accept my blessings,
Your Mother[25]

Written to Kamala Sengupta [undated]
My dear daughter Kamala,

Keep some religious books with you and read them when you have time and opportunity. Always meditate on the form of God and repeat His name. Whatever divine form you like, meditate on that form. As it is not possible to have holy company always, so study the holy books. Thus the mind becomes pure and perfect. Don't yield to laziness, which ruins both the body and the mind. While working with the hands, repeat God's name mentally. If you don't feel any urge to repeat the mantra, force yourself to practise it. It will definitely purify your mind. Do not worry. Just call on God. He is compassionate and loving. If you call on Him whole-heartedly, His grace will dawn on you. Don't be afraid. Keep on calling on God; you will witness His infinite grace.

Please accept my affectionate blessings,
Your well-wisher Mother[26]

Written on (7 Bhadra) August (year ?) from Calcutta: to a woman now unknown
My dear daughter,

I am sorry to hear the news from your letter. What can you do? This is the way of this world. There is no other escape from suffering other than taking refuge in God. Always call on Him and cry to Him. He will make everything right. It is inevitable to go through pain and suffering in this world, but one can attain peace by becoming absorbed in His name.

Please accept my blessings,
Your Mother[27]

Letters Described in Reminiscences

Brahmachari Gopesh, later Swami Saradeshananda, lived in Jayrambati for some years as an attendant of Holy Mother. He wrote down many letters for Holy Mother. He published summaries of some of these letters in his book *Sri Sri Mayer Smritikatha*:

Swami Brahmananda once wrote to Holy Mother with great humility asking for permission and blessings for the inauguration of the Bhubaneswar Math. Holy Mother expressed her joy and blessed the function, praying that it would be carried out with great success by the Master's grace.

Swami Premananda was critically ill in Deoghar and in a long letter asked for Holy Mother's blessings. The grief-stricken Mother wrote to him expressing her great concern and prayed to the Master for his welfare.

Once Swami Saradananda asked Brahmachari Ganen to send some money to the Mother in Jayrambati, and the brahmachari reported that it had been sent. When Saradananda learned a few days later that the money had not yet been sent, he was extremely disturbed. He sent an urgent letter to the Mother expressing his sorrow and begging for her forgiveness. The Mother wrote him back that the money was not urgently needed, so it was all right. She sent her blessings.

Swami Prajnananda wrote to the Mother from Mayavati describing its panoramic view. He also informed her that tigers come to the ashrama at night. The Mother was alarmed and expressed her concern.

Ramakrishna Basu, Balaram's son, wrote to the Mother about his mother's last illness, passing away, and shrāddha ceremony, and asked for the Mother's blessings. She expressed her sorrow, and blessed him for his welfare.

Holy Mother had some disciples who were in prison because they were connected with the Indian freedom movement. When they wrote to the Mother, the police opened their letters, read them, and then stamped them. When she held those letters, the Mother would look at the police stamp with tearful eyes and sometimes express a word or two against the government's unjust actions.

Devotees wrote to her for advice on their various problems. Mrinalini, Aurobindo Ghosh's wife, wrote a long letter about her relationship with her husband. She was one of Mother's initiated disciples and she sent some money for the Mother's service. Another woman wrote that her husband had come to dislike family life, and he wanted to become a monk. He wanted to send her and the young children to her father's home. When Holy Mother listened to this letter, she became very sad and said: "Look, it is unfair and awful! She is a young woman. Where will she go with these little children and what will she do?" Then she said firmly: "Write to him forbidding him to give up his family now. Let him first raise the children. Let him earn money to take care of their food and shelter. Afterwards let him decide."

Another devotee wrote to the Mother that sometimes he had to lie at his work, so he was considering giving up his job. If he did, though, he would be unable to support his family as he had no other source of income. Perplexed, he sought the Mother's advice. The Mother listened to the letter and then paused for a while. She asked her attendant: "Please write to him and tell him not to resign from his job." The young attendant hesitated to write this, wondering why the Mother should have given such advice when the disciple wanted to follow the path of truth. But the Mother explained: "Today he is afraid to speak a little untruth. But if he left his job, he would fall into pecuniary distress, and he would not be afraid to steal or even rob others." The Mother repeated the last sentence a couple of times. The attendant was amazed to observe the Mother's far-sightedness and her anxiety to protect her disciple.

Another devotee wrote to tell the Mother that there was a shrine in their home with pictures of the Master and the Mother. Every day they would worship, offer food, and do the vesper service. One evening his young daughter put the incense holder under the altar and a cloth hanging down from the altar caught fire and burnt everything, including the pictures of the Master and the Mother. This is very inauspicious. Afraid, he asked the Mother for assurance and blessings. The Mother was dismayed. She said: "This kind of worship and Arati [vespers] are not to be treated lightly. One should do it carefully. This kind of ritual is appropriate for the Math and ashrama." In answer to the letter, the Mother advised him to be careful in the future and bestowed her assurance and blessings upon him.[28]

Swami Arupananda was a disciple and an attendant of the Mother. He read many letters to the Mother and recorded her answers and comments in his reminiscences, which are excerpted here.

Udbodhan: 1 May 1912

In the morning I went upstairs to read letters to Holy Mother. She was seated near the door of her room.

Disciple: "The daughter of a devotee has written from her father-in-law's place that she would like to come here to see you. She has sent you her salutations. She has further requested you to be careful so that her husband's relatives might not know about her writing to you."

Mother: "Then do not write any reply to her. She wants me to conceal it from her relatives. I do not know such a game of hide and seek. At Jayrambati, Yogendra, the mailman, used to write letters for me. Many complained, saying, "Does the mailman see our letters?" They did not like my asking a man in a humble position to write my letters to them. Why not? There is no deceit in me. Anybody who likes may see my letters."

Another devotee inquired as to when Holy Mother would return to Jayrambati. I asked her, "May I tell the devotee that you will return there in autumn at the time of the Jagaddhatri Puja?"

Mother: "Oh, no, no! Can one be sure of it? As to where I shall be, that remains entirely in the hands of God. Today a person is, and tomorrow he is not."

Disciple: "O Mother, why should you talk like that? It is because you are alive that so many people are able to see you and get peace of mind."

Mother: "Yes, that is true….Alas, how fond they are of me. I am also very fond of them. My child, I bless you from my heart that you may live long, attain devotion and enjoy peace."[29]

In the course of a letter written from Jayrambati to a devotee on 18 September 1913, Holy Mother wrote: "There is no happiness whatever in human birth. The world is verily filled with misery. Happiness here is only a name. He on whom the grace of the Master has fallen alone knows him to be God himself. And remember, that is the only happiness."

A monastic disciple went to Rishikesh and visited the Mother at Jayrambati on the way. A few days later, he wrote to the Mother, saying, "Mother, once you said that I would get the vision of the Master in the course of time, but that has not happened as yet." Hearing the contents of the letter, the Mother said to the disciple, "Write to him: 'Sri Ramakrishna has not gone to Rishikesh for your sake or simply because you are there.' This boy has become a monk. What else is he to do but call upon God? The Lord will reveal Himself to the devotee when it is His sweet will."[30]

Date unknown; Udbodhan House

A poor young man came a couple of times to Holy Mother for initiation, but unfortunately it did not work out because the Mother was ill. He wrote: "Please do not refuse me anymore. It is with great difficulty that I go over there. Please let me know whether I will be initiated the next time I come." Listening to the letter, the Mother said: "When I am not well, whoever comes for initiation will have to go back. And when I am well, I may not invite people for initiation. People get a favourable opportunity according to their destiny and past karma. Some come many times but do not see me because either I am ill or for some other reason. It is their bad luck. What can I do? You may say that it means a great deal of expense for him, and everybody does not have money. A guru may turn someone back several times, but a true seeker comes back even begging money from others. The truth is this: He who is really eager to cross this ocean of the world will tear the bonds of maya and none can bind him. Financial difficulties, awaiting a reply, and the fear of going back without initiation — these are mere excuses. Anyway, nowadays I feel better, so please write to him to come."

A woman wrote to the Mother: "Mother, I am young. My father-in-law and mother-in-law will not allow me to go to you. How can I go against their will? It is my desire to receive your blessing." The Mother asked the disciple to write to her: "Child, you need not come here. Call on the Lord who pervades the entire universe. He will shower His blessings upon you."[31]

30 September 1918; Udbodhan House

It was morning. The Mother was cutting fruit for worship. The disciple was reading her a letter written by a devotee. He had written under such strain that it seemed as if he were piqued with God. The Mother dictated the reply: "The Master used to say, 'Sages like Shuka and Vyasa were at best big ants.' God has this infinite creation. If you do not pray to God, what does it matter to Him? There are many, many people who do not even think of God. If you do not call on Him, it is your misfortune. Such is the divine maya that He has thus made people forget Him. He feels, 'They are quite all right. Let them be.'"

Later, the above devotee arrived and the disciple said to the Mother, "Mother, it is this devotee who wrote you that letter." The Mother said: "Is it so? I see he is a good boy." Then she said to the devotee: "You see, it is the nature of water to flow downwards, but the sun's rays lift it up towards the sky; likewise it is the very nature of the mind to go to lower things, to objects of enjoyment, but the grace of God can make the mind go towards higher objects."[32]

Udbodhan Shrine

The Mother was seated on her bedstead. The disciple was reading to her letters from her devotees. Krishnalal Maharaj was also there. The letters contained such statements as "The mind cannot be concentrated," etc. The Mother listened to these and said in a rather animated voice: "The mind will be steadied if one repeats the name of God 15,000 or 20,000 times a day. It is truly so. O Krishnalal, I myself have experienced it. Let them practise it first; if they fail, let them complain. One should practise japa with some devotion, but this is not done. They will not do anything. They will only complain, saying: 'Why do I not succeed?'"[33]

Facsimiles of Holy Mother's Letters

In this section are reproduced two letters that we have reason to believe were written by Holy Mother herself.

The following letter was written to Nishikanta Majumdar of Dhaka. He framed the letter and kept it on his altar. His daughter, Bina Das, said that her parents were the Mother's disciples and they told her that the letter was written by Holy Mother herself.

Sri Sri Hari
6 Agrahayan
Monday

My dear son,
   I have received your letter. Please accept my blessings. Call on the Master; he will do everything for you. All are well here.

Your Mother[34]

The following letter was written to Jatindra Nath Ghosh of Khulna on 11.3.1915. The style and language of the letter appear to be Holy Mother's, but we cannot confirm that she wrote it.

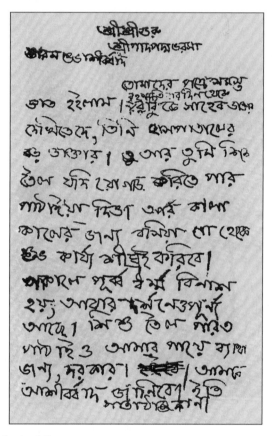

Refuge at the feet of the guru
My dear,

I learned everything from your letter. An English doctor is now treating Radhu since last Thursday. He is the top doctor in the hospital. If you could find some shishu* oil, please send it to me. One should perform good works whenever possible without waiting for an auspicious or inauspicious time. The bad time destroys past samskaras, and the vision of God comes from virtuous deeds. If possible, please send some shishu oil, which I need for my leg pain.

Please accept my blessings.
Your Mother[35]

*Shishu is a small dolphin, and its oil is used externally for rheumatism.

The period of Ramakrishna's ministry was six to seven years, and the number of his disciples, devotees, and admirers might be close to a hundred. On the other hand, Holy Mother's ministry took place over a period of 34 years, and her disciples and devotees numbered in the thousands. Brahmachari Akshaychaitanya recorded in *Sri Sri Mayer Padaprante*, Part 2, the number of the Mother's initiated disciples as 1,176, but that does not seem to be a complete list. It is amazing how the Mother, a village woman without formal education, kept in touch with her many disciples and devotees through correspondence. Those who wrote down the Mother's dictation may not have known elegant language, correct spelling, or how to form nice sentences, but the recipients of those letters felt Holy Mother's heartfelt love, blessings, and divine presence through those words. Most of the letters were short and to the point, and they were written on postcards, not on stationary. Holy Mother acknowledged gifts from her devotees; she inquired about their welfare, and answered their spiritual questions. She showered her infallible blessings upon them. Blessed are those devotees who received letters from Holy Mother, the spiritual companion of an avatar.

Sarada Devi at Jayrambati, 1913.

28
Untold Stories
of Jayrambati

Snehena badhnāsi mano-asmadiyam
doshān asheshān saguni karoshi;
Ahetunā no dayase sadoshān
svānke grihitvā yadidam vicitram.
— *A Hymn by Swami Abhedananda*

Mother, you have bound our hearts to you with affection; you have turned all of our vices into virtues; despite our shortcomings, you have taken us on your lap out of mere compassion. How wonderful is your divine play!

Holy Mother grew up in nineteenth-century Bengal and followed the ancient Indian traditions that closely controlled women's lives. Before marriage, girls freely and fearlessly moved around their parents' homes and the villages of their birth. They talked loudly, wore casual clothing, mixed freely with neighbours, and did not follow formalities or suffer restrictions. But when they married, they moved to their husbands' homes where they were required to speak softly, wear more formal attire, and observe their husbands' family traditions and formalities. They could not travel alone or mix freely with others, and they were required to veil their faces.

In Jayrambati, Holy Mother was known as "Saru," "Sari," or "Sarada," and she was simply a village girl, the daughter of Ramchandra and Shyamasundari. In Kamarpukur, however, she was the wife of Ramakrishna, a shy daughter-in-law in the Chattopadhyay family. In Kamarpukur — and later in Dakshineswar and Calcutta — she wore a long veil and could not speak openly or travel freely. She silently served others and acted as a mother and a guru. In Jayrambati she was a daughter first, and only secondly a mother and guru. Holy Mother made many trips to Jayrambati from Calcutta to enjoy this freedom.

It is said in the scriptures: *Nistraigunye pathi vicharatām ko vidhi ko nishedhah* — That person is free from injunctions and prohibitions who walks on the path of Nirguna Brahman. It is difficult for a free soul to follow the minute details of social customs and rules. Holy Mother always felt a natural attraction towards her humble thatched hut in Jayrambati with its mud walls and floor. There was no running water, modern toilets, or paved roads in her village, but its air was clean and it was surrounded by trees and meadows. It seems that the Mother sometimes got bored and tired of living confined within the four walls of Udbodhan House in Calcutta. One of the main causes of her rheumatism was lack of physical movement, which started in Dakshineswar where she lived like a caged bird. Although Jayrambati was infested with malaria and dysentery and lacked good food, medicine, and the amenities of city life, still, she pined for her native village.

Once the Mother told Swami Arupananda: "You see, here [in Calcutta] I always move carefully and speak cautiously because people get offended easily. I would rather live happily in Jayrambati than in Calcutta. In Jayrambati I can say what is on my mind without reservation, and others reciprocate in the same way. Neither do they mind anything nor do I. There is no misunderstanding. But the people of Calcutta get hurt if words are used a little improperly."[1]

Ashutosh Mitra recorded an interesting incident: "During the worship in Udbodhan, we heard the Mother speaking to the Master, 'I understand that you like the sandesh and rasagollas of Calcutta and don't care for the plain food and the water from the big pond of Jayrambati.' We knew that the Mother was preparing to visit Jayrambati and her resolve would not be altered by anyone's request."[2]

It is said that the Master once told her, "This Jayrambati will ruin your life."[3] And actually the Master's words came true, when towards the end she contracted kala-azar there.

Holy Mother loved to be independent and self-reliant. She could not bear to be a burden to others. Before 1915, when her new residence in Jayrambati was built, she lived with her brothers' families when in Jayrambati. She helped them financially and served them with much physical labour. She was never a burden to them; rather they became a burden to her. In fact, without her help, their households would have been in a pitiable condition. She carried their burden till the end. Once she remarked: "I am paying their debt."

But the Master's disciples adored her and looked after her with great love and respect. They never took advantage of her. The Master told her to look after the people of Calcutta, so she lived in Calcutta and helped them spiritually. The disciples tried their utmost to make her life comfortable wherever she was.

Although Udbodhan House was Holy Mother's home in Calcutta, she considered it to be an ashrama for the monks. She made sure that her relatives and dependants did not inconvenience them.

She may also have felt uncomfortable accepting service from the monks for long periods, and went to Jayrambati with her family and companions from time to time to give them a break.

Swami Parameswarananda described Jayrambati during Holy Mother's time:

> At that time, Jayrambati was also called "Tentulmuri." There were only a few literate persons in Jayrambati and even they lived mostly in Calcutta or somewhere else. The condition of the village was very bad and the roads were horrible. The main road passed through the middle of the village. There was a ditch in the road and during the rainy season, the ditch filled with water and flooded the houses on the southern side of the village. The water level of the Punyapukur and the road was the same. The road was so muddy that sometimes cows got stuck in it and people had to lift them up with bamboo poles.
>
> Only the Banerjee family of the village tried to maintain their prestige and culture to some extent. There was only a little scope to learn reading and writing in the kindergarten school. Only three or four people had some kind of job; the rest lived by farming. There were factions and enmity among the villagers. Under such village circumstances, the Mother lived with such a low profile that no one knew who she was. The villagers called her "Sister," "Aunt," or "Mother," and she loved them equally. Still they disturbed her by demanding money under various pretexts. Even the leaders of the village would ask her for money during the public worship of the village.[4]

Nowadays one can go from Vishnupur to Jayrambati within an hour by car or bus, but it was not easy to travel to Jayrambati during Holy Mother's time. When the train service connected to Vishnupur, Holy Mother would take an overnight train from Calcutta to Vishnupur and then travel the final 28 miles by bullock cart, which took 10 to 12 hours. In the early days she had no devotees in Vishnupur, so she would halt near Lalbandh Lake and her attendants would cook some food for her in a roadside inn.

In 1909 Swami Sadananda, a disciple of Vivekananda, stayed for a couple of months in the house of Sureshwar Sen in Vishnupur. Sureshwar, his brother Boshiswar, and the entire family became ardent followers of

Ramakrishna and Swami Vivekananda. From 1911 onward, Holy Mother usually rested in the Sen family's home during her journey to Jayrambati.

Ramakrishna once told her, "Hello, Vishnupur is a hidden Vrindaban; you must see it." At that time the Mother did not realize that she would have to pass through Vishnupur many times, so she said: "I am a woman. How can I see that place?" The Master replied: "No, my dear, you will see it." One day the Mother visited the Sarvamangala temple on the bank of the Lalbandh and then exclaimed: "Truly, the Master's words have come true today."[5]

It was a tedious journey to cover the final distance from Vishnupur to Jayrambati. Bullock carts were constructed of bamboo strips. The driver spread some hay on the cart to cover the bamboo strips and the passengers spread a blanket or a cotton sheet over the hay. There was a canopy over the cart and the passengers sat or lay down in the shade with their luggage. The bullock cart moved slowly over the undulating, unpaved road with a constant jerking motion.

When Holy Mother travelled, she and her attendants stopped along the way to cook food at roadside inns or drink water from ponds. During these breaks in the journey, Holy Mother rubbed her knees with a little mustard oil to get some relief from rheumatic pain.

Beginning in 1911, the Mother made Koalpara another halting place between Vishnupur and Jayrambati. There, her devotees built Jagadamba Ashrama for her.

Once when Yogin-ma was going to Jayrambati with Saradananda, she remarked: "Look, it is easier to go to Gaya and Varanasi than to come to Jayrambati."

Saradananda gravely replied: "Is Jayrambati a less holy place than Gaya and Varanasi?"[6]

Sarala (later Bharatiprana) recalled a journey with Holy Mother to Jayrambati: "When I went to Jayrambati with the Mother, the bullock cart jolted right and left, and sometimes moved backwards. One day I mentioned to Holy Mother, 'People are going to Varanasi and Vrindaban in such comfort, and how difficult it is to come to your birthplace.' She replied: 'This is the way it goes, my child. A pilgrimage is always full of hardship, but the result is the same.' Only two persons could travel in one bullock cart. I sometimes would get down from the cart and walk three-fourths of the way to Jayrambati. Nowadays how easy it is to go to Jayrambati."[7]

Jayrambati was truly a remote village, and during the rainy season people suffered from malaria and dysentery. Mail was delivered twice a week from the Anur post office. Once the Amodar River was flooded and mail delivery was cut off. Saradananda did not get any news about the Mother for a long time, so he sent a man from Calcutta to Jayrambati. When the man saw that Holy Mother was suffering from dysentery, he wrote a letter to Saradananda and posted it at the Kotalpur post office, which is nine miles away. Saradananda immediately sent Dr. Kanjilal and Sister Sudhira to look after Holy Mother and eventually she got well. We complain about even a little discomfort, whereas the Mother endured many physical problems without disturbing others. She was the embodiment of fortitude.

Swami Saradeshananda left this eyewitness account of her motherly concern:

> The Mother used to live in Jayrambati like a daughter of her father's house. She wore no veil or purdah here and she talked with people without hesitation. For that reason, her children flocked there to meet her. In Udbodhan, the monks and devotees served and looked after her; whereas in Jayrambati, the Mother was busy taking care of the monks and devotees. She collected the groceries, cooked the meals, fed the devotees, cleaned their eating place, and arranged their rest. Those who came from far away, she kept at her place at least for a couple of days. She was always anxious to make them comfortable. She enquired about their home and family, listened to their tales of joy and sorrow, expressed her sympathy and empathy, and gave them spiritual advice. She acted as a mother — a true mother. When the devotees were about to leave, she became sad and tears trickled from her eyes. She continued watching them till they were out of her sight. That picture of the Mother remained engraved forever in the hearts of those devotees.[8]

Holy Mother's Daily Life

It is amazing how the Mother lived harmoniously with her young nieces, sisters-in-law, the women devotees, and also the young monks and male devotees in the small living quarters of Jayrambati. Although all were her children, she kept an eye on the men and women devotees so that they did not mix or talk freely. Her male attendants and devotees stayed in the front cottage and the women in the back cottages. During meals, the Mother would call the men devotees, feed them, and talk to them, but she did not allow them to linger. She reminded them: "Whatever we might be, my children, we have female forms."[9] The Mother made a special effort to instill monastic ideals in the hearts of her young attendants.

One hundred years ago (in 1915) the Mother was still living in her physical body on this earth and lived in Jayrambati and Calcutta. Though we were not fortunate enough to see her divine play, her disciples left their reminiscences for us. We can now visualize her daily routine, how she cooked and cut vegetables, what she ate and what her favourite dishes were, how she talked to and initiated the devotees, how she dealt with her relatives and disciples, how she suffered from malarial fever and rheumatic pain, how she travelled by train and bullock cart, her meditation and ecstasy, and so on.

It is natural for the devotees to know the Mother's daily routine in Jayrambati. Saradeshananda gave this eyewitness account:

> Early in the morning, the Mother would get up, wake the Master, and put his picture on the altar. After bathing, she prepared the things necessary for the Master's worship, cut the fruits, and got the *naivedya* [food offering] ready. She then performed the worship and afterwards distributed the prasad to all members of the household. Afterwards she went to the kitchen to help the cook: she chopped vegetables and even cooked some items. Some women devotees helped her. When the food was ready, she offered it to the Master. As long as she was physically able, she distributed the food to the devotees and removed their leaf plates. Later, sitting on the veranda, she watched her children eat and instructed the servers to give more food to some of them. After lunch she served them betel rolls; she loved to see the disciples chewing betel after a nice meal. Sometimes she shared some of her food with her brother's family. After lunch the Mother cleaned her teeth with tobacco powder and answered the questions of the devotees. Then she would go rest.[10]

Swami Saradeshananda recorded what Holy Mother generally ate in Jayrambati:

> The menu was like the menu of an ordinary middle class family. Breakfast: puffed rice; Lunch: rice, urad dal, poppy-seed curry, a hot vegetable curry, chutney, and sometimes spinach, another vegetable dish, boiled vegetables, a fried dish, occasionally fish for the devotees. Previously the Mother used to cook and also serve. Later, she instructed her attendants about how to set the leaf plates and asanas properly, i.e., maintaining equal distance from one another and an equal water level in all glasses. When the food was ready, she called the monks and devotees to come and eat so that flies would not sit on the food. If anyone was late, she waved the corner of her upper cloth to drive the flies from the food. She joyfully watched her children eat and asked the server to give more to some of them. Supper: chapati [a type of flatbread], a vegetable curry, milk and molasses. The Mother used to make the dough and flatten the chapatis. When the food was ready, she offered it to the Master and then covered the dishes so that

they would remain warm. Some evenings Aunt Bhanu would massage the Mother's feet. If she was tired, she would lie down on the veranda and ask her attendant to rub garlic oil on her legs. When the disciples had finished their japa and meditation, the Mother called them for supper. The Mother protected the food with a stick so that Radhu's cat would not eat it. There was an oil lamp flickering on the dark veranda and the Mother sat with her back against the wall and her legs extended. No one knew where her mind roamed in that silence.[11]

The Mother was very concerned that the monks and devotees in Jayrambati not suffer from lack of food. The Mother first fed the men devotees in Jayrambati and then she ate with the women. If any monk went to run errands, she did not eat until he returned, even if it was late.

Some devotees sent money regularly to Holy Mother for her living expenses. Saradeshananda described Holy Mother's spirit of detachment:

> The mailman came with a money order. The Mother affixed her left thumb impression on the receipt and someone attested it: 'Left thumb impression of Sri Sarada Devi.' Then the mailman counted the money and handed it over to the Mother, who put it in a box in her room. She then gave some refreshments to the mailman, talked to him a little, and bade him good-bye. No one knew who had sent the money or how much. Later, at her leisure, she gave the money order coupon to her attendant and asked him to write a letter of acknowledgement with her blessings to the sender. If the attendant received the money order, she asked him not to count the money, saying: "My child, the tinkling sound of the coins generates greed in the minds of human beings. And the money has such power that even a wooden doll opens its mouth to take it."[12]

Swami Gauriswarananda recalled:

> The Mother managed her living expenses, but she never had much money on hand. She opened her box and gave me money for marketing. She would give me almost all of the money in the box and say: "Buy one rupee's worth of oil, one rupee's worth of flour, two rupees' worth of ghee, and so on." I said: "Not that way, Mother. Let me write down what you tell me. Then I shall buy the things by weight: five seers of one item, two-and-a-half seers of the other, and so forth. It will be more economical." Delighted, the Mother said: "My son, buy things according to your calculation. I don't know how to calculate money that way." At times when all the money was spent, she would say: "Well, Indu will be sending money in a few days; then we can buy things in large quantities." Indu, a Ranchi devotee, used to remit 15 rupees on the first or second day of every month.[13]

The devotees often presented Holy Mother with delicious fruit, fancy sweets, and fine clothes; she accepted them with joy and blessed them. But this was only for the satisfaction of the devotees; she had no attraction at all for those things. The Mother wore saris that were suitable for middle-class women, and she used them till they were torn. Sometimes she wore patched saris and distributed the new ones that she received to the poor and the needy.

Surendranath Gupta, a disciple from Assam, wanted to buy a fancy silk sari for the Mother. When she heard that it cost 80 rupees, she flatly refused to accept it. Realizing her devotee's eagerness, she asked her attendant to write to him: "If you want to spend that money, you should instead buy a piece of land that will serve the monks and the devotees."[14]

Holy Mother's New Residence

In the early days of Holy Mother's ministry she lived in a thatched hut that was located on her brother Prasanna's portion of the family land. Although Holy Mother bore almost all of the household expenses, she lived with her brother's family with great hesitation. One day she lamented: "I feel that I should take my children and live under a tree."[15]

As the number of her disciples increased, it became difficult to accommodate them. Moreover, Holy Mother needed freedom to conduct her spiritual ministry. Eventually Prasanna's wife remarked: "Why is there so much tumult in my house? I don't like it."

Prasanna said to Holy Mother, "Sister, it will not be possible for you to continue staying in this cottage. You had better arrange another dwelling place."[16] As soon as Swami Saradananda and M. heard about this, they quickly had the Mother's new home built.

In 1915 a piece of land was purchased from her brothers at the southwest corner of Punyapukur. Keshavananda drew up plans for a residence composed of four mud cottages with thatched roofs. Construction of Holy Mother's new residence began in April 1915 and was completed in May 1916. The cost of construction was 1,900 rupees. M. donated 500 rupees and Saradananda collected the remaining funds. Arupananda and the monks of Koalpara supervised the construction.

After the residence was built, Holy Mother and Radhu lived in the main cottage, which was also used as the shrine. In this cottage, Holy Mother initiated many devotees and gave monastic vows to brahmacharis and sannyasins as well. The hut adjacent to Holy Mother's cottage was her kitchen and the opposite cottage was for her niece Nalini. Another cottage, facing west, was for the monks and male devotees.

During the rainy season, the courtyard in front of Holy Mother's cottage

Above: Opening ceremony for Sarada Devi's new cottage (below) in Jayrambati, 15 May 1916. Dimensions: 18' 11" x 8' 5"; height 8'; veranda 6' wide; one door and two windows; earthen floor, mud walls and a thatched roof.

became so muddy that it was hard for her to walk on it. Narayan Iyenger (later Swami Srivasananda) offered money to cover it with concrete, but Holy Mother objected, saying: "My son, it is not necessary to put concrete on the courtyard. The people will comment that we have a lot of money."[17] After the Mother left Jayrambati the last time for Calcutta, the floor of her cottage was paved with cement, but she never again lived there.[18]

The inauguration ceremony for the house was held on 15 May 1916. The monks of Koalpara Ashrama bought the necessary supplies according to Holy Mother's instructions. But then a couple of wealthy householder devotees took control of the ceremony and began ordering the monks around. The monks were hurt and they did not come to Jayrambati on the inauguration day. Holy Mother inquired about them repeatedly, but no one knew why they did not attend.

When Brahmacharis Rajen and Barada later came with groceries for the Mother, Nalini asked them why they had not attended the inauguration. They tried to avoid answering directly, but Nalini surmised the reason and told Holy Mother. Holy Mother also learned that those wealthy devotees were planning to take her to Calcutta via Garbeta instead of Koalpara, which was her usual route. She firmly said: "These are all self-proclaimed leaders! The boys of Koalpara maintain the centre for me and the devotees. They do everything for me. Day and night they do whatever I need. Sometimes they even carry devotees' luggage if no porter is available. Without any authority, these devotees have hurt my boys' feelings with uncalled-for remarks. X. is planning my Calcutta trip via Garbeta, crossing rivers and canals. Who has authorized him to do so? The Koalpara boys are my right and left hands. Whatever others may suggest, I shall always travel via Koalpara."[19] Holy Mother's reassurance uplifted the monks' spirits.

Saradananda could not attend the inauguration ceremony of the new residence because he had to go to Varanasi and Vrindaban on urgent work for the Ramakrishna Mission. On 25 May he returned to Calcutta. Swami Arupananda wrote to Saradananda describing the inauguration and informing him of Holy Mother's wish that he come to Jayrambati to see the new residence. On 2 July 1916 he went to Jayrambati and was pleased to see the Mother in her new home. The Mother now decided that her new residence, as well as Punyapukur and some other land, should be registered as an endowment for the Goddess Jagaddhatri. The trustees of Belur Math would be responsible for its maintenance.

On 6 July 1916 Saradananda left for Koalpara, accompanying Holy Mother and her companions on the way to Calcutta. On the evening of

7 July a subregister from Kotalpur came to Koalpara to register the trust
deed. Swami Ishanananda wrote:

> We were amazed, observing Swami Saradananda's love, sincerity, and
> thoughtfulness in performing the Mother's work. It was arranged that the
> subregister would come by palanquin to Koalpara in the evening for the
> registration. At the courtyard of the Mother's cottage, the swami spread
> a carpet, put a bolster on it, and had at hand a pack of cigarettes, a betel
> roll, and a hand fan. After a while, the subregister arrived and alighted
> from the palanquin. He was a Muslim, 27 or 28 years old. The swami was
> quite heavy and over 50. But the swami got up and received him cordially.
> When the subregister sat, the swami began to fan him. We took the fan
> from him and he offered a cigarette, tea, and betel roll. The subregister
> did not know the swami, but felt a little embarrassed seeing our respect
> for him. The subregister asked the Mother a few questions and she softly
> answered sitting on the veranda. She then put her thumb impression on
> the document and it was registered. The swami served refreshments to
> the subregister and walked him to his palanquin. When he left, the swami
> felt a great relief that an important task had been accomplished. It was a
> great lesson for us seeing the swami's humility in performing the Mother's
> work. The next day the Mother and her companions left for Calcutta and
> arrived at Udbodhan on 8 July 1916.[20]

Holy Mother had strong common sense and kept a keen eye on every
detail. When the new residence was completed, the Union Board imposed
a tax of four rupees and collected the money from Jnanananda. Holy
Mother was then in Calcutta. The next year when the village watchman
came to collect the tax, the Mother said to him: "Why have you imposed
such a large tax on this property? Try to reduce it. I shall be able to pay
this tax, but during my absence how will these monks pay the tax? They
maintain themselves by begging for food and clothing."[21]

The Mother did not stop there. On 19 March 1918 she wrote a letter to
Prabodh Chandra Chattopadhyay, one of her disciples and the headmaster of Badanganj High School.

> My son,
> Perhaps you know that the Union Board has imposed a four-rupee tax
> on this property for the village watchman. It seems too high, so yesterday
> I sent a letter to Shambhu Babu [Shambhu Roy, president of the Union
> Board] through Brahmachari Gopesh. I mentioned in that letter that this
> property had been dedicated to God and I am not the owner. Moreover,
> I am not a permanent resident of Jayrambati and this property does not
> have any income. The monks and brahmacharins who live here as care-
> takers are not supported by this property. Under such circumstances it

is not possible to pay this permanent heavy tax. I somehow manage my household expenses by the voluntary contributions of the devotees. There is no income from this property.

In reply to this letter, Shambhu Babu said that he had already told you to write a letter to the district magistrate. I don't know whether you have done anything in this respect. I hope you will take action as soon as you receive this letter. Please do what is right. Shambhu Babu further said that it should be mentioned in the application that this is a "Religious Institution." It has no income. It is maintained with the help of the generous public.*

With blessings,
Your Mother[22]

Holy Mother can no longer be seen with our physical eyes, as she is now residing on a spiritual plane. But we can visualize her divine play in this world by meditating on the reminiscences of her given by those blessed ones who lived with her. Different attendants of the Mother recorded their accounts of her life from their various perspectives, and these accounts help us to visualize how she lived, worked, and interacted with people. In fact, all these details help to make a biography living, and this is why we are including in this book all the relevant reminiscences of her.

Swami Ishanananda described the Mother's daily routine in her new residence in detail:

As per her usual habit, the Mother would get up at three o'clock in the morning. After washing, she would pick up the Master's picture from the bed and wipe his face with a piece of wet cloth. Some days she would hum a couple of lines from a Hindi bhajan: "In the morning Mother Kaushalya awoke Ramachandra and asked her son to do good to men, sages, and gods." She then began to practise japa sitting on her bed, and later she would lie down. If Radhu's child cried in the other room, she brought the baby in with her. When the Mother got up and opened her door, we would get up and practise japa sitting on her floor. Some days she would ask us to repeat a certain mantra of a certain deity. After sunrise the Mother would drink ayurvedic water made from soaked coriander, jute leaf, and gram. She then began to cut vegetables, and others joined her. At that time newcomers would come to bow down to her and she talked to them. The Mother would feed the gram that had been soaked overnight to her pet parrot named Gangaram. As her body began to be feeble due to old age, she took makaradhwaj** with pomegranate juice in the morning. The Mother

---

* The Mother paid the tax for two years, and then from the third year on, the property was exempted.
** An ayurvedic medicine

would send us to collect more vegetables and other groceries from the markets of neighbouring villages, as there was no market in Jayrambati.

The Mother dictated the grocery list and then brought the money from a box in her room. Whenever she received any money, she touched it to her forehead and put it in the box and when taking it out she again did the same. She gave me a maximum of 50 rupees at a time for shopping. The money was arranged in piles of 10 rupees [not paper money]. We generally found in her box 15 to 20 rupees, one thermometer, a small pair of scissors, a bundle of thread, and some small cloth bundles. These small cloth bundles contained different items, such as a little clay from the Simhavahini temple, a little opium that the doctor prescribed for her stomach, dry rice prasad of Lord Jagannath, six or seven strands of the Master's hair, and a small piece of the asana on which the Master sat during meals in Dakshineswar. When she was cleaning the box while leaving Jayrambati for the last time, she gave the last bundle to me and said, "You keep this one with you."

At nine o'clock in the morning, the Mother would bathe in the pond, or sponge herself with warm water if she was not well. Afterwards she worshipped the Master and Gopala. Later, she gave initiation if there were any candidates. She then distributed the prasad to the devotees on *sal* leaves. If there were not sufficient fruits and sweets, she would make some halwa [farina pudding] and offer it to the Master. The Mother ate a little puffed rice and drank a glass of rock candy syrup that had been offered to the Master. She then cut vegetables and supervised the cooking in the kitchen. She prepared betel rolls with thin slices of betel nut, fennel seed, and other spices, as she had been taught by the Master. During this time her attendant read the devotees' letters to her and she dictated the answers.

About one o'clock in the afternoon, the cook would inform the Mother that the food was ready for offering. After washing her hands and feet, she carried the *Panchapatra* [puja utensil] and addressed the Master: "Food is ready. Please come and eat." It seemed the Master was going with her to the kitchen. Some rice and vegetables were placed on a stone plate and the Mother offered them to the Master. She then arranged food for Radhu and her son and asked the monks and devotees to sit on the veranda for their meal. She sat on one side of the veranda, extending her legs, and watched them eat. Occasionally she cooked one or two dishes and served them, before she ate. The Mother was bilious and suffered from a burning sensation in her body, so she preferred food that had a cooling effect on her system, such as *urad dal* [lentil], poppy seed curry, and so on. For dessert she would mix rice with milk and eat some; the leftovers were distributed among the disciples as prasad. After lunch, the Mother cleaned her teeth with tobacco powder.* She then took some rest and some days visited her brothers' households to inquire about them.

---

*She actually cleaned her teeth after each meal.

At four o'clock in the afternoon, the Mother went to the pond and washed her sari. She then sat to cut vegetables for dinner and told her attendants the menu and how many people they would feed that night. At that time Aunt Bhanu and other village women would come to her and she would inquire about their welfare. She always gave them some sweets and fruits. The villagers sincerely loved and respected her and called her "Aunt" or "Mother." In that gathering the Mother talked about the Master and shared her life stories, and the village women also told many funny stories.

In the evening, the Mother performed arati, waving an oil lamp and burning camphor. She then sat for meditation on her bed. Towards the end, her body was weak, so she would lie down after a while but she continued doing japa. Some evenings I would read *Sri Ramakrishna Kathamrita,* part three, to the Mother. She was absorbed listening to the descriptions of Dakshineswar and the Master's talks and teachings. Sometimes she said: "Aha! It seems so real, as if the Master were talking right now in front of us. I am getting goose bumps." At that time the out-of-town devotees sat near her and talked to her openheartedly. They said: "When the Mother is at Calcutta we do not get the opportunity to talk to her so freely and intimately. For that reason the Mother comes here for us, bearing so much hardship."

After arati her attendants made chapatis with five pounds of flour. The cook only prepared rice and dal. At night the Mother ate four luchis [fried bread], one vegetable dish, and drank milk. The attendants prepared sago or barley for those who had a fever. After finishing the evening work, Mandakini, the Mother's woman attendant, rubbed medicated oil on the Mother's feet. The Mother did not feel any shyness in front of Hari and me, as we were very close to her. We also rubbed her feet and back with that oil. Her body was very tender. She would get pain if we pressed too hard, so we were extremely careful in serving the Mother. She used to say: "Barada and Hari are not my sons; they are my two daughters. They are my right hand and left hand in Jayrambati. It is hard for me to function here without them."

Some days the Mother asked me to sing some devotional songs. On days when Surabala and Radhu were out of control, the Mother requested me to sing this song: "Mother, this world is your crazy market place. Whom should I praise?" As she listened to this song, the Mother laughed with joy and then lamented, "My son, my household is indeed a crazy market place." If I were out doing some errands in the morning, I read her mail in the evening, and she dictated her answers.

One day I went on reading letters, but she just listened and kept quiet. Finally she said: "He who has money should give to charity for a noble cause. And he who has nothing should repeat the mantra." She continued:

"It means very little to God if one thinks, 'I have repeated the mantra so many times and practised so much austerity.' If Mahamaya, out of compassion, unlocks the path, then one can realize God. O human beings, take refuge in the Divine Mother, then only will She graciously open the path."

At nine o'clock the Mother offered supper to the Master. If the Mother was ill, or for some other reason could not offer the food, I or Hari, and sometimes Nalini, would offer the food to the Master. The Mother taught us a special mantra for offering food to the Master. Then the Mother took her supper — a couple of luchis with milk — in her room. After arranging for Radhu and the others to go to bed, she went to bed at eleven o'clock at night.[23]

Police Surveillance

Police officers would come to Holy Mother's home in Jayrambati and also Koalpara Ashrama every evening and write down visitors' names and addresses and the purpose of their visits. Even Swami Saradananda had to furnish all this information to the police, which bothered Holy Mother.

Brahmachari Jnan had lived in Jayrambati for a few years and then contracted malaria. He went to Katihar for a change and lived with Dr. Aghorenath Ghosh, a disciple of the Mother. Dr. Ghosh's two younger brothers belonged to the Revolutionary Party and had run away. Thinking that Jnan was associated with them, the police wanted to arrest Brahmachari Jnan and keep him in detention. Dr. Ghosh was a high-ranking government officer and stood security for him. The police allowed Jnan to be free on the condition that whenever required, the doctor would present him before the police.

After some months, Jnan decided to return to Jayrambati and left Katihar. Holy Mother was then staying at Jagadamba Ashrama. She was happy to see Jnan, who had fully recovered from his ill health. But she knew that he was still under police surveillance, and that the doctor was standing security for him for a heavy amount. The ashrama members were against Jnan's staying there. They advised him to return to Katihar until the police freed him unconditionally. They feared that his stay would increase police surveillance on Jayrambati and the Koalpara ashramas.

However, Holy Mother said: "Whatever is to happen will happen by the will of the Master. My son will stay with me." Finally the monks and Swami Saradananda, who happened to be at Koalpara, convinced Jnan that for the good of Dr. Ghosh and the ashrama, he should return to Katihar. Jnan went to the Mother and explained the whole situation. He told her that Swami Saradananda approved the plan. When Jnan left, the

Mother felt so pained that she cried profusely and it took several days for her to calm herself.[24]

A few months after this incident, a police officer from the Shiromani-pur police station came to Jayrambati to inquire about Brahmachari Jnan. Holy Mother had gotten the news from the village watchman the day before, but she was not worried at all. The next morning Manindra Babu, a lawyer from Arambagh who was also a disciple of Holy Mother, came to Jayrambati. In the afternoon the police officer came. Manindra received him cordially, talked to him honestly, and supplied the information that he requested. Meanwhile Holy Mother served *halwa* and other sweets as refreshments, even including a betel roll. The police officer respectfully took the dust of the Mother's feet and left.[25]

This kind of police harassment and surveillance created an uncertain and fearful atmosphere in Koalpara and Jayrambati. The Mother was unhappy seeing her innocent children being ill-treated by the police.

Swami Nikhilananda described two incidents of police harassment:

A disciple of Holy Mother, a quiet and spiritually minded young man, was harassed for nothing by the police. One day as he came out of the shrine room after meditation, the police arrested him and took him away without giving him time to take refreshment. Holy Mother was very sad to hear about it and said: "This was certainly an unjust action on the part of the English. He is one of my good children, and for nothing he is being harassed. He could not take even a little prasad. Will the British rule last long?"

Another disciple of the Mother was interned with the present writer [Swami Nikhilananda]. Unable to bear the rigours of internment, he committed suicide. After the writer's release he told the Mother about the young man's death. With a sigh she said: "O God, how long will You put up with the iniquity of this government?"[26]

Bibhuti Ghosh, an ardent disciple of the Mother, knew Bholanath Bandyopadhyay, the deputy superintendent of police in Bankura. Bibhuti was a school teacher in Bankura and he visited Holy Mother every weekend. He arranged for Bholanath to visit Holy Mother's ashrama in Jayrambati. The officer first came to the Shiromanipur police station and then by palanquin to Jayrambati. Many monks and devotees received him cordially and showed him around. He saluted the Mother with folded hands, and the Mother blessed him, saying, "May you attain devotion." Holy Mother arranged for refreshments of jilipis and sweets on her veranda. While eating, Bholanath asked the Mother with a smile, "Are you afraid, Mother, of this police inquiry?"

"Why would she be afraid?" Bibhuti said. "There is nothing to fear."
Holy Mother replied: "Yes, my son, I am scared."

Bholanath said: "Mother, what should you be afraid of? Can you tell me that any innocent devotee has been harassed? Police try to locate political suspects. Don't worry anymore. I shall arrange everything before I leave the police station."

While Bholanath was leaving, the Mother again blessed him, saying: "My son, may you live long." Afterwards there were no more police inquiries or harassment of the Mother's ashramas in Jayrambati and Koalpara.[27]

The Mother's Love for the Villagers

Most people first think of their own self-interests and then think of others; whereas divine beings always look after others, forgetting themselves. Divine beings are the embodiments of unselfishness, love, and compassion. They can enter the hearts of sufferers, relieve them from their pain and agony, and show them the way to overcome their problems.

Nivarani Dasi, or Nibu-jhi, was 24 years old when her husband, a roofer, fell from a roof. His back was broken, and he became bedridden. He asked Nibu-jhi to go to Holy Mother for help. The Mother consoled her, saying: "My child, danger comes to everyone in this world, but one should not be disheartened. Your husband is now not well, so you must find a job and take care of him till he recovers from his injury. Everything will be all right when his injury is healed. Pray to the Master wholeheartedly. Everything will be fine." Holy Mother gave Nibu-jhi some puffed rice and molasses and said: "Take this food and share it with your husband." She also gave Nibu-jhi a new sari because hers was torn.

One day, sometime later, Holy Mother said to her: "Nibu, Shashi has left his job. Will you work for me?" Nibu-jhi faithfully served the Mother as a maidservant from that time on.

Nibu recalled:

I lived with the Mother and worked with her, but unfortunately I did not recognize her divinity. We knew her as our "Bamundidi." She worked in the cowshed, cleaned the cow dung, and gave fodder to the cows; she operated the husking machine and made rice; she mopped the mud floor with cow dung and mud paste; she cooked and distributed food to the devotees. Her disciples and devotees called her "Mother," so I began to call her that also.

Gradually her household began to grow and she moved from her brother's house to her new house. I cut vegetables with the Mother and removed the seeds from tamarinds. Even in her old age, she was never idle. She never asked anyone to do a certain job twice. If that person did not do the work the first time, she herself would do it. Her brothers were not practical and they quarrelled among themselves, but they were afraid of their sister.

Once an earthen tub cracked that was used for the cows' drinking water. When the cowherd told us of this, the Mother asked me, "Nibu, bring the tub to me and I shall repair it."

I asked, "Is that a woman's job?"

Mother: "Do what I say. Bring the tub and collect some mud from the pond."

I brought some clay from the edge of the pond and told her that the tub was irreparable and should be thrown away. The Mother did not listen to me. She began to repair it and asked me to bring some more clay. Finally, she succeeded. I exclaimed: "My goodness! Mother, you have fixed it so quickly! How did you do it?"

She answered with a smile: "You said that it could not be done. Now see! It is repaired." I was dumbfounded.

So many devotees visited the Mother every day. Some days she would tell me: "Nibu, wash my feet; they are burning. People commit sins and dump them on me. I am dying from this pain." Her rheumatism was aggravated. I brought *akanda* leaves, heated them by the side of the wooden stove, and pressed them on her knees. This gave her some relief.

The Mother was truly a goddess. I did not recognize her true nature, but I served her and she took my service. Now I think of her and am waiting for her call.[28]

Holy Mother did not like for the monks to offer a higher price for milk because it would drive up the cost and deprive the poor children of the villagers. Once Holy Mother's attendant Jnanananda told the milkman: "I shall pay one rupee for eight seers of milk, but it must be pure." When Mother heard about it, she scolded Jnanananda, saying: "What is this, Jnan? Here one can buy 16 seers of milk with one rupee so even poor people can afford to buy milk. Now you have doubled the price! It is a common practice for the milkmen to mix water with the milk. If you increase the price for milk, they will add more water to get more money."[29]

One of Holy Mother's disciples once said: "When the Mother is not in Jayrambati, the poor people suffer. When the Mother is there, she buys their milk and the vegetables they grow around their thatched huts or on the roofs. They get a little money, which helps them to buy some other things. When the Mother goes to Calcutta, nobody buys their products. For that reason, the Mother returns to Jayrambati again and again."[30]

Although Holy Mother never studied Vedanta philosophy, she knew practical Vedanta very well — she practised and taught it throughout her life. Ramakrishna once said: "One cannot practise religion on an empty stomach." Religion does not function well if the masses are poor. Accordingly, Holy Mother sought to reduce the poverty in her village by creating jobs. She attracted many devotees — doctors, lawyers, teachers, businessmen, and others — to her remote village. She was the mother of a large household.

Once a wealthy devotee arranged to have a well dug on her property so that the villagers could have pure drinking water. She engaged unemployed Muslims to build and repair the cottages at her residence, and she bought their fruit, vegetables, and molasses. She hired palanquin bearers, bullock cart drivers, and horse carriage drivers for herself and her devotees. She hired poor women from the village to carry luggage for devotees, to make puffed rice, and to husk rice for her household. She gave jobs to women as cooks and maidservants, and provided them with room and board. She also bought milk from the local milkmen; sweets from the confectioners; and rice, dal, oil, and spices in large quantities from markets in neighboring villages. During Jagaddhatri Puja and at other festival times, she hired priests, musicians, yatra parties, and snake charmers to entertain the villagers.

Holy's Mother's Anger

As a human, Holy Mother sometimes suffered worry and anxiety. She also lost her temper, but only momentarily. Sarala described the Mother's anger at Radhu: "Once in Jayrambati I saw the Mother terribly angry. She was mad at Radhu, who was then 15 or 16 years old. Radhu was running away and the Mother ran after her to punish her. The Mother's hair was disheveled in her excitement and she threatened Radhu, saying, 'Today I shall beat you vigorously — let me see who can protect you?' I was extremely frightened and was wondering what would happen. Then the Mother caught Radhu and the latter began to laugh. Do you know what the Mother did then? She gently spanked Radhu's back, as if caressing her. I witnessed her terrible anger melt away in the twinkling of an eye. I could not help myself and said to her: 'Well, Mother, what have you done? You were so angry and now this is the outcome!' The Mother was also laughing by then, and said: 'It is enough. If I punished her, could anyone protect her?' Her anger was like a performance."[31]

Holy Mother's Compassion for the Poor

"Next to love, sympathy is the divinest passion of the human heart," wrote Edmund Burke.[32] Only a generous heart suffers for the misfortunes of others, and only a great soul can absorb another's pain and grief.

In his memoirs, Swami Ishanananda told the story of Lakshmi Das, whom Holy Mother called "Majhi Bau" because her husband was a *majhi* (a boatman):

> One day I returned to Jayrambati from Koalpara with an elderly woman porter, who carried a heavy load of groceries. She put down the load from her head and bowed down to the Mother. The Mother asked, "Majhi Bau, why have you not come here for a long time?" The woman replied in a piteous voice: "Mother, I am now in great difficulty. I move around various places to earn my livelihood. That is the reason your devotees do not find me to carry their luggage to your place. A few days back, my younger son passed away."
>
> At this the Mother exclaimed, "What do you say, Majhi Bau?" Immediately the Mother's eyes moistened. Having the Mother's empathy, that woman gave way to her grief and cried out loudly. The Mother sat down near her, pressed her head to a post of the veranda, and began to cry loudly. Hearing her cry, all the men and women of the household rushed there and were dumbfounded seeing that sight. Thus some time passed. When the intensity of their grief subsided a little, the Mother asked Mandakini to bring some coconut oil. When it was brought, she poured it on the woman's head. After having oil rubbed on her head, that woman calmed down as it has a cooling effect. The Mother then gave her puffed rice and molasses as refreshments and bade her farewell with tearful eyes, saying: "Majhi Bau, come again." It was evident how that woman had been consoled by the compassionate conduct of the Mother.[33]

Lakshmi (Majhi Bau) and her husband, Jogindra Das, had their home in Haldi, a village close to Jayrambati where many low-caste people lived. Jogindra was the head of Holy Mother's palanquin bearers and he used a rowboat to catch fish in the Amodar River. One night Jogindra was drunk and beat his wife. The next morning she went to the Mother and complained against her husband. Immediately, the Mother called for Jogindra and asked angrily, "Why did you beat your wife?"

He replied: "Didi [Revered Sister], I have no son. My family line will be extinguished. I beat her out of frustration."

The Mother firmly told him: "Never raise your hand to your wife and never abuse her verbally. You are unhappy because you have no son; she is equally unhappy. What can she do?" Ashamed, Jogindra stood there with his head down.

Then the Mother said: "Go home. I tell you, by the grace of the Master, you will have a son. But never beat your wife."

Through the blessing of Holy Mother, Majhi Bau and her husband,

Jogindra Das, had a son and afterwards another son.* The Mother named him Shantiram, or Shanti, and arranged for his rice-feeding ceremony with the Master's prasad. She also gave the baby two silver bangles. When Shantiram was a little boy, he and his parents would visit Holy Mother, who gave the boy various sweets and puffed rice to eat.

Jayrambati did not have a market, so people would go to Haldi to buy groceries and cloth. It is said that during the early days, when the Calcutta devotees came to Jayrambati, the Mother went to Haldi along with one or two companions in the early hours of the morning to buy groceries. Before the devotees got up, the Mother had returned to her cottage. When Shanti was ten years old, the Mother left Jayrambati for the last time. He recalled: "That picture of the Mother's departure is still vivid to me. She was in my father's palanquin, and Barada Maharaj followed her on foot. She went to Vishnupur via Sihar. The Mother worshipped Shantinath Shiva with sweets and then distributed prasad to us. Then her palanquin left for Koalpara and I returned home. It was the last time I saw the Mother."[34]

One year there was a drought in the Jayrambati area and the rice fields were almost dry. After bathing in the pond, Holy Mother went to the Simhavahini temple, bowed down, and prayed: "Mother, if there is no rain, my children will not have any food. How can I watch my children starve? The children will come to me and say, 'Mother, we have no food to eat.'" Holy Mother returned to her cottage and began to worship the Master. Immediately there was the sound of rumbling in the clouds and then a torrential rain. The farmers' crops were saved.[35]

Holy Mother and the Minstrels

In 1917, Jagaddhatri Puja was held in Holy Mother's new residence at Jayrambati for the first time. The Mother herself prepared everything needed for the Divine Mother's worship. Brahmacharis Rajen and Barada came to Jayrambati from Koalpara the day before the ceremony to help. The morning of Jagaddhatri Puja, Holy Mother went to the altar and prayed to the Divine Mother that the worship would be accomplished without any problems. After the worship, homa fire, food offering, and arati, the Mother again came to bow down to the Divine Mother. She also bowed down to the priest and the priest's prompter. All of the devotees and the villagers had a sumptuous feast of *prasad*, which made the Mother happy.

*Jogindra had six children: First two daughters, then two sons, and then two more daughters.

The next morning Lalu of Satbere Village came to Jayrambati. He was a fisherman and also a folk singer. He bowed down to the Mother and said: "Aunt, I want to sing Baul songs this evening in front of the deity." Holy Mother discouraged him, saying: "No, my child, that is not possible. It will create a lot of problems for me. Where shall I get a canopy and light? I cannot arrange those things." But Lalu was insistent: "Aunt, I shall gather everything. You will not have to worry at all."

Late that afternoon Lalu arrived, carrying a broken tin trunk on his head and a drum on his back. When Holy Mother saw him, she said: "Lalu, people will make fun of you. You should sing a couple of devotional songs to Mother Jagaddhatri with the monks, and then leave after having prasad." Lalu would not listen to her. He set up some bamboo poles in the front courtyard and tied a torn jute cloth to them as a canopy. He hung a kerosene lantern on a post. He then marched through the village beating his drum and announcing the performance. When he returned to the courtyard, he began beating his drum with great enthusiasm in front of the deity. An audience gathered. He opened his trunk, took out his cloak, his anklets, and his *ektara* (a one-stringed instrument). However, when he pulled out his cloak, a few cockroaches fell off. Nalini shouted: "You wretch, do not sing here. You have come here to release your cockroaches! Close your trunk right now and leave."

Lalu paid no heed to Nalini. He shook his cloak a few times and put it on. He then began to play his ektara and sing this song:

> He is really a fool who thinks that the world is real.
> Think — who is your father and uncle in this world?
> You are now smoking tobacco through your hubble-bubble,
> Which is making the bubbling sound.
> When you lose your teeth in old age,
> You will have to eat puffed-rice powder.

Lalu entertained his audience by singing a few more humorous and devotional songs. Holy Mother and the villagers laughed heartily.[36]

Shortly before Durga Puja every year, the minstrels of Bengal, known as Bauls, go from door to door singing Agamani songs. Agamani is a kind of popular devotional song based on the stories of Shiva-Parvati and associated with Durga Puja, which is held in autumn. The songs tell the story of Parvati, also called Uma, who was married to Shiva. When she went to her husband's house after the wedding, her mother, Menaka, was worried about her because Shiva was known as a poor beggar. In autumn Menaka asked her husband to bring Parvati home, but Parvati stayed for only three days. This visit is celebrated as Durga Puja. The songs composed about her return to her parental home are known as Agamani songs.

Once a village minstrel began to sing an Agamani song while sitting near the entrance to the Mother's courtyard. Ashu saw the Mother seated near the door, listening to this song:

> Go, go, O my husband Giri, please bring Gauri [Uma], who is in distress.
> In my dream I heard from the sage Narada that Uma cried, saying, "Ma, Ma."
> Your son-in-law is a bhang-addict* beggar, and my Gauri is a golden daughter.
> Her husband sold all of Uma's beautiful clothes and jewellery and enjoyed bhang.

When the song was over, the Mother remained seated, motionless. The minstrel asked for a few coins, but she could not answer. Ashu gave him four pice and he left. Ten minutes passed; still Holy Mother did not move. Ashu asked her to go to her room, but she did not respond at first. When requested a second time, she said: "Let us go. Now everything is distasteful to me." After a while she got up and sat on the floor in her room. Ashu observed her abstracted mood. Soon she exclaimed: "How many days more to go? A long time has passed." Gradually she became normal and began to rub oil on her body and left for her bath. Probably that song reminded her of her true nature.[37]

Love always Triumphs

Malaria, typhoid, pneumonia, dysentery, and cholera were the main killers in Bengal in the early twentieth century, as they are in many poverty-stricken rural areas today. Mosquitoes, flies, and polluted drinking water are the main carriers of those diseases. Mosquitoes multiply in the stagnant water of village ponds, and the filth washed by rain from the bushes around the ponds pollutes the water. Villagers often bathe and wash their clothes in the same water that they use for cooking and drinking.

In Holy Mother's time, Jayrambati had no doctors, and medicine was not easily available. Holy Mother suffered from malaria many times in Jayrambati, and Saradananda would send doctors and medicine from Calcutta for her treatment. These doctors were often alarmed when they saw the Mother's emaciated body, and they would bring her back to Calcutta to recoup her broken health.

Swami Parameswarananda recalled:

*Bhang is marijuana.

Amodar River, north of Jayrambati, where Sarada Devi bathed.

Men and women bathed in Banerjee's Pond, which is located on the south side of Jayrambati village. The villagers used that water for drinking also. I used to bathe in the Amodar River at the northern part of the village. One could find pure clean water by digging into the sandbank of the river by hand. I decided to collect that water for the Mother to drink, so I carried a pitcher with me when I went for bathing. I collected that clean water and put the pitcher near the Master's altar in her room. I said: "Mother, you worship the Master with this water and then use it for drinking."

I thought that the Mother would be pleased with that water, but she scolded me instead. She said: "Who has asked you to bring this water? I have not asked you. I drink the sweet water of Banerjee's Pond. Don't bring it again." Later I noticed that the Mother used the water I had brought for worshipping the Master and she drank it also. The next day I thought: since the Mother was drinking this water, I should bring it again, though she forbade me. This water is undoubtedly purer than the water of Banerjee's Pond. So I took the pitcher to the river as before, collected the water in the same way, and brought it to the Mother. Seeing the water, the Mother angrily said: "Why have you brought this water? Who has asked you to bring it? I forbade you, and still you are bringing the water. I am satisfied with this local water. Will you not obey me? Do not bring water anymore." I kept quiet, but I noticed that she used that water again.

The next day I brought water from the sandbank of the Amodar River and placed the pitcher once more near the altar of the Master. This time the Mother became very much irritated and told me: "I am forbidding you repeatedly and still you are bringing the water! Will you not listen to me?" Observing that the Mother was enjoying the water, I emphatically replied: "Mother, I go to bathe in the river every day and I will bring water for you. If you wish, drink it; otherwise, don't drink it. But I will bring water every day." At this, the compassionate Mother told me in an affectionate voice: "My son, you are bringing that water and I am drinking it with great relish. This water is really good for my health. I forbade you because I did not want you to suffer from carrying this water such a long distance." I deeply felt her motherly affection and compassion.

On one other occasion I disobeyed the Mother. Mandakini, an attendant of the Mother, was suffering from pneumonia with a high temperature, chills, and chest pain. I said, "Mother, let me arrange for Manda's stay in a nearby neighbour's cottage, which will be convenient for looking after her." The Mother replied: "No, she has come to serve me. Where will she go? She will stay in my room." Manda made her bed on the floor between the Master's altar and the Mother's cot. It became inconvenient for the Mother to get up and down from her cot and perform worship to the Master. Moreover, her rice, dal, puffed rice and other groceries were in her room, and she would meet the devotees there also.

I could find no solution, so I went to Koalpara Ashrama and informed Swami Keshavananda of the situation. He agreed to look after the treatment and nursing of the patient. On my way back to Jayrambati I arranged for a palanquin and bearers in Haldi Village and asked them to come to the Mother's house the next morning. All these arrangements were made without consulting the Mother. When Holy Mother saw the palanquin in the morning, she asked me with wonder: "My son, who is going by palanquin?" I replied: "Mother, we have decided to send Manda to Koalpara Ashrama, where she will get treatment. Swami Keshavananda has taken responsibility for her treatment and diet. There will be no difficulty."

Hearing this, the Mother angrily said: "Why have you brought the palanquin without asking me? She has come to serve me. Where will she go? She will stay here. Who has given you permission to bring the palanquin?"

Determined, I said: "Mother, I will not listen to your order. I am sending her to Koalpara."

Holy Mother replied, "Then, you won't obey my order?"

"No, Mother, I won't listen to your order in this respect. Moreover, Radhu's son comes to your room, and this is not good for him."

The Mother did not say anything. I asked Manda to get ready, which offended her immensely. Her desire was to stay with the Mother all the time. Although there was great difficulty with her staying in Jayrambati, she preferred to be near the Mother if she were to die. She was reluctant to move anywhere else and she, too, was mad at me.

When the Mother went to Punyapukur, a pond, I told Manda: "You have come to serve the Mother and now you are thinking only of yourself. Can't you feel the Mother's difficulties?" As soon as the Mother returned, I kept quiet. Again when the Mother went out, I insisted: "If you do not want to give trouble to the Mother, please get in the palanquin. Don't delay anymore. You will have to go to Koalpara." Reluctantly she got up from her bed and got into the palanquin.

As soon as she left, we cleaned the Mother's room and slowly the bad odour of the patient disappeared. Later, the Mother told me: "It is good that she was sent to Koalpara. She had a desire to stay with me. She came to serve me, so I forbade you from sending her against her wishes." After a few days Manda was cured of pneumonia and returned to Jayrambati.

I felt guilty that I had disobeyed the Mother — my guru. Later, I told my story to Swami Saradananda, and he reassured me: "There is no fear. You disobeyed the Mother for her own welfare. Remember, whenever you disobey the Mother, let there be no self-interest in your mind. Let your actions be for her service and convenience."[38]

The Story of Jadu

In 1911 Holy Mother returned from her South Indian pilgrimage and went to Jayrambati for Radhu's wedding. Swami Saradananda, Yogin-ma, Golap-ma, and others were present during the marriage ceremony. The Mother was pleased and relieved when Radhu was married and went with her husband to Tajpur. The evening when the newly married couple left, Swami Saradananda was in a jovial mood. He praised Brahmachari Jadu for his untiring work in arranging Radhu's marriage. Swami Isha-nananda recorded:

> There was a heavy rain and thunderstorm in the evening and Brahma-chari Jadu prepared a smoke for Sharat Maharaj. Imitating the East Bengal accent, the swami humorously said: "Jodo, if you can collect 108 *podyo** now and offer them at the feet of the Mother, then you will receive her unlim-ited grace and blessings in one day and you will achieve the result of your daily worship with *podyo*. You are a *Bangal* [a man of East Bengal known for tenacity] and this will be a test of your devotion and enthusiasm."
>
> Although Jadu had worked hard for Radhu's wedding, disregarding the rain and muddy roads, he had picked some lotuses every day from a pond and offered them at the feet of the Mother. When Sharat Maharaj made that comment, Jadu immediately left in search of more lotuses. It was pitch dark and raining heavily, with lightning and thunder. Concerned, Sharat Maharaj got up and called him: "O Jodo, O Jodo, please come back." But the stubborn Jadu did not pay any heed to that call.
>
> Holy Mother finished her kitchen work and was seated on her cot with her feet dangling. Someone told her about this incident but she did not say anything. After an hour Jadu returned, drenched with rain, with 108 lotuses from a pond one mile away. He offered those lotuses at her feet and bowed down to her. The Mother blessed him by placing both of her hands on his head. Sharat Maharaj remarked: "Well, let His will be done. I hope he does not get sick." I heard that after some time, Jadu contracted malaria, and after suffering for a while, he passed away in full conscious-ness in the hospital of the Ramakrishna Mission at Kankhal.[39]

The Story of Banku

Once a young monk asked Bhai Bhupati, a devotee of Ramakrishna, "Could you tell us what made the Master most happy?"

He replied: "The Master became very happy when a person renounced *kamini-kanchan* [lust and gold]." Similarly, Holy Mother was pleased when she found someone who had renounced hearth and home to become a monastic.

---

*According to the colloquial language of East Bengal, Jadu is pronounced as Jodo, Padma as Podyo. Padma means lotus.

Banku, also called Bankim, was Holy Mother's second cousin, so in Hindu society she was considered his aunt. Banku's mother died when he was young; he was raised by his mother's aunt and grandmother in his native village of Pukure, a couple of miles south of Jayrambati. From his childhood, Banku had a sweet, melodious voice and was drawn to music. When he grew up, he learned to sing the stories of the Ramayana, and he gathered together a professional singing group. Banku charmed his audiences by singing different episodes from the Ramayana. He also performed *lila kirtan* (songs on an avatar's life) and danced with anklets and a *chamara* (a yak-tail fly whisk). Banku became famous in the Jayrambati area. Holy Mother was fond of him and once arranged for him to perform Ramnam kirtan in her residence. One day Banku suddenly disappeared.

One morning Satish Biswas, one of Holy Mother's neighbours, saw Banku at the Amodar River. He had become a monk. Satish brought Banku to his home so that Holy Mother and the villagers could see him. Holy Mother generally did not visit the homes of other villagers. Brahmachari Gopesh (later Swami Saradeshananda) was a friend of Banku, so he accompanied Holy Mother to see him. Many people were there, including Satish's aunt Bhanu. When Bhanu saw Holy Mother, she said to Satish: "O Satish, you have great fortune today that the Mother has come to your house. Please give her a seat and bow down to her." Satish's wife spread a carpet on the mud floor of their veranda and Holy Mother sat there, dangling her legs. She wore a sari with a thin red border and a little veil on her head. Her hands were on her lap and her hair hung over her right shoulder. Her face was serene and joyful. There were sacks of paddy by her side. It was as if Mother Lakshmi were seated at the house of a fortunate householder.

Banku bowed down to Holy Mother with great devotion and stood in front of her. She graciously blessed him and remarked: "Banku has become a monk — very good, very good. He made the right decision." Banku remained silent. He had long hair and he wore a long cloak and wooden sandals. He carried a brass water pot in one hand and a staff in the other. Banku's aunt Bhavini Devi began to cry when she saw him in monastic dress. Some villagers disapproved of Banku becoming a monk because they wanted him to remain a professional singer. However, Holy Mother supported Banku and praised his monastic life. She said: "It is good that Banku has become a monk. What is in this physical body? See how I am suffering from rheumatism. This body is so impermanent that finally it ends up as four pounds of ashes. It is wonderful that Banku has become a monk and gone to the path of God. He has made the right decision." All of the villagers listened quietly to the Mother's remarks.

Holy Mother invited Banku to her home and asked Gopesh to accompany him. After returning to her cottage, Holy Mother served refreshments to Banku and asked him to have lunch with her. After lunch she told Banku that he could stay with her as long as he wanted.

Banku was not well, but he recovered under Holy Mother's care. Although he generally practised silence, from time to time he talked to Holy Mother and Gopesh. In the morning and evening he would sing some Baul songs according to his mood. Gradually he got well and then early one morning he disappeared. No one knew where he went.[40]

Gauri-ma's Surprise Visit

Once Gauri-ma went to see Holy Mother in Jayrambati. She went to Koalpara from Vishnupur and continued to Jayrambati with Brahmachari Barada as a guide. They arrived at the Amodar River in the late afternoon and waited till it was dark before continuing to Holy Mother's cottage. Gauri-ma asked Brahmachari Barada to wait outside. She then stood at the threshold and imitated a beggar's voice, calling out: "Mother, may I have some alms?" Radhu's mother, Surabala, came out and inquired: "Who is there?" Gauri-ma repeated: "Mother, may I have some alms?" Surabala cried out in fear when she saw Gauri-ma in the dark and ran to Holy Mother. Immediately the Mother came out from her room and said in a firm tone: "Who is there?" Gauri-ma replied: "Mother, I am a night-beggar. May I have some alms?" Although it was dark, Holy Mother recognized Gauri-ma's voice and said: "O Gaurdasi, please come in. When did you arrive?"[41] It was a joyful reunion.

Holy Mother and the Village Caste System

Ramakrishna said: "The caste system can be removed by one means only, and that is the love of God. Lovers of God do not belong to any caste. The mind, body, and soul of a man become purified through divine love....A brahmin without this love is no longer a brahmin. And a pariah with the love of God is no longer a pariah. Through bhakti an untouchable becomes pure and elevated."[42] As the Master accepted and instructed all, so did Holy Mother. She accepted all as her own children and did not care for the discrimination of the rigid caste system. She indiscriminately initiated many people, including those of the low castes. Some of her non-brahmin disciples helped with her household work and also helped the cook in the kitchen. But the orthodox, narrow-minded brahmin villagers in Jayrambati and surrounding villages, and even her own brother Kalikumar did not approve of her catholic views.

As a result, the social leaders of the Jayrambati area directly and indirectly put pressure on Holy Mother. They also collected a heavy subscription on the occasion of her Jagaddhatri Puja or any function in her family, which they spent during their public festivals. Holy Mother told them: "If you need any money for the public Shitala worship or Yatra performance, I shall contribute. But why are you unreasonably demanding? I am forbearing your unjust demands, but in the future my children will not tolerate them." The Mother protested to the leaders of the village, but when one of her disciples wanted to take action against them, she said: "They behave like animals. It is a misuse of energy to fight with them. My son, we must hiss but not bite, or they will take advantage of us."[43]

Once during Jagaddhatri Puja, Holy Mother's brother Barada was distributing food to a group of villagers that included brahmin landlords from Jibta village. One of the monks who was not a brahmin by birth put some ashes from the homa fire on Barada's forehead. According to strict caste rules, the food being served was then considered polluted. Immediately the brahmins in the group stood up to leave, with their food unfinished. Their leaving would have been very inauspicious for the puja. Holy Mother rushed to them and humbly requested that they finish their meal. Finally they penalized Holy Mother 25 rupees and sat down again and ate the food.

This news reached Calcutta. A few days later, Lalit Chattopadhyay came to Jayrambati with a gramophone and a pistol. Every day Lalit played gramophone records in Holy Mother's living room to entertain the villagers. The people of Jayrambati had never seen a gramophone and were amazed to hear music coming from a machine. One day the landlords from Jibta who had penalized Holy Mother came to hear the gramophone. Lalit played a couple of records for them, but then he took out his pistol. He said angrily: "Those who have collected a fine from the Mother, please beg forgiveness from her and return the money, or I shall shoot you."

Holy Mother, her sisters-in-law, and some other women were outside the room listening to the gramophone. When Lalit got up with his pistol, the Mother tried to stop him. But the heroic devotee said to her: "Mother, now I am your terrible child. I shall not listen to you. These people think that you are helpless and live in Jayrambati with no one to protect you. They must beg forgiveness from you and from me too." The landlords begged forgiveness from the Mother and returned the money.[44]

Chapter 5 describes the beginning and tradition of the Jagaddhatri Puja in Jayrambati. This annual worship of the Mother of the Universe was closely connected with Holy Mother. Every autumn the monks and devotees participated in this event, and Holy Mother's presence created an ethereal mood. She seldom missed Jagaddhatri Puja in Jayrambati. Holy Mother even prolonged the festival by keeping the image of Goddess Jagaddhatri for three days so that the people of Jayrambati and its adjoining villages could enjoy food, music, and yatra performances longer.

One evening after vespers, the monks and devotees began to sing some devotional songs in Prasanna's parlour, including the following:

Do not worry about the vision of the Mother.
She is the Mother of everyone, not simply of you and me.
She is the Mother of the untouchables as well as brahmins.
If one calls on the Mother once, his life never goes in vain.
To hear the call "Mother, Mother," from the children,
The Divine Mother remains behind the door,
Because if they see Her, they will not call Her anymore.
If the Mother were cruel, She would not give birth to children.
The world would become barren, and people would suffer without food.
When you perspire profusely, who is the air that cools you?

The devotees joyfully clapped their hands and repeated some lines from the song. Holy Mother listened attentively. That night Holy Mother told Brahmachari Barada: "Aha, that song was simply captivating. It is true that devotees have no caste. All children are the same to me. I wish I could feed them from the same plate. But this wretched country has such pride regarding caste. In any case, there is no problem regarding puffed rice [because it is not cooked food]. Tomorrow early in the morning, go to Kamarpukur and buy two seers (four pounds) of jilipis from the shop of Satya Maira."

The next morning at nine o'clock Barada went to Kamarpukur and bought the jilipis. The Mother offered some to the Master, and then arranged them around heaps of puffed rice on a big plate. She sent this to the devotees in Prasanna's parlour. A dozen monks and devotees joyfully began to eat breakfast as Holy Mother stood in another room and watched.[45]

Observing people coming from various places in India to visit Holy Mother, the villagers gradually realized that devotees are in a special class. One day some children were playing in front of her cottage as Holy Mother was seated on the veranda. Seeing some new people, a boy asked, "Who are they?"

The other boy replied, "They are devotees."

"What is their caste?"

The other boy replied wisely, "Don't you know? They are devotees."

As she listened to the boys' conversation, Holy Mother remarked: "Look, anything that comes from the mouths of children becomes true. They understand perfectly that devotees form a separate caste."[46]

Holy Mother's Low-Caste Disciples

One morning a young schoolboy from the Garbeta area came to meet Holy Mother at Jayrambati. He was a Bagdi, which was a low caste. At noon he asked Holy Mother to give him initiation. She listened to his background and was hesitant to initiate him in her village. She said: "Well, you have your family guru; you can have initiation from him. You are young, so don't be in a hurry for initiation. Moreover, at present my health is not good and I have too many problems here. It would be better if you could come to Calcutta for initiation."

The boy replied: "Well, Mother, I understand that you are hesitant to be a Bagdi's mother. But in the Telo-Bhelo meadow, you didn't hesitate to become a Bagdi's daughter."*

Holy Mother smiled but said nothing. Later she said to him: "My child, tomorrow morning take your bath and wait. After my worship, someone will call you."

The next morning after her worship, Holy Mother initiated the boy. At that time, her brother Kalikumar was buying groceries in Haldigram, and Nalini had gone to take her bath. Holy Mother was concerned about how they would react if they came to know about the initiation. However, it went off without any difficulty. Holy Mother was extremely careful to avoid confrontation with her conservative family members.[47]

Bhusan Chandra Puila was another disciple of Holy Mother who belonged to the Bagdi caste. Bhusan recalled his initiation: "In the afternoon, I went to Jayrambati with my uncle Shivadas Dalui and his uncle Jatindra Dalui. I asked for initiation from the Mother, but she declined. I told her, 'Mother, you had a Bagdi father, so why are you hesitant to accept Bagdi children?' At night when she asked us to have prasad, I said, 'If you do not initiate us, we shall not eat.' We did not eat that night, and neither did the Mother. The next morning Uncle Prasanna came to us and said, 'Sister has asked you to have a bath and go to her for initiation.'"[48]

---

*He was referring to the incident when Holy Mother was confronted by the Bagdi robber. She had said to him, "Father, I am your daughter Sarada."

Swami Parameswarananda told this story: "It was long after the incident at Telo-Bhelo. The Mother was then in Jayrambati. A young Bagdi man came and asked the Mother, 'Please initiate me.' I was present. The Mother said, 'I am not well; it is not possible for me to initiate you.' That young man thought that the Mother was reluctant to initiate him because he belonged to the low Bagdi caste. Piqued, he said in a harsh tone: 'I see that you could be a daughter of a Bagdi, but you don't want to be the mother of a Bagdi. I have come from Telo Village. Please know that your robber-father is my father.' When she heard this, the Mother was pleased and initiated him despite her illness."[49]

Holy Mother's Farsightedness

Sudhir Chandra Samui was born in Jayrambati. His father was an illiterate farmer, and his grandmother was one of Holy Mother's maids who mopped the floor and washed the clothes. Holy Mother told her to send her grandson Sudhir to school. He later graduated from the University of Calcutta and became the headmaster of Deopara Champamani High School. He wrote in his memoirs:

> At that time there was no school for the children in Jayrambati village. The Mother arranged to start a primary school for them. The Mother had deep feelings for the poor farmers of the village. Once she asked Bibhuti Ghosh, a disciple of the Mother: "Bibhuti, it would be wonderful if a dam could be built on the Amodar River to divert some water to Aher [a big lake that is now called Mayer Dighi]. That will help the farmers to irrigate their fields during the drought."
>
> I have seen Amzad, a robber of Shiromanipur, who came to see the Mother from time to time. We were afraid of him. I saw the Mother receive him with affection and feed him.
>
> At that time there was no good facility for drinking water in the village. The villagers bathed and washed clothes in the same pond where they collected drinking water. The Mother arranged through Swami Saradananda to dig a well in the village so that the people could have good drinking water.
>
> During Jagaddhatri Puja the Mother would arrange a big festival and feed the villagers. She supervised the whole affair. She had unbounded love and affection for the villagers. My uncle Ramendra Ghosh looked after the Mother's cows. Once he was bitten by a snake. The village doctor and Bibhuti tied his hand so that the poison could not spread, and the doctor cut the spot to take out the poisonous blood. The Mother rushed there and said to them: "What are you doing? Take Ramendra to the temple of Simhavahini, give him the Mother's bathing water to drink, and apply the

mud of the temple on his wound. He will be all right." It was done and Ramendra recuperated within two or three days.

On some auspicious occasions, the Mother and Aunt Bhanu went to the Amodar to bathe. Seeing the farmers working in the fields, the Mother commented: "These people work so hard but do not get square meals every day." The place where the Mother took her bath is now called "Mayer Ghat."[50]

Holy Mother's Illness and Recovery

In the fall of 1917 after Jagaddhatri Puja, Holy Mother suffered from malaria off and on. In January she became bedridden. When this news reached Calcutta, Swami Saradananda left for Jayrambati on 21 January 1918 accompanied by Dr. Satish Chakrabarty, Dr. Kanjilal, Yogin-ma, Golap-ma, and Sarala. When Holy Mother saw so many people arriving at Jayrambati, she said to Brahmachari Barada: "My son, so many of them have come to look after me. Please receive Kedar's permission for you and Rajen to stay here for a few days, buy groceries, and do errands for them."

Dr. Kanjilal gave homeopathic medicine to Holy Mother that slowly cured her fever. The presence of her dearest ones gave her joy and strength. Swami Saradananda was in a great mood. Every day the party would bathe in the Amodar River. On the bank of the river there was an amalaki tree. There Brahmachari Bimal (later Swami Dayananda) would read a couple of verses from the Bhagavad Gita, and Saradananda would explain them, which enthralled the audience. Yogin-ma repeated 10,000 japa every day there without changing her position. Barada brought pure drinking water from the river in a pitcher back to Holy Mother's residence, and the Mother served them prasad. Saradananda, Yogin-ma, and Golap-ma returned to Calcutta, but Holy Mother wanted to stay in Jayrambati, so Brahmachari Bilas and Sarala stayed a few days more.

One day in February 1918, Brahmacharis Rajen and Barada went to Jayrambati with groceries. When they were about to return to Koalpara that evening, they saw the Mother seated on the veranda, stretching her legs. Rajen said to her: "Mother, previously I had deep concentration in japa and meditation, and I experienced great joy. But now I am engaged in various activities, and I am unable to concentrate. I am unable to practise japa and meditation sufficiently."

The Mother replied calmly: "My son, in the beginning if you do not get a little taste in spiritual life, how will you pass the rest of your life? For that reason, the Master gave you a little intoxication, but now he is making you do his work. After you have accomplished the necessary tasks, he will bestow on you higher realizations. You will attain bliss. Don't worry.

Now do his work; you will get spiritual experience later. The Master exists. Don't forget him. Think of him and do your duties."[51]

As the Mother did not go to Calcutta, the monks requested that she visit Koalpara. She agreed, and in the middle of March 1918, she went to Koalpara and stayed a few days in Jagadamba Ashrama. One afternoon Holy Mother suddenly lost outer consciousness, saying, "Master." Kedar's mother said that the Mother was in samadhi. Other women sprinkled water on her head and eyes and fanned her. When the Mother regained her consciousness, Nalini asked, "Aunt, what happened?" The Mother tried to hide it, saying: "It is nothing. Perhaps I became dizzy while trying to thread a needle."

Later Holy Mother described her samadhi to Brahmachari Barada: "After my illness in Jayrambati I went to Koalpara with a weak body. One afternoon I was seated on the veranda. Nalini and others were sewing something nearby. It was very hot and the sun was scorching. I saw the Master enter through the main door, come into the shade of the veranda, and lie down on the cold muddy floor. When I saw that I hurriedly tried to spread the upper part of my sari on the floor, and then I lost outer consciousness. Kedar's mother and others raised an uproar. I told them: 'It was nothing. Perhaps I got dizzy while passing thread through the eye of a needle.'"[52] Holy Mother also told Barada that whenever she was very ill and thought of the Master, he always appeared before her.

Holy Mother was gaining strength day by day in Koalpara, and the monks and devotees were happy to have her with them. One day Prabodh Chattopadhyay of Shyambazar came to visit her. She said to him: "Hello, Prabodh, what is the news of the war [World War I]? What destruction of human lives! Nowadays people have invented so many weapons to destroy people, and also so many machines, telegraphs, aeroplanes, and so on. Look, Rasbihari left Calcutta yesterday and reached here today! We used to go to Dakshineswar on foot and with so much hardship!"

Excited, Prabodh praised Western science and technology. He gave examples of a few scientific inventions. The Mother agreed and then said: "But, my son, despite those amenities, the scarcity of food and clothing has increased. Previously there was not so much suffering for want of food." Prabodh could not argue.[53]

While they were talking a hailstorm started, and the Mother's women companions began collecting hailstones putting burlap sacks on their heads. Overjoyed, they gave some chunks of hail to Holy Mother and she ate them. On that hot day, everyone enjoyed putting pieces of ice in their mouths. The next day the Mother had a fever, perhaps because she had eaten the hailstones. Her temperature rose to 103° and her hands and feet began to burn. Delirious, she was calling "Sharat, Sharat." A letter was sent to Sharat Maharaj in Calcutta describing the Mother's physical condition and remittent fever. A cable also was sent on 10 April 1918.

Saradananda immediately sent Dr. Kanjilal along with Parameswarananda and Bhumananda. Dr. Kanjilal gave medicine to Holy Mother but her fever did not subside. Delirious, the Mother said, "Has Sharat come?" If the attendant asked, "Mother, shall we ask him to come?" She replied, "No, my son, it will be hard on him to come in this hot summer weather." Dr. Kanjilal was alarmed that his homeopathic medicine was not working.

News was again sent to Saradananda. Immediately he left for Jayrambati, bringing his brother Dr. Satish Chakrabarty (an allopathic doctor) and Yogin-ma. They took the night train, and arrived at Koalpara on 17 April 1918 at one-thirty in the afternoon by horse carriage from Vishnupur. Without changing his clothes, Saradananda rushed to Holy Mother's room and saw that she was restless and stretching out her hands for relief. Her temperature was very high and the burning sensation was unbearable. She was not fully conscious. The doctor told Saradananda that when the Mother's temperature increased, she enjoyed touching something cool to get relief from the burning sensation.

Saradananda had a bulky body and had just arrived from a long journey on a hot summer day. His clothes were wet with perspiration, so his body was cool. He sat on the cot near the Mother's head, lifted his shirt and T-shirt, and placed her hands on the lower part of his chest. Holy Mother felt the coolness and opened her eyes. When she saw Sharat, she said: "Ah! My whole body has become cool. Sharat's body is like a cold stone."

Saradananda said: "Mother, we have come. Now you will get well soon."[54]

Holy Mother replied: "Yes, my son, I shall get better soon." The Mother's temperature became normal the next day, and a few days later she began eating solid food. On 21 April Dr. Kanjilal returned to Calcutta.

Day by day the Mother's health was improving and she was gaining strength in Koalpara. Saradananda and others were optimistic. One day after the vesper service, the Koalpara monks asked Saradananda to sing some songs about the Master. He sang a song composed by Girish Ghosh* and another that he had written.** He also taught the local monks the aratrika hymns to the Master according to the tune sung in Belur Math.

* *Dukhini brahmani kole* — Who is lying in the lap of a poor brahmin woman...?
** *Oi stimita chita sindhu* — Who is that divine child arisen from cosmic consciousness...?

During that joyful period, sad news arrived in Koalpara: Swami Prajnananda had passed away. He was a revolutionary who had become a disciple of the Mother and then president of Advaita Ashrama. He was a brilliant thinker and a great writer. Grief-stricken, Saradananda remarked: "Prajnananda was a gentleman." The swami considered a man a "gentleman" who could talk rationally without losing his temper in adverse and hostile situations.[55]

Nalin Bihari Sarkar recorded how Holy Mother sought divine help during her illnesses: "Once the Mother was suffering from terrible malaria at Jayrambati just prior to her last illness. I was massaging her feet. She said to me: 'Look, my son, I have been praying for the last few days, but there has been no response. How much I have wept; still none came to help me. At last the Divine Mother Jagaddhatri came today. But her face resembled my mother's face. Now I shall recover from my illness....My son, this time I have suffered too much. Only after much prayer did I see Jagaddhatri today. I am going to be cured this time also. Don't be afraid, my child. If you call on God earnestly, He will definitely protect you in all situations.'"[56]

Holy Mother Returns to Calcutta

One morning Saradananda bowed down to Holy Mother and said: "Mother, this time we shall not return to Calcutta without you. You will have to come with us." She did not object. She only said: "But, my son, before I go to Calcutta, I shall restart my journey from Jayrambati." On 29 April Saradananda arranged a palanquin for the Mother, and everyone went with her to Jayrambati. The villagers came to see her and said: "Mother, we almost lost hope that we would see you again. We are extremely happy that you are well."

"This time I really suffered from a terrible fever," she replied. "Sharat, Kanjilal, and others came. I got well by the grace of Mother Simhavahini. Sharat is asking me to go to Calcutta. If all of you approve, I shall go and recuperate there." Everyone consented.[57]

When Holy Mother was sick in Koalpara, Radhu left for Tajpur with her husband. Now the Mother sent Brahmachari Barada to Radhu to ask if she wanted to go with her to Calcutta. Radhu came to Jayrambati to meet Holy Mother but declined to go with her to Calcutta. The day before Holy Mother left Jayrambati, Brahmachari Barada caught some fish from the Punyapukur. Saradananda encouraged him to catch more. Then he suggested that Barada show those fish to Holy Mother and invite all members of her family for lunch. Holy Mother's brothers had high regard for Saradananda. Knowing that it was Saradananda's wish, the Mother was very pleased. It was a grand feast. The Mother stood near the door and watched them eat with great joy.

On 5 May 1918 Holy Mother left Jayrambati by palanquin. She stopped in Koalpara that night. Saradananda and others continued to Vishnupur by bullock cart, but a horse carriage was brought from Vishnupur for the Mother because her body was weak. On the sixth morning she left Koalpara and arrived at Sureshwar Sen's house in Vishnupur by eleven o'clock that morning. The next day, on 7 May 1918, Holy Mother and her party left Vishnupur by train and reached Udbodhan at eight o'clock that night.

Sarala recalled details of the trip:

A date was fixed for our return to Calcutta. From Jayrambati the Mother left by palanquin and we went by bullock cart to Koalpara, where we halted a day. Revered Sharat Maharaj hired two horse carriages from Bankura paying 30 rupees, so that the Mother might not suffer during the journey to Vishnupur. A bullock cart was arranged for Nalini, Maku, and Mandakini. A bed was made by placing a box between the seats of the horse carriage and some pillows were put on one side so that the Mother could comfortably recline on it. The Mother commented: "Look, what a beautiful arrangement Sharat has made." On her way the Mother stopped at one place. At that time there was no horse carriage in that area; so hearing the noise, the villagers assembled on both sides of the road. The carriage arrived at Vishnupur at eleven o'clock in the morning. Sureshwar Sen's house was in a lane, decorated with banana trees, mango leaves, and auspicious paintings on the ground. Devotees were assembled on both sides of the lane, as if they were waiting to worship a divine image. The Mother got down from the horse carriage and reached Sureshwar's house by a palanquin. The Mother entered her assigned room, took out the Master's picture from the tin box, worshipped him, and offered *naivedya* on *sal* leaves. She then said: "I am hungry. Please serve me food." The next day we left Vishnupur at eleven o'clock in the morning and reached Howrah after evening. A carriage was waiting and we safely reached Udbodhan House.[58]

29
Udbodhan:
The Mother's House

Prasida mātah vinayena yāce
nityam bhava snehavati suteshu;
Premaika-bindum cira-dagdha-citte
vishinca chittam kuru nah sushāntam.
— *A Hymn by Swami Abhedananda*

Be gracious, O Mother, we humbly beseech you, who are ever affectionate to your children. Please soothe our burning hearts by pouring one drop of your infinite love into them.

Ramakrishna said to Holy Mother: "Look at the people of Calcutta; they are like worms squirming in darkness. You must bring light to them." In 1909, when Udbodhan House was built in North Calcutta, Holy Mother began to fulfill the Master's command in earnest. People came to her for spiritual awakening not only from Calcutta, but also from all over India, and even from Europe and America. In fact, Udbodhan House, which is also called Mayer Bari, or "Mother's House," became an oasis for suffering souls and seekers of God.

Many important events are connected with Udbodhan House. Several distinguished people met Holy Mother in this house. For example, Aurobindo Ghosh, one of the greatest Indian revolutionaries, met the Mother there on a Sunday in 1910 and sought her blessing. His wife, Mrinalini Devi, and his mother also came to Udbodhan House to receive the Mother's blessing. Three young men who were connected with the freedom movement in India, regularly visited the Mother in Calcutta. They later became her disciples and joined the Ramakrishna Order, eventually becoming Swamis Prajnananda, Chinmayananda, and Atmaprakashananda. Also, Sister Nivedita and Sister Christine often visited Holy Mother in Udbodhan House. The Mother initiated innumerable devotees there.

The name of Holy Mother's Calcutta house is very significant. Swami Vivekananda started three journals during his lifetime: *Brahmavadin* (in 1895) in English, *Prabuddha Bharata* (in 1898) in English, and *Udbodhan* (in

Udbodhan House, Sarada Devi's Calcutta residence.

1899) in Bengali. The Bengali word *udbodhan* means "awakening." These journals were meant to disseminate the message of Ramakrishna and the universal teachings of Vedanta. Swamiji wanted to use the Udbodhan magazine to awaken the divine consciousness that lies dormant within human beings. Perhaps Swamiji had an intuition that one day Holy Mother would awaken the spiritual consciousness of many people from Udbodhan House.

Inspired by Swamiji, Swami Trigunatitananda bought a press to publish *Udbodhan*. Besides the journal, the publication office produced Swami Vivekananda's works in English and Bengali. Until 1908 Udbodhan Press did not have a permanent home; it functioned from a devotee's house or in rented office space.

Swami Vivekananda wrote to Swami Shivananda from America in 1894: "We must first build a Math for the Mother....I shall show how to worship the living Durga and then only shall I be worthy of my name. I shall be relieved when you have purchased a plot of land and established there the living Durga, the Mother."[1] The wish of a knower of Brahman is always fulfilled. Saradananda was fortunate to be able to fulfill Swamiji's wish and at the same time to give Udbodhan Press a permanent home.

Udbodhan Press operated out of Girindralal Basak's house at 14 Ramchandra Maitra Lane in North Calcutta for some time, but he died in 1906. On 18 July 1906, Kedar Chandra Das donated a small piece of land on Gopal Neogi Lane in Baghbazar to build a publishing house for Udbodhan Press. There were 2,700 rupees in the publication fund, so it was suggested that a tiled shed be built on the donated land in Baghbazar. Saradananda decided to build a two-storey brick building instead. The first floor would house the Udbodhan publication office and a shrine; the second floor would contain living quarters for Holy Mother and her companions.

Construction began in late 1907, but soon ran into difficulties. The publication fund was enough to pay only for the foundation of the building, so Saradananda borrowed 5,700 rupees from different devotees. But that was still not enough. Some distinguished devotees then came forward to complete the project. Udbodhan Press moved to its new home in November 1908.

Description of the Mother's House

Udbodhan House, or Mayer Bari, is now a branch of Ramakrishna Math. The centre is located at 1 Udbodhan Lane in Baghbazar. Originally there were six rooms on the first floor, three rooms on the second, and one room on the third floor to the right side of the staircase. The main entrance is to the north, and next to the kitchen there is a small back door to the south. A narrow lane (Gopal Chandra Neogi Lane) runs behind the house. At the left side of the entrance, there is a small room, which was occupied by Saradananda. It was his parlour and office, as he was the general secretary of the Ramakrishna Order till 1927. He wrote most of *Sri Sri Ramakrishna Lilaprasanga* (*Sri Ramakrishna and His Divine Play*) in this room from 1909 to 1919, and thus paid off the loan assumed for building Udbodhan House.*

To the right of the entrance, there are two rooms — one for the Udbodhan publication office and the other for workers and the Mother's monastic attendants. At night, the monks slept on the floor of these two rooms. The other three rooms at the back were used as the kitchen, the storeroom, and the men's dining room. Saradananda and the men devotees ate downstairs and the Mother and her women companions ate upstairs in the room adjacent to hers. The small room below the marble staircase was used as a storeroom for the shrine.

On 18 December 1909, a small plot of land adjacent and to the east of the house was purchased for 1,850 rupees. In 1915 an addition was constructed there, with one room on the first floor and another on the second. A narrow wooden staircase attached to the eastern wall connected the two. The men's bathroom was below the staircase, and another bathroom was to the left of the main staircase. The Udbodhan publication office was moved to the lower room of the new section and the upper room became Saradananda's bedroom. The swami stayed in his office from morning till night and went to sleep after supper.

During this period another room was constructed on the third floor, to the north of the staircase. Holy Mother used to sit on the cement roof next to this room and dry her hair in the sun. She was very happy there because she could see the pinnacles of the Kali temple of Dakshineswar. The panoramic view of the Ganges from the roof of Udbodhan House brought back sweet memories of her days with the Master in Dakshineswar.

Ramakrishna's picture had been installed on the marble altar on the east side of the upstairs shrine room** and was worshipped daily. Sister Nivedita made a silk canopy that used to be hung over the altar. Holy

---

*Once Saradananda said: "I took a loan of 11,000 rupees for building the Mother's house. It was a heavy burden on my shoulders. I paid off the debt by selling books. This Udbodhan House was built to keep Mother in Calcutta. She was our focal point, and centred on her I did all my work in a joyful mood." SDA (*see References*), 131
** The dimensions are 24'0" x 9'8".

Mother faced north while worshipping the Master with the altar to her right. She always carried with her the photograph of Ramakrishna that he had once worshipped at Dakshineswar. This photograph was kept on a silver throne when she was in Udbodhan along with the other photograph of the Master on the right side of the altar. Presently, those two pictures of the Master are kept just as they were during the Mother's time.

There was a narrow balcony* to the north of the shrine room. In a room adjacent to the shrine there were two beds: one for Holy Mother and another for her niece Radhu. When she saw this arrangement Holy Mother said: "I can't live separated from the Master; it is not proper."[2] Then both beds were moved to the west side of the shrine room. After the first night, Holy Mother said that two beds made the room too crowded and Radhu could sleep on one side of her bed, which was larger. At her request, the smaller bed was removed from the shrine room. The room adjacent to the shrine became Holy Mother's storeroom. Golap-ma, the Mother's nieces, and other women companions lived in the southern room on the second floor, just to the right of the main staircase and next to the women's bathroom. The women also stayed in rooms on the third floor. Yogin-ma lived in her father's home at 59/1 Baghbazar Street, but came to Udbodhan House every day to help the cook cut vegetables and to serve the Mother.

A Divine Environ

When the construction of Udbodhan House was completed, it was decided that the Mother and her companions — Radhu, Maku, Nalini, Surabala, Golap-ma, Mandakini, and others — would live upstairs and the monks and the publication office would be downstairs. When Radhu was married in 1911, her husband, Manmatha, lived on the third floor of the house from time to time. A couple of monks had concerns about a married couple living together in the same house with monks, especially as Udbodhan House was a branch of the Ramakrishna Math.

Swami Asitananda wrote that Saradananda heard about the controversy but did not say anything. Swami Brahmananda, the president of the Order, was then in South India. When news of the controversy reached him, he wrote: "My goodness! Who is raising questions about the Mother's companions living in Udbodhan? The Mother and all her companions are welcome in Udbodhan House. Wherever the Mother stays, that place is Varanasi, Vrindaban, and the land of liberation. The Mother's

*The dimensions are 24'0" x 2'10".

Sarada Devi worshipping in the Udbodhan shrine, 1909.

In the inset photograph, her right hand is offering the flower and her left hand is ringing the bell.

presence will open the door of liberation there." Swami Brahmananda had such a forceful personality that no monk of the Ramakrishna Order contradicted him.[3]

The Mother's Routine and Method of Worship

Every morning when she was at Udbodhan House, Holy Mother would walk through the back door to the Ganges to bathe with Golap-ma or another female companion. Thus she avoided the gaze of the public. As she got older, she bathed in the Ganges on alternate days only because of her rheumatism. During her early days at Udbodhan House, she bathed at Raj Ghat; later on, she bathed at Durgacharan Mukherjee's ghat.

After bathing, Holy Mother filled a small pitcher with Ganges water, poured some at the bottom of a banyan tree by the side of the road, and bowed down.[4] She always followed local customs. After bathing one day, she gave a banana, a mango, and a pice coin to the priest of the ghat and said: "I am offering this fruit to you, but the fruit of this gift is also yours."[5]

When we read the Bible, we find that the teachings or stories of Jesus were recorded differently by Matthew, Mark, Luke, and John. The wording in each gospel is different from the others; some stories have more detail than others. We observe the same thing in the reminiscences of the Mother's disciples. Her main disciples saw her daily life and her method of worship in Udbodhan House from their own perspectives. Different eyewitness accounts are presented in this chapter so that the reader can see a complete picture of the Mother's divine play.

Ashutosh Mitra described the Mother's daily routine:

> She got up very early in the morning. After bathing and changing clothes, she would repeat her mantra with her rosary. She performed the worship of the Master at eight in the morning and then drank a glass of rock candy syrup. After lunch she took a little rest and at four in the afternoon she changed her clothes and repeated her mantra. She cleaned her teeth with tobacco powder (roasted Matihari tobacco leaf mixed with ashes of hay) four times a day — in the morning, after lunch, in the afternoon, and after supper.[6]

Swami Asitananda recorded Holy Mother's method of worship:

> At the beginning of her worship, the Mother would take a wet towel and rub the Master's picture from the head to the feet gently and carefully, so that the Master might not get any pain. She knew that the Master's body was very soft and that once his finger was cut while breaking a luchi in Dakshineswar. She then decorated the face and body of the Master's

picture with sandal paste using a bel leaf stem. During the worship she took flowers dipped in sandal paste from the flower tray and placed them at the feet of the Master very gently and artistically. She also offered tulsi and bel leaves. She did not spend much time repeating various mantras. It is natural for people to become hungry after bathing, so she then offered food to the Master. At that time she was in an exalted mood and could see that the Master was taking the essence of the food. When asked about her food offering, she said: "I don't know why you do not see it, but I see Gopala, wearing anklets, sitting on the asana and drawing out the essence of the food. A light comes from the Master's eyes and absorbs the inmost substance of the food." When Holy Mother rang the bell during worship, its sound was soft, sweet, and rhythmic, overwhelming the people there. It was a divine sight to see the Mother's worship.[7]

Sarajubala Sen left this eyewitness account of the Mother's food offering:

Golap-ma came to the roof and asked the Mother to make the offering of food in the shrine room. The Mother came down from the roof. I followed her after a while to the shrine room. Like a bashful young bride, she was saying to Sri Ramakrishna in a soft voice, "Come now; your meal is ready." Then she came to the image of Gopala and said, "O my Gopala, come for your meal." I was just behind her. Suddenly she looked at me and said with a smile, "I am inviting them all to their noonday meal." With these words, the Mother entered the room where the food was offered. Her earnestness and devotion made me feel that the deities listened, as it were, to her words and followed her to the offering room. I was pinned to the floor with wonder.[8]

In the middle of 1909 Holy Mother contracted chicken pox and became very weak. She was quarantined in her room. Within a few weeks she recovered and began to worship the Master as usual. Swami Saradananda then engaged Swami Shantananda to assist Holy Mother. Shantananda recalled:

We used to arrange flowers and cut fruit for worship. The Mother always wanted to perform the Master's worship by herself except when she was not well. If we tried to clean the shrine floor, she would forbid us to do so and did it herself. The Mother's method of worship was unique. After sitting on the asana she did *ācamana* [purification by sipping water]. She then gave the Master a bath by dripping a couple of drops of Ganges water on his picture with a copper spoon. She carefully and gently wiped the water off with a soft towel, put a dot mark on his forehead with sandal paste, and slowly placed the picture on the throne. Then she put the images of

Gopala and other deities in a copper basin and gave them a bath together, wiped them dry, and placed them on the altar. She offered worship articles, decorated the Master with flowers and a garland, offered *naivedya* [fruit and sweets], and finally merged into meditation. She remained absorbed in that state for an hour. Someone had to touch her body to awaken her. Thus after finishing worship, she distributed the prasad in leaf bowls to everyone present. She gave more prasad to the servants and the household cook, remarking: "They work hard so they should have more good food." After taking a little prasad, she would go for a bath in the Ganges* with Golap-ma or someone else. She returned within an hour and Golap-ma would carry a pitcher of water for the next day's worship. Afterwards the Mother would sit in the room adjacent to the shrine and prepare betel rolls for offering to the Master.

When the cooked food was ready, the Mother went to the shrine and offered it to the Master. We used to have our prasad in the big room to the right of the staircase, and the Mother and the women devotees had their prasad in the room adjacent to the shrine. After lunch, the Mother took some rest, changed her cloth and washed it. At four o'clock she roused the Master from rest and placed the picture on the altar. The Mother gave darshan on Tuesdays and Saturdays from five to six o'clock. She sat on her cot, dangling her legs, covering herself with a chadar. The devotees would come one after another, bow down to her, and leave. Any person with a question would come at the end, and the Mother talked to that person. It was the Mother's order that every devotee should have some prasad before they left Udbodhan. One day there was a shortage of prasad, so I suggested that it would be enough if they got a small amount each. Immediately the Mother said: "No, no. You go to the market, buy some sweets, and I shall offer them to the Master. If the devotees eat well, they will feel an attraction for the Master, and thus they will develop devotion."[9]

Swami Arupananda wrote a detailed description of Holy Mother's routine:

Holy Mother got up at three o'clock in the morning, looked at the image of the Master, and chanted the names of the deities. Then she bathed and changed her clothes. She took the Master's picture from his shrine bed and put it on the altar, then sat and repeated her mantra. She had a habit of getting up very early in the morning in Dakshineswar, and she followed that habit all through her life. If she was not well, she would get up at the same time, then after bathing she would lie down again. She said: "Wherever I live, I hear the sound of a flute exactly at three o'clock in the morning." She always maintained her routine. Her body did not know what laziness was.

---

* It seems that previously she took her bath in the Ganges very early in the morning. This story comes from later in her life.

Later in the morning the Mother arranged the flower tray and other worship ingredients, cut fruits for the offering, and then sat for worship at eight o'clock. Later the women devotees helped her in the puja arrangements, but she tried to do everything by herself. Towards the end when the Mother lived in Udbodhan, the monks performed the daily worship. When she worshipped, she finished within an hour and then distributed the prasad on *sal* leaves. The Mother did not like it if a monk lingered over the worship and chanted hymns for a long time. Once she remarked: "Let him finish the worship first and offer food to the Master, and then let him chant as long as he likes. What is this? It is too late for people to have breakfast." The Mother always preferred to finish work quickly, at the regular time.

After lunch the Mother would lie down for a little rest. At that time some women devotees would come to see her because they had to return to their homes by four or four-thirty. At that time, while lying down, the Mother would talk to them. Soon she would get up. After three-thirty she would again go for a wash and change her cloth. She would then offer refreshments to the Master and repeat her mantra. Meanwhile other women devotees came and she talked to them and answered their questions. At five-thirty, when the men devotees visited her, she sat on her bed dangling her legs, her head and face covered with a chadar. During summer one of her attendants or a known devotee would stand nearby and fan her. The men devotees would bow down to the Mother one after another, and if someone asked her "How are you?" she answered either by nodding her head or saying a word or two softly. Then the attendant would loudly repeat what the Mother had said. If someone had any specific question, that person would come last. If Holy Mother knew the person, she would speak audibly, but if Holy Mother did not know the person, or if that person was elderly, Holy Mother would speak softly and the attendant would repeat her words aloud.

In the evening after finishing japa, the Mother would lie down on the floor to rest. At that time her attendant Mandakini or some other woman devotee would rub her legs with medicated oil for her rheumatic pain. After offering food to the Master, the Mother would eat a couple of luchis with curry and a bowl of milk as a light supper and go to bed by eleven o'clock.[10]

Shrine Service

Holy Mother was very particular about the Master's service. She saw the Master living in the picture and she wanted the monks and devotees to perform their duties in the shrine perfectly and carefully. One evening she said: "New devotees should be given the privilege of service in the shrine room. Their new zeal makes them serve the Lord carefully. The others are tired of service. Service, in the real sense of the word, is not a joke. One should be extremely careful about making one's service perfectly flawless. But the truth is, God knows our foolishness and therefore He forgives us."

The Mother told a woman devotee standing near her to be careful to pick the right kind of flowers, to make the sandal paste without leaving any hard particles in it, and to not pick worm-eaten bel leaves for worship. She also cautioned her not to touch any part of her body, her sari, or her hair while working in the shrine. "One must work in the shrine room with great attention," she said. "Offerings and the rest should be made at the proper time."[11]

Happiness and Misery

On 25 September 1910 Arupananda asked Holy Mother an important question: "Mother, if there exists a being called God, why is there so much suffering and misery in the world? Does He not see it? Has He not the power to remove it?"

Mother replied with this story:

Creation itself is full of misery and happiness. Could anyone appreciate happiness if misery did not exist? Besides, how is it possible for all persons to be happy?

Sita once said to Rama, "Why don't you remove the suffering and unhappiness of all your subjects? Please make all the inhabitants of your kingdom happy. By your mere will, you can easily do it."

Rama said, "Is it possible for all persons to be happy at the same time?"

"Why not?" asked Sita, "Please supply from the royal treasury the means of satisfying everyone's wants."

"All right," said Rama, "your will shall be carried out."

Rama sent for Lakshmana and said to him, "Go and notify everyone in my empire that everyone may take whatever he wants from the royal treasury."

At this, the subjects of Rama came to the palace and told him what they wanted. The royal treasury began to flow without stint. When everyone was spending his days joyously, through the maya of Rama, the roof of the building in which Rama and Sita lived started to leak. Workmen were sent for to repair the building. But where were workmen to be had? There was not a labourer in the kingdom. With the absence of masons, carpenters, and artisans, all buildings fell into disrepair, and work was at a standstill. Rama's subjects informed the king of their difficulties. Finding no other help, Sita said to Rama: "It is no longer possible to bear the discomfort of the leaking roof. Please arrange things as they were before. Then everyone will be able to procure workmen. Now I realize that it is not possible for all persons to be happy at the same time."

"Let it be so," said Rama. Instantaneously all things were as before and workmen could once more be engaged.

Sita said to Rama, "Lord, this creation is your wonderful sport!"

No one will suffer at all times. No one will spend all his days on this earth in suffering. Every action brings its own result, and one gets one's opportunities accordingly.[12]

Happiness and misery are part of human life. There is no one in this world who is always happy or always miserable. The secret of happiness is renunciation. Holy Mother was the embodiment of renunciation. And she taught it through her life and actions. Sometimes we see a person's greatness in small things. Sarala, one of the Mother's attendants, told the following story: "In Udbodhan there was only one broken comb. We all — Holy Mother, Radhu, Maku, and I — used to comb our hair with that one comb. One day Nalini told the Mother, 'Aunt, you have so many devotees and they always ask you what you need — then why don't you ask them for a new comb?' The Mother replied with a smile, 'Look, we are managing well with this broken comb.'"[13]

Holy Mother at the Circus

On Christmas Day in 1918 Holy Mother went to see Wilson's Circus in the Maidan (a large park) with her nieces and devotees, a trip that was arranged by her disciple Lalit Chattopadhyay. Kartik (later Swami Nirlepananda), a grandson of Yogin-ma, recorded his account of the trip:

The First World War had just ended and the English people were cele-brating their victory. Moreover it was Christmas Day. Radhu, Maku, and Nalini wanted to see the circus and they asked the Mother's wealthy devo-tee Lalit Babu to take them to it. Lalit said to them that if they could make the Mother agree to go with them then he would arrange everything. The nieces rushed to their aunt and demanded that she go with them. The Mother finally agreed. When Sharat Maharaj heard about it, he cautioned Lalit: "Since the Mother has agreed, I have nothing to say. You are a mature person and not a boy. Please carefully consider the gravity of the situation. Don't be carried away by momentary excitement. Who will be responsible if the Mother is hurt? Do you dare to take Holy Mother on an outing on this crowded festival day?"

Lalit replied: "Maharaj, the Mother does not go anywhere without your permission. Please give me permission and I will take the responsibility. Be assured that I will look after the Mother's comfort with all my might. I am taking the entire risk upon my shoulders."

Dr. Kanjilal's car was always available for the Mother, but she was reluc-tant to go by motor car, so Lalit hired four horse carriages. The circus was held in the southern part of the Maidan, near Victoria Memorial Hall. Lalit bought expensive tickets for the Mother and her companions. The Mother was pleased to go to the circus.

It was a cold winter day. The Maidan was very crowded and festive. Music was playing and the whole place was flooded with light. When the circus was over that evening, the large crowd was jostling to leave the Maidan. Lalit was running around attempting to get a horse carriage, but he failed. The Mother was calmly standing in the open Maidan on that cold evening. The distance from the circus tent to Dharmatala Junction was nearly half an hour's walk. It was hard for the Mother to walk such a distance as she had rheumatic pain. But without any complaint the veiled Mother slowly limped all the way holding the hand of Golap-ma, her bodyguard. The Mother was a little afraid that Sharat, her loving caretaker, would be angry at Lalit.

As I used to sleep at night in Sharat Maharaj's room, the Mother said to me: "You see, my son, Lalit was not at fault. He was helpless. He tried his utmost but could not get a single carriage. What could he do? Please explain the whole situation to Sharat nicely, so that Lalit will not get scolded." What sympathy, compassion, and love the Mother had for her heroic devotee Lalit! Finally, she got into a carriage and we all returned to Udbodhan House.

Sharat Maharaj was anxiously awaiting the Mother's return. He was smoking a hubble bubble and was deeply concerned about the Mother's safety. As soon as we arrived at Udbodhan House, a devotee cross-examined me in front of Sharat Maharaj. When I told the whole story about the Mother being inconvenienced, Sharat Maharaj could not bear it. He roared like a tiger and reprimanded Lalit right and left, saying, "You are a fool!" Embarrassed, Lalit kept his head down. The Mother did not go to Sharat Maharaj's room. When Lalit came upstairs, the Mother caressed his head and back, blessed him profusely, so that his feelings might not be hurt. At last she said to him: "My son, Sharat said the right thing. Henceforth, do everything after considering the pros and cons." The Mother was an embodiment of compassion.[14]

Sarala (later Bharatiprana) recalled some details of that trip to the circus: "We watched the circus in Maidan till nine o' clock. The Mother was as jubilant as a girl as she watched the various performances. It was quite late at night, so a horse carriage was not available. Lalit Babu brought a taxi but the Mother refused to ride. Once when she had ridden in a taxi, a dog was run over. From then on she stopped riding in taxis. Lalit Babu begged her, saying: "Mother, I am not finding any horse carriage here. Please get in the taxi and the driver will drive very slowly." But the Mother said: "No, try again. You will find a carriage." Lalit Babu went quite a distance and fortunately got a phaeton. We returned late to Udbodhan House in that carriage."[15]

Lalit: A Heroic Devotee

Swami Nirlepananda told a wonderful story of Holy Mother's love for her devotee Lalit. Previously Lalit used to drink and lead a wanton life, but by the grace of the Mother his life was changed. He and his wife, Dasi, had lost several children and were nearly mad with grief. After taking refuge in the Mother, Lalit built a charitable dispensary at Jayrambati. He made every effort to make the Mother's life comfortable both in Jayrambati and Calcutta. One day he said proudly to Nirlepananda: "Long before the Udbodhan House was built, the Mother came to the house I rented in Shankharitola. I had an oil painting made of the Mother and I asked her to worship her own picture in my shrine with flowers and sandal paste.* She did, and then she initiated me."

One day Lalit invited Radhu's husband, Manmatha, and Kartik, who was then a college student, for lunch. Lalit's wife was extremely shy and avoided men she did not know. When the two young men knocked at the door, she did not open it. Manmatha was headstrong and he felt humiliated because Lalit would not receive him. He returned to Udbodhan House with Kartik.

When Lalit returned home, his wife told him what had happened, and he immediately rushed to Udbodhan House and complained to the Mother: "Mother, you should scold these two young boys. I just went to buy some sweets from the market. You know your daughter-in-law's bashful nature. They did not even wait a little, though I returned soon." Lalit felt terrible thinking that he had humiliated his guru's relative. He burst into tears. The Mother consoled him, saying: "My son, I shall send them to your house right now and they will eat there. Don't worry. You go home and make things ready. What trouble inviting these boys!"

The Mother did not say anything to Manmatha but privately called Kartik to the northern balcony and scolded him, saying: "You are a college student and you have this kind of intelligence? Why did you not wait till Lalit's return? It is Sunday and there was no hurry. Manmatha is headstrong and foolish. I can't say anything to him." She then called Sharat Maharaj and said: "My son, you take these two boys, go to Lalit's

---

*In 1923 when the Mother's temple was built in Jayrambati, Swami Saradananda installed this painting of the Mother on the altar. During the Mother's centenary in 1953-54, this picture was replaced with a marble image, and the picture was removed to the shrine bedroom of Jayrambati.

home, and have lunch there. Please calm down Lalit." Sharat Maharaj obeyed the Mother's order. Overwhelmed with joy, Lalit remarked: "Am I an ordinary devotee? Look, the Mother is holding my hand."

Lalit had a large moustache like the German emperor, Kaiser Wilhelm II, so Swami Brahmananda called him "Kaiser," and the monks and devotees called him "Kaiser Chatterjee."[16]

The Story of Swami Purnananda

Swami Purnananda went to medical school, but he later took initiation from Swami Brahmananda and became a monk. He lived in Udbodhan House when the Mother was there. To control his restless mind and improve his patience, Brahmananda told Purnananda: "You must repeat your mantra 10,000 times every evening. Count them. If you make a mistake in counting, start over; otherwise an ogress will swallow the results of your japa." According to his guru's instruction, Purnananda steadily began to repeat the mantra with deep concentration. Some days when he lost count, he had to start again. When the supper bell was rung during his japa, he did not go to the dining room with the other monks. This created a problem in the household because someone needed to wait with his food till late at night.

One day the Mother asked him: "My son, why are you so late for supper?" Touched by the Mother's affectionate words, Purnananda burst into tears. He told her what Swami Brahmananda had said to him. When she heard this, she laughed loudly and said: "Rakhal said that an ogress would swallow the result of your japa? Look, my son, you are young and your mind is restless, so Rakhal gave you that instruction to make your mind calm and one-pointed. I assure you that you will not have to be afraid of finishing your japa. When the bell is rung, please come and eat your supper. Later you can complete your japa at your convenience." Thus the Mother's assurance freed him from anxiety, and from then on Purnananda ate supper regularly with the monks.[17]

Nafar Chandra Kole

Late one evening in November 1918, Nafar Chandra Kole, a wealthy man from Koalpara, came to Udbodhan House and met Swami Saradananda on an urgent matter. He desperately wanted to see the Mother. The swami called Brahmachari Barada who was then setting the Mother's mosquito curtain. When Barada came downstairs, Saradananda asked him to inform the Mother that Nafar Chandra Kole urgently wanted to see her. When Holy Mother got the news, she told Barada to ask Nafar to see her upstairs. Nafar went to the Mother, prostrated before her, and said with tearful eyes: "Mother, I am wretched. I came to see you because I am in great danger. Recently four of my grandchildren died of influenza, and a couple of other granddaughters and a grandson are now suffering. Mother, you must bless me so that my lineage will not die off. Please tell me whether my grandson will live."

The Mother consoled him, saying: "What are you so afraid of? You are fortunate, a wealthy man." But Nafar held both her feet and said piteously: "Mother, may I not lose my grandson in my old age — this is my prayer."

The Mother said gravely: "Don't be anxious. Please get up. Well, I shall pray to the Master for you."

"Mother, I have come to *you* for help," insisted Nafar.

She then reassured him, saying: "Don't be afraid. You will not have that misfortune." With the Mother's blessings, Nafar went to Saradananda downstairs. The Mother asked Brahmachari Barada to give Nafar a couple of sweets as prasad. Afterwards she said to Barada: "This old man possesses a lot of money. But still, in his old age he is afraid that his dynasty will come to an end. Just see, my son, there is no peace in this world. His eldest daughter-in-law is the daughter of Shambhu Roy of Jibta village. Perhaps she sent this old man to me." The Mother's blessing answered his prayer.[18]

The Blessed Slum Dwellers

Holy Mother's room was the shrine as well as her bedroom and her parlour. She had no privacy, so from time to time she walked on the roof. She seldom visited devotees' homes in Calcutta. When she bathed in the Ganges, she left by the back door, not the main entrance, where Saradananda and other monks lived and worked in the publication department. By contrast, the elderly Golap-ma, caretaker of the Mother, moved around everywhere in the house. Sometimes the Mother sat alone on the northern balcony of her room and repeated her mantra in the evening or gave a private interview.

In front of Udbodhan House there was a large slum. The inhabitants came from various parts of India and earned their livelihood by hard manual labour. When Holy Mother was in Calcutta, they could see her from their huts when she went out onto the balcony to the north of her room. The slum dwellers loved and respected Holy Mother. Sometimes Holy Mother watched the poverty-stricken people of the slum from her balcony.

One day a woman from the slum entered the Mother's house with her sick child and prayed with tearful eyes for her blessing. The Mother looked intently at the child for a while and then reassured the woman: "Don't worry, my child. Your son will be all right." She took two pomegranates and some grapes, offered them to the Master, and then handed them to that woman, saying, "Please feed these fruits to your ailing son." Holy Mother's compassion and empathy brightened that poor woman's face. She bowed down to the Mother and left. Shortly afterwards, her son regained his health.[19]

One of the men who lived in the slum had a mistress and they lived together. Once the mistress became seriously ill. Referring to her illness, the Mother said: "He nursed her with such great devotion. I have never before seen anything like it. He has shown a real spirit of service. What intense feeling!"[20]

One afternoon the Mother was seated on her balcony, repeating her mantra when she heard a man verbally abusing his wife, and slapping and kicking her. The woman had a child in her lap. She fell down with the child from the veranda to the courtyard. Still the man went on kicking her. The Mother could not bear it. Although she was extremely shy and usually spoke softly, she now stood at the balcony's iron railing and cried aloud in a tone of sharp reprimand: "You rogue! Are you going to kill the girl outright? I am afraid she is already dead!" Hardly had the man looked at the Mother when he became as quiet as a snake before its charmer. He released the woman, bent his head down, and went back into their room. The Mother's compassion made the woman burst into loud sobs. Filled with gratitude, she looked at the Mother with tearful eyes. The Mother learned that the woman had not cooked a meal on time. Soon after, the man went out to console his wife. When the Mother saw this, she returned to her room.[21]

Saralabala Sarkar wrote: "The Mother enjoyed the sun while sitting on her northern balcony. She loved to watch the young children playing. One day a man began to beat his wife with a stick and she was crying loudly. Seeing it from the balcony, the Mother got up and her veil dropped from her head. The sweet-tongued Mother shouted to that man: 'You rogue, give up your stick. Beware! Don't hit her anymore.' Getting that severe scolding, the man was embarrassed. He dropped the stick, saluted the Mother with folded hands, and ran away. Previously he used to beat his wife from time to time, but thenceforth he never hit her again."[22]

Although the Mother did not leave her house often, she saw from her upper balcony what was going on in the world. There were some houses of ill-fame in the slum below. Sarajubala Sen once recalled: "The Mother was on the balcony and laughing. She called me: 'O my daughter, come here. Be quick.' As soon as I went to her, she said: 'Look, look, that man is peeping through the windows of the prostitute's house. He runs from window to window, but he can't get in. Look, what infatuation! What animal instinct! That poor fellow hears the music inside the room, but he cannot get inside. Ah, he is dying of anxiety and restlessness.' The way the Mother described that man's condition, I could not check my laughter. Both of us laughed and laughed, and then went back into her room. I said: 'Mother, it would be wonderful if a person developed that kind of eagerness and restlessness for God!'"[23]

The next day Sarajubala came and found the Mother on her balcony, repeating her mantra. Holy Mother said to her: "You have come. Please sit down." She then finished her japa and touched the rosary to her forehead. She pointed to the slum and said: "Look, these people work very hard the entire day for their livelihood, and now they are relaxing with their families. Blessed are the poor in spirit!"

Sarajubala commented: "This reminded me of what I read in the Bible, Jesus' own words: 'Blessed are the poor in spirit, for theirs is the kingdom of heaven.' Today I heard the same words from the mouth of the Mother."[24]

Being Mahamaya herself, Holy Mother watched the play of maya from her balcony.

Motivated Prayers

Human beings have desires, and their happiness and misery depend on whether those desires are fulfilled. When human efforts fail, they seek divine help.

Dr. Mahendralal Sarkar, one of Ramakrishna's physicians, was an M.D., but he practised homeopathic medicine. Similarly, the Mother's main physician was Dr. Jnanendra Nath Kanjilal, an M.D. who practised homeopathic medicine. He and his first wife Hemaprabha and second wife Surupasundari were disciples of the Mother.* Whenever the Mother was sick in Jayrambati or Koalpara, he always went there and treated her. When the villagers learned that Dr. Kanjilal was a famous doctor from the Calcutta Medical College, they also came to get treatment from him. The Mother commented: "My qualified and talented son has come, so the

---

*Dr. Kanjilal first married Hemaprabha but they were separated. He then married Surupasundari, and when she died he went back to live with Hemaprabha. (vide *Mayer Katha*, 71)

people come to get help from him." This made the Mother happy. In gratitude the villagers would bring various presents and food to Dr. Kanjilal. Before he left Jayrambati the doctor would give the villagers his sample patent medicines to use when needed.[25]

The Mother was compassionate towards poor people and could not bear to see them suffer from want of food and clothing. Sometimes she blessed devotees by saying: "You will never suffer from lack of food." She would also say, "The Master told me that those who would chant his name would never suffer from lack of food."

Holy Mother was very fond of Dr. Kanjilal. One day his second wife, Surupasundari, bowed down to her and said: "Mother, please bless us so that your son may have a good income." The Mother looked at her and said: "My daughter, how can I bless you that way? That would mean that people would get diseases and suffer so that your husband would make more money. My child, I can't bestow that kind of blessing. Let all beings be healthy and happy."[26]

Sarajubala Sen recalled: "One evening two pretty young women had been taking Holy Mother into their confidence on the northern porch of her room when I suddenly presented myself there, not finding her anywhere else. I heard the Mother saying to them: 'Lay the burden of your mind before the Master. Tell him your sorrows with your tears. You will find that he will fill your arms with the desired object.' I could at once understand that the women were praying to be blessed with children. They were abashed at the sight of me. My state of mind was even worse. A few months later, I again met those women in the house of the Mother. I was glad to find that their cherished desire was going to be fulfilled soon."[27]

On the evening of 6 August 1918, some women came to pay their respects. They bowed down to the Master in the shrine, and then Nalini introduced them to Holy Mother. One of them had come to Calcutta for medical treatment. The doctor had diagnosed a tumour in her abdomen and she was to have an operation. She was very anxious. Holy Mother did not allow the women to touch her, though they begged her to let them take the dust of her feet. They pointed to the sick woman and said: "Please bless her so that she may be cured. May she be able to pay her respects to you again." The Mother answered them by saying: "Bow down before the Master and pray to him sincerely. He is everything."

After they had left, Holy Mother told her attendants: "Please sweep the room and sprinkle it with Ganges water. It is now time for the Lord's food offering." After saying that, she lay down on the bed and said to a devotee: "My child, please fan me a little. My whole body is burning. My salutations to your Calcutta! People come here and lay before me a catalogue of their sorrows. There are many who have committed sinful acts. There are still others who have had 25 children! They weep because ten of them are dead! Are they human beings? No! They are veritable beasts. No self-control. No restraint....People have been streaming here today since four o'clock in the afternoon. I cannot bear their misery anymore."[28]

It was the evening of 22 August 1918. Exhausted, Holy Mother was lying on her bed. A brahmachari came upstairs and told her that a certain woman devotee wanted to see her. Reluctantly she sat up. Soon a well-dressed woman entered the room and bowed to her, touching her feet. She said that her husband had been suffering from diabetes and his feet were swollen. The doctors said it was a dangerous disease. She prayed to the Mother for her husband's recovery. Holy Mother replied: "I do not know anything, my child. The Master is everything. If he wills, your husband will be all right. I shall pray to the Master for him."

Reassured, the woman said: "I am now very happy, Mother. Sri Ramakrishna can never disregard your prayer."

No sooner had she left the room than Holy Mother lay down again and said to a devotee: "Let anybody come, whoever that person may be. I am not going to get up again. What trouble it is, my child, to get up again and again with my aching feet. Besides, I feel a burning sensation in my whole back, caused by a rash. Please rub it with the medicated oil."

The Mother continued: "Her husband is dangerously ill. She came here to pray to God for his recovery. Instead of being prayerful and penitent, she has covered herself with perfumes. Does this become one who comes to a shrine? Ah, such is the nature of your modern people!"[29]

Family Problems

A perfect marriage is rare in this world. A married couple who were longtime devotees of Ramakrishna quarrelled from time to time. It is said that the Master tried to help them reconcile their differences. After the Master's passing away, the Mother became the couple's mediator. One morning the husband beat his wife badly and she took refuge with the Mother in Udbodhan House. Holy Mother told her attendants to inform her as soon as the woman's husband came. Four days passed, but the husband did not show up. He sent his second son to bring his mother home, but Holy Mother would not let her go. Finally one evening the husband came himself, and Holy Mother summoned him upstairs. She told him through an attendant: "You are an old man now. Is this kind of behaviour seemly? Your eldest son now has three degrees and may be married soon; your daughter-in-law will inherit this kind of abuse. Please don't abuse your wife anymore. Promise?" The husband agreed to follow the Mother's advice. She further said: "Your wife is a good-natured woman. Do not hurt her. Does she do anything for herself? Her only shortcoming is that she gives away lavishly. What to do? Please take good care of her." The couple returned home and from then on had no more quarrels.[30]

Change Your Word, Change Your World

Words have great power. Once a blind man was seated on the sidewalk with a placard that read: "I'm blind. Please help." It was seldom that anyone put a coin into his tin can. Then one woman on her way to work stopped and wrote on the opposite side of the placard with a marker: "It's a beautiful day, but I can't see it." The blind man felt the woman's shoe before she left. Soon many passers-by began to drop coins into his container. The blind man heard those sounds, and knew that it was full. At the end of the day the woman returned and stood before the blind man. The blind man touched her shoe and recognized her. He asked, "What did you write?" The woman replied: "I wrote the same thing in different words."

Sarajubala Sen wrote: "Late one evening a beggar was heard calling out in the lane. He was crying: 'Radha-Govinda, O Mother Nandarani! Please be kind to the blind.' When she heard his voice, the Mother said: 'This beggar passes through the lane almost every night. At first he cried, "O Mother, please be kind to the blind." But Golap one day rightly said to him: "Please utter the name of Radha-Krishna — names of God. This will serve the double purpose of uttering the holy name and also of reminding the householders of God. Otherwise day and night you will think only of your blindness." Since then, the blind man, while passing through this lane, shouts the name of God. Golap gave him a piece of cloth. He also gets alms in other forms.'"[31]

Bhumananda recalled:

In Udbodhan House one day Golap-ma scolded a maidservant and then came upstairs. When Holy Mother heard her loud voice, she inquired, "Golap, what happened?"

Golap-ma replied: "Mother, you do not see any fault in others. So it is fruitless to say anything to you."

The Mother said in a sweet and soft voice: "Golap, is there any dearth of people in this world who see faults in others? If I do not see their faults, will the world stop functioning?"

"Mother, this is your house," Golap-ma responded. "If you say some-thing, they will listen; but who is going to listen to me?"

The Mother gravely replied: "This house belongs to my children. The Master got it for them so that they could live here. Well, why don't you go to Sharat [Saradananda] and say whatever you have to say?" Golap-ma remained silent."[32]

Compassion for the Poor

It was 30 September 1918, Maha-ashtami, the second day of Durga Puja. Many devotees assembled in Udbodhan House to pay their respects to Holy Mother. Sarajubala Sen recorded:

> It was the time of the noonday worship when a party of three men and three women from a distant part of the country came to pay their respects to Holy Mother. They were very poor, all their possessions consisting of one piece of cloth each. They had begged for their passage money to Calcutta. One of the party — a man — was having a private talk with the Mother. There seemed to be no end to the conversation. The time for the noon food offering was passing, and the Mother was supposed to offer it. The Mother's attendants became annoyed. One of them said to the dev-otee in unmistakable language, "If you have anything more to say, you better go downstairs and talk to the monks." But the Mother said firmly: "It does not matter if it gets late. I must hear what they have to say." She continued to listen to him with great patience. In a whisper she gave him some instructions. Then she sent for his wife as well. We inferred that they must have experienced something in a dream. Later on we came to learn that they had received a sacred mantra in a dream. After about an hour they took prasad and left. The Mother said: "Alas, they are very poor! They have come here with great hardship."[33]

There is a saying: "The measure of love is compassion; the measure of compassion is kindness." Many people came to the Mother for peace and consolation. In 1913 a middle-aged man came to the Mother with his grief-stricken daughter who was 17 years old. He said: "Mother, this is my daughter. She had a baby girl who died this morning. She is overcome with grief, so I have brought her to you for consolation."

Holy Mother asked the girl to come near her, but when the girl extended her hand to touch the Mother's feet, the Mother remarked: "How can you touch me? You are now in the period of mourning."* At this, that girl's sad face became even more gloomy. She drew back and felt helpless. Seeing

---

*According to the Hindu custom, the mourning period continues for 11 days. During that period one is not supposed to perform any ritual or touch a deity.

her sorrowful face, the Mother exclaimed with great empathy: "Ah, my child! You are grief-stricken and have come to me for solace, and I hurt you. Set aside that custom, my child. Bow down and touch my feet."

She moved close to the girl, who then fell at the Mother's feet, crying. Holy Mother touched her head and blessed her. She again consoled her, saying: "Have devotion for the Master. Please open your heart to him whenever you have pain and suffering." She continued: "Ah, she has just gotten a shock. Is it possible for her to be calm today?" The girl's father was standing near the door. After a while the father and the daughter gathered themselves to some extent, bowed down to the Mother, and left.[34]

Actresses Visit Udbodhan House

As the sun shines on everything equally, so God's love flows evenly towards saints and sinners. Krishna says in the Gita: "I am the same towards all beings; to Me there is none hateful or dear. Even the most sinful man, if he worships Me with unswerving devotion, must be regarded as righteous; for he has formed the right resolution. He soon becomes righteous and attains eternal peace. Proclaim it boldly, O son of Kunti, that My devotee never perishes."[35]

Ramakrishna told his devotees: "All the sins of the body fly away if one chants the name of God and sings His glories. The birds of sin dwell in the tree of the body. Singing the name of God is like clapping your hands. As, at a clap of the hands, the birds in the tree fly away, so do our sins disappear at the chanting of God's name and glories."[36]

What a reassuring message! Tarasundari and Tinkari — two superstars of the Calcutta theatre — had heard Ramakrishna's message. Though the two actresses had not met Ramakrishna, they had heard his message through Girish Chandra Ghosh, their director and mentor. Later they visited Holy Mother at Udbodhan House and received her blessing.

One's birth is in the hands of Providence, but one's karma is one's own responsibility. These actresses were born in the red-light district of Calcutta and did not know who their fathers were. Their mothers were active in the world's ancient profession, and they grew up in misery and poverty. Orthodox society shunned them; they were not even allowed a formal education. But the acting talent of Tarasundari and Tinkari enabled them to overcome all these obstacles. Their self-effort and sincerity, patience and perseverance, passion and ambition led them to the pinnacle of success in life. A blazing fire cannot be hidden, nor can a great talent.

Tarasundari and Tinkari sometimes visited Holy Mother at Udbodhan House but they never entered the Mother's room where the Master's

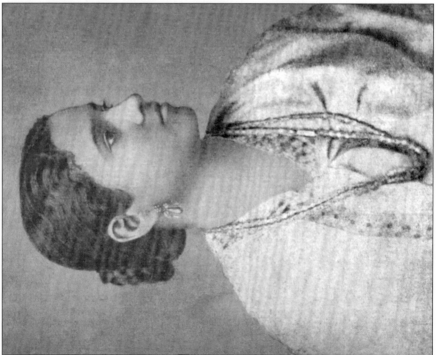

Actresses in Girish Ghosh's theatre. Left: Tinkari. Right: Tarasundari.

shrine was located. Instead, they bowed down to the Master and Holy Mother from outside the door. Holy Mother loved them and always asked them to stay for lunch. Afterwards, she would give them each a betel roll. One day after they left, the Mother remarked: "These girls have genuine devotion. Ah! Whenever they call on God, they do it with one-pointed minds."[37]

During Holy Mother's last illness, Tarasundari visited her quite often. Swami Ishanananda recalled:

> One day at noon, Tarasundari, the famous actress of the Star Theatre, came to visit Holy Mother. Mother's body was very weak, so she was lying on the floor of her room surrounded by some women. Tara bowed down to her and sat down outside her door. She spoke to the Mother softly and with great reverence. Mother said: "You act very well in the theatre. It is hard to recognize you when you appear on the stage with your costume and makeup. Why don't you recite something for us?" Tara sometimes acted in the role of a man. She saluted the Mother with folded hands and then recited a part of the heroic role of Prabir in the play *Prabir-Arjun* [actually Jana]. Afterwards the Mother said to her, "My child, come another day." Tara again saluted the Mother and left with some prasad in hand.
>
> Another afternoon Tara unexpectedly arrived in a taxi and brought four or five baskets of gifts: sweets, curd, mangosteens, oranges, bananas, grapes, pomegranates, pineapples, and other fruit; as well as flowers and bouquets of tuberoses; saris for Mother, Radhu, Maku, and Nalini; and woollen shoes for Radhu's and Maku's children. Mother had a slight fever and she was in bed. Tara bowed down to her from outside the door. Mother asked me to put the gifts in the middle room. When Tara left with some prasad, Mother asked me to distribute some of the things to Radhu, Maku, and other workers of the household. [38]

Sometimes an exciting and glamorous life is also exhausting and stressful. To refresh herself, Tarasundari often visited Holy Mother or the Master's disciples. Swami Parameshananda recalled:

> One afternoon at two o'clock Tarasundari came to visit Swami Sarada-nanda at Udbodhan House. She brought a large quantity of sweets and fruit to offer to the Master, and I put them in the storeroom and gave her a small carpet on which to sit on the upper floor near the steps. She pushed away the seat and sat on the bare floor. Swami Saradananda was then resting, so I asked her to wait.
>
> I had seen Girish's play *Prafulla* at the Star Theatre and I told her that I had seen her performance in that play.
>
> Tara replied: "Swami, I am glad that you enjoyed the women's perfor-mances in the play. They act in such a way that the audience feels that they

are like goddesses. You are a young monk, so you don't know what a sinful life they have led. As they act, tears flow through one eye and a smile shines through the other."

I asked: "Why don't you recite something for us?"

Tara then began to recite some lines from a tragedy and tears trickled from her eyes. Her sari even became wet. She then recited a portion of the title role from Girish's play *Jana*. When Arjuna killed Jana's son, Prabir, in battle, her heart was devastated by grief and she cried profusely. Afterwards, Jana wanted to take revenge. Like the Greek goddess Nemesis, she roared and burst into loud laughter. The whole house reverberated with the sound of that laughter. Thus Tara demonstrated how actresses can cry and laugh alternately.

When Swami Saradananda heard the noise, he got up and washed his face in the bathroom to get ready to receive his visitors. When I entered his room, he asked, "Who has come?" I told him that it was the actress Tara and recounted my conversation with her. The swami then said to me, "Well, you have learned a wonderful lesson from her." He then instructed me to send Tara's offerings of fruits and sweets to the Kali temple.

I took Tara to Swami Saradananda. She bowed down to him, and sat near the threshold of his room. Swami Saradananda always saluted women by bowing his head. When they began to talk, I left the room.[39]

Girish inspired many actors and actresses and told them about Ramakrishna, Holy Mother, and the disciples of the Master. Tinkari met Holy Mother for the first time when she went with Tarasundari to Udbodhan House in Calcutta. Holy Mother had seen Tinkari perform in *Vilwamangal Thakur*. Ashutosh Mitra recalled the visit:

Tinkari, the famous actress, came to visit Holy Mother, and Sister Lakshmi asked her to sing a song. Tinkari said hesitatingly, "What kind of song shall I sing for you?"

Holy Mother replied: "It will be wonderful if you sing that song of Pagalini [from *Vilwamangal*]." Tinkari had performed in that role. She got ready to sing.

It was nine-thirty. We were busy working downstairs. Suddenly we heard Tinkari's sweet and melodious voice singing to the *Chayanat* tune, "He [Krishna] travels holding my hand." We stopped our work and went upstairs to listen to her sing. Sharat Maharaj was writing something; he dropped his pen and became absorbed in the music. Yogin-ma was cutting vegetables; she also went upstairs. The cook and servants also stopped what they were doing and went upstairs to listen to the song.

When I went upstairs I noticed that Holy Mother had finished her worship and was listening to the song, sitting on the floor. Tinkari sat on the little veranda near the entrance to the Master's shrine. We felt that her overflowing devotion was reverberating throughout the entire house through her singing:

"He [Krishna] travels holding my hand.
Wherever I go, He follows me,
Even if I don't ask Him to."

Holy Mother looked at the Master's photo and then closed her eyes. After a while she opened her eyes, but we felt she was indrawn. Her eyes were open but she was not seeing anything. Tinkari continued:

"He wipes my face with great care,
And intently looks at my face.
When I smile, He smiles; and when I cry, He cries.
How lovingly He takes care of me."

The whole house was completely still, as if no one were there. Everyone was overwhelmed and absorbed in an exalted mood. Was it the influence of Tinkari's singing or Holy Mother's spiritual power? Who could say? Tinkari finished the last lines of that song:

"So I came to know: who says that the Precious One does not exist?
Come and see for yourself whether it is true or false.
He is talking to me with great love."

Holy Mother expressed in an ecstatic mood: "Ah! Ah!"

Tinkari finished her singing. Holy Mother remained in that condition for a while, and silence prevailed. Then she wiped her eyes and said to Tinkari, "What a beautiful song you have sung today, my child!"[40]

Strange Visitors

One day a seemingly mad woman entered the Mother's house singing softly and playing the cymbals. Without anyone's permission, she walked up the staircase. Saradananda saw her and said to Ashu: "Look, a mad woman has gone upstairs. Watch her." Ashu immediately went to the second floor and saw the Mother welcoming the woman, saying, "Please come, my daughter." The woman did not bow down to the Mother or even talk to her. She stood outside the shrine and began to sing. She wore a torn sari and her hair was dry, dishevelled, and filthy. Sometimes she knelt down and sometimes she sang with folded hands and then raised both hands. As long as she sang, she did not open her eyes. Although her body was dirty and ugly, her voice was very sweet. She sang this song in the mood of a gopi:

My friends, dress me — all of you dress me properly,
I want to be a yogini — I shall renounce everything for my beloved Krishna.
I shall put on an ochre robe and earrings made of conch-shells;
Thus, in the garb of a yogini, from place to place I shall wander,
Till I see my cruel Hari.

If Krishna does not come to Vraja,
All my youth and beauty will be meaningless like a broken piece of glass.
Friends, decorate me like a nun, I can't stay at home anymore.
I shall go to every home of Mathura and search for my beloved Krishna;
If anybody stops me, I shall kill myself and blame that person as my
    murderer.
I can't bear anymore. Dress me like a yogini.

When the mad-looking woman finished singing, Holy Mother gave her a new sari, but she would not accept it. Holy Mother asked the woman to eat something, but she would not eat. When she left, Holy Mother remarked: "What intense renunciation! She does not want to eat or take anything. I think she will soon give up her body."[41]

Once a young man came to Udbodhan House to bow down to the Mother. All of a sudden he began crying as he held her feet. Holy Mother was embarrassed, and her attendant asked the young man to leave. Another devotee said to the attendant: "Please let him express his wishes to the Mother. She is not your exclusive property."

The attendant replied, "Sir, don't you see this man is creating a disturbance?"

The Mother tried to console the man: "My son, be calm. Tell me what you want."

The man said, "Mother, be gracious unto me — be merciful."

The Mother caressed his head and said: "My child, you have my grace. Please be calm." The man controlled himself and then went downstairs with his friend to see Swami Saradananda. Later on, Saradananda said with a smile: "The people of East Bengal are a little emotional. Some people explode with emotion."

Once a devotee from Jessore went to bow down to the Mother, hiding a knife in his pocket. After bowing down to her, he showed the Mother his knife and said, "Please show me your true form." When the Mother remained silent, he said: "If you do not show your true form, I shall stab myself."

Alarmed, the Mother got up and grabbed his knife, saying: "Give up this knife. What form do you want to see?"

She pointed to her face and said, "Now see this form."

The man saw something and calmed down. One can achieve many things through the power of emotion, but emotionalism is merely ludicrous.[42]

Once in August Holy Mother went to visit Mother Kali at Kalighat in South Calcutta. After worshipping Mother Kali, she was walking to visit

Nakuleshwar Shiva. On the way a bhairavi, clad in ochre robes, with a trident in hand, blocked her way. She looked at the Mother's face for a while and then began to sing an *Agamani* song composed by Girish. Motionless, the Mother stood there on the street. The pilgrims and beggars crowded around to hear the bhairavi sing:

> O my daughter, Uma, tell me how did you stay in your husband's home?
> So many people say so many things, and those talks make me living-dead.
> It is hard for a mother to bear that my son-in-law lives by begging.
> If Shiva comes to pick you up this time, I shall tell him that you are not at
> home.

When the song ended, the Mother asked Ashu to give the nun a little money, but she would not accept it. She said: "Mother, one should take the right thing from the right person. I shall take that thing which I am supposed to receive from you. Mother, go where you are going." The Mother began to walk. From behind her the bhairavi collected the dust of the Mother's feet from the street, put it on her head, and left.

When Holy Mother arrived at the Nakuleshwar temple, she did not go inside. Instead, she asked Nalini, Radhu, Surabala, and Golap-ma to go inside the temple, but she stayed outside, sitting at the entrance. She was extremely indrawn. When it was time to return home, Golap-ma had to call her a few times before she got up and entered the carriage. She was still distracted. She did not say a single word during the journey. After returning to Udbodhan House, the Mother asked, "Who is that bhairavi?"

Ashu replied, "Perhaps she was connected with Girish's theatre, and has now become an ascetic."

"Oh," said the Mother and then remained silent.[43]

On 30 September 1918, the second day of Durga Puja, a woman dressed in an ochre cloth offered flowers at the Mother's feet and placed two rupees there. Holy Mother said: "My goodness! Why should you do that? You have put on the ochre cloth and wear rudraksha beads on your arms. Who has initiated you?"

The woman replied: "I am not initiated. I put on the ochre cloth on my own. I am practising some sadhana but I am not getting any peace."

Holy Mother scolded her: "Without initiation and spiritual experience, you have put on this sacred cloth! This is not proper. The robe you have put on is very holy. I was about to salute you with folded hands. First realize God. One should acquire spiritual power; then all will come and bow down to you. My child, it is not easy to wear the ochre cloth. These boys of the ashrama have renounced everything for the Master; they are entitled to wear the ochre cloth."

"I wish to be initiated by you," the woman replied.

"How is it possible? I am not well," Holy Mother said.

The woman humbly begged for initiation, and Golap-ma supported her. After a while it seemed that the Mother yielded a little, and she said, "We shall think about it later."[44]

Basudevananda as a Worshipper

When Holy Mother was in Jayrambati, or when she was not well, a monk would perform the worship at the shrine in Udbodhan House. In May 1918, Swami Basudevananda was sent from Belur Math to Udbodhan House to serve as a worshipper. He found various deities on the altar, including the Master's picture, Mother's Gopala, Maku's Radha-Krishna, Yogin-ma's Gopala and Baneshwara lingam, and another Kali image. When the Mother returned from Jayrambati, Basudevananda asked her: "Mother, how shall I perform worship to all these deities?"

"How do you worship now?" she asked.

The swami replied that he had learned some mantras from his grandmother when he was at home and he still used those mantras. The Mother then instructed him: "Worship all these deities with the seed mantra of your Chosen Deity. He has become all gods and goddesses. First take the seed mantra, then add a particular deity, and finally add *namah* [meaning "salutation"]. If you have an inclination to worship any god or goddess, you can worship the image of the Master. Your Chosen Deity and the Master are the same, and he has become all gods and goddesses."[45]

One day Basudevananda was sitting in Holy Mother's room making sandal paste for worship. The Mother was doing japa on her rosary. Seeing nobody else around, Basudevananda asked her: "Mother, sometimes I feel weakness in my mind."

She put her rosary down and said to him: "Don't pay any attention to those things. That kind of weakness looms in everyone's mind except the Master's. Has any great soul ever been born who has not experienced that kind of weakness? It is a great lesson when a seeker understands that he has a weakness in his mind and tries to rectify it. At that time the Divine Mother becomes propitious and opens the door for him. When a man has good thoughts for some days, he thinks that he has achieved everything and gives up sadhana. From time to time the Master reminds monks in this way that their sadhana is not yet over. He does this by creating lower thoughts in their minds. Why does the Master do that? To destroy pride.

As long as you are alive, be careful and surrender to the Master. Some evil elements are still around. They will jump on you when they find an opportunity. The ego generates all sorts of worthless and bestial thoughts. One should hold the attitude of self-surrender till death. Once even the Master absorbed the onslaught of lust in his body, so one should not be proud that one has conquered lust."[46]

One afternoon Basudevananda was putting the picture of the Master on the altar after his noon rest. The Mother was seated on her cot. Yogin-ma asked Basudevananda, "Hello, how do you like Udbodhan House?"

The swami replied: "The work here is very monotonous. When the Mother is not here, from time to time I feel dry. Moreover, there is no one here to teach the scriptures."

Holy Mother said: "How can the Master's service be dry? You should reflect upon the cause of dryness. The human mind becomes accustomed to a certain condition, and when it goes to another situation, it feels uncomfortable and it longs for the previous condition. At that time one should pray to the Master. You will see that he will make your mind joyful. In the beginning of spiritual life, it is not good to study and discuss the scriptures day and night; this makes the mind dry. If you study and meditate on the Master's divine play, you will notice that your mind will be saturated with sweetness and joyfulness. The mind becomes peaceful when one hears Sharat's *Lilaprasanga* and M.'s *Kathamrita*. You should also read Akshay's *Punthi*.* Whenever I have a little time, I like to listen to it."[47]

Once Basudevananda and other monks were making a lot of noise downstairs. Golap-ma became upset and said to Holy Mother: "What is this? You have no control over these boys. The Master would discipline his disciples. No one could misbehave even slightly."

The Mother replied: "What can I do? I don't see any fault in others, so how can I discipline them? Moreover, I am their Mother. How can I punish them? I receive them and clean away their dirt and impurities. They are all the Master's children. Is it so easy to punish them? He has his own way of making everything right. His overwhelming love will set them straight. Our Master was the embodiment of love. There was no harshness or rudeness in him. When people say, 'Well, God will give the result of that person's karma,' I then pray to the Master, 'Master, do good to both the ignorant and the intelligent.' I tell the boys: 'Don't harbour ill-feeling for others. Don't pray to God to take action against

---

*Holy Mother is referring to *Sri Ramakrishna and His Divine Play*, *The Gospel of Sri Ramakrishna*, and *A Portrait of Sri Ramakrishna*.

others. Rather, pray for the welfare of the oppressor.' God's judgement is well-balanced and there is not the slightest mistake in it. There is no end to His mercy."[48]

Once Swami Basudevananda fell ill with influenza. He said to Holy Mother: "Mother, generally the mind is restless. Now that I have this terrible physical discomfort, it is hard to concentrate on God."

The Mother replied: "My son, learn to divide the mind in two parts — discreet and indiscreet. The discreet mind is like the parents and the indiscreet mind is like the children. Parents are always watchful over their children. You should scold and punish the mind if it does anything wrong, as parents scold naughty children. Thus if you continue to practise this for some days, you will notice that the mind will come under control. If a bad habit takes root in the indiscreet mind for many days, then a hundred scoldings cannot uproot it. At that time pray to the Master to change the weak mind. There is no other way. He is God. He can do anything. He can recast the old mould into a new one. As a potter gives shape to raw clay, the Master could give shape to human minds according to his wish. He could build a human character according to his will."[49]

Blessed Are the Simple and Sincere

A young vagabond named Chandra Mohan Datta came to Udbodhan Publication Office one day looking for work. He sat on the outside veranda and fortunately met a man named Mohan, who worked for the household. Chandra learned from Mohan that Udbodhan House was an office of the Ramakrishna Mission and some monks lived there. Chandra asked, "May I meet the head of this centre?" Mohan asked him to wait. He soon came back and said: "Please come. The Mother has asked me to take you to her."

Chandra was a little perplexed to learn that women also lived in this Mission Office. However, he went to the upper floor to see Holy Mother. Chandra recalled: "At the first sight of the Mother, I felt that she was my own. Her eyes were so calm, as if compassion were dripping from them. I bowed down to her and she blessed me by touching my head. She inquired about me in detail — my name, where I lived, who else lived with me, and so on." The simple-natured Chandra opened his heart to Holy Mother, describing his pain and agony, his brother's ill-treatment of him, and how he was desperately looking for a job.

The Mother listened to his story and then asked affectionately: "Are you ready to do any kind of work or would some kinds of work affect your prestige?"

Chandra replied: "I shall be doing my Mother's work. Where does the question of prestige come in?"

Pleased, the Mother said: "Some of my monastic children and a few women live in this house. We need someone to do our shopping. My son Sharat decides whether to give an appointment. Go with Mohan and meet him."

Mohan said to Saradananda: "Maharaj, the Mother has sent this gentleman to you. She has mentioned that if you consider it necessary, you may appoint him to do our shopping."

Smiling, Saradananda said: "Who am I to appoint? You have already come to me with an appointment letter."

He then said to Kishori, another worker: "You said that you needed another person to help. Train this young person to serve that purpose."[50]

Chandra was hired at a salary of ten rupees per month to buy groceries every morning with Mohan and to pack and sell books published by Udbodhan Office. Whenever there was a festival in one of the Ramakrishna ashramas, Chandra carried books to sell from a stall. Thus he was instrumental in spreading the Master's message and increasing the income of the Udbodhan Publication department.

"When an individual takes a sincere step, then all gods attend, and his single deed is sweet,"[51] said Henry David Thoreau. The Mother's heart melted as she observed Chandra's sincerity and loving service. She initiated him and sanctified his rosary. She also asked him to do some small errands for her. One day she said to him: "Do you know why I have some of my work done by you? When I am no more, the memory of all this work will bring solace to you."

Another day she said to him: "My children will not be born again. You too will not be born. This birth is your last birth." Tears of gratitude trickled from Chandra's eyes. Saradananda heard the Mother's blessing to Chandra and joyfully told him: "Well, so you have managed to attain your end! You have accomplished the sole purpose of life merely by doing some odd jobs for her, for whose favour Brahma, Vishnu, and Shiva are engaged day and night in such arduous austerities. Go now, romp about free of care."[52]

Once a terrible flood in East Bengal swept away Chandra's house, leaving his parents, wife, and children homeless. When the news reached Chandra, he felt helpless. He did not say anything to the Mother or the monks. He was so depressed that he could not eat or sleep. The all-knowing Mother learned about Chandra's situation and said to him: "My son, no one has any hand over Providence. Don't be broken-hearted. Go to your home and take steps to put everything in order. What will you gain from worrying? Why are you not eating properly?"

Chandra replied tearfully: "Mother, what can I do there? Our home and everything we own has been swept away. We need a lot of money to restore everything. Moreover, I don't even have any travel money."

The compassionate Mother said: "I know your situation. Take this money and go home. This money will cover your travel and repairs to your house. But don't tell anyone that I have given you money. Tell others that your house has been inundated by a flood so you are going home."[53] Saying so, the Mother handed Chandra a bundle of notes that were tied up in the corner of her sari. Chandra was overwhelmed by the Mother's unselfish love, compassion, and generosity.

Later, according to Holy Mother's instructions, Chandra rented an apartment in Bosepara Lane near Udbodhan House and brought his wife and children from Dhaka. But the owner of the house was rude to the children and they could not play freely. When the Mother heard about this, she asked Saradananda to have a house built for Chandra and his family. The swami always obeyed the Mother's command. He bought a piece of land for Chandra on Bosepara Lane and built a small house with brick walls and a tin roof. This made the Mother happy. Holy Mother also initiated Chapala, Chandra's wife.

One day the Mother gave a handful of rice to Chandra and said: "Tie this up in a piece of cloth and place it in the earthen jar in which you store rice. There will never be want of rice in your household."[54]

30
The Divinity
of Holy Mother

Devim prasannām pranatārti-hantrim
  yogindra-pujyām yugadharma-pātrim;
Tām sāradām bhakti-vijñāna-dātrim
  dayā-svarupām pranamāmi nityam.
  — *A hymn by Swami Abhedananda*

I always salute Sarada Devi, that gracious Goddess who removes the sufferings of those who bow down to her, who is worshipped by the masters of yoga, who is the very personification of spirituality for this age, who is the giver of devotion and wisdom, and who is the embodiment of compassion.

According to the Hindu scriptures, when God incarnates as an avatar, his Shakti also incarnates with Him as his spiritual consort. Krishna said in the Gita: "Whenever there is a decline of dharma [righteousness] and a rise of adharma [unrighteousness], I incarnate myself."[1] In the Chandi, the Divine Mother said: "Whenever the demoniacal powers try to disrupt or destroy this world, I shall incarnate and destroy those enemies of divine beings."[2]

Some religions believe only in the Fatherhood of God, but Hinduism asserts both the Fatherhood and Motherhood of God. Brahman is consciousness and devoid of form, so It can manifest as male or female. In the Brihadaranyaka Upanishad it is said that the Creator was not happy because He was alone. "He desired a mate. He became the size of a man and wife in close embrace. He divided this body into two. From that division arose husband and wife."[3] This concept is symbolized by the Hindu deity Ardhanārishwara, one half of whose body is female and the other half male. Moreover, this deity has become manifest as Rama and Sita, Krishna and Radha, Buddha and Yashodhara, Chaitanya and Vishnupriya, and Ramakrishna and Sarada — all divine beings who have taken human form.

Marble image of Sarada Devi in Jayrambati, installed in 1953, during her centenary.

Holy Mother was a *devi*, a goddess, but she took on a human form to fulfill her divine mission. Her birth, conduct, and actions were divine, but she concealed her divinity. Ramakrishna once humorously said that she was like a cat covered with ashes. Although she was surrounded by her family, monks, and devotees, and behaved like an ordinary woman, she could not hide her divinity completely. From time to time she revealed her true nature to some of her close disciples and devotees.

Holy Mother Reveals Herself

One way to recognize divine beings is when they speak about themselves; otherwise it is not possible for ordinary human beings to comprehend the infinite Lord. In the tenth chapter of the Gita, before Krishna reveals his divine manifestations, Arjuna says to him: "You are the supreme Brahman, the supreme abode, the supreme purifier, the eternal divine Being, the primal God, unborn and omnipresent. So say all the sages, including the divine sages Narada, Asita, Devala, Vyasa; you also say so unto me."[4] Other avatars or divine incarnations also declared their divinity to their disciples. Krishna said: "Fools disregard me when I assume a human form; for they are unaware of my higher nature as the supreme Lord of all beings."[5]

At many points in this book I have related important incidents pertaining to Holy Mother's divinity. Chapter 2 narrates the divine circumstances surrounding Holy Mother's conception. Chapter 3 describes the period in Kamarpukur after her wedding when eight young girls — the eight confidantes of the Divine Mother — accompanied her. Chapter 5 describes in detail Holy Mother's encounter with the robber in the meadow of Telo-Bhelo, and how the robber and his wife saw Mother Kali in her. Chapter 11 tells how Holy Mother took her terrible form of Bagala to subdue crazy Harish who was threatening her.

Ramakrishna was fully aware of Holy Mother's divinity. When he spoke about her to his disciples, he said: "She is Saraswati, the goddess of learning. She has assumed a human body to impart wisdom to human beings; but she has hidden her celestial beauty lest people, by looking at her, should befoul their minds with sinful thoughts."[6] When Hriday was jealous of Holy Mother and treated her rudely, the Master cautioned him, saying: "Look here, you may insult me, but don't hurt her feelings. If He who dwells in this [*meaning himself*] hisses, you may somehow get by; but if He who dwells in her hisses, no one — not even Brahma, Vishnu, or Shiva — will be able to protect you."[7]

In 1910 Surendranath Sarkar went to Kothar, in Orissa, to receive initiation from Holy Mother. After the ceremony, he said to her: "Mother, the devotees call you Kali, Adyashakti, and Bhagavati. It is mentioned in the Gita that the sages Asita, Devala, Vyasa, and others considered Krishna to be Narayana Himself. Krishna *himself* confirmed this to Arjuna. The word 'himself' strengthened the statement. I believe whatever I have heard about you. Yet, if you substantiate those statements about yourself, then I will be free from doubt. I want to hear from you directly whether this is true or not."

Holy Mother replied: "Yes, it is true."[8]

On 4 September 1918, the Mother told Sarajubala Sen: "People call me Bhagavati, the goddess. I think that it must be so. So many incredible things have happened in my life! Golap and Yogin are witnesses of those events. If I think: 'Let this happen, or I shall eat this,' immediately God makes those things possible."[9]

In 1919, one evening in Jayrambati, Brahmachari Barada read some letters from devotees to the Mother. One woman devotee wrote a letter glorifying Holy Mother with various hymns. After listening to the letter, the Mother remarked: "Look, sometimes I wonder. I am Ram Mukhopad-hyay's daughter and many women of my age live in Jayrambati. How am I different from them? Devotees from various places come and bow down to me. On asking them I learn that some are judges and some are lawyers. Why do they come here?" She remained silent for a while. Then Barada asked, "Well, Mother, don't you remember your real nature at all times?"

Holy Mother replied: "How can it be possible, my son? If it were so, how could I perform all these activities? But you see, in the midst of all these activities, whenever I wish, inspiration comes in a flash. Then I understand the whole play of Mahamaya."[10]

Lavanya Chakrabarty recorded in his reminiscences:

> In 1912 at Lakshmi Nivas in Varanasi I met a woman with a veil near the main door. Looking at her face, I asked: "Are you the Mother?"
> "Yes, my son, I am your mother."
> "My mother!"
> "Yes, I am the Mother of you all."
> "Our Mother!"
> "Yes, my son, I am the Mother of the Universe."
> A devotee asked, "Mother, people call you Bhagavati."
> Holy Mother replied, "It does not matter what others say. I tell you myself that I am Bhagavati."[11]

One day Holy Mother referred to Ramakrishna as Bhagavan, God Himself.

A disciple asked her, "If the Master is Bhagavan [God], then what are you?"

"Who else am I?" the Mother replied without any hesitation. "I am Bhagavati, the Divine Mother of the Universe."[12]

Someone asked: "Mother, your relations have such close association with you. Why do they not gain any spiritual wisdom?"

Holy Mother replied: "They are like bamboo and silk-cotton trees. They may grow near a sandal wood tree, but they do not get its essence."

A woman devotee asked her, "Why can't we perceive you as the Divine Mother?"

Holy Mother replied: "Can everybody recognize divinity? There lay a big diamond at a bathing place. People thought it was an ordinary stone and rubbed the soles of their feet against it after finishing their baths in order to remove dry skin. One day a jeweller went there, saw the precious stone, and realized that it was a valuable diamond."[13]

On 1 February 1907, Swami Arupananda interviewed Holy Mother in Jayrambati:

> Arupananda: "Mother, people say that our Master is God Eternal and Absolute. What do you say about it?"
> Mother: "Yes, he is God Eternal and Absolute to me."
> Arupananda: "It is true that to every woman her husband is God Eternal and Absolute. I have not asked the question in that sense."
> Mother: "Yes, he is God Eternal and Absolute to me as my husband, and in a general way as well."
> Arupananda thought that if Sri Ramakrishna was God Absolute, then Holy Mother must be the Mother of the Universe. She must be the same as the divine consort, like Sita and Rama, Radha and Krishna. So he asked her: "If that is so, then why do I see you preparing *chapatis* like an ordinary woman? It is maya, I presume. Isn't that so?"
> Mother: "It is maya indeed. Why, otherwise, should I be in this state? I could be in *Vaikuntha* sitting next to Narayana as Lakshmi." Then she continued: "You see, God loves to sport as a human being. Krishna was born as a cowherd boy and Rama as a son of Dasharatha."
> Arupananda: "Do you remember your real nature?"
> Mother: "Yes, now and then I do. At those times I say to myself: 'What is this that I am doing?' Then I look at the house, children, and other family members (*gesturing towards them with her palm*), and forget my real self."[14]

Holy Mother was so humble and self-effacing that she could not bear it if someone praised her. Arupananda reminisced: "One morning I was reading aloud to the Mother and to several devotees on the porch of her room at Jayrambati. I was reading a life of Sri Ramakrishna entitled *Ramakrishna Punthi,* written in verse. In the chapter on her marriage with Sri Ramakrishna, the author eulogized her greatly and referred to her as the 'Mother of the Universe.' As I read that passage, the Mother left the porch."[15]

Vaikuntha, a disciple of Holy Mother from Cuttack, visited her at Kamarpukur. Ramlal and Lakshmi were also there. Before he left, Vaikuntha bowed down to Raghuvir in the shrine and then to Holy Mother. Suddenly she said: "Vaikuntha, call on me." The next moment she controlled her feelings and said: "I mean, call on the Master. That will serve your purpose." Lakshmi heard Holy Mother's remarks and said: "Mother, what do you mean? This is not fair. What will the devotees do if you hoodwink them in this way?"

"Why? What have I done?" Holy Mother asked.

Lakshmi replied: "A minute ago you said to the devotee, 'Call on me.' Now you say, 'Call on the Master.'"

Holy Mother responded, "If a person calls on the Master, is there anything more for him to do?"

Lakshmi said, "Mother, it is not proper to delude your children."

Then Lakshmi said to Vaikuntha: "Look, today I have heard something new from the Mother: 'Call on me.' Never forget her words. Is the Master different from the Mother? You call on the Mother. You are very fortunate that the Mother herself has said this to you. You pray only to the Mother." Then turning to Holy Mother, Lakshmi asked: "Mother, did I say right?" Holy Mother tacitly approved.[16]

Sarala (later Bharatiprana) recalled: "One day at Jayrambati, vexed with her relatives, the Mother said to them angrily: 'Do not torture me too much. If He who dwells inside this body hisses but once, not even Brahma, Vishnu, or Shiva will be able to save you.' On another occasion she said to me, referring to Radhu's torment of her: 'Look here, child, this body is a divine body. How much more torture can it bear? Can a human being, unless he be God, put up with all this? Let me tell you something. No one will understand me as long as I am alive. They will know only afterwards.'"[17]

It is by God's grace alone, not self effort, that human beings can have the vision of God. In the Gita, Krishna told Arjuna: "You cannot see Me with these eyes, so I give you a divine eye." Then only could Arjuna behold Krishna's cosmic form.

In 1965 at Trichur Pravrajika Dhiraprana asked Pravrajika Bharatiprana about her experiences with Holy Mother. Bharatiprana remained silent for some time and then said:

> I knew and felt Holy Mother to be my very own mother. I was not aware of her divinity. One day the Mother showered her grace on me and revealed a glimpse of her real nature. She was drying her hair on the roof of Udbodhan House. I went there to do some work, and she asked me to bring some flowers. When I brought them, the Mother indicated that I should offer those flowers at her feet. While doing so, I saw that the Mother's body became vast. I was bewildered and did not trust my eyes. Overwhelmed by that divine sight, I offered those flowers at her feet and prostrated fully. After a while the Mother assumed her normal form. Only then did I realize that the Mother of the Universe manifested Herself in Holy Mother.[18]

Nilima Mukhopadhyay recorded another story of Holy Mother's divinity that she had heard from Bharatiprana. Nilima asked: "What did you think about Holy Mother?" Bharatiprana replied: "I did not experience anything in particular. I lived with her as a child would with its mother. Her love was fathomless. But yes, one day I was taken aback. On that day unexpectedly many devotees came to the Mother's house for prasad, and we became anxious about how to feed such a crowd. I hurriedly went to the Mother and informed her of the situation. She got up and said encouragingly: "Everything will be all right. Let us go to the kitchen and see." The Mother entered the kitchen and saw the food. She then took a spatula and stirred each container. Amazingly, all the devotees were satisfied with that food. Then it suddenly dawned on me: "Well, is Holy Mother then Goddess Annapurna Herself?"[19]

One day in Jayrambati, Swami Tanmayananda worshipped the Mother's feet, as she was his guru. Then when he put her feet on his head, she said: "My foolish child, one should not put another's feet on the head because the Master dwells there."

"Mother, I have not seen the Master," Tanmayananda replied.

"The Master is God Himself."

"If the Master is God, then who you are?"

"Who else am I?"

"If you wish, you can show me the Master."

"When the Master touched Naren [Vivekananda], he was so scared that he cried out. Practise spiritual disciplines and you will see him."

"What is the need of spiritual disciplines for a person who has a guru like you?"

Holy Mother explained: "Yes, that's true. But you see, one might have all kinds of food at home, yet one must cook it and eat the food. He who cooks earlier, gets his food earlier too. Some eat in the morning, some in the evening, and yet some starve because they are too lazy or afraid to cook."[20]

Swami Maheswarananda recalled:

> Once at Koalpara Ashrama a distinguished devotee [Narayan Iyenger] came to bow down to Holy Mother. He had learned that the Mother got a burning sensation if someone touched her feet. So he said: "If we touch the Mother's feet and that causes pain to her, then we should not do it."
>
> The Mother replied: "No, my son, we have come only for that purpose. If we do not absorb and digest others' sins and sufferings, who else will? Who else will bear the burden of the sinners and sufferers? If good souls touch my feet, I don't feel pain. When some people touch my feet, I get a burning sensation. Of course, my son, you may touch my feet when you bow down."[21]

Holy Mother was the embodiment of purity, and she had the power to purify others. One night in Jayrambati, her cook said that she had touched a dog and needed to bathe.*

Holy Mother said: "It is rather late in the evening. Don't bathe now. Wash your hands and feet and change your sari."

The cook objected, "Oh, that won't do!"

Holy Mother responded, "Then sprinkle some Ganges water on your body."

But even that did not satisfy the cook's fastidious nature. Finally the Mother said: "Then touch me."[22]

One day in Udbodhan House a woman disciple named Sailabala Chaudhury said to the Mother: "You are Mahamaya. You have deluded us and made us involved with our father, mother, husband, and children." Immediately the Mother replied: "Don't say that I have kept people deluded. I feel a terrible pain when I see the sufferings of worldly people. What can I do, my child? They don't want liberation."

Another day Sailabala asked the Mother: "You have instructed me in how to repeat the Master's mantra, but how should I think of you?"

She replied: "You may think of me as Radha, or in any other way that appeals to your mind. It will be enough if you think of me even as your mother."[23]

Although Holy Mother's divinity could manifest itself spontaneously, she could also withdraw it quickly. Although she tried to hide her divinity, her devotees now and then realized her real nature.

Swami Ritananda reminisced: "One day in Jayrambati when the

---

* In India some dogs are strays and are not clean, so orthodox Hindus bathe if they touch them.

Mother was sweeping the veranda of her old cottage with a broom, a beggar loudly called from outside, 'Mother, please give me some alms.' The Mother soliloquized: 'I can't do any more. I can't finish my work with innumerable arms.' Saying so, she stopped and put one hand on her knee. I was seated nearby and eating puffed rice. She looked at me and said with a smile: 'Look, I have only two arms, and I say that I have innumerable arms!' Smiling, the Mother continued her sweeping."[24]

Once, not long after Ramakrishna's death, Holy Mother was travelling to Jayrambati from Kamarpukur. Shivaram, the Master's nephew, was then a young boy. He was travelling with the Mother and carrying her bundle. As they neared Jayrambati, Shivaram thought of something and stopped. The Mother was surprised and asked him to keep up.

Shivaram replied, "I shall move only if you tell me something."

"What?"

"Will you tell me who you are?"

"Who else am I? I am your aunt."

"Then you can go by yourself. You are near your home. I won't go with you."

"Don't be silly. Who do you think I am? I am a human being, your aunt."

"Very good. Then why don't you go on by yourself?"

The sun was about to set. Seeing Shivaram standing still in the meadow, Holy Mother said: "People say I am Kali."

"Are you really Kali? Is it true?"

"Yes," Holy Mother replied.

Shivaram was pleased and said: "Let us go then."[25]

It was the spring of 1920. Holy Mother was leaving Jayrambati for Calcutta, so Shivaram came from Kamarpukur to see her. He arrived at Jayrambati around noon and informed the Mother that he would stay there that day and return to Kamarpukur the next day. After lunch the Mother told him to rest and go back to Kamarpukur in the afternoon with some fruits to offer to Raghuvir, their family deity. Shivaram replied that he had done the worship for that day; he had even finished the evening worship and put the Lord to bed. Stunned, the Mother said: "What is this? If Raghuvir and Shitala are worshipped in this way during your lifetime, then imagine what will happen when your children take charge! Have you not heard how my father-in-law worshipped Raghuvir with great respect and devotion?"

Shivaram replied: "Aunt, it will be fine. It is only a matter of one day. Today I want to stay with you." After saying that, Shivaram went to take rest in the parlour with the monks.

Meanwhile Holy Mother made a bundle of fruit and vegetables. She had Brahmachari Barada call Shivaram at four o'clock. The Mother said to him: "Raise Lord Raghuvir from bed and perform the vesper service and the food offering. Whatever you have done is like giving a noon rest to the deity. Don't worry. When you come to Dakshineswar, you will see me."

Then the Mother told Barada: "Carry this bundle and go with Shibu. Go with him up to Amarpur on the other side of the Amodar River and then come back." With tearful eyes Shivaram bowed down to the Mother and left with Barada. On the way he did not say a single word. After arriving at Amarpur, Barada handed over the bundle to Shivaram and returned to Jayrambati.

In the late afternoon the Mother began to cut vegetables for dinner. Barada was seated near her. Suddenly Shivaram came back with the bundle in hand. He prostrated at Holy Mother's feet and said tearfully: "Mother, tell me what will happen to me? I want to hear it from you."

Mother replied: "Shibu, get up. You have nothing to worry about. You have served the Master so much. He loved you dearly. You have no more to fear. You are already free even in this life."

"Mother, please take all my responsibility for this life and the next," Shivaram said. "You told me about your true nature previously. Please confirm that once more now."

Holy Mother was trying to console Shivaram by caressing his head and chin, but was a little perturbed by his overwhelming emotion. She said calmly and gravely: "Yes, I am that Kali." Shivaram then knelt down before her and chanted this salutation mantra: "O Consort of Shiva, the most auspicious of all auspicious beings! O Doer of all actions! O Refuge of all! O three-eyed goddess of golden complexion! O Power of Narayana, I salute You again and again." Holy Mother touched his chin with her fingers and kissed them, and then blessed him by touching his head.

Shivaram was overwhelmed with joy. He took his bundle and stick and got ready to leave. Again Holy Mother asked Barada to carry the bundle up to Amarpur. Barada obeyed the Mother and followed Shivaram. A great commotion was going on in Barada's young mind about Holy Mother's divinity. After leaving Jayrambati, Shivaram said to Barada: "Brother, the Mother is Kali Herself. She can change human destiny. One can attain liberation by her grace. Do you understand? Brother, you are blessed. Hold onto her firmly."[26]

Holy Mother was generally reticent to speak about her divinity, but she revealed her true nature to some of her close disciples who were

pure, sincere, and devoted to her. At the same time she was an embodiment of humility and considered herself to be a servant of the Master.
While giving initiation to her disciples, she would point to the Master's
picture and say, "He is your guru." During Holy Mother's last illness,
an elderly woman devotee was praising her, saying: "Mother, you are
Jagadamba — the Mother of the Universe. You are everything."

Holy Mother told her abruptly: "Keep quiet! You are calling me
'Jagadamba!' I am gratified that the Master graciously gave me shelter at
his feet. 'You are Jagadamba, you are such and such!' You had better leave
this place."[27]

Although she did not disturb the sincere faith of anyone, she could not
tolerate flattery.

In December 1910, Holy Mother went to Kothar, in Orissa, to recuperate from an illness. She was accompanied by some monks and devotees.
The party stayed at a house that Balaram's family owned. One noon when
everyone else was resting, the Mother left her room and sat on a veranda,
her legs extended in front of her. Ashu was with her and watched her as
she sat deep in thought. Her eyes were wide open, but indrawn. In an
abstracted mood, the Mother said:

> "This repeated journey to the earth! Is there no escape from it? Wherever
> there is Shiva, there is Shakti. They are always together. It is the same Shiva
> again and again, and the same Shakti too. No escape.
>
> "People do not understand how much the Master suffered for their
> sake. All those austerities! Did he need them for himself? Still he per-
> formed them for people's welfare. Can they themselves practise spiritual
> disciplines? Where is the power, the vigour? That is why the Master did all
> that. Do you know that song?"
>
> "Which one?" asked Ashu.
>
> "'Behold, the Lord of the lowly has come for the lowly!' Really my chil-
> dren are beggars. Can He remain still if they call on the Mother? At once
> the Lord comes down."
>
> "Is Chaitanya also God?"
>
> "Yes, yes. It is the same God. He comes down again and again. It is the
> same moon that shines night after night. No escape. He is in the clutches
> of His creatures. They are His own. Who will look after them if not He?
>
> "He said: 'Whenever you call on Me, I shall appear before you.' Remem-
> ber this and never forget it. If you call on Him, you will realize Him. He is
> the Wish-fulfilling Tree."
>
> "I know only my Mother."
>
> "It is the Master who taught the name of Mother. Did people know
> before that God is Mother? It is Her creation. She gives birth to all beings

and again swallows them. To swallow means to give liberation. It is all Her sport, Her play."[28]

Brahmachari Bimal (later Swami Dayananda) was the regular worshipper in Udbodhan House. One day after the worship, he went to bow down to the Mother. She pointed to the pictures of Kali and the Master, then pointed to herself and remarked: "All three are one."[29]

In 1896, during Durga Puja, Holy Mother was staying on the third floor of a rented house in Baghbazar. Its first floor was a turmeric warehouse and the second floor was occupied by Holy Mother's male attendants. Kumudbandhu Sen recalled:

> During Durga Puja the monks and devotees bowed down to Holy Mother and offered flowers at her feet. On Ashtami, the second day of worship, while we were waiting on the second floor M. [Mahendra Nath Gupta] arrived. Golap-ma called out, "Those who want to see the Mother, please come." One by one, we went upstairs with flowers and offered them at her feet. But M. remained on the second floor. I asked, "Master Mahashay, will you not go to see the Mother?" Smiling, he replied, "I have already seen her." Surprised, I said: "Well, you have come just now. When did you see her?" He replied softly, "In the Siddheshwari Kali temple in Baghbazar." "Mother, did not go there. I have been here since yesterday." M. again said, "I have seen her there." He then began to sing:

> > Can one be joyless if one's Mother is blissful?
> > The Divine Mother keeps Her child in bliss in this world and the next.
> > The blissful Mother Tara ever fills the mind with bliss.
> > O Mother, I pray: May my mind be attached to Your blessed feet.[30]

Manifestation as a Devi

Some of Holy Mother's disciples and devotees saw in her different forms of the Divine Mother, including Bagala, Kali, Jagaddhatri, Sita, Radha, and so on. She took those forms out of compassion or out of necessity — never to demonstrate her power. The contrast between Ramakrishna's and Holy Mother's manifestation of divinity is that the Master could not suppress his samadhi or control how he revealed himself in various divine forms, whereas the Mother had full control. In this connection Swami Premananda wrote in a letter: "The Master was endowed with the power of knowledge and we witnessed many times his ecstasy and samadhi. But what of the Mother? She held these powers suppressed within herself. What superhuman power she had!"

In this section we shall reproduce a few eyewitness accounts of Holy Mother's divinity.

Manoranjan Chaudhury of Noakhali (now in Bangladesh) was very devoted to Mother Kali. He read the first part of *Sri Ramakrishna Kathamrita* (*The Gospel of Sri Ramakrishna*) in Bengali by M. and then came to Calcutta. He first visited Dakshineswar and Belur Math, and then met M., who suggested that he go to Jayrambati to meet Holy Mother. Manoranjan took the train for Vishnupur and then went to Jayrambati. He was overwhelmed with joy and asked for the Mother's grace. The next morning the Mother was waiting for him after she finished her worship.

Manoranjan reminisced: "As soon as I arrived, the Mother asked, 'Do you want initiation?' I replied, 'Mother, I know nothing about it. Do as you wish.' Pointing to the Punyapukur, the Mother said, 'Go, have a bath in that pond and then come back.' I hurriedly dipped in the pond and returned to the Mother. M. had told me to bring a thin red-bordered cloth, one rupee, and a few hibiscus flowers, which I presented to the Mother. The Mother initiated me with a mantra and taught me how to repeat it on her own fingers. Pointing to the picture of the Master, she said, 'He is your Ishta, your Chosen Deity.' After initiation I bowed down to the Mother. When I raised my head, I did not see her. Instead I distinctly saw Mother Kali seated in place of Holy Mother. Once again I fell at her feet, and then lost outer consciousness."[31]

Swami Haripremananda, a disciple of Holy Mother, recalled:

Let me tell you of an incident concerning Holy Mother. I don't remember the date or year, and I don't feel they are important. Radhu, Holy Mother's niece, had been suffering from a chronic disease for a long time. As a result, her body was reduced to a skeleton. She did not have strength even to speak. Whenever she tried to speak, only a croaking sound came from her throat. Holy Mother was very compassionate to her. She said to me: "Hari, I shall take Radhu to Bankura. Please come with me. Vaikuntha [Holy Mother's disciple] lives in Bankura. He is an allopathic doctor, but practises homeopathy. He has a wonderful reputation."

I said: "Do you mean Vaikuntha Maharaj, Swami Maheswarananda?"

"Yes, yes. You lived in Bankura town. You must know him."

"Yes, Mother, I know him very well. He is the head of the Bankura centre. He is an excellent homeopath."

"Yes, you are right. I am talking about him."

I accompanied Holy Mother and Radhu to Bankura. At that time there were not many rooms at the Bankura centre. There was no accommodation for outsiders, especially women. So a two-room apartment was rented for Radhu's treatment. Radhu stayed in one room, and Holy Mother and myself in the other.

One evening Doctor Maharaj [Swami Maheswarananda] came and

left after seeing Radhu. There was a small stool in our room; Mother was seated on it. On my own, I began to gently massage Mother's feet. They were wrinkled and dry. Moreover, her body was then lean and thin. While massaging her feet, a question arose in my mind: "Is Mother truly the Mother of the Universe? Could the Divine Mother have such wrinkled feet with visible veins?" Although the question was in my mind, I did not express it. I continued to massage her feet.

Gradually a mysterious change occurred. I felt that her feet were no longer the emaciated feet of an old woman; they were the well-developed feet of a young woman. There was a lantern nearby and in the light I clearly saw two beautiful feet outlined with a stripe of red paint [alta], toes fully developed and close to one another, and exquisite half-crescent toenails. There were also golden anklets adorned with gems and jewels. I wondered whose feet these were that I was massaging!

Astonished and dumbfounded, I slowly shifted my gaze from Mother's feet to her face. I saw the form of Goddess Jagaddhatri with a golden complexion, three eyes, and four arms, adorned with many ornaments. She wore a crown on her head and held weapons in her hands. A magnificent lustre emanated from her body. Before I saw that form completely, I lost outer consciousness, saying, "Mother, Mother."

I don't know how long I stayed in that condition. When I regained consciousness, I found Holy Mother caressing my back with her hand and saying, "O Hari, O Hari, what has happened to you? Get up, get up!" I got up and saw again the old, emaciated Mother looking at her sick niece.

This is our Mother of the Universe — Mother Sarada — the spiritual consort of Bhagavan Sri Ramakrishna! Victory to the Mother! Victory to the Master![32]

Swami Arupananda narrated the following incident, which took place in Jayrambati:

Arupananda: "Mother, shall I pass my whole life in this way — constructing houses, marketing, keeping accounts? What shall I gain from doing such work?"

The Mother calmly replied: "Well, my son, what else do you want to do? In this age, Swamiji has inculcated these works as the means of God-realization. If you perform this work without any motive and as worship, you will attain liberation. What else do you want to do? Do you want to practise austerities in the solitude of the Himalayas? There you will find the monks fighting among themselves over a piece of bread or a blanket! Will the Lord appear before you if you go to the mountains and forests and sit there with closed eyes? Is there any better path than the path of action that has been delineated by Swamiji? While working, think that you are working only for God and are serving Him. The work that you are doing here is truly my work. Rasbihari, look at me."

Rasbihari [Arupananda] looked at the Mother's face and saw a luminous goddess seated in front of him in place of the plain and elderly woman who had been talking to him. Her entire form was radiant with an effulgent light. Rasbihari could not keep looking at that luminous form. Struck with awe and fear, he closed his eyes. Immediately he heard the familiar voice of the Mother: "O Rasbihari, what happened to you? Why have you closed your eyes? Look — look at me." Rasbihari opened his eyes and saw Holy Mother sitting in front of him as before — the same familiar look with the usual sweet smile on her face.[33]

Towards the end of his life Arupananda related another experience to a monk in Varanasi:

I was in Jayrambati. The Mother's new house was then under construction. Brahmachari Hemendra and I were looking after the construction work. The Mother was living in one of the cottages of Uncle Prasanna, her brother. Sometimes her brothers argued with us, complaining, "You are giving everything to our sister and depriving us." Thus one day a quarrel ensued and I was irritated. Perturbed, I went straight to the Mother. She was standing on the veranda of Uncle Prasanna's house, facing the courtyard and holding onto a post with her left hand. Agitated, I said to her: "Mother, there is so much quarrelling, bickering, and disturbance that I cannot work here anymore." Saying this, I sat on the veranda of a thatched hut opposite her cottage. The Mother remained standing there and calmly said: "If you cannot work here, that is fine. Here things go on in this way." I saw her look vacantly towards me. Immediately I saw that her standing form became illuminated and a halo appeared around her body for a while. The Mother did not say anything else. This vision calmed my agitation instantly. A complete change took place in my mind and I thought: To whom did I say that I won't do your work? I left and began to work again with great enthusiasm and respect. I saw this clearly with my open eyes in broad daylight."[34]

Vaikuntha (later Swami Maheswarananda) of Bankura was an allopathic doctor, but later began to practise homeopathy because it was less expensive for poor people who could not afford to buy allopathic medicines. He was a reputable and successful doctor, and Holy Mother had tremendous faith in him. He used to put the first dose of medicine on the patient's tongue and then give the patient the rest of the doses in small packets to take later. Once the Mother was suffering from dysentery in Jagadamba Ashrama, Koalpara. Vaikuntha came from Bankura to treat her. He opened his homeopathic medicine box and came forward to put a drop of medicine on the Mother's tongue. But just as he was about to administer the medicine, he became confused and dumbfounded. He kept on looking at the Mother's face.

The Mother said: "O Vaikuntha, give me the medicine." Vaikuntha was startled and his hand began to shake. Instead of dropping the medicine on her tongue, he put the medicine phial back in the box and prostrated at her feet. The Mother asked: "What happened, Vaikuntha? Will you not give me the medicine?" Still shivering, Vaikuntha said: "Yes Mother, I shall give the medicine. But what have I seen, Mother?" Without answering the question, she changed the topic and said: "My son, I am suffering from dysentery. Please give me some medicine quickly." Vaikuntha put some of the medicine into the Mother's hand and asked her to swallow it. Later Vaikuntha said that he had seen the face of the goddess Jagaddhatri in the Mother's face, so he did not dare put medicine directly in her mouth. Afterwards, he always gave medicine to the Mother in tiny paper packets.[35]

Chandra Mohan Datta wrote in his reminiscences:

Holy Mother graciously revealed her true nature to me. She made me understand that she was a goddess of heaven, born as a human being to deliver us. I sometimes accompanied the Mother to Jayrambati. Once the Mother was returning to Calcutta and we were travelling by bullock cart via Koalpara. On the way to Vishnupur, the bullock cart stopped and the Mother took a little rest under a roadside tree. Suddenly a desire came to my mind to see the true form of the Mother. Seeing her alone under the tree I beseeched her: "Mother, you love me like your own son. It is through your benevolence alone that I maintain myself and my family. You protect us from all danger and adversity. Still I have an unfulfilled desire. If you fulfill that, I shall have nothing left to wish for." The Mother wanted to know about that desire. I said, "My last desire is to see your true form." The Mother did not agree to this. Observing my repeated earnest entreaties, she reluctantly agreed and said to her companions: "You go away a little. I shall have a private talk with him."

She said to me: "Look, you alone will see it and no one else. Don't be afraid of seeing my true form, and don't divulge to others what you will see as long as I am alive." Saying so, the Mother assumed her true form in front of me. It was the form of the Divine Mother Jagaddhatri. I was petrified with fear by seeing that divine luminous form. An ethereal glow emanated from her body, illuminating the area. My eyes were dazzled by the brilliance of the glow. I further saw Jaya and Vijaya [two companions of Jagaddhatri] flanking the Mother. My whole body began to tremble and did not stop. I could not stand steadily. I fell at her feet. The Mother then withdrew the form of Jagaddhatri and resumed her usual human form.

She stroked me with her hand, and slowly my shivering stopped. When I regained my normal state, she said again: "Don't tell anyone what you have seen as long as I am alive." I asked the Mother: "Who are your Jaya and Vijaya?" "Golap and Yogin," she replied.[36]

Basana Nandi was born near Kamarpukur, probably in 1899. She was married when she was 7 years old, but her husband died shortly thereafter. When she was 13, Holy Mother hired her to do some household work, such as cleaning the dishes and clothes, sweeping and mopping the floor, and so on. In the evenings she also massaged the Mother's feet to relieve her rheumatism. Basana recalled:

One day in Jayrambati I wanted to go to a neighbouring village to attend a Puja festival. But the Mother would not allow me to go alone. That night when I was massaging her feet with oil, she told me: "The thing which you are eager to see, you will see here." While massaging her feet, I fell asleep. Suddenly my sleep broke and I saw a bright light all around. I have never seen such an effulgent light. I saw the living goddess Jagadhatri in the midst of that light. It was a beautiful and benign form of the Divine Mother. But I did not see the Mother. Frightened, I cried "Mother, Mother," and ran out of the room. But I did not see the Mother outside either. I returned to the room and found the Mother sleeping on her bed. There was no more blazing light. Instead, a dim kerosene lantern was lit in a corner. I called out to the Mother and she asked, "What have you seen?" I told her what I saw. Smiling, she said: "What you have seen is true. I am Jagaddhatri, Durga, Lakshmi, Saraswati, and Kali."[37]

Lalmohan Das, known as Lalu, was a fisherman who lived in Satbere Village, close to Jayrambati. When he had time off from fishing, he learned Baul songs from Baral Master, who was a worshipper of Kali. Lalu bought a Baul costume, anklets, an ektara (a stringed instrument), and a small tabor (a drum). With permission from Holy Mother, he sang Baul songs during the Jagaddhatri Puja in Jayrambati. Lalu used to call Holy Mother "Aunt." His wife and four sons were also devoted to her.

The Mother always had many visitors, and Lalu used to supply fish and vegetables for them. During one of the festivals, the swamis of Jayrambati asked Lalu to catch fish from Punyapukur, which belonged to the Mother. Lalu went with his party and dropped a long net in the water. The Mother and her nieces came to the eastern ghat to watch.

Lalu reminisced:

Although I was busy in the water pulling the net, my eyes from time to time were on Aunt. I saw her walking on the east side of the pond along with two women* wearing the same bordered saris and similar veils. I did not see their faces but it seemed that their faces were similar to Aunt's. I was startled. I was about to go to Aunt, but suddenly a big fish escaped by jumping over the net. Again I concentrated on setting the net. We caught some small fish and but could not get the big one for Aunt.

Later one day when she was alone I asked her: "Aunt, the other day when you came to see our fishing with your nieces, I saw two women with you, who seemed to be of your age and of a similar appearance and had similar clothing." Without assigning any importance to my question, she said: "Who else was with me? Leaving Radhu and Maku, I went to the Bel-tala to get some *Gime* spinach." I said, "No, Aunt, when you were going to the Bel-tala I saw two women — one was in front of you and the other in back." Smiling, Aunt said: "Lalu, you have too much bile in your stomach. You should drink some rock candy syrup." Saying so, Aunt entered her room. Again I saw two women — one in front of her and the other behind her. I cried out, "Aunt!" She answered from the room, "Lalu, wait for some prasad." She returned and gave me some sweetened puffed rice and fruit. Aunt never revealed her divinity, but I will never forget those two scenes. From then on, I had no doubt that Aunt was not a human being; she was truly a goddess.[38]

Aghoremani, a childhood friend of Holy Mother, recalled: "Once during the Jagaddhatri Puja in Jayrambati, Ramhriday Ghoshal of Haldepukur Village was present. He saw Holy Mother meditating in front of the goddess Jagaddhatri in the shrine. For a long time, he looked at the face of the image and then at the face of Holy Mother. Back and forth went his gaze and he could not find any difference between them. Stupefied and frightened, Ramhriday left."[39]

Holy Mother was seen in her Jagaddhatri form by several of her disciples and devotees. But what about her other divine forms? While in Rameswaram, as soon as she saw the image of Lord Rameswar, she exclaimed: "I see it is just the same as when I first placed it here." She remembered that she was Sita in one of her previous incarnations. The porter of the Vishnupur railway station recognized Holy Mother as Sita and received initiation from her.

After Ramakrishna's passing away, Holy Mother went to Vrindaban for a pilgrimage. There she experienced the mood of Radha and restlessly searched for Krishna in the groves of Vrindaban. Later she told a devotee that she had been Radha in a previous incarnation.

Durga Puri narrated the following incident:

*Those two women were Jaya and Vijaya, two companions of the Divine Mother.

Once a Vaishnava priest of the Shitala temple in Garpar, East Calcutta, asked Gauri-ma to accompany him to Vrindaban, the place of Radha and Krishna. She told the priest: "Well, one day I shall show you the living Radharani." The priest did not understand Gauri-ma's hint. Then she went to Udbodhan and told Holy Mother what she had said to the priest. As soon as Holy Mother heard the word "living Radharani," she protested, saying: "Shame on you! Why did you say that, Gaurdasi? Radha was Chinmayi, consciousness personified."

"You are also the same," remarked Gauri-ma. After a few days Gauri-ma accompanied the priest to Udbodhan, who at first saw the Mother as an ordinary woman. However, he bowed down to the Mother and then raised his head to see her face. Overwhelmed, he kept on looking at the Mother's face. He then folded his hands and repeated three times: "Vande Rādhām ānandarupinim — I salute Radha, the embodiment of bliss."[40]

It is well known that the Mother encountered a robber at Telo-Bhelo and that she addressed him as father. One day Ashu asked the Mother: "What did the robber see in you?"

"He told me that he saw Kali in me," Holy Mother replied.

Ashu responded: "Then you revealed yourself to him as Kali? Don't hide it, Mother. Please tell me."

"Why should I show him? He told me what he saw."

"Well, Mother, you showed him [that you were Kali]. The robber did not see any other woman. He saw only you. Whether you admit it or not, it is self-evident that you showed him."

"Well, you may say whatever you like," Holy Mother said, and smiled.

"Mother, I don't want to see your Kali form," said Ashu. "I am happy to see you in this form. You are my mother and I am your son."

"Very well, my son. I am relieved. I will not have to stand and stick out my tongue."[41]

After Ramakrishna's passing away, Holy Mother stayed in Kamarpukur for a year. In Chapter 11, we related how she was pursued by Harish, who had become crazy, and how she escaped by punishing him and assuming a divine form. Later one day Ashu asked the Mother: "Mother, did you take the form of Bagala at that time? I have heard this from the monks in Belur Math."

Holy Mother replied: "Who knows, my child? I was then not myself."

Ashu said: "You don't like to be caught. You are like a cat covered with ashes — so no one can recognize its true form."

The Mother smiled.[42]

In Chapter 26, we described how Surendranath Sen went to ask for

initiation from Swami Vivekananda, but Swamiji refused and told Surendra that the person who would initiate him was greater than himself. At
that time Surendra was very disappointed. However, he received a mantra from a goddess in a dream, and he reported this to Swamiji.

Swamiji explained the dream: "The Master used to say, 'A divine dream
is true.' It is called attaining perfection through a dream. Go on repeating
this mantra. You will attain everything. You will not have to do anything
else."

"I don't believe in dreams," Surendra replied. "A dream is just a baseless thought."

Swamiji said: "In fact, this dream is true. Go on repeating the mantra, and then you will see: the goddess who gave the mantra will appear
before you in a physical form. She is an incarnation of Bagala and is now
in the form of Saraswati."

"I don't understand what you mean," said Surendra.

Swamiji reassured him: "You will understand in time. You will see that
the external form is calm and benign but the inner form is formidable.
The form of Saraswati is very calm and serene."

Surendra replied, "I don't believe all these things."

"Whether you believe it or not, go on repeating the mantra. It will do
you good," Swamiji advised.[43]

Surendra never repeated the mantra that he received in his dream. But
later, when he was initiated by Holy Mother, he was amazed to discover
that the dream-mantra and the Mother's mantra were the same. He then
realized the truth of Swamiji's words.

Prabodh Chandra Chattopadhyay was the headmaster of Badanganj
School and a disciple of the Mother. He related this incident:

> Once when Shivaram was away from his home in Kamarpukur, his wife
> arranged their daughter Panchi's marriage with a young man after con-
> sulting with the wealthy and influential Laha family. Ramlal, Panchi's
> uncle, was not in favour of the marriage because the boy belonged to a
> low-caste family. With Ramlal's permission, Prabodh and Jnanananda
> quietly escorted Panchi to Holy Mother in Jayrambati. The Mother heard
> the whole story. Prabodh told the Mother that if this marriage did not go
> through, the Laha family might be upset and prevent the Master's temple
> from being built in Kamarpukur. Then Prabodh casually remarked that
> it might not matter if the temple was not built in the Master's birthplace.
>
> Irritated, the Mother said sharply: "What do you mean? The birthplace
> of the Master is a holy place — the most sacred spot for pilgrims. It is not
> proper to speak that way."

Expressing his apprehension, Prabodh said: "I wonder, if Shivaram's wife becomes angry about the marriage affair, would she set fire to the Master's cottage?" Immediately the Mother's mood changed and she said: "That would be wonderful. It would fulfill the Master's wish. He loved cremation grounds — the whole place would be a cremation ground." Saying so, the Mother burst into harsh laughter. Gradually her voice became louder and grew into a roar. This dreadful laughter continued for a few minutes. Prabodh and the others were stupefied. A little later the Mother became normal again.[44]

During World War I, the Mother was in Jayrambati. One day she asked someone to read the news of the war to her. She listened for ten minutes and learned about the massive destruction in Europe. Suddenly her mood changed. She began to laugh "Ho–Ho–Ho" in a soft voice. Then she started to laugh loudly "Ha–Ha–Ha–Ha", and that roar of laughter shook the cottage. Golap-ma and Yogin-ma were present. They prayed to her with folded hands: "Mother, restrain, restrain yourself."* Gradually the Mother became normal again.[45]

Once there was a performance of the play *Daksha-Yajna* at Balaram's house. Holy Mother, Gauri-ma, Golap-ma, Yogin-ma, and many other people were there. In this story, a daughter of King Daksha, Sati (Parvati), married Shiva against her father's wishes. The King held a sacrifice and invited the gods, but did not invite Shiva and Sati. The sage Narada carried the news to Shiva and Sati, who lived on Mount Kailash. Sati was upset. She went to the top of the mountain and found that her sisters were going to her father's place with their husbands. She lamented: "Ah me! All my sisters are going, but not me." The audience was touched by Sati's grief. This scene roused the Mother's memory of her divinity. She heaved a sigh and tearfully blurted out: "Ah me! All my sisters are going, but not me."

Immediately her companions' attention fell on her and Gauri-ma said: "What happened, Mother? Now you can't hide your real nature anymore." Embarrassed, the Mother asked her to keep quiet.[46]

During Holy Mother's early days in Jayrambati she had heard all kinds of uncharitable remarks about Ramakrishna from the villagers. They said that the Master was crazy, that he walked around naked in the temple garden of Dakshineswar, and so on. Her mother, Shyamasundari, also

---

*According to the Hindu tradition, the Divine Mother has two aspects: benign and destructive. She plays in both ways. To those who are evil-minded, she appears before them as a destructive force. Perhaps these two incidents roused in her mind the play of destruction.

from time to time lamented that she had married her daughter to a madman. Hearing her husband being criticized again and again, one day Holy Mother became enraged. She told her mother: "Look, don't say that my husband is mad. I caution you. Once I gave up my body listening to the criticism of my husband.* Do you want to see that happen again?" Observing her normally calm daughter's terrible form, Shyamasundari was stunned and fearful. From then on she never criticized her son-in-law in front of her daughter.[47]

Once there was a famine in Bankura, and the Ramakrishna Mission conducted relief work there. At that time a monk visited the Mother in Jayrambati and related to her the pitiable condition of the people in Bankura. After listening to the sad story, the Mother waved her hand and said, "My son, by the grace of Mother Simhavahini, Jayrambati Village is not affected by famine."

The monk replied: "Mother, I don't understand Mother Simhavahini. It is because of you this village is well protected." The Mother remained silent.[48]

A devotee once asked her: "Mother, some say that you are Kali, some say you are Durga, and others say you are Jagaddhatri. I shall believe you if you say yourself who you are."

Holy Mother replied: "Yes, my son, what those people say — I am that."[49]

Holy Mother Speaks the Truth

Holy Mother's life was based on truth, so everything she said came true. During Durga Puja one year, Girish's sister came to see the Mother in Udbodhan. She was extremely generous and devoted to the Mother. After the puja, Holy Mother was planning to go to Varanasi, so she was busy arranging her things, moving from room to room. At last Girish's sister said: "Mother, may I take leave now?" Absentmindedly the Mother said: "Yes, go." The woman hurried down the stairs. As soon as she left, the Mother said to herself: "What a foolish thing have I done! Did I say to her, 'Go?'** Never before have I said such a thing to anybody. And, alas, she never came back. I do not know why such words came out of my mouth."[50] Girish's sister passed away that very night.

Surendranath Roy of Barisal was a doctor who had contracted

---

*Sarada Devi reminded her mother Shyamasundari that in the past she was Sati, who gave up her body when her husband Shiva was criticized by her father Daksha.
**The Indian custom is to say to one who is taking leave, "Come again." It is very inauspicious to say "Go" to anybody.

tuberculosis while treating his patients. He was bedridden and throwing up blood. At last he lost hope for his life and wrote a letter to Holy Mother, who was his guru: "Mother, I have this terrible disease and I shall not live long. I have a desire to see you once more before I die. I am very sick and too weak to visit you. But if you wish, please come to Barisal and see me. Please come."

Holy Mother sent him one of her photos and a bound volume of *Udbodhan* magazine (1319-1320 BE). She wrote to him: "My son, don't worry. Your disease will be cured. It is not possible for me to go such a distance. See my photo, which I am sending to you, and read this volume of *Udbodhan*."* Surendra felt the Mother's presence in that photo and kept it near his head. Gradually he was cured of that disease.[51]

One year there was a terrible drought in the Jayrambati area and the crops were withering away. The farmers were helpless, so they went to Holy Mother and prayed: "Mother, there is no possibility of having any crops this year. We and our children shall all die without food." Observing their agony, the Mother's heart melted. She went to see the field with the farmers and was very much perturbed. She looked all around and fervently prayed to the Master: "Alas! Lord, what have you done? Will these people die without food?"[52] The Mother's prayer and blessing were infallible. That very night there was a downpour. The farmers had a record harvest that year.

Holy Mother's Divinity Is Hidden

One needs to practise tremendous spiritual disciplines before one is able to recognize an avatar. If God and the Divine Mother do not reveal their true nature, no one can understand them. One realizes God by His grace only. The Katha Upanishad says: "The Atman is attained by him alone whom It chooses."[53] Krishna also said in the Gita: "Veiled by my maya born of the gunas, I am not revealed to all."[54] It is true: A prophet is not honoured in his own country.

Hardly any villagers in Jayrambati understood the divinity of Holy Mother. People from far off places came there and worshipped the Mother as the Devi, whereas the villagers looked on her as their aunt or sister. One day a village woman said to the Mother, "People from distant places come to see you, but why can't we recognize your true nature?"

The Mother replied: "It does not matter whether you understand me. I am your friend — that is enough."

The village watchman, Ambika Bagdi, once said to Holy Mother:

* *Sri Ramakrishna Lilaprasanga* was being published serially in *Udbodhan* at that time.

"People call you Devi, Bhagavati, and so on, but we don't understand those things at all."

Holy Mother replied: "It is not necessary for you to understand those things. You are my Brother Ambika and I am your Sister Sarada."[55]

Thus the Mother played her divine role through both self-revelation and self-concealment.

Those who were pure, simple, sincere, and devoted understood the Mother's extraordinary nature to some extent — but most of the villagers of Jayrambati saw her as Ramchandra Mukhopadhyay's daughter. One day she made a comment: "These people cannot understand who I am."[56]

The Mother's Omniscience

God is omniscient, omnipotent, and omnipresent. Holy Mother was endowed with all these characteristics, but she did not manifest them all at once. She knew everything collectively (*sarvajna*) as well as individually (*sarvavit*). She was aware of the past, present, and future of her disciples, and she guided them on the path of blessedness. She did not embarrass them by revealing their shortcomings in front of others. Fault-finding was not in her nature. She removed her disciples' fear and delusion by reassuring them with her motherly love and affection. Many of them were overwhelmed when they witnessed her divine power.

Vedanta says that the absolute truth is beyond mind and speech, but it is not beyond reason. Human beings are guided by faith and reason, in other words, by the heart and the intellect. The intellect clears the path of truth and the heart pushes forward along it. Blaise Pascal said, "We know the truth, not only by reason, but also by the heart." People invariably fail when they try to understand the truth only through reason, because the intellect has limitations. Truth stands the test of experience. There are some episodes of the Mother's life that we cannot explain, but we shall present them to the readers and let them come to their own conclusions.

In the early days when Holy Mother was staying at the nahabat in Dakshineswar, Yogin-ma would visit her and the Master once a week. Yogin-ma used to worship Lord Shiva in her Calcutta residence every day, and she used bilva leaves for the ritual. She would pick fresh bilva leaves from the Dakshineswar garden and carry them to Calcutta, but by the time of worship, the leaves were dried up. One day the Mother asked, "Yogin, do you worship using dried bilva leaves?"

Surprised, Yogin-ma replied: "Yes, I do, Mother. How did you know about it?"

The Mother calmly said: "During my meditation this morning, I saw you worshipping with dried bilva leaves."[57]

On the evening of 20 September 1918, Sarajubala Sen came to Udbodhan House. Mandakini was rubbing oil on Holy Mother's back. Nalini and other women were also near the Mother. The Mother was then praising Yogin-ma's and Golap-ma's visions and spiritual experiences. Nalini asked: "Aunt, I hear so many people get deep meditation and visions, but I don't experience anything. I have been living with you for such a long time, but what have I achieved?"

Holy Mother replied: "Why do you not get these experiences? People have experiences because they have so much devotion and faith. Look, one needs faith and devotion. What do you have?"

Nalini said: "Aunt, people say that you are omniscient. Is it true? Well, could you tell me what is in my mind?"

Holy Mother smiled. When Nalini insisted, the Mother said: "They say that out of their devotion." Then she continued: "I am nobody. The Master is everything." She folded her hands and bowed to the Master's photo, and said, "All of you pray to the Master, 'Let there be no ego in me.'"

A woman from Dhaka then said: "My son says: 'What shall I say to the Mother? She is Jagadamba, the Mother of the Universe. She knows what is in every mind.'"

Sarajubala replied: "Many of us address the Mother as the Divine Mother of the Universe, but the Lord alone knows the extent of our conviction. When sceptics like us proclaim her divinity, it is a sort of parrotry."

Holy Mother smiled and said, "You are right, my child."

Sarajubala continued: "The Mother is a veritable goddess. If the Mother does not make us understand this out of compassion, is it possible to comprehend that? Utter absence of egotism is the convincing proof of the Mother's divinity. A human being is full of ego. Every day we see hundreds of people prostrating themselves before the Mother and calling her 'goddess Lakshmi, Mother of the Universe.' Were she a mere human being, she would be puffed up with pride. Has a human being the power to withstand so much honour?"

Pleased, the Mother looked upon Sarajubala, her eyes full of grace.[58]

Prafulla Gangopadhyay recalled:

One day while offering food to the Master, I saw a current of light falling on the offering from his picture. Referring to this, I asked the Mother: "Mother, is this vision of mine true or a fantasy? If it is a fantasy, please do something so that I can be free from it."

After a brief pause, Holy Mother replied: "No, it is not a fantasy, my son. You have seen right."

"Do you know what I see?" Prafulla asked.

"Yes, I do."

"Does the Master accept the food that I offer to him? Do you also accept the food that I offer to you?"

"Yes."

"How can I understand this?"

Mother replied: "Well, have you not read in the Gita that God accepts the fruit, flowers, water, and other things that are offered to Him with devotion?"

Surprised, Prafulla exclaimed: "Are you then God?"

At this, Holy Mother burst into laughter.[59]

It was 13 November 1913. After the vesper service, the Mother lay down on her bed in Udbodhan House. Yogin-ma was also there. The Mother was a little drowsy. Suddenly she got up and said: "Is Purna dead, Yogin?"

Yogin-ma was amazed to hear this question and asked, "Who has told you this, Mother?"

The Mother replied: "I was asleep. Suddenly I heard someone saying, 'Purna is dead.'"

Yogin-ma then confirmed: "Yes, Mother, Purna died this afternoon. I did not tell you, Mother." That evening the Mother talked about Purna and expressed her sorrow.[60]

Some days after Lalmohan (later Swami Kapileswarananda) received initiation from the Mother, a doubt arose in his mind: "What have I done? Alas, I took initiation from a woman." Gradually this created severe mental anguish. Finally he decided that he would give up the mantra if the Master did not remove his mental conflict. The next day Swami Premananda sent Lalmohan to Udbodhan House from Belur Math with milk for Holy Mother. As soon as Lalmohan bowed down to her, she said to him: "Look, I did not give you the mantra. It was the Master who gave it."

A few days later, that doubt cropped up again. He thought: "I shall believe that the Master has given me the mantra only if Haren Babu tells me that he has received power from the Mother." Some days later during the Master's birthday festival, Haren Babu went to Udbodhan House, bowed down to the Mother, and then went to Belur Math. He told Lalmohan, "Today I have received a special power from the Mother." Thus Lalmohan became free from doubts.[61]

Kshirodbala Roy was a young widow from Sylhet who came to

Udbodhan House for initiation from Holy Mother. Her brother-in-law was a disciple of the Mother. It was decided that she would receive initiation the next day. Her brother-in-law was to escort her. But that evening the Mother told him that Kshirodbala would be sick the next day, so the initiation would take place on the following day. After returning from Udbodhan, Kshirodbala was sick with dizziness. Despite her illness, she made herself ready. However, her brother-in-law did not show up. Then at noon he came and told Kshirodbala what the Mother had said the previous evening.

The next morning Kshirodbala and her brother-in-law went to Holy Mother. She brought fruit and sweets, flowers and bel leaves, and a new sari for the initiation. She saw Holy Mother waiting for her near the door. Immediately Holy Mother took her to the shrine and asked her to sit on an asana. Kshirodbala had tied two rupees in the corner of her cloth for her return carriage fare. When Kshirodbala was about to sit on the asana, Holy Mother said: "My child, you have come to take shelter in the Master, who renounced lust and gold. There are two rupees tied in the corner of your sari. Take them out." Immediately, Kshirodbala removed those rupees and put them on the floor near the wall. Then the Mother initiated her, and reassured her, saying: "Don't be afraid. Now you have been reborn. I have absorbed the results of your karma done in past lives. You are now pure and sinless."[62]

Gokuldas De met Holy Mother in Udbodhan House in 1909 when he was a student. He asked Swami Saradananda for a picture of the Mother. The swami told him that he could have one if he would worship it every day. Gokuldas decided not to take the picture because he was then studying for a B.A. degree in Rangoon, Burma. When he returned to Rangoon after his vacation, he became seriously ill and almost lost hope for his life. However, he experienced the Mother's presence and gradually recuperated from that illness. In October 1911 Gokuldas took a break from his studies and returned to Calcutta. During this time M. taught him how to chant the Gita and the Chandi. Gokuldas continued to visit Holy Mother regularly in Udbodhan. He felt that it was through her grace that he had recovered from his illness.

One day he went for a walk on the bank of the Ganges and found the Mother sitting on the lower step of the ghat repeating her mantra. From a distance he began to recite a hymn from the Chandi in a low voice: "O Mother, you are pleasing, yea more pleasing than all the pleasing things and exceedingly beautiful. You are indeed the supreme Goddess, beyond the high and low."[63] Holy Mother turned towards Gokuldas, raised her hands and blessed him, and again became absorbed in japa.[64]

One evening, while massaging the Mother's feet with medicated oil for her rheumatism, Swami Arupananda silently prayed to have the Mother's disease in his own body so that she would be cured. The Mother smiled a little and then said to him: "My son, what are you thinking? You live long. I am old. How much longer shall I live? You should not think like that. May the Master grant you a long life." Saying so, she put her hand on Arupananda's head and blessed him.[65]

Lalit Mohan Saha of Dhaka recalled: "In 1918 [while living in Calcutta] I was suffering from terrible restlessness of the mind. I was piqued and decided not to visit the Mother anymore. But my friends persuaded me to go to Udbodhan House. There I saw many devotees waiting to bow down to the Mother. They bowed down one after another, and she did not say a single word to anyone. At last when I bowed down to her, she affectionately asked, 'My son, are you keeping well?' In a piqued voice, I answered: 'Yes, Mother, I am fine.' The Mother smiled and said to me: 'What is this, my son? This is the mind's nature. Simply because of it, should you behave this way?'"[66]

In 1914, Mahendra Nath Gupta of Barisal received initiation from Holy Mother, and then in 1915 he went to Jayrambati to see her. Mahendra reminisced: "I had a desire to offer flowers and sandal paste at the Mother's feet. I wondered where I could get those things in this unfamiliar place. Meanwhile, a niece of the Mother brought flowers and sandal paste to me and conveyed her message that if I wanted to offer these, I should go to her now and offer them."[67]

Swami Tanmayananda recalled: "One day on my way to Jayrambati from Koalpara I was thinking that I would be very happy if I could give a little personal service to the Mother. When I arrived there, I found the Mother seated with her legs stretched out in front of her. A cup of oil was on the ground next to her. I began to rub one of her legs with the oil. The Mother said: 'Look, I feel acute pain in this leg. Rub oil on this leg and put some pressure on it.' I massaged her leg for 25 minutes. Finally, the Mother said: 'Are you satisfied now? I shall now go to bathe, and then I shall have to worship the Master. Take your lunch here before you leave.'"[68]

One afternoon Prafullamukhi Basu, a woman disciple, saw Mandakini changing the covers of the Mother's quilt and mattress. A thought flashed through her mind: "I wish I could give this service to the Mother." When Mandakini left, the Mother entered the room. When she saw her bed, she remarked: "Just see, my daughter, how she has muddled everything! She has reversed one cover for the other. My child, change the covers and make the bed again." Thus the Mother fulfilled Prafullamukhi's unexpressed wish.[69]

Swami Bhumananda recalled: "One day Golap-ma was cutting vegetables and remarked, 'The Mother gave me liberation today.' We asked, 'What happened, Golap-ma?'

"Golap-ma told us: 'The other day a nun came from Varanasi and begged for money to pay her guru's debt. The Mother never asks for money from anyone, nor does she ask anybody to give money to someone. But she whispered to me: 'Golap, what is the necessity of keeping those ones [gold coins]? Why don't you give them to this nun?' Dumbfounded, I asked, 'What are you talking about, Mother?' She replied, 'Well, I am talking about the wealth that you have been holding onto all these years like a miser.' In fact, I had saved three gold coins in my house secretly for many years. I brought them from my home and gave them to the nun. Now my mind is light and carefree.'"[70] Golap-ma's financial condition was poor, so she had kept those three gold coins in case of any difficulty. But the omniscient Mother released her from attachment to them so that she could depend wholly on God.

Giver of Liberation

Liberation is the final goal of human life. All beings consciously or unconsciously seek freedom, because freedom is the nature of the soul. According to Vedanta, there are three kinds of liberation: *jivan-mukti*, or liberation while living in this body; *videha-mukti*, or liberation upon leaving the body; and *krama-mukti*, or liberation while passing through the higher realms. The scriptures say *jnānāt moksha*, that is, liberation is possible through the knowledge of Brahman. This knowledge does not come until a person is completely free from desire. And all desires originate from ignorance. As day and night can never be together, so the knowledge of Brahman, or God, and the desire for the world cannot dwell simultaneously in the human heart. Ramakrishna said: "God cannot be realized if there is the slightest attachment to the things of the world. A thread cannot pass through the eye of a needle if the tiniest fibre sticks out."[71] So, human beings are born again and again in this world to fulfill their desires.

In Jayrambati on 5 January 1910, Mother said to Arupananda:

As long as a person has desires, there is no end to his transmigration. It is desire alone that makes him take one body after another. There will be rebirth for a person if he has even the desire to eat a piece of sandesh. It is for this reason that a variety of foodstuffs are brought to Belur Math [so that monks can satisfy all their desires for food]. Desire may be compared to a tiny seed. It is like a big banyan tree growing out of a seed that is no bigger than a dot. Rebirth is inevitable as long as one has desires. It is like taking the soul from one pillowcase and putting it into another. Only one or two people out of many can be found who are free from all desires. Though one gets a new body on account of desire, yet one does not completely lose spiritual consciousness if one has merits from a previous birth to one's credit.[72]

Holy Mother never read Vedanta philosophy, but her teachings beautifully concurred with the conclusions of Vedanta. According to Vedanta, the desire for progeny, the desire for wealth, and the desire for name and fame bind a soul. The soul is released when the cessation of desire, the dissolution of the mind, and illumination take place simultaneously.

On 26 May 1911 in Jayrambati, Arupananda had a wonderful conversation with Holy Mother regarding bondage and liberation.

Arupananda asked, "Will sannyasins who profess the ideal of Vedanta attain nirvana?"

"Surely," Holy Mother replied. "By gradually cutting off the bonds of maya, they will attain nirvana and merge themselves in God. This body is, no doubt, the outcome of desire. The body cannot live unless there is a trace of desire. All comes to an end when one gets rid of desire completely."

"Well, Mother, the Master used to say that Ishwarakotis can come back to the relative plane of consciousness even after the attainment of nirvana; others cannot do so. What does that mean?"

"The Ishwarakoti, even after the attainment of nirvana, can draw his mind back from it and direct it to the ordinary plane of consciousness."

"How can the mind that has merged itself in God be brought back again to the world? How can one ever separate a jar of water from the water of the lake it has been poured into?"

"Not everyone can do so. Only a paramahamsa can. A hamsa [swan] can separate the milk from a mixture of water and milk and then drink only the milk."

"Can everyone be rid of desire?"

"If they could, then this creation would come to an end. The creation continues because everyone cannot be free from desire. People with desire take birth again and again."

"Suppose a man gives up his body while standing in the waters of the Ganges."

"Freedom from birth is possible only when there is no trace of desire. Otherwise, nothing else is of any avail," Holy Mother concluded.[73]

The Divine Mother holds the key to liberation. In the Chandi, even the gods praise Her: "O, Mother, Thou art the great primal energy, the source of infinite strength. Thou art the seed of the world, and illusion divine. Thou hast enchanted the whole universe, O Goddess supreme, by Thy deluding charms. And yet being propitious, Thou bestowest liberation upon human beings."[74]

Ramakrishna said enigmatically on different occasions that Holy Mother had the power to give liberation. In Varanasi, Golap-ma said to Brahmananda, "Rakhal, the Mother asks why a devotee propitiates Shakti, the Divine Mother, at the beginning of worship." Brahmananda replied: "It is because the key to the knowledge of Brahman is in the Divine Mother's custody. There is no way to commune with Brahman unless the Mother graciously unlocks the door."

Holy Mother emphatically reassured her disciples: "The Master promised me, 'To those who take refuge in you, I shall appear at their last moment and escort them by the hand.' Don't be afraid, my son. Always remember the Master is behind you, and so am I. Whatever you do and wherever you go, the Master will come during your last moments to take you to his abode. God gave you hands, feet, and other senses to function in this world, so it is natural that they will act according to their nature. The senses have their way."[75]

One day a disciple said to Holy Mother: "The Master said that those who accepted him as their spiritual ideal would not be born again. Again, Swamiji said that no liberation is possible without being initiated into sannyasa. What, then, is the way for householders?"

The Mother replied: "Yes, what the Master said is true. What Swamiji said is equally true. Householders have no need of external renunciation. They will spontaneously get internal renunciation. But some people need external renunciation. Why should you be afraid? Surrender yourself to the Master, and always remember that he stands behind you."[76]

One day, Holy Mother placed her hand on her chest and told Swami Kamaleswarananda: "If I go to the Master, you too will certainly go to him."[77]

Swami Vijnanananda told this incident to Swami Parameshananda: "One day the Master appeared before me and said: 'Peshan, you talk only about me and give my name to people. Give her [Holy Mother's] name also and talk about her. How will people get liberation if they do not know her? She is the giver of liberation.' From then on, Swami Vijnanananda would initiate his disciples with the mantras of both the Master and the Mother."[78]

Indubhusan Sengupta, a disciple of Holy Mother, asked: "Mother, is it true that those who have received spiritual initiation from you will not be born again?"

Holy Mother replied: "Yes, it is true. They will not have to come to this world again. Know for certain that there is someone always behind you."[79]

Umesh Chandra Datta wrote in his reminiscences of Holy Mother:

Once I asked: "Mother, the Master said that for those who had taken refuge in him, this would be their last birth. What will happen to those who have taken refuge in you?"

She replied: "What else will happen, my son? The same thing will happen here too."

I asked: "Mother, what will happen to those who have received initiation from you, but who do not practise japa and meditation?"

Mother: "What else will happen? Why do you worry so much? Fulfill all the unfulfilled desires of your mind. Later you will enjoy eternal peace in the abode of Ramakrishna. The Master has created a new realm for all of you."

Another day I asked her about liberation and devotion. The Mother said: "As regards liberation, it can be given at any moment, but God does not want to give devotion so easily." Saying so, she left immediately. She uttered those words in such a way that it seemed as if the gift of liberation was in the palm of her hand."[80]

One morning in Udbodhan House, the Mother was talking with Arupananda and Lalit Chattopadhyay. Regarding spiritual life, she said: "The way is extremely difficult, like the sharp edge of a razor." She paused a while, then continued: "But he has kept you in his arms. He is looking after you."

Arupananda: "But we are not aware of it."

Mother: "That is why you are all miserable."

Lalit: "The Master will take us in his arms after death. Is there anything great in that? If he would only do so while we are in this body."

Mother: "He is holding you in his arms even in this body. He is above our head. Truly he is holding you."

Arupananda: "Does he really hold us? Is it true?"

Holy Mother said firmly: "Yes. Really. Truly."[81]

On different occasions Holy Mother said of some people that their present birth would be their last. In April 1912, Surendra Chakrabarty, a disciple, came to Udbodhan House and said to the Mother: "Mother, we are deprived of the vision of the Master." She replied: "You will get it in due course. This is your last birth. Nivedita said, 'Mother, we too are Hindus; but due to our karma we have been born as Christians.' This is their last birth too."

Hearing the Mother's occasional remarks about the last birth, Arupananda asked her: "Mother, what is the true meaning of the term 'last birth'?" The Master told some people that it would be their last birth; you are also saying the same thing."

Holy Mother replied: "The 'last birth' means that a person will not have to return to this world again and go through the cycle of birth and death." Arupananda wanted to verify this, so he asked: "Then, does 'last birth' mean nirvana?"

Holy Mother replied: "Of course it does. In some cases, their minds will be free from desire just prior to death."[82]

Once in Udbodhan House, Golap-ma cleaned the toilet and then after changing her cloth, she began to cut fruit for offering. Nalini could not bear it. She asked Golap-ma to bathe in the Ganges, but Golap-ma ignored her. Later the Mother commented: "How pure Golap's mind is. How high-souled she is. Therefore, she does not discriminate so much between pure and impure things. She does not bother about rules regarding external purity. This is her last birth."

The Mother also said of Gauri-ma: "Gaurdasi serves the girls whole-heartedly in her ashrama, and when they are ill, she bathes them with her own hands. She did not do such things when she was with her family, but now the Master is making her do all types of karma because this is her last birth."[83]

The concept of "last birth" is a controversial topic. According to the Katha Upanishad, "When all the desires dwelling in the heart fall away, then the mortal becomes immortal and here attains Brahman."[84]

Krishna says in the Gita: "At the time of death, a person who leaves his body remembering me alone, he attains my being. Of this there is no doubt." (8:5)

Buddha said that nirvana is possible when a person becomes free from desire.

Ramakrishna said, "For those who come *here*, it will be their last birth." The word *here* may be interpreted as referring to God. When a person realizes God, his heart becomes illumined and all desires disappear, so he will not have to come back again. Holy Mother was omniscient and she knew the destiny of each individual. She reassured her disciples that the Master would come to receive them at their time of death.

Sarada Devi at Jayrambati, 1913.

31
The Human Aspects
of Holy Mother

Gunahina-sutān aparādha-yutān
  kripayādya samuddhara moha-gatān;
Taranim bhava-sāgara pārakarim
  pranamāmi parām jananim jagatām.
— *A Hymn by Swami Abhedananda*

Out of your grace, redeem your child, who is full of faults and has fallen into delusion. You are the ship that takes people across the ocean of worldliness; I salute you, Supreme Mother of the Universe!

God incarnates in every age to demonstrate how to live as a human being. Only a human being can manifest the nine kinds of *rasa* (sentiments or moods), which we find in a traditional Indian drama: *sringara*, erotic; *vira*, heroic; *karuna*, compassionate; *raudra*, angry; *adbhuta*, marvellous; *bhayanaka*, terrible or dreadful; *bibhatsa*, monstrous; *hasya*, humorous; and *shanta*, peaceful or calm. We see various characters in the divine dramas of the avatars who perform roles according to these rasas. Ramachandra, Krishna, Buddha, Jesus, Chaitanya, and Ramakrishna acted in the main roles, but a skillful actor or actress can make even a small role lively and earn high praise from the audience. All roles in a drama are equally important and worthy of a talented actor or actress.

Playwrights base their characters on people whose lives are eventful and successful, glorious and famous, adventurous and courageous, heroic and patriotic, talented and creative, historic and religious, or perhaps endowed with eternal values and motivated by public interest. Holy Mother's life demonstrates almost all of these characteristics, so her divine drama is interesting, intriguing, and inspiring.

It is worth seeing how a divine being acts in the role of an ordinary person. If a poor person acts in the role of a king onstage, he will have to forget his poverty; otherwise his performance will not be natural and convincing. Again, if a teetotaler performs in the role of a drunkard, he must forget himself in order to perform that role properly. Identification with the role and forgetfulness of one's own individuality are essential for an adept actor. If avatars do not forget their divinity while acting on the world stage, they will not be able to perform convincingly as human beings.

Like everyone else, Holy Mother ate, slept, walked, worked, talked, laughed, cried, suffered from disease and grief, and passed through worries and anxieties. At the same time, she was unique. She responded to worldly circumstances like ordinary people, but the moment she focussed her mind on her true nature, she realized that she was acting on a stage and the world was not real.

Human beings live full-time in the domain of maya, but the Mother lived sometimes in the domain of maya and sometimes in the realm of divinity. She could move from one realm to the other at will. Ramakrishna explained this phenomenon: "Everyone is under the spell of this world-bewitching maya. When God assumes a human body, He too comes under the spell. Rama wandered about weeping for Sita. 'Brahman weeps, entangled in the snare of the five elements.' But you must remember this: God, by His mere will, can liberate Himself from this snare."[1]

Ramakrishna succinctly described the human aspect of God: "The Nitya and Lila are the two aspects of Reality. God plays in the world as Man for the sake of His devotees. They can love God only if they see Him in a human form; only then can they show their affection for Him as their Brother, Sister, Father, Mother, or Child. It is just for this love of the devotees that God contracts Himself into a human form and descends on earth to play His lila....It is because through a human body one can hear His words. He sports through it. He tastes divine bliss through a human body. But through His other devotees, God manifests only a small part of Himself."[2]

Swami Parameswarananda recalled: "We have seen the Mother's two aspects: human and divine. When she was in the ordinary human plane, she followed social rules and norms and experienced pain and suffering, grief and affliction like ordinary people. Her extraordinary divine aspect was hidden beneath an ordinary human appearance. But amidst the hustle-bustle of her household, her mind always remained calm and focussed upward. She was completely detached. When she remembered her true nature, she dwelt in a higher realm that was beyond the reach of ordinary human beings."[3]

Because Holy Mother was a world teacher, every one of her actions and words has deep significance. Wherever she lived, her all-inclusive love made that place and its people her own. She had a special love for her small, poor village of Jayrambati. Once while she was leaving for Calcutta, her aunt said to her, "Sarada, do come again."

"Of course, I will come," replied the Mother.

She then took some dust from the mud floor and touched it to her forehead, quoting a Sanskrit verse: *Janani janmabhumishcha swargādapi gariyashi* – "Mother and motherland are superior even to heaven." As we have mentioned earlier, her life in Calcutta was not as free as her life in Jayrambati. In Calcutta she lived upstairs in Udbodhan House and once a day she went to have her bath in the Ganges. Seldom did she go out for sightseeing or to visit a devotee's house. However, she was always busy with her worship and spiritual ministry. Those who could not go to Jayrambati came to her Calcutta residence for initiation and spiritual instruction.

We have described the Mother's daily routine in Jayrambati (*See Chapter 28*) and in Calcutta (*See Chapter 29*). In this chapter we shall depict her human qualities so that ordinary people can relate to her.

One morning in Jayrambati, Holy Mother was helping to husk paddy, which she did almost every day. Swami Arupananda asked her, "Mother, why should you work so hard?"

"My child," she said in reply, "to make my life a model, I have done much more than is necessary."[4]

Her pure, perfect, and unselfish life is an ideal model for human beings. She left a mould for her children, and it is now up to us to cast our lives in that mould.

Holy Mother's Daily Life

The greatness of a person can be ascertained through his or her small actions. In day-to-day life, everybody follows a routine. The Mother also followed a routine. She got up early in the morning, bathed, cleaned her teeth with tooth powder, meditated and repeated her mantra, worshipped the Master, had breakfast, cut vegetables, cooked food for her household, and served the devotees.

When she was a little girl, she helped her mother with household work and cared for her four younger brothers. Swami Parameswarananda tells us that as a girl, the Mother bathed in the Amodar River. She carried puffed rice and fried eggplant or potatoes in a cloth with her and after bathing she shared them with her brothers like any other village girl. Imagining the Mother seated under a tree on the bank of the Amodar River eating puffed rice is a scene for meditation.

Fancy breakfast food was not available in Jayrambati. When Holy Mother started to give initiation, she would buy jilipis or make halwa and serve it to the devotees with puffed rice. In her old age, when she had lost a few teeth, she would put some puffed rice in the corner of a cloth, pound it with a pestle, and make it into powder so that she could eat it.

There was no running water or electricity in Jayrambati during Holy Mother's time. The Mother carried a water pitcher on her waist from the pond or river, like other women, and lit her house at night with oil lamps and kerosene lanterns. One can imagine Holy Mother meditating in her mud hut at night with the flickering flame of the oil lamp sending light dancing on the Master's photograph.

All the year round Holy Mother used to wear a sari without a blouse or petticoat. She did not wear shoes. During winter she might put on a cha-dar, but she had no other warm clothing. Once in Udbodhan House, at a devotee's request, she wore a warm undershirt for a few days, but then she gave it away. She did not have an umbrella to protect herself from the scorching sun or the torrential rain in her primitive village.

Observing Birthdays

Village people seldom celebrate birthdays, especially if there are sev-eral children in a family. But they observe the birthdays of avatars, gurus, and holy persons. In 1918 the devotees observed Holy Mother's birthday in Udbodhan House. Swami Ishanananda reminisced: "After I offered a flower at her feet, she blessed me by touching my head and said: 'Now offer flowers on behalf of all the people of Jayrambati and Koalpara ash-ramas. Tarak [Swami Shivananda] could not come from Belur Math, so offer flowers on his behalf and also on behalf of all of my children, known and unknown.' Then she fervently prayed: 'Master, please look after their welfare in this life and the next. I am the Mother of all. What more shall I say?'"[5]

Swami Parameswarananda recalled: "Once the Mother was staying with Radhu at Koalpara. I expressed a desire to observe the Master's birthday in Jayrambati, and the Mother approved of this. She gave me five rupees for expenses. The celebration was done on a grand scale and many people were fed. Hearing about the celebration later, Holy Mother remarked: 'As long as I am alive, it is not necessary to go to excess.'[6]

"Another time in Jayrambati a devotee began to practise spiritual dis-ciplines vigorously. The Mother told him: 'You do not have to practise so many spiritual disciplines here. Eat, relax, and enjoy this place.'[7] Similarly,

Jesus said: 'Son, be of good cheer!...Can the children of the bridal chamber fast while the bridegroom is with them?'"[8]

In 1919, Holy Mother's birthday was observed in Jayrambati. Swami Saradananda sent a sari and a chadar to her from Calcutta. The Mother put on the sari and worshipped the Master and then sat on her cot holding Radhu's child on her lap. The monks and the devotees offered flowers at her feet and she blessed them, saying, "I wholeheartedly pray to the Master for the welfare of all of you."[9] The monks, devotees, and members of her brothers' families enjoyed the grand feast.

Travelling

Nowadays people go to Jayrambati easily by car, bus, or train. In her early days, Holy Mother travelled on foot; later she used various kinds of transport, such as bullock carts, palanquins, horse carriages, boats, steamers, trains, and automobiles. One can visualize the Mother walking 64 miles from Jayrambati to Dakshineswar, carrying a small bundle containing clothes, a towel, hard molasses, and some puffed rice in a small cloth bag. She bathed in roadside ponds, lakes, or rivers and drank water from them. She would bring a few rupees to buy food along the way and to pay the ferrymen as she crossed the five rivers between Jayrambati and Dakshineswar. The meadow of Telo-Bhelo is blessed by Holy Mother's feet.

Every human mind is more or less curious — that is the basis of all education. Holy Mother was not a cloistered nun; she loved people and enjoyed visiting holy people and holy places. She went on pilgrimages to both North and South India. While living in Calcutta she used the horse carriage of Nivedita's school on holidays to visit the museum, the zoo, the Hog Market, and the park, and she went to the botanical garden in Shibpore. She got down from her carriage and saw these places of interest with great enthusiasm.

Joy and Sorrow

Happiness and misery rotate in a cyclic order. No human being is always happy or always miserable. It seems that God offers the results of peoples' karma on an installment basis by giving suffering and happiness alternately.

Every human being laments when a loved one dies. When the Master passed away, Holy Mother cried out, saying: "Mother! O Kali! What have I done that you have departed, leaving me alone in the world?" However, she accepted death as inevitable for every human being. No one can alter the decree of Providence. Like other mortal beings, she cried when

those closest to her died — her mother, her uncle, Yogananda, and Premananda. She lamented the passing of Nivedita, Swami Vivekananda,
Swami Ramakrishnananda, and her close relatives. She had an affectionate and motherly heart, and she cried for suffering humanity.

However, Holy Mother said that the Master had placed a pitcher of
bliss in her heart when she was at Dakshineswar. She might have been
tossed by the pairs of opposites — happiness and misery — like other
human beings, but a current of bliss always flowed within her. Sometimes
she was humorous and laughed heartily. Humour absorbs the shocks
of life, eases tense situations and family friction, and brings a smile to
gloomy faces.

Once in Jayrambati, Surabala, who was mentally unbalanced, wanted
to play cards. She asked Holy Mother to play with her. Holy Mother and
Ashu took one side and Surabala and Nalini the other. Holy Mother and
Ashu won six times. Surabala became upset, threw down the cards, and
blurted out: "Sister-in-law, you will always win and we shall always lose.
I won't play anymore." Holy Mother replied: "We are sattvic and follow
the spiritual path, so we must win."[10] Surabala made a sound of disgust
and left. The Mother laughed.

Once the Mother was suffering from malaria and the doctor prescribed
sago for her diet. After drinking the tasteless sago, the Mother addressed
her disciples, "Hello, it seems you have no devotion for my prasad today!"

Another day the Mother was seated on a cot in her brother Prasanna's
room, with her feet dangling. Prakash Maharaj, a monk, offered flowers
at her feet and bowed down. He prayed, "Mother, please don't make me
wander around anymore in my spiritual journey." She replied: "My son,
all these years you forgot me and moved around. Should I not now make
you wander a little?"[11]

Swami Gauriswarananda recalled: "Once a swami brought a huge bel
fruit from Varanasi to Jayrambati for the Mother. She kept it under her
cot. One day she was cutting vegetables on the veranda of Nalini's room
and I was cutting them along with her. When the vegetables were cut,
she asked me to fetch the bel. I had never seen such a huge bel before,
and thinking it to be a pumpkin, I went back to say that there was no bel
fruit under the cot. The Mother said: 'I put it there myself. Where would
it go? Look carefully.' I went back, checked the place, and reported, 'No,
Mother, there is no bel there.' Then she asked, 'What is there?' 'A pumpkin,' I replied. She laughed and said, 'Bring that pumpkin here.' As soon
as I picked it up I realized that it was a bel. Seeing me with the bel, the
Mother laughed heartily."[12]

Once in Udbodhan House, Nalini said to Holy Mother: "Please set my mind right. I have no peace of mind. I don't want to live anymore. I shall leave everything to you in my will. After my death you dispose of everything according to your wishes."

Holy Mother laughed and asked, "When are you going to die?" Then she gravely said: "You had better go home quietly. Don't create mischief in this holy place." Then she continued: "If your mind does not become free from restlessness living in this spiritual atmosphere surrounded by monks and devotees, then what do you want? What a wonderful life you have! You have no trouble or responsibility here. You could have made the best of this life. You do not realize the value of this place now, but you will learn it when I depart. You have a sinful mind and that is why you have no peace. You are leading a lazy life and you do not do any work. That is the reason your brain is overheated. Can't you think a good thought? Oh, what an impure mind you have!"[13]

Fear and Anger

Although Holy Mother was a divine being, she experienced fear and anger like an ordinary person.

Holy Mother was afraid of ghosts. One night in Udbodhan House she asked one of her disciples: "Are you afraid of ghosts?"

"We are children of the Divine Mother," he replied. "What can they do to us?"

"But I am afraid of ghosts," said Holy Mother.

"Yes, I know," the disciple responded. "You are frightened by your own goblins and imps."*

Holy Mother laughed and said: "You are right, my child. They are terrible; they shrivel up my innards and make them stick to my belly."[14]

Holy Mother was also afraid of having surgery. While she was in Puri, she had an abscess on her foot, which a doctor lanced quickly without warning her. From then on she avoided allopathic doctors and surgeons. Once in Udbodhan House she was suffering from a toothache, and Saradananda brought a dentist to extract her tooth. Holy Mother hid when the dentist arrived.

Golap-ma said to Saradananda: "The Mother is afraid of any kind of surgery. Her system is not like ours. Is there no medicine to get rid of a toothache?"

Saradananda replied: "If the fearless Mother is afraid, what can I do? Medicine cannot stop this kind of pain. I brought the dentist so that she

* Referring to her troublesome relatives.

would not have to suffer for long."

"We should not do this if the Mother does not want it," said Golap-ma.

Finally, Saradananda apologetically sent the dentist back, saying that they could not find Holy Mother.

The whole house was thoroughly searched again. Finally, someone found Holy Mother lying under her cot covered with a chadar. Her tooth-ache slowly subsided.[15]

Sarala (later Bharatiprana) described the Mother's fear of surgery: "If anyone had any cut or wound, the Mother would apply a coating of clay from Mother Simhavahini's temple. Once Yogin-ma had an abscess, and the Mother applied that clay to it. After some days when she heard that the wound needed surgery, she was concerned. She exclaimed: 'Oh Yogin, I hear the doctor is going to cut your abscess. What will happen? It is strange that Simhavahini's clay did not cure it. My Lord, what will happen? Is surgery necessary?'

"It was unbearable for the Mother to see other people in pain. During Yogin-ma's operation, the Mother went to the shrine and began to repeat her mantra. When the surgery was over, I gave the news to the Mother and she was relieved. She asked: 'Is it done? Is Yogin well? Did she suffer from pain?' Then she went to Yogin-ma, caressed her head, and inquired: 'Is it too painful, my dear? How are you now?'"[16]

The Mother was very angry when the Bankura police arrested a young woman named Sindhubala, who was pregnant, considering her to be a political suspect. On another occasion Holy Mother lost her temper when she saw from the balcony of Udbodhan that a man was beating and kick-ing his wife in the slum area.

Jewellery and fancy clothes may enhance a young woman's beauty temporarily, but modesty and purity keep her beauty alive forever. Holy Mother was the embodiment of modesty. According to the custom for conservative Hindu and Muslim Indian women at the time, she wore a veil over her face in front of most male disciples and visitors — even the Master's disciples. Swami Ishanananda recalled:

> Sometime in the spring of 1919, the Mother was at Jayrambati. One noon Radhu, Maku, and Nalini were talking boisterously and acting shame-lessly. The Mother said to her nieces: "What are you doing? Don't you have any sense of decency and respect? Women should not behave immodestly. They need to be careful in their bearing and maintain self-respect. There is a saying: 'If a woman's cloth is above her knees, she is as good as naked though she is wearing a sari five yards long.' Women must maintain their modesty and dignity." Then one of the nieces spoke out, "Aunt, the Master

said, 'One does not succeed so long as one has these three: shame, hatred, and fear.'" Immediately the Mother said: "No, that is not so. The Master said that to those who were intoxicated with God. I say that it is necessary to have a sense of shame, hatred, and fear — especially for women."[17]

Ramakrishna's and Holy Mother's teachings are not contradictory; rather, they are complementary. Ramakrishna's advice is for those who are already established on the divine plane, and Holy Mother's instructions are for those who are working towards that state. People are like saplings, which need a fence to protect them; otherwise cows will eat them. But big trees do not need any fence. Good and evil cannot touch illumined souls because they transcend the pairs of opposites. But those who are seekers of God and have started their spiritual journey should discipline themselves and be careful.

It seems that the Mother meant that a woman must protect her character and dignity by all means. This is also applicable to men. Both men and women should be modest, avoid evil company, and be careful about losing their purity or chastity. No one respects an immoral, shameless person. Holy Mother recalled: "Lakshmi used to imitate the singers of the day, singing and dancing before the Master, displaying all their gestures. Once, the Master said to me: 'That is her mood. Be careful that you do not lose your modesty by trying to follow her example.'"[18]

In the Ramayana, when Ravana kidnapped Sita and tried to tempt her, she said: "You are a sinner. I hate you. You may kill me, but my mind will never think of any other person than Rama." Behind this kind of hatred, there is moral strength and courage. Similarly in the Mahabharata, the unrighteous Dushashana tried to humiliate Draupadi by forcefully taking off her sari in the court of the Kauravas. Draupadi prayed to Krishna for help. Krishna then supplied an infinite length of fabric for her sari to protect her modesty. The chaste Draupadi's anger and hatred was partly responsible for the destruction of the Kuru dynasty. One should show anger and hatred if someone tries to destroy one's pure character, modesty, and spirituality.

Regarding fear, the Mother did not mean fear of a robber, tiger, snake, or death. She meant fear of losing one's dignity, of scandal, and of public disgrace.

About the Mother's shyness, Sarala wrote: "In Udbodhan, during the Mother's last illness, a monk came to see her. She was sleeping and the monk began to massage her feet. There was no veil over the Mother's head at that time. After the monk left, the Mother scolded me, saying:

'There was no veil over my head. Why did you not arrange it? Am I dead? I am still alive and you are looking after me in this way?'"[19]

Hunger and Thirst

As an embodied being, Holy Mother experienced hunger and thirst like an ordinary person. In 1887, when the Mother was 34 years old, she went to Kamarpukur with Yogananda and Golap-ma. They travelled by train to Burdwan and then walked 30 miles because they did not have enough money to hire a bullock cart. After walking 16 miles, the Mother was hungry and totally exhausted. Golap-ma managed to make some khichuri in a roadside inn. After finishing the meal, the Mother exclaimed: "Golap, what nectar you have prepared!"

Once in Jayrambati the Mother was very ill from malaria. Swami Saradananda, Yogin-ma, and Golap-ma brought a doctor from Calcutta with fruit, special diet, and medicine. Holy Mother had an aversion to the food and special diet that Saradananda had brought from Calcutta. One day Keshavananda's mother came from Koalpara to see Holy Mother. She brought some *mayna-kota** for her, thinking that it would awaken her taste buds and bring back her appetite. Every morning and every evening before going to bed, Saradeshananda inquired about Holy Mother's needs. One morning the Mother said to Saradeshananda: "My son, I feel hungry. Could you feed me?" She then whispered something to her attendant, Mandakini, who was lying on the floor. Mandakini left the room for a bit, and then brought some mayna-kota in a cane bowl. Holy Mother asked Saradeshananda to feed it to her. Perplexed, the swami worried that the food would be bad for her. But when the Mother insisted, he began to feed her. The Mother's face was beaming with joy and satisfaction like an adolescent girl. She then drank a glass of water. The swami put the Mother back to bed, covering her with a chadar.[20]

Disease and Pain

Once one of Holy Mother's disciples remarked: "No human body is perfect. Even if a young and healthy person's body is checked by a doctor, he will find some abnormality somewhere in that person's system." Avatars also suffer from physical ailments and pain. Buddha died of blood dysentery. Ramakrishna suffered from fevers and dysentery, and he died of cancer. Sometimes people ask, "Why do avatars get diseases?" Avatars absorb people's sins and bad karma, and that is why they suffer.

* Parched rice powder mixed with roasted sesame powder, a little chili powder, and salt.

Moreover, every mortal being goes through six stages: it is born, lives, grows, changes, decays, and dies. There is no exception to this natural law.

Holy Mother had a weak stomach, and she suffered from rheumatism throughout her life. At various times she had episodes of malaria, dysentery, chicken pox, headache, toothache, inflammation of the eye, and prickly heat (miliaria, also called *ghamachi*). She died of *kala-azar* (also called leishmaniasis).

Once in Jayrambati, the Mother saw her emaciated body reflected in a pond and wanted to give it up. During that illness her eyes swelled and she had blurred vision. But she recuperated by the grace of Mother Simhavahini (*See details in Chapter 5*).

The villages of Bengal are notorious for malaria because mosquitoes breed in large numbers in ponds full of hyacinths. Many people die from malaria every year. Holy Mother suffered from this illness many times in Jayrambati. Dr. Kanjilal and Dr. Satish Chakrabarty often came from Calcutta to treat her.

One day in Jayrambati, the Mother was sitting on the couch preparing betel rolls. Swami Arupananda said to her: "In the future many people will practise spiritual disciplines to propitiate you."

Holy Mother answered with a laugh: "What do you say? People will say, 'Our Mother had rheumatism and limped when she walked.'" Then she continued: "This illness is a blessing in a way. When the Master was lying ill in Cossipore, he said: 'Those who came with selfish motives have left me, saying: "If he is an incarnation of God, how can he be sick? This is all maya." But those who are my own, their hearts break when they see my suffering.'"[21]

During Holy Mother's time there was no electricity in Udbodhan House. She used a palm-leaf hand fan during the summer. During heat waves she would get prickly-heat rash. At such times she was terribly uncomfortable. Once she was considering applying sandal paste on her body but feared that the paste would give her a cold. Her disciple Sarajubala suggested that she use talcum powder to relieve the rash. Although it was a cosmetic item at that time, the Mother agreed to use it. The next morning Sarajubala sent the powder. Holy Mother applied it and enjoyed some relief. When Sarajubala came to Udbodhan House that evening, Holy Mother said to her: "Look, I used your powder and the prickly-heat has subsided in some areas. Please apply some to this area that is aggravated. The itching also is much reduced. Sharat is also suffering from prickly heat. It would be nice if someone applied this powder to his body."

Sarajubala said: "My goodness, who is going to tell him to use it? It is a luxury item used by fashionable people." Holy Mother laughed when she heard this.[22] In fact, the Mother did not care for luxury at all.

The Mother had long, thick hair. In Jayrambati she bathed either in the pond or in the Amodar River, and in Calcutta she bathed in the Ganges or used tap water. She was careful to dry her hair in the sun; otherwise she would get a headache. In Dakshineswar she took a bath early in the morning and her hair remained wet all day because her hair was twisted in a bun and covered with a veil. In the early afternoon, when there were no people around and the temple workers took their rest, she would sit on the steps of the nahabat to dry her hair. In Jayrambati, she moved around with her hair loose and without a veil, so her hair dried quickly after her bath. In Calcutta she sat on the roof to dry her hair. Sarajubala recorded: "I found the Mother on the roof drying her hair. When she saw me, she said: 'Take the cloth off from your head and dry your hair. Don't keep your hair wet because the water soaks into the head and ruins the eyesight.'"[23] This may have been a village belief.

Favourite Foods

There is a saying in Sanskrit, *bhinna rucirhi lokāh* — "Taste changes from person to person." Everyone is brought up eating certain types of food, and food habits differ from person to person, place to place, and country to country. For example, menus and delicacies are different even between Bankura and Calcutta, East Bengal and West Bengal, North India and South India, China and America. Holy Mother loved the local food of Jayrambati village and the surrounding district of Bankura.

Ashu Mitra made a list of the Mother's favourite foods:

Fruit: mangoes, jackfruit, rose-apple, *jāmrul*, lichi, mangostein, and papaya.

Vegetables: *sajinā, kalmi* (an edible aquatic plant), āmrul (a kind of sour spinach), *jhinge, dhudhul, patal*, potatoes, and pumpkin.

Dal (pulses): urud, chānā, arhar, and moong dal.

Fried and boiled foods: *bara* (balls made from lentil paste), fried egg-plant, *phulari* (made from lentil paste), *chira bhaja* (fried flattened rice), *papadam* (a type of fried cracker), steamed *posta* (poppy seed paste), *mocha* (boiled banana flower), poppy seed curry, and hog plum and poppy seed chutney.

Desserts: *tilkutā* (a sweet made with sesame seed), *chānār murki* (a sweet made with cheese), *gajā* (a sweet made with flour), *pātisāptā* (a kind of cake made with rice powder, milk, and coconut).

On Ekadashi days, the eleventh day of the lunar fortnight, the Mother did not eat rice. Instead, she ate *luchis* (fried bread), *rādhā-ballabhi, chana dal,* or *dhonkā* (a kind of curry made of lentil paste), farina pudding or milk pudding made with oranges (*kshir-kamlā*).[24]

Swami Arupananda also listed Holy Mother's favourite foods:

> The Mother preferred sweet-sour mangoes rather than extremely sweet mangoes, such as *pearafuli, langra,* and *alfonso.* Among the spinaches, she liked gram spinach and radish spinach. As she sometimes suffered from dysentery, Kaviraj Durgaprasad Sen asked her to eat āmrul spinach [a sour spinach] as an antidote. Swami Premananda supplied āmrul spinach from Belur Math. She loved fried things, such as *beguni* — fried eggplant dipped in batter, *phulari* made from lentil paste, hot lentil *barā* — a lentil chop fried in oil, potato chop, *jhuri-bhājā* — a kind of crisp snack made of lentils, and other fried things. For lunch she liked thin urad lentils and barbecued *posta* paste, which were her favourite dishes in Jayrambati. She ate bitter squash curry [*sukta*], mixed vegetable curry [*chachari*], and vegetable soup mixed with a little lime juice. For dessert, she liked *rātābi sandesh* [a dry sweet made of cheese] and *rasapuli* [a ball made of sweet potato and soaked in syrup], and a sweet ball made of moong dal. Finally, she would drink a cup of milk after lunch and after supper. She would mix some of her milk with rice and give it to the devotees as prasad. In the afternoon the Mother did not have any refreshments. For supper, she had two or three luchis, a little vegetable curry, and some milk.[25]

Criticism of Holy Mother

Buddha said in the *Dhammapada* (verse 228): "There never was, there never will be, nor is there now, a man who is always blamed or a man who is always praised." Those who have many faults see faults in others. This is like a strainer mocking a needle because it has a hole. Even perfect God-men were criticized by ordinary people. Once a Christian made a remark about Buddha: "I like everything about him except his death because he was not crucified." Holy Mother prayed to the Lord that she might not see faults in others, and her prayer was answered. Her life was so pure, loving, and transparent that she was considered to be *ajatashatru*, a person who has no enemies.

The Mother's main critics were her own relatives. Her brother Kali complained when Holy Mother spent money on festivals and devotees instead of giving it to him. Radhu's mother, Surabala, did not want young men to become monks. When they came to Holy Mother, she would say to them: "Look, this person whom you call the Mother is snatching you away from your biological mother. She will make you a monk and force you to abandon your hearth and home." The Mother listened to her sister-in-law's warnings and smiled.

The members of the Roy family in Jibta were the wealthy landlords in the Jayrambati area. One of the young men of that family went astray because of evil company, and his father was very sad because he could not reform his son. One of his relatives suggested that he send him to Holy Mother in Jayrambati for spiritual advice. Terrified, the wealthy man said: "I would rather set apart some of my property for my son to squander and live in his own way than send him there."[26] Anyone who wants to do good in the world will have to face criticism. Once a young devotee received sannyasa from Holy Mother, but his mother came and asked the Mother to send her son back home. She said that he was the only wage earner and the whole household depended on him. Moreover, he had a wife and a son. The Mother listened to her and expressed sympathy, but did not agree to make him go back home. Holy Mother said firmly: "He has chosen the right path for himself. He has already made provision for the maintenance of you all. I have heard there is someone to look after you. So I will not ask him to return to his home." Although the mother could not take her son back home, the Mother's blessings reassured her and she returned home with great hope. On Holy Mother's advice, the young monk maintained a good relationship with his mother as long as she lived.[27]

A disciple often brought a heavy load of groceries on his head to Holy Mother from a market six miles away. One day when the disciple was coming to Jayrambati with groceries he met a middle-aged man in a neighbouring village whom he knew. The man remarked: "Ah, this boy is so deluded by maya!" After arriving at Holy Mother's house, the disciple bowed down to the Mother and told her what the man had said. Immediately Holy Mother's face became grave and she said: "My son, this type of person is like a worm crawling in samsara. People like this are steeped in worldliness. They cannot understand or appreciate any kind of spiritual service. They never attain love for God. They come into the world, undergo all its sufferings, and then die. Thus they rotate through life again and again. After passing through endless sufferings of many births, when their minds turn towards God, His grace dawns. Only then do they attain liberation."[28] The disciple listened to the Mother in utter astonishment.

Pique and Childlike Behaviour

It is natural to experience emotions, wounded feelings, pique, discontent, and bitterness, and for our behaviour to change according to our experiences. When a grown-up person plays with a child, that person's childlike nature arises from within and he or she also behaves like a child.

Holy Mother was a mature, wise woman and a guru to her disciples. But from time to time her childlike nature manifested and she acted accordingly. Once in Jayrambati there was no cook, so Nalini was making the chapatis. Holy Mother and Saradeshananda were rolling the dough. While baking the chapatis over a fire, Nalini remarked: "Aunt, your chapatis are not puffing up well." Holy Mother became as annoyed as a little girl. She set aside the rolling pin and said: "Well, here is your rolling pin. If my chapatis are not properly flattened, I will not roll anymore." Saradeshananda reassured the Mother and fervently begged her to roll more chapatis. Holy Mother said: "I have been rolling chapatis all my life, and today this girl says that my chapatis are not up to the mark."

Saradeshananda said: "Mother, your chapatis are fine. How does Nalini know which ones are yours and which ones are mine? We are putting our chapatis on the same plate. She is blaming you for nothing. Mother, you are rolling very well." Holy Mother was mollified and began to roll chapatis again.[29]

Swami Gauriswarananda recorded a similar incident:

One day in Jayrambati there were a good number of male devotees but not a single woman devotee. The Mother gave me a large quantity of flour that I kneaded into dough. Mother said to Nalini: "You bake the chapatis; Rammay [later Gauriswarananda] and I will roll them out for you." The Mother rolled one chapati at a time on her small marble *chaki* [disc] with a small rolling pin of ebony, while I rolled three at a time on a large wooden chaki with a thick wooden rolling pin. The work was going on quite smoothly. Nalini suddenly commented, "Aunt, Rammay's chapatis are puffing up better than yours." No sooner had she uttered these words than the Mother set aside the chaki and the rolling pin, and stopped working. In a wounded voice, she said: 'Here I am, grown so old after having rolled chapatis all my life, and Rammay, a mere child born the other day, rolls them better than I do! I'm not going to roll any more chapatis. Let him do it.' So there sat Mother, her chaki and rolling pin set aside. I too set aside my chaki and rolling pin and got up. I told the Mother: 'If you don't roll chapatis, I won't either. I am leaving.' The Mother realized that if both of us did the work together, it would be done quickly and there would not be any delay in offering food to the Master and serving the prasad to the devotees. So she resumed rolling chapatis. I challenged Nalini: 'Two of us are together supplying chapatis to you. How could you tell the Mother's from mine? Can I ever roll chapatis better than the Mother? Why do you make unnecessary comparisons?'"[30]

As Holy Mother was always surrounded by people in Calcutta and Jayrambati, she sometimes went to relax in the secluded Jagadamba Ashrama, which was located in Koalpara. Swami Parameswarananda recalled: "While living in Jagadamba Ashrama, the Mother sometimes behaved like a young girl. A swing was set up there. Occasionally the Mother enjoyed swinging, and the devotees would push her. The women devotees would also swing and let Holy Mother push them. Thus in that joyful atmosphere, the Mother would get some rest."[31]

Ashu Mitra wrote: "One day in Jayrambati, the Mother went to the pond to bathe. She carried a pitcher of water on her waist, like other village women. When I asked whether she knew how to swim, she replied that when she was young she learned to swim like other village girls. They turn their pitchers upside down and then hold onto them and paddle."[32]

Swami Gauriswarananda recalled: "After a meal, the Mother would give me two betel rolls to chew at a time. She would comment to the women around her: 'I do enjoy the sight of Rammay after he has had betel rolls. His complexion is dark and his lips become crimson with the pigment of betel leaves. It seems to me that black charcoal cakes are on fire."[33]

Caring for and Raising Children

Because Holy Mother was the eldest of her siblings, she had helped her mother raise her brothers and do the housework. When her brothers were married, she looked after her young sisters-in-law as if they were her own daughters. When they were pregnant or ill, the Mother cared for them. When her brother Abhaycharan died, she looked after his mentally unbalanced wife, Surabala, and her young daughter, Radhu. Holy Mother raised Radhu and sent her to school, tried to discipline her, initiated her, took her on pilgrimages, arranged her marriage, and even looked after her child, Banabihari. She took the child on her bed and sang lullabies to him. Similarly, she looked after her other nieces, Nalini and Maku, and Maku's child, Neda.

Swami Parameswarananda reminisced: "The Mother decorated Banabihari like baby Gopala. She put collyrium on the edge of his eyelids and a dot of sandal paste on his forehead, and she tied a tuft of hair on the top of his head. She also fed Banabihari like baby Gopala. In fact, that child looked like baby Krishna."[34] Because Radhu and her mother, Surabala, were not capable of taking care of the boy, the Mother took responsibility for him. She sometimes received her visitors with the child on her lap.

Swami Saradeshananda recalled:

Once on the Mother's birthday, many disciples and devotees came to Jayrambati to pay their respects. They offered flowers at her feet and she blessed them. It was a festive occasion. A feast had been arranged. Some devotees were singing in the parlour and the Mother was cutting vegetables. She then cooked some soup and other things in a small wooden stove for her sister-in-law, Indumati, who had given birth to a child [Vijay] just a few days previously. She was lying in and not feeling well. There were no other women in her household, so the Mother had to look after her. A festival was going on celebrating the Mother's birthday, but she was unattached, like water on a lotus leaf.[35]

Once a young monastic disciple cut a finger on his right hand while doing some work in Jayrambati. It was difficult for him to eat. He was using a spoon with his left hand and somehow managing. When Holy Mother saw this, her heart melted. She sat near the disciple and fed him with her own hand. As long as it took his hand to heal, the Mother fed him as a loving mother feeds her child. This grown-up disciple was touched, having been fed by the Mother.[36]

Holy Mother as Singer and Storyteller

Ramakrishna said that Holy Mother was Saraswati. She had come to impart knowledge. According to the Hindu tradition, Saraswati is the goddess of learning and music, so she is depicted as holding a book in one hand and a vina in the other. Holy Mother did not go to school or take music lessons. From her childhood she listened to Baul songs, songs from the Ramayana, songs on Manasā, *tarjā* (a kind of contest of songs composed extempore), songs from *yātrās*, and kirtan sung for 24 hours at a time. Village children learned nursery rhymes, folk rhymes, and stories from their grandparents and other older relatives. The Mother remembered those songs and stories. Moreover, when she married Ramakrishna, she learned many songs from him. Later, Holy Mother remarked: "Ah, what a great singer the Master was! His voice was so sweet. While singing he was one with his song. His voice is still ringing in my ears. When I remember it, other voices appear so flat. Naren also had a melodious voice. Girish had a sweet voice, too."[37]

In the nahabat at Dakshineswar, Holy Mother and Lakshmi heard many songs from the Master's room, and at night they would sing those songs. One day the Master heard them singing as he walked towards the Panchavati. Yogin-ma recalled: "The Mother had a good, musical voice. One night she and Lakshmi were singing in low voices. It was very resonant and reached the Master's ears. The next day he said: 'Last night you were singing very well. That's good, very good.'" Thus the Master encouraged Holy Mother to sing. Singing is a wonderful way to commune with God.

Sometimes during the evenings in Jayrambati, Holy Mother told stories and nursery rhymes to Radhu, Maku, and Nalini. One day Radhu complained that she had already heard those rhymes, and asked Holy Mother to sing a song. At Radhu's request the Mother sang a song from *Chaitanya Lila* by Girish Ghosh:

> O Keshava, bestow thy grace upon thy luckless servants here!
> O Keshava, who dost delight to roam Vrindaban's glades and groves!
> O Madhava, our mind's Bewitcher! Sweet One, who dost steal our hearts,
> Sweetly playing on thy flute!
> Chant, O Mind, the name of Hari, Sing aloud the name of Hari,
> Praise Lord Hari's name. [38]

As did Ramakrishna, Holy Mother encouraged monks and devotees to sing devotional songs. Sarajubala wrote:

> This evening there was Kali kirtan in Udbodhan House. The monks of Belur Math took part in it. The music commenced at half past eight in the evening. All of the women devotees sat on the upper veranda to hear the music. I was rubbing oil on the Mother's feet and could hear the songs from her room. Now and then the monks sang some songs that the Master had sung. Excited, the Mother remarked: "The Master sang this very song!" The monks were singing:

> > The black bee of my mind is drawn in sheer delight
> > To the blue lotus flower of Mother Shyama's feet,
> > The blue flowers of the feet of Kali, Shiva's Consort,
> > Tasteless, to the bee, are the blossoms of desire.

> The Mother became restless. Tears flowed from her eyes. She said to me: "Come, dear. Let us go to the veranda and listen to this song." When the kirtan ended, I bowed down to the Mother and returned home.[39]

Some evenings after vespers, Holy Mother sent her attendant to ask Saradananda to sing some songs. He had drums and a tanpura in his parlour downstairs. At the Mother's request, the swami would sing in his melodious voice:

> Behold my Mother playing with Shiva, lost in an ecstasy of joy!
> Drunk with a draught of celestial wine, She reels, and yet She does not fall.

And also:

> In dense darkness, O Mother, thy formless beauty sparkles;
> Therefore the yogis meditate in a dark mountain cave.
> In the lap of boundless dark, on Mahanirvana's waves upborne,
> Peace flows serene and inexhaustible.[40]

Some mornings the Mother would hum songs after meditation. Swami Ishanananda mentioned that while awakening the Master from his night rest, she hummed a couple of lines from a Hindi bhajan:

> In the morning, the Mother Kaushalya awoke Ramachandra,
> And she asked her son to do good to men, sages, and gods.[41]

In 1912 when the Mother was in Varanasi, Swami Shantananda recorded that the Mother sang this song early in the morning:

> The blissful garden of Shiva is Varanasi,
> Where the Mother Annapurna dwells gracefully.[42]

When actresses from Girish's theatre came to visit the Mother, she asked them to sing some songs. They joyfully entertained Holy Mother and her companions as well as the monks in Udbodhan House.

Holy Mother was a wonderful storyteller and had a fantastic memory. She could relate in detail the stories of her personal life and the events of the Master's life to her disciples and devotees. Swami Saradananda received the Mother's accounts about the Master while writing *Sri Ramakrishna and His Divine Play*.

Holy Mother as a Householder

As God is neither a monk nor a householder, so Holy Mother was neither a nun nor a householder. She represented both ideals. The most vital things needed to make family life joyful are mutual love and respect, patience and forbearance, detachment and devotion to work, adjustment and forgiveness, selflessness and sympathy, joyfulness and spirituality. These twelve qualities are essential for a happy home. The Mother upheld her household with these qualities, so wherever she lived, peace and joy prevailed.

Holy Mother made people her own with her divine love, compassion, and sweet words. One day at Jayrambati, someone used harsh words when speaking to Surabala. At this, the Mother remarked: "One should not hurt others even with words. One must not speak an unpleasant truth if it is not necessary. By indulging in rude words, one's nature becomes rude. One's sensitivity is lost if one has no control over one's speech. The

Master used to say that one should not ask a lame person how he became lame."[43]

Swami Ishanananda recalled:

One morning in Jayrambati while the Mother was rubbing her body with oil, someone was sweeping the courtyard. After the work was done, that person threw the broomstick aside. At this the Mother said: "What is this? You have thrown away the broomstick with such disrespect when the work is done. It takes the same amount of time to put it gently in a corner as it does to throw it aside. One should not trifle with a thing though it may be very insignificant. If you respect a thing, the thing also respects you. Will you not again need that broomstick? Besides, it is also a part of this family. From that standpoint also, it deserves to be treated with respect. Even a broomstick should be treated with respect. One should perform even an insignificant task with respect."[44]

To make Holy Mother's life comfortable, devotees bought land from her brothers and built a house for her. They also bought a paddy field for her so that she might not suffer from lack of food. Lalit Chattopadhyay bought an adjacent pond called Punyapukur so the Mother would not have to go far to wash her clothes and dishes. These basic things are essential in village life.

The Mother was neither extravagant nor stingy, but she was frugal. Some devotees gave her money every month to maintain her household as she had to look after her nieces, disciples, and visiting devotees who came to her for initiation. She had her disciples buy paddy during the harvesting season because it was cheaper then. She purchased groceries from a distant market at a wholesale rate. She vehemently opposed the tax that was imposed on her house, arguing that it was a religious institution. She acted as a prudent householder.

Swami Saradeshananda wrote: "Every year at the proper time, the Mother arranged to have the annual necessities such as rice, pulses, molasses, and other things bought from the market when they were at the cheapest rate. Again, before the rainy season, the Mother arranged to collect firewood for cooking and to repair doors and windows, the mud walls and the thatched roof. She kept an eye on every little thing.

"She could not bear any waste. She asked her attendants to collect cow dung and dry the patties in the sun to use for fuel. When parcels came from Calcutta and other places, she asked that the boxes and wrapping papers be saved to use later. The peelings from vegetables and fruits, and the foamy water from boiled rice, were given to the cows; leftover rice and dal were given to beggars or to the cows."[45]

The saying, "Waste not, want not" is very true. The less we waste, the less we lack in the future. The volume of food wasted in Western countries could feed all the poor people of the Third World.* Rammay (later Swami Gauriswarananda) often came to visit Holy Mother from Badanganj High School and stayed with her over the weekends. One Saturday a woman devotee cooked a gourmet dish called *bhuni-khichuri* for lunch, and the Mother saved some for Rammay. When he came in the afternoon, the Mother gave him that food to eat. He ate some and was about to throw away the leftovers. The Mother told him, "My son, don't throw away such good food." She asked him to call a poor woman who lived nearby, and she joyfully took away the remaining food. Then the Mother said: "One should have one's due. What men can eat shouldn't be wasted on cattle; what cattle can eat shouldn't be thrown away to dogs. What cattle and dogs can't eat can be given to the fish in the ponds. Nothing should be wasted."[46]

Prabodh Chandra Chattopadhyay was the headmaster of the Badanganj High School and also a disciple of the Mother. Whenever he visited the Mother in Jayrambati he would bring expensive fruits, sweets, and other things in a large basket. Holy Mother told him: "My son, I have everything by the Master's grace. I have no needs. You are a householder and you have spent so much money on me. You will have to look after your wife, your children, and their educational expenses; and you have spent so much money for these gifts." Prabodh was a little hurt. Understanding his wounded feelings, the Mother said: "Listen, my son, why I have said this. You are a householder; you need to save something. If you have no savings, how will you serve the monks? The monks do not earn money. They live on the financial help of the householder."[47] Prabodh was touched by the Mother's farsightedness and her affection for him.

In Calcutta, the monks took care of the groceries and household affairs while Holy Mother took care of the devotees' spiritual welfare. But her vigilant eyes were everywhere. Sarajubala recorded:

*Regarding the waste of food in America, an article published in the *New York Times* on 18 May 2008 stated: "Americans waste an astounding amount of food — an estimated 27 percent of the food available for consumption, according to a government study — and it happens at the supermarket, in restaurants and cafeterias and in your very own kitchen. It works out to about a pound of food every day for every American....In 1997, in one of the few studies of food waste, the Department of Agriculture estimated that two years before, 96.4 billion pounds of the 356 billion pounds of edible food in the United States was never eaten. Fresh produce, milk, grain products and sweeteners made up two-thirds of the waste."

One day after lunch, the Mother lay down and was about to fall asleep. A servant from Balaram's family called on her and left a basket of custard apples in the shrine for the offering. Then he took the empty basket downstairs and asked the monks what he should do with the basket. They told him to throw it out in the lane. When the Mother overheard this, she left her bed and went to the porch. She looked at the lane and said to me: "Look there. How beautiful that basket is! They have asked him to throw it away! It does not matter to them in the least. They are all monks and totally unattached. But we cannot allow such waste. We could at least use the basket for keeping vegetable peelings." She asked someone to fetch the basket, wash it, and keep it for future use. I learned a lesson from her words, but we are so slow to learn.[48]

It is customary in Bengal to eat various kinds of cakes on the last day of the Bengali month of *Paush,* which falls in the middle of January. One year on that day in Jayrambati, Holy Mother husked paddy to make fresh rice, then washed black lentils vigorously in the pond. She asked Nalini and Surabala to grind the soaked rice and lentils into a paste with a pestle and a stone slab. After finishing her bath and worship, she went to the kitchen and made various kinds of cakes (*saruchakli, puli, rasabara,* and *patisapta*) and rice pudding for the rest of the day. She offered the dishes to the Master and served the prasad to the devotees and relatives, who enjoyed those delicious cakes immensely. She said to Ashu: "I have made a large quantity and saved some for tomorrow. These cakes become tastier when they are kept overnight. You will enjoy them again tomorrow."[49] Ashu was touched, observing how the Mother had worked hard the entire day to serve everyone.

Humility and Sympathy

Pride makes people artificial, and humility makes them genuine. As God is egoless, so a realized soul must be egoless. Humility is the test of spirituality.

Ramakrishna demonstrated his humility by cleaning the toilet of the Dakshineswar temple garden and the drain of the sweeper Rasik. He also swept the garden path and acted as a gardener. Holy Mother washed the clothes of her devotees, cooked for them, mopped the floor of her home in Jayrambati, swept the courtyard, and did many so-called menial tasks. As a divine being and the wife of Ramakrishna Paramahamsa, she did not need to perform the duties of a maidservant and cook. However, the performance of such activities was necessary for the Mother to present herself as a role model for her disciples and future generations.

Towards the end of her life, Holy Mother became feeble, so an elderly brahmin woman was hired to cook for her large household in Jayrambati. Holy Mother used to call her "Aunt." It is customary to pay respect to the seniors on the last day of Durga Puja; so when Holy Mother was about to bow down to the brahmin cook, she said: "What is this, Mother? You are the Mother of the Universe and all people bow down to you. I am an ordinary woman. I can't accept your salutation." But the Mother insisted. She bowed down to her and said: "It is perfectly all right. You are my aunt."[50]

Sympathy exists in all hearts but it may not manifest in all of them. Holy Mother's sympathy always flowed towards everyone around her, and it manifested through her love and service. Earlier we described her sympathy for actresses, who had questionable character. Their glamour and riches could not give them peace, so from time to time they visited the Mother in Udbodhan House.

According to the Kaushitaki Upanishad (3:8), whomever the Indwelling Self wishes to uplift from this mundane world, It make that person do good deeds. To uplift some poor and neglected souls, Holy Mother sometimes accepted personal service out of compassion. One day she told a little boy: "My son, please pick some flowers for me. You are my jewel." The boy refused, but Holy Mother insisted. Finally, that boy picked some flowers for her worship. Though Holy Mother had several attendants, she asked one poor elderly village woman to massage her feet with oil. The woman said that she was too tired from working the whole day and needed to rest. Holy Mother pleaded: "Look, my child, give me a little massage for my feet. What else can you do?" The woman yielded at last.[51] This is the way the Mother sometimes bestowed her grace on some souls without letting them know about it.

Love and Compassion

Without love and compassion, human beings are like beasts. These two noble qualities make life smooth and joyful. They exist in every human heart to differing degrees. That person is great whose love and compassion are focussed on others. Through love and compassion, one can get rid of selfishness, which is a sin. Jesus taught his disciples to love their neighbours and to treat others like the Good Samaritan, who rescued a wounded man by the side of the road. Buddha, Ramakrishna, and other great teachers taught their followers to love and serve people with their hearts and souls. Holy Mother was the embodiment of love and compassion, and these qualities were manifested in all her actions and dealings with people.

Although Holy Mother followed the social customs of her time, she did not approve of all of them. For example, orthodox Hindu widows of Bengal led a very austere life during Holy Mother's lifetime: they ate one strict vegetarian meal a day, fasted on the Ekadashi day, shaved their heads, did not put oil on their bodies, wore a plain white sari, practised spiritual disciplines, and so on. Holy Mother herself did not follow such strict rules. After the Master's passing away, she ate vegetarian food and wore a plain white sari with a thin red border, and did not shave her head.

Due to social pressure, some widows practised such rigorous austerities that it seemed they would kill themselves. The Mother advised one such widow, "At night, first offer chapatis, milk, fruits, and sweets to the Master and then eat them." According to the custom of those times, a widow was not supposed to eat cooked rice twice a day. The Mother modified the rule for the sake of that widow's fragile health.

Kshirodbala Roy, a young widow from Bangladesh, came to Udbodhan House for initiation. She was a very austere woman and observed the local customs to excess. She recalled:

> Staring at me intently, the Mother asked, "My child, what do you take on Ekadashi day?" I replied, "Formerly I used to eat sago, but learning that it is adulterated with various other things, I don't take it now." As soon as she heard this, the Mother said, "No, no, I say you should take sago; it will keep your body cool." Then with deep sorrow in her voice the Mother said: "Child, you have been practising much austerity. I say, don't do it any further. Your body has almost turned into a piece of wood. How will you perform spiritual practices if your health is broken, my child?"
>
> She asked whether I used oil. I said, "I haven't used it ever since I was widowed." On hearing this the Mother said: "The use of oil keeps the head cool. Therefore use oil." I said: "As I have not used it for a long time, I have begun to hate the feel of it. I shall not be able to use oil, Mother." Golap-ma said, "Though she is very young, she has ruined her health by fasting and practising other austerities." Gauri-ma said, "Dear, why have you cut off your hair?" I said, "Widows in our part of the country do not grow their hair." Gauri-ma replied: "Without hair, one's eyesight deteriorates. Since you have dedicated your body to Sri Krishna, how does your hair belong to you, dear?" Yogin-ma then said: "This body is the temple of God. It is wise to keep it fit." But the Mother said: "You have done well. Keeping one's hair gives rise to a feeling of fashionableness to some extent, for one has to take care of it. So what you have done is right. You have overcome the craze for luxuriant locks, and you have also come here. You have now achieved that for which you lived so austerely. Now, I say, don't indulge

in such austerities any longer. You will have initiation tomorrow. Come here at eight o'clock in the morning. It will be nice to take a holy dip in the Ganges and to see Mother Kali on the day of initiation."[52]

Once, when the Master was still alive, Yogin-ma took her widowed aunt to Dakshineswar. It was an Ekadashi day and she was fasting, taking neither food nor water. She had fasted the previous day also. When this elderly woman arrived at the nahabat, she was gasping and could not stand erect. The Mother held her and asked, "Shall I give you a little sherbet?" The woman refused because she was fasting. After a while the Mother and Yogin-ma took her to the Master's room. While going up the steps, she almost fell. Immediately the Master came forward and held out his hand to her. The Master asked: "Why is she gasping?" Yogin-ma explained the situation. Then the Master said to Holy Mother, "Why did you not give her a little sherbet?" The Mother replied that she had offered it, but the widow refused to take it. The Master then took some sugar from his shelf, mixed it with some Ganges water, and said to the woman, "Please drink." She looked at the Master's face and then drank without another word. She said gratefully: "Father, my heart is cool now."[53] Ramakrishna and Holy Mother never encouraged the mortification of the flesh. One cannot concentrate on God if one suffers from hunger pangs. The Master said: "Religion is not possible on an empty stomach." Holy Mother also said: "First calm your body with food and drink and then call on God." This is a very practical teaching.

Holy Mother's sister-in-law Surabala was very sad after her husband's death and decided to eat only boiled rice and ghee once a day and strictly observe the Ekadashi fast without even drinking water. The Mother told her: "Don't torture yourself. Please drink water. Look, if the soul wants to eat something, one should offer it; otherwise fasting becomes a harmful act. The soul cries out, saying, 'She has deprived me of food.'" Holy Mother, Yogin-ma, and Golap-ma did not fast completely on the Ekadashi day; they ate luchis, fruit, and sweets.

Holy Mother had a very soft corner in her heart for the poor and downtrodden people of society. Kshirodbala Roy recalled:

One day a woman vendor came to Udbodhan to sell blankets. She wanted one rupee four annas for one blanket; Nalini began to bargain with her and offered one rupee. After a while, the Mother said to Nalini: "Why are you haggling so long for four annas? Shame on you! This poor woman carries her merchandise on her head and moves from door to door to earn a little money, and you are detaining her such a long time. Moreover, you don't need a blanket; still you want to buy one. It would be better to buy one blanket for her [Holy Mother was pointing to Kshirodbala], as she sleeps only on a blanket, and she has only one. She is content with only one blanket and never asks for anything from anyone."[54]

Kshirodbala was touched by the Mother's compassion and also amazed by how the Mother kept track of her needs.

Love is the cement that connects human hearts. A loveless life is dull and dreary, boring and tiresome, heavy and burdensome, painful and unpleasant. Tennyson said: "It is better to have loved and lost, than never to have loved at all." Holy Mother taught a naughty little girl who had given her family a great deal of trouble how to love. Mukulmala, a granddaughter of Bhavanath Chattopadhyay, regularly came to Udbodhan House with her parents, and the Mother always gave her plenty of sweets to eat. The Mother initiated her when she was 9 years old. Once, when Holy Mother was about to leave for Jayrambati, she said to the girl: "Darling, you have been visiting me a long time. Do you love me?"

"Yes, I love you very much."

"How much?"

The girl stretched her arms as wide as she could and said: "That much."

Holy Mother asked: "Will you still love me when I am away at Jayrambati?"

"Yes, I will love you just the same. I shall not forget you."

"How shall I know it?"

"What should I do to make you know?"

"I shall be sure of your love for me if you can love everyone at your home."

"All right, I will love all of them. I will not be naughty anymore."

"That's very good. But how shall I know that you will love everyone equally, and not some more or some less?"

"What should I do to love everyone equally?"

"Let me tell you how to love everyone equally. Do not demand anything of those you love. If you make demands, some will give you more and some less. In that case you will love more those who give you more, and less, those who give you less. Thus your love will not be the same for all. You will not be able to love everyone impartially." The little girl promised to love everyone without demanding anything in return. Her family reported that from that time forward her behaviour was exemplary.[55]

32
Two Flowers
on One Stem

Vāgarthau iva sampriktau vāgartha pratipattaye;
Jagatah pitarau vande pārvati-parameshvarau.
— *Raghuvamsham by Kalidasa*

As the word and its meaning are interconnected and one cannot exist without the other, so the Divine Mother Parvati and the Supreme Lord Shiva are eternally connected like power and the possessor of power. I bow down to the Parents of the Universe.

It is impossible for the limited human intellect to comprehend the infinite God. We can try to understand something of God by reading descriptions in the scriptures and by observing the lives of avatars, saints, and god-like souls. In this chapter we shall learn what Holy Mother said about Ramakrishna, which will help us visualize how these two divine beings interacted and played their divine roles in this world. Though they had separate names and separate forms, essentially, they were one substance — pure consciousness — and they were aware of this.

The Shvetashvatara Upanishad says that the same Brahman manifests in this universe through multiple names and forms: "Thou art woman, Thou art man; Thou art the youth and the maiden too. As an old man Thou totterest along on a staff; it is Thou alone who, when born, assumest diverse forms."[1]

According to nondualistic Vedanta, Brahman (the Absolute) becomes Purusha and Prakriti through Its power of maya, but the two are always interconnected. *Shakti shaktiman abhedah* — The power and the possessor of power cannot be separated. It is like fire and its power to burn, or milk and its whiteness. The dualistic Vaishnava tradition says that Krishna is the only Purusha and all males and females in the universe are in the domain of Prakriti. Ramakrishna said: "It is Brahman alone that appears as Ishwara, maya, living beings, and the universe.... That which is Brahman is also Shakti, Kali."[2]

Two in One, a painting by Bijali, an American devotee (*Courtesy: Vedanta Society of Southern California*).

On 16 October 1883, Ishan Mukhopadhyay said to the Master that according to the Chandi, "Brahman alone is the Primal Energy. Brahman is identical with Shakti."

The Master replied: "It will not do simply to express that idea in words. Only when you assimilate it will all be well with you."[3]

This type of discussion on Brahman-Maya, Shiva-Shakti, Purusha-Prakriti is mysterious to us. We read or hear these words but cannot comprehend their relationship till we unveil the mystery through the experience of Oneness. The lives of Ramakrishna and Holy Mother can help us understand to some extent how God and the Divine Mother, Shiva and Shakti, Purusha and Prakriti, function on the dualistic plane.

In *Bodhasara,* Narahari Acharya used an analogy to explain this phenomenon: When a newly married bride goes to her husband's home, she is so shy that she wears a veil and cannot talk to her husband in front of anyone. But she feels united with him through her heart and loves to see him through her veil. Similarly, when duality dissolves in the heart of a spiritual aspirant, he experiences union with the Atman or God. But with a view to playing or interacting with God, he separates himself from the Divine and begins to worship Him with love and devotion. In fact, before illumination, duality is delusion and bondage, but after illumination, duality is sweet and beautiful.

It is for the sake of the Atman, or the Self, that every human being loves someone or something. This Atman pervades every being and every thing, so through it people feel connected to their husbands, wives, children, money, home, and so on.

According to the Vedantic tradition, one can establish a relationship with God in three ways: first, *tasyi-vāham* or "I am His" (third person); second, *tavai-vāham* or "I am Yours" (second person); and third, *tvame-vāham* or "I am You" (first person). In the first kind of relationship, devotees look upon God as separate, though God is invisible. They pray for God's favour. This is the beginning of religion. In the second, devotees feel that God is near and dear, and they behave with God like a close relative. In the third, devotees lose their self identity, and their egos merge into God-consciousness. The two become one; the lover and the Beloved are lost in love. This is called *samadhi* or divine communion.

The great devotee Hanuman described this relationship: "O Lord, when I identify myself with the body, I am your servant. When I consider myself to be an individual soul, I am part of you. And when I look upon myself as the Atman, I am one with you. This is my firm conviction." This statement is the best explanation of the different phases of spiritual consciousness.

Ramakrishna knew who Holy Mother was, and Holy Mother knew Ramakrishna's true nature. Once Naresh Chandra Chakrabarty, one of Holy Mother's disciples, went to Jayrambati. Wishing to accept his worship, the Mother said to him: "I love yellow flowers, and the Master loves white flowers. Please get both kinds of flowers from Kishori." Naresh rushed to Kishori (later Swami Parameswarananda) and got the flowers from him, and then returned to find the Mother waiting at the same spot. Following the silent instructions of the Mother, Naresh offered yellow flowers at her left foot and white flowers at her right foot. Naresh then fervently prayed: "Mother, I offer to you the results of all my actions in this earthly life and also hereafter."[4]

Swami Gambhirananda wrote: "By accepting his worship that day, the Mother disclosed indirectly to him the truth of the unity of Shiva and Shakti in her holy person. She wanted the white flowers for the snow-white Shiva who was identical with Sri Ramakrishna, and the yellow ones for the golden-coloured Shakti as embodied in herself."[5]

One day in Dakshineswar, the Master was seated on his small cot and Holy Mother was sweeping his floor. Holy Mother asked the Master, "Who am I to you?" Without a second thought the Master replied, "You are my Blissful Mother."

Swami Parameswarananda recorded: "Once a disciple asked the Mother, 'How do you regard the Master?' She remained silent for a while and then gravely answered, 'I regard him as my son.' Another day the Mother said to me: 'Know for certain that the Master and I are one. Don't see us separately.'"[6]

One day in Dakshineswar, Hriday jokingly asked Holy Mother, "Aunt, don't you call the uncle 'father'?"

Immediately she replied: "Why do you speak of him as father only? He is my mother, father, friend, relative, and everything else."[7]

From Ramakrishna's viewpoint, Holy Mother was the Mother of the Universe; and from Holy Mother's perspective, Ramakrishna was the embodiment of all gods and goddesses.

In Jayrambati on the morning of 8 June 1913, Surendranath Bhaumik and Dr. Durgapada Ghosh came to the Mother and bowed down to her. They had been visiting and were to take their leave that afternoon. She blessed them by placing her hands on their heads and then she asked them to take their seats. After a brief conversation, Surendra said to the Mother: "Mother, while worshipping the Master I find one difficulty. Suppose a devotee has a general belief that his Ishta-Devi [the chosen goddess] and the Master are one and the same. He worships the Ishta-Devi through the image of the Master. Afterwards he surrenders the fruits of his japa to the image of the Master, uttering the words, 'O Maheshwari [the supreme goddess], through thy grace,' and so forth. This creates confusion in my mind."

Holy Mother said with a smile: "Don't worry, my child. Our Master alone is Maheshwara [the supreme god] as well as Maheshwari. He alone is the embodiment of all the deities. He alone is the embodiment of all mystic syllables. Through him one can worship all gods and goddesses. You can address him as Maheshwara as well as Maheshwari."[8]

As Yogin-ma observed Holy Mother's involvement with her brothers, nephews, and nieces, one day a doubt about the Mother's renunciation cropped up in Yogin-ma's mind. In a vision, Ramakrishna said to her: "Do not doubt her [Holy Mother]. Know that she and I are one."[9]

On 31 January 1913, Sarajubala asked a few questions regarding spiritual practices. Holy Mother replied: "Do not make any distinction between the Master and me. Meditate on and pray to the particular aspect of the Divinity revealed to you. Meditation begins in the heart and ends in the head. Neither mantra nor scripture is of any avail; bhakti, or devotion, alone accomplishes everything. The Master is everything — both guru and Ishta. He is all in all."[10]

On another occasion in Jayrambati, the Mother initiated a devotee and asked him to offer all his karma, virtues and vices, merits and demerits at the Master's feet. She then gave him a mantra and pointed out the Master as his guru. The devotee was a little confused. Because Holy Mother had given him the mantra, he thought she should be his guru. The devotee did not realize that the Mother and the Master are one. Then he asked, "How shall I think of the Master?"

The Mother gravely replied: "The Master is all — Purusha and Prakriti. If you meditate on him, you will achieve everything." She then said to a woman devotee: "All gods and goddesses exist in the Master — even the goddesses Shitala, Manasa, and others."[11]

Swami Basudevananda recalled: "When the Mother was in Udbodhan, she used to drink the *charanamrita* [holy water] of the Master after the worship. One day someone brought the charanamrita of Siddheshwari Kali at Baghbazar and I carried both to her in two different containers. She was on the veranda and asked what I had brought. I said, 'Two kinds of charanamrita in two containers.'

She said: 'Both are the same. Mix them together.'

'All right, I shall do so from tomorrow.'

She gravely said: 'No, mix them together right now.' Immediately I mixed them and the Mother drank the charanamrita. Then, with a smile, she put her hand on my head and blessed me."[12]

Although he was established in Advaita, or nondualism, the Master experienced dualism, qualified nondualism, and nondualism as complementary, not contradictory. The different philosophies are like different pictures of the sun. The Master enjoyed God through various moods — shanta, dasya, sakhya, vatsalya, madhura, and so on.* Holy Mother was like the Master in this respect. Although she was established in Advaita, she used to worship the Master, Gopala, and other deities regularly. We have already mentioned that the Mother began to worship a picture of the Master at the nahabat during the Master's lifetime, and the Master himself worshipped the same picture. Later, wherever she went, she always carried that picture of the Master in a small tin box and worshipped it every day. This indicates that it is Holy Mother who first introduced the worship of Ramakrishna. It is said that Vishnupriya made an image of Chaitanya from a piece of margosa wood and was the first to worship her husband during his lifetime.

We have already described Holy Mother's mode of worship, which was informal and full of affection and devotion. She considered the Master to be her father, mother, husband, friend, and also her beloved God. Her disciples observed her interaction with the Master during the worship. When she was alone in Kamarpukur, the Master would now and then appear in a vision and ask her to make *khichuri* and cheese and offer them to him. Once during Jagaddhatri Puja in Jayrambati, Holy Mother performed her daily worship in her room early in the morning. Then she addressed the Master and said: "Look, today is the Mother's worship in our house. Please eat quickly. I shall have to go there."[13]

When she wanted to go to Jayrambati from Calcutta, she would talk to the Master during the worship: "Now you will have to go to Jayrambati. I see you like the good food of Calcutta and do not like the water of the big pond of Jayrambati and the tulsi leaves."[14] During her final departure from Jayrambati in February 1920, she stayed one night at Jagadamba Ashrama in Koalpara. At five o'clock in the morning, Brahmachari Barada saw that the Mother had finished her worship and was offering sweets and fruits to the Master. She then wrapped up the Master's picture in a cloth, put it in her trunk, and said to the Master: "Get ready. We will have to start now."

---

*Shanta [peace and serenity], dasya [attitude of the servant towards the master], sakhya [attitude of friendship], vatsalya [attitude of a parent towards a child], and madhura [attitude of a lover towards the beloved].

We see only the picture of Ramakrishna in our shrines, but the Mother saw the living Master there. When Swami Arupananda asked if the Master dwelt in the picture, she replied: "Of course he does. The body and the shadow are the same. And what is his picture but a shadow?"[15]

The Mother saw the Master not only in the waking state but in the dream state also. Once in Jayrambati someone worshipped the Master at noon. After lunch the Mother went to bed to take some rest. In a dream, she saw the Master lying on the floor. She asked, "Why are you lying on the floor?" Her sleep broke. She looked at the altar and found that some flowers were touching the Master's picture and some ants were crawling over his picture. She immediately removed those flowers and cautioned the worshipper to be more careful in the future.[16]

On another occasion the Mother told Sudhira about a cosmic experience: "Once I was in such a state that I could not remove the ants from the naivedya [food offered to Ramakrishna]. I felt that the Master was eating that food [through the ants]."[17]

In 1911, Dr. Lalbihari Sen went to Jayrambati and fell ill there. During his convalescence, the Mother gave him a little khichuri. The doctor hesitated to eat it, fearing that the food might harm him. But the Mother assured him, saying: "It will not do any harm to you as the Master himself has partaken of it."

The doctor asked: "Can one see the Master?"

The Mother replied: "Yes, one can see him. Nowadays, he sometimes asks for khichuri and cheese to eat."

Once a monk in Koalpara said to Holy Mother, "I offer food to the Master, but I don't know whether he accepts it or not."

The Mother emphatically replied: "Surely he does eat it, my son. If you offer the food to the Master wholeheartedly, he will eat it."[18]

Once when Radhu was ill, Holy Mother stayed for some days at the boarding house of Nivedita's School on Bosepara Lane. Sarala (later Bharatiprana) was assigned to serve Radhu. One day Holy Mother asked her to make the food offering to the Master. Sarala did not know the mantras used for the food offering, and she told this to the Mother. The Mother said: "Look, my daughter, consider the Master to be your very own. Tell him: 'Master, please come, sit down. Here is the food, please eat it.' At that time think that the Master has come and sat down and is eating the food. There is no need to utter mantras when you offer food to your dearest ones. These kinds of formalities are to show honour and respect to distinguished relatives and guests when they visit your home. They are not necessary for your own people. The Master will accept your offering according to your attitude."[19] Holy Mother also taught Sarala a mantra for the food offering.

People may become confused as they read Holy Mother's various statements made to her disciples on different occasions. Ramakrishna said that Satchidananda alone is the guru. He could not bear it if anyone called him a guru. Similarly, Holy Mother did not promote herself as a guru. She always stressed to the devotees that the Master was all in all. She told Swami Kapileswarananda, "Look, I have not given you the mantra; it is the Master who has given it to you." After initiating Swami Sadhanananda in Jayrambati, Holy Mother showed him the Master's picture and said, "The Master is your guru."

Sadhanananda asked: "Mother, you are saying that the Master is the guru. Who are you?"

Holy Mother humbly replied: "My son, I am nobody. The Master is the guru and the Ishta."[20]

Another time, after initiating a disciple, Holy Mother pointed to the Master's picture and said, "He is your guru."

The disciple replied, "Yes, Mother, he is the guru of the universe."

Holy Mother then pointed to the picture of Bhavatarini Kali and said, "She is your Chosen Deity."

The disciple asked, "Mother, why should I worship an invisible deity and leave behind the visible one?" He was asking why it was necessary to worship an image of the Divine Mother when Her living presence was in Holy Mother. Observing the sincere devotion of her disciple, Holy Mother smiled and said, "All right, my son, let it be."[21]

One day Ashu asked: "Mother, do you still see the Master every day? Does he eat from your hand?"

Holy Mother replied: "Are we separate?" Embarrassed, she pressed her tongue between her teeth and then said, "See what I have said inadvertently."[22]

To those who thought the Master and Holy Mother were separate, Swami Premananda would say: "Those who consider the Master and the Mother to be different are ignorant of their true nature. In fact, the Master and the Mother are the obverse and reverse of the same coin."[23]

Some considered those who received the mantra from the Master to be of a higher rank than those who received the mantra from Holy Mother. Swami Vijnanananda told Akshaychaitanya: "There is no difference between receiving the mantra from the Master and the Mother. Are the Master and the Mother different? I sometimes give the Mother's mantra to devotees."[24]

After Holy Mother's passing away, Josephine MacLeod asked M. about Holy Mother, "What was she to you?"

M. replied: "The same as Sri Ramakrishna, God-incarnate on earth. He and Holy Mother are one in the same way that Christ said, 'I and my Father are one.' The Master said, 'Brahman and Shakti are one.'"[25]

On 19 March 1917, Holy Mother wrote to her disciple Manada Shankar Dasgupta: "If you have a keen desire to meditate on my form, do it. There is no difference between me and the Master. The only difference is between the two forms. The Master dwells inside my body."

On 13 April 1917, she wrote to Manada again: "The Master and I are one."

Manada went to Holy Mother and asked, "Mother, is it necessary to repeat the Master's name during my spiritual practice?"

"Yes, you must repeat the Master's mantra," she replied

"Why is this necessary? You and the Master are the same."

Holy Mother quickly corrected him: "My son, although we are one, I can't advise my disciples to give up the Master."[26]

Once in Koalpara Holy Mother talked about the Master to her disciples. Keshavananda lamented his bad luck that the Master had left this world before he could see him. The Mother consoled him by pointing to herself and saying: "The Master dwells in this body in a subtle form. The Master himself told me, 'I shall live within you in a subtle form.'"[27]

Swami Saradananda wholeheartedly believed that Holy Mother's will was God's will. He never tried to change the Mother's will; he obeyed Holy Mother completely. He used to say, "Are the Mother and the Master different?" Once someone asked Saradananda, "Do you respect the Mother because she is the wife of your guru?"

The swami replied: "No, we respect her because she and the Master are one and the same. However, there is one difference: we could argue with the Master, but that is not possible with the Mother."[28]

"I Incarnate in Every Age"

Krishna declared in the Gita that God incarnates in every age. In *The Gospel of Sri Ramakrishna*, in some places Ramakrishna gave distinct hints about his reappearance, and in other places he was more indirect.

On 24 December 1883, the Master told M.:

I shall have to be born once more. Therefore I am not giving all knowledge to my companions. (*With a smile*) Suppose I give you all knowledge; will you then come to me again so willingly?[29]

On 9 August 1885, the Master said to Mahimacharan:

It will be sufficient for the youngsters who come here if they know only two things. If they know these, they will not have to practise much discipline and austerity. First, who I am, and second, who they are. Many of the youngsters belong to the inner circle.

Those belonging to the inner circle will not attain liberation. I shall have to assume a human body again, in a northwesterly direction.[30]

In 1895 Swamiji wrote a letter to Swami Ramakrishnananda from America: "The Satyayuga [Golden Age] started the day Ramakrishna was born as an Incarnation."[31]

The Holy Mother concurred, saying: "The Satyayuga began with the birth of the Master. Many luminaries have accompanied him....Countless ordinary people take birth and die; but the foremost ones come with the avatar for the sake of his mission."[32]

People expect peace and happiness in a golden age; but within 28 years of Ramakrishna's passing away, the first world war took place and millions of people were killed. When Holy Mother was asked about this, she responded that the storm comes before the rain. Storms obscure people's vision by blowing dust, breaking trees, and destroying homes. Then the rain comes and settles the dust so that people can see clearly again. Similarly, at the advent of an avatar, terrible disasters occur, clearing all unrighteousness, falsehood, hypocrisy, greed, and evil from society. At that time the realm of dharma, or righteousness, becomes manifest.

As the Master incarnates in every age, Holy Mother also incarnates along with him to establish the eternal religion and benefit humanity. Nalin Bihari Sarkar of Midnapore once asked Holy Mother, "Mother, did you come with all the avatars?"

"Yes, my son," she replied.[33]

Ramakrishna never directly stated when he would return, as far as the record shows. Some people said he would come 100 years after his death, and some said after 200 years. It seems that he may return soon because at present the world is in deep turmoil, crushed by violence, hatred, and war. People are hungry for peace and joy. Ramakrishna said: "Wherever there is any trouble in the Divine Mother's empire, I shall have to rush there to stop it, like a government officer."[34] So God must be born in every age to accomplish His mission of serving suffering humanity.

On different occasions, Holy Mother made various statements about the Master's return. Once she recalled: "The Master said he would come again after 100 years. Meanwhile, for those hundred years he would live in the hearts of those who love him. Standing on the semicircular veranda at Dakshineswar, the Master said this, pointing towards the northwest. I told him I would not come again. Lakshmi also said she would not come again, even if she were chopped into shreds like tobacco leaves! The Master laughed and said: 'How can you avoid coming? Our roots are twined together like the kalmi plant. Pull one stem and the whole clump comes forward.'"[35]

Holy Mother also said: "The Master said that he would dwell in the hearts of his devotees for a hundred years in his subtle body. He further said that he would have many devotees among the white people."[36]

Neither *The Gospel of Sri Ramakrishna* nor *Sri Ramakrishna and His Divine Play* includes any direct statement from Ramakrishna concerning how he will return. However, M. recorded that on 15 March 1886, Ramakrishna said: "A band of minstrels [Bauls] suddenly appears, dances, and sings, and it departs in the same sudden manner. They come and they return, but none recognizes them."[37]

On 9 February 1912 Gauri-ma said: "The Master will come back twice and once as a Baul."

Holy Mother: "Yes, the Master said to me, 'You will carry my hubble-bubble.' I might have to cook in a broken pan and he will eat from a stone plate. He will travel continually without caring for his surroundings."[38]

Holy Mother continued: "[After the Master's passing away] we went to Vrindaban by train. Latu, Jogin, and Kali got down from the train. Golap was passing the luggage to them from the train. Golap handed Latu's hubble-bubble to me while I was getting down. Lakshmi reminded me, 'Aunt, here you have fulfilled the Master's words that you would carry the hubble-bubble.' Immediately I said, 'Master, here I fulfilled your words.' Saying so, I dropped the hubble-bubble on the ground."[39]

On 12 May 1913, Swami Arupananda told Holy Mother that a devotee from Ranchi had had a vision of the Master. He had seen the Master wearing an ochre cloth and wooden sandals, and holding tongs.

Arupananda asked, "Mother, why did the Master have wooden sandals and tongs?"

Holy Mother: "Those are the signs of a monk. He said that he would come back as a Baul. The Bauls wear a long robe, grow a beard, and tie their long hair on their heads in a bun."[40]

Brahmachari Akshaychaitanya wrote in his book *Sri Sri Sarada Devi*: "The Holy Mother said to Nikunja Devi [M.'s wife]: 'One day the Master said: "I know who you and Lakshmi are, but I shall not tell you. To repay my debt to you, I shall be born as a Baul and make you my companion."'"[41]

Once an attendant of the Holy Mother said to her, "I heard that you and the Master will come back as Bauls."

Holy Mother replied: "Well, you will not escape either. Those who have come this time will have to come the next. Have you seen the moon in the sky? Does the moon rise alone? It rises along with the stars."

The attendant said joyfully, "Mother, we are all ready to come back because we will be with you."[42]

Swami Nikhilananda wrote:

To her [Holy Mother], God was both Pure Spirit, or Brahman, and also the Universal Energy, or Shakti, and Sri Ramakrishna was the Divine Incarnation of modern times. "The Master is the embodiment of all deities and of all mantras," she said. "Really and truly, one can worship through him all gods and goddesses." And she continued: "Sri Ramakrishna assumed this human body to remove the sorrows and sufferings of others. He moved about in disguise, as a king walks through his capital. The moment he became known, he disappeared." On another occasion Holy Mother said: "He who has prayed to the Master even once has nothing to fear. By praying to him constantly, one obtains ecstatic love through his grace. This love is the essence of spiritual life. The Master used to say to his devotees: 'I have made the mould; now you may cast the image.' To 'cast the image' means to meditate on the Master, to think of the various incidents of his life. Contemplate the great sufferings the Master had to undergo because of taking upon himself the results of the bad karma done by others, and then you will find that your body and mind have been purified. Your grief and misery will disappear if you only remember how the Master, though Divinity Itself, suffered for the sake of others and yet did not miss even for one moment the ecstatic joy he experienced from the contemplation of the Divine Mother." Thus she advised her disciples to meditate on Sri Ramakrishna and repeat his name. Through his grace every desire of the seeker would be fulfilled. Those who pray to him, the Mother taught, "will never suffer from want of food or other physical privations, and will also easily gain love and knowledge of Brahman."[43]

Holy Mother witnessed the Master's divine play. She knew how he had practised his superhuman sadhanas, and was fully aware of his divine mission in this world. In 1919, after Durga Puja, Keshavananda came to Jayrambati from Koalpara to pay his respects to Holy Mother. In the course of their conversation, Keshavananda asked her, "Mother, was it for the establishment of the harmony of religions that the Master came this time?"

Holy Mother replied: "Look, my son, it never occurred to me that the Master practised all religions with the intention of preaching the harmony of religions. He was always absorbed in God-consciousness. The way the

Christians, Muslims, and Vaishnavas practise spiritual disciplines and realize God, the Master also practised those paths in the same way, and thus he enjoyed the divine play of God in various ways. He was completely oblivious of how days and nights would pass. But you see, my son, in this present age he set the ideal of renunciation. How many people recognized him as God? People were attracted to his renunciation. Only a few in his inner circle realized him as God. Has anyone ever witnessed such natural renunciation? What you have mentioned about the harmony of religions is also true. In every incarnation a particular ideal is emphasized and other ideals remain dormant."[44]

Holy Mother's Advice to Monks

Ramakrishna was a monk and Holy Mother lived like a nun, although she took no formal vows. Their teachings to monastics were very similar. Both emphasized renunciation, discrimination, purity, and humility, which are indispensable in monastic life. Like Ramakrishna, Holy Mother cautioned her monastic disciples again and again about lust and gold, which bind the soul.

St. Paul wrote to the Corinthians: "If people cannot control themselves, they should marry, for it is better to marry than to burn with passion."[45] Regarding monastic ideals, Holy Mother was uncompromising and she rebuked any monk she saw deviating from them. She frankly told a monk: "After receiving the ochre cloth, don't get involved with women. It is better to marry than to form a group of monks and nuns living together, as some Vaishnava sects do."[46]

A monk was sick and staying at a devotee's house, but Holy Mother did not approve of it. She said to Brahmachari Barada: "I understand he was ill. But why did he live with a householder? There are monasteries. A monk must not lower the ideal of renunciation. Even if a wooden image of a woman lies upside down on the road, he must not turn it the other way, even with his foot, to look at its face. It is dangerous for a monk to save money. Money can create all kinds of trouble, even endanger one's life."[47]

To Brahmachari Ashok, who inherited a lot of money, Holy Mother said:

Had your father not left any money for your mother, I would have asked you to earn money and look after her comfort. Through the grace of the Master, that obstacle has been removed. Just see that the money left at her disposal is not wasted. Make some arrangements for it, and look after her as much as you can. Is this a small advantage for you? One cannot earn money in strictly honest ways. Money always taints the mind. For this reason, I ask you to settle the financial affairs of your mother as soon as possible. Such is the fascination for money that if you involve yourself too much with it, you will feel attracted to it. You may think you are above money and that you will never feel any attraction for it because you have once renounced it. You may further think that at any moment you can leave it behind. No, my child, never harbour this thought in your mind. Through a tiny little loophole, the thought of money will enter into your mind and then strangle you gradually, quite undetected. You will never know it. Especially as you are from Calcutta, you know how money can draw people into reckless ways of living. Settle your mother's affairs as soon as possible and then run away from Calcutta....The Master could never bear to touch money. You are all out in the world, taking his name on your lips. Always remember his words. Money is at the root of all the disasters you see in the world. Money may lure one's mind into other temptations. Beware![48]

It is said that Brahmachari Ashok did not obey his guru and eventually had to leave the Order.

Holy Mother's Advice to Householders

Holy Mother did not give discourses to householders. Instead, she demonstrated the ideal householder's life. Her life was her message. However, the following are some examples of Holy Mother's advice to householders:

"The aim of life is to realize God and remain immersed in contemplation on Him. God alone is real and everything else is false. God is one's very own. This is the eternal relationship between God and His creatures. One realizes God in proportion to the intensity of one's feeling for Him. He who is really eager to cross the ocean of the world will somehow break his bonds. No one can entangle him."[49]

"Holy men are born on earth to show people the way to God. They teach each person differently. There are many paths leading to the same goal. Therefore the teachings of all the saints are true."[50]

"The path leading to Brahman is very difficult. It is quite natural for a man to forget God. Therefore whenever the need arises, God becomes incarnated on earth and shows the path by practising spiritual disciplines Himself. This time, too, God has shown the example of renunciation."[51]

"Many think of God only after receiving blows from the world. But blessed indeed is he who can offer his mind, like a fresh flower, at the feet of the Lord from his very childhood. One should practise renunciation in youth. In old age the body deteriorates and loses strength. The mind does not possess vigour. Is it possible to do anything then?

"Today the human body is; tomorrow it is not. Even the shortest span of life is beset with pain and misery. He who is able to renounce all for God's sake is a living God....It is the body that changes. The Atman always remains the same. Lust and gold must be renounced. The Master used to say, 'I can cover the whole village of Kamarpukur with gold; but what good will that do?

"Everything is illusory — husband, wife, even this body. These are the great shackles of maya. Unless you can free yourself from these shackles, you will never be able to cross to the other shore. Attachment to the body, this identification of the self with the body, must go. What is this body, after all, my child? It is nothing but three pounds of ashes when it is cremated. However strong or beautiful this body may be, it ends up in those three pounds of ashes. Yet people are attached to it. What maya!"[52]

"One must experience the effects of one's past actions. None can escape them. But japa minimizes their intensity. For example, a man who, as a result of his past karma, is destined to lose his leg, may instead suffer from the prick of a thorn in his foot.

"If you love a human being, you will have to suffer for it. He is blessed, indeed, who can love God alone. There is no suffering in loving God. Be devoted to God and take shelter at His feet. It is enough to remember that there is someone — call Him Father or Mother — who is always protecting you."[53]

"God is purity itself and cannot be realized without the practice of control of the body and mind. Can anyone destroy lust altogether? A little of it remains as long as one has a body; but it can be subdued, just as a snake can be subdued by means of dust.* If you are constantly in contact with objects of enjoyment, you are likely to succumb to their influence....Don't be afraid. In this Kaliyuga, mental sin is no sin. Free your mind from all worries on that score. You need not be afraid.

"The Master used to say that truthfulness alone is the austerity of the present age. One attains God by holding to the truth."[54]

"My child, it is good to be active. Bless me that I may work as long as I live. One must always do some work. Only through work can one remove the bondage of work. Total detachment comes later. One should not be without work even for a moment. Work helps one to fend off idle thoughts. If one is without work, such thoughts rush into one's mind."[55]

"Be devoted to God and take shelter at His feet. Blinded by egotism, people think of themselves as independent agents in regard to their work. They do not depend on God. God protects one who relies on Him. How little intelligence a man possesses! He may want one thing, but asks for another. He starts to mould an image of Shiva and often ends by making the likeness of a monkey! It is therefore best to surrender all desires at the feet of God. Let Him do whatever is best for us. But one may desire devotion and nonattachment. These are not harmful desires."[56]

*Referring to the charmed dust used by the snake-charmers of India.

They Worshipped Each Other

Both Ramakrishna and Sarada knew their true nature was undivided, pure consciousness, and that their bodies were made of maya. But during their divine play on this earth their spiritual relationship was a mystery to most people. They literally worshipped each other. Swami Vishuddhananda, a disciple of Holy Mother, once explained this mystery:

> The Master said to Holy Mother: "The Mother who is in the temple is the same Mother who gave birth to this body and is now living in the nahabat, and She is the same Mother who is now massaging my feet." It seems to me that the Master saw Holy Mother from three angles: He gave advice to Sarada as a disciple; he allowed her to serve him as a devoted wife; and he worshipped her as the veritable Divine Mother of the Universe.
>
> Holy Mother also served and worshipped Ramakrishna as her husband, guru, and Ishta [Chosen Deity].
>
> Some people ask me, "Who is greater — the Master or the Mother?" I answer: "Please think carefully. The Master worshipped the Mother and she gracefully accepted that worship. Now you decide yourself."
>
> During the incarnations of Rama and Krishna, the Shakti was not properly honoured, but rather humiliated. In Ramakrishna's incarnation, however, he worshipped his own Shakti and placed Her in the highest position by this worship. Moreover, he made Bhairavi Brahmani his guru. This is the age of the Motherhood of God.[57]

"Thy Will be Done"

Ramakrishna and Holy Mother were divine beings and they were endowed with the power to change their own destinies as well as the destinies of others. Although out of compassion they vicariously took some devotees' bad karma on themselves and suffered, they did not use that power for themselves to get rid of their own sufferings. They completely surrendered their destiny to God's will.

When Shashadhar Tarkachudamani asked the Master to apply his will-power to cure his cancer, the Master replied: "As a pandit, how can you make such a suggestion? This mind has been given up to God once and for all. How can I withdraw it from Him and make it dwell on this cage of flesh and bones?" Similarly when someone said to the Mother, "Mother, if once you say, 'Let the disease be cured,' it will definitely be cured." Holy Mother replied: "My child, can I say such thing? Whatever is the will of the Master that will happen. What more can I say?" Someone insisted, "Mother, please say once, 'Let the disease go,' and it will go away." She humbly replied: "I cannot say that. Let the Master's will be done."[58]

33
Further Glimpses
of Holy Mother

Pavitram charitam yasyāh pavitram jivanam tathā;
Pavitratā-svarupinyai tasyai kurmo namo namah.
— *A hymn by Swami Abhedananda*

She whose life's story is pure, whose character is pure, who is the very embodiment of purity, to that Holy Mother we offer salutations again and again.

G reatness knows itself. In this world some are born great, and some achieve greatness through hard work. It is wrong to believe that money makes a person great; it is the person who makes himself or herself great. In fact, it is the inner noble qualities of a person that make him or her great.

In the Chandogya Upanishad, Narada practised many spiritual disciplines and was endowed with vast learning, yet he was mentally afflicted on account of his ignorance of the Self. So he went to the sage Sanatkumara, a knower of Brahman, to learn the knowledge of the Self. Sanatkumara gave Narada 21 instructions and lifted his mind from the lower to the higher plane, and finally to the highest point, the Infinite.

Sanatkumara described the Infinite thus: "The Infinite is bliss. There is no bliss in anything finite. Where one sees nothing else, hears nothing else, understands nothing else — that is the Infinite. The Infinite is immortal."

Narada asked, "Venerable sir, in what does the Infinite find Its support?"

Sanatkumara replied, "*Sve mahimni* — In Its own greatness."[1]

Holy Mother was born with divine greatness, and she shone in her own greatness. What makes a person great? In this world people become great by vast learning, physical beauty, enormous wealth, overwhelming oratory, striking leadership, scientific invention, marvellous adventures, attractive acting, prolific writing, wonderful singing, skilled dancing, astonishing bravery, spectacular athletic skills, and so on. Holy Mother

Sarada Devi at Jayrambati, 1918.

did not gain greatness through any of the above, yet she shone in her own glory.

What made her great? Her maternal affection for humanity attracted people; her pure character and glowing renunciation were awe-inspiring; her simplicity and modesty were majestic; her passion for truth and self-control were overwhelming; her sympathy and empathy touched many suffering and bereaved hearts; her compassion and forgiveness saved many wayward souls; her patience and perseverance were phenomenal; her conversations and manners were sweet and dignified; her common sense and skill in action set the example for others; her practical advice on the worldly plane and spiritual advice on the spiritual plane were extremely effective; and her sense of duty and unselfish service were the model for all.

Holy Mother was the Divine Mother, and she was endowed with all divine qualities. Wherever she lived, she created such a spiritual atmosphere that everyone around her felt they were living in a blissful abode.

Swami Nikhilananda, a disciple of Holy Mother, gave us a description of Holy Mother's physical appearance:

Holy Mother was well built for a Hindu woman of Bengal. She had a fair complexion and was of medium height, though in several of her photographs she gives the impression of being rather tall. The soles of her feet were ruddy. Her thick black hair, which Yogin-ma used to braid, almost reached her knees. Before Sri Ramakrishna's death she usually wore a white sari with a wide red border. She also wore some gold jewellery that the Master had given her: two bracelets for her upper arms, bangles for her wrists, a necklace, earrings, and a nose ring. When the Master gave her these ornaments he said to Hriday, jokingly: "I suppose that's all there is to my relationship with her." As already mentioned, after wearing them a short while, she discarded most of them. After the Master's death she wore a single gold bracelet on each wrist. Speaking of her own appearance, she once remarked: "I was rather pretty in my youth. Later I became a little stout." Women often were struck by her physical beauty. As Golap-ma said, she looked like a goddess. While meditating, she appeared radiant. Swami Premananda's mother once asked her: "Mother, where did you get such celestial beauty and charm?" Once Sri Ramakrishna compared her to Saraswati, a goddess of exquisite beauty and grace. Her fair complexion later became somewhat dark. By the time she was 50, when most of her disciples saw her, she had again become slim from repeated attacks of malaria at Jayrambati, and she appeared pale. Towards the end of her life she developed a slight stoop and often limped because of rheumatism.

Holy Mother's immaculate purity, her unceasing meditation and prayer, her all-embracing compassion and utter selflessness, endowed her with the delicacy and tenderness of a maiden, a subtle grace and quiet dignity, and withal guilessness and simplicity. Her innate motherliness put visitors at ease. To a person coming to her for the first time, she conveyed the feeling that she had been eagerly waiting for him. Holy Mother always inspired reverence but never gave a feeling of remoteness. During her later years, on rare occasions, a superficial observer would be deceived by her unassuming manner....

Holy Mother, unlike any other orthodox Hindu widow, wore, after the Master's death, a sari with a narrow red border, using it as skirt, blouse, and veil. Before strangers she covered herself practically from head to foot with an additional white cotton chadar. Once, during the cold season, she was given a thin woolen undershirt. She expressed pleasure at this gift and used it for three days. On the fourth day she took it off and said to the devotees: "Is it proper for a woman to wear a shirt? I put it on for three days just to please you." ...Holy Mother observed some of the caste rules. Like a Hindu widow, she was vegetarian, but again unlike a Hindu widow, she did not cut her hair, she wore gold bracelets, she wore a sari with a narrow red border, and ate a light supper at night.[2]

Ashu Mitra wrote: "We always saw the Mother wearing a sari with a narrow red border. Most of the devotees would supply that type of cloth for her. She wore two diamond-cut gold bangles on her wrists and a rudraksha rosary strung on a gold chain around her neck. There were 108 small rudraksha beads in that rosary, which was made during the time of Swami Yogananda. By the time we knew her, those rudraksha beads were worn out and the chain was broken. So a new rudraksha rosary with a gold chain was made for her. She wore an iron ring on the middle toe of each foot to relieve her rheumatism."[3]

Generally biographers write about noteworthy events, marvellous achievements, and amazing stories that take place in the public life of great personalities. They skip the daily routine, trifling events, and relationships with friends and family. As a result, readers do not get a full picture of that person.

As human beings, we relate to the human aspects of divine personalities. Otherwise how could we understand the infinite Lord? It is impossible to comprehend God with our impure minds and puny intellects. The Mundaka Upanishad describes the Cosmic Being: "The heavens are His head; the sun and moon, His eyes; the four quarters of the earth, His ears; the revealed Vedas, His speech; the wind is His breath; the universe, His heart. From His feet is produced the earth. He is indeed the inner Self of all beings."[4] When we read this verse, we become afraid to love that Supreme Being, whose eyes are the sun and the moon. We cannot imagine approaching Him or establishing a relationship with Him. For that reason, we need Rama, Krishna, Buddha, Jesus, Ramakrishna, Holy Mother, and other great teachers of the world, who can speak to our hearts and guide us along the path of blessedness.

This chapter provides some further glimpses of Holy Mother that reveal some facets of her private life, her interpersonal relationships, her love and concern for others, her surroundings, her methods of teaching, and so on. These brief and seemingly insignificant incidents draw us close to the Mother, and we get a chance to see her human side vividly. Observing all these things, we feel that she is not a goddess sitting in heaven but a human being like us moving on this earth. To a lover, every detail of the beloved's life is important because it brings more familiarity, feeling, awareness, love, and joy.

"The Light Shineth in Darkness"

Jesus said: "I am the way. I am the light. Those who follow me shall not walk in darkness."

John wrote: "The light shineth in darkness and the darkness comprehended it not."[5]

Holy Mother's life is the beacon light in this age, but few people understood her during her lifetime. Now her exemplary life stories and inspiring teachings are spreading throughout the world. People of the East and the West are receiving solace and succour from her divine life.

In the fall of 1914, Nilkanta Chakrabarty visited Jayrambati with his wife and a relative. He had already been initiated by Holy Mother and during this visit, Holy Mother initiated his wife. While in the area, they also wanted to see the Master's birthplace in Kamarpukur. In the morning Holy Mother sent with them some fruit and vegetables for offering to Raghuvir, the family deity. Shivaram, the Master's nephew, received them cordially, fed them, and showed them the places connected with the Master. In the afternoon, he showed them Manik Raja's mango orchard, where the Master used to play with his friends when he was a boy.

Nilkanta recalled:

We spent a long time with Shibu-da in the mango orchard listening to stories of the Master. We left Kamarpukur in the late afternoon and arrived in Jayrambati in the late evening. From a distance, we saw a person standing with a kerosene lantern in hand on the road near the Banerjee's pond on the southern outskirts of the village. When we drew close, we saw an incredible sight that overwhelmed us with wonder and joy. We remained speechless. As we were late, the loving and compassionate Mother was concerned. She was standing on the village road alone waiting for us. I exclaimed, "Mother, you are here!" She replied in her affectionate and calm voice: "My son, I was anxious about you. You are from a far-off place [Gharinda in Bangladesh]. The night is very dark. There is every possibility of going in the wrong direction. I asked someone to go to the crossroads, but he declined. So I have come here myself to wait for you." We were dumbfounded. Is there anything to compare with this love? I feel that she is my eternal mother — my mother of birth after birth — my own mother.[6]

The Wonder of Wonders

Sometimes an artist is amazed when she sees her own wonderful painting because while working on it, she forgot space and time and became identified with it. When she returns to the conscious plane, she sees the wonders in her artwork. Although Holy Mother was the Mother of the Universe, sometimes she was bewildered by the things of this world. However, she enjoyed her ignorance as a human being.

In March 1881, she came to Calcutta from Jayrambati with her mother and her brother Prasanna, staying briefly at an apartment that Prasanna rented in Kansaripara. She recalled: "I had never seen a water tap before I first came to Calcutta. I went to the bathroom, turned on the water tap, and heard a hissing sound like a snake coming through it. Terrified, I ran from the bathroom and told the ladies: 'Please come and see! A snake entered the pipe, and it is making a hissing sound.' They laughed and said: 'Look, there is no snake there. Don't be afraid. The air pressure makes that hissing sound before the water comes.'* I laughed heartily with them."[7]

Now and then Holy Mother acted like a simple and unsophisticated village girl. As people enjoy a child's innocence, so the disciples and devotees were delighted by Holy Mother's charming ignorance regarding worldly affairs. Swami Gauriswarananda wrote: "At that time there were few educated people in Jayrambati. Two or four among the women could write their names in Bengali. Holy Mother said: 'A girl has been married to a boy in the Banerjee family. She is from Calcutta, and she knows how to wind a watch.'"[8] The Mother was amazed that the girl was so intelligent that she could wind a watch. In Jayrambati, she had never seen any woman with a B.A. or M.A degree, or a girl wearing a wrist watch.

---

* In Calcutta during Holy Mother's time, the corporation supplied water four times a day at certain hours. Those who had underground tanks and pumps collect that water in overhead tanks and use it throughout the day; people who could not afford to collect the water in tanks had access to it at those four stipulated times only.

As mathematics perplexed the Master, so machinery puzzled Holy Mother. Swami Saradeshananda wrote:

The Mother had the power to completely transform the human heart, the subtlest mechanism, with a mere glance, but it was a very difficult task for her to handle the simple mechanism of a hurricane lantern. In Jayrambati she had an antique hurricane lantern and its chimney was protected by a wire net. It was extremely difficult for her to remove the chimney from the hurricane lamp for cleaning, to open the cap and fill it with kerosene, and to wind the knob to set the wick. So she would ask someone to clean the hurricane lantern. She was more accustomed to using an oil lamp on a stand and a small kerosene lamp. She praised the skill and cleverness of the women who handled the hurricane lantern. She said: "Oh, how many things they know! How quickly they set the kerosene lamp right!"[9]

But Holy Mother loved to learn new things (*See Chapters 2 and 27 for details on how she learned to read and write*). Swami Gauriswarananda recalled:

When the Mother had completed the lessons of Part 1 of *Varna Parichay* [the primary book] and had just gone on to learn the first line of Part 2 — *aikya* [unity], *manikya* [jewels], *kuvakya* [bad or obscene words] — Hriday snatched the book from her hands, declaring: "Too much learning is not good for women. It has an adverse effect on their character, leading them to enter into clandestine correspondence with men and read plays and novels." Such was the state of the Mother's education. What was wonderful, however, was the Mother's consummate mastery of spiritual knowledge despite being hardly literate. I was only an adolescent then. The Mother's education being limited to "*kuvakya*," I used to have misgivings about her ability to answer the varied questions that devotees, monks, and brahmacharins brought to her. I wondered why they did not take their queries to the venerable swamis at Belur Math — Swamis Brahmananda, Shivananda, Saradananda, and others — who were adept in the scriptures. But the Mother never told them, "Go to Rakhal, Tarak, or Sharat" for the answers to their questions. She used to listen to everyone's questions, and her answers were such that all their doubts were resolved. Being too young, I neither understood their questions nor the Mother's answers to them, but I saw that all the questioners went away obviously satisfied.

Whenever copies of the *Udbodhan* and *Tattwamanjari* magazines arrived, the Mother would inquire, "Is there any article by Sharat?" If so, she would ask me to read it aloud. Once a Sanskrit hymn was published in the *Tattwamanjari*. When I read it out to her, the Mother said, "Translate it for me into Bengali." I did not know the meaning of the word "*deshikendram*" and some other words, and there being no dictionary at hand, I said: "I do not know the meaning of some words. I shall ask the meanings from our Sanskrit teacher in the school, and then I shall tell you." She, however, did not give up. "Tell me as much as you have understood," she persisted.

The Mother was a perfectionist and she had a keen eye for details. One day I sprinkled water on sal-leaf plates, shook them, and then placed them on the veranda for lunch. Watching me work, the Mother said: "Oh, no, my son. My children will eat on them. First wash those leaf plates nicely; otherwise there will be dust on them. When I was well, I used to wash each leaf and wipe it with a cloth." Another day I was placing the asanas at mealtime. The Mother saw it from the veranda and told me, "The asanas are not set straight." I rearranged them a little; even then she said, "No, they are not straight yet." When I could not find my mistake, she came forward and set them correctly. Then I saw that all the asanas had been placed parallel to each other, equidistant, their fronts presenting a straight line.[10]

Ashu Mitra wrote about an interesting event: "Once we printed some photos of Holy Mother (size 12" x 15") from the studio of a European photographer. I gave one copy to the Mother to see; she took it with both hands and then touched it with her forehead. Seeing her childlike action, I suppressed my laughter. When she returned the photo, I asked her, 'Mother, whose photo is this?' Like a simple girl, she replied: 'Why? It is my picture.' I laughed. She asked, 'Why are you laughing?' I replied, 'Why did you salute it by touching it to your head?' She also laughed and finally said, 'The Master also dwells in it.'"[11]

Holy Mother's Language

We do not have any recordings of Holy Mother's voice, but several disciples and devotees wrote down many of her teachings and also their reminiscences of her. From their memoirs we have come to know that Holy Mother spoke to the Calcutta devotees in formal Bengali mixed with colloquialisms and used the rural language of the Jayrambati area when she was with her relatives and people from the village. Before we discuss the charm of Holy Mother's language, it is important to understand the difference between colloquial Bengali and the formal, literary language.

Children learn their colloquial mother tongue from their parents, friends, and relatives, but they learn the formal, literary version from books and from teachers in school. Since Holy Mother never learned formal Bengali in a school, her language was simple and sweet. Her words were clear and charming; her examples were apt and beautiful; her descriptions were poetic and graphic; her ideas were profound and meaningful; her style of conversation was original and captivating.

Her pronunciation was like that of the people of the Bankura district of Bengal. For example, she pronounced "N" in place of "L": she said "Natu" in place of Latu; "Kishtanal" for Krishnalal; "Kanjinal" for Kanjilal; "Nalit" for Lalit. People all loved her endearing mispronunciations. She also used pet names for her closest disciples. For example, she called Jogin Maharaj "Chele [boy] Jogen." Yogin-ma was "Meye [girl] Jogen," and Gauri-ma was "Gaur-dasi." She addressed her male disciples and devotees as "Baba" meaning "my son" and her female disciples and devotees as "Ma" or "Meye," meaning "My child, or daughter." She always called the Master's monastic disciples and her monastic disciples by their premonastic names. She explained to Swami Avyananda: "You see, I am their mother. It hurts my heart to say their monastic names."[12] She always referred to Ramakrishna as "Thakur," meaning "Master."

Sometimes the Mother's sentences were short and cryptic, mixed with elegant and colloquial Bengali phrases. Some of her village patois was not clearly understandable to people from Calcutta. Yet her words were forceful and powerful, her conversations sweet and charming, and her teachings meaningful and inspiring because she spoke only the truth — and truth is ever fresh and never becomes old. Although the Mother's teachings are almost a hundred years old, they still inspire millions of people all over the world.

We may translate her conversations and teachings into English and make an effort to convey the meaning to the readers, but it is almost impossible to express the beauty and mood, the similes and metaphors, and the idioms and proverbs of her language. Some writers have tried to translate the teachings of the Mother literally, but those translations are not always understandable and readable, especially to Westerners. Of course, no translation can do full justice to the original.

Some Original Expressions of Holy Mother

Holy Mother was not a literary person, but some of her words and similes, comments and descriptions were original and profound. It is extremely difficult to translate her words and expressions into English, and it is impossible to convey the flavour, freshness, and beauty of her original language.

Here we cite some examples:

In 1899 when Swami Yogananda passed away, Holy Mother cried out, "A brick has come out of the building; now the whole thing will come down."

In 1911 when Swami Ramakrishnananda passed away, the grief-stricken Mother said: "Alas, Shashi is gone. My back is broken."

In 1911 when Nivedita died, she expressed her grief by saying, "All creatures cry for a great soul."

In 1918 when Premananda died, the Mother lamented, saying: "Baburam was dearest to my heart. All the energy, devotion, and wisdom of Belur Math were embodied in my Baburam and walked there on the bank of the Ganges."

Ashu once fell sick in Jayrambati and Holy Mother took care of him. Deeply moved, he asked, "Mother, shall I receive your affection all through my life?"

She replied, "Yes, my son, in my love there is no ebb tide or flood tide."

Observing the greed and selfishness of her family members, she one day exclaimed: "Look, I am a lotus that has bloomed in this dump site."

About Swami Saradananda, she remarked: "Sharat is like my Vasuki*, engaged in thousands of activities. Whenever rain pours, he spreads his umbrella to protect me."

One year on Gurupurnima, the monks and brahmacharins came to pay their homage to Holy Mother at Udbodhan House. She remarked upon seeing them: "Look at the power of the Master! These boys have been attracted by him. When the sun rises, the moon fades. During the full moon, only the big stars are visible and they flicker dimly. When the moon sets, people see the sky studded with stars."[13]

Storytelling is an art. It conveys events in words and images. Like an expert storyteller, Holy Mother gave Ashu a vivid description of her journey through Telo-Bhelo and her encounter with a robber in February 1877:

> The mother of Bhushan Mandal [Satyabhama] and some women planned to bathe in the Ganges on an auspicious occasion. I insisted that they accompany me. They would return to Jayrambati after their holy bath while I would stay with the Master at Dakshineswar. Lakshmi and Shibu also went with us. From Kamarpukur we reached Jahanabad [now Arambagh]. Still there was daylight, so my companions did not stop there and moved onward. They said that they would be able to cross the Telo-Bhelo meadow before evening. But I could not keep pace with them. My feet were aching and I was exhausted. I followed slowly behind them, as I was not accustomed to walking like them. I was limping and moving alone across that desolate and extensive meadow. I had heard during my childhood days that the meadow was infested with robbers. It was dusk. I continued to move forward. I had an eerie sensation in my body. Suddenly in that dark

---

*A mythical thousand-hooded snake. It is said that he protected the new-born baby Krishna from rain by spreading his huge hood over him.

evening I saw a man coming towards me. He had shaggy hair and silver bangles on his wrists; he was tall and thin and held a staff in one hand. I came to a stop and I had goose bumps all over my body. The man belonged to the *Bagdi* caste. Like a rude robber, he asked me in a harsh voice, "Who are you?" and then stared at me with his mouth open. Meanwhile, his wife arrived. When I saw a woman, I gained some strength. I said: "Father, I am Sarada. I am your daughter. I am going to your son-in-law. My companions have gone forward without me. Please escort me to them."[14]

Stories have to be told and retold or they die. Holy Mother immortalized her "Robber Story" with her own words. In Chapter 5, this story has been narrated elaborately by Swami Saradananda.

Three Types of Teachings

Holy Mother's teachings are both concise and precise. She did not use many parables, stories, or scriptural quotations, but referred to her own experiences. She often quoted sayings of Ramakrishna. Manada Shankar Dasgupta, a disciple and biographer of Holy Mother, classified the Mother's teachings into three groups: First, short and clear; second, the gospel of hope and fearlessness; third, simple and classic. Here are some examples from each group of teachings:

1. Short and clear

Questioner: "Mother, how shall I meditate?"

Mother: "Just think of the Master."

Questioner: "How shall I practise spiritual disciplines?"

Mother: "My son, at the end, the mind becomes the guru. Sadhana means to keep the mind on God and to be absorbed in Him. Repeat His name."

Questioner: "Is it of any use merely to repeat His name without intense devotion?"

Mother: "Whether you jump into the water or are pushed into it, your cloth will get drenched. Meditate every day. Constant meditation will make the mind one-pointed."

Questioner: "What is the goal of human life?"

Mother: "The goal of human life is to realize God and to be absorbed in Him."

Questioner: "The Master used to say: 'I have made the mould; now you may cast the image.' What does this mean?"

Mother: "To 'cast the image' means to meditate on the Master, to think of the various incidents of his life."[15]

2. The gospel of hope and fearlessness

Questioner: "Mother, I cannot concentrate my mind in meditation at all."

Mother: "It does not matter much. Look at the picture of the Master and that will be enough. One should cultivate constant recollectedness."[16]

Questioner: "I cannot calm my mind and concentrate."

Mother: "The mind will be steadied of itself if aspirants repeat God's name 15,000 or 20,000 times a day. I myself have experienced it."[17]

Questioner: "My mind becomes restless now and then. It craves enjoyment. That frightens me."

Mother: "Don't be afraid. I tell you that in this Kali Yuga mental sin is no sin. Free your mind from all worries on this account."

Questioner: "However I may try to remove evil thoughts, I do not succeed."

Mother: "This is the result of what you have done in your past life. Can anyone altogether destroy lust? A little of it remains as long as one has a body. But it can be subdued, as a snake can be subdued by charmed dust."[18]

Holy Mother said to a disciple: "Do not fear, my child. Always remember that the Master is behind you. I am also with you. As long as you remember me, your mother, why should you be frightened? The Master said to me, 'At the end of their life, I shall certainly liberate those who come to you.'"[19]

3. Simple and classic

Questioner: "Mother, the mind is very restless. In no way can I steady it."

Mother: "As the wind removes the cloud, so the name of God destroys the cloud of worldliness."[20]

Questioner: "Mother, I have practised austerities and japa so much, but I have not achieved anything."

Mother: "God is not like fish or vegetables that you can buy for a price."[21]

Questioner: "How can one realize God — through worship, japa, or meditation?"

Mother: "God is realized only through His grace. Nonetheless, one must perform japa and meditation, for they remove the impurities of one's mind. As one gets the fragrance of a flower by handling it, or the scent of sandalwood by rubbing it against a stone, similarly, one becomes spiritually awakened by continuously contemplating the Divine. But you can become illumined right now if you become desireless."[22]

To a restless disciple who wanted to return the mantra, Holy Mother said: "Look here, my child, the sun dwells high in the sky, and water remains on the earth. Does the water have to shout at the sun and ask: 'O Sun, please take me up?' It is the very nature of the sun to take up the water in the form of vapour. Let me assure you that you will not have to practise any discipline."[23]

Questioner: "Does the Master really live in the picture?"

Mother: "Of course he does. The body and the shadow are the same. And what is his picture but a shadow? If you pray to him constantly before his picture, then he manifests himself through that picture."[24]

A Nun in White Clothing

Ramakrishna took monastic vows from Tota Puri performing the viraja homa and became a paramahamsa sannyasin, but he used to wear a white cloth with a thin red border all through his life. Only on a few occasions did he wear an ochre cloth at the request of the devotees. Holy Mother did not take monastic vows, but she led the life of an ideal nun. She was Kaushambi, or Durga, who was married yet had unbroken chastity. Holy Mother wore a red-bordered white cloth as her husband had. She gave initiation, brahmacharya vows, and informal sannyasa, giving the ochre cloth to some of her disciples, as Ramakrishna had. However, after bestowing the ochre cloth, Holy Mother asked her disciples to take formal sannyasa and receive their monastic names from the Master's disciples.

Holy Mother's teachings are permeated with renunciation. Once a woman devotee asked Holy Mother to order her daughter to marry. The Mother replied: "Is it not misery to remain in lifelong slavery to another and always dance to his tune? Though there is some risk in being a celibate, still, if one is not inclined to lead a married life, one should not be forced into it and subjected to lifelong worldliness. Those girls who are drawn to the ideal of complete renunciation should be encouraged to lead a celibate life."[25]

Apart from her life of renunciation, she performed the duties of a wife and mother. Swami Nikhilananda wrote:

Holy Mother, in a unique way, fulfilled the duties of wife, mother, and nun. There have been before in the world the ideal wife, the ideal mother, and the ideal nun, but a combination of the three in one person is rare indeed. Holy Mother was wedded to Sri Ramakrishna at the age of five, lived with him as long as he lived, and ministered to his physical needs in the best tradition of a Hindu wife. She was his companion in spiritual life. She demonstrated that wifely devotion and love are possible without demanding physical satisfaction from one's mate. In spite of her marriage, she remained a nun, pure in body and mind, and in uninterrupted communion with God. Though she had no children of the flesh, she had many of the spirit. Like an earthly mother, she looked after her disciples' physical comfort. But unlike an earthly mother, she was totally unattached in her love and expected no return from it. Truly Sister Nivedita declared that Holy Mother was Sri Ramakrishna's last word on the ideal of Indian womanhood. But why of Indian womanhood alone? She can very well represent the universal ideal of womanhood.[26]

Holy Mother's Visit to a Devotee's House

Holy Mother seldom visited her devotees in Calcutta; instead, they came to see her in Udbodhan House. Holy Mother was very fond of Sarajubala Sen and her sister Sumati. One day Sarajubala invited the Mother to visit their Ballygunj residence in South Calcutta, and the Mother accepted her invitation. Sarajubala's account reminds us of the story of Martha and Mary in the Bible.

> May 1914: The Mother will come to our Ballygunj house today. We have been making preparations since yesterday. We bought a new carpet seat and a new set of white marble plates and bowls for her use. I could not sleep all night for joy, thinking of the Mother's visit. It was arranged that she would come in the afternoon. In case she changes her mind, Shokaharan [Sumati's husband] has gone to the Mother's house at Baghbazar in the morning and is waiting there with the carriage. We also have finished our household work and made ourselves ready to receive her. I arranged the Mother's carpet, placed flowers all around, sprinkled Ganges water in all the rooms and doorways, strung garlands of flowers, and placed two large bouquets on either side of the Mother's seat.
>
> As the day advanced, we were waiting eagerly for the Mother's arrival. Finally the blessed moment arrived. Hearing the sound of the carriage, we all went downstairs. When the carriage stopped, I noticed the Mother affectionately looking at us with a smiling face. As soon as she got down from the carriage, we rushed to take the dust of her feet.
>
> Golap-ma, Surabala, Nalini, Radhu, and four or five monks and brahmacharins came with the Mother. We took the Mother upstairs and bowed down to her. She inquired: "Have you all finished your meal? I tried to be as quick as possible, but somehow could not manage to get here earlier than this." Saying so, she touched my chin and kissed her fingers. I could not sit near her; I rushed to the kitchen to make the food ready. Most of the dishes were already prepared.
>
> They were playing a gramophone upstairs. In between my various tasks I went upstairs and found the Mother extremely delighted to be

listening to the songs on the gramophone. She exclaimed like a happy girl: "What a wonderful machine has been invented!" It was a hot summer day. The Mother lay down on a fine mat on the veranda and others were seated around her. We served ice water in a stone bowl and the Mother sipped that cold water from time to time. Seeing me, she called, "My child, have a little ice water." I took some as her prasad and then ran back to the kitchen. Today I was trying to finish quickly, yet still could not get everything done.

In the evening, all items of food were arranged in the adjacent room. The Mother asked Golap-ma to offer the food to the Master, but she replied: "Mother, you offer it. Why should I when you are present?" Then the Mother sat on the asana to offer the food and commented: "Ah, how beautifully all these dishes have been arranged!" Thus she expressed her joy like a girl and filled our hearts with delight. After the food offering, the Mother and others sat to have the prasad. The Mother finished her supper first and then sat on a cane chair on the veranda. She called to me, "My child, give me a betel roll." I was then serving food to Golap-ma and others. I hurriedly carried a betel roll to her. I felt ashamed that she had to ask for it. I told Sumati: "Could you not wait with a betel roll near the door? You see how busy I am."

After a while, the Mother went to the washroom downstairs and I accompanied her with a lamp. The garden in this part of the house is somewhat desolate. There were rows of crotons on either side of the pathway. The Mother affectionately told me: "Ah, you could not find time to sit near me. Come to Udbodhan House soon and bring your mother as well." My mother came to visit me and she was fortunate that she saw Holy Mother at our home.

It was time for the Mother to depart. She was reluctant to ride in the motor car because once when she went to attend the chariot festival at Mahesh, a dog was run over by the car. But Baghbazar was a long way off and it would be very late and uncomfortable unless they went by car. Finally, the Mother agreed to the devotees' request to use the car. She bowed down to the Master several times, blessed us, and then got into the car.[27]

Holy Mother from Different Points of View

If a man loses a hand or a foot, or an eye or an ear, he can function without much difficulty. But his life stops if he loses his memory. Human beings live in this world with their memories of happiness and misery. Holy Mother's disciples and devotees left us their memoirs so we could visualize her life from different angles. Although these stories and episodes may seem small and insignificant to the general reader, they are extremely important and inspiring to her devoted children. We were not fortunate enough to live with her, but we can feel her presence by meditating on these incidents of her divine drama.

Sarajubala recalled:

> I was not able to visit Holy Mother for some days on account of the pressure of my school duties. No sooner had I saluted her today than she began to show her love for me in countless ways. Bhudeb [Mother's nephew] was reading the Mahabharata. He was a mere boy and therefore could not read fluently. The Mother also had her other duties to attend to. It was almost evening. She said to Bhudeb, pointing to me: "Give her the book. She will read it quite easily. The reading cannot be stopped without finishing this chapter." It was her order, so I began to read the Mahabharata. Never before had I read a book in her presence. At first I felt a sort of shyness, but somehow I finished the chapter. The Mother saluted the book with folded hands. We then went to the shrine to witness the evening worship. The Mother took her seat and soon became absorbed in meditation.[28]

A devotee of the Master, Tejchandra, and his wife often visited the Holy Mother at Udbodhan House, and she was very fond of them. Tejchandra died on 16 September 1912. Holy Mother told the following story about him:

> He who eagerly prays to God will see Him. The other day Tejchandra passed away. What a sincere soul he was! The Master used to frequent his house. Someone had deposited 200 rupees with Tejchandra. One day he was robbed of that amount by a pickpocket in the tramcar. He discovered the loss after some time and suffered terrible mental agony. He came to the bank of the Ganges and prayed to the Master with tears in his eyes, "O Lord, what have you done to me?" He was not rich enough to make up that amount from his own pocket. As he was thus weeping, he saw the Master appear before him and say: "Why do you weep so bitterly? The money is there under a brick on the bank of the Ganges." Tejchandra quickly removed the brick and really found there a bundle of banknotes. He narrated the incident to Sharat [Swami Saradananda]. Sharat said: "You are fortunate to get the vision of the Master even now."[29]

Swami Arupananda recalled how the Mother served her disciples: "I had a severe headache. I went to the Mother's room in the afternoon and told her about it. She said, 'It is probably due to the heat.' She then mixed some ghee and camphor, and making a paste of it, applied it to my forehead with a gentle massage. 'Whenever the Master had a headache, he applied this medicine,' she said.

"I started feeling a little better after a few minutes of massage, and came downstairs. After some time, the headache really disappeared. I went and told the Mother, 'The headache is hardly there, Mother.'"[30]

In November 1908, a devotee went to Jayrambati for initiation. Afterward, he and some other devotees went to visit Kamarpukur. Unfortunately this devotee had a heated exchange with a swami there. On his return to Jayrambati, Holy Mother's brother Barada reported this to her. She cautioned the devotee: "Know that one has to be careful about these three things: First, a house situated on the bank of a river. At any time the river may destroy the house and sweep it away. Second, a snake. You must be very careful when you see one, for there is no knowing when it will bite you. Third, a monk. One word or thought from a monk may do harm to a householder. When you see a monk, you should show him respect. You should not slight him with disrespectful words."[31] These valuable words of the Mother guided the devotee all through his life.

It is said that only a good student can be a good teacher; and a good teacher learns continuously so his or her teachings remain always fresh. Ramakrishna said: "As long as I live, so long do I learn." Sarajubala recorded how Holy Mother learned various things in her village.

Regarding creation, one night the Mother said: "In the beginning of creation, the Creator made human beings with the quality of sattva. As a result, they were born with divine knowledge. In no time, they understood that the world was not real. So they immediately renounced the world and followed the path of God-realization. They practised severe austerities, attained liberation, and merged into the divine. The Creator then found that the purpose of His creation had not been realized — those wise ones were unfit to continue the play in the world. So the Creator added rajas and tamas to sattva and created human beings with those three qualities. Thus His play in the world continued nicely." Then she cited a beautiful rhyme regarding creation. She continued: "My daughter, in our youth we learned so many wonderful things from seeing the *yatras* [dramas] and listening to the narrators of mythological stories. Nowadays we seldom hear those things."[32]

Sometimes Holy Mother tested the faith of her disciples. Sarajubala recorded:

One day I went to Baghbazar and found Holy Mother resting after her lunch. She was gracious enough to ask me to fan her. Suddenly I heard her speaking to herself: "Well, you all have come here. But where is the Master?"

I said in reply: "We could not meet him in this life. Who knows in which future birth we shall be able to see him? But this is our greatest good fortune: that we have been able to touch your feet."

"That is true, indeed," was the brief remark of the Mother. I was rather amazed by this avowal. Very seldom did she speak of herself in such a way.[33]

In Jayrambati, Holy Mother had a hard time finding flowers for worship. The villagers grew vegetables around their houses rather than flowering plants. Swami Gauriswarananda wrote in his reminiscences:

I had a passion for gardening right from my childhood. In Jayrambati sometimes the Mother did not have any flowers to worship with. She would offer only *tulsi* leaves, *durva* grass, *bel* leaves, and sandalwood paste to the Master, addressing him: "Master, not a single flower could be procured today. Be pleased to accept these." I had planted some flowering trees — jasmine, red oleander, marigold, hibiscus, *dopati, tagar*, and several others. How delighted the Mother was with those flowers! One day I discovered the Mother digging at the roots of the jasmine plant after her noon rest. I snatched the spade from her hands, saying: "I shall attend to this. You don't have to do it." She said: "You do everything for the plant because I am very fond of jasmine. And now that it is the season for these flowers to bloom, I was digging the soil so that it can be watered well." When the first oleanders blossomed, she did not let anyone pick the flowers, even for worship. She would say: "Let Rammay come and see how beautifully his shrub has blossomed! He himself will pluck the flowers. Only then shall I offer them to the Master." Such boundless love! On Saturday as soon as I came and greeted the Mother, she led me by the hand to the shrub and exclaimed: "Look, such beautiful flowers your shrub has borne! Such sweet fragrance too!" She handed me a basket. I gathered the flowers and brought them to her. Only then did she worship the Master with them.

One day I took to her a lime plant that I had grown by grafting. There were seven or eight limes on it. The Mother was delighted and kept saying to everyone: "Just see how clever the boy is! He has grown the graft so well that is already bearing fruit!" Another day I had broken off a large branch of an amalaki tree with fruit on it and given it to the Mother. She was displeased and forbade me to break off branches of fruit-bearing trees with fruit on them, in particular amalaki trees. This amalaki tree stood on the bank of the Amodar River. Revered Sharat Maharaj, Yogin-ma, and Golap-ma used to meditate under it. Sharat Maharaj used to chant the Gita too. "Thirty-three crores of gods and goddesses dwell under an amalaki tree," the Mother said. She added, "Japa and meditation practised under the amalaki tree yield greater results." Later she directed me to save the leaves on that branch for the purpose of worship, remarking, "These leaves are also used for worship like bel leaves."[34]

The Last Story of a Nepali Nun

Ashu Mitra wrote a fascinating story concerning the Nepali nun who met the Mother in Varanasi and who suggested that Holy Mother practise the panchatapa (*See Chapter 10*) to assuage the grief that she felt after Ramakrishna's passing.

With permission from Holy Mother, one of her attendants (whom we can assume was Ashu himself) went on pilgrimage to Badarika Ashrama, in the Himalayas. Ashu went with another monk, who was the Mother's disciple but not a member of the Ramakrishna Order. They first went to Rishikesh and stayed at Kailash Math. One early morning he heard a woman crying pitifully from a nearby cottage. Out of curiosity, he entered the cottage and found a dying woman there. She kept calling out, "Mother, you have not yet sent your disciple!" As soon as she saw Ashu standing at the door, she said: "Finally you have come! Please come close and sit down. Do what I say — there is not much time left." Ashu was dumbfounded. She said: "Don't doubt me. You can verify this with Holy Mother. She promised that she would send one of her disciples to me during my last moments. Now do what I say: Under my pillow are 40 rupees and a notebook. When I die, immerse my body in the Ganges with the help of other monks. On the fourth day, use that money to arrange a feast for the monks. Memorize the contents of the notebook within three days and then immerse it in the Ganges. Use the mantras in that notebook for the good of others and never for your own benefit."

Ashu ran back to Kailash Math to find his companion. He left a message for him saying that he would not be able to go to Badarika Ashrama and that he should go on by himself.

When he returned to the cottage a few minutes later, Ashu saw that the woman's last moment had arrived. She passed away, saying, "O Mother, O Mother." He immersed her body in the Ganges with the help of some monks from the Kailash Math. He then went to Kali Kalmi Baba's ashrama and gave 40 rupees to the abbot there to arrange a feast. He stayed in the ashrama, memorized the mantras in that notebook, and then dropped it in the Ganges after three days. He then wrote a letter to Holy Mother asking for her permission to visit Jayrambati, but did not get a reply within six days. So he went to Jayrambati and reported the whole story to her.

After hearing the tale, the Mother said: "Yes, she made me promise that I would send one of my disciples to her at her last moment. This girl was very good. She knew various kinds of rituals. While I was in Varanasi, she used to visit me, and she suggested that I perform the panchatapa."[35]

Holy Mother's Teachings

In Shankara's introduction to his commentary on the Gita, he describes how a divine incarnation works in this world: "The Lord — the eternal possessor of knowledge, sovereignty, power, strength, energy, and vigour — brings under His control His own maya, which consists of the three gunas. And then through that maya He serves human beings out of compassion without any purpose of His own."[36]

The unmotivated action of an illumined soul, according to Vedanta, is called *ābhāsa*, a show. An illumined soul knows that he or she is not the doer or enjoyer of that action. The illumined soul is free from ego, devoid of desire, and does not covet the results of actions. As an instrument of God, that person serves others unselfishly.

Holy Mother's life was her message. She was born to be a teacher, so all her actions and words were meant for the good of humanity. Holy Mother taught the ancient teachings of practical Vedanta — renunciation, discrimination, purity, faith, devotion, meditation, control of the mind, austerity, skill in action, self-effort, and so on. All these teachings are scattered throughout this book, but in Chapter 26 we cited many of her teachings in question-and-answer form. In Chapter 32, we mentioned some of her teachings that echoed the Master's. Now we shall present some of her teachings as recorded by a few of her close monastic disciples.

Swami Parameswarananda recorded:

Once the Mother was seated surrounded by several women devotees. Suddenly she said: "Well, I have seen so many *sadhus*, but there was none who could compare with the Master." A devotee replied: "Mother, how can there be any comparison with the Master? He came to deliver people and those sadhus came to be delivered. So the Master was unique." Silently supporting her statement, the Mother's face glowed with a smile.

One night at Jayrambati I was massaging the Mother's feet. Referring to the bickering and disorderliness in Koalpara Ashrama, I asked her: "Mother, we have renounced hearth and home and everything in the name of Sri Ramakrishna. We have come to work for him. Then why is there so much quarreling and friction among ourselves?" The Mother replied: "Look, my son, the source of trouble is seeing faults in others. Once this happened to me and I saw faults in others. And I could not get rid of it. Finally I prayed to the Master earnestly: "Master, may I not see faults in others. May I see only their good qualities." From then on that attitude completely disappeared from my mind. If I would see a little good quality in anybody, I saw it in a magnified way. If you want peace, don't see faults in others."

Just before her final departure from Jayrambati, the Mother instructed me about the annual Jagaddhatri Puja and the future of her new house.* The Mother said: "Procure the annual consumption of rice, fire wood, and other basics. Then there will be no problem for other things." We used to live in Jayrambati as members of the Mother's family.

At the request of her disciples, the Mother came to Koalpara Ashrama for a few days' rest. The Mother asked me to take responsibility for cooking, though I had no knowledge of it. One day I was cutting vegetables, sitting near the Mother. Finding her alone, I asked: "Mother, how can one attain the knowledge of Brahman? I see various things with my physical eyes. How can I understand through discrimination that everything is Brahman? How can one have this experience of oneness? In the beginning, should one practise focusing on each object [in one's meditation], or does it [meaning the experience of oneness] come spontaneously? I am confused. Again, after studying Swamiji's books, it seems that there cannot be any liberation without the knowledge of Brahman." The Mother answered gravely: "It is a difficult path. It takes a long time to reach the goal when practising that path of sadhana. Call on the Master, depend on him, and he will make you know everything. What will you gain by worrying about all those things? You will achieve everything by the Master's grace."

Another day I privately asked the Mother: "Mother, my mind is very restless. I can't calm it. How can I control the mind?" She replied: "My son, Sharat and Rakhal also say that it is difficult to control the mind." After a brief pause, she said: "Call on the Master and he will make things favourable."

Once in the course of conversation I said to the Mother: "Mother, the condition of my mind is sometimes so restless that I get scared I might be drowned in maya." The Mother emphatically said: "What do you say, my son? Why will you drown? You are the Master's child and my child also. You will never be drowned. The Master will always protect you. You have read in the Master's book that a frog cannot escape if it is caught by a cobra. The Master is holding you."

On another occasion, the Mother assured a disciple: "Even Providence does not have the power to destroy my children." And again, "Those who come here,** this will be their last birth."

One night the Mother was resting on the veranda of her new house, and we went to bow down to her. She began talking to us: "Look, X made such a remark! He says that these boys are moving from one ashrama to another ashrama out of greed for good food. Why would my children and the Master's children suffer from lack of food? They will never suffer from want of food. I prayed to the Master: 'Master, may my children never

---

* The Jayrambati house later became a monastery.
** Meaning those who take refuge in Holy Mother.

suffer from lack of food.'" She briefly paused and then said agitatedly: "He says that my children move about from ashrama to ashrama because they are gluttons! Why will they not eat well? Those who have attachments will suffer."

When the Mother initiated a young man into sannyasa, he said to her: "Mother, please instruct me now how I should lead my life." The Mother replied: "May the Master protect you. He will protect you. Call on him. He does everything. You all work for him. Never look at a woman even if she is made out of clay."

The Mother handed over an ochre cloth to a brahmachari and then said with a smile: "Now you will be able to sleep happily. Whether you achieve anything or not, from now on you will be able to sleep without disturbance."

Another day in the course of conversation the Mother said: "Look, you follow this instruction from the Master, 'Adjust according to time, to person, and according to place and circumstances.' Then you will never be cheated or confused. And always give honour to respected persons."

Another time a couple who were devoted to the Master came to the Mother and prayed: "Mother, please bless us so that we might not get entangled in worldly maya. May we practise celibacy and lead a pure life." The Mother replied with a smile: "What do you say, my children? If you do not have children, how will the number of my devotees increase?"

One day after finishing the daily worship, the Mother was seated on her asana. Her mind still had not returned to the earthly plane. Suddenly one of my brother disciples asked, "Mother, how do you look on the Master?" She remained silent for a while and then gravely answered, "I look on him as my child." The questioner was astounded. The Mother merged into deep silence, and I became speechless.[37]

Swami Ishanananda also recorded a few of Holy Mother's teachings:

"There is no wealth equal to contentment, and no virtue equal to forbearance."

"Forget your individuality and try to realize your true nature."

"How can any harm come to one who always thinks of his or her Chosen Deity?"

"Do you know how one can develop equal love for all? Do not expect anything from the one you love. Only then can one love everyone equally."

"Look, is he a human being who has no compassion in his heart?"[38]

Holy Mother was the ultimate authority for the Ramakrishna Order. In case of doubt, dilemma, problem, or crisis, the monks sought her advice, and the omniscient Mother offered solutions. Swami Saradeshananda described her advice as concise and clear, discreet and practical, affectionate and compassionate. Above all, she taught through her exemplary life. Swami Saradeshananda's record illustrates this:

A head of a centre could not control the junior monks who were the Mother's disciples, so he sought the Mother's advice. She said: "The boys have become monks to call on God and make their lives blessed. They are doing their best for the ashrama and will always do so. They are now grown up. Their minds and intellects are developed, and they are aware of right and wrong, good and bad. Under such circumstances if they proceed to work independently, you should not be an obstacle to their path. However, if you stop them, they will not be able to continue working permanently under you, going through mental privations. If you find any difficulty in getting your work done, you will have to respectfully explain the entire situation to them. They have been obeying you all along and will also do so now. One can accomplish everything by love. You cannot make a person work by force or by duplicity."[39]

A brahmachari from the Garbeta Ashrama was traveling around, collecting money for the ashrama. One day he came to Jayrambati. Holy Mother always felt perturbed whenever someone came to that area to raise money in the name of the Master or in her name. Nonetheless, she fed that brahmachari affectionately and enquired about his visit to Jayrambati. She then told him: "My son, the poor people of these villages somehow survive with great difficulty by farming. It is not right to collect money from these people. If you appeal to them for money in the name of the Master, they will consider him disgusting."[40] The term "fund raising" always created an uneasy feeling in the Mother's mind.

Indiscriminate mixing with worldly people and engaging in gossip with them lead to one's degradation. Holy Mother always cautioned her disciples against this danger. Once she sent one of her disciples on an errand to a neighbouring village. He finished his work, spent a long time there, and then returned to the Mother. She later learned that the disciple had finished his errand quickly. He then stayed to chat and got entangled in an unfortunate situation. Saddened, the Mother firmly told him: "Whenever you go on an errand, as soon as it is done, return immediately. It is seen that some people dig for earthworms on the shallow surface, but then they dig deeper and face a snake."[41]

It is human nature to create big problems out of petty matters. The Mother always taught her disciples to have patience and forbearance and to endure everything calmly. She quoted the Master: "Sha, Sha, Sa — forbear, forbear, forbear! He who forbears, survives; and he who does not, perishes." She said: "One suffers as a result of one's own karma. So instead of blaming others, one should pray to God, depend on His grace, and bear those sufferings calmly under all circumstances."[42]

Once in Jayrambati, Holy Mother was rearranging something in her room by pushing a heavy table when the top of it came off and fell on her foot. She was badly injured and her foot was bleeding from a deep cut. It was painful and she sat down, holding her foot, with tears trickling from her eyes. Everyone present rushed to help her. The doctor came from the dispensary, applied medicine, and bandaged the wound. Holy Mother blamed herself: "I thought that I could clean the room nicely by moving the table, but while lifting its heavy top, it fell on my foot. I will have to bear the result of my karma. I could have easily asked someone to move it. Just now a boy came from Koalpara with groceries. He ate refreshments, talked to me, and then left. He could easily have moved that table for me. But I wanted to do it myself, and as a result I was injured. I will have to go through this suffering in accordance with my destiny." Nalini gently reprimanded the Mother for her action. The Mother kept quiet. Gradually her pain subsided. She then said to Saradeshananda: "My son, don't write about this accident to Sharat in Calcutta. He will be anxious and immediately send someone here, and there will be a commotion. That person will go through trouble to come here unnecessarily. This wound is not very serious; it will heal easily." Holy Mother had an independent nature and she never blamed others for her sufferings.[43]

When Swami Vivekananda first introduced philanthropic activities in the Ramakrishna Mission, some monks thought that these activities did not conform to the ideal of Ramakrishna. But Holy Mother reminded them: "All work belongs to the Master. My children, work for the Master. Otherwise, who will feed you? If you go on begging for food from door to door in the sun, you will get dizzy. If you do not eat well, you will be sick. Don't listen to those who doubt the activities of the Ramakrishna Mission. Work well, eat well, and meditate on God."

The Mother always encouraged her devotees and disciples to practise japa and meditation. But she kept a vigilant eye on them and cautioned them not to overdo spiritual practices. She forbade them to practise too much austerity, and at the same time she did not like too much luxury regarding food and clothing.

Those who had an opportunity to live in the company of the Mother realized that she taught them strength of character for building their lives, renunciation, forbearance, self-control, spiritual sadhana, firm faith in God under all circumstances, steadiness, devotion, and dependence on God. She did not care for emotional outbursts among her disciples. Rather, she wanted them to be balanced, calm, steady, and resolute.[44]

Swami Basudevananda recorded the following teachings of Holy Mother:

> In 1918 a devotee asked the Mother: "Why do I have bad thoughts in my mind?"
>
> Holy Mother replied: "It is the natural tendency of the mind to go downwards. People build a dam to save water by tremendous effort, but sometimes the dam breaks and the water goes away. Still people try to keep the dam intact. Let me tell you, holy company and spiritual talk help the mind to move upward. Moreover, even the mind of an ungodly person changes by the grace of a holy man. A greedy man went to a holy man in Vrindaban to learn how to make gold and received a philosopher's stone from him. Later, that man developed dispassion for wealth and received divine knowledge from the holy man. Thereafter, he threw away that stone. In the disguise of a monk, a hunter went to catch birds and observed their simple and fearless nature. This generated renunciation in him, and he gave up that cruel profession. So I tell you: Have the company of the holy whenever you have an opportunity. If holy company is not available, read holy books. The mind becomes pure by discussing the lives of great souls. Look, the movement of water is always downward; but the scorching sun evaporates the ocean water as vapour, which rises up and is blown away by the wind to the top of the mountains. There it becomes snow; then it melts as water, and flows through springs and rivers and helps humankind."[45]

Shivarani Sen, a young devotee, recorded the following teachings in her reminiscences:

> The Mother's words were very sweet. One day she told me: "My child, never sit idle. Always do some work. If you do not engage yourself with some work, bad thoughts will crowd into your idle mind."
>
> Another day she said to an elderly woman: "During your journey, if you see that someone has fallen on the road, you are supposed to lift that person up. One should not move forward, seeing someone fall on the path." I did not understand then the purport of the Mother's statement. Later I realized that the Mother meant all people walking towards God knowingly or unknowingly. Those who fall from that path should be helped by others to get up and move forward. The Mother demonstrated this ideal in her life. She uplifted many sinners, destitute, and depressed men and women in this world, and gave them shelter. Blessed are those strayed and lost children who got shelter with the Mother!
>
> The Mother was very shy. If boys were 15 or 16 years old, she considered

them as men and wore a long veil in front of them. She said: "Modesty is the best ornament of women. Women do not look good without shyness and decorum." One day she said to a young beautiful bride: "When you go out, always dress yourself by covering your body well. Then others will think that someone is escorting you."

The Mother's mind was always saturated with the thought of Sri Ramakrishna, and this was revealed through her actions and words. One day she said to my grandmother: "Remember the Master in every step of your life. Then you will never feel any suffering as suffering. Who does not encounter pain and suffering in life? They are part of life. If you chant his name and take refuge in him, the Master will give you strength. Pain and suffering will not be able to torment you."[46]

Kumudbandhu Sen was a disciple of Swami Brahmananda. He was also well known to Holy Mother and the Master's disciples. One day he told Holy Mother that he could not concentrate his mind well during meditation — his mind was fickle and unsteady. The Mother smiled and replied: "Oh, that is nothing — that is the nature of the mind, just like that of the ears and eyes. Meditate regularly. The Name of God is more powerful than the senses. It will be all right in time, if you practise regularly. Always think of the Master, who is looking after you. Don't be worried about your lapses."

Kumud asked, "Mother, bless me that I may practise regularly."

Holy Mother responded, with a kind smile: "Be sincere in your practice, words, and deeds. You will feel how blessed you are! His blessing is always on all creatures of the earth. It is needless to ask for it. Practise meditation sincerely and then you will understand His infinite grace. God wants sincerity, truthfulness, and love. Outward verbal effusiveness does not touch Him. Observe punctuality of time in your practice. Take His name and utter the mantra while concentrating your mind with all your might. If you exert yourself sincerely, banish all other thoughts, and pray to Him from the core of your heart, then your call will be responded to and your prayers granted through His grace."[47]

One day in Udbodhan House, Holy Mother was talking with some women about the simplicity and purity of children. She said: "God always dwells in the hearts of children. He manifests in the highest degree in them because they are simple and pure. So the Master used to say: 'If children sincerely call on their mother, she rushes to them, leaving all her work. Similarly, God surely appears to that person who wholeheartedly calls on Him.' You see, when you are extremely busy with your household work and one of your children loudly cries, 'Mother, Mother,' don't you drop what you are doing and hurry to take that child on your lap?"

The Mother's guileless way of speaking made the women laugh. The Mother asked with a smile, "Did I not say the right thing?" They answered, "Yes, you did, Mother."

A woman asked: "Mother, all children do not have the same desire to learn. Some children lack liveliness and eagerness. How can we enhance the natural curiosity in their minds so that they can develop normally?"

The Mother answered with a smile: "What do you mean? You have become a mother and now you expect me to know what is going on in your children's minds? Listen. One should communicate with them in a simple and intimate way. Chat with them. You should allow them to play with children of their own age. Never scold them too much and never physically abuse them. If you reprimand them severely or beat them, they may be frozen with fear and will run away from you. They will understand easily if you lovingly help them understand. Never refuse to answer their questions by rebuffing them or threatening them. If you scold and intimidate them, they will be afraid to ask questions, which will impede the natural development of their minds."[48]

Is there any easy way to keep the mind focussed on God in the midst of worldly responsibilities? This is a universal question. A woman devotee asked: "Mother, we are doing our household duties day and night, and we become tired, fulfilling the orders and desires of everybody around us. We don't even get five minutes a day to call on the Master. What will happen to us? Will he not bestow any mercy on us?"

Holy Mother responded: "Surely the Master will bestow his grace on you, my child. He is all-knowing. He dwells in the hearts of all. He will definitely know if there is any sincere longing in you. Moreover, do you yourself do the household work, my child? It is the Master who makes you do everything. This world belongs to him. Nothing happens without his wish. Even the leaves of the tree do not move without his will. 'No action can be performed without the wish of Krishna.' Know for certain that it is the will of God that such longing has dawned in your heart. Those who love God, He protects them. Whether you love Him or not, He loves you. In this world, there are monks and householders. God thinks more about householders. The Master used to say, 'A monk is *supposed* to call on God, but there is a heavy load of 20 maunds on the back of the householder.' So he thinks of the householder more. Have a little recollectedness of the Master. Call on him with a longing heart. Think of and reflect on him. At the end of the day call on him shedding two tears. My child, what do you have other than those two teardrops? Everything in this world belongs to him, but those two teardrops are yours. Please offer them to the Master. He will be tied by your love. My child, don't be afraid. This time the Master came to make an easy path to realizing God."

A woman devotee said: "Mother, I have no peace of mind. I am fully consumed by domestic problems and sufferings. When I come here I get a little peace talking to you."

Seeing her tears, the Mother said: "You are forgetting, my child, that everything is happening by the will of the Master. It is by his will that you have come to me. Love God and teach your children also to love Him. Let them learn to love God, knowing He is their own. When a *jiva* comes to the world, that person comes with his or her past karma. So we see that some people love God from their early years. Some grow up and then go astray. Everything happens as a result of one's past karma. But out of grace, God changes one's destiny. He changes what He had ordained for that person, and that is why He is called *kapal-mochan*, the dispeller of destiny. As everything is in His hands, so one should surrender oneself to Him."[49]

One day while sitting on the northern veranda of Udbodhan House Holy Mother and Sudhira were talking about a person of the Nivedita School. The Mother said:

> People do not scrutinize their own minds; they only see others' faults. If they see their own faults and try to rectify them, then the tendency of seeing faults in others will not rise. Mahamaya created this tendency in the human mind. People magnify their own qualities: they make their mole hills into mountains and others' mountains into mole hills. They are thoroughly occupied with their own so-called greatness and have no time to think of others. If one remembers that everyone belongs to the Master, then one cannot help but love all. Once I was in such a condition that I could not remove the ants from the Master's *naivedya;** I felt as if the Master were eating [through the ants]. One relishes gossip and criticism when one does not see the Master in all. As long as one does not try to make spiritual progress oneself, one's mind will be constantly agitated with others' affairs.[50]

A lady came to Udbodhan House and informed the Mother that some of her relatives were passing through a difficult time. She asked: "Mother, doesn't the Master see the sufferings of these people? Why does he not prevent them?"

Holy Mother replied: "Does anything happen without the will of God? Even a leaf on a tree does not move without His wish. According to His

* Food offered during worship.

will, this universe and all beings are functioning. Can a material object function if there is no consciousness behind it?"

The woman asked, "Is God fully aware of these sufferings?"

"When a person does anything wrong, does he or she always remember it?" Holy Mother responded. "God made the law: Each action has its own effect. He is conducting this world with this law."

"Then how can human beings escape from the grinding results of their terrible actions? Is there no forgiveness in God regarding this law of karma?"

Holy Mother replied: "Is it possible for you to survive without His forgiveness? Can you see the karma of your innumerable past lives? If so, you would not ask this question. Even Arjuna did not know the karma of his past lives, what to speak of ordinary human beings. He who has made the law can change it also. Moreover God has given human beings the tendency towards good karma; and good karma reduces the impact of bad karma. He gave human beings the freedom to perform good and bad actions — that is the reason His *lila* is continuing. Although He has given us a little freedom, the main key is in His hand. Both good and bad are in front of you: you select. This is the way He plays. The play cannot continue if someone does only good or only bad. In a game of hide-and-seek the running about soon stops if in the beginning all the players touch the 'granny.' Her pleasure is in continuing the game. There are many methods mentioned to counteract the results of bad karma in the scriptures, such as rituals for peace [*shanti swastyana*], sacrifice [*yajna*], charity [*dana*], austerity [*tapasya*], and so on. It is God who prescribes these methods."

"Many people perform those rituals but we do not always see the results," the woman commented.

Holy Mother replied: "If a ritual is performed correctly, the result is bound to come. It takes time to yield the results of one's actions. One cannot get a ripe mango as soon as the blossom appears on the tree. It takes time for the bloom to develop as a mango. Does the chariot descend from heaven the moment you have finished a sacrifice? Let me tell you one thing: If you want to escape the results of good and bad karma, then chant God's name, repeat your mantra, worship the Lord, and read the scriptures. Always discriminate between the real and the unreal. Good karma subdues bad karma, but cannot destroy it. The good and bad karmas of an individual soul are destroyed only by chanting God's name, which also purifies the mind. Then one can know one's true nature."[51]

Above: Panoramic view of Jayrambati with Punyapukur.
Below: Shantinath Shiva Temple, Sihar.

34
Farewell
to Jayrambati
(27 January 1919 to 27 February 1920)

Kripām kuru mahādevi suteshu pranateshu cha;
Charanā-shraya dānena kripā-mayi namostu te.
 —*A hymn by Swami Abhedananda*

Bestow your grace on your children, O great Goddess! And on those who salute you, by giving them refuge at your feet, O compassionate One! Salutations to you!

Saint Ambrose said: "If you are in Rome, live in the Roman way; if you are elsewhere, live as they do there." The ability to adjust to circumstances is essential to living a happy and peaceful life. Holy Mother repeatedly told her disciples to adjust according to time, place, and person.

Holy Mother played her divine drama mainly from two stages: Jayrambati and Calcutta. In Jayrambati she lived among poor and unsophisticated villagers, while in Calcutta she was surrounded by wealthy and sophisticated city people. However, nothing affected her because her mind dwelt above the pairs of opposites, such as happiness and misery, luxury and poverty. She truly loved her village of Jayrambati because she enjoyed more freedom there than in Calcutta.

In the first 33 chapters of this book, we have presented to the reader the immortal saga of Holy Mother from 1853 to 1918. From 27 January 1919 to 27 February 1920, Holy Mother lived in Koalpara and Jayrambati, where her life story had begun 66 years previously. Although part of this last period of the Mother's life has been mentioned in Chapter 19, we shall recapitulate some incidents here for the continuation of the story.

Holy Mother's niece Radhu was pregnant and suffering from neurosis. She could not bear the noise in Calcutta, so the Mother decided to move to Jayrambati with her. Early in the morning of 27 January 1919,

Holy Mother left Udbodhan by horse carriage with Radhu and Radhu's mother, Surabala, as well as Maku and her son Neda, Nalini, and Mandakini Roy (a widowed disciple and attendant of the Mother), Brahmachari Ganen, Dwijen (later Swami Gangeshananda), and Brahmachari Barada. Holy Mother and her female companions travelled by train in a reserved second-class compartment and the men went by inter class. They spent two nights at Sureshwar Sen's house in Vishnupur. On the 29th, they left for Jayrambati, taking six bullock carts. It was decided that after resting in Koalpara for a couple of days, the party would continue to Jayrambati. However, Radhu had slept well for two nights in that quiet village and wanted to remain. Holy Mother consulted with her brother Kalikumar and others, and they suggested that it would be good for Radhu to stay in Koalpara rather than continue on to Jayrambati. Accordingly, Radhu and Holy Mother lived at Jagadamba Ashrama in Koalpara for six months (29 January to 22 July 1919).

During this period, Holy Mother was passing through a hard time: Nalini and Maku were jealous of Radhu and left for Jayrambati, where Maku's son Neda died from diphtheria on 20 April 1919. Holy Mother discouraged devotees from visiting her in Koalpara. As Radhu's mental illness and pregnancy worried her, she wrote to Saradananda and asked him to send Sarala (later Bharatiprana), who was an experienced nurse in the female ward of the Ramakrishna Mission Home of Service in Varanasi, to Koalpara as soon as possible. Saradananda immediately wrote to Swami Kalikananda asking him to release Sarala and send her to Calcutta. The next day, before leaving Varanasi, Sarala went to Turiyananda and told him that she was going to Holy Mother to care for Radhu. Turiyananda said to her: "You are going to the Mother? Very well. The great Divine Mother is engaged in doing good to humanity. We are trying our utmost to raise our minds to this chakra [pointing to his throat], and she has brought her mind down forcibly to that centre, saying, 'Radhu, Radhu.' Try to understand this great mystery! Victory to the Mother, the great Primordial Power!"[1]

Sarala arrived in Koalpara during the first week of April 1919 accompanied by Ruma Devi, who wanted initiation from the Mother. Dr. Matilal (later Swami Prabuddhananda from Mayavati) accompanied them. They arrived at Koalpara via Vishnupur. Sarala saw that Holy Mother was lying down on the floor with a low temperature. When Holy Mother saw Sarala, she said: "My child, I am happy that you have come. Look at my condition! I am lying down, helpless. Look after Radhu. I am relieved that you are here."[2] She greeted Ruma and told her that Saradananda had written to her asking for Ruma's initiation. She agreed to initiate her as soon as she was well.

Ruma was born in Garbiang, a village in the Himalayas between Mayavati and Kailash, and she spoke Hindi. She came from a respectable and spiritual family. She had read about Ramakrishna and Holy Mother and had received a mantra in a dream. When the Mother learned that Ruma planned to return to her home with Dr. Matilal, the Mother initiated her on the same day despite her illness. After initiating her, she said to Sarala: "This girl followed my instructions well. Where is Kailash and where is Koalpara! My child, see how the Master attracts people!"[3] Ruma had knit a woolen rug for the Mother and now presented it to her. She cried profusely as she left and the Mother blessed her.

Sarala recalled: "Radhu was suffering from neurosis and wouldn't move out of the thatched hut adjacent to the cowshed. Despite Radhu's mental state, we were happy to be with the Mother at Koalpara. One day a bird sat on the branch of a tree near our room. Like an innocent girl, the Mother asked the bird, 'O bird, could you tell me whether Radhu will have a boy or a girl?' The bird cried out, 'Khoka, Khoka, Khoka.'* Pleased, the Mother said to us that Radhu would have a son."[4]

In spite of the fact that she was staying in that remote village of Koalpara, Holy Mother's life was eventful. Keshavananda's mother was an elderly woman and hard of hearing, but she was devoted to the Mother. She got all kinds of news about the Mother from her youngest daughter-in-law and believed the gossip that she heard. Holy Mother did not approve of this. One afternoon, Keshavananda's mother said that Kishori's wife, Yugal, had stolen Holy Mother's footprint. There was a big commotion. That evening, Holy Mother said to Brahmachari Barada: "Tomorrow go to the market and buy some cloth and a bottle of *alta* [red paint] and give it to Kedar's mother. Let me fulfill their desire." The next day Barada went to Kotalpur and bought some fine bleached cloth and a bottle of alta. He cut that cloth into 32 pieces and gave it to Keshavananda's mother to make the footprints. Within a couple of days, Holy Mother's footprints were taken and distributed among the devotees. They were the last footprints taken while she was alive.[5]

After the Master passed away, when Holy Mother was alone in Kamarpukur, she felt helpless because she had no children to look after her. Then the Master appeared to her and said: "Well, you are thinking of children. I have left you many of them, all jewels."[6] Saradananda was one

---

*Khoka means "little boy."

of those jewels. His love and devotion, faith and respect for Holy Mother were truly second to none. Although he was physically in Calcutta, his mind was focussed on the Mother's health and welfare and her needs. That is why the Mother used to say affectionately, "Sharat is the bearer of my burdens." The following excerpts from Saradananda's letters show how seriously he bore the responsibility for Holy Mother and her family affairs, and sought to make her daily life smooth and pleasant.

19 February 1919: Mother, please accept our countless salutations. I am getting all news of you from Kedar [Keshavananda]. I am concerned about Radhu. I pray to the Master for her quick recovery. I have already sent some lemons and pomegranates; and yesterday *Madhyam Narayan* oil [an ayurvedic oil] has been sent. I have sent Rs. 25 to Kedar for your expenses in Koalpara and today I am remitting another 25 rupees. Please let me know whether I should send some money for your personal expenses. I learned from Kishori's letter that you had asked for a lavatory to be built in Jayrambati. I asked him and Kedar to send me an estimate as soon as possible."

25 February 1919: "Dr. Suresh Bhattacharya, Dr. Bipin Ghosh, and Dr. Durgapada Ghosh treated Nalini [Mother's niece], but her condition did not improve. According to their suggestion we have brought a Western woman doctor who is now treating her. She will be able to return to Jayrambati after two or three weeks. We pray to the Master so that Radhu can get rid of the neurosis."

27 February 1919: "I have sent 50 lemons and 13 pomegranates by postal parcel. The shipping cost is high, so I did not send you earlier. However, we shall send more as soon as you finish those. Please ask Kedar and Kishori to complete the construction of the lavatory in Jayrambati before the rainy season. There is a famine all around now. We are not getting sufficient funds for relief work. We are doing some relief work in Bankura and Manbhum districts. Today I learned from the letter of Kedar that Radhu had a little temperature. We are concerned about her. Please take care of yourself. If your health is good, then we shall be able to maintain our strength, confidence, and composure, and Radhu will be taken care of properly."

21 March 1919: "I have asked Dr. Vaikuntha of Bankura to go to Koalpara whenever you need him [for Radhu's delivery]. Tomorrow Nalini is going to Jayrambati with Kalo, a son of Sureshwar Sen of Vishnupur. I am sending with her pomegranates, patal [a vegetable], lemons, and sweets. Please don't neglect your body, and eat at the right time. If you are ill, the whole arrangement will be jeopardized. I heard you had some pain for a couple of days. Now how are you? Your Western woman devotee's daughter's marriage date has been fixed for two months from now, and

the bridegroom is a nice person. She conveyed her pranam to you and asked me to inform you."

17 April 1919: "Mother, please accept our respectful pranams. I have heard your body is still weak. There is a possibility of relapse of fever if you work hard and do not eat timely. Please take care of yourself. Devamata has written a letter to you from America, which I am sending to you. Paramananda has sent 66 rupees for you [from Boston]. Shall I remit it now?"

29 April 1919: "We are shocked to hear the news of the death of Neda [Maku's son], and we understand you are afflicted immensely. It is all the Master's play, and we understand it very little. I am sending 150 rupees per month for your household expenses in Koalpara."[7]

On 9 May 1919, Radhu gave birth to a son in a natural way without much difficulty. It was a great relief to the Mother. The Mother named the boy Banabihari — an epithet of Krishna that means "he who roams in the forest."

On 23 July 1919, Holy Mother moved to Jayrambati with all her companions, and she lived there till 27 February 1920. Radhu was weak and bedridden most of the time. According to custom, six months after Banabihari's birth, Holy Mother arranged his rice-feeding ceremony (*annaprashan*) and fed many people.

Holy Mother knew that her days were coming to an end, so she began making arrangements for the future. She said to Parameswarananda: "You stay in Jayrambati. If you live here, then I will feel a great relief."

He replied: "Mother, I feel hesitant to live here long. I heard that one should not stay at the house of one's guru more than three days."

Holy Mother reassured him: "Don't worry. I am asking you to stay here."[8]

Swami Parameswarananda obeyed the Mother's order and looked after the Mother's temple in Jayrambati until his death in 1978.

Narayan Iyenger (later Swami Srivasananda) proposed that the courtyard of the Mother's new house be cemented because during the rainy season that area became muddy. When Parameswarananda informed the Mother about Narayan's proposal, she said: "No, my son, it is not necessary to cover the courtyard with bricks and cement. People will say that we have a lot of money."[9] The swami understood that she wanted to live just like the other villagers in Jayrambati.

Parameswarananda recalled:

Many devotees would come to visit the Mother in Jayrambati. She would arrange for their stay and food with great care. She could not bear it that they should be inconvenienced while living with her. We saw the Mother roaming in the village and collecting vegetables and milk for tea for her visiting devotees. It was a sight to see. We read in the scriptures that only the devotees yearn for God, and here we witnessed the Divine Mother had descended on the earth, longed for the devotees, and served them. This truth we realized by meditating on the *lila* of the Master and the Mother. Sri Ramakrishna would climb on the roof of the mansion and cry: "O devotees, where are you? Please come." Thus many devotees came to Dakshineswar. In Jayrambati, we have seen that the Mother would wait for the devotees, and if there was no devotee on a particular day, she would lament: "Well, today no devotee has come." It is amazing that shortly after that a couple of devotees would arrive. The Divine Mother herself descended to earth to deliver people, so she eagerly waited for her children.[10]

In August 1919, there was heavy rain in Jayrambati. In the evenings after japa and meditation, Holy Mother would ask her disciples to sing some devotional songs in the parlour, or she would ask them to read the Bengali *Sri Ramakrishna Kathamrita* to her. Swami Ishanananda wrote:

> For the last few days we have been reading the *Kathamrita* — Part 3. After listening to the reading, one day the Mother said: "How wonderfully Master [*meaning M.*] kept everything in his memory and then wrote it down so beautifully. Listening to the conversations of the Master, it seems that those are taking place right now in front of us. What a vivid description! And the Master's words go straight to the mind and stick there. Nowadays so many people are drawn to the Master by reading and listening to the *Kathamrita*. They are getting peace. The Master's words are infallible."
>
> I commented: "Mother, all the advice and ideas of the Master are so beautiful! They fill the mind with joy."
>
> The Mother said: "You are right, my son. If anyone can comprehend even a little of these teachings, that person's life will be blessed."[11]

One noon during this period, Ishanananda was preparing betel rolls with Holy Mother and asked her: "Mother, when you encountered the robber in the Telo-Bhelo meadow, were you afraid?" She was hesitant to say anything because she didn't want to expose Lakshmi, Shibu, and the others who had left her alone. Maku insisted, "Aunt, tell us the story."

Holy Mother said: "Yes, I was terribly afraid. My heart was palpitating. The moment that man came near and asked, 'Who are you?', immediately from the bottom of my heart, I said, 'Father, I am your daughter,' and I became like his daughter. Then that robber became somewhat puzzled. He said, 'Don't be afraid, my child.' Meanwhile, his wife arrived." When Maku asked her to continue the story, the Mother said: "What happened then is all written in the book. I cannot tell it anymore."[12]

The Mother's Last Jagaddhatri Worship

After the rainy season in 1919, the Mother was suffering from malaria off and on. Her health broke down. She was weak and thin. When fall came, she got ready to perform Jagaddhatri Puja. Parameswarananda went to Calcutta to buy various things according to Holy Mother's instructions. When he was leaving to return to Jayrambati, Saradananda told him, "Please tell the Mother that her health has deteriorated from several attacks of malaria, so immediately after the worship she should come back to Calcutta." Parameswarananda reached Jayrambati with a bullock cart loaded with the articles for worship. He saw that the Mother's health was very poor, yet she had constant visitors. According to her instructions, the clay image of the deity was made and other necessary items and groceries were purchased locally.

Parameswarananda recalled:

I observed that the Mother was indrawn most of the time. On previous occasions, she had asked us to do things, but this time it was different. Now, she demonstrated how to do a particular thing, and then said, "In the future follow this method." It seemed to me that she was making arrangements for the future when she would not be with us. When she was telling us repeatedly, "You will do it this way," a doubt came to our minds and we felt uneasiness. The articles of worship were kept in the houses of Kali and her other brothers. She ordered me to move everything to her new house. It seemed that she was cutting all connections with her brothers.

The day before the worship, I asked the Mother in the evening, 'Who will do the *alpana*?* Shall I call the aunts?"

"No, don't call them. You are my sons and you are my daughters. You do the *alpana*." I had learned how to draw in school, so I painted the floor of the shrine. Delighted, the Mother called the ladies: "See how beautifully he has painted the floor. Can you do it like he does?" The Mother showed me how to set the plates of *naivedya* and what kind of utensils would be used for offering food and drink to the deity. She also told me how the naivedya would be distributed among the priest, the mantra prompter, and others. She also mentioned what was to be given to the image maker, drummer, and others.

Before the worship began, the Mother received the priest and the mantra prompter with humility, offering them each a cloth, sacred thread, betel leaf, and betel nut. The *mangal-ghat* [consecrated pitcher] filled with water from Banerjee's pond arrived, accompanied by musicians, and was placed at the front of the altar. The priest invoked the prana in the deity with the mantras and began the worship. The Mother bowed down to

*An auspicious painting made with paint from rice powder.

Mother Jagaddhatri encircling the corner of her upper sari around her neck. The deity was worshipped three times and the ceremonies continued till four o'clock. In between the worship ceremonies, the Mother offered flowers. When the *homa* began, the Mother sat and watched the *purnāhuti*. Then the priest sprinkled the peace water from the *mangal-ghat*. The Mother and all the devotees received that holy water and bowed down to the deity. After the first worship, the prasad was served to the brahmins and then to other people. After the vesper service, puffed rice, luchi, and sweets were offered to the Goddess Jagaddhatri. The worship continued for another two days. On the third day, before the immersion ceremony, an earring was taken from the image according to custom, and the Mother whispered into the ear of the deity, asking her to come back the next year.

The Mother always loved to listen to yatra performances based on the Puranas, and she arranged one every year. The villagers also enjoyed these performances. Before the worship of Mother Jagaddhatri, the Mother said to me, "Take these hundred rupees and arrange for the yatra performance of Anukul Mandal for two nights." When we had booked the performance, Uncle Kali said to the Mother: "Sister, I have financial problems, and you are spending money for a yatra." Disgusted, the Mother said to me: "My son, it is not possible to do anything for Kali. Return that money to me." I returned the money to her. I was sad that the Mother would not hear the yatra performance. The Mother also purchased three and a half acres of paddy field for the annual celebration of Mother Jagaddhatri."[13]

Holy Mother's health was failing day by day. Previously when Narayan Iyenger had offered money to pave the courtyard of her house with cement, she declined. He offered again to complete the project before Holy Mother left for Calcutta. This time she said to Parameswarananda, "Since Narayan is asking again and again, let him pave the courtyard with cement."[14] Then she pointed out a small section of the courtyard that should not be cemented because a wooden stove* would be made there for cooking during Jagaddhatri Puja and for making puffed rice. She also forbade paving the floor of her bedroom with cement.

Seeing Ramakrishna in Every Being

The culmination of the Vedantic experience is to see God in every being and every thing. This realization takes place when a person's individuality dissolves and his or her I-consciousness becomes one with the Cosmic

---

*A temporary wooden stove for cooking during the festival time is made by digging a hole in the ground.

Consciousness. The Mundaka Upanishad uses an analogy to describe this experience: "As flowing rivers disappear into the sea, losing their names and forms, so a wise man, freed from name and form, attains the Purusha, who is greater than the Great."[15] Ramakrishna had such experiences, one of which he described to Holy Mother, saying: "I am glad you are here. I feel as if I am going to a faraway country across the water — very far away." The Master also said to M. and Hirananda: "The Indivisible Satchidananda — I see It both inside and outside. You all seem to me to be my kinsmen. I see you all as so many sheaths [referring to their bodies], with the heads moving."[16]

In Jayrambati, Holy Mother had a similar experience of Oneness. Parameswarananda described this:

> The Mother's health was not good and her mind was indrawn most of the time. She was performing all her duties in the household but the focus of her mind was towards the Infinite. One day we arranged the *naivedya* in the shrine and the door was open. Niranjan, a greedy boy from the Banerjee family, cast a hungry look towards the food. Holy Mother told me: "The look of that boy has made the food bad. It cannot be offered to the Master. Prepare fresh food for the Master." When the fresh naivedya was ready, the Mother offered it to the Master.
>
> Another day I saw that boy on the veranda. Before offering the naivedya to the Master, the Mother gave some of it to that boy to eat. Surprised, I asked her: "Mother, the food has not yet been offered to the Master, and you have given some of it to that boy?"
>
> She replied, "My son, the Master also dwells in him." I became apprehensive but could not say anything.
>
> On another day she took some food from the offering plate and gave it to Gangaram, her pet parrot. I protested: "Mother, what are you doing? The naivedya has not yet been offered to the Master, and you have given some to Gangaram."
>
> She replied: "It is all right, my son. The Master dwells in the bird."
>
> One evening she poured some milk into the Master's bowl and asked me to drink from it. Dumbfounded, I asked her, "Mother, how can I drink the milk from the Master's bowl?"
>
> She said: "The Master exists inside you. I am telling you to drink." I protested several times, but she insisted that I drink milk from that bowl.
>
> One night her attendant had no pillow, and she gave her own pillow to her attendant to use. When I protested, she said: "My son, it is all right. The Master also lives in her."
>
> I was perturbed when I observed the Mother's mood. She was seeing the Master in every being. I thought that she would probably depart from this world soon.[17]

The Mother's and the Master's Birth Anniversary

Although Holy Mother was suffering from malaria off and on in Jayrambati, she tried to make her disciples and relatives happy. She knew her days were drawing to an end, so she shared herself with these people as much as she could. As mentioned before, during the last part of October 1919, the Mother arranged the rice-feeding celebration for Radhu's son and held a feast for her relatives and the villagers. Holy Mother's birthday — the last birthday that she celebrated — was on 13 December 1919. When Parameswarananda asked about arrangements for her birthday, she said: "Invite the monks and devotees and the families of Kali, Barada, and Prasanna." Kali wanted the occasion to be celebrated on a large scale and said to her, "Sister, we should invite the villagers and beggars."

Holy Mother replied: "Let me feed the people in my household. Later I shall consider your suggestion."

On her birthday, she took a sponge bath with tepid water and put on a sari sent by Saradananda. She performed the Master's worship, and then sat on her bed with her feet dangling, holding Radhu's baby on her lap. The devotees put a vermilion mark and sandal paste on her forehead and placed a garland around her neck. Then they came one by one, bowed down to her, and offered flowers at her feet. She blessed everyone, saying: "I pray to the Master for your welfare." Generally Holy Mother could not eat before feeding the disciples and devotees. But on that day, after the food offering to the Master, she ate at the request of her disciples, as her health was poor. Then the devotees and villagers had their prasad.[18]

Jamini Devi recalled: "I put a dot of sandal paste on the Mother's forehead, a garland around her neck, and offered flowers at her feet. After bowing down I looked at her face and saw a beautiful divine form in place of her old form. I can't describe that celestial form in human language. After a short while, she became as usual and said, 'My child, now bow down.'"[19]

That afternoon Holy Mother had a relapse of her fever. Her attendants informed Saradananda in Calcutta that her condition had worsened and local treatment had produced no result. In between bouts of fever, Holy Mother initiated some devotees who had come from far-off places. Her compassion was welling up for those who were suffering. She was distributing her blessings so quickly, it was as if she would burn away, like camphor.

In February 1920, before the Master's birthday, Kali went to Holy

Mother and said: "Sister, because you are present this year, we must observe the Master's birthday on a grand scale and feed many people. Moreover, many relatives will come from other places to see you. We shall buy sufficient food and other things so there will be no shortage."

The Mother said slowly: "Look, brother Kali, I don't have your devotion and strength to observe the birthday festival of the Master on a grand scale. Whatever vegetables and other foods are available in the local market, buy them and arrange the feast. As you see, my health is declining day by day."

Kali took charge of the Master's birthday festival, which fell on 21 February 1920. After the worship, prasad was distributed among the monks, relatives, and villagers. It went off smoothly. In the late afternoon, Holy Mother felt weak, so she lay down with Radhu's baby inside the mosquito curtain. Ishanananda read some devotees' letters to her and then rubbed her feet. When the baby began to cry, Holy Mother asked Ishanananda to take him to Radhu. The baby was on the other side of Holy Mother, and Ishanananda was hesitant to step over her. However, she insisted, so he obeyed and then bowed down to her. She blessed him and said: "There are many rules in the Vaishnava scriptures regarding proper and improper service to the guru. It is a sin to step over the guru, walk over his shadow, disobey his command, and even to step over his things. But let me tell you what the real services to the guru are: one should be humble towards the guru, should sincerely and affectionately serve the guru, do the guru's work as instructed, and please the guru in all ways. The guru becomes angry if the disciple opposes his or her will and acts egotistically. It is a great mistake to make the guru angry."[20] Holy Mother then explained that it was hard for her to get up, so she had asked him to step over her body to pick up the baby.

One evening at eight o'clock, Holy Mother was seated on her veranda. Parameswarananda was massaging her feet with medicated oil for her rheumatism, and she was talking about the Master. Meanwhile, a young woman entered the house and began to cry loudly. Her husband had died suddenly. He had been highly educated and had a high position in his office. The young widow sat on the veranda. She held Holy Mother's feet, and her tears wet them. Overwhelmed by her heart-rending sobs, Parameswarananda said, "Mother, this girl is deeply hurt."

Mother replied, "My son, let her cry." Tears trickled from the Mother's eyes also. Amazed, Parameswarananda thought that the Mother would console her. Instead, she let her cry. He did not realize that the Mother was absorbing her grief. After some time, the woman stopped crying.

When she stopped crying the Mother said to her, "My child, have a little prasad and drink some water."

Amazed, Parameswarananda saw that the woman was now completely free from grief. Her experience with Holy Mother had shown her the impermanency of the world and her face was radiant with serenity.[21]

Towards the end of January 1920 Naresh Chandra Chakrabarty, a disciple of the Mother, went to Jayrambati with two devotees for their initiation. The Mother told them: "I am very sick. I can't initiate you now." The devotees began to cry, and Naresh again requested that she initiate them. Holy Mother replied, "This body can no longer accept the burning sensation [that people's sins produce]."

Naresh humbly asked, "Mother, if you do not show your grace, where will they go?"

She finally agreed to initiate them. She told Naresh: "Their bodies are very impure. Ask them to stay here for three nights. If anyone stays here for three nights, his body will be pure because this place is the abode of Shiva."[22] Holy Mother initiated them three days later.

The Last Journey to Calcutta

Swami Saradananda was hearing news of Holy Mother's poor health from various sources, and he was concerned. He wrote to Holy Mother and also sent messages through other people requesting that she come to Calcutta for treatment. At last she agreed to come. However, Saradananda was called to Varanasi to look after an urgent matter concerning the Ramakrishna Mission there. He stayed in Varanasi from 25 November 1919 to 20 January 1920, and then went to Bhubaneswar to see Swami Brahmananda on 6 February. He returned to Calcutta on 17 February.

Holy Mother refused to go to Calcutta during Saradananda's absence. She told her attendants: "If Sharat is not there, my going to Calcutta is out of the question. Who else can take care of me? Who can carry my burden and problems except Sharat?"[23] At last Saradananda fixed the Mother's departure date for 24 February 1920 and sent Swamis Atmaprakashananda, Bhumananda, and Boshiswar Sen to Jayrambati. They arrived there on 21 February.

The disciples then began packing for Holy Mother and the companions who would go with her to Calcutta. She did not have much luggage. Generally, she carried a few saris, a towel, a blanket, a mosquito curtain, tooth powder, a little dry mud from Mother Simhavahini's temple, and her little tin box, which contained the Master's picture wrapped up in a cloth and some precious mementos. It was decided that Parameswarananda

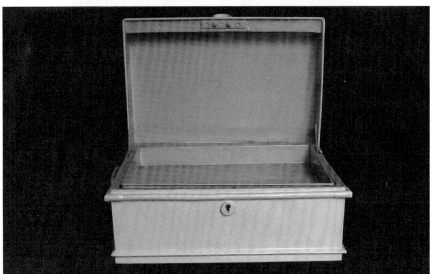

Above: Ramakrishna's picture (*now in Udbodhan shrine*), which Sarada Devi worshipped and carried during her travels.
Below: The tin box (*now in Belur Math museum*) in which she carried the picture.

and Haripremananda would stay in Jayrambati to look after the Mother's house, while Ishanananda accompanied her to Calcutta.

Parameswarananda described the plans:

The date of the Mother's departure for Calcutta was 24 February 1920. It was planned that the Mother would go by palanquin via Sihar, and others would cross the Amodar River by a small boat and then go by bullock cart. They would have lunch at Koalpara Ashrama and then after resting, they would start for Vishnupur. In the morning, the Mother finished the worship, wrapped the Master's picture and put it in her tin box. She then added her jewellery and money and closed the box. She ate a little breakfast. Before leaving, she remembered that some leftover rice from the previous night was soaking in water, and she wanted to give it to a poor woman. She said to me, "This rice will be wasted, so let me give it to that woman."

I said: "Mother, I shall give it to her. You will not have to do it."

She said, "No, my son, I shall give it to her."

After giving the rice to the woman, the Mother went to Punyapukur to wash her hands. Her foot slipped and she almost fell. Somehow she controlled her balance and said to me: "My son, I was about to fall. You see, this body is very weak." She sat down and took a little rest.

Men and women of Jayrambati came to see the Mother off and said to her with tearful eyes: "After recovering your health, please come back soon. Don't forget us."

The Mother replied: "Everything is the will of the Master. Can I ever forget you?" Then her attendants came one by one and bowed down to her. She gave me one of her used silk cloths and gave a chadar to Brahmachari Hari. Her palanquin was kept on the shore of Aher Lake, which is on the western outskirts of the village. The Mother asked me to carry her tin box and I put it on my head. She walked behind me and the villagers followed her. Meanwhile, a white-breasted kite flew over the Mother's head. When I saw it, I said to her, "Mother, the journey will be auspicious." She replied indifferently, "Yes, my son." Hari carried a pan and a jug of water mixed with turmeric.* When the Mother reached her palanquin, Hari washed the Mother's feet with that water and dried them before she entered the palanquin. I privately told Hari to save that water. But when I stepped away, the Mother said to Hari, "I walked over this dirty street, so throw that water away." Hari told her that I had asked him to save it. The Mother insisted that he throw it away. When I came back I found that the pan was empty. I was disappointed as I wanted to save that auspicious water.

The Mother entered the palanquin and I placed the box inside it. We followed her. When the palanquin reached the Shantinath Shiva temple in Sihar, the Mother got down and asked Brahmachari Barada to buy

---

*Turmeric can be used as an antiseptic.

some sweets. She offered them to Lord Shiva and distributed the prasad to everyone present. She then bowed down to a brahmin who was a relative on her Mother's side. She returned to the palanquin. When she reached the edge of Sihar village, she asked the bearers to stop. She put her hand on my head to bless me, and then affectionately said: "You have come quite a distance. Now go back. Hari will be with you. Please eat well. After reaching Calcutta, I shall write to you." Barada followed the Mother on his bicycle. Gradually the Mother's palanquin disappeared from sight and I returned to Jayrambati with a heavy heart.[24]

We cannot resist including these details of the Mother's life because they were so beautifully, meticulously, and graphically recorded by her disciples. We are eternally indebted to them. Moreover, these precious eyewitness accounts are very helpful for meditation on the Mother, who is now beyond name and form. Every tiny thing about the beloved is important to the lover. Now we shall present the vivid account of Brahmachari Barada (later Swami Ishanananda), who accompanied Holy Mother on her last journey from Jayrambati to Calcutta:

> After returning from Varanasi, Swami Saradananda fixed the date of the Mother's return to Calcutta and then sent Swamis Atmaprakashananda, Bhumananda, and Boshiswar Sen to Jayrambati to escort the Mother. It was decided that Radhu, her son, and her mother; Maku and her son; Nalini; Mandakini, a brahmin widow who took care of Radhu's son; and I would go with the Mother. Swami Parameswarananda and Hari would remain in Jayrambati.
>
> The Mother's body was very weak. Two days before the departure, she went to bow down to Mother Simhavahini. She was terribly exhausted when she returned home and later said, "I perspired like one on one's deathbed."
>
> The departure time was eight o'clock on the morning of 24 February 1920. Two palanquins were hired — one for the Mother and another for Radhu and her son — to take them up to Vishnupur. I was to follow the Mother on my bicycle and the others would go by bullock cart after crossing the river. The palanquins would take an eight-mile detour via Sihar and Shiromanipur to Koalpara.
>
> The night before the journey, the fickle Radhu suddenly announced that she would not go by palanquin with her son. The Mother tried to convince her, but she would not change her mind. The Mother waited till the next day, thinking that Radhu would change her mind. But in the morning before departure, when Radhu had not yielded, the Mother said: "Let Radhu go with her son by bullock cart, and Maku and her son will go by palanquin with me."

We carried the luggage to the other side of the Amodar River and loaded it into the bullock cart. After returning to the Mother's house, I saw that many men and women of the village had come to see the Mother off. They plaintively said: "Aunt, please come back soon after recuperating. Don't forget us for a long time."

The Mother replied in a choked voice: "Everything is the will of the Master. Can I forget you?" It was a wonderful scene of mutual love and respect. Everyone bowed down to her, and at last Swami Parameswarananda and Hari bowed down. The Mother gave a cloth to the swami and a chadar to Hari, and blessed them by touching their heads.

The Mother then bowed down to the Master, put his picture in her tin box, and tied a cloth around it. After crossing the threshold, she saluted Mother Simhavahini with folded hands and saluted other deities of the village. Her palanquin was waiting on the shore of Aher Lake, which is to the west of the village. Mother Simhavahini is the presiding deity of the village, so the Mother did not board the palanquin within the village.* The Mother began to walk westward and saw Uncle Prasanna's wife waiting in front of her door. She held a jug of water and a pan; her intention was to wash the Mother's feet before she got into the palanquin. The Mother told the aunt: "Subasini, you will not have to carry the water and pan. Give them to Hari. He will wash my feet." Accordingly, she handed the jug and pan over to Hari; and she also walked to the palanquin with the Mother carrying a glass of water, some sweets, and a crushed betel roll.

On the way, the Mother saluted Yatrasiddhi Roy Dharma Thakur, the presiding deity of the Ghosh family, situated in the western part of the village. When she came close to the palanquin, the Mother touched the ground with both hands. Facing the village, she said: "One's Mother and one's birthplace are higher than heaven." Thus saluting the village, she got inside the palanquin, but she kept her feet out for Hari to wash in the pan. Aunt Subasini then gave the sweets and water to the Mother, a little of which she took, and then she chewed the crushed betel roll.

The bearers lifted the palanquin and moved towards Sihar. The villagers watched the Mother's departure intently and with tearful eyes. I followed the palanquin riding on my bicycle. The Mother asked the bearers to stop near the Shantinath Shiva temple at Sihar. She got down and went to a nearby pond, where she washed her hands and feet. Then she bought two rupees' worth of sweets — sandesh, sugar, and nabat. Entering the temple, she bowed down to Lord Shantinath and offered the sweets. Many men, women, and children of Sihar came to see the Mother. She distributed that sweet prasad to all. She ate a little and gave some to us. Then she tied a

---

* In those days it would have been considered disrespectful to the deity for a person to use such a conveyance within the village, as only a deity would be carried in that way.

little prasad in the corner of her cloth for Radhu. We reached Koalpara by eleven o'clock in the morning. All of the bullock carts had arrived before us.

We were unloading the luggage at Koalpara when a mosquito curtain was found to be missing. Bhumananda privately told me that by mistake he had left the money bag, containing the travelling funds, on the cornice of Uncle Kali's parlour. Immediately I went back on my bicycle, hid it in the bushes by the river, and crossed the Amodar River. I got the money bag and returned to Koalpara. The Mother listened to the whole story and commented: "I see these are all inauspicious signs."

It was decided that the bullock carts would leave Koalpara that very evening for Vishnupur after supper. The Mother and Maku would start the next morning by palanquin, and I would follow them by bicycle.

In the morning when I arrived at the Jagadamba Ashrama, the Mother had already finished the worship with flowers and sweets and was wrapping the Master's picture with a cloth. Then while placing it in her tin box, she addressed the Master: "Please get ready. Now it is time to depart." When she saw me, the Mother said: "Barada, you have come? Why are you so late? Soon it will be hot. Take this flower for the journey." She touched that flower on her head, handed it over to me, and said, "Tie it in the corner of your cloth." I did as she asked. She then repeated a mantra while touching my head and chest and affectionately touched my chin. She then bade farewell to all and entered the palanquin.

All these days she was using a stick for walking because of weakness. That stick belonged to her brother Prasanna. She now gave the stick and also a mosquito curtain to Swami Ritananda to give to Prasanna. She said to him, "My son, I am leaving Sharat behind."[25] He did not understand the implication of her words.*

I rode my bicycle behind the Mother's palanquin. After leaving Kotalpur, the Mother looked out from the palanquin and called to me: "Barada, always stay near us and go carefully. All of Radhu's and Maku's jewellery is in a box in Maku's palanquin." When I heard this, I was a little concerned. I said to Joge Dule, who was devoted to the Mother and was the leader of the bearers of Haldigram Village: "Look Joge, the Mother is a little afraid. Be alert, especially in the jungle section near Vishnupur."

Joge replied: "What are you saying, brother? We are sixteen** and each one of us has a bamboo staff hidden under the palanquin. No robber can do any harm to the Mother while we are alive. Don't be afraid." I was relieved by Joge's words.

---

* This was Holy Mother's final departure from Jayrambati, so she returned what she had borrowed from her brother. She also assured her disciple Ritananda that Sharat would look after him after she was gone.
** There were eight bearers for each palanquin.

When we arrived at Jaipur, the Mother asked the bearers to stop the palanquin. She got down at the roadside inn where we had cooked food and eaten during her last journey to Jayrambati. When she saw the inn's dilapidated condition, the Mother remarked, "Ah, this is our inn!" The Mother sat on a blanket under a tree next to the inn and said to me, "Feed the bearers." She then took two rupees from her box and asked me to buy puffed rice for them. Of course I also had some money with me for travelling expenses. The bearers enjoyed the refreshments.

The Mother warmed up milk for Maku's child and then washed her hands and feet in a nearby pond. Then she said to me: "Buy some puffed rice for me. Let me eat something. And buy puffed rice and some fried things for you and Maku." When I brought all those things, the Mother had a few bites and then gave the rest to us, saying, "I can't eat any more." When the bearers finished their refreshments, the journey continued.

The distance between Jaipur and Vishnupur is eight miles and both sides of the road are covered with dense jungle. After crossing four miles, we reached Tantipukur where there was a shop by the side of the road. Seeing that shop from the palanquin, the Mother told me: "Barada, ask the bearers to stop here. My feet are numb from sitting in the palanquin. Buy a pice worth of oil from that shop and bring it to me in a sal leaf. I shall rub my feet with that oil."

I was a little scared because I saw that nearly 30 poor labourers were talking about something near that shop. I told her: "Mother, there are some strange people there. Please don't get down from the palanquin. You stay inside and I will bring the oil." At that time Maku cried out: "Brother, I am thirsty from eating puffed rice. I want to drink some water."

The Mother said, "Go to that pond and drink water."

I said: "How can she drink that water? It is bad water."

The Mother said: "So many passers-by drink that water; you go and drink that water. Nothing will happen. Barada, you go with her."

I first brought oil for the Mother and then escorted Maku to the pond. Again our journey continued.

As the Mother sat in the palanquin, she continued rubbing oil on her outstretched legs and enjoying the wonderful scenery of the sal forest on both sides of the road. At about two o'clock in the afternoon we reached Sureshwar Sen's house in Vishnupur. All of the bullock carts had arrived at eight o'clock in the morning. Swami Atmaprakashananda and others learned that we had puffed rice on our way, and that was why we were late. They laughed because they knew that people from Bankura are excessively fond of puffed rice.

Sureshwar Sen was no more. He had passed away a few months earlier, but his sons and his brother Boshiswar arranged everything just as Sureshwar had done. He had been a wonderful host to the Mother. The

Sarada Devi at lunch at Sureswar Sen's house in Vishnupur, February 1920. This is the last photo taken of Holy Mother during her lifetime. Left to right: Sarada Devi, Surabala (inside), Jamini, Maku, Nalini, Nandarani, and Mandakini.

Mother lamented: "Ah, whenever I came here, Suresh would stand in front of this cottage with folded hands waiting for orders. He would not even come onto the veranda. What wonderful devotion he had! Suresh was like a second Girish."

At noon when the Mother and her women companions sat on the veranda for their noon meal, Boshiswar took a group photograph. It was the last photo of the Mother taken during her lifetime.

That day and the next we stayed in Vishnupur. Then on the third day we had an early lunch and went to the railway station. According to the Mother's directions, we all bought third-class tickets and travelled to Calcutta in the same compartment. When we arrived at Howrah Station, we saw Kiran Datta's phaeton waiting for the Mother.* Brahmachari Ganendra, Dr. Durgapada Ghosh, and others were at the station to receive the Mother. We hired another four horse carriages and reached Udbodhan House around ten o'clock that night [27 February 1920].[26]

---

*According to Swami Saradananda's diary: "Friday, February 27, 1920. Sri Sri Ma reached here [Udbodhan] 9 p.m. (night) in Dr. Kanjilal's motor."

35
Return
to Her True Abode
(27 February 1920 – 21 July 1920)

Sarve kshyanta nichayāh patanāntah samuchrayāh;
Samyoga viprayogānta maranātam cha jivitam.
Kālah karshati bhutani sarvāni vividhānyuta;
Na kālasya priyah kashchit na dveshyah kurusattama.
  —*Mahabharata*, Stree Parva, 2:3,8

Vidura to Dhritarashtra: "Everything is subject to destruction; everything that is high is sure to fall down. Union is sure to end in separation; life is sure to end in death. Death drags all creatures down, even the gods. There is none dear or hateful to death, O Kuru chief."

The life of every human being is a story, and every human story has a beginning and an end. The stories of ordinary human beings end as soon as they die. They remain in the memory of their relatives and friends for a short while, but gradually they pass into oblivion. Divine stories continue eternally, like the flow of a river. Stories of divine beings such as Rama, Krishna, Buddha, Jesus, Ramakrishna, Sarada Devi, and others continue throughout the ages because their life stories enter into the realm of human imagination. People keep them alive in their hearts through meditation and by practising their teachings in daily life, so their stories remain ever fresh.

At the advent of an avatar, or divine incarnation, a renaissance occurs, a new civilization begins, and a cultural revival takes place. Although Christ's public life lasted only three years, his contribution to the world of thought and culture has lasted for more than 2,000 years. His life and teachings still inspire countless artists in every field — painters, sculptors, architects, poets, writers, musicians, actors, and dramatists. The avatars who lived before Christ — Rama, Krishna, and Buddha — continue to inspire writers and artists all over the world. Now in this present age, the

Above: Sarada Devi's room and shrine at Udbodhan House, Calcutta.
Below: View of the slum from Sarada Devi's northern balcony. The tall buildings did not exist in Sarada Devi's time.

inspiring and fascinating life stories of Ramakrishna and Sarada Devi are in the domain of human imagination and they are spreading all over the world. Although their physical forms have disappeared, their spirit has entered into the veins of humanity.

Holy Mother arrived in Calcutta on 27 February 1920 to enact the last part of her divine play. This portion lasted for 4 months and 21 days, and we shall watch it now with heavy hearts and tearful eyes.

The disciples of the Master watched his last act for 10 months and 21 days as he suffered from cancer. People ask: If they are divine beings, why do they suffer? The answer is simple: They take the sins of others upon themselves to deliver sinners from the results of their karma. For this reason they are called saviours. In Christianity, this is called "vicarious atonement." Christians believe that Christ suffered in order to take the sins of humanity upon himself. In Hinduism, the avatar is *patit-pavan*, the purifier of souls, and *kapal-mochan*, one who has the power to wipe out another's karma.

On 27 February 1920, Holy Mother arrived at her Calcutta residence after nine o'clock in the evening. There was no electricity in Udbodhan House at that time. When Yogin-ma saw Holy Mother in the light of a hurricane lantern, she exclaimed: "What sort of Mother have you brought here, Barada? Her complexion has become almost black. She is nothing but skin and bones. We never thought she was in such a bad state." The next morning, Swami Saradananda got all the news of the Mother's journey from Jayrambati to Calcutta. He learned that she had arrived late in Vishnupur because she had taken a break at Jaipur to feed the palanquin bearers. The swami was pleased, and commented: "Well, how can they carry the palanquin for 24 miles from Koalpara without eating something?"

Barada said: "The Mother herself gave that instruction. She also ate some puffed rice, as did we."

"Very well," Saradananda said, and he smiled.

Holy Mother's Medical Treatment

After Holy Mother arrived, Swami Saradananda and a medical team began her treatment with great hope and expectation. The Mother was not sent to a hospital, but all the best doctors in Calcutta were engaged one after another, and they came to Udbodhan House to treat her to the best of their ability. Holy Mother's burning fever rose and fell and rose again, but she silently endured it all without complaint. Saradananda was extremely concerned about the Mother's delicate health and carefully followed the doctors' advice. He and the Mother's disciples took turns feeding and nursing her with great love and care, thus fulfilling Ramakrishna's prophecy that many people would come to look after her.

The following is a chronology of Holy Mother's treatment:

February 28 to 11 March 1920: Dr. Jnanendra Nath Kanjilal, a disciple of the Mother, began to treat her. He was an allopathic doctor but he also practised homeopathy. He had treated the Mother previously, so he knew her system. Under his homeopathic treatment, her fever subsided on the fourth day, but on the seventh day it again rose to 101°. Saradananda called in a new doctor.

12 March to 7 April 1920: Kaviraj Shyamadas Vachaspati, a famous ayurvedic doctor, began to treat the Mother. His treatment showed some result after a week and the Mother had no fever for the next 15 days. The monks and devotees were joyful, and they began to visit the Mother again. Unfortunately, the fever returned. In addition, Vachaspati's treatment featured a decoction made from indigenous herbs that were so bitter that the Mother's whole mouth was affected. She lost her sense of taste and had no appetite. When Vachaspati was informed of this, he said that this was the only medicine prescribed in his ayurvedic scriptures for the Mother's disease. Saradananda turned to an allopathic doctor.

8 April to 30 April 1920: Dr. Bipin Bihari Ghosh, a cousin of Swami Premananda, began to treat the Mother. He was an allopathic doctor, but his medicine could not bring the Mother's fever down. On 10 April, the Mother had some stomach pain, and Dr. Haran Chandra Bandyopadhyay gave her a medicine that provided relief.

Dr. Bipin Bihari Ghosh left for Ghatshila, and during his absence, Dr. Durgapada Ghosh, Dr. Satish Chakrabarty, and Dr. Kanjilal treated the Mother. On 13 April Dr. Suresh Chandra Bhattacharya came to see the Mother. When Dr. Bipin Bihari Ghosh returned on 15 April, he changed the prescription after consulting with Dr. Durgapada Ghosh. Dr. Bipin Ghosh insisted on a Soamin injection for Holy Mother.

Saradananda then consulted with the medical team and decided to bring in a specialist, Dr. Pranadhan Basu, a famous allopathic doctor who was also a Bengali Christian.

On 28 April, the Mother's blood was tested by Dr. J.M. Dasgupta. No bacteria or kala-azar* cells were found.

---

*Kala-azar is a slow-progressing, fatal disease caused by a protozoan parasite of the genus *Leishmania*. In India, *Leishmania donovani* is the only parasite that causes this disease. Its main symptoms are a recurrent fever, loss of appetite, weakness, pallor, weight loss with progressive emaciation, and enlargement of spleen and liver. Anemia develops rapidly.

1 May to 31 May 1920: Dr. Pranadhan Basu arrived and began to treat the Mother with special care. He charged 16 rupees for a house call and 5 rupees for taxi fare. Saradananda called on Dr. Suresh Chandra Bhattacharya and Dr. Nilratan Sarkar to assist in diagnosing Holy Mother's illness. On 16 May, Dr. Basu declared that the Mother had kala-azar, or Black Fever, and suggested that she be given an injection. Ishanananda wrote: "In the evening, Dr. Nilratan Sarkar came and examined the Mother and also declared that she had kala-azar. Observing the Mother's physical weakness, he said it would not be possible for her to bear the strong injection of medicine. So the treatment continued as usual. Dr. Sarkar did not change her diet."[1] Dr. Shyamapada Mukherjee gave Holy Mother injections of Soamin on 22 and 25 May 1920.

Swami Ishanananda wrote a touching story about Dr. Pranadhan Basu:

In the evening Dr. Pranadhan Basu, a Christian physician, came to see Holy Mother. After examining her, the doctor went to Sharat Maharaj's room downstairs. [One afternoon Tara, an actress, brought the Mother gifts of fruits, sweets, and flowers.] Mother asked me: "Barada, you carry Tara's tuberose flowers, sweets, and the remaining things to the doctor's car. The Christian people love flowers." The doctor prescribed some medicine and a proper diet and received his fee and taxi fare from Lalit Babu, who was Mother's disciple. While getting into the car, the doctor saw baskets full of fruits, sweets, and flowers. He asked who had given all these things. Sharat Maharaj replied: "Mother has presented you with those things." Pleased, the doctor left Udbodhan.

The next day Dr. Basu was in the Mother's room in Udbodhan and saw Sri Ramakrishna's picture and other pictures on the altar. Curious, he asked Saradananda downstairs, "Who is this patient that I have been treating all these days?"

Saradananda: "You are treating Sri Ramakrishna's wife. She is the Mother of the Ramakrishna Order."

Dr. Basu: "Who provides all these expenses for the treatment?"

Saradananda: "Some generous devotees."

Dr. Basu: "My goodness! Why did you not tell me earlier?"

After prescribing medicine and diet, the doctor was about to leave, and Sharat Maharaj offered money as usual for his fee and taxi fare. The doctor humbly said: "You have made your life blessed by serving her all through your life with steadfast devotion. Please allow me to serve her a little in the last part of my life." He said this with great feeling from his heart. From that day on, Dr. Basu never took any money for his visits to the Mother. Even when Dr. Bipin Ghosh took over the treatment, Dr. Basu came regularly to Udbodhan and joined in the discussion with the Mother's medical

Above: Rasbihari (Swami Arupananda) and Sarajubala Sen, the main recorders of Sarada Devi's gospel.
Below: Sarala (Pravrajika Bharatiprana), an attendant
of Sarada Devi and the first president of Sarada Math.

team. One day Dr. Basu wanted to know about Sri Ramakrishna, so Saradananda presented him a set of *Sri Ramakrishna Lilaprasanga* [*Sri Ramakrishna and His Divine Play*].[2]

1 June to 17 July 1920: The allopathic treatment had failed, and Saradananda wrote in his diary on 1 June 1920: "Doctors seem to have come to their tether's end with regard to the case of Holy Mother. So Kaviraj* Rajendra Nath Sen was called in today and given charge of her case."[3] Kaviraj Shyamadas was not well, so Kaviraj Rajendra Sen and Kaviraj Kalibhusan Sen took over the Mother's case and began ayurvedic treatment. Kaviraj Shyamadas later returned to join the medical team. Shyamadas's student, Ramchandra Mallick, came every day and prepared medicine for Holy Mother.

18 July to 20 July 1920: Dr. Kanjilal treated Holy Mother with homeopathic medicine during the Mother's last few days.

Saradananda engaged Sarala (later Bharatiprana) as the main nurse for the Mother, and she was helped by Mandakini, Golap-ma, Yogin-ma, some girls from Nivedita's School, and the Mother's monastic attendants, including Ishanananda, Shantanana, Saradeshananda, and Arupananda. Sarala recalled:

> Within a couple of days of the Mother's arrival from Jayrambati to Udbodhan, Sharat Maharaj appointed me to serve her. Seeing the Mother's health deteriorating day by day, I was pained and sometimes I cried. One day I said to the Mother, "Mother, if you leave, I shall not live anymore." She replied: "Surely, my child, you will come to me in the end. But you will have to do some of my work, before you return to me."
>
> Radhu and her son, Nalini, Surabala, Maku, and others had come to Calcutta with the Mother. The Mother had been fond of Maku's son Neda, who died some 10 months previously. Because seeing Maku might remind the Mother of his death and cause her pain, Maku and Nalini did not want to stay at Udbodhan. Sharat Maharaj arranged for them to stay at the home of Balaram's family.
>
> The Mother had a high temperature every day, and eventually that fever turned into kala-azar. I used to feed her, make her bed, give her medicine, and perform other personal services. Mandakini helped me. Sharat Maharaj brought all the best doctors of Calcutta to treat the Mother. Apart from medical treatment, there were rituals and japa-yajna performed in Udbodhan to counteract ominous influences. Despite all kinds of treatment and nursing, however, the Mother was becoming weaker and more emaciated day by day. She had lost all taste for food and could not eat

* "Kaviraj" is an honorific title used for practitioners of ayurvedic medicine.

properly. From the middle of June, she was almost bedridden. In spite of her ill health, one day she looked at my arms and said: "Sudhira has given you three thin bangles, which I don't like. Let me get well; I shall have four thick bangles made for each of your arms." I told her: "That will be fine, Mother. First get well soon, and then I shall be happy."

One day she remarked: "If I had a small stick, I could go to the bathroom while supporting myself on it." The next day, it was found that someone had left a stick in the corner of the room. It was just the right size and the Mother used it to get to the bathroom.

The Mother's temperature began to rise. She was having chills and fever two or three times a day. She was really weak. One day she said to me: "Now I find I can't get to the bathroom on my own anymore. I shall have to manage everything in my room. Please put the Master's shrine in another room. Remove the cot from my room and make the bed on the floor." [On 17 June 1920] the Master's shrine was moved to a room on the third floor. The Mother was having a terrible burning sensation all over her body, so Sister Sudhira arranged for the girls of Nivedita's School to come to the Mother and fan her by turns. Bani, Gita, Kanak, Shiva, and others fanned the Mother from morning until evening, and at night, Aunt Prafulla and Sister Chapala fanned her.

At that time the Mother was under ayurvedic treatment, and her food was cooked with firewood. The Mother did not relish food at all. Every day she ate a little poppy seed preparation, and she liked āmrul [a kind of sour spinach] chutney. Fresh āmrul spinach came from Belur Math every day. She ate very little rice. The ayurvedic doctor said that the Mother could have any food she liked. The more milk she could drink, the more strength she would gain. But an equal amount of water should be added to the milk. Then it should be boiled over firewood until the water portion was evaporated. We served that milk to the Mother. Her hands and feet were swollen, so her food was cooked without salt. We kept some powdered rock salt in a glass container that we mixed with her food before she ate. During her meals, we set several pillows on the bed for her to recline upon, and put a towel on her lap. Her food plate was on the floor, and I fed her a little at a time. Sometimes the Mother could eat by herself holding a small bowl in her left hand. But because of her weakness, she could not hold the bowl long.

I would feed milk to the Mother and check her temperature with a thermometer. Sometimes she refused to drink her milk. At that time I would say, "Shall I call Sharat Maharaj?" Then like a little girl, she drank the milk. Her last serving of milk was at 11 o'clock at night. One night she flatly refused to take the milk. I said to her, "Shall I call Maharaj?" She said: "Call your Maharaj. I shall not drink the milk." Everyone had gone to bed, so I did not call Sharat Maharaj. As soon as I came back to the Mother's room, she said, "Did you not call him?" I went to his room and made a little noise near his head. He immediately got up. I told him everything, and he came to the Mother's room and stood near her head. There was an oil lamp inside the room and a hurricane lantern outside.

The Mother asked, "Has Sharat come?"

I replied: "Yes, Mother. He is standing near your head."

Mother: "Come, my son. Come and sit down." She said: "You see, my son, she called you at this time and gave you so much trouble."

Sharat Maharaj gently caressed the Mother's head for a while and then asked, "Mother, will you drink a little now?" When the Mother said "yes," Maharaj suggested, "Let Sarala feed you."

Mother said: "No, I won't drink from her hand. She only says day and night, 'Mother, eat; Mother, eat.' And she puts a stick* in my armpit. She has learned only those two things. I won't eat from her hands. You feed me."

Maharaj's hands were shaking and he became nervous. I decided, however, that I would not feed the Mother. Let Maharaj feed her. When the Mother talked about me to Maharaj, I was hurt but I kept a smile on my face. I brought the hurricane lamp near the bed and poured milk into the feeding cup. Maharaj began to feed her the milk little by little. Then he said, "Mother, please take your time and then drink again [*Ma, ektu jiriye khan*]."

Mother said: "See, how sweet his words are — 'Mother, take your time and then drink again!' Can't they talk like that?"

When the Mother had finished drinking, Maharaj dropped the mosquito curtain, tucked it under her mattress, and said, "Mother, let me go now."

Mother said: "Yes, my son. Ah, how much trouble I have given you this night. Please go and sleep now, my son. Durga! Durga!"

Previously the Mother had worn a long veil in front of Sharat Maharaj and she seldom talked to him directly, which had hurt his feelings. Sometimes he would say with a smile: "It is as if I am her father-in-law!" In those days the daughter-in-law wore a veil in front of her father-in-law. Later Sharat Maharaj said: "With a view to removing my pain and wounded feelings, the Mother took my service that way."

The next day I said to Sharat Maharaj: "It seems that the Mother is a little irritated with me. I shall no longer give her the milk or check her temperature with the thermometer. But I shall arrange everything from behind the scenes."

Sharat Maharaj: "But you will have to feed the main meal."

I said: "Yes, Maharaj, I shall feed the Mother solid food and do other things. Let someone else give her the milk and use the thermometer."

That day passed and the Mother watched everything. The next morning I finished my work and then I said to Mandakini: "My clothes are dirty.

* Referring to the thermometer.

I am going to the boarding house at Nivedita's School to hand over these clothes for washing. After my return, I will feed the Mother lunch." When I left, the Mother asked Mandakini, "Where has Sarala gone?"

Learning that I had gone to the boarding house, she said: "Has Sarala then left, being mad at me?"

Mandakini: "No, Mother, Sarala is not mad at you. She has gone to give her clothes for washing. She will be back to feed you your lunch."

Mother: "No, Sarala must be mad at me and has left."

When I returned, Mandakini told me everything. As soon as I entered the room, the Mother asked me to come near and then said: "My daughter, are you angry with me?"

"No, Mother, why should I be angry with you?" I replied.

She said: "Then why are you not giving me milk and putting the stick under my armpit? Look, my child, sometimes I am a little irritated from suffering constantly with this disease. Sometimes I say something, but I do not mean it. Don't be angry with my words, my child." Saying so, she put my head on her chest and showed her affection. I then cried.[4]

During her prolonged illness, Holy Mother developed a repulsion towards food. She did not relish the doctors' diet and her food intake was very small. She used to eat a small quantity of rice for lunch. One day Dr. Kanjilal was present when the Mother was eating. Seeing the big quantity of rice on the plate, he told Sarala in front of the Mother: "You should not serve the Mother. Tomorrow I shall bring two nurses to serve her. You need not do anything."

The Mother heard the doctor and told Sarala later: "Ha! Does he think that I will take service from those girls with boots on? It is not possible. You serve me as usual. Why does Kanjilal make so much fuss over my eating rice? Do I relish rice? He does not know." Within a few days, the Mother completely stopped eating rice. One day she said to Sarala: "Just see, the other day Kanjilal was annoyed at my taking rice. From that day on my desire to eat rice has disappeared."[5]

Sometimes the Mother would call Sharat Maharaj and complain like a little girl: "My son, I can't take this bitter medicine anymore. You rub my back with your cold hand."[6] Thus the Mother took some personal service from Swami Saradananda.

Shanti Swastyayana, a Ritual to Remove Obstacles and Bring Peace

When human efforts fail, people resort to divine help. When Holy Mother's medical treatment was not bearing any result, Saradananda had the Mother's horoscope examined by some noted astrologers.[7] They suggested performing the traditional Shanti Swastyayana, a kind of ritual and prayer to remove obstacles and bring physical, mental, terrestrial, and supernatural peace. Accordingly, Saradananda instructed Swami Vishweswarananda to perform this ritual for 15 days (from 14 to 28 May) in a room on the third floor of Udbodhan House.

Vishweswarananda worshipped five forms of the Divine Mother — Kali, Tara, Bhuvaneswari, Chinnamasta, and Kamala. He also worshipped five planets in order to propitiate them. Moreover, Saradananda arranged the recitation of the Chandi at the Siddheshwari temple in Baghbazar.[8] In addition to performing these rituals, the Mother's devotees and disciples prayed and repeated mantras for her recovery.

Swami Saradeshananda later wrote:

> Apart from medical treatments, there were performances of rituals propitiating the deities, stars, and planets, and there was a homa fire for the recovery of the Mother. Sometimes she felt a little better, but there was no lasting effect. Every day a monk [Saradeshananda] brought fresh flowers and spotless bel leaves from Belur Math for the ritual and homa, and fresh lemons for the Mother. One morning when Saradeshananda arrived at the shrine of Udbodhan, he found that Kapil Maharaj [Swami Vishweswarananda] was very much disturbed. The *ghat* in which he was performing the special ritual had all of a sudden sprung a leak that morning. Everyone was sad and anxious. They replaced it with a new one, but unfortunately that one also was leaking. Kapil Maharaj hurriedly went to a shop and bought a new one after carefully examining it. After cleaning and filling it with water, it was placed on the altar. Thus, the worship was delayed. This day they were having a special worship and homa for the guardian deity of the Mother's destiny. This sudden mishap created deep concern in the minds of all. When a monk told the whole story to Yogin-ma, she said with a deep sigh: "Yes, my child. I understand it all. It is not the jar that has developed the leak; we have lost favour with fortune."[9]

When this ritual had no effect, some disciples earnestly prayed to Holy Mother: "Mother, if you say once, 'Let this disease be cured,' it will definitely go away."

The Mother replied: "Can I pray such a thing, my child? Whatever is the wish of the Master, that will happen. What more can I say? Whenever the Master takes me, I shall go."[10]

In addition, Holy Mother indicated to those close to her that she would soon depart from this world. One day when Gauri-ma came to see her, she said: "My time has come to go. When I die, keep a little relic of my body in your ashrama." Another day, she said to someone: "Do not grieve. I shall have to go."[11]

Towards the End

During her last pilgrimage in Varanasi, when Surabala had cursed her, "Sister-in-law, you die," the Mother remarked: "Surabala does not know that I am deathless." Holy Mother was not afraid of death at all. She silently forbore all suffering and continued to help others.

On the morning of 8 March 1920, Swami Brahmananda came to see Holy Mother. She was a little better. The Mother was silent and Brahmananda was sad and grave. This was his last visit; he left for Bhubaneswar on 26 March. On 19 March, Swamis Shivananda and Vijnanananda came from Belur Math. On 12 May, Swami Shivananda returned. The Chariot Festival was held on 18 June, and Swami Shivananda came again to see the Mother. Swami Ishanananda wrote: "Mahapurush Maharaj quite often came from Belur Math to Udbodhan by boat. He discussed the Mother's physical condition and treatment with Sharat Maharaj and then returned to the Math. He did not go upstairs to disturb the bedridden Mother because he did not want to make her feel uncomfortable."[12] Many monks from different centres of India visited the Mother during this period. Some slept in the courtyard due to the shortage of space.

As there was no electric fan or air conditioning in Udbodhan House, Holy Mother suffered from the summer heat. Her suffering was made worse by her fever and excessive bile secretion. Most of the time someone fanned her with a palm-leaf fan. Every day, Swami Shivananda selected some monks and sent them to Udbodhan House from Belur Math to serve the Mother although the Mother had sufficient attendants there.

Kaviraj Shyamadas noticed that the Mother's hands and feet were swollen. He changed the medicine and prescribed *punar-nava* spinach and āmrul spinach so that the Mother would get back her appetite. Those types of spinach were not available in Calcutta, but when the news reached Belur Math, the monks searched and found some in the flower garden of the monastery and in some other places. At Swami Shivananda's instruction, every morning a brahmachari crossed the Ganges to take fresh spinach to Udbodhan. The monk bowed down to the Mother, got news about her physical condition, and reported to Shivananda when he returned to Belur Math.[13]

Holy Mother's visitors were strictly restricted. Only the monks and close disciples and devotees could see her, and only from outside her room. No one was supposed to touch her feet. A few sincere people who came from far away saw the Mother after getting permission from Saradananda.

Sometimes it is wrong to keep a patient isolated in a room because that makes the patient more depressed. If a patient is surrounded by loved ones, that patient feels joy and hope inside, and knows there are people who care for him or her. Sometimes we think that patients should not talk because it will make them weaker. Of course there are some visitors who talk about worldly things or about their problems and those kinds of people make the patient tired and bored. These sorts of visitors should be barred. But it is good for patients to talk to those whom they love and with whom they are well acquainted. They relieve the patients' suppressed pain and agony.

Saradeshananda had lived with the Mother as an attendant for a long time in Jayrambati, and she was very fond of him. There was no room for him to stay at Udbodhan House, so he travelled from Belur Math to Udbodhan every day to see her. After seeing her, he bowed down to the Master's image in her room, prayed to him for the Mother's recovery, and returned to Belur Math. He had a great desire to talk to her and serve her during this critical time. One day at noon, the swami went upstairs on an errand and peeped through the slightly opened door. The Mother saw him and called him inside. She asked her female attendant to give him the fan and then leave them alone. The doctor had instructed that she sit reclining on a bolster for an hour after lunch and then lie down to sleep. Saradeshananda began to fan her gently, and the Mother talked to him from time to time. She broke her drowsiness talking to her dear disciple. The whole of Udbodhan House was quiet because most people were resting after lunch. Holy Mother told Saradeshananda that despite all kinds of treatment, there had been no good results so far. He consoled her: "Mother, you will be all right by the grace of the Master. Please don't worry."

There was no sign of any sorrow or worry in the Mother's eyes, face, or words. Seeing her disciple's sad face, the Mother pressed her foot with a finger and said, "Look, here is a pitting edema." The swami looked at the hollow on the Mother's foot intently. Then the Mother said, "My son, you check with your own finger."

Saradeshananda knew that he was not supposed to touch the Mother's feet. However, because the Mother was asking him, he touched the hollow lightly. Not satisfied, the Mother said with a smile, "My son, press it hard and check for yourself." So he pressed hard on the Mother's foot and he saw the pitting edema. The way the Mother looked at the hollow in her foot, it seemed as if it were not her foot but someone else's. It took a long time for that hollow to vanish because of her anemia and edema. Then the Mother changed the topic and talked about other things. After an hour, the Mother lay down and slept for a short while. The swami continued to fan her. When she woke up, she wanted to rinse her mouth. The swami brought a pan and water. There was a half-chewed betel roll in her mouth, which she spit out first and then rinsed her mouth. The swami took the pan outside on the veranda and washed it. Just then it struck him that he had lost something valuable that day — the Mother's prasad.

Holy Mother then wanted to drink some water and the swami gave her a glass, but it was difficult for her to swallow. He rubbed her back gently with his left hand and rubbed below her throat with his right hand. Holy Mother looked at her disciple graciously and drank slowly. The disciple was overjoyed that the Mother had fulfilled his desire by taking personal service from him.

Later that afternoon, Holy Mother was seated on her bed when an attendant came and asked her something. The Mother gave Saradeshananda a key and instructed him to take some money from the tin box in which she used to carry the picture of the Master. Many memories flooded the swami's mind. When at four o'clock another attendant came to take over the duty, Saradeshananda left with a heavy heart.[14]

One afternoon in the middle of March 1920, Lakshmi, Ramlal, and Ramlal's daughter Krishnamayi came to see Holy Mother. They were on their way to attend a festival at the Archanalay in Entally. Ramlal bowed down to the Mother and then went downstairs to meet Saradananda. Lakshmi entertained the Mother and her companions by singing and acting, performing the way she used to in front of the Master at Dakshineswar. In the course of conversation, Lakshmi raised the issue of the future temple at the Master's birthplace and the family property in Kamarpukur. Holy Mother described her proposal to Lakshmi, who related it to Ramlal and Saradananda. Both of them approved her plan for the future temple at Kamarpukur (*See Chapter 24 for details*). Holy Mother was always courteous and loving towards the Master's relatives. After they left, the Mother said to Ishanananda: "While talking to Lakshmi I forgot to give her a sari and some money. You go to Entally and see the festival at Archanalay, and then give this cloth and money to Lakshmi. They decorate the Master beautifully at Archanalay."[15] Ishanananda followed the Mother's order.

We have mentioned in Chapter 20 that the place where Holy Mother was born was purchased from her three brothers in the early part of 1920. Each of them received a fair price for the land plus 100 rupees extra. In February 1920, Holy Mother requested that a well be dug in the southeast corner of that plot, and then she left for Calcutta. Swami Parameswarananda was the caretaker of Holy Mother's house in Jayrambati. He could not figure out exactly where the Mother was born, so he wrote to her at Udbodhan House: "Mother, we are unable to pinpoint the spot of your birth. It would be wonderful if you could tell us how we can determine that spot."

She wrote back from Calcutta: "When I was born, a Bagdi woman of Jayrambati was present. She is still alive. If you ask her, she will be able to locate the exact spot where I was born."

Swami Parameswarananda recalled: "This Bagdi woman lived in the southern part of Jayrambati village. We found her and asked her about the Mother's birthplace. That old lady said, 'If you give me five rupees then I shall tell you.' When we agreed to pay her the money, she said: 'Saru [Sarada] was not born in this place.* Saru was born in a thatched hut where Bhavini's** kitchen and cowshed exist now.' This statement created confusion. When I informed Swami Saradananda of this, he wrote to me, 'If that plot of land is available, please try to buy it.'"[16] This land was purchased after the Mother's passing away by paying 300 rupees each to Prasanna, Kali, and Surya (the Mother's cousin).[17] Holy Mother's temple was built there and dedicated in 1923 by Swami Saradananda.

Last Spiritual Ministry

Although Holy Mother was gravely ill, she continued to bestow grace on seekers of God.

In April 1920, Priyangbada Majumdar came from Mymensingh (now in Bangladesh) with her relative Durgesh Das to see the Mother. When the Mother learned that she had come from such a distance, she initiated her from her bed, despite her attendant's protests.[18]

Nalinikanta Basu was a disciple of the Mother, and his wife Chapala wanted initiation. Holy Mother had earlier asked her to wait. They lived in Jessore (now in Bangladesh). In May, Chapala realized that the Mother was not well, so she talked to Lakshmi, the Master's niece, who agreed to give her initiation. When Chapala reported this to the Mother, she said: "I shall initiate you. The husband and wife should have the same guru." When her attendant objected, the Mother said, "Look, she has come from

---

*Meaning the plot of land that had been purchased from Holy Mother's brothers.
**Bhavani was one of Holy Mother's maternal cousins.

such a distance!" In the middle of May 1920, the Mother initiated Chapala without any formality. Chapala at first thought that perhaps Holy Mother had not initiated her properly. Immediately the Mother said: "My daughter, go to the shrine and bow down to the Master. Don't worry. You will achieve everything from this initiation." All doubts were dispelled from her mind, and she returned home with a joyful heart.[19]

God makes everything favourable for those who are sincere and who long for God. Binaybala Sen had heard about Ramakrishna and Holy Mother in her husband's home in Dhaka (now in Bangladesh). Knowing that the Mother was in Calcutta, she came to her father's house in South Calcutta. After a long search, she reached Udbodhan House one afternoon. At that time no attendant was guarding Holy Mother's door, so she went straight upstairs. When Holy Mother saw Binaybala, she said: "My child, you have come to me for the mantra. Go to the bathroom. Wash your hands and feet and come to me."

Binaybala said, "Mother, I have not brought anything for initiation."

Holy Mother replied, "You don't need all those things." Holy Mother then initiated Binaybala.

One day towards the end of the Mother's life, Binaybala came to see the Mother. Again there was no attendant with her. When Binaybala entered the Mother's room, she said: "My daughter, you have come. Sit down. I am very ill; perhaps this body will not last long. My attendants may come at any time. My feet are aching. Give a little massage to my feet." Binaybala was overwhelmed by the chance to serve Holy Mother.[20]

Mahamaya Mitra, a sister of Kalipada Ghosh, had met Ramakrishna and had free access to the Mother. One day she brought Hiranmayi Ghosh, her nephew's wife, to the Mother. When Hiranmayi approached the Mother for initiation, she recommended that she have initiation from Lakshmi. However, when Hiranmayi tearfully bowed down to the Mother, Holy Mother put her hand on her head and whispered the Ishta mantra into her ear.[21] Thus till the end the Mother bestowed grace upon the sincere seekers of God.

Swami Ishanananda wrote: "Towards the end, the Mother could not sit long because of her weakness. But I saw her repeating her mantra while she was lying down."[22] The compassionate Mother repeated the mantra for the welfare of her children.

Many devotees, disciples, and newcomers wanted to see the Mother, but Swami Saradananda strictly restricted her visitors. One day a devotee went to bow down to Holy Mother, but then he grabbed her feet and put them on his chest. "What is this?" Holy Mother cried out. Her attendant immediately took that devotee downstairs. Another day an unknown woman came and begged Saradananda to allow her to see Holy Mother. Observing her earnestness, the swami asked a monk to escort her to the Mother and then bring her back downstairs. That monk called a brahma-chari to take the woman upstairs and then got involved with his own duties. The woman went upstairs on her own and grabbed the Moth-er's feet, beginning to cry. Yogin-ma shouted out, "Sharat, whom have you sent?" Immediately a monk went upstairs and brought that woman downstairs. Golap-ma commented: "It is easy to worship a stone image of God because it does not talk. But it is difficult to worship the human-God, who speaks."[23] Later on it was decided that the devotees could see her only from outside of her room.

Holy Mother's Bereavement

As day and night rotate, so do happiness and misery, laughter and tears, birth and death. This is the way God has created the world. He does not want human beings to have only happiness or only misery, so they are tossed about by these pairs of opposites. After going through these experiences, people realize that permanent happiness is not possi-ble in this world; it is possible only in God. The Upanishad says: *Bhumaiva sukham nālpe sukhamasti* — Bliss is only in the Infinite and not in the finite. Then human beings finally turn their minds to the Infinite God.

Like other human beings, Holy Mother experienced joy and grief. When we observe the Mother crying after losing her dear ones, we find consolation and strength in similar situations thinking of her human aspect. We also understand the teaching of the Gita (2:27): "Death is cer-tain for the born. Rebirth is certain for the dead. You should not grieve for what is unavoidable."

Towards the end of her life Holy Mother endured the loss of three of her dearest ones: Latu, or Swami Adbhutananda; Ramakrishna Basu, the son of Balaram Basu; and her third brother, Barada.

Holy Mother was very fond of Latu, the Master's guileless and unso-phisticated disciple, whom she had known since her early days in Dakshineswar. At that time, the Mother was performing all of the house-hold work by herself. To ease her burden, the Master engaged Latu to help her cook by making dough, cleaning, and cutting vegetables. Many years later, during Holy Mother's last illness in Udbodhan House, Shantananda came to visit from Varanasi, where Latu had been staying. Holy Mother asked him and others about Latu, and she was told that he was not well. Latu had developed a small blister on his right ankle that developed into gangrene. The doctors performed surgery, but Latu died on 24 April 1920. Saradananda forbade everyone from telling Holy Mother of his death given her critical condition. However Golap-ma could not keep anything secret. When the Mother asked about Latu one day, Golap-ma told her, "Latu passed away 10 days ago." At this, the Mother burst into tears. That afternoon her temperature rose.

Ramakrishna Basu was a disciple of Holy Mother, and his family greatly supported the Ramakrishna Order. Holy Mother stayed in their house on many occasions, and many monks also lived there from time to time. Ramakrishna Basu fell ill with appendicitis. Though the best doctors treated him, it was of no avail. He died on 14 May 1920. Golap-ma reported this to the Mother and again she cried. Saradananda wrote in his diary: "H.M's fever rose to 100°. She had a bad night with indigestion and wind etc. all due to hearing the sad news about Ram."[24]

Holy Mother learned that her brother Barada was seriously ill with pneumonia, so she sent a postal money order for his treatment. He died on 20 June 1920. Before Holy Mother learned this, she said to her attendant: "Is Barada gone? I saw him standing near the railing looking at me."[25] She asked Brahmachari Barada to send more money for her brother's treatment. Saradananda forbade him to send the money, and also forbade him to tell Holy Mother of her brother's death. Observing Barada's delay, the Mother forcefully ordered him to send the money order that very day. Golap-ma then told the Mother that her brother had passed away. She cried out and began shaking. Her attendants fanned her and rubbed her eyes and mouth with wet hands. Saradananda was very concerned. Yogin-ma consoled her, saying: "Mother, your temperature has been high for the last few days, so Sharat did not inform you. He was waiting to tell you when your temperature went down. Brahmachari Barada sent that 20 rupees to Kishori [Swami Parameswarananda] for the *shrāddha* ceremony."[26] The Mother cried off and on for a couple of days and asked for some more money to be sent for the *shrāddha*.

These bereavements greatly affected Holy Mother's health. Her condition deteriorated rapidly and her temperature rose to 102° during the afternoons, causing a burning sensation and restlessness. She began to say: "Take me to the bank of the Ganges. I shall feel cool there."[27] Accordingly, Saradananda began to search for a suitable house near the Ganges in Cossipore or Dakshineswar. Someone also suggested taking the Mother to Varanasi. However, the doctors forbade them from moving her in her present condition. Her attendants then began to bring ice, cover it with a towel, and place her hands on it. This gave her a little relief.

Sarajubala's Reminiscences

Holy Mother was very fond of and free with Sarajubala. She visited Holy Mother five times during her last illness, and she recorded these visits in her reminiscences. Here we reproduce some excerpts:

24 March 1920: Holy Mother was extremely unwell, having been in the grip of malarial fever for a long time. I prostrated myself before her, and she blessed me by placing her hand on my head. She asked me how I was. I offered her a little money for her expenses, and she accepted it. At the sight of her emaciated body, I lost all power of speech. I looked at her face wistfully and thought, "Alas, how pale and weak her body is."

The Mother was so weak that she felt it painful even to utter a word. I was seated on the floor. In the meantime, Rasbihari Maharaj came up and asked me not to talk much with her; but the Mother now and then asked me about various things. I gave her short replies.

30 March 1920: I went to pay my respects to Holy Mother after five or six days. She had had no fever for the previous two or three days, but she was much worried on account of Radhu and her incapacity to look after her little child. The Mother lay down on her bed and asked me to rub her feet. While rubbing them, I asked her whether I could speak to her about something and if it would inconvenience her. The Mother said: "No, not at all. Say what you want to."

I told her about some experiences I had had, and at this the Mother remarked: "Ah, my daughter, can one experience such bliss every day? Everything is real. Nothing is untrue. The Master is all — he is Prakriti, he is Purusha. Through him you will achieve everything."

I: "Mother, one day while doing japa with great concentration, a long period of time passed quite unobserved. I therefore had to get up and attend to my household duties without carrying out the other items of spiritual practices that you had instructed me to do. Was it wrong on my part to have done so?"

Mother: "No, no. There is nothing wrong in it."

I: "Someone told me that while meditating at dead of night, he hears a mystic sound. Generally he experiences it as coming from the right side of the body; sometimes, when the mind is working on a lower plane, it comes also from the left side."

Mother (*after thinking a while*): "Indeed, the sound comes from the right side. Only when there is body-consciousness does it come from the left side. Such things happen when the power of the kundalini is awakened. The sound that comes from the right side is the real one. In time, the mind itself becomes the guru. To pray to God and meditate on God for even two minutes with full concentration is better than doing so for long hours without it."

I did not feel inclined to question the Mother on the significance of body-consciousness, for the Mother was not doing well.

I was about to leave. Instantly the Mother raised her head from the pillow and said, "Well, my daughter, I have raised my head." She did so because it is not the custom for a devotee to bow down to one lying down. When I bowed down, she said: "Come again. Come a little earlier in the evening. Can't you finish your household duties a little earlier and come?"

Then, uttering the name of Durga as a prayer for my safety, she bade me adieu. Even after I had come to the veranda, I heard her uttering the name of Durga in a compassionate tone. What unbounded love! So long as we were with her, we forgot all the sorrows and suffering of worldly life.

Undated: The Mother's illness showed no signs of improvement. Her body was getting weaker and weaker. I went to see her one afternoon. She was about to go for her evening wash. She asked me to help her get up. She said, "I am getting a fever very often, and the body has become very weak." She got up with great effort. Then she said to me: "Look, someone has kept a stick near the door. I had been thinking for a few days that if I could get a stick, then I could move myself a little with its support. Look, the Master has just supplied this one for me." The Mother showed the stick to me. Then she said with a smile: "I asked everyone who had left this stick here. But no one could tell me."

Undated: Another day I went and heard the Mother's monastic disciples saying: "This time when the Mother gets well, we won't allow anyone to get initiation from her. Mother, you have all this suffering because you are taking the effects of others' sins." At this, the Mother said with a smile: "Why? Did the Master come this time to eat only rasagollas?" Everyone was speechless. Mother, how wonderfully you expressed your compassion through these few words!

14 April 1920: The evening aratrika [vesper service] in the shrine was over. The Mother was feverish. Rasbihari Maharaj was rubbing her hands and Brahmachari Barada her feet. They were taking her temperature, and the Mother was lying with her eyes closed. I stood by her side. Once the Mother asked, "Who is there?" Rasbihari Maharaj replied to her in a low voice, "Saraju is here." I heard that the temperature was 100.1°.

Sister Sudhira was giving a treat to the girls of Nivedita's School, as it was the Bengali New Year's Day. Sarala, the disciple who was attending the Mother, had gone to the school. The Mother asked Brahmachari Barada to bring Sarala back, for she had to feed Radhu's child. It was not yet time to feed the child, but as he was crying, Radhu wanted to feed him just then. The Mother tried to dissuade her. This only enraged Radhu, who began to abuse the Mother. She said: "May you die, and I shall light your funeral pyre!" We were deeply pained to hear this. The Mother was so badly ill, and Radhu was abusing her in such a fashion at that time! Radhu, however, went on shouting out many more abusive words. Such conduct on her part was seen quite frequently. The Mother, who had unbounded patience, had put up with such behaviour on all occasions. But this time, because of her protracted illness, she got annoyed and remarked: "You will realize the consequences of your words later! What a sad plight you will be in after my death; you will understand! I do not know how many kicks and thrashings with broomsticks are in store for you! Today is the first day of the year. I sincerely wish that you may die first, and then I shall follow you with a peaceful mind."

At this, Radhu became still more irritated and abusive. After a while Sarala arrived and fed the child. The experience of that day cast a gloom over my mind. The Mother said to me: "Fan me, my child. Radhu's torment is burning my whole body." Then she asked me to rub her feet. Meanwhile Rasbihari Maharaj entered and began to drop the mosquito curtain. So I took leave of her, and the Mother said by way of bidding farewell, "Come." This was the last command and last word I heard from her.[28]

During the Mother's last illness, my husband used to visit her every day. One day he said to her, "Mother, will you not give me something?" She asked him to call on Sharat Maharaj. When Sharat Maharaj arrived, she asked him to bring scissors. When he brought the scissors, the Mother took them and cut a few hairs from her head. She then said to Sharat Maharaj: "There is an empty casket in that niche. Please bring it to me." When Maharaj brought the casket to her, she put those hairs in it. She handed it over to my husband and said: "This container is a *siddha-yantra* — holy and auspicious. You can worship all gods and goddesses on it. There is no necessity to perform worship with pomp. The worship should be sattvic. Repeat your Ishta-mantra and give a bath to the container with Ganges water. If that is not available, then use the tap water. Perform mental worship."

My husband took the container on his head and came home barefooted. According to the Mother's instruction, he worshipped that holy container all through his life. The Mother told me and my husband: "Those who have taken refuge in the Master will never suffer from lack of plain food and clothing." This siddha-yantra of the Mother is the refuge of our family. The Mother and the Master provided not only for our food and clothing but also took responsibility for our spiritual life.[29]

Mahamaya Cuts Her Maya

Attachment invariably brings pain. Ordinary people are attached to their family and friends, money and possessions, home and other things, so it is painful for them to leave this world when the God of Death summons them. Ramakrishna explained: "Entangled creatures, attached to worldliness, talk only of worldly things at the hour of death. What will it avail such men if they outwardly repeat the name of God, take a bath in the Ganges, or visit sacred places? If they cherish attachment to the world within themselves, it must show up at the hour of death. While dying they rave nonsense. Perhaps they cry out in a delirium, 'Turmeric powder! Seasoning! Bay leaf!' While dying they think of their wives and children, and weep, 'Alas! What will happen to them after my death?'"[30] That is why ordinary people marvel when they see the death of a death-less One, an illumined soul.

Holy Mother began to make herself ready for her departure from the world stage by cutting off all ties and attachments. Swami Saradananda once remarked about the Mother's greatness and power: "I have never seen such attachment, and again I have never seen such detachment in my life."[31]

Brahmachari Gopesh (later Saradeshananda) described the Mother's spirit of detachment: "I was very much surprised to hear the Mother's remark about her dead brother. Just a few days earlier Uncle Baradaprasad had died. Holy Mother was extremely grief-stricken and cried profusely. But she overcame that grief very quickly. When I went to see her, she said to me without any emotion, 'My son, did you hear that Barada passed away?' At first I failed to understand whom she was talking about because it was beyond my imagination that she could relate the news of her dear brother's death without any grief. Noting my vacant look, she said: 'Fudi's [Kshudi's] father, from Jayrambati.' I was very sad to hear the news, but greater than my sadness was my astonishment at her lack of emotional attachment."[32]

The devotees observed that Holy Mother was becoming indifferent towards her relatives and family affairs. One day a devotee said to her: "Mother, your health has deteriorated badly. I have never seen your body so weak."

She replied: "Yes, my son, it has become very weak. It seems whatever work of the Master that was to be done by this body is over. Now the mind longs for him only, and nothing else. Just see, how much I loved Radhu, and how much I have done for her happiness and comfort; but now my mood has changed. When she comes near me, I feel disgusted. I think: why is she here trying to drag my mind down? The Master kept my mind down all these years with these family ties and attachments to his work. Otherwise, would it have been possible for me to stay in this world when he left?"[33]

Holy Mother was also very fond of Gauri-ma, as she lived with her for some time during her stay in Dakshineswar. The Mother initiated Gauri-ma's adopted daughter Durga, who later became Gauri-ma's successor and head of Sri Saradeshwari Ashrama. Towards the end, when the Mother was weak and had no inclination to talk, Gauri-ma and Durga visited the Mother every day on their way back to their ashrama after their bath in the Ganges. Swami Ishanananda wrote:

> Every day Gauri-ma would talk to the Mother and fan her a little. Today Gauri-ma went upstairs as usual and bowed down to the Master. But when she came to bow down to the Mother, she said: "Don't touch me. Why do you come every day to bother me? What for? What to see?" At this, Gauri-ma was shocked and she said in a pained voice: "Mother, you are ill and bedridden. We have no peace of mind. We want to be with you all the time, but we don't always find the leisure. So we come to see you once a day." The Mother replied: "What do you expect from me? I can't put up with any more irritation." Then observing Gauri-ma's sad face, the Mother said: "If you come, don't enter my room. Just look at me from outside the door. Don't make me talk."
>
> Gauri-ma was stunned and tears trickled from her eyes. The Mother did not say anything more. Gauri-ma remained speechless and left that day with tearful eyes. From the next day on, Gauri-ma sat every morning for an hour outside the Mother's room, watching the Mother and weeping silently. She then left after bowing down to her. The Mother noticed this but did not relent. Some days Gauri-ma and Durga would come to visit the Mother in the afternoon and leave after inquiring about her health.[34]

Holy Mother had not been able to get good drinking water in Jayrambati, so a devotee gave money to dig a well. The well was completed after Holy Mother had left for Calcutta. Swami Parameswarananda sent the first water taken from the well in a bottle to Calcutta through Brahmachari Hari. Holy Mother joyfully drank a little water from her birthplace. Hari said: "Mother, Brother Kishori has covered the floor of your room with concrete. The next time when you come to Jayrambati, you will not find any difficulty."

Holy Mother replied: "Why did Kishori remove the mud from my room and pave it with cement? I love my mud floor. What was the need to do all these things? Does Kishori think I will ever go there again? I won't live there anymore."[35] Thus she severed her connection to her sweet home, Jayrambati.

Now came Radhu's turn. Holy Mother decided to tear the last bond of maya. Some days before her passing away, she said to Radhu: "Look here, Radhu, I want you to return to Jayrambati. Don't stay here any longer." Then she told her attendant Sarala, "Tell Sharat to send her to Jayrambati."

Sarala asked: "Mother, why are you sending them to Jayrambati? Will you be able live without Radhu?"

Holy Mother said firmly: "Certainly. I have withdrawn my mind."

Sarala reported this to Yogin-ma and Swami Saradananda. Yogin-ma went to the Mother and said: "Mother, why are you asking Radhu and others to leave?"

Holy Mother replied: "Yogin, she shall have to live at Jayrambati hereafter. Hari is returning there. Send her and others with him. I have withdrawn my mind. I don't want her here anymore."

Yogin-ma objected: "Mother, don't say that. If you detach your mind, how shall we live?"

"Yogin, I have cut the chain of maya," Holy Mother responded. "No more of this."

Yogin-ma could not reply; she reported the whole thing to Swami Saradananda. He said with a deep sigh: "Now it will be impossible to keep the Mother on earth any longer. As she has detached herself from Radhu, there is no hope whatsoever." Sarala was there. He said to her: "See if you can direct her mind again to Radhu." But the effort was futile. Understanding their intention, the Mother clearly said: "Know once and for all that the mind which has been withdrawn will not come down again."[36]

Holy Mother's mind was soaring high to the Infinite, so the world of maya became distasteful to her. Swami Ishanananda recorded the Mother's mental state at that time:

The Mother said to me: "Why did Radhu, Nalini, and others not go to Jayrambati with Hari? You take them back to Jayrambati. None of them needs to stay here." When I informed Sharat Maharaj of this, he could not decide what to do. We could not figure out why the Mother was asking Radhu and others to be sent to Jayrambati, especially Radhu, whom she loved so much and could not bear separation from. Even while she was ill, she looked after Radhu and her son. The Mother was now so irritated with her nieces that Nalini and others were frightened to go near her. Helpless, Maku wept in a quiet corner. Nalini said: "If our presence hurts our aunt, we had better go away to our village. But I don't know what our village people will say. They will criticize us for leaving her at this time." Sharat Maharaj tried again to persuade the Mother and said: "Mother, these girls feel bad at the thought of going away when you are so ill. Let them stay a while; they will go back to Jayrambati when you recover a little."

The Mother persisted: "It would have been better if you had sent them away. All right, but let them not come near me. I do not want to see even their shadow. I have cut off all attachments."

Meanwhile it was necessary to send the brahmin woman, the caretaker for Radhu's son, back to Jayrambati. Yogin-ma suggested, "Let Barada go for a couple of days to take her home."

The Mother said: "How can the work here be done without Barada? Also, he is very young and won't be able to take her home carefully. Ask Rajen to take her home. Barada can teach weaving at Nivedita's School as his substitute for an hour every day. If he teaches in the late afternoon, it will not be much of an inconvenience." From the next day, according to the Mother's wish, I went to the Nivedita School for some days and showed the girls how to weave.

Like other days, after lunch I was one day alone with the Mother and stroking her feet. Radhu was sleeping in the next room with her son. Waking from his sleep, the boy crawled to the Mother's room. He came near her bed and was trying to climb on her chest. Seeing this, the Mother said: "I got rid of all attachments for you. Go. Go away. I have no attachment to any of you. You will not succeed anymore." Then the Mother said to me: "Barada, pick up this child and take him to the other room. I do not relish this any longer." I picked up the boy and took him to his grandmother.[37]

During one of her previous illnesses, Holy Mother had remarked: "Maybe I shall have to suffer again like this." Thus she indicated that she would be born again for the good of humanity. This time she created a bond of illusion with Radhu so that she would continue her divine play in this world after Ramakrishna's passing away. Holy Mother's last words to Radhu were: "I have cut the string. How can you bind me? Do you think I am a human being?"

Radhu later said to Akshaychaitanya: "I knew the Mother as my own aunt. I never knew that she was a goddess but thought she was a human being."[38] There is a saying, "One knows the value of a tooth only after one loses it." Afterwards Radhu tearfully understood whom she had lost.

A few days before she passed away, Holy Mother said to Arupananda, "As one tears a straw, I have torn my attachment for Radhu."

Arupananda said earnestly: "Mother, you can live if you wish."

"Who craves death?" came the quick reply. Holy Mother had surrendered her will fully to the Divine Will and seemed to be awaiting the Master's final call. Again and again she said, "I shall go when the call comes."[39]

Handing Over Responsibility

Holy Mother's condition was deteriorating quickly. Her body was thin and emaciated, and it appeared to melt into the bed. The physicians gave up hope and told Saradananda that those who wanted to see her should come soon. Monks and devotees began to flock to Udbodhan from far and near.

Five days before Holy Mother passed away, a woman called "Annapurna's Mother" came to see her. She stood at the door, as no one was allowed to enter the sickroom. When the Mother turned on her side, she saw Annapurna's Mother and motioned to her to come near. She came in, bowed down to the Mother, and said with tearful eyes: "Mother, what will happen to us?" In a feeble voice the compassionate Mother said to her: "Why should you be afraid? You have seen the Master. What should frighten you?" Then she added very slowly and softly: "Let me tell you something. My child, if you want peace, then do not look into anybody's faults. Look into your own faults. Learn to make the world your own. No one is a stranger, my child; the whole world is your own." This was Holy Mother's last message to suffering humanity.[40]

Sarala recalled: "Towards the end Holy Mother became like a little girl and would frequently say, 'Let me go, let me go.' One day she said to me, 'My child, it is time for me to go.' When Lalit Babu came to see her, the Mother said to her beloved disciple, 'Lalit, let me go.' Lalit Babu said: 'Mother, are we giving you too much trouble that you want to leave us?' The Mother replied: 'No, my son, how can you give me pain and trouble? Whatever work the Master assigned to me, that is done. What else?' Lalit said tearfully, 'Mother, if you depart, how shall we live in this world?' The Mother replied: 'Why should you be afraid, my son? The Master exists and he will look after you.'"[41] Thus the Mother reassured her disciples before leaving the world.

When the Master's altar was on the east side of her room, the Mother had slept with her head towards the Master. But when the shrine was shifted to the third floor, she lay with her head towards the Ganges, which was to the west. At about half-past eight in the morning, two or three days before the final day, Holy Mother asked Bibhuti Ghosh to call Saradananda. He went downstairs and said, "Maharaj, the Mother is calling you." "I am coming right now," said the swami. Bibhuti hurriedly went upstairs and saw that the Mother's eyes were wide open and unblinking. He told her that the swami was coming. She asked Bibhuti to fan her forcefully. Saradananda came in, knelt on the left side of the Mother's feet, and was about to stroke her hands when Holy Mother caught the swami's right hand under her left hand and said: "Sharat, I am leaving. I leave Golap, Yogin, and others behind. You look after them." Saying so, the Mother immediately withdrew her hand. Swami Saradananda controlled his tears with great effort, got up, tiptoed backward, and left the room.[42]

End of the Divine Play

Holy Mother enacted her divine play on this earth for 67 years and 7 months, and her main stages were Jayrambati, Kamarpukur, Dakshineswar, and Udbodhan House in Calcutta. Who were the main characters in her drama? Her noble parents, her greedy and selfish brothers, her dependent and helpless nieces, her unstable sister-in-law Surabala, and her difficult niece Radhu; Ramakrishna and his disciples, especially Vivekananda, Brahmananda, Yogananda, Trigunatitananda, Saradananda, Adbhuta-nanda, M., Girish, Nag Mahashay, and other devotees; her close compan-ions: Yogin-ma, Golap-ma, Gauri-ma, Gopal-ma, Lakshmi, and Nikunja Devi; her own disciples, including Arupananda, Ishanananda, Sarade-shananda, Parameswarananda, Keshavananda, Gauriswarananda, Vidy-ananda, Virajananda, Pravrajika Bharatiprana, Sarajubala, and Sudhira; her Western devotees: Nivedita, Sister Christine, Devamata, Josephine MacLeod, and Sara Bull; Sagar Santra, her robber father of Telo-Bhelo and his wife; her roofer Amzad, a bandit from Shiromanipur; the actresses Tarasundari and Tinkari; and even the minstrels Lalu and Haridas; the mailman Yogendra, and the watchman Ambika of Jayrambati. Blessed are these people and other nameless disciples and devotees who were the supporting actors and actresses of Holy Mother's divine drama. It is through their interaction and dialogue with Holy Mother that we are able to visualize her play vividly even after nearly a century.

Swami Arupananda, an attendant and disciple, described the Mother's last days:

> All efforts seemed to be futile. The Mother's disease advanced day by day. Her temperature would rise three to four times a day. The excessive bile secretion during the fevers gave her a terrible burning sensation. The Mother would say, "I would dip my body in the cold water of a pond covered with algae." We would place our hands on some ice and then pass them over her body. When her temperature was high, she sometimes lost outer consciousness. It was summer. I brought some ice from a dis-tance. When I returned, I saw that the Mother was restless because of the unbearable burning sensation. I covered that chunk of ice with a cloth and placed the Mother's hand on it. Getting some relief, the Mother cried out,

"O Rasbihari, where did you get such a wonderful thing?" Those who had cool bodies, the Mother would touch when she felt the burning sensation. After going through this prolonged illness, she became like a little girl. She was tired of lying down all the time. One morning she asked me to hold her and help her sit. Sarala was there. We put several pillows at her back and helped her to sit, and we passed our hands over her face, hands, and feet, which made her calm.

In the morning I used to collect information about the Mother's physical condition before I went to the office of the ayurvedic doctor. She never forgot to tell me, "Before you go, have your lunch, or it will be too late." When the ayurvedic doctors — Kaviraj Kalibhusan Sen, Kaviraj Ram Chandra Mallick, and Kaviraj Rajendra Nath Sen — visited her, she asked us to serve them refreshments — sandesh, mangoes, and other things. When Dr. Kanjilal, Dr. Durgapada Ghosh, and Dr. Shyamapada Mukhopadhyay came to check her condition, she inquired about their welfare. One day the Mother's two disciples from Arambagh — Prabhakar Babu and Manindra Babu — came to visit her. She talked to them with a feeble voice: "How are you, my children? Shall I live? I can't eat anything. I feel weak. My brother Barada has died." Then she asked, "Have you gotten any rain?"

Manindra Babu replied, "No, Mother, we did not get any rain."

The Mother asked, "Will you get prasad here?" Manindra Babu said, "Yes, Mother." Manindra Babu had sent tender palm fruits [which have a soothing effect] for the Mother through Ramani, a woman devotee. The Mother said: "I don't remember when Ramani came. I was not conscious because of the fever. Please tell her not to mind." When Swami Shantananda arrived from Varanasi, the Mother asked, "How is Latu?" She heard earlier that Latu Maharaj was not well. Latu Maharaj had died, but no one had told her.

Mandakini and Sarala served the Mother wholeheartedly. When the Mother was healthy, she was reluctant to accept anyone's service, so no one got a chance to serve her. One day after having her meal at 11 o'clock, the Mother was lying on her bed on her side. I began to fan her so that she could sleep comfortably. After five minutes, the Mother told me: "My son, no more fanning is necessary. Your hand is aching."

I said: "No, Mother, my hand is not aching. I shall stop when I have pain."

After a while the Mother said with closed eyes: "My son, your hand will get pain. Please stop. I am going to sleep." Still, when I did not stop, the Mother said: "My son, my sleep is not coming thinking that your hand will get pain. You stop fanning. Let me sleep without worry."

Finally I stopped fanning. The Mother was quiet. I did not get a chance to serve her for more than 10 minutes.[43]

The curtain of the last scene in the Mother's divine drama was about to drop. Kala-azar consumed her life slowly over a period of several months. The doctors lost hope. The devotees kept hope alive till the end, but no one can withstand Providence. Swami Ishanananda left a record of the Mother's last days:

Sister Sarala, Mandakini, Brother Rasbihari, and I were sharing the responsibility for the Mother's care. Mahamaya Mitra and the girls of the Nivedita School (Gadai, Malati, Sulata, Nandarani, Pakhi, Mira, and Sudhira) fanned the Mother by turns. Brother Rasbihari took care of the doctors and medicine. Someone brought fresh milk from Dr. Kartik's house at five o'clock in the morning, and I boiled that milk over a wood-burning stove, adding an equal amount of water and evaporating the water portion. According to the ayurvedic doctor's instruction, I prepared whey from some of the milk, and also barley for the Mother's diet. Generally my duty at noon was to be with the Mother and look after her. When the doctors came, she asked me to give them prasad. Sister Sarala prepared rice and administered the medicine and food at the right time. Mandakini washed the Mother's clothes, cleaned the utensils and room, and fanned her. M. sent his wife, Nikunja Devi, to serve the Mother. She helped in the kitchen and fanned the Mother in the evening. M. came to see the Mother every evening.

Holy Mother's childish petulance went on. One morning she said to me: "My son, don't go away from me. Always stay here. Sarala bothers me very much: always the same stick [thermometer] and the same word, 'eat.' I will not eat anything from her hand nor allow her to come near." She began to show this annoyance more and more. Sharat Maharaj was worried. In the morning he came to the Mother, sat near her bed, took her hand on his lap, and began to stroke her head and brush the hair away from her forehead. He said to her in a wheedling voice, as if she were a child: "Mother, Sarala is very much hurt. She will not put the stick under your arm again. This is your eating time. Who will feed you?" Sharat Maharaj said to me: "Barada, bring the milk in the feeding cup. This time I shall feed the Mother." The Mother said: "Why should you take the trouble? Barada will feed me. Bring the milk, Barada, I will drink it." As soon as I poured the milk into her mouth, the Mother gave a start: the milk was a little too hot. Lest Sharat Maharaj and I feel badly about it, she said: "Never mind, cool the milk a little. Barada can feed me very well." This mood of the Mother continued for a couple of days. Sharat Maharaj changed our duties. Sister Sarala prepared the food, and I and Mandakini fed her.

That noon Sharat Maharaj called me into his room and stroking my head tenderly told me: "Barada, you are very fortunate. Today the Mother on her own took the food from you and thus made you her real attendant.

Serve the Mother carefully. Learn all the details well from Sarala." At this time the Mother used to eat soft boiled rice, milk, boiled ripe mango, and sugar mashed together. After a couple of days when the Mother's mood became calm, we started to do our work as before.[44]

As it is impossible for the snow-clad mountain to lose its coolness, or the blazing fire to lose its heat, so it was unthinkable for Holy Mother to hurt anyone. Sarala mentioned earlier how she was hurt by the Mother and after a while how her wounded feeling melted away when the Mother took her head on her bosom as a blessing. Tears flowed from Sarala's eyes and she resumed her usual duties.

Towards the end, the Mother hurt Sarala's feelings a couple of times, which was extremely unusual for her. We do not know why, but we can guess. Perhaps Holy Mother was a little irritated by her prolonged illness; or, as Sarala was her main caretaker, the Mother wanted to eradicate her ego forever. Ramakrishna smashed M.'s ego so that he could be the recorder of his gospel. Perhaps the Mother hurt Sarala so that she could dive more deeply within her inmost self. Holy Mother knew that in the future Sarala would have a great responsibility — she would be the head of her Order, Sarada Math. Holy Mother had tremendous love for her and faith in her capabilities. In this world a person shares joy and success with those whom he or she loves most and also tries to release their stress and agony.

The Mother was tired of eating a bland diet and she lost the ability to taste anything. One day she asked her attendant to give her some puffed rice and fried gram, which she had eaten in her village as refreshments. The attendant obeyed the Mother's order, but informed Swami Saradananda about it. The swami knew that this food would be like poison to her, so he immediately went to the Mother. When she saw him, Holy Mother hid the bowl behind her back like a little girl. The swami told her, with folded hands, "Mother, I am begging you to give me that bowl." She handed it over without protest. For her own welfare, Saradananda took food out of her mouth, and this pained him greatly. After Holy Mother passed away, Saradananda overcame that sorrow by feeding Swami Brahmananda some puffed rice and fried gram.*

*Swami Bhumananda's eyewitness account: After the Mother's passing away, Swami Brahmananda came to visit Udbodhan House. Sharat Maharaj bowed down to Maharaj and said: "Maharaj, when the Mother was ill, one day she was about to eat puffed rice and fried gram. Hearing that news I went to her, begged that food from her, and did not allow her to eat it. Today I want to feed you puffed rice and fried gram, and thus I shall fulfill my wish of feeding the Mother. Maharaj said with a smile: "All right, bring puffed rice and fried gram and I shall eat it." (*continued*)

Swami Saradeshananda described Holy Mother during her last days:

The Mother's health had completely broken down. She could not move. The Master's altar had been removed from her room and she was lying on a mattress on the floor. We had all lost hope and were anticipating the worst at any moment. Early one evening I went to find that the Mother's women attendants had helped her to sit up and were supporting her. With their help, the Mother raised her hands and bowed down towards the Master. Her beautiful round arms, which had bestowed on us so many boons and assurances, were now reduced to mere skin and bones. I could not keep looking at them for long. Those hands by which the Mother had blessed her children, served prasad and food to them with love and affection — now what awful condition they were in! Those beautiful bangles, which the Mother had always worn, had now become so loose that they were tied to her wrists with strings. Seeing this, Balaram's daughter had a pair of bangles made, fit for a small girl, and put them on the Mother's wrists instead. They were with the Mother till the very end and even when the last rites on her pure body were performed.[45]

Towards the end, monks and devotees rushed to Udbodhan House from near and far to have a last glimpse of Holy Mother. But they all assembled downstairs because no one was allowed to see her. When Holy Mother's attendant informed her of the innumerable visitors, the compassionate Mother said in a feeble voice: "My child — those who have come to see me, those who have not, and those who will come in the future — tell them that my love and blessings will be bestowed on each of them."[46]

During her final three days, Holy Mother seldom uttered a word and always remained indrawn. She felt annoyed if anyone tried to draw her out. Gradually she lost the power of speech. Towards the end she said to Brahmachari Barada: "Barada, fan me. Don't go away from me." When Barada wept, the Mother consoled him, saying: "Sharat is there. Why should you be afraid? The Master always exists. He will look after all — here and hereafter."[47]

Sarala recalled Holy Mother's last moment:

(*continued from previous page*) Maharaj began to joyfully eat puffed rice and fried gram, and Sharat Maharaj tearfully watched, placing both hands on his chest. When Maharaj finished eating, Sharat Maharaj's face beamed with joy. Sharat Maharaj told us many times: "The Master and the Mother dwell in Maharaj. You must know that by serving him, you are serving the Master and the Mother." We had a glimpse of the truth of this statement that day by observing Sharat Maharaj's satisfaction in feeding puffed rice and fried gram to Maharaj. — *Swami Saradananda: Jeman Dekhiachi* by Swami Bhumananda, 262-63

From the morning of her last day, the Mother's breathing trouble started. During the previous day, my stomach had been upset and I felt very weak. But Sharat Maharaj asked me to eat rice and soup in the Mother's room and stay with her. Her breathing difficulty was so intense that it was hard to look at her face. One could hear that breathing sound from the first floor to the third floor. Her eyes were swollen. The cause of this horrible suffering was that she had initiated many people without any discrimination and had absorbed their sins. The whole of Udbodhan House was packed with monks and devotees. Sister Sudhira and I remained seated near the Mother's feet the entire night. Yogin-ma brought a small jar of water and asked me to dip the Mother's toe in it to sanctify the water. While she was breathing, I began to put Ganges water into her mouth, drop by drop. Gradually the sound of her breathing became fainter and fainter. Finally it stopped. It was after 1:00 a.m., 4 Shravan 1327 B.E.[48]

Swami Saradananda wrote in his diary: "Tuesday, July 20, 1920. — Holy Mother in peace and glory of Maha-Samadhi at 1-30 a.m. (night)."* According to the Hindu calendar the day begins at sunrise, whereas according to the Gregorian calendar, it begins at midnight. So by the Gregorian calendar, Holy Mother passed away at 1:30 a.m. on Wednesday, 21 July 1920.

Swami Nikhilananda wrote: "On 21 July 1920, about one o'clock in the morning, it became evident that Holy Mother's last moments were at hand. The attendants began to chant the Lord's name. Half an hour later, the Mother breathed deeply several times and entered into deep samadhi. Peace-eyed slumber settled over her body, which, though ravaged by a long illness, suddenly relaxed and gave out a celestial light. Many of her devotees were deceived by this radiance and thought she was still with them."[49]

Swami Arupananda said:

What a wonder! As a result of prolonged suffering, the Mother's body was completely emaciated and reduced to only skin and bone, pale and worn out; and thus it looked at the time of death. When her prana [life-force] vanished from the body, Sharat Maharaj asked her women attendants to replace her cloth with a new one, make a new bed, and place her body on it. Incense was lighted near her bed. Grief-stricken, all sat around the Mother's body. Suddenly someone saw that the Mother's face had become radiant and a halo appeared around it. He cried out, 'Look,

*The next day as the General Secretary of the Ramakrishna Order, Saradananda wrote a short note to all the centres: "Yesterday our Most Venerable Mother journeyed to Kailasa [the abode of Shiva]. Please perform special worship to the Master and the Mother on the thirteenth day."

look, the Mother's face has become illumined.' Everyone cast a glance on the Mother's face. Wondering, they were looking at one another and asking themselves: 'From where has this radiance suddenly appeared? We have never seen such a thing before!' Everyone's heart burst into delight and astonishment. They began to sing bhajans, especially songs glorifying the Divine Mother.[50]

At that time there was no telephone in Udbodhan House. Swami Saradananda immediately sent Bibhuti Ghosh to Belur Math with the sad news; Swami Shivananda sent most of the monks to Udbodhan House to see her and to bring her body to Belur Math. They arrived in the early dawn. It was a sight to see: Swamis Saradananda, Nirmalananda, Dhirananda, and other monks, M., Shantiram Ghosh, Kiran Datta,* Dr. Durgapada Ghosh, Yogin-ma, Golap-ma, Mahamaya Mitra, Sudhira, and other women devotees stood encircling the Mother silently with folded hands. Barada continued fanning her. Grief-stricken, Saradananda went to his room and lay down on his stomach, pressing his face into the pillow. Ishanananda wrote: "In the morning the Mother's face became very serene and the colour of her body gradually turned bright. Yogin-ma called Sharat Maharaj to see it. Maharaj came, saw the Mother's divine body, offered a handful of flowers at her feet, and bowed down."[51]

Swami Gauriswarananda reminisced: "After the Mother's passing away, Sharat Maharaj left her room, went downstairs to his room, and cried. After some time Yogin-ma called him from upstairs, 'Sharat, come upstairs and see.' 'What more is there to see?' replied Sharat Maharaj with tearful eyes. Yogin-ma answered, 'See what you have never seen before in your life.' He went upstairs and was dumbfounded to see the Mother's luminous face. He bowed down, touching his head to her feet, and then returned to his room downstairs."[52]

Sarala said: "It was heartbreaking to see the Mother's face when she was ill, and now her face revealed a dazzling beauty — exactly like the face of Mother Durga in an image. We dressed her in a silk cloth with a thin red border."[53]

Two photographs were taken of the Mother's body: The first one was taken in her room without any people around her. She is seen lying down on her bed. Her face and feet are visible. The second picture was taken downstairs in the courtyard of Udbodhan House. The Mother is seen lying on a cot covered with flowers. Her serene face shows that she has

---

*According to Brahmagopal Datta, his father, Kiran Chandra Datta, gave money to Swami Dhirananda to buy sandalwood and ghee for the Mother's cremation. *Sri Sri Mayer Padaprante*, 3:708

Sarada Devi in mahasamadhi in the Udbodhan House courtyard, 21 July 1920.

Persons identified in this group from left to right: 1. Boshiswar Sen,
2. Swami Avyaktananda (Manoranjan), 3. Swami Nikhilananda (Dinesh),
4. Tridivdev Biswas (Panchu, a nephew of Boshi Sen), 5. Rajeswar Sen (Bhola, a
nephew of Boshi Sen), 6. Mukunda Saha, 7. Swami Asitananda (Satu), 8. Swami
Sambidananda (Jogen), 9. Swami Shantananda (Khagen), 10. Nalinikanta
Bose, 11. Bipin Roy Chaudhury (father of Swami Akunthananda), 12. Swami
Maheswarananda (Vaikuntha), and 13. Swami Ishanananda (Barada).

just gone to sleep. Some of her disciples and devotees are standing on the other side of the cot. Brahmachari Barada is holding a palm-leaf fan. Swamis Shantananda, Maheswarananda, Avyaktananda, Boshi Sen, and others are visible in the picture. The Mother's disciples put red paint on the soles of her feet and made many footprints as mementos.

In the morning, a large crowd poured into Udbodhan House. The Mother's body was brought downstairs and placed on a cot that was beautifully decorated with flowers and garlands. The devotees came one after another, bowed down to her, and took their last view of the Mother.

At 10:30 a.m. the monks and devotees lifted the Mother's cot on their shoulders and began to walk from Baghbazar to Belur Math via Baranagore. Swami Saradananda led the funeral procession barefoot, and hundreds of monks and devotees followed him. It was a hot summer morning. Swami Maheswarananda, who was Mother's disciple and physician, was a tall man. He held an umbrella above the Mother's face to protect her from the sun. Some parts of Cossipore Road were paved with big pieces of stone and some parts with asphalt. All of the monks and devotees walked barefoot, so they got blisters because of the heat. But they did not feel any pain, as they were experiencing an indescribable ecstatic joy.

The monks and devotees sang devotional songs (*Ramnam Sankirtan*) throughout the journey. On the way, many other people joined the procession with flowers and incense. Finally the procession reached Kutighat in Baranagore, on the east bank of the Ganges. A big boat from the monastery was waiting to receive the Mother's body, and several rented boats were also there to ferry others. Swami Sankarananda was the helmsman of the Mother's boat, and other monks rowed it to Belur Math on the west bank.

From the Form to the Formless

The Infinite God becomes finite by assuming a human body, and all bodies — divine, human, or animal — are subject to destruction. There is no exception to this law of nature. Holy Mother cast off her human form and returned to her true abode, the formless, all-pervading consciousness. Because the mind has a form, it cannot think of that which is formless. Although Holy Mother's human form no longer exists, the photographs taken of her during her lifetime are now objects of our meditation.

Swami Ishanananda wrote in his reminiscences: "Towards the end, the Mother always expressed her eagerness to go near the bank of the Ganges. She said: 'Take me to the bank of the Ganges, and there I will cool myself.' When her body was brought to Belur Math, different monks suggested different spots for the Mother's cremation. But Mahapurush Maharaj rejected their suggestions, and selected the particular spot where her temple now exists. He said: 'Holy Mother will be at peace watching the holy river Ganges. She will bestow eternal peace upon humanity.'"[54]

Swami Saradeshananda left a written portrait of Belur Math before the Mother's body arrived there and afterwards:

Swami Shivananda was gravely pacing back and forth on the upper floor of the Math building. Sometimes he looked at the Ganges, Dakshineswar, Cossipore, or Udbodhan from the upper veranda and then again returned to his room. Only he knew what was going through his mind. Still it was dark. When there was a little brightness in the east, Bhuban Babu, an old devotee, bowed to Swami Shivananda and said: "Maharaj, the Mother is shining in Udbodhan. A divine light has been seen radiating from her face. Seeing her, no one can tell that she has left us. All grief goes away upon seeing her face."

The Master's worship and food offering were arranged quickly. Swami Subodhananda was running around and supervising everything. Before the arrival of the Mother's body, the Master's worship service and food offering needed to be finished. There was a picture of Holy Mother in the Master's bedroom at Belur Math. Lakshman Maharaj, the worshipper, asked permission from Mahapurush Maharaj and then placed the Mother's picture at the left side of the Master's on the altar. He decorated the Mother's picture with flowers and a garland. From that very day the Mother's daily worship began publicly at Belur Math.

About noon, the Mother's body arrived at Belur Math by boat. Her body was smeared with sandal paste and perfume and the cot was beautifully decorated with flowers and garlands. The Mother's women devotees with tearful eyes bathed her body by dipping it in the Ganges, and then dressed her in a new cloth. After that, her body was brought to the courtyard near the steps of the Master's temple [the old shrine]. A monk performed the worship and arati by waving a lamp with five wicks. Many footprints of the Mother were taken. Then her body was carried to the funeral pyre, which had already been set up with sandalwood on the spot where the present temple exists. Swami Saradananda circumambulated the Mother's body and set the wood on fire. Swamis Shivananda, Subodhananda, Nirmalananda, M., and many of the earliest men and women devotees surrounded the funeral pyre and watched that wonderful cremation. Swami Nirmalananda chanted some Vedic hymns. The blazing fire engulfed the Mother's body and everyone offered incense, *aguru* [perfume], and camphor as oblations. The cremation ended very quickly. To extinguish the fire, everyone began to bring water from the Ganges in earthen pots. Then it began to rain, and Swami Saradananda asked everyone to stop bringing water. A small shower extinguished the funeral pyre and cooled the children of the Mother from the summer heat. A few monks gathered the Mother's relics and ashes in a copper vessel. It was amazing that there were not many relics of the Mother's body; most of them were reduced to ashes. The copper vessel was carried into the Master's shrine and placed in front of the Mother's picture. There was a special food offering to the Master with luchis, a vegetable curry, and rasagollas, which were afterwards distributed among all present.

In the evening a disciple [Swami Saradeshananda himself] burnt incense on the spot where the Mother's body had been cremated. From the next day on, Swami Subodhananda designated a brahmachari to burn incense there every day.[55]

Swami Bhuteshananda saw Holy Mother when she was alive, and he also saw her body in the courtyard at Udbodhan House after she had passed away. He followed the funeral procession along with the monks. He related a slightly different story, with some additional information: "We crossed the Ganges by boat and came to Belur Math. At that time the Ganges was just east of the Nagalingam tree, which was to the south of Swamiji's room and was planted by Swami Brahmananda. There was a slope in that area down to the Ganges. The Mother's boat was anchored there and her body was carried to a spot under the mango tree in the courtyard. The monks and devotees paid their last homage to the Mother. Then her body was carried to the place where her temple exists. There was no ghat there, but the bank was even and parallel to the Ganges. The women devotees gave the Mother a bath there. The funeral pyre was arranged with the sandalwood on the spot where the Mother's temple exists at present. Brother Ramlal, the Master's nephew, was invited to set fire to the funeral pyre, but he was not available, so his brother Shivaram set the fire as a part of the ritual."[56]

Swami Atmaprakashananda was in the procession and he recalled: "A bath was given to the Mother's body at the old ghat of Belur Math. I heard from Yogin-ma and Golap-ma that the Mother's body was soft and flexible. It was very unusual, because a dead body generally becomes stiff and inflexible. Her divine body was consigned to the fire at 3:00 p.m."[57]

Sarala (later Bharatiprana) reminisced:

The Mother's cot was carried to the Kutighat at Baranagore via Cossipore. Golap-ma and Yogin-ma forbade me to join the funeral procession, saying, "What will you see there?" But Sister Sudhira grabbed my hand forcibly and dragged me in the procession. At that time loud Hari-Sankirtan [devotional music] was going on. My mind was blank. I walked to Kutighat with

Above: Sarada Devi's birth anniversary festival at Belur Math in 1937.
Below: Panoramic view of Belur Math on the Ganges.

the group. There the monks and devotees carried the Mother's body to a big boat. The women devotees boarded a small boat, which went along with the big boat. At 2:00 p.m. we reached Belur Math and the Mother's body was taken to a spot under the mango tree in the courtyard. The monks worshipped the Mother's body and offered food. Her body was taken to the Ganges to be bathed. Some women held a cloth to block the view. Sister Sudhira and I took the Mother's body in the Ganges and gave her a nice bath with the water. Lately due to the excessive burning sensation of her body, the Mother would often say: "Take me to the Ganges. Take me to the Ganges." This time I felt the Mother's body was light and soft. We removed the cloth she had on and dressed her again in a new silk cloth with a narrow red border. Again the monks carried her body under the mango tree. And again they performed arati with light and incense. I watched everything but my mind was so numb that I felt nothing. The funeral pyre was arranged where the present temple of the Mother exists. It was hard for me to watch. I lay down behind Sister Sudhira. The Mother's body was placed on the sandalwood pyre and Sharat Maharaj and other monks circumambulated the pyre and offered bel leaves, incense, and bdellium on it. Sister Prabodh grabbed my hand and lifted me up, saying, "Look, how beautiful it looks." I saw the flames of the blazing fire rising high. At that time there were no trams and buses like at present, so there was not much of a crowd. The blazing fire consumed the Mother's body. I did not see the Mother's body on the pyre because I kept my eyes down, thinking that there was no need to see that painful scene. When it was over, we encircled the pyre and offered oblations three times. It was amazing that there was rain on the other side of the Ganges but not on this side.[58]

The all-devouring Agni, the god of fire, consumed Holy Mother's mortal form. Swami Bhuteshananda said: "After the cremation, the monks and devotees poured Ganges water over the slow-burning fire. I also poured water. Some monks gathered the Mother's relics and ashes, and then the devotees began to collect the relics. Swami Saradananda, leaving his natural gravity, loudly said: 'Let me remind those who are collecting these relics and ashes: if they cannot maintain their sanctity and do not worship them daily, great harm will befall them.' Hearing the swami's grave warning, the devotees returned those relics to the funeral spot."[59]

Swami Saradananda recorded in his diary: "Wednesday, 21 July 1920. — Procession to Belur Math via Baranagore at about 10:30 a.m. and the Yajna at about 3:00 p.m. A heavy shower ended the ceremony at about dusk.

"Sunday, 1 August 1920. — Especial puja of the R. K. Order at Belur and Calcutta Maths on account of the Ascension of H. M."[60]

Sarada Devi's shrine at Belur Math, built on her cremation site.

Mother! O Mother!

When Holy Mother passed away, Swami Brahmananda was in Bhubaneswar. On 21 July around 1:30 a.m. Brahmananda was seated in his easy chair, covered with a shawl. He was grave. He asked Nirvanananda: "What is the time now? I don't know why my mind is so restless for the Mother. I don't know how she is doing."

"Maharaj, will you not sleep?" Nirvanananda asked.

The swami did not answer. "Shall I bring a smoke?" The swami remained silent. Nirvanananda left the room. The next morning, Maharaj was pacing on the veranda restlessly and did not go out for his usual walk. That very day a telegram came from Swami Saradananda with the news that the Mother had passed away at 1:30 a.m. Brahmananda's face became swollen with grief. He simply lay down. After a while, he got up and said to his attendant: "I shall eat only *havishanna*.* Those who are the Mother's disciples should eat *havishanna* once a day and not wear shoes." The swami did not speak for three days. He ate *havishanna* for twelve days, and he went barefoot. Then one day he said, "All these days we were protected by a big mountain."[61]

Just after the cremation, Swami Shivananda said to the monks and devotees at Belur Math: "The Divine Mother Sati's body was divided into 51 pieces and fell in 51 places throughout India. Those places became Shakti-pithas or Devi-tirthas. And today that very Sati's entire body has become mixed with the ground of Belur Math, so you can imagine what a great and holy place Belur Math is!"[62]

A couple of days after the Mother's passing away, a respected couple who were the Mother's disciples came to Belur Math. They had come from far away to see Holy Mother, but their hopes were dashed to pieces. Swami Shivananda consoled them, saying: "The Mother is now all-pervading. One can now see her in everything and every being. Anyone who calls on her wholeheartedly will see her. Previously she lived in a particular place. Now she is everywhere. Do not grieve. Call on her with a sincere and longing heart, and she will reveal herself to you."[63] Swami Shivananda's message touched many grieving hearts.

Regarding Ramakrishna's passing away, Romain Rolland wrote: "The man himself was no more. His spirit had departed to travel along the path of collective life in the veins of humanity."[64] Similarly, when the Mother's

---

*According to the Hindu custom, when parents die, the son observes rituals for a minimum of eleven days, including offering prayers and water to the departed one. The bereaved son also eats havishanna (boiled rice with ghee), wears one cloth, goes barefoot, does not shave, sleeps alone, studies the Gita and Upanishads, and so on.

earthly life ended and she merged into the Divine, her spirit began to spread in the East and the West. The following two letters testify to the Mother's divine influence, permeating the minds of two important persons — one of the East and one of the West — who knew her intimately.

M., the recorder of *The Gospel of Sri Ramakrishna*, received immense love and grace from the Master and the Mother. Holy Mother initiated him, his wife, and all his children. A little over a year after the Mother's passing away, he wrote a letter of consolation to Umesh Chandra Datta, a fellow disciple.

Calcutta
Durga Puja 1328 (1921)

Dear Umesh,

Upon receiving your letter I realized that we have truly lost our Mother. Alas, one year has passed since she disappeared from us. There is a saying that children pass through a hard time for a year after losing their mother. However, here is a song:

> Mother! Mother! My boat is sinking here in the ocean of this world;
> Fiercely the hurricane of delusion rages on every side!
> Clumsy is my helmsman, the mind; stubborn my six oarsmen, the passions;
> Into a pitiless wind I sailed my boat, and now it is sinking!
> Split is the rudder of devotion; tattered is the sail of faith;
> Into my boat the waters are pouring! Tell me, what shall I do?
> For with my failing eyes, alas! nothing but darkness do I see.
> Here in the waves I will swim, O Mother, and cling to the raft of Thy name!

Now where is the way out? When a mother spanks her children, they cry, saying "Mother, Mother," to go back to her lap. The children's only resort is to cry and call out "Mother, Mother," like kittens. Let her will be done.

What more shall I write to you? Your condition and my condition are the same. Now the only thing we can do is to call "Mother, Mother." Today is *Bodhan*, the awakening ceremony of the Divine Mother who has come to receive worship in Bengal as Durga — the same Mother who took human form and thought of our welfare till 21 July last year. Is she not thinking of us now? It is impossible for Holy Mother to forget us.

The other day I had a dream. The Mother said to me: "As you saw me when I gave up the body, that body was made of maya. Look, I still remain in the same form."

Affectionately,
Srima (M.)[65]

Miss Josephine MacLeod was a wonderful American devotee and very dear to Holy Mother, who called her "Jaya." When the Mother passed away, Jaya was staying in England with her niece Alberta. After receiving the sad news, she wrote to Swami Saradananda.

15 August 1920
Halls Croft
Stratford-On-Avon

Dearest Saradananda,

First from dear Mrs. Sevier, other from Boshi [Sen] after he returned from the cremation at the Math that have I heard of Holy Mother's death on July 21st! And so that brave quiet strong soul has gone out, having left to modern Hindu womanhood the ideal of the great place that woman is to take in the next 3000 years! To me her life is one of intense encouragement — gathering all of us under her sheltering and understanding life, creating new precedents, as new needs arise, self-reliant — direct — wise! Oh, what an example each of us can make of her! She created new precedents — so must we — not hers — but our own! In no other way can the world's problems be solved.

Yours in sincerity and affection,
J. MacLeod[66]

Conclusion

In one sense Holy Mother's biography ends here, yet in another sense it begins here, as she has entered into the minds of innumerable people around the world.

Shortly after Holy Mother's passing, hundreds of people who knew her personally began to record their reminiscences; some of her disciples and devotees wrote biographies and articles about her, composed poems and songs about her, and spoke about her privately and publicly for more than half a century after her passing away. Now Holy Mother has been enshrined in millions of homes and has entered the hearts of millions and millions of people all over the world. People are now meditating on her divine form, repeating her name, praying to her for solace and succour, getting inspiration from her immortal life and message, and thus glorifying the greatness and divinity of Holy Mother.

The play of divine beings never stops. Only the fortunate ones witness it. Swami Shantananda, an attendant of Holy Mother, narrated how, long after her passing away, he received a command from Holy Mother that reassured him of her living presence. He said that during her lifetime the

Mother had once told him how to receive her command:

> If there is any crisis in your life, remember me. Isolate yourself from others for a few days and practise japa and meditation intensely. Pray wholeheartedly and ask me, "Mother, what shall I do?" During that period, eat less and keep your body and mind pure. Try to maintain silence and speak only if it is absolutely necessary. Don't let other people know what you are doing. Continue your prayer and sadhana in this way with a one-pointed mind. Never lose patience. If you see that you are not receiving my command, still you should not give up hope. If you find that no response is coming, then know for certain that your mind has not risen high enough to receive my command. You will definitely receive my command if you call on me with wholehearted faith and devotion.[67]

This is truly a gospel of hope for children of the Mother. The compassionate Mother left clear and simple directions for us to reach her when we are buffeted by tension and anxiety, temptation and frustration, trials and tribulations, crisis and depression — when we can find no way out from the turbulent ocean of maya.

Holy Mother was infinite. No biographer can write her complete biography. When Swami Saradananda visited Varanasi after the Mother had passed away, some elderly monks said to him: "Please write a biography of Holy Mother so that future generations might understand her life correctly. You have performed a great service for the world by writing the biography of Sri Ramakrishna. It would be wonderful if you were to write the Mother's life." Instead of responding directly, the swami recited this song in Bengali:

> I was amazed to witness the play of the playful Mother,
> But now I wonder whether to laugh or cry.
> So long did I live near her and follow her steps,
> Yet I failed to understand, and now acknowledge my defeat.
> Various are her actions in this world, destroying and creating.
> All this is child's play to her — this much I have understood. [68]

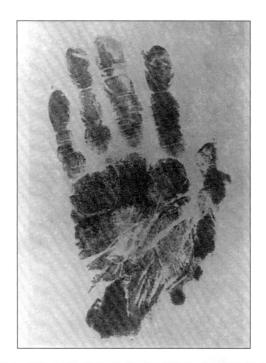

Sarada Devi's handprint and footprints.

Above: Painting by Franz Dvorak, Czech artist (1862–1927).
Below: Bronze bust by American sculptor Malvina
Hoffman (1885–1966).

Epilogue

Jananim sāradām devim rāmakrishnam jagadgurum;
Pādapadme tayoh shritvā pranamāmi muhurmuhuh.
— *A hymn by Swami Abhedananda*

I salute the Divine Mother Sri Sarada Devi and Sri Ramakrishna,
the Guru of the world. Taking shelter at their lotus feet, I bow down
to them again and again.

We have made a long journey with Holy Mother, following
her divine drama with innumerable characters over a period
of nearly seven decades. Readers might be curious to know
what happened after her passing away to some of the people who performed important roles in Holy Mother's play. Blessed are those souls
who recognized the Mother's divinity by her grace; and equally blessed
are they who recognized her as human. We can see the Mother's divine
and human aspects through them. They all left their wonderful experiences and fascinating stories, which are now objects of meditation for us.

Holy Mother's Nieces

Appendix 5 presents Holy Mother's family tree, which will help the
reader to visualize her connection with her close relations. Holy Mother's nieces Nalini, Sushila (known as Maku), and Radharani (known as
Radhu), revealed her human aspects. Though they had their sweet and
loving aspects, these women were often jealous, angry, selfish, sensitive,
narrow-minded, and quarrelsome. Nalini had a hysterical mania for
cleanliness and purity, and the others had a strong attachment to worldly
life. One should not be upset by the strange behaviour of these women
and their ill-treatment of their aunt because they were acting in their roles
to glorify the life of the Mother. In Holy Mother's divine drama they represented people who are endowed with more or less similar traits. It is
worth noting how Holy Mother lived harmoniously among these complex characters, how she tackled their problems and maintained her sanity. Her teachings to her nieces are meant for all human beings who have
similar problems. Her love and compassion, forbearance and forgiveness
conquered their hearts, and despite their shortcomings, they knew that
their aunt was their all in all.

When Holy Mother passed away, her nieces' miserable condition was like that of the relatives of Krishna when he departed from the world. Uddhava described it to Vidura: This world is unfortunate, and more unfortunate are the people of the Yadu dynasty. As fish do not recognize the glory of the full moon as long as they see its reflection in water, considering it to be only one among themselves, so did the Yadus fail to realize Lord Hari [God], who was living with them. It is amazing that they did not know Krishna was the Lord of all beings, but under the influence of maya, some looked upon him as the chief of their dynasty, some as a relative, some as a friend, and others as an enemy.[1]

Nalini

Holy Mother's oldest brother's name was Prasanna and his wife was Ramapriya. They had two daughters, Nalini, who was born probably in the early 1890s, and Maku, who was born in 1896. In 1900, Nalini was married to Pramatha Nath Bhattacharya of Goghat, a village a few miles from Jayrambati and near Kamarpukur. Holy Mother helped organize Nalini's marriage ceremony. But Nalini never developed a relationship with her husband's family. Quite often she left her husband's home and returned to her parents in Jayrambati.

Prasanna was working as a priest in Calcutta and had rented a tiled house in the Simla area. His wife, Ramapriya, his daughters, and Nalini's husband were living with him there. During this time Pramatha became very ill with what the doctor diagnosed as double pneumonia. Holy Mother was then living at M.'s house, and she visited Pramatha a few times. According to her instructions, M. and Swami Saradananda engaged a doctor for Pramatha. This doctor later became her disciple. Pramatha recuperated and later returned to Goghat. In 1905, Ramapriya died of cholera in Jayrambati. Prasanna was working in Calcutta, so Nalini and Maku became members of Holy Mother's household. Following his wife's death, Prasanna married a woman named Subasini. Nalini and Maku did not like their stepmother, so they remained with Holy Mother. Nalini avoided going to her husband's home because the family was poor and she was not treated well there. One day her husband came with a bullock cart to pick her up, but she closed the door and would not come out. The Mother asked her to go with her husband, but she threatened to commit suicide if she was forced to go. Pramatha left, disappointed.

Nalini and Surabala, the wife of Holy Mother's youngest brother (Abhaycharan), lived with the Mother. They quarreled and fought most of the time; their relationship was like that of a snake and a mongoose. Observing Nalini's low self-esteem, Holy Mother sometimes gave her some responsibilities to make her feel a little important. However, this encouraged her bossy tendency, and she sometimes quarreled with Mandakini, the Mother's attendant. Nalini was always jealous of Surabala's daughter, Radhu, because the Mother paid more attention to her and spent a lot of money on her. Sometimes Nalini tortured herself to get more attention and favour from the Mother. She was quite a character, but the Mother forgave all her shortcomings and treated her as her own daughter. She travelled with the Mother back and forth between Jayrambati and Calcutta.

Nalini was present when the Mother passed away. Afterwards, she moved into the Mother's house in Jayrambati. She lived there for a few years but was not happy. Swami Parameswarananda asked Swami Saradananda to arrange for Nalini to stay at Udbodhan House, but instead the swami made arrangements for her to live at the boarding house of the Nivedita School in Calcutta. Nalini died in 1928 or 1929. According to an eyewitness account, she pitifully cried to Holy Mother during her last illness, saying "Aunt, take me with you. I can't bear any more suffering, and people do not care for me." During her last moment, instead of 'aunt' she said: "Mother, take me; Mother, take me." And thus Nalini breathed her last.

Nalini played her role very well in the divine drama of Holy Mother. Through her, we have received some wonderful teachings of the Mother, such as what to pray for (desirelessness), how to offer food to the Master, and how to serve food to others (Amzad), how to live harmoniously in family life, and so on.[2]

Sushila (Maku)

In 1908, when Maku was 12 years old, Holy Mother arranged her marriage to Pramatha Nath Chattopadhyay, the son of Vaidyanath Chattopadhyay of Tajpur, a village a few miles from Jayrambati.

Maku lived with her husband for some time, but mostly she lived with Holy Mother in Jayrambati and also in Calcutta. In fact, her husband also sometimes stayed in Jayrambati. While in Calcutta, the Mother sent Maku and Radhu to the Missionary Girls' School, where they learned how to read and write. Sometimes the Mother dictated answers to devotees' letters to them. They also read books to Holy Mother at her request. They looked upon Holy Mother as their own mother and she tried to fulfill their demands.

One year during Durga Puja, Brahmachari Barada bought cloths for her nieces, but they did not like the coarse cloth made in India. Instead they wanted fine cloths made in England. So to make them happy, the Mother asked another attendant to buy English cloths for them.

In 1919 at Vishnupur, an astrologer read Maku's palm and predicted that her children would not survive long enough to see each other. Maku was scared and related this prediction to the Mother with tearful eyes. The Mother then asked the astrologer how to counteract that bad omen, and she had the rituals he recommended performed according to his instructions.

Both Radhu and Maku were pregnant and staying with the Mother in Koalpara. Without asking the Mother's permission, Nalini left for Jayrambati with Maku and her son Neda. Holy Mother lamented. Neda developed diphtheria. Although the Mother and Swami Saradananda arranged for Neda's treatment, he passed away in Jayrambati. The Mother was fond of Neda and cried for him. She remarked: "This boy was a great soul, a fallen yogi in his previous birth. This was his last birth."

Once Maku was suffering from a high fever and crying for her mother. Holy Mother asked her stepmother to look after her. But while Subasini was rubbing Maku's forehead, Maku was searching for the Mother. When she saw her, Maku said, "Mother, don't leave me." Holy Mother consoled her, saying, "No, I shall not go away." With the Mother's blessing, Maku recovered quickly. One day Maku said to the Mother: "Aunt, so many people come to you and receive initiation, and then they get rid of their grief and suffering. Why don't you initiate me? It will protect me from danger and remove all my bad omens."

"We shall see," replied the Mother.

The next day when the Mother sat for her worship, Maku went to her and said, "Aunt, please initiate me, or I shall kill myself by hitting my head in front of you." Seeing her intense desire, the Mother initiated her. This was the first time the Mother initiated one of her relatives. Later she initiated Subasini, Radhu, Manmatha (Radhu's husband), Bhudeb (Kalikumar's son), and his wife Prabhavati.

On 24 February 1920, when Holy Mother was leaving Jayrambati for Calcutta for the last time, two palanquins were hired — one for the Mother and the other for Radhu and her son. But Radhu preferred to go by bullock cart with her son, so the Mother arranged the other palanquin for Maku and her son. During the last five months of Holy Mother's life, Maku lived at Udbodhan House with other relatives. Towards the end, the Mother cut all her family ties and asked her nieces to return to Jayrambati. The women felt helpless and Maku cried bitterly. At Saradananda's request, Holy Mother reluctantly agreed to let them stay in Udbodhan House.

After the Mother's passing away, Maku returned to Jayrambati along with Nalini, Radhu, and others.

Maku's husband, Pramatha, was an intelligent student and passed the matriculation examination. He was in good health but had once injured his right leg, so he limped a little. When the financial condition of his family deteriorated, the Mother arranged a job in the railway for him through one of her disciples, who was in a high position in the railway department. Pramatha eventually became the station master at Raniganj. As Maku mostly stayed with the Mother, Pramatha visited her occasionally during his leave. After the Mother's passing away, Maku moved in with her husband at Raniganj. Maku's second son was born during the Mother's lifetime, but he died within a few years. Her third son also died at a very young age. Grief-stricken, Maku asked her husband to perform a special homa ritual so that their children might survive. In 1923, Maku had a daughter named Anandamayi and in 1928 she gave birth to a son she named Shambhuchandra. She tied onto the boy's wrist an auspicious amulet with eight metals that she had collected from the homa fire.

In 1930, Maku died from typhoid at the age of 34. Her two children were very young, so to look after them, Pramatha married Annapurna, a girl from Anur. Annapurna had three sons by Pramatha — Dulal, Mukti, and Alok. But Annapurna also died young. Anandamayi then raised her brothers. Pramatha retired from his job and settled in Tajpur, his native village, where he died in 1956 at the age of 72.

The Mother's wonderful teachings to Maku regarding renunciation and modesty are recorded in various places in this book. She told Maku: "If you want peace, don't see faults in others. Always try to maintain calmness of the mind. Pray to the Master for good, pure thoughts and guidance."[3]

Radhu

Radhu played a special role in Holy Mother's life, as the Mother repeatedly told the devotees. Radhu was born in 1900 after her father's death. Her mother, Surabala, was almost insane. (*See Chapters 18 and 19 for details on Radhu's life.*) Holy Mother raised Radhu, sent her to school, arranged her marriage, and looked after her son. Radhu was the Mother's constant companion for 20 years. The Mother dictated letters to Radhu, and sometimes Radhu read books to the Mother.

Holy Mother would have preferred that Radhu serve the Master instead of getting married, but Surabala insisted on Radhu's marriage. Holy Mother reluctantly arranged to have her married to Manmatha Nath Chattopadhyay of Tajpur, a village a few miles from Jayrambati. Maku's husband Pramatha and Radhu's husband Manmatha were cousins. The Mother sent Gauri-ma to Tajpur to get information about the bridegroom and his family. She met Manmatha, then a teenage boy, on the street when he was carrying some mangoes. Radhu was 11 years old when the wedding was held on 10 June 1911.

Manmatha was born into a wealthy family, so he never tried to earn money and support himself. He spent his time playing cards and singing songs. He was fond of music, so the Mother bought a harmonium for him. He was whimsical, humorous, and immature. When he was young, he made a mini zoo at his house, collecting a peacock, a cockatoo, a rabbit, a mongoose, a white rat, a pigeon, and other animals. He also loved trees and plants and made a garden. He stayed mostly with Radhu and thus became a member of the Mother's household in Jayrambati and Calcutta. When the income from their land decreased, Manmatha's family fell into a financial crisis. As she did for Pramatha, the Mother arranged a job for Manmatha in the railway, but he had no desire to work.

According to Radhu's horoscope, she was supposed to become a widow; but the Mother initiated Manmatha and thus overturned the decree of Providence.

After Holy Mother passed away, Radhu moved to the Mother's new house in Jayrambati with her son, as the Mother herself had arranged. When the Mother registered her property in Jayrambati in the name of the goddess Jagaddhatri, she specified that Radhu would be the caretaker of the goddess and live in the room of her new house that faced south; and Nalini would live in the room that faced north. The parlour would be occupied either by a monk from Belur Math or by a worker, and the annual Jagaddhatri Puja would be held in that parlour. Swami Saradananda was to send 30 rupees to Radhu every month for living expenses.

Swami Parameswarananda wrote: "After the Mother's passing away, it was hard to recognize Radhu's son, Banabihari. The boy became ill and day by day became more emaciated. His behaviour became very strange. The Mother used to decorate him with sandal paste and collyrium and he looked like Baby Gopala. When he crawled and later walked, he looked as beautiful as Gopala. One day I said to the Mother, 'Mother, you have brought the living Gopala by worshipping the image Gopala.' The Mother replied: 'You are right, my son. The worshipper brings the deity to the world. As long as the worshipper stays, the deity stays.'

"I realized the truth of the Mother's words when Radhu returned to Jayrambati with her son after the Mother's passing away. Banabihari was restless and greedy. He had lost all his charm. He suffered from illness for sometime and then died."[4]

After the Mother's passing away, Manmatha visited Bibhuti Ghosh in Bankura, a great devotee of the Mother, to ask him for financial help. Manmatha stayed often at the Ramakrishna Ashrama there. Bibhuti helped him to open a bookshop in Bankura, but Manmatha could not manage it. Later at Radhu's request, Swami Saradananda gave some money to Manmatha to open a shop in Tajpur, and somehow he earned a little money to support himself.[5]

Radhu eventually went to live with her husband in Tajpur. All through her life, Radhu had been well protected by the Mother, as if shielded by the Himalayas. Now she began to face the reality of life. When Radhu had ill-treated the Mother, Holy Mother predicted a sad life waiting for her. Radhu's happiness was shattered when she began to live with her husband. Holy Mother died on 21 July 1920, and Radhu wrote two letters to Bibhuti Ghosh from Tajpur:

Sri Hari, Tajpur, 31 August 1920
Revered Bibhutidada,

How are you? I received your letter. It would be wonderful if you visit me once a month. My husband has started to fight with me. He is beating me every day and abusing me verbally. Please take leave and come for a day or two; otherwise he might kill me. I consider you like my father and mother, so I inform you of all my sufferings. Please leave your work and rescue me from this place. Please don't forget me. I have no more patience. I am getting punishment every day. Please take me away from this place. Accept my pranam.

Your sister,
Radharani

Tajpur, Sunday, 14 December 1920
Revered Bibhutidada,

Please accept my hundred salutations. Perhaps you have received my previous letter. You wrote to me that that you would come and take me away from this place but you did not come. Perhaps I did many wrongs to you. Kindly come here and see me. I am passing my days with terrible suffering. You have not even written a letter to me. The Mother has gone, so you have forsaken me. I write considering you as my parent. Will you not look after me anymore? Please write a letter to your wretched sister.

Let me know whether you are coming or not. I beg you to come and take me away from this place. My husband agreed to send me right now from this place, but who will take me? Kishori Maharaj [Swami Parameswarananda] says: "Where will you stay in Jayrambati? Why don't you adjust to your husband?" Will you not show any mercy on me? I beg at your feet. Please come and write to me as soon as you get this letter.

Awaiting your reply,
Radhu

It seems that towards the end of 1920, Bibhuti brought Radhu to Jayrambati from Tajpur. By the Mother's grace, Radhu escaped widowhood but could not avoid unhappiness in her marriage. Within nine months after the Mother's passing away, in April 1921, Manmatha took a second wife, Hiranmayi. This was a blow to Radhu. She began to realize what she was missing. She began to live alone in Jayrambati, but from time to time Manmatha visited her when he needed money. He took a share of the pension that Swami Saradananda provided for her. The shameless Manmatha used and abused Radhu for his selfish purposes. In 1926 Radhu had a daughter named Nirmala, but Manmatha never looked after her. Swami Parameswarananda and Swami Atmabodhananda raised Nirmala and arranged for her to be educated in the Nivedita School in Calcutta. Sarala (later Bharatiprana) also looked after her. When Nirmala was grown up, Swami Parameswarananda arranged her marriage with Vaidehi Nandan Mukhopadhyay of Raghubati.

Swami Ishanananda wrote about Radhu's last illness:

It was July-August 1940 [Bhadra 1347 BE]. The Mother's dearest Radhu was living in the Mother's room at Jayrambati. She had been suffering from malaria for some time, so she was brought to the boarding house of the Nivedita School in Calcutta for treatment. Swami Atmabodhananda [the head of the Udbodhan centre] engaged a doctor, who suspected the disease to be tuberculosis. The swami informed Priya Maharaj [Swami Atmaprakashananda], head of the Ramakrishna Mission Home of Service, Varanasi. He quickly rented the second floor of a house near the hospital and sent a cable to send Radhu immediately. Swami Atmabodhananda asked me to accompany Radhu and a woman attendant from the Nivedita School to Varanasi. After arriving there, Radhu was X-rayed. The report revealed that both of her lungs were considerably affected. She had a 102° temperature and was coughing constantly. There was no hope for survival. Priya Maharaj took good care of her, providing nursing, diet, and treatment. I had a return ticket to Calcutta valid for 12 days, so on the final day I went to Radhu and said: "Radhu, I am leaving for Calcutta today. You stay here and don't worry. Priya Maharaj has arranged everything for you. When you get well, I will take you back to Jayrambati." Radhu's temperature was rising. Priya Maharaj, an attendant, and I were then in the room.

Although Radhu was weak, she spoke out in an animated voice: "Ah, Gopal-da, shame upon your intellect! You may hide it, but I know what disease I have. I have contracted tuberculosis. Does anybody survive this disease? You are telling me that I will go to Jayrambati after recovery!" I said: "Radhu, don't think about all those things. Priya Maharaj has arranged your treatment and nursing. If you need anything, the swami will provide. Don't worry." Radhu replied: "Gopal-da, you are just trying to console me. You are leaving me in Varanasi, because you think that if I die here I will get liberation. Have you got this kind of knowledge after living with the Mother for such a long time? The Mother took responsibility for me, arranged everything for me from my very birth, and even left her own room in Jayrambati for me. She is my only refuge. Has she not arranged for my liberation? If I die even in a dump, liberation is in my palm by the grace of the Mother. Brother, you don't need to worry about that." Tears trickled from the eyes of Priya Maharaj, and I stood there with my head bent down. Radhu continued: "The Mother had already arranged the place where I will die. You don't have to think about that."[6]

Usharani Devi recalled:

Satyen Maharaj [Swami Atmabodhananda] sent Radhu to Varanasi for treatment during her last illness. Priya Maharaj looked after her needs and treatment, and Sarala served her wholeheartedly. Radhu stayed at Varanasi for two months. Sarala cooked various dishes for her and we would carry food to her every day at 11:00 a.m. People generally know that Radhu had misbehaved with the Mother, but towards the end, her mind was absorbed in the Mother. I told Sarala, "Have you seen what a change has come over Radhu?" Sarala remarked: "It was bound to happen. Radhu came to bring the Mother's mind down to the earthly plane. For that reason she had to play the role of a crazy woman. Now her acting is over. What else will she do but call on the Mother?" Radhu was anxious to return to Jayrambati and said, "I don't want nirvana, dying in Varanasi. I want to go to the Mother." Sarala consoled her, saying: "Stay here. You will get well." Relentlessly Radhu said to Sarala: "No, I don't want to stay here although you are taking care of me well. I want to go to the Mother. Why should I die here and attain nirvana? Let Satyen Maharaj and Priya Maharaj die and attain liberation. I must go to the Mother, and I will not stay here anymore." Addressing Brahmachari Gagan (later Swami Ritananda), Radhu said, "Brother, why don't you escort me to the Mother's house in Jayrambati?" Because of her insistence, Gagan Maharaj accompanied Radhu to Jayrambati and she died there within two weeks.[7]

When Radhu returned to Jayrambati, Manmatha's other wife, Hiran-mayi, cared for Radhu during that brief period. She also looked after Rad-hu's daughter, Nirmala, when she was young.

Swami Ishanananda mentioned that Radhu returned to Jayrambati and lived in the Mother's room. She passed away on 23 November 1940 at 9:00 a.m., at the age of 40, consciously thinking of Holy Mother. Victory to the Mother and blessed is her Radhu![8]

In 1961 Manmatha died at the age of 65; and in 1985, Hiranmayi died at Tajpur at the age of 75.

Yogin-ma

According to Hindu mythology, Jaya and Vijaya are two of the Divine Mother's women attendants. When She incarnates in this world, Her attendants come with Her. Holy Mother said that Yogin and Golap were her Jaya and Vijaya.

Yogindra Mohini Biswas, or Yogin-ma, was born on 16 January 1851 in Baghbazar, North Calcutta. Her family's home was very close to that of Balaram Basu, one of Ramakrishna's householder disciples. When Yogin-ma was seven she was married to Ambika Charan Biswas, the adopted son of a rich and prominent family of Khardah, a village 12 miles north of Calcutta.

Although child marriage was then customary, Yogin-ma did not go to live with her husband's family at the time of their wedding. Only after she had grown up did she go with great hopes and expectation to Khardah to join Ambika Charan. But to her dismay she very soon discovered that this rich young man was a drunkard and libertine. Although Ambika Charan had inherited much property and wealth from his father, he squandered it in a very short time. Yogin-ma lived with him for a few years and tried in vain to change his life. She bore him a daughter named Ganu and a son who lived only six months. But patience has its limits. Disgusted with her husband's immoral life, she at last severed her relationship with him and returned to her parental home, bringing her daughter.

In 1882, at the age of 31, Yogin-ma met Ramakrishna for the first time at Balaram Basu's house. Balaram often went to Dakshineswar by boat and would invite other devotees to go along with him. Yogin-ma went with him a few times, and then she started to visit the Master with other devo-tees. After sometime Yogin-ma met Holy Mother. The two were immedi-ately drawn to one another. They were about the same age. Holy Mother once said, "Yogin is my Jaya — my friend, companion, and attendant." When Ramakrishna passed away in August 1886, Yogin-ma was staying at Kalababu's Kunja, a retreat house in Vrindaban belonging to Balaram's family. She was overwhelmed with grief when she learned of the Master's passing. Holy Mother joined her there soon after.

In 1893 Holy Mother and Yogin-ma performed the *Panchatapa,* the austerity of five fires, at Nilambar Babu's garden house near the present Belur Math. Holy Mother used to tell the women devotees: "Yogin and Golap have practised so much spiritual discipline. It will do you good to talk about it amongst yourselves."

Sarala reminisced:

> Yogin-ma was a great sadhika, or spiritual aspirant. She practised japa and meditation intensely. Quite often she experienced samadhi. We saw her staggering while she walked from the Ganges ghat to the Mother's house. She went to the Ganges early in the morning and after her bath she practised japa till ten o'clock. Then she went to the Mother's house. Her eyes were red. She put down her asana and then said in loud voice, "Where is the royal princess [Holy Mother]?" Her first task was to bow down to the Mother. She would be annoyed if she could not see the Mother, and if the Mother was a little late, she would remark with a wounded heart, "Hello, daughter of a wealthy person, will you not show your face?" So before Yogin-ma's arrival, the Mother would wait for her. She told us in a low voice: "Look, Yogin will come any moment now. She practises japa and meditation intensely for a long time. That is why her head gets heated."
>
> After bowing down to the Mother, at ten-thirty she took her breakfast — rock candy syrup, fruit prasad and tea. She was a light eater. Afterwards, she helped the cook cut vegetables. Sometimes the Mother asked her to have lunch prasad at Udbodhan, but she refused as her mother was at home. After returning home she cooked whatever she had arranged beforehand. She offered that food to the Master and ate with her mother. After lunch she took a little rest and then read some religious books. In the late afternoon she visited Balaram's house, where several monks stayed. Before dusk she returned to Udbodhan, changed her sari, and began Arati. I generally lit the *pancha-pradip;** otherwise she did this herself. She waved the lamp for a long time before each picture in the shrine room. Our hands would ache after ringing the bell for so long. The Mother also sat there and Yogin-ma waved the lamp in front of her. At night she offered the food to the Master and then she returned home after eating some offered luchis and farina pudding. As long as the Mother was alive, that was Yogin-ma's routine. After the Mother's passing away, she lived in Udbodhan for the rest of her life.[9]

Holy Mother had great regard for Yogin-ma's judgement and consulted

---

*A brass oil or ghee lamp with five wicks.

her not only about domestic matters but about spiritual affairs and even mantras.

Holy Mother's passing away in 1920 created a tremendous void in Yogin-ma's mind. Yogin-ma longed to join her and the Master. One day in Udbodhan House a young monk noticed Yogin-ma's poor health and expressed his sympathy. She looked at the portrait of the Mother and then said tearfully: "What can I do, my child? Truly, my health is completely broken down. She left, breaking my everything." She remained silent, gazing at the picture of the Mother from her bed.[10]

Yogin-ma suffered from diabetes during the last two years of her life. Although her austere body became weak and fragile, her mind was always alert, and she never forgot her blessed association with Ramakrishna, Holy Mother, and her fellow direct disciples of the Master. She often went into bhava samadhi, sweetly uttering the words: "Ha Gopala! Ha Gopala!"

For two or three days before she passed away, she lay speechless and refused to take even a little liquid. Swami Saradananda asked the doctor who was attending her to examine her to see if she was in a coma, as can happen to diabetics. The doctor checked carefully, but could not find any symptoms of coma. The swami was then assured that the Master's words had come true — that Yogin-ma would give up her body in a state of jnana, that is, she would merge into Brahman.

On Wednesday, 4 June 1924, at 10:25 p.m., when all the activities of the monastery were over, Yogin-ma passed away in Udbodhan House, next to the room where the Holy Mother had lived. Swami Saradananda sat near her head at the time of her death and repeated Ramakrishna's name, while a monk recited a passage from the second chapter of the Bhagavad Gita. The monks carried Yogin-ma's body to Kashi Mitra's cremation ground on the bank of the Ganges and cremated it in accordance with the Hindu custom, with the chanting of Vedic mantras.

Sarala recalled Golap-ma's reaction to Yogin-ma's death: "I was seated quietly when Golap-ma came to Yogin-ma's room and said: 'Yogin is gone. Actually she came to the Master before I did, so it is natural that she should go to him before I go.' Saying these few words, she went back to her room and sat there quietly the whole night. She neither lay down nor did anything else. The monks returned at 3:00 a.m. after the cremation was over."[11]

Golap-ma

Golap Sundari Devi, known as Golap-ma, was born in a brahmin family of North Calcutta, sometime in the 1840s. She was at least 10 years older than Holy Mother. Her parents arranged her marriage to a poor brahmin when she was young, but her husband died after a few years, leaving her with two small children, a son and a daughter. When Golap-ma's son was still very young, he also died, and her mainstay in life then became her daughter, Chandi. She was a charming, beautiful, and well-mannered girl. When she grew up, Golap-ma arranged her marriage to Saurindra Mohan Thakur, an eminent and wealthy landlord of Calcutta. But fate was again cruel to Golap-ma. Chandi died prematurely, creating a tremendous void in her mother's life.

Golap-ma cried and cursed herself but could find no cure for her grief. Yogin-ma, a neighbour, came to her aid. Seeing Golap-ma's terrible suffering, Yogin-ma took compassion on her and one day in 1885 took her to Ramakrishna at Dakshineswar.

Sarala reminisced: "Golap-ma's daughter Chandi was a beautiful girl. Seeing her beauty, Raja Saurindra Mohan Thakur married her, spending a lot of money. Chandi would visit her mother from time to time during the day. She sent a pension to her every month. Chandi died after giving birth to two sons and one daughter. The sudden death of Chandi was a terrible blow to Golap-ma. She almost lost her mind. Sometimes she would sit alone on the bank of the Ganges. During this time Yogin-ma met her and took her to Sri Ramakrishna. Then the Master introduced her to the Mother, saying, 'This girl will stay with you and serve you.'"[12]

Golap-ma later described her first meeting with the Master: "When I first went to the Master I was tormented with grief for my daughter, Chandi. Yogin took me to him. He touched my head and removed all the grief from my heart. It was amazing. In a moment, my mind became calm and serene. I immediately laughed like a *jnani*. I felt that I had come to this world to act in a play. Who is whose mother and who is whose daughter? In my childhood I had played with cloth dolls, and after that I played with flesh-and-blood dolls. This world is nothing but a play with dolls, so why should I cry for my daughter? It is a glorious thing to cry for God. Such was the power of the Master!"[13]

After Golap-ma had unburdened her heart to Ramakrishna, he said in an ecstatic mood: "You are fortunate. God helps those who have no one to call their own." After a few visits Ramakrishna introduced Golap-ma to Holy Mother, saying: "You should feed this brahmin girl well. Sorrow is assuaged when the stomach is full." Ramakrishna knew that when he was gone Holy Mother would need a companion, so one day he spoke to her about Golap-ma: "Keep your eyes on this brahmin woman. She will live with you permanently." Holy Mother gave shelter to Golap-ma, who thenceforth began to stay with her off and on in the nahabat.

Golap-ma was the Holy Mother's Vijaya and followed her like a shadow for 36 years. She went on several pilgrimages with Holy Mother to different holy places in India, including Deoghar, Puri, Prayag, Hardwar, Rameswar, Kailoar, Kothar, and other places. Golap-ma also accompanied her to Jayrambati and Kamarpukur many times. Holy Mother used to say: "I cannot go anywhere without Golap. I feel secure when she is with me." Whenever they went somewhere by carriage, Golap-ma held the Holy Mother's hand as they got in and out. When they walked anywhere, Holy Mother walked behind Golap-ma like a bashful new bride. In the Mother's Calcutta household, Golap-ma acted as a supervisor and also protected Holy Mother from emotional and temperamental devotees. Without a thought for herself, Golap-ma faithfully and joyfully served the Master, the Mother, and her devotees over a period of 36 years.

Holy Mother passed away on 21 July 1920, and Golap-ma lived for four years after that. She continued her service as usual, but she greatly missed Holy Mother. She had a little heart trouble and some minor complications, and gradually her health began to fail. One day Golap-ma told some women devotees, "Yogin died in the bright fortnight, and I shall go in the dark one."

Sarala reminisced:

Golap-ma was broken-hearted at the death of Yogin-ma. While living in Udbodhan I used to go to the Nivedita School to give some classes, and Golap-ma would keep food for me. Once I had severe food poisoning. Seeing me ill, Golap-ma's palpitations began. She was scared that I might die. However, Dr. Durgapada Ghosh treated me and I recovered. He suggested to Sharat Maharaj that I should go to Varanasi for a change. Golap-ma again became worried and said, "If she goes to Varanansi, who will look after me?" I said to Sharat Maharaj, "I shall not go to Varanasi."

Golap-ma lived in the southern room on the second floor. The day before her passing away, she was gasping. The ayurvedic doctor came and predicted, "Probably she will not last the night." In the afternoon she felt a little better. There was a big picture of the Mother in her room. Facing the picture, she prayed to the Mother with folded hands, "Mother, tomorrow is your birthday, please keep me fit." Despite her physical discomfort, she continued repeating: "Jai Ramakrishna! Jai Ramakrishna!"

On the Mother's birthday, there was a 16-item worship in Udbodhan and many people took prasad. In the morning, Golap-ma felt a little better and told me: "Sarala, today you will not have to serve me. You work for the Mother." She said to Sharat Maharaj: "Sharat, make my bed today in the corner of the Mother's room and I shall sit there." Accordingly Sharat

Maharaj made her bed, piling several pillows at her back. The Mother's worship was completed smoothly, and Swami Basudevananda came from Belur Math and informed Golap-ma that the worship went off well there. At four o'clock in the afternoon, Golap-ma said that she was not feeling well. I said: "You did not eat anything the whole day. Now eat some prasad." I gave her a chunk of orange and she ate it. Facing the Mother's picture, she said: "Mother, your worship is over. Now you do whatever you want to do." Immediately she started to gasp for air and gradually the gasping increased. But in between gasps she continued to utter, "Jai Ramakrishna! Jai Ramakrishna!" I could not hold her as I was exhausted. At midnight Sharat Maharaj took over the duty and asked me to lie down in the next room. It was December in a cold winter. After a few hours I again took over the duty and sent Maharaj to rest. Thus the night passed.

In the morning Golap-ma said to me: "Ask the cook to prepare some rice and soup quickly for the Master." According to her instruction, the food was offered to the Master and everyone had prasad. That afternoon Golap-ma breathed her last, uttering, "Jai Ramakrishna! Jai Ramakrishna!" The monks carried her body for cremation to Kashi Mitra's cremation ground. The next day I left Udbodhan House and went to the Nivedita School.[14]

A few days before her death, Golap-ma said to Swami Basudevananda: "It seems to me that this body will not last long. Quite often I see a girl wearing an ochre cloth and a rudraksha garland and carrying a trident come out of my body. Then I look at this body and it seems to be dead."[15] Golap-ma died at Udbodhan House, at 4:08 p.m. on 19 December 1924.

Sarala reminisced about Yogin-ma and Golap-ma, Holy Mother's two faithful companions: "Yogin-ma and Golap-ma were highly advanced in spiritual life, but each had her own unique way of revealing this. Yogin-ma liked to be absorbed in japa and meditation, while Golap-ma liked to be involved with service to Holy Mother and to the devotees. Golap-ma would enquire after minute details as to whether the pillows of the monks were covered or not. Like Jaya and Vijaya, they always accompanied Holy Mother. They made all efforts to ensure that her household ran smoothly. I have learned so much from them, and have received such a wealth of blessings, love, and goodwill, that I shall never be able to express in words."[16]

Aunt Bhanu

Aunt Bhanu was the Mother's childhood companion. Her proper name was Managarabini, which the villagers had abbreviated into Mani and then into Bhani. Holy Mother's devotees converted it into Bhanu. According to the village relationship, the Mother used to call her *pisi*, meaning aunt. Thus she became Bhanu-pisi, or Aunt Bhanu. Holy Mother and Bhanu were more or less the same age, and were close friends and neighbours. Holy Mother's father was the family priest of Kshetra Biswas, Bhanu's father.

When she was young, Bhanu was married to a man from Phului-Shyambazar. She had a daughter who died at a young age. Bhanu became a widow at the age of 20 and took shelter in her father's house. She was deeply religious and followed the Vaishnava tradition, against her brother's wish.

Whenever Ramakrishna came to Kamarpukur from Dakshineswar, he also visited Jayrambati, and thus he eventually met Bhanu. At that time the villagers considered the Master to be crazy, but Bhanu recognized him to be a great soul. Bhanu felt a divine attraction for the Master, so she visited him quite often. Other village women also came to see the Master. He told funny jokes to the village girls. Some laughed and some went away. Those who were genuine seekers remained, and the Master then talked to them seriously about spiritual life. To test Bhanu's sincerity, the Master teased her by saying, "Your brother Gaur is coming." That made her nervous. Then the Master told her: "You cannot realize God as long as you have shame, hatred, and fear." He also gave her some advice: "When your brother tries to punish you, raise your hands and dance, saying, 'Bhaja mon Gaur-Nitai — O my mind, worship Gaur and Nitai.' Then your brother will think you are crazy and will not bother you." The simple Bhanu followed the Master's advice and it worked.

Bhanu spun thread on a spinning wheel to support herself. Sometimes the Master visited her cottage and sang funny songs to the sound of her spinning wheel. Bhanu sometimes stayed with Holy Mother in Calcutta. After listening to the story of how the Master sang to the whir of Bhanu's spinning wheel, Nivedita got a spinning wheel and asked Aunt Bhanu to sing the songs to her. Nivedita was delighted to hear them.

During the Master's time, Bhanu's parents were in good financial condition. They had several cows and Bhanu prepared many milk products for the Master. Once while returning from Jayrambati to Kamarpukur, the Master asked Bhanu for a betel roll. She immediately went to make the betel roll, but the Master left for Kamarpukur without waiting. When Bhanu returned, she found the Master gone. It is considered inauspicious to call to a person from behind, so she ran to catch up with him. After walking some distance, the Master looked back and saw Bhanu following him. Surprised, the Master said: "Aunt, you have come such a distance!" She said, "You asked for a betel roll, so I have brought it for you."

The Master said with a smile: "You will succeed; you will succeed; you will succeed."

Bhanu understood that the Master had blessed her and that she would succeed in her spiritual disciplines. After taking the betel roll from her hand, the Master said to her: "Because you are a woman and have come alone such a distance, your people may scold you. Now do one thing: Buy an earthen pot from the house of a potter on the way back and take it home with you. They will think that you went to the potter's house."

Bhanu considered that incident to be significant in her life. Later, when devotees came to Jayrambati, she invited them into her cottage, fed them fried gram, fried sweet palm cake, and offered a betel roll. Then she would tell stories of the Master and the Mother. Holy Mother's devotees who came from distant places loved Aunt Bhanu. Forgetting food and rest, she entertained them by singing the songs that the Master had sung, and also kirtan that she had learned in her early years.

Observing that the local villagers were not interested in the Master, Bhanu lamented: "People come from Vishnupur, Tamluk, and other distant places, but our local people are ignorant about the Master. It is true: there is a shadow under the oil lamp."

In 1917, when a large number of devotees began to visit Jayrambati, Aunt Bhanu was in her late sixties. She had a slim body with a dark complexion. She was simple and always cheerful, and her dealings with people were frank and loving. She behaved like a gopi of Braja, and she sometimes sang and danced. She gestured with her hands when she spoke and was fond of talking about the Master, Holy Mother, and spiritual topics.

She worshipped Ramakrishna every day. If she went anywhere, she entrusted her picture of the Master to Indumati, Barada's wife, and told her how to perform the worship: "Pick up two tulsi leaves and offer them at the feet of the Master, saying: '*Tulsipatram Ramakrishnaya namah.*'"

Bhanu had sincere devotion for Holy Mother. When the Mother was in Jayrambati, Bhanu visited her in the evenings and talked about their early lives together and about God. Sometimes she rubbed the Mother's feet with medicinal oil. After receiving prasad from the Mother, Aunt Bhanu returned to her home with the light of an oil lamp. She was very concerned when the Mother was not well. She said that she had seen the Mother one day as a goddess with four arms. She was convinced that the Master was Lord Shiva. She told the Mother, "When you sing I hear the Master's voice."

Holy Mother replied: "I don't know, Aunt. You know all those things."

"The Master dwells in you," Bhanu replied.

When the Mother went on pilgrimage, Bhanu sometimes accompanied her. In 1912, the Mother took Bhanu along on her last visit to Varanasi where they stayed at Lakshmi Nivas, a house near the Sevashrama. One day Swami Brahmananda came to bow down to the Mother and began to joke with Aunt Bhanu. She, too, was very humorous and sang a song about Gopala:

Who has domesticated this black cat [Krishna] in our area?
O Lalita, catch him for me [Radha].
He has eaten curd, broken the jar, and wiped his face on the blanket.

While listening to Bhanu's song, Brahmananda became absorbed in ecstasy and tears poured from his eyes, wetting his shirt. The Mother saw this and later said to Bhanu: "Aunt, you are not an ordinary person. Rakhal is like an ocean and you have violently stirred him."

Once Holy Mother went with a woman and Brahmachari Gopesh to attend a 24-hour kirtan in the house of a villager who lived on the other side of Jayrambati. It was late in the evening. They saw from a distance, a dancing light coming towards them. When it came near, the Mother saw a lamp on the head of a person. The Mother recognized her and exclaimed, "Aunt!" Bhanu then came down to her normal state. She was returning home, intoxicated from the kirtan. She had put the lamp on her head and held it with her right hand, as if it were a pot; her left hand was on her waist and she was dancing to the melody of the kirtan. Both laughed. Then Holy Mother bowed down at the shrine of the villager, briefly listened to the kirtan from a distance, and returned home.

Holy Mother was very fond of Bhanu and praised her devotion. Once when Bhanu was very ill, the Mother went to see her. She said: "Aunt, you also are leaving me? If you go, with whom shall I talk?" Bhanu replied that everything was in Holy Mother's hands. Without saying anything, the Mother left. That evening Bhanu had a vision: she saw the Mother standing outside her room. The Mother extended her hand and put *charanamrita* in her mouth, and then said, "Aunt, please drink." Gradually Bhanu recovered. Bhanu was convinced that Holy Mother had saved her life. When she told this to the Mother, she replied, "Aunt, it is the will of the Master." [17]

Bhanu said: "One day, with open eyes, I saw the Mother as a devi with four arms. When she was facing me I saw her as Sarada with two arms, and when I was behind her I saw her with four arms." [18]

After the death of her parents, Bhanu's financial condition deteriorated. In this world, poverty pounds human beings. But it could not touch

Aunt Bhanu's mind because it was steeped in devotion — intense love for Ramakrishna and Sarada. Bhanu died not long before the Mother's passing away.[19]

Annapurna's Mother

The woman called "Annapurna's Mother" lived in Nakuleshwar Bhattacharya Lane, Kalighat, in South Calcutta, and her actual name is not known. Her husband died when she was young, and then her daughter Annapurna died. She could not cope with this grief, and she lost her mental balance. One day she went with Vijay Krishna Goswami to Dakshineswar to see Ramakrishna. She sang songs for the Master and developed *madhura bhava*, or the lover-beloved relationship, with him. Holy Mother fed her and took care of her when she visited Dakshineswar.[20] Later she visited the Master a few times in Cossipore. Gradually she recovered her mental health and often visited Holy Mother in Udbodhan.

On 31 January 1913, Annapurna's Mother brought a young woman to the Mother in Udbodhan for initiation. She said: "Mother, this girl has been pestering me to be taken to receive initiation from you. I could not ignore her. Therefore I have brought her to you."

Holy Mother replied: "How will it be possible to give initiation today? I have already taken my breakfast."

"But the girl is fasting," she responded. "It does not matter at all if you have eaten anything or not."

"Is she ready for initiation?"

"Yes, Mother. She has come fully prepared for it."

The Mother agreed. After the initiation was over, Annapurna's Mother began to talk about the girl and said: "She is not an ordinary girl. After reading about Sri Ramakrishna, she became eager to practise spiritual disciplines. She cut her long hair, dressed herself as a man, and set out on a pilgrimage....Later her father went there [to Vaidyanath] and brought her back home."

The Mother heard these words in silence and then remarked, "Ah, what devotion."

After the noonday meal the Mother asked her new disciple to rest for a while. She obeyed the Mother for a short time and then left the room and went to the porch. Holy Mother remarked: "She is restless." The Mother learned that the girl's husband was living alone and earning very little money, so she was living with her parents. Her husband visited her on weekends. Annapurna's Mother reported to the Mother that the girl had said to her husband: "You are not my husband. The Lord of the world alone is my lord." The Mother kept quiet, making no comment.

In the afternoon, Annapurna's Mother entered the room and said: "Mother, I saw you in a dream asking me to take your prasad, which would cure me of my disease. But Sri Ramakrishna forbade me to eat prasad from anyone. Still, I shall be glad if you will kindly give me a little of your prasad." Holy Mother refused to do so, but the woman began to insist upon it.

"Do you want to disobey Sri Ramakrishna?" Holy Mother asked.

Annapurna's Mother replied: "Sri Ramakrishna's words were applicable as long as I made a distinction between him and you. But I now realize you and he are identical. So please give me your prasad."[21]

Holy Mother yielded. A little later Annapurna's Mother and the young woman left.

Holy Mother gave her last important message "how to attain peace of mind" to Annapurna's Mother (*See Chapter 35*).

Sarala Devi (Pravrajika Bharatiprana)

Sarala was born in July 1894 in Guptipara, a small town in the Hooghly district on the bank of the Ganges. Her parents were Rajendra Nath Mukhopadhyay and Sushila Devi. At a young age she moved to Calcutta to be educated and lived with her mother's family. She first entered a missionary school; later, when Sister Nivedita's school at 17 Bosepara Lane opened in 1902, she enrolled there. She met Swamiji a few times with Nivedita and later said: "I was then a little girl, so I don't remember much about Swamiji. I remember only that he had gorgeous, well-built features and large, beautiful eyes."[22]

As was customary at the time, she was married as a child. However, she had no interest in family life. She was close to Sister Sudhira, who was a teacher in Nivedita's school, so in 1911, with Sudhira's help, Sarala ran away from her family. She moved from place to place. Holy Mother initiated her on Buddha Purnima [the full-moon day of Buddha's birthday] in 1911. In 1913, Holy Mother told her: "My child, how long will you move around in this way? Now you stay here and that will help me."

One day Swami Brahmananda asked Sister Sudhira to recruit a young woman to be a nurse in the women's section of the Ramakrishna Mission Home of Service in Varanasi. Sudhira was Sarala's guardian and wanted her to be able to support herself, so Sudhira arranged for Sarala to be trained as a nurse in Lady Duffrin Hospital in Calcutta. Golap-ma, who was very orthodox, objected because Sarala was a brahmin and would have to care for people of all castes, but Holy Mother said: "What is wrong? She will come back and serve us." The Mother blessed Sarala by putting her hand on her head and saying, "My child, don't be afraid."

Sarala trained from 1914 to 1917 and became a registered nurse. Holy Mother's blessing was fulfilled. Later Sarala was blessed to care for Holy Mother, Radhu, Yogin-ma, and Golap-ma. After the Mother passed away, when Sarala went to bow down to Swami Shivananda, he said: "My goodness! Your hands should not touch my feet; rather, put your hands on my head. We should cover your hands with gold. You have served the Mother of the Universe with those hands."

Swami Saradananda was very fond of Sarala and he instructed her to live in Varanasi and practise spiritual disciplines. He also initiated Sarala into Tantric sannyasa and gave her the name Sri Bharati. She was absorbed in sadhana in Varanasi for 27 years.

From 1953 to 1954, during the centenary of Holy Mother, the Ramakrishna Mission decided to establish Sarada Math for women; and on 2 December 1954, Sarada Math was inaugurated in Dakshineswar. Swami Sankarananda, president of the Ramakrishna Order, initiated Sarala and some other women into brahmacharya in 1953 and into sannyasa on Holy Mother's birthday on 1 January 1959. Sarala received the name Pravrajika Bharatiprana and became the first president of Sarada Math. She then began to initiate devotees, and she also travelled to various parts of India to establish branches of Sarada Math.

From 2 December 1954 to 30 January 1973, Bharatiprana lived mainly in Dakshineswar, where she manifested her ideal life to the nuns over a period of 18 years. Her steadfast devotion, austerity, humility, punctuality, renunciation, and love inspired all those who came in contact with her. She passed away on 30 January 1973. Her body was cremated at the Cossipore cremation ground, near the place where Ramakrishna's body had been cremated.

The Fortunate Dacoit Baba

Chapter 5 introduced the robber who encountered Holy Mother in 1877 in the Telo-Bhelo meadow while she was going to Dakshineswar. The Mother addressed him as "Father" and his wife as "Mother," and they treated her as their own daughter. Readers may be curious to know more about this ruthless robber's background as well as his transformation. Professor Tarit Kumar Bandyopadhyay, a native of Telo Village, wrote a short biographical sketch in his Bengali book, *Sri Sri Ma O Dakat Baba*. The following information is taken from that book.

Sagar Santra and his wife, Matangini, lived in Telo Village. Sagar was likely born in 1849. He got his name because he was born on the day of Makar-sankranti, an auspicious day when millions of people bathe in Ganga-sagar, the confluence of the Ganges and the Bay of Bengal. It is also said that he got that name because he had a gigantic body like a sagar, or ocean.

He was very tall, with a robust body. He had a dark complexion and bushy hair. His upper body was usually bare and all his strong muscles were visible. No one dared to argue or fight with him. He could eat a lot — in one sitting, he could eat three or four pounds of rice. In his youth his family was poor, so he sometimes worked as a day labourer. He asked his employers not to throw away the foamy water from their rice, and he drank it to satisfy his hunger. He also ate leftover rice that was preserved in water at night. Every night after supper at ten o'clock he would rinse his mouth with a loud noise. All the villagers knew that Sagar had finished his meal.

Every morning he practised physical exercises, such as pushups, sit-ups, and so on. He was a skilled fighter with bamboo sticks. He could whirl his bamboo stick around with such speed that he blocked brickbats or stones thrown at him. During exhibition fights with sticks, Sagar could whirl his stick for a couple of hours at a stretch with tremendous speed. People were afraid when they saw his gigantic figure, skill, strength, and energy.

Wherever he went, he tied his bushy hair up with a thin towel and carried his bamboo stick. At noon before bathing, he massaged his body with oil and sat in the sun for some time rubbing his bamboo stick with oil. On one wrist he wore a bangle that had been offered to a deity.

Sagar was also an expert tree climber. In summer, many people made their living by producing molasses from palm juice. They collected the juice by making cuts in the small palms and setting earthen jars below the cut. Juice would drip throughout the night. Very early in the morning when people were still asleep, Sagar would climb the trees and steal the palm juice, which he drank.

Sagar was an expert fisherman. When the Damodar and Mundeshwari rivers flooded during the rainy season, Sagar caught fish with a fishing net, a bamboo trap, and a fishing rod. Sometimes he spent the entire night fishing. In the morning, he would send his wife to sell his catch in the neighbouring villages. When the water subsided, Sagar cultivated the land and grew rice in the rainy season and legumes in the winter.

Sagar also worked for the wealthy Ghosh family of Telo Village, who owned vast tracts of land. Jadugopal Ghosh had two sons, Shashibhushan and Nityagopal. Shashibhushan married Jugalkishori, who came from the Palit family. She inherited some land from her father, but her brother claimed it. As a result there was litigation and bad feelings between the Ghosh and Palit families that turned into a feud. Both parties hired fighters to take possession of the land. As Sagar was a guard for the Ghosh family, he gathered a group of fighters and attacked the fighters of the Palit family. The Palit fighters could not withstand Sagar's skillful attack and they ran away. Thus Sagar protected the property of his employer.

When he retired from his job, he began to steal rice from others to support his family and from time to time rob also. Though Sagar sometimes stole from others, he was not a professional robber. Sagar and his wife were devoted to the Divine Mother, and he took a leading role in the public worship of the village. During the annual Kali Puja festival, a yatra was performed in the village for several nights. There was a yatra party in Telo Village, and Sagar acted as the demon Kamsa in *Krishna Lila* and Yama (the god of death) in a play on *Sati-Behula*. Sagar also sang and composed songs.

He and his wife had four children: The first was a daughter who died shortly after birth; the second was a son named Behari; the third was a son named Mehari who died at a young age; and the fourth was a daughter named Durgabala.

According to the Ramakrishna Punthi, Sagar sang to Holy Mother when he and his wife escorted her to Tarakeswar. Generally the robbers worked in gangs and did not take their wives during attacks. It seems Sagar and his wife were returning from somewhere to their village when they saw Holy Mother on the road in 1877. At that time Sagar and Matangini had lost their first daughter and had no other children. It seems their parental instincts welled up when they saw the Mother alone and helpless on the road. So instead of returning home, they devoted themselves to helping Holy Mother. Later both of them visited Dakshineswar and met the Master. They received the Master's and the Mother's blessings.

Sometime in April or May 1910, Sagar climbed up a bel tree to cut a branch and fell from the tree. He later died of a head injury sustained in the fall. Matangini then developed a mental illness and died ten years after her husband. Holy Mother addressed the robber couple as "father and mother" and changed their lives.[23]

On 3 May 1977, on the spot where Holy Mother spent the night in an inn with her robber parents 100 years earlier, the villagers of Telo-Bhelo built a temple and installed an image of the Mother. Swami Parameswarananda, a disciple of the Mother, dedicated this temple and established Telua Ramakrishna-Sarada Sevashrama.[24]

Holy Mother's Temple at Belur Math

After Holy Mother's passing away, Swami Saradananda had two important tasks to do in her memory. He had two temples built: One was on the spot in Jayrambati where Holy Mother was born in 1853, and the other was where her body was cremated at Belur Math in 1920. Some of the Mother's disciples and devotees came forward to fund these projects. It is amazing that Holy Mother's temple was the first built among the four temples at Belur Math — even before that of Ramakrishna. Holy Mother's temple was consecrated on her birthday, 21 December 1921. Since the Mother loved the Ganges, her temple faces this sacred river. Moreover, before his passing away, Ramakrishna had told her in an abstracted mood: "Look at the people of Calcutta; they are like worms squirming in darkness. You must bring light to them. This is not my burden alone. You, too, shall have to share it."[25] Holy Mother is facing eastward across the Ganges, towards Calcutta, as the Master wished.

Three Other Temples at Belur Math

The following are short histories of the other three temples at Belur Math:

Swami Vivekananda's temple stands on the spot where Swami Vivekananda's mortal remains were cremated on 5 July 1902. It was consecrated on his birthday on 28 January 1924. The temple has in its upper storey an alabaster OM (in Bengali characters). Beside the temple stands a bel (bilva) tree in the place of the original bel tree under which Swami Vivekananda used to sit and near which, according to his wish, his body was cremated.

Swami Brahmananda's temple stands on the spot where his body was cremated on 11 April 1922, and it was dedicated on his birthday on 7 February 1924. Swami Brahmananda was the spiritual son of Ramakrishna and the first president of the Ramakrishna Math and Mission.

Ramakrishna's temple was originally conceived by Swami Vivekananda, and it was dedicated on 14 January 1938 by Swami Vijnanananda. It enshrines the sacred relics of Ramakrishna. On 9 December 1898, long before the temple was built, Swami Vivekananda installed the relics of the Master at Belur Math. Architecturally, this temple has an important place among modern temples of India. It incorporates the motifs of various religions, thus symbolizing the harmony of religions taught by Ramakrishna.

Holy Mother's Temple at Jayrambati

The omniscient Mother knew that in the future her children would visit Jayrambati on pilgrimage, so before she passed away she arranged to purchase from her brothers the plot of land where she was born (*See Chapters 20 and 34 for details*). Holy Mother told her disciples in Jayrambati: "In the future, during my absence the Master's disciples and devotees will come here. And if they have to go from door to door for a little food and beg for shelter from the villagers — it will be unbearable for me. Henceforth you make some arrangements here so that they will find shelter."[26] To fulfill Holy Mother's wishes, Saradananda came forward to build her temple in that remote village. Swami Parameswarananda and a group of monks overcame many difficulties and had the temple built within two years.

When the Jayrambati temple was under construction, an old gentleman at Udbodhan House asked Swami Saradananda: "Maharaj, is it right to build the Mother's temple before the Master's temple?" The swami replied: "You will get an answer if you ask this question to the Master and the Mother. Only this much I can say, that if we had had your suggestion before we undertook this project, perhaps it would have been otherwise."[27] Everyone laughed and the gentleman was embarrassed.

The sanctuary of the Jayrambati temple is 33 feet, 6 inches long and 19 feet, 6 inches wide. The front veranda is 10 feet wide, the back 9 feet, and each side 8 feet 9 inches wide. The dome is 45 feet high. Some masons from Calcutta and local workers built the temple.

Holy Mother's temple was dedicated on 19 April 1923 (Akshay Tritiya, Thursday, 6 Vaishakh 1330 BE). Swami Vishweswarananda, a disciple of the Mother, performed the ritual and Swami Saradananda installed on the altar an oil painting of the Mother that she herself had worshipped and had installed at Lalit Chattopadhyay's house. The festival continued for four days; thousands of people came from various parts of the country and the neighbouring villages.

During Holy Mother's centenary celebration in 1953-1954, the front natmandir was added and a marble statue of the Mother was installed. The oil painting was moved to her bedroom in the temple.

Swami Nikhilananda, a disciple of Holy Mother, wrote: "Three shrines now stand as memorials to Holy Mother, all erected by the loving care of her beloved child Swami Saradananda. One is the Udbodhan, where she spent the last 11 years of her active life. The second, a white temple, stands on the bank of the Ganges at Belur Math where her body was consigned to fire. The third, another white temple, has been erected on the site of her birth at Jayrambati. From the top of this temple flutters a flag emblazoned with the simple word 'Ma,' reminding her devotees from far and near of her repeated assurance that she would stand by them till their hour of liberation and recalling to them her words of benediction: 'I am the Mother of the virtuous; I am the Mother of the wicked. Whenever you are in distress, say to yourself: "I have a mother."'"[28]

Appendix 1

The First Three Photographs of Holy Mother*

We are thrilled to see the wonderful photographs of Holy Mother, but we never think to inquire about when, where, and by whom these photos were taken. Many Indians are idealists who do not pay much attention to the nitty-gritty of history, whereas Westerners more often seem to be realists who appreciate the value of history.

In 1968, Swami Ishanananda, a disciple of Holy Mother who had been her attendant for 11 years, gave a photograph of Holy Mother (the front-facing, worship pose) to Advaita Ashrama. That photo was an original print that had been in Sister Nivedita's possession. At that time the author was staying at Advaita Ashrama to supervise the publication of Ishanananda's book *Matri Sannidhey* (*In the Company of Holy Mother*). Ishanananda told the monks of Advaita Ashrama the following story about the first three photographs taken of Holy Mother:

"The photo of the Mother with her eyes cast down was her first photo. Though very shy, the Mother sat to be photographed, covering her right arm. She was then in an ecstatic mood. The photographer took a photo when she was in that condition. He then loaded the second glass negative in his camera and was waiting for the second exposure. After some time, the Mother realized that the photo had been taken, so she asked Golap-ma, 'Is it over?' Mrs. Ole Bull asked the Mother to sit a little longer because she wanted to have a front-view picture with the Mother's feet visible. The Mother agreed. Nivedita arranged the Mother's sari and hair, and the photographer took a second shot, which is now worshipped everywhere. Finally, Nivedita wanted to be photographed with the Mother, and that was the third exposure."[1]

In Hollywood, on 27 December 1947, Swami Krishnananda showed his photo collection to Josephine MacLeod. When she saw the front-facing

*Translated from a Bengali article by Swami Chetanananda published in *Udbodhan*, 108:9.

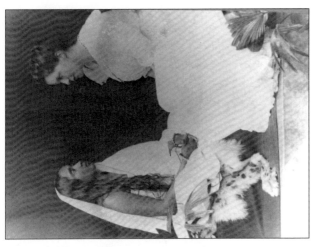

First three professional photographs of Sarada Devi at 45 years old, Calcutta, November 1898.

pose of the Mother, Miss MacLeod reminisced, which Krishnananda recorded on a gramophone disc: "Yes, it is a very nice picture. How did you [Krishnananda] make this picture coloured? Well, these records have to be kept somewhere. You know, Sarada Devi had never been seen by a man [whom she did not know] in her life. They [Sara Bull and Nivedita] said to her, 'We want a picture of you.' So I said to her, 'Would you pose?' and she replied, 'Oh, yes.' And she sat there as if she had done nothing else but pose all her life. That utter control. Such poise. There she is. That photo was taken because we wanted her to. But she didn't care for the pomp of it all."[2]

In 1910, when Holy Mother saw a photo of herself in Udbodhan, she said to Swami Arupananda, her attendant: "Yes, this is a good picture, but I was stouter before it was taken. Jogin [Swami Yogananda] was very ill at that time. I became emaciated with worry. I was very unhappy then. I would weep when Jogin's illness took a turn for the worse, and I would feel happy when he felt better. Mrs. Sara Bull took this photograph. At first I did not agree to it; but she insisted and said, 'Mother, I shall take this picture to America and worship it.' At last the picture was taken."[3]

Swami Vidyatmananda, Pijush Kanti Roy, and Swami Sattwananda did some research on the first three photographs of Holy Mother, and their findings were published in *Vedanta in the West* (172:March-April 1965) and *Udbodhan* (94:4 and 94:5; 97:9 and 97:12; 102:5). All three persons agreed that these photos were taken in November 1898 [when Holy Mother was 45 years old] by Mr. Harrington, an English photographer. But the researchers held different opinions regarding the order in which the first and the second photographs were taken. Vidyatmananda and Roy concluded that the downward-looking pose of the Mother was taken first, but Sattwananda heard from Arupananda that the front-facing pose was taken first.

The next question: where were these three photographs taken? At that time Holy Mother lived in a rented house at 10/2 Bosepara Lane, Calcutta. The Mother and Golap-ma lived on the second floor. Yogin-ma stayed with the Mother during the day and returned to her home at night. Swami Yogananda, Brahmachari Krishnalal, and a brahmin cook lived on the first floor and looked after the Mother. For the first eight or ten days of Holy Mother's residence, Nivedita stayed in one of the rooms on the first floor, and then she moved to a rented house at 16 Bosepara Lane.

Nivedita described the situation: "It was a strange household, of which I now found myself a part. Downstairs, in one of the guard-rooms beside the front-door, lived a monk [Swami Yogananda], whose severe austerities, from his youth up, had brought him to the threshold of death from consumption in the prime of manhood. To his room I used to go for Bengali lessons. In the kitchen behind, worked a disciple [Krishnalal] of his, and a brahmin cook: while to us women-folk belonged all above stairs, with roofs and terraces, and the sight of the Ganges hard by."[4]

Swami Bhumananda wrote: "The Mother was to come to Calcutta, so a house was rented at 10/2 Bosepara Lane, Baghbazar. The picture of the Mother which is found now in almost every home was taken in this house." Ashutosh Mitra, a biographer of the Mother, also wrote: "The Mother's first photo was taken at 10/2 Bosepara Lane." Swami Arupananda said that those photos were taken on the roof of that house.

After scrutinizing the three photos, it seems clear that they were indeed taken on the roof of Holy Mother's residence. Nivedita described the roof of the Mother's place. No shadows are visible in the photos, so they must have been taken in open daylight without a flash. The field camera used glass plates. The background of all three photos was a black curtain hung on a wall. In the picture of Holy Mother with Nivedita, the curtain does not cover the entire wall. A wooden cot is set in front of the background and a carpet or dark blanket is spread over the cot. There is a striped deer skin on the blanket and the Mother is seated on it. Two earthen tubs with palms are set on the floor, one on each side of her. The right-hand tub is not visible in the first two pictures, but both are visible in the picture with Nivedita. Part of the deer skin is hanging from the cot. Nivedita sits sideways on the cot facing Holy Mother, her dress covering her legs.

Now here is another question: Who arranged Holy Mother's sari and hair? Swami Gambhirananda wrote: "Sister Nivedita set the Mother's hair and upper cloth." Pravrajika Muktiprana wrote: "Mrs. Ole Bull set the position of the Mother's veil and hair." Swami Vidyatmananda said that both Nivedita and Sara Bull worked on the Mother's sari and hair when she sat on the asana. It seems that Nivedita was very free with Holy Mother, so she took the active part and Mrs. Bull helped her. All these arrangements were done before the photographer, Mr. Harrington, arrived. Careful study of these photos reveals that a cloth or a chadar has been wrapped around the Mother's chest. This is clearly visible in the photograph taken with Nivedita. Holy Mother wore a plain, red-bordered sari without a blouse under it like other women. When she went out or received visitors, she covered her upper body with a chadar. It seems that Nivedita had used a safety pin to attach the border of her sari to the cloth under her right armpit, and then artistically placed the folds of her sari. One can see these folds clearly in the front-facing photo of the

Mother. Holy Mother's long black hair was then placed over her right shoulder, covering her collar bone and the safety pin. Thus the Western women lovingly decorated this living goddess, and the photo is now worshipped by innumerable people all over the world.

All three pictures were taken at one sitting. The question arises concerning the order of the first two pictures. The present writer agrees with Swami Ishanananda's, Swami Vidyatmananda's, and Pijush Roy's opinion: first, the Mother's downward-looking pose (a side view); second, the front-view pose that is now worshipped; third, the pose with Nivedita.

When the side view of Holy Mother was taken, she was undoubtedly indrawn and in an ecstatic mood. There is no shyness on her face. A couple of toes on her left foot are visible but her entire right foot is covered by her sari.

When the front-view photo of Holy Mother was taken, she had assumed an awakened and compassionate form. The Western women brought Holy Mother's mind down from the spiritual realm to the earthly plane and arranged her hair and clothes. The Mother sat up straight. Some toes of both feet are visible. Nivedita saw how Ramakrishna sat for his shrine photo, so perhaps she placed the Mother's hands in a similar fashion. Or, Holy Mother herself could have held her hands that way. The position of Holy Mother's veil is the same in all three photos. In the first picture, her right upper arm is covered, but not in the second picture. A garland of rudraksha beads is around her neck, and diamond-cut bangles are on her wrists. In the second picture, Holy Mother's right eye is a little more open than the left. Her long black hair reaches her lap. Sara Bull wanted a picture for worship, so this second picture was taken.

The second photo of the Mother is really incomparable. In this picture, the Mother's face is beaming with simplicity and purity, compassion and grace, self-control and nobility, affection and love. It is as if the compassionate Divine Mother, giver of liberation, is looking with open eyes towards the world to bless humanity and deliver individual souls from bondage. In this picture, the Mother is not indrawn or unconscious. She is alert and awake.

In her third picture, with Nivedita, Holy Mother is fully present. She was very fond of Nivedita and very affectionate to her. She called Nivedita "Khooki," or Little Girl, and said of her, "Her outside is white and the inside is also white." So to fulfill the request of her dear Khooki, Holy Mother agreed to be photographed with her. Both sat on the same cot, face to face. This picture is very informal and the look that they exchange is ethereal. It is as if Holy Mother is pouring bountiful love and affection through her eyes on Nivedita, and she is receiving it with awe and joy.

In conclusion, in the first picture, the Mother is indrawn; and in the second and third pictures, she is fully awake. One should remember that the photos were taken in sequence, in a short time. It is more rational to accept indrawn-awake-awake rather than awake-indrawn-awake.

Holy Mother once said, pointing to herself: "Know that this body is divine. The shadow and the person are identical." So all the pictures of Holy Mother can be objects for our meditation.

*   *   *

There are nearly 35 photographs of Holy Mother: some were taken by Brahmachari Ganendranath, some by Boshi Sen, and some by professional photographers including Van Dyke and B. Datta. Ashutosh Mitra wrote in his book *Sri Ma* that on some afternoons Holy Mother went to different places in Calcutta in the horse carriage of the Nivedita School. One day in 1905, she was taken to the studio of the Van Dyke Company on Chowringhee Road, in Calcutta, and a photograph was arranged and paid for by Swami Virajananda. Another day Ashu took the Mother to B. Datta's studio on Chitpore Road. Four photographs were taken, but one was rejected. B. Datta also took some photos of the Mother at Udbodhan House. The remaining photos were taken by Ganendranath and Boshi Sen at Jayrambati, Vishnupur, and Udbodhan House.

Appendix 2

Swami Saradananda's Diary[*]

[*Swami Saradananda's personal diary describes Holy Mother's last days in Udbodhan House.*]

Friday, February 27, 1920 — Sri Sri Ma reached here at about 9 p.m. (night) in Dr. Kanjilal's motor.

Saturday, February 28, 1920 — H.M. under Dr. Kanjilal's treatment.

Sunday, February 29, 1920 — Went to Math for Sri R.K. Anniv-celebration and returned at about 5:30 p.m. Annada M. Roy paid a cheque for Rs. 2,000/- for Jayrambati and Bhubaneswar account. Paid cheque to Ganen for realisation and deposit in current account of the Tata Bank.

Monday, March 1, 1920 — Sri Sri Ma better though suffering slight rise of temperature in the afternoon.

Tuesday, March 2, 1920 — Sri Sri Ma almost the same.

Wednesday, March 3, 1920 — H. M. better and free from fever.

Thursday, March 4, 1920 — H.M. same.

Friday, March 5, 1920 — H.M. had fever up to 101° temp. in the afternoon.

Saturday, March 6, 1920 — H.M. better but not free from fever.

Sunday, March 7, 1920 — H.M.'s temp. normal in the afternoon.

Monday, March 8, 1920 — Maharajji [Swami Brahmananda] arrived at Howrah by the Puri Express at 7:30 a.m. and went directly to Belur Math. H.M.'s morning temp. 97.6°. H.M. evening temp. 99°

Tuesday, March 9, 1920 — H.M's morning temp. 99.2° H.M.'s evening temp. 99.6°

*Brahmachari Prakash, *Swami Saradananda* (Basumati Sahitya Mandir: Calcutta, 1935), 303-09.

Wednesday, March 10, 1920 — Bura Baba's cook etc., sent per Baradakanta of Kankhal (Mukti-Chaitanya) to Benares. Watch regulation (hearing gun fire). Maku and Nalini arrived here from 57 Ramkanta Bose Street (Balaram-Mandir) with Gauri-ma to stay here.

Thursday, March 11, 1920 — H.M. same.

Friday, March 12, 1920 — Kanjilal went to Math for abhisheka. H.M.'s fever rose higher. Shyamadas Kaviraj's treatment began.

Saturday, March 13, 1920 — K's abhisheka day. Went to the Math at night to witness.

Thursday, April 8, 1920 — H.M. not better with Kaviraji treatment; so Dr. Bipin took up her case from today.

Saturday, April 10, 1920 — H.M. suffering from pain in the stomach. Dr. Haran's medicine relieved her.

Sunday, April 11, 1920 — Satish came on leave from Sirgoja.

Monday, April 12, 1920 — Bipin [Dr.] absent at Ghatsila, so Drs. Durga [Durgapada Ghose] Satish [Satish Chandra Chakrabarty] and Kanjilal [Jnanendra Nath Kanjilal] treated Mother.

Tuesday, April 13, 1920 — Dr. S. Bhattacharjee [Suresh Chandra Bhattacharjee] came to see Mother.

Thursday, April 15, 1920 — Dr. Bipin [Bipin Bihari Ghose] returned from Ghatsila — came to see H.M. and altered prescription with Durga.

Monday, April 19, 1920 — Drs. Satish, Durga, and Haran came to see H.M.

Friday, April 23, 1920 — Aristochin stopped; but H.M. felt worse for it.

Saturday, April 24, 1920 — Latu Maharaj entered Maha-Samadhi at 12 noon at Benares. Drs. Bipin and Durga altered prescription for H.M.

Sunday, April 25, 1920 — H.M. same.

Wednesday, April 28, 1920 — Blood exam. of H.M. by Dr. J. N. Dasgupta.

Friday, April 30, 1920 — Dr. Bipin suggested and insisted on Soamin injection for H.M.

Saturday, May 1, 1920 — Dr. P.D. Bose [Pranadhan Bose] called for H.M.

Wednesday, May 5, 1920 — Ramkrishna Basu ill.

Saturday, May 8, 1920 — Dr. Bipin declared Ram's case to be appendicitis. — Dr. P.D.B. kept Mother without medicine.

Sunday, May 9, 1920 — Ram under Drs. Bipin and Brown's treatment. H.M. without medicine.

Monday, May 10, 1920 — Ram little better. Dr. P.D.B. came and kept H.M. without medicine.

Tuesday, May 11, 1920 — Dr. P.D.B altered medicine for H.M. Ram's illness increased and his case was declared to be hopeless in the evening.

Wednesday, May 12, 1920 — Drs. Brown, Bipin and Bhattacharjee consulted about Ram and decided to inject strychnine-digitalis to improve his pulse. They declared the case to be hopeless, for operation cannot be done on account of general weak condition and weakness of heart. Dr. Kanjilal took up the case. S. Shivananda came from the Math.

Thursday, May 13, 1920 — Ram's case became worse from afternoon.

Friday, May 14, 1920 — Ramkrishna Basu died at 3:45 p.m. H.M.'s fever rose to 100° — she had a bad night with indigestion and wind etc. — all due to hearing the sad news about Ram. Shanti-Swastyayana begun for H.M.

Saturday, May 15, 1920 — H.M.'s indigestion and wind persisted. Dr. P.D. Bose came in the afternoon. Fever rose to 99.2°

Sunday, May 16, 1920 — Fever rose to 100° at 11 p.m. — the morning temp was 97.6° — P.D. Bose, Durgapada and Dwijen came in the morning. P.D. Bose declared H.M.'s case to be K. Ajar [kala-azar] and talked about injection and Dr. Brahmachari [U. N. Brahmachari]; left very sad and disappointed at the news. What to do next?

Monday, May 17, 1920 — H.M.'s morning temp. 99.2° — it rose to 99.8° at 10 a.m. Kanjilal came in the morning en route for Dakshineswar with his wife and daughter. Told him P.D.'s opinion of H. M.'s case.

Thursday, May 20, 1920 — Sponging given with rice diet to H.M. — fever rose to 100° in the evening.

Friday, May 21, 1920 — Rice diet given to H.M. — fever rose to 100.6° at 6 p.m. becoming 98.2° at 11 p.m. — Another rise at about 3 a.m.

Saturday, May 22, 1920 — Soamin injected by Shyamapada [Dr. Shyamapada Mukherjee] at 11:30 a.m.

Tuesday, May 25, 1920 — 2nd injection of soamin at 10:30 a.m. — fever rose to 100° at 2 p.m. and to 101.4° at 7 p.m. due to what — Astami? injection? or both? Feeling disappointed.

Wednesday, May 26, 1920 — P.D. Bose came at 10:30.

Tuesday, June 1, 1920 — Doctors seemed to have come to their tether's end with regard to the case of Holy Mother. So Kaviraj Rajendra Nath was called today and given charge of her case.

Saturday, June 5, 1920 — Sudden ailment (personal) about six ounces of blood out of the urethral passage at 10:30 a.m. and relief felt by it! Told Dr. Sashi [Sashi Bhushan Ghose] of it in the afternoon, who advised urine examn.

Sunday, June 6, 1920 — Urine examn. result good — Nothing serious then? Told Dr. Kanjilal who was at a loss to understand but gave a dose of medicine. Sanyal [Vaikuntha Nath] returned from Velpukur.

Thursday, June 17, 1920 — Sri Sri Ma very ill with indigestion and inflammatory pain in the stomach. Very serious condition — but Kaviraj says it will pass over.

Monday, July 19, 1920 — 1st tooth fallen [Saradananda's].

Tuesday, July 20, 1920*. — Holy Mother in peace and glory of Maha-Samadhi at 1:30 a.m. (night).

Wednesday, July 21, 1920 — Procession to Belur Math via Baranagore at about 10:30 a.m. and the Yajna (oblation in fire) at about 3 p.m. A heavy shower ended the ceremony at about dusk.

Sunday, August 1, 1920 - Especial puja of the R.K. Order at Belur and Calcutta Maths on account of the Ascension of H.M.

Monday, August 2, 1920 — Especial puja at the [Nivedita] School.

---

*According to the Hindu calendar, the day begins at sunrise, so it is mentioned "Tuesday, July 20"; but according to the Gregorian calendar it was "Wednesday, July 21, 1920".

Appendix 3

Swami Nirlepananda's Diary*

[The last days of Holy Mother in Udbodhan House, from the diary of Swami Nirlepananda, a grandson of Yogin-ma. Translated from Bengali.]

1920

26 February [actually 27]: The Mother arrived with her companions at Udbodhan from Jayrambati at 8:45 p.m.

3 March: The Mother had a temperature every day. Hot weather.

4 March: Dol Purnima [a spring festival]. The Mother's temperature continued. All are concerned and there is no joy in anyone's mind.

8 March: Swami Brahmananda came to see the Mother in the morning. The Mother was a little better. This was her last meeting with the Master's spiritual son. The Mother was silent and Maharaj was sad and grave.

14 March: Mother is not well. Ayurvedic treatment begins.

19 March: In the afternoon, Swamis Shivananda and Vijnanananda came to see her.

26 March: Swami Brahmananda left for Bhubaneswar.

27 March: Annapurna Puja. The living Annapurna is bedridden.

2 April: Swami Vijnanananda came to see the Mother.

15 April: Kaviraj Shyamadas Vachaspati came.

26 April: Dr. Satish Chandra Chakrabarty and Dr. Kanjilal checked the Mother, as her condition was not good.

1 May: Dr. Pranadhan Basu took charge of the Mother's treatment from Dr. Bipin Ghosh.

*Swami Nirlepananda, *Ramakrishna-Saradamrita* (Karuna Prakashani: Calutta, 1968), 208-11.

2 May: Dr. Nilratan Sarkar came to see the Mother as her condition deteriorated.

12 May: Ramakrishna Basu [Balaram Basu's son] is in critical condition. The Mother's fever continued.

14 May: Ramakrishna Basu passed away at 3:45 p.m.

17 May: Regarding the Mother's treatment, there is no shortage of money or any lack of effort. It was in M.'s note that there was a shortage of money during the last days of the Master in Cossipore. Shashi Maharaj fed the Master one orange [off season] for three days.... There was no electricity in Udbodhan. The Mother's luminous body lighted the place, and now that light is on the way to extinction. Many devotees are sad.

22 May: Dr. Shyamapada Mukherjee gave an injection to the Mother.

1 June: Snanyatra, the foundation day of the Dakshineswar Kali Temple. The Mother's condition is the same.

5 June: Many monks began to visit the Mother. The house is small but packed with devotees. Some are sleeping in the courtyard of Udbodhan House.

11 June: The Mother has nausea, and the girls of the Nivedita School are attending her at night by turns.

17 June: It is unbearable to see the Mother's suffering. Her condition is critical. Many doctors and Kaviraj are visiting her. The Master's shrine along with the throne was transferred from the Mother's room to a room on the third floor. The Mother's cot has been removed from her room and a thick bed has been set on the floor. Her head is towards the altar. Kala-azar has jumped on the malaria and made the Mother's body emaciated.

18 June: Chariot festival. A signal for the Mother's departure. Mahapurush Maharaj came at night to see the Mother.

19 June: The Mother felt a little better, and Kaviraj prescribed rice and soup.

26 June: Tulsi Maharaj came to see the Mother. The medicine of Kaviraj Rajen helped a little.

5 July: The Mother's condition deteriorated. Her voice is very feeble and hard to understand. She is thirsty.

9 July: Very weak. She is reluctant to eat.

14 July: High temperature. At night she lost outer consciousness for some time.

16 July: Critical condition. She did not have outer consciousness for some time.

19 July: The ayurvedic treatment was replaced by homeopathic treatment. Heavy rain, as if all of Nature were crying.

20 July: Oxygen was administered at 11:00 p.m.

21 July: The Mother merged into Brahman at 1:10 a.m. [actually 1:30 a.m.]. The world lost the Divine Mother. Her divine body was carried from Baghbazar to Baranagore by the monks and devotees. A long procession started towards Belur Math. Her body was covered with heaps of flowers and garlands. Her forehead was tinged with vermillion. There was nonstop singing of Ramnam along the procession. The Mother's Sharat [Swami Saradananda], with his heavy body, was in front of the procession, barefoot. The last chanting for a departed person of the Ramakrishna Order, "Hari Om Ramakrishna, Hari Om Ramakrishna," continued uninterruptedly. When the procession arrived in Baranagore, flowers were showered from the upstairs of a house owned by Narayan Datta, a devotee. The Mother's body was taken to Belur Math by boat, crossing the Ganges. The Mother's body was bathed and dressed by her women disciples and the girls of Nivedita School. The funeral pyre with sandalwood and ghee was ignited at 2:00 p.m. The final oblation was done at 5:00 p.m. Nirvana. Then came a shower as if the vast space shed quiet tears. Returned to Udbodhan by boat at 7:00 p.m.

22 July: Sharat Maharaj said: "The Mother has gone. Her life will show light and give peace to the devotees forever."

Appendix 4

Journeys of Ramakrishna and Holy Mother between Kamarpukur – Jayrambati and Dakshineswar – Calcutta

Professor Tarit Kumar Bandyopadhyay made a chart detailing Ramakrishna's and Holy Mother's travels between the Kamarpukur-Jayrambati area and the Dakshineswar-Calcutta area.* We are grateful to Professor Bandyopadhyay for furnishing this thoroughly researched information, and we provide it in this appendix to help the reader visualize how Ramakrishna and Holy Mother made the long journeys on foot, by bullock cart, by palanquin, by boat, by steamer, and by train.

Telo-Bhelo route, 64 miles: Holy Mother walked from Jayrambati to Baidyabati via Arambagh-Tarakeswar, and then travelled by boat to Dakshineswar. This route passed through 61 villages (from Jayrambati) and crossed five rivers — Amodar, Dwarakeshwar, Mundeshwari, Damodar, and Ganges. Holy Mother once encountered a robber on this route.

Burdwan route, 101 miles: Sarada Devi walked from Jayrambati to Burdwan via Uchalan, a distance of 34 miles, or took a bullock cart, and then travelled to Calcutta by train for 67 miles. This route passed through 17 villages and crossed the Damodar River.

Ghatal route, 68 miles: In 1870s there was a steamer service between Calcutta and Ghatal. In July 1877, Holy Mother travelled with Ramakrishna and Hriday along this route. They went by steamer from the Armenian Ghat at Calcutta and stopped at Bandar, and then took a boat to Bali-Dewanganj. In Dewanganj, they stayed at Banshidhar Modak's house for three days, and finally either walked or went by palanquin the last eight miles to Kamarpukur.

*Tarit Kumar Bandyopadhyay, *Sri Srima O Dakat Baba*, Dev Sahitya Kutir Pvt. Ltd. (Calcutta, 1994), 45-49.

Vishnupur route, 153 miles: Holy Mother took a train from Calcutta to Vishnupur, a distance of 125 miles, and then went to Jayrambati by bullock cart or palanquin for 28 miles.

Ramakrishna's Journeys from Kamarpukur to Calcutta–Dakshineswar

Trip	Year (English/Bengali)	Route
1	1852 / 1259	Telo-Bhelo
2	1855 May / 1262 Jaishtha	Telo-Bhelo
3	1860 December / 1267 Agrahayan	Telo-Bhelo
4	1867 December / 1274 Agrahayan	Burdwan
5	1873 / 1279	Burdwan
6	1876 February / 1282 Magh	Burdwan
7	1876 September / 1283 Aswin	Burdwan
8	1877 September / 1284 Aswin	Burdwan
9	1878 September / 1285 Aswin	Burdwan
10	1880 October / 1287 Kartik	Burdwan

Ramakrishna's Journeys from Dakshineswar to Kamarpukur

Trip	Year (English / Bengali)	Route
1	1854 September / 1261 Aswin	Telo-Bhelo
2	1858 September / 1265 Aswin	Telo-Bhelo
3	1867 May / 1274 Jaishtha	Telo-Bhelo
4	1873 March / 1279 Phalgun	Burdwan
5	1876 January / 1282 Paush	Burdwan
6	1876 July / 1283 Ashar	Ghatal
7	1877 July / 1284 Ashar	Ghatal
8	1878 July / 1285 Ashar	Ghatal
9	1880 February / 1286 Magh	Burdwan

Sarada Devi's Journeys from Kamarpukur-Jayrambati to Dakshineswar-Calcutta

Trip	Year (English / Bengali)	Route
1	1872 March / 1278 Chaitra	Telo-Bhelo
2	1874 April / 1281 Vaishakh	Telo-Bhelo
3	1876 March 17 / 1282 Chaitra	Telo-Bhelo
4	1877 February / 1283 Magh	Telo-Bhelo
5	1881 March / 1287 Phalgun	Telo-Bhelo
6	1882 January / 1288 Magh	Telo-Bhelo
7	1884 January / 1290 Magh	Telo-Bhelo
8	1884 January / 1290 Magh	Telo-Bhelo
9	1885 March / 1291 Phalgun	Burdwan
10	1888 May / 1295 Vaishakh	Burdwan
11	1890 February / 1296 Magh	Burdwan
12	1893 July / 1300 Ashar	Burdwan
13	1894 January / 1300 Magh	Burdwan
14	1894 September / 1301 Phalgun	Burdwan
15	1895 February / 1301 Phalgun	Burdwan
16	1896 April / 1303 Vaishakh	Burdwan
17	1897 May / 1304 Vaishakh	Burdwan
18	1898 March / 1304 Chaitra	Burdwan
19	1900 October / 1307 Aswin	Burdwan
20	1904 February / 1310 Magh	Burdwan
21	1906 April / 1312 Phalgun	Vishnupur
22	1907 September / 1314 Aswin	Vishnupur
23	1909 May / 1316 Jaishtha	Vishnupur
24	1910 July / 1317 Ashar	Vishnupur
25	1911 November / 1318 Agrahayan	Vishnupur
26	1913 September / 1320 Aswin	Vishnupur
27	1916 July / 1323 Ashar	Vishnupur
28	1918 May / 1325 Vaishakh	Vishnupur
29	1920 February / 1326 Phalgun	Vishnupur

Sarada Devi's Journeys from Dakshineswar-Calcutta to Kamarpukur-Jayrambati

Trip	Year (English / Bengali)	Route
1	1873 October / 1280 Kartik	Telo-Bhelo
2	1875 September / 1282 Aswin	Telo-Bhelo
3	1876 November 8/ 1283 Agrahayan	Burdwan
4	1877 August / 1284 Ashar	Ghatal
5	1881 March / 1287 Phalgun	Telo-Bhelo
6	1883 June / 1290 Ashar	Telo-Bhelo
7	1884 January / 1290 Magh	Telo-Bhelo
8	1884 July / 1291 Shravan	Burdwan
9	1887 September / 1294 Bhadra	Burdwan
10	1889 February / 1295 Magh	Telo-Bhelo
11	1890 November / 1297 Kartik	Burdwan
12	1893 October / 1300 Kartik	Burdwan
13	1894 April / 1301 Jaishtha	Burdwan
14	1894 October / 1301 Kartik	Telo-Bhelo
15	1895 May / 1302 Jaishtha	Burdwan
16	1896 November / 1303 Agrahayan	Burdwan
17	1897 July / 1304 Ashar	Burdwan
18	1899 October / 1306 Kartik	Burdwan
19	1901 April / 1308 Chaitra	Burdwan
20	1905 May / 1312 Jaishtha	Vishnupur
21	1906 September / 1313 Bhadra	Vishnupur
22	1907 November / 1314 Kartik	Vishnupur
23	1909 November / 1316 Kartik	Vishnupur
24	1911 May / 1318 Jaishtha	Vishnupur
25	1913 February / 1319 Phalgun	Vishnupur
26	1915 April / 1322 Vaishakh	Vishnupur
27	1917 January / 1323 Magh	Vishnupur
28	1919 January / 1325 Magh	Vishnupur

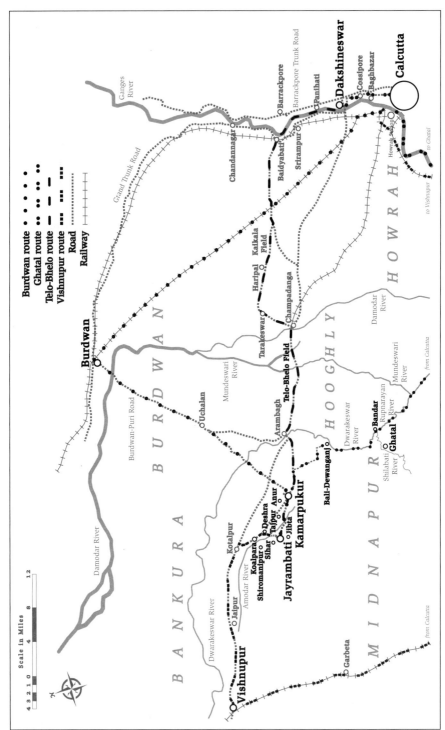

Map showing the routes Sarada Devi took between Jayrambati-Kamarpukur and Dakshineswar-Calcutta.

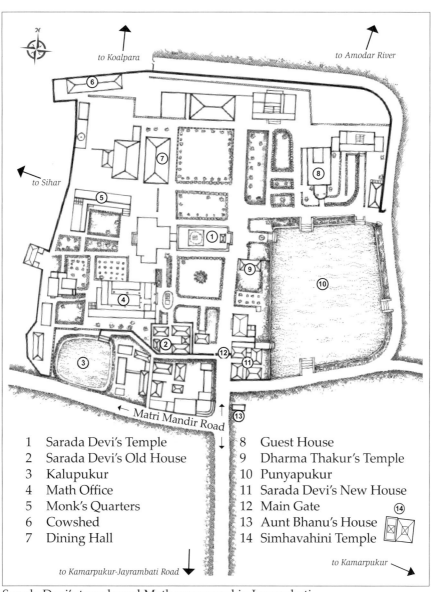

Sarada Devi's temple and Math compound in Jayrambati.

1 Sarada Devi's Temple
2 Sarada Devi's Old House
3 Kalupukur
4 Math Office
5 Monk's Quarters
6 Cowshed
7 Dining Hall
8 Guest House
9 Dharma Thakur's Temple
10 Punyapukur
11 Sarada Devi's New House
12 Main Gate
13 Aunt Bhanu's House
14 Simhavahini Temple

to Koalpara

to Amodar River

to Sihar

Matri Mandir Road

to Kamarpukur-Jayrambati Road

to Kamarpukur

Appendix 5

The Family Tree of Holy Mother

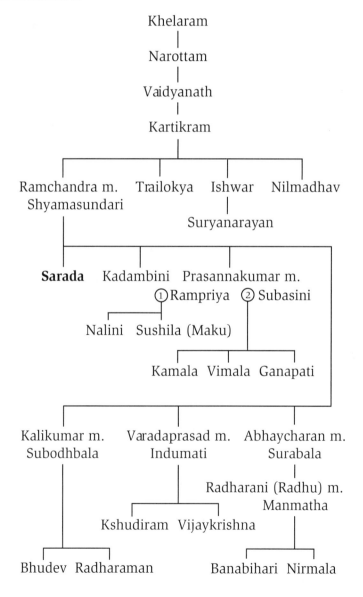

Khelaram
|
Narottam
|
Vaidyanath
|
Kartikram

Ramchandra m. Shyamasundari   Trailokya   Ishwar   Nilmadhav

Suryanarayan

Sarada   Kadambini   Prasannakumar m. ①Rampriya ② Subasini

Nalini   Sushila (Maku)

Kamala   Vimala   Ganapati

Kalikumar m. Subodhbala   Varadaprasad m. Indumati   Abhaycharan m. Surabala

Radharani (Radhu) m. Manmatha

Kshudiram   Vijaykrishna

Bhudev   Radharaman   Banabihari   Nirmala

Sri Sarada Devi: A Chronology

1853: Born in Jayrambati on Thursday evening, 22 December (8 Paush 1260, Krishna Saptami Tithi). Sarada was the first child of Ramchandra and Shyamasundari Mukhopadhyay.

1859: Marriage to Ramakrishna in May (end of Vaishakh 1266); and first visit to Kamarpukur (Ramakrishna's home).

1860: Second visit to Kamarpukur in November-December. Sarada lived with Ramakrishna for a few days and then returned to Jayrambati.

1864: Terrible famine in the area of Jayrambati. Sarada fanned hot food for the hungry people so they would not burn their mouths when eating it.

1866: Third visit to Kamarpukur in May. Eight celestial girls (companions of the Divine Mother) accompanied Sarada when she went to the Haldar-pukur for a bath. She returned to Jayrambati after a month.

1866-67: Fourth visit to Kamarpukur in December-January. Sarada stayed a month and a half. Ramakrishna and his mother, Chandramani, were then in Dakshineswar.

1867: Ramakrishna came to Kamarpukur with Hriday and Bhairavi Brahmani and stayed from May to November. Sarada visited Kamar-pukur for the fifth time and stayed for seven months. She received secular and spiritual training from Ramakrishna.

1872: First visit to Dakshineswar with her father, Ramchandra, via Telo-Bhelo in March. Fever on the way and vision of Mother Kali. Shodashi Puja on the night of Phalaharini Kali Puja (5 June).

1873: Illness in Dakshineswar. Returned to Kamarpukur and then Jayrambati in October via Telo-Bhelo. Death of Ramakrishna's brother Rameswar.

1874: Sarada's father, Ramchandra, died on 26 March. Second visit to Dakshineswar via Telo-Bhelo in April.

1875: Severe attack of dysentery during the rainy season. Returned to Jayrambati in September via Telo-Bhelo. Again attacked by dysentery and eye problem; got medicine from Mother Simhavahini through vision.

1876: Suffered from malaria and was treated at Kayapat-Badanganj. Third visit to Dakshineswar in March via Telo-Bhelo. Lived some days in the thatched hut built by Shambhu Mallick and then moved to the nahabat to serve Ramakrishna, who was then suffering from dysentery. Observed Savitri Vrata on 22 May. Returned to Jayrambati on 8 November via Burdwan.

1877: Ramakrishna's mother, Chandramani, died on 13 February in Dakshineswar. Shambhu Mallick died. Fourth visit to Dakshineswar in March via Telo-Bhelo. Encountered a highwayman. Returned to Kamarpukur with Ramakrishna and Hriday in July by steamer and boat via Bali-Dewanganj. In September, Ramakrishna returned to Dakshineswar and Sarada to Jayrambati. Her mother, Shyamasundari, had a vision of Mother Jagaddhatri and performed Her worship with Sarada'a help.

1878-80: Lived in Jayrambati.

1881: Fifth visit to Dakshineswar, with Shyamasundari, Lakshmi, and others, via Telo-Bhelo in March. Hriday treated them poorly and they left Dakshineswar on the same day with heavy hearts, returning to Jayrambati via Telo-Bhelo. In May, Hriday was dismissed from the temple for his misconduct.

1882-83: Sixth visit to Dakshineswar via Telo-Bhelo in March 1882. Served the Master till June 1883 and then returned to Jayrambati via Telo-Bhelo.

1884: Seventh visit to Dakshineswar via Telo-Bhelo. In January, Ramakrishna broke his arm. Holy Mother started her journey at an inauspicious time (Thursday afternoon), so the Master asked her to return home and start her journey again at an auspicious hour. She left the next day via Telo-Bhelo. After a few days she returned to Dakshineswar via Telo-Bhelo. This was her eighth visit. The Master sent her back to Kamarpukur in July to attend his nephew Ramlal's wedding. Everyone in her party went to Burdwan by train and then by bullock cart to Kamarpukur.

1885: Ninth visit to Dakshineswar in March 1885 via Burdwan. Ramakrishna developed cancer in April and was moved to Balaram's house in Calcutta for treatment on 26 September. On 2 October Ramakrishna was moved to the house at Shyampukur. A few days later, Holy Mother moved to Shyampukur and began cooking a special diet for the Master. On 11 December, she moved with the Master to the Cossipore garden house.

1886: Holy Mother went to Tarakeswar and prayed to Lord Shiva for the Master's recovery. The Master instructed her to look after the people of Calcutta and to live in Kamarpukur after his passing away. He passed away on 16 August at 1:02 a.m. When the cremation was over, Holy Mother tried to remove her bangles, as was customary for a Hindu widow, but the Master appeared before her and forbade her from removing her bangles. On 18 August 1886, Holy Mother, accompanied by Golap-ma, Lakshmi, and Latu, paid a visit to Dakshineswar and returned the same evening to Cossipore. She left Cossipore on Saturday, 21 August. Balaram invited her to stay in his Calcutta home. The Master's relics were installed at Kankurgachi Yogodyana on Janmashtami, 23 August. Holy Mother left for pilgrimage on 30 August with Golap-ma, Lakshmi, Nikunja Devi (M.'s wife), Jogin, Kali, and Latu. Visited Vaidyanath, Varanasi, Ayodhya, and Vrindaban, where she stayed for one year. She initiated Jogin (first disciple) according to Ramakrishna's instruction.

1887: On 31 August Holy Mother returned to Calcutta after visiting Hardwar, Jaipur, and Prayag. She lived at Balaram's house until she moved to Kamarpukur in the middle of September, travelling via Burdwan. In Kamarpukur she suffered from poverty and loneliness. Ramakrishna appeared and reassured her. According to M.'s diary she lived in Kamarpukur from September 1887 to May 1888 and visited Jayrambati from time to time.

1888: In June the devotees brought Holy Mother to Calcutta via Burdwan and rented Nilambar Mukherjee's house at Belur, where she stayed nearly six months. On the roof she had nirvikalpa samadhi. Swami Abhedananda composed a hymn (*Prakritim paramam* etc.) on Holy Mother, recited it to her, and received her blessing. On 5 November she left for Puri with several monks and devotees by steamer to Chandvali, then by motor boat to Cuttack, and finally by bullock cart to Puri. Her party lived at Kshetrabasi Math from 9 November 1888 to 9 January 1889.

1889: Holy Mother returned to Calcutta on 12 January. She visited Kalighat on 22 January. On 5 February she left for Antpur, Premananda's birthplace, with some disciples and devotees of the Master. On 12 February she returned to Kamarpukur via Tarakeswar and Telo-Bhelo by bullock cart and stayed till February 1890. During this period, Harish, a mentally unbalanced devotee, disturbed her; but Harish left when Niranjanananda and Saradananda reached Kamarpukur.

1890: Holy Mother returned to Calcutta in February via Burdwan and stayed in a rented house belonging to Raju Gomastha in Belur, near the Ganges. On 4 March she moved to M.'s house in Calcutta and then on 25 March went to Gaya with Swami Advaitananda to perform rituals for Ramakrishna's mother, Chandramani Devi, and also visited Bodhgaya.

On the way she stopped at Vaidyanath. On 2 April she returned to M.'s house and then moved to Balaram's. Balaram passed away on 13 April. In May she moved to a rented house in Ghusuri that was close to a cremation ground near Belur. In July Vivekananda went to her and sought her blessing to travel as an itinerant monk. In August Holy Mother suffered blood dysentery and in September she moved with Golap-ma to a house belonging to Saurindra Mohan Thakur in Baranagore. There Girish Chandra Ghosh met Holy Mother for the first time. After recovering from an illness, Holy Mother moved to Balaram's and then in October went to Kamarpukur-Jayrambati via Burdwan.

1891-92: In the early part of 1891 Girish visited Holy Mother at Jayrambati with Niranjanananda, Subodhananda, Bodhananda, and others. On 10 November Saradananda and others attended Jagaddhatri Puja.

1893: Vivekananda sought Holy Mother's blessing for his departure to the West on 31 May. She and her party returned to the rented Nilambar Mukherjee's house at Belur via Burdwan in July. Practised Panchatapa (austerity of five fires) with Yogin-ma on the roof. Left for Jayrambati in October via Burdwan and arranged Jagaddhatri Puja.

1894: Returned to Calcutta in January via Burdwan and went to Kailwar in Bihar with Krishnabhavini (Balaram's wife), Golap-ma, Saradananda, Yogananda, and others. Stayed there for two months. Returned to Jayrambati in April via Burdwan. Returned to Calcutta in August via Burdwan and stayed with Balaram's family. At an invitation from Matangini (Premananda's mother), she attended Durga Puja at Antpur. Returned to Kamarpukur-Jayrambati with Yogin-ma and Golap-ma in October via Telo-Bhelo.

1895: Returned to Calcutta with her mother and two of her brothers in February via Burdwan, and then left for pilgrimage. Yogin-ma, Golap-ma, and Yogananda accompanied her. Visited Varanasi, Vrindaban (where she stayed for two months), Prayag, and Gaya. Returned to Calcutta in April. Stayed with M.'s family for a month and then left for Jayrambati on 13 May via Burdwan. Visited Kamarpukur in November.

1896: Returned to Calcutta in April via Burdwan and stayed one month at Sharat Sarkar's house at 59/2 Ramkanta Basu Street. Trigunatitananda read a letter from Vivekananda to her, and she was happy to hear news of his work. Moved to a rented house on Sarkar Bari Lane with Golap-ma and Gopal-ma and stayed six months. The first floor was a turmeric warehouse. In November after Kali Puja, left for Jayrambati via Burdwan.

1897: Vivekananda returned from the West to Calcutta on 20 February and then in March went to Darjeeling for a rest. Holy Mother returned to Calcutta via Burdwan in April. On 29 April Swamiji met her at 10/2 Bosepara Lane, Baghbazar. After receiving her blessings, Swamiji inaugurated the Ramakrishna Mission at Balaram's house on 1 May. Holy Mother left for Jayrambati on 21 June via Burdwan.

1898: Ramakrishna Math moved from Alambazar to Nilambar Mukherjee's house in Belur on 3 February. The Belur Math property was registered on 5 March. Holy Mother returned to Calcutta via Burdwan in March and stayed at 10/2 Bosepara Lane. On 14 March Swamiji visited her with some monks and devotees. On 17 March, Nivedita, Sara Bull, and Josephine MacLeod visited and had refreshments with her. In April Vijnanananda began supervising the construction of Belur Math. On 7 April Holy Mother visited Belur Math. Nivedita, Mrs. Bull, and Miss MacLeod were staying there, and they cordially received her and showed her around. In October, Swamiji returned from Amarnath and visited the Mother on Maha Ashtami at Baghbazar with Brahmananda and Saradananda. Holy Mother visited Belur Math on 12 November, the day before Kali Puja, and then returned to Calcutta with Swamiji, Brahmananda, Saradananda, and others. The next day she blessed the opening ceremony of the Nivedita School at 16 Bosepara Lane. The first three photographs of Holy Mother were taken in November under the arrangement of Sara Bull. The consecration ceremony for Belur Math was held on 9 December. On 20 December the Mother visited Belur Math to see the new Belur monastery and shrine.

1899: On 2 January, the Ramakrishna Math was moved from Nilambar Mukherjee's house to Belur Math. On 13 March, Holy Mother worshipped Ramakrishna at the Nivedita School and in the evening visited the Chatterjee Nursery with the students. On 15 March, she worshipped the Master at Belur Math on the occasion of Ramakrishna's birth anniversary. Yogananda died on 28 March. Nivedita and Sadananda began plague relief efforts in Calcutta on 31 March. On 20 June, Holy Mother arranged a feast for Swamiji, Turiyananda, and Nivedita, who left for the West in the evening. On 2 August, Holy Mother's younger brother, Abhaycharan, died. On 30 October, she left for Jayrambati via Burdwan.

1900: Radharani (Radhu) was born in Jayrambati on 26 January. Holy Mother suffered from cholera in Kamarpukur and returned to Calcutta in October with Radhu, Surabala, Uncle Nilmadhav, and Aunt Bhanu via Burdwan. They stayed at 16 Bosepara Lane. On 9 December Swamiji returned from the West.

1901: Holy Mother attended Ramakrishna's birth anniversary at Belur Math on 24 February. She attended the first Durga Puja at Belur Math from 18 to 22 October and stayed at Nilambar Mukherjee's house.

1902: While in Calcutta, Holy Mother had a vision concerning Radhu's future. In April, she left for Jayrambati via Burdwan with Radhu, Surabala, and Nilmadhav. Had another vision concerning Radhu in which Ramakrishna told her: "Take her as a support. She is Yogamaya." Vivekananda passed away on 4 July at Belur Math.

1903: Lived in Jayrambati.

1904: Returned to Calcutta via Burdwan with Radhu and others on 14 February and lived in a rented house at 2/1 Baghbazar Street. Niranjanananda passed away on 9 May. Holy Mother attended the Chariot Festival at the Archanalay in Entally and then attended Janmashtami at Kankurgachi. In the middle of December she went to Puri by train with devotees and many relatives, including her mother and brothers. The party stayed at Kshetrabasi Math. Holy Mother suffered from an abscess that needed surgery. Visited Jagannath and other temples.

1905: Returned from Puri to Calcutta during the third week of January. Holy Mother's uncle Nilmadhav died in March. She was photographed in April at B. Datta's studio in Chitpore, and in May at Van Dyke's Chowringhee studio. In May she left for Jayrambati by train via Vishnupur. On subsequent trips to Jayrambati and to Calcutta, she always travelled by train via Vishnupur. Her brother Prasanna's wife Ramapriya died, and Holy Mother took responsibility for her two daughters, Nalini and Sushila (known as Maku).

1906: Shyamasundari died in January. Holy Mother returned to Calcutta in April. Gopal-ma passed away on 8 July. Kedar Das donated a piece of land to Belur Math on 18 July. Saradananda began plans to build a house for Holy Mother's permanent residence and the Udbodhan publication office. Holy Mother returned to Jayrambati in September before Jagaddhatri Puja.

1907: Despite her poor health, she returned to Calcutta to attend Durga Puja at Girish's invitation in September. Stayed at Balaram's house. Returned to Jayrambati on 11 November. Construction of Udbodhan House (The Mother's House) began.

1908: Construction of Udbodhan House was finished at the end of the year and the publication office moved there on the first floor.

1909: Attended Ramakrishna's birth anniversary in Kamarpukur. On 23 March Saradananda left for Jayrambati with Yogin-ma, Golap-ma, and Bhumananda at Holy Mother's invitation to help partition her family property. After finishing the task, Saradananda left for Calcutta on 22 May with Holy Mother and others. She entered Udbodhan House, her permanent Calcutta residence, on 23 May. Contracted chicken pox in June. Attended the Janmashtami festival at Yogodyana on 6 September. Left for Jayrambati on 16 November. Swami Advaitananda passed away at Belur Math on 28 December.

1910: Holy Mother returned to Calcutta in July. Seeing her poor health, Krishnabhavini (Balaram's wife) suggested that she accompany her to Kothar in Orissa, where her family had a retreat house. Holy Mother agreed. On 5 December, she left Calcutta with Radhu, Surabala, Golap-ma, and some monks, as well as Krishnabhavini's family.

1911: Holy Mother stayed at Kothar 66 days, and her health improved. Expressed a desire to visit Rameswaram. Ramakrishnananda planned a pilgrimage for South India. Holy Mother left Kothar with a large party on 8 February. The party rested at Berhampore and then continued to Madras. They arrived on 11 February and stayed at Sundar Vilas, opposite to the Ramakrishna Math. Left for Madurai on 11 March by a night train. The next day visited the Meenakshi temple and other places. The party went by train to Mandapam, then by steamer to Pamban, and finally by train to Rameswaram. Worshipped Lord Shiva with 108 gold bel leaves and visited the Raja of Ramnad's treasury. After spending three days in Rameswaram, the party returned to Madras via Madurai. Went to Bangalore by train on 24 March and stayed three days. Returned to Madras on 28 March and left for Puri on 1 April. On the way, the party stopped at Rajahmundry and the Mother bathed in the Godavari River. Left Rajahmundry on 4 April and reached Puri on the same day. On 10 April, the party left for Calcutta. They arrived on 11 April. The Master's disciples held a reception at Belur Math. On 12 May, Holy Mother saw Nivedita for the last time and then left for Jayrambati on 17 May. Radhu's wedding was held on 10 June. Ramakrishnananda died on 21 August and Nivedita died on 13 October. Installed pictures of Ramakrishna and herself in the shrine of Koalpara Ashrama. Returned to Calcutta on 24 November.

1912: Girish died on 9 February. Attended Durga Puja at Belur Math from 16 to 20 October and stayed in Sonarbagan House (now Leggett House). Holy Mother left for her last pilgrimage to Varanasi on 5 November and stayed at Lakshmi Nivas. Visited Vishwanath, Annapurna, and other important places. On 9 November, visited the Ramakrishna Sevashrama and donated ten rupees. Went to see Sarnath with her companions. Observed her birthday on 30 December.

1913: Returned to Calcutta on 16 January. Left for Jayrambati on 23 February and rested at Koalpara Ashrama. Kalikumar's son Bhudeb was married on 7 May. Holy Mother suffered from dysentery in July. Saradananda sent Dr. Kanjilal to treat her and Sudhira to care for her. Holy Mother returned to Calcutta on 29 September.

1914: Holy Mother remained in Udbodhan House for the whole year. Asked Keshavananda to build a house for her in Koalpara as a place for her to rest between Jayrambati and Calcutta. Moreover, she wanted to stay away from her brothers' squabbling. With the help of local workers, the monks built a residence that contains three rooms plus a kitchen, and a toilet. Later it was named Jagadamba Ashrama.

1915: On 10 January, Trigunatitananda died in San Francisco. In the evening of 15 January, Saradananda read to Holy Mother the first part of *Lilaprasanga,* which describes the Master's early life. On 19 April, Saradananda accompanied her to Jayrambati. Preparations were made to build a new house for the Mother in Jayrambati. A piece of land was purchased from the Mother's brothers at the southwest corner of the pond called Punyapukur. Keshavananda drew the plan and four mud cottages were built at a cost of 2,000 rupees. This residence is now called The Mother's New House. Punyapukur was purchased for Holy Mother by Lalit Chattopadhyay. In September, she came to Koalpara with Radhu, Maku, and Nalini and stayed 15 days. Gauri-ma visited Jayrambati.

1916: Holy Mother entered her new house in Jayrambati on 15 May. On 2 July, Saradananda went to Jayrambati and was pleased to see the Mother in her new house. On 6 July, he accompanied her to Koalpara Ashrama. At her request, the new house and a paddy field were endowed to the Goddess Jagaddhatri. This was registered on 7 July. That evening, Holy Mother and her party left for Vishnupur. They arrived in Calcutta on 8 July. Attended Durga Puja at Belur Math from 3 to 6 October and stayed at the Sonarbagan House.

1917: Holy Mother left for Jayrambati on 31 January. Stayed at Jagadamba Ashrama for a couple of days. In November, Jagaddhatri Puja was held at the new house. In the fall, the Mother suffered on and off from malaria.

1918: Holy Mother had a high temperature on her birthday, 4 January. On 21 January, Saradananda went to Jayrambati with Dr. Kanjilal, Dr.

Satish Chakrabarty, Yogin-ma, Golap-ma, and Sarala. She was cured by Dr. Kanjilal's treatment. Police harassed visitors to the Koalpara and Jayrambati ashramas. Bibhuti Ghosh approached a high-ranking police officer and stopped the harassment. Holy Mother moved to Koalpara in March and had a relapse of malaria. A cable was sent to Saradananda on 10 April and Dr. Kanjilal left for Koalpara on the same night. On 17 April, Saradananda, Dr. Satish Chakrabarty, and Yogin-ma arrived. On 21 April, Holy Mother's fever abated and she ate solid food. On 29 April, Saradananda accompanied the Mother to Jayrambati and then left for Calcutta on 5 May. They arrived at Udbodhan on 7 May. Premananda died on 30 July. On 31 December, Holy Mother moved to Nivedita School's boarding house with Radhu, who was pregnant and suffering from neurasthenia. Radhu could not bear any noise.

1919: On 27 January, Holy Mother left for Jayrambati with Radhu and reached Koalpara on 29 January. Radhu preferred to stay at the solitary Jagadamba Ashrama. Holy Mother arranged various kinds of treatment for Radhu. On 20 April, Maku's son Neda died. On 7 May, Radhu gave birth to a baby boy whom Holy Mother named Banabihari. She moved to Jayrambati on 23 July. Her birthday festival was on 13 December, and in the afternoon she had intermittent fever.

1920: On 24 February, Saradananda sent Bhumananda, Atmaprakashananda, and Boshiswar Sen to bring Holy Mother to Calcutta. All arrived at Udbodhan on 27 February. Holy Mother's last days and the detailed medical treatment have been recorded by Saradananda (see Appendix 2) and Nirlepananda (see Appendix 3). On 24 April, Adbhutananda passed away. On 14 May, Balaram's son Ramakrishna Basu died. On 20 May, Holy Mother's brother Baradaprasad died. On 21 July at 1:30 a.m., Holy Mother entered into Mahasamadhi, and her body was cremated at Belur Math on the same day.

Glossary

Abhaycharan, or **Abhay:** Holy Mother's youngest brother. He died before his wife, Surabala, gave birth to their daughter, Radhu.

Abhedananda, Swami (Kali): A disciple of Ramakrishna who accompanied Holy Mother during her 1886 pilgrimage. He wrote a hymn to Holy Mother, worked in Europe and America, and established Ramakrishna Vedanta Math in Calcutta.

Achalananda, Swami (Kedarnath): A disciple of Vivekananda who helped to establish the Ramakrishna Mission Home of Service in Varanasi.

Adbhutananda, Swami (Latu): A disciple of Ramakrishna and attendant of Holy Mother.

Advaitananda, Swami (Senior Gopal): A disciple of Ramakrishna and attendant of Holy Mother.

Aghoremani Devi: *See* Gopal-ma.

Ambika: A watchman in Jayrambati.

Amzad: A Muslim robber who took refuge in Holy Mother. He helped construct her new cottage in Jayrambati.

Annapurna's Mother: She sometimes visited Ramakrishna in Dakshineswar and Cossipore. She was close to Holy Mother. (*See* Epilogue.)

Arupananda, Swami (Rasbihari): A close disciple and attendant of Holy Mother.

Ashu, or **Ashutosh Mitra:** *See* Satyakama, Brahmachari.

avatar: A deity born as a human being; a divine incarnation.

Baburam: *See* Premananda, Swami.

Bagala: A fierce aspect of the Divine Mother.

Balaram Basu: A wealthy householder devotee of Ramakrishna.

Banabihari, or **Banu:** Radhu's son.

Barada, Brahmachari: *See* Ishanananda, Swami.

Baradaprasad, or **Barada:** One of Holy Mother's younger brothers.

Basudevananda, Swami (Harihar): A disciple of Holy Mother and worshipper in Udbodhan House.

Baul: An itinerant minstrel of Bengal.

bhairavi: A Tantric nun.

Bhanu, Aunt (also known as **Managarabini** or **Bhanu-pisi): Holy** Mother's childhood friend. (*See* Epilogue.)

Bharatiprana, Pravrajika (Sarala): A close disciple of Holy Mother who tended her during her final illness. (*See* Epilogue.)

Bhumananda, Swami (Brahmachari Jnanananda): Author of *Sri Sri-mayer Jivan Katha.*

Bibhuti Ghosh: A close disciple of Holy Mother from Bankura.

Boshiswar Sen: A brother of Sureshwar Sen of Vishnupur.

Brinde, or **Binodini Dasi:** A maidservant at the Dakshineswar temple complex.

Bull, Sara, or **Mrs. Ole Bull:** An American disciple of Vivekananda who donated funds to acquire the Belur property in 1898.

chadar: A lightweight shawl.

chamara: A fan used in worship.

chana dal: Chickpea stew.

chapati: Hand-made Indian bread, similar to a tortilla.

charanamrita: Sanctified water.

Christine, Sister (Christine Greenstidel): One of Vivekananda's American disciples. She taught at Sister Nivedita's school for girls.

dakshina: An offering given to a priest officiating at a puja.

darshan: Being in the presence of a deity or a holy person.

Devamata, Sister (Laura Glenn): An American disciple of Swami Para-mananda who served Holy Mother during her stay in Udbodhan House.

Dhirananda, Swami (Brahmachari Krishnalal): Initiated by Holy Mother; he attended Swami Vivekananda and assisted Swami Yoga-nanda in serving Holy Mother.

dhoti: A man or boy's garment made of one long piece of cloth.

Durgacharan, or **Nag Mahashay:** A staunch devotee of Ramakrishna and Holy Mother.

Durgapada Ghosh: A doctor and disciple of Holy Mother.

Ekadashi: The eleventh day after the new or full moon; a day of fasting for many Hindus.

Gagan: *See* Ritananda, Swami.

Ganendranath, Brahmachari (Ganen): A disciple of Holy Mother who took many photos of her.

Gauri-ma, or **Gaurdasi:** A devotee of Ramakrishna who sometimes stayed with Holy Mother. She established Sri Saradeshwari Ashrama.

Gauriswarananda, Swami (Rammay): A close disciple of Holy Mother who served her in Jayrambati.

ghat: A ceremonial pitcher that has been consecrated for worship.

Girijananda, Swami (Girija, also **Tarun):** A disciple of Holy Mother.

Glenn, Laura: *See* Devamata, Sister.

Golap-ma: Golap Sundari Devi, a devotee of Ramakrishna and attendant of Holy Mother. (*See* Epilogue.)

Gopal, Senior: *See* Advaitananda, Swami.

Gopal-ma: Aghoremani Devi, a devotee of Ramakrishna who had visions of her Chosen Deity, Baby Krishna.

Gopesh: *See* Saradeshananda, Swami.

Greenstidel, Christine: *See* Christine, Sister.

guna: A fundamental principle of nature. *See* sattva, rajas, and tamas.

Haldarpukur: A pond in Kamarpukur.

Haripremananda, Swami (Hari): A disciple and attendant of Holy Mother.

harital: A yellow mineral.

homa: A fire ceremony.

Ishanananda, Swami (Brahmachari Barada): A close disciple and attendant of Holy Mother during the last 11 years of her life. The author of *Matri Sannidhey* (*In the Company of Holy Mother*).

Ishwar: Paternal uncle of Holy Mother.

ishwarakoti: A godlike soul.

jiva, jivakoti: An ordinary soul.

Jnanananda, Brahmachari: *See* Bhumananda, Swami.

Jnanananda, Swami (Brahmachari Jnan): An attendant of Holy Mother in Jayrambati.

Jogin: *See* Yogananda, Swami.

Kadambini: Sister of Holy Mother. She died in her youth.

Kali: *See* Kalikumar.

Kalikrishna: *See* Virajananda, Swami.

Kalikumar, or **Kali:** One of Holy Mother's younger brothers.

Kanjilal, Jnanendra Nath: A doctor and disciple of Holy Mother. He was her main physician.

kaviraj: An ayurvedic doctor.

Kedar or **Kedernath Datta:** *See* Keshavananda, Swami.

Kedarnath: *See* Achalananda, Swami.

Keshavananda, Swami (Kedarnath Datta): A close disciple of Holy Mother who established Koalpara Ashrama.

Khagen: *See* Shantananda, Swami.

khichuri: A dish made of rice and lentils.

Kishori: *See* Parameswarananda, Swami.

Krishnabhavini: Wife of Balaram Basu.

Krishnalal, Brahmachari: *See* Dhirananda, Swami.

Lakshmi: Daughter of Rameswar and niece of Ramakrishna.

Lalit Chattopadhyay: A heroic and devoted disciple of Holy Mother.

Latu: *See* Adbhutananda, Swami.

Leggett, Betty: An American devotee of Vivekananda and sister of Josephine MacLeod.

luchi: A type of fried bread.

MacLeod, Josephine: An American devotee of Vivekananda who became close to Holy Mother.

Mahendra Nath Gupta, or **M.:** Recorder of *The Gospel of Sri Ramakrishna*.

Maheswarananda, Swami (Vaikuntha Maharaj): A disciple of Holy Mother and a physician who practised both allopathic and homeopathic medicine.

Maku, or **Sushila:** A niece of Holy Mother and a daughter of Prasanna. (*See* Epilogue.)

Mandakini, or **Manda:** A young widow from Nabasan Village and an attendant of Holy Mother.

Matangini: Wife of Sagar Santra, Holy Mother's dacoit father from Telo Village.

nahabat: A concert tower at Dakshineswar where musicians performed.

naivedya: Food offered during worship.

Nalini: A daughter of Prasanna and niece of Holy Mother. (*See* Epilogue.)

Narayan Iyenger: *See* Srivasananda, Swami.

Neda: A son of Maku and a great nephew of Holy Mother.

Nikunja Devi: M.'s wife and a disciple of Holy Mother.

Niranjanananda, Swami (Niranjan): A disciple of Ramakrishna.

Nivedita, Sister (Margaret Noble): An Irish disciple of Vivekananda who started a school for girls in Calcutta. Holy Mother was extremely fond of her and blessed her school.

paddy: Unprocessed rice.

panchatapa: An austerity involving five fires. The spiritual aspirant sits under the blazing sun, surrounded by four fires, and repeats mantra from dawn to dusk.

Parameswarananda, Swami (Kishori): An intimate disciple of Holy Mother. Author of *Sri Sri Ma O Jayrambati*.

pinda: Food offered at a funeral ceremony.

Prabodh: A disciple of Holy Mother and headmaster of Badanganj High School.

Pranadhan Basu: A Christian doctor who treated Holy Mother at Udbodhan House, refusing to be paid.

pranam: To bow down or prostrate oneself.

prasad: Food that has been offered to a deity or a holy person.

Prasanna, or **Prasannakumar:** One of Holy Mother's younger brothers.

Premananda, Swami (Baburam): A disciple of Ramakrishna who was close to Holy Mother.

puja: Ritualistic worship.

purnāhuti: The final offerings made into the fire during a homa ceremony.

Radhu, or **Radharani:** A niece of Holy Mother and daughter of Abhay-charan and Surabala. (*See* Chapter 19 and Epilogue.)

rajas: The active quality, or guna.

Rajen, Brahmachari: *See* Vidyananda, Swami.

Ramchandra: Father of Holy Mother.

Ramlal: A son of Rameswar and nephew of Ramakrishna; also a priest of the Kali temple in Dakshineswar.

Rammay: *See* Gauriswarananda, Swami.

rasagolla: A moist sweet made from cheese.

Rasbihari: *See* Arupananda, Swami.

Ritananda, Swami (Gagan): A disciple of Holy Mother.

sadhu: A holy person or spiritual aspirant.

Sagar Santra: Holy Mother's dacoit father from Telo Village. (*See* Epilogue.)

samskara: A tendency or habit inherited from a previous life.

sandesh: A dry sweet made of cheese.

Saradananda, Swami (Sharat): A direct disciple of Ramakrishna and devoted caretaker of Holy Mother. Author of *Sri Ramakrishna and His Divine Play*.

Saradeshananda, Swami (Gopesh): A close disciple and attendant of Holy Mother. Author of *Sri Sri Mayer Smritikatha* (*The Mother as I Saw Her*).

Sarajubala Sen: A close disciple of Holy Mother and a recorder of her reminiscences.

Sarala: *See* Bharatiprana, Pravrajika.

sari: A woman's garment made of one length of cloth.

sattva: The peaceful or spiritual quality, or guna.

Satyakama, Brahmachari (Ashutosh): A younger brother of Swami Tri-gunatitananda and a disciple and attendant of Holy Mother. Author of *Srima*.

Shakambhari: Wife of Rameswar and sister-in-law of Ramakrishna.

Shantananda, Swami (Khagen): A close disciple and attendant of Holy Mother.

Sharat: *See* Saradananda, Swami.

Shivaram: A nephew of Ramakrishna and godson of Holy Mother.

shrāddha: A ritual held for a departed soul.

Shyamasundari Devi: Mother of Holy Mother.

Srivasananda, Swami (Narayan Iyengar): A high-ranking official in Mysore who was initiated by Holy Mother with his wife and daughter. Holy Mother gave him an ochre cloth and advised him to take formal vows after retiring; in 1934 Swami Shivananda gave him the vows of sannyasa.

Sudhira, Sister (Sudhira Basu): A sister of Swami Prajnananda (Debabrata Basu). She was a teacher at Sister Nivedita's school and ran the school from 1914 to 1920. She received initiation from Holy Mother and became one of her closest disciples.

Surabala: Wife of Abhaycharan, sister-in-law of Holy Mother, and mother of Radhu. She was known as "Crazy Aunt."

Sureshwar Sen: He and his family were disciples of Holy Mother. While travelling to Calcutta via Vishnupur, Holy Mother stayed in their home.

Sushila: *See* Maku.

tamas: The inactive or inert quality, or guna.

tanpura: A stringed instrument used as a drone.

tapasya: Austerities.

Trailokya Nath Biswas: A son of Mathuranath Biswas and grandson of Rani Rasmani, the founder of Dakshineswar Temple.

Trailokya: Paternal uncle of Holy Mother.

Vaikuntha: *See* Maheswarananda, Swami.

Vidyananda, Swami (Brahmachari Rajen): A disciple and attendant of Holy Mother. He built Mother's temple in Jayrambati and was its first caretaker.

Virajananda, Swami (Kalikrishna): A disciple of Holy Mother whom she initiated in 1893. He was given sannyasa by Vivekananda in 1897.

yatra: A dramatic performance with music and dance, usually performed outdoors.

Yogamaya: Shakti, or the Divine Mother.

Yogananda, Swami (Jogin): A disciple of Ramakrishna and an attendant of Holy Mother.

Yogendra: The mail carrier at Jayrambati.

Yogin-ma, Yogindramohini Biswas: A disciple of Ramakrishna and a close companion of Holy Mother. (*See* Epilogue.)

References

We have provided exhaustive references so that readers know the sources of incidents, episodes, reminiscences, and utterances. Following is a list of abbreviations for important sources that have been frequently cited:

Abbr. Title

AK   Abhaya Dasgupta, ed., *Sri Sri Saradadevi: Atmakatha*, Ramakrishna Mission Institute of Culture: Calcutta, 1994

BS   Pravrajika Nirbhayaprana, ed., *Bharatiprana Smritikatha*, Sarada Math: Dakshineswar, 1988

DP   Swami Saradananda, *Sri Ramakrishna and His Divine Play*, trans. by Swami Chetanananda, Vedanta Society: St. Louis, 2003

GHM   Her Devotees and Children, *The Gospel of the Holy Mother Sri Sarada Devi*, Ramakrishna Math: Chennai, 2004

HMN   Swami Nikhilananda, *Holy Mother*, Ramakrishna–Vivekananda Centre: New York, 1962

MD   Swami Chetanananda, ed., *Matri Darshan*, Udbodhan Office: Calcutta, 1987

MJ   Swami Parameswarananda, *Sri Srima O Jayrambati*, Matri Mandir: Jayrambati, 1971

MJKB Swami Bhumananda, *Sri Sri Mayer Jivan-katha*, Sri Ramakrishna Sarada Math: Calcutta, 1986

MK   *Mayer Katha* (in one volume), Udbodhan Office: Calcutta, 2004

MSI   Swami Ishanananda, *Matri Sannidhey*, Udbodhan Office: Calcutta, 1969

MSS   Swami Saradeshananda, *Sri Sri Mayer Smritikatha*, Udbodhan Office: Calcutta, 1982

RG   M., *The Gospel of Sri Ramakrishna*, trans. Swami Nikhilananda, Ramakrishna–Vivekananda Centre: New York, 1969

RSD   Monastics, Devotees, and others, Swami Purnatmananda, ed., *Reminiscences of Sri Sarada Devi*, Advaita Ashrama: Calcutta, 2004

SB   Purva Sengupta, ed., *Srima Bhashita*, Ramakrishna Mission Institute of Culture: Calcutta, 2011

SDA   Brahmachari Akshay Chaitanya, *Sri Sri Sarada Devi*, Calcutta Book House: Calcutta, 1972

SDG   Swami Gambhirananda, *Srima Sarada Devi*, Udbodhan Office: Calcutta, 2008

SDM   Manada Shankar Dasgupta, *SriSrima Saradamani Devi*, Calcutta, 1956

SDT   Swami Tapasyananda, *Sri Sarada Devi: The Holy Mother*, Ramakrishna Math: Chennai, 1958

SDTC *Sri Sarada Devi, The Holy Mother: Her Teachings and Conversations*, Swami Nikhilananda and Swami Adiswarananda, Skylight Paths Publishing: Vermont, 2004

SGW *Sri Sarada Devi: The Great Wonder*, A compilation, Ramakrishna Mission: New Delhi, 1984

SMA   Ashutosh Mitra, *Srima*, Calcutta, 1944

SP   Swami Purnatmananda, ed., *Sri Sri Mayer Padaprante*, Udbodhan Office: Calcutta (Vol. 1:1995; 2:1995; 3:1997; 4:2003)

SS   Swami Lokeswarananda, ed., *Shatarupe Sarada*, Ramakrishna Mission Institute of Culture: Calcutta, 1985

Introduction

1. Swami Bhumananda, *Swami Saradananda: Jeman Dekhiachi* (Udbodhan Office, 1928), 296; Brahmachari Prakash, *Swami Saradananda* (Basumati Sahitya Mandir: Calcutta, 1936), 202–03
2. HMN, 3–4
3. SDT, 73
4. HMN 257; *The Complete Works of Swami Vivekananda*, Advaita Ashrama (Calcutta, 1969), 482
5. MK, 350; AK, 74
6. HMN, 270
7. Ibid., 159; MK, 96
8. Thomas and Thomas, *Great Philosophers*, (Bharatiya Vidya Bhavan: Bombay), ix

Chapter 2
Birth and Early Life of Sarada Devi

1. SDG, 14
2. SDG, 14–15; SDA, 5
3. AK, 3
4. Ibid., 4
5. HMN, 22; SDA, 13
6. AK, 4–5
7. Krishna Chandra Sengupta, *Sri Sri Lakshmimani Devi* (Cuttack, 1943), 11
8. Ramakrishna Mission Institute of Culture (Calcutta 2006), *Mayer Chithi*, 3, 79 (*See details in Chapter 27*).
9. SDG, 18–19
10. Ibid., 19
11. SDG, 20, AK, 6–7

Chapter 3
Marriage and Early Years

1. HMN, 25–26
2. Adapted from *Sri Sri Ramakrishna Punthi*, Akshay Kumar Sen (Udbodhan Office: Calcutta, 1949), 52–54
3. AK, 8; SDA, 17; HMN, 28
4. DP, 326
5. AK, 9; HMN, 31
6. SP, 2:432
7. AK, 10–11; HMN, 31–32
8. AK, 10–11
9. AK, 11; HMN, 32
10. SDG 29
11. AK, 9
12. AK, 9–10; HMN, 30
13. HMN, 30

14. SP, 3:689
15. MK, 27
16. Ibid., 195
17. DP, 344; AK, 11; HMN, 32

Chapter 4
Journey to Dakshineswar
1. HMN, 34
2. SDG, 34
3. HMN, 35
4. SP, 3:682–83
5. DP, 344
6. AK, 12
7. SDG, 35
8. GHM, 324
9. MK, 226–27
10. SP, 3:690
11. DP, 348

Chapter 5
Awakening of Divinity
1. DP, 326
2. Ibid., 348
3. AK, 45
4. HMN, 40
5. DP, 349
6. Ibid., 349
7. MJKB, 25–26
8. DP, 350–51
9. AK, 16
10. SP, 3:689–90
11. AK, 17; HMN, 44–45
12. AK, 18
13. Ibid., 18
14. HJKB, 27–28
15. AK, 17
16. DP, 368–69
17. MK, 43; SDTC, 87
18. MK, 254; AK, 19–20
19. SDM, 33
20. Swami Prabhananda, Amritarup Sri Ramakrishna (Udbodhan Office: Calcutta, 1991), 30–31
21. MK, 43
22. Ibid., 229
23. Amritarup Ramakrishna, 28
24. Prakash, Swami Saradananda, 203

25. SP, 2:433
26. SDA, 41
27. DP, 876–79
28. SDA, 44
29. Swami Prabhananda, Journeys with Ramakrishna (Ramakrishna Math: Chennai, 2001), 151–52
30. SDM, 49
31. MK, 254–55; AK, 20–21
32. SDA, 39
33. MK, 229
34. HMN, 52
35. MK, 229
36. Ibid., 131–32
37. SDM, 66
38. DP, 554
39. HMN, 53
40. Ibid., 53–54
41. SDM, 50
42. Swami Chetanananda, ed., Swami Subodhanander Smritikatha (Udbodhan Office: Calcutta, 2005), 249

Chapter 6
With Ramakrishna in Dakshineswar
1. AK, 30–31
2. Swami Gambhirananda, Holy Mother Sri Sarada Devi, (Ramakrishna Math: Chennai, 1955), 101–02
3. MK, 64
4. Swami Chetanananda, ed., Ramakrishna as We Saw Him (Vedanta Society: St. Louis, 1990), 33–34
5. Ibid., 354
6. Swami Chetanananda, They Lived with God (Vedanta Society: St. Louis, 2006), 182–83
7. Swami Chetanananda, How to Live with God (Vedanta Society: St. Louis, 2008), 216
8. HMN, 76
9. SDM, 57
10. Ibid., 84
11. DP, 465
12. HMN, 65
13. Ibid., 80

14. *Ramakrishna as We*, 26
15. SDT, 67–68
16. HMN, 59–60
17. Swami Jagannathananda, *Srima–Katha* (Udbodhan Office, Calcutta, 1953), 1:176
18. MK, 207
19. HMN, 71–72
20. *They Lived with God*, 378
21. Swami Chetanananda, *God Lived with Them* (Vedanta Society: St. Louis, 1997), 189
22. Ibid., 487
23. SDM, 57
24. HMN, 71
25. SP, 4:905
26. HMN, 57–58; AK, 33
27. *They Lived with God*, 317; SDM, 78
28. *They Lived with God*, 182
29. MK, 246
30. RG, 594
31. Ibid., 572
32. AK, 54
33. AK, 54
34. *Vedanta Kesari*, December 2003: 477–79; *Amritarup Sri Ramakrishna*, 29–30
35. *Vedanta Kesari*, Dec. 2003, 479; *Amrita-rup*, 33
36. SDG, 65
37. *Ramakrishna as We*, 445–46
38. DP, 161
39. MK, 22
40. Ibid., 62–63; HMN 75; RG, 59
41. SDM, 82; HMN, 76
42. SDG, 88
43. SDM, 74
44. MK, 296
45. SDG, 88
46. HMN, 76–77
47. SDG, 86; MK, 33
48. SP, 4:1006–07
49. RG, 210
50. MJKB, 52–53
51. MK, 132; HMN, 77
52. SDG, 87
53. Ibid., 86
54. Ibid., 85; HMN 70
55. Ibid., 84–85
56. Ibid., 89; HMN 78
57. HMN, 78–79
58. MK, 134
59. SDG, 90
60. SP, 4:892
61. HMN, 79
62. HMN, 80
63. *They Lived with God*, 81
64. SP, 4:1146–47
65. Ibid., 4:1150–51
66. Ibid., 4:1151–52
67. Ibid., 4:1148
68. Ibid., 4:1152–54
69. Ibid., 4:1154–55
70. Ibid., 4:1155–56
71. Ibid., 4:1156–58

Chapter 7
Holy Mother's Reminiscences of the Master

1. MK, 141–42
2. Swami Chetanananda, ed., *Ramakrishna as We Saw Him* (Vedanta Society: St. Louis, 1990), 19–31

Chapter 8
Farewell to Dakshineswar

1. DP, 867
2. Ibid., 868
3. Ibid., 856
4. Ibid., 862
5. Ibid., 863
6. Ibid., 693
7. MK, 133
8. *They Lived with God*, 382
9. MJKB, 73
10. *Sarada* (Yogeswari Ramakrishna Math: Howrah), 7:240
11. DP, 875

Chapter 9
In Shyampukur and Cossipore

1. MK, 215
2. DP, 873, 879–80
3. DP, 923
4. HMN, 89
5. MJKB, 85

6. MK, 42; *God Lived with Them*, 190
7. *God Lived with Them*, 250–51
8. MK, 66, 213
9. *God Lived with Them*, 451–52
10. MK, 216–17
11. *Ramakrishna as We Saw Him*, 446
12. Ibid., 446
13. RG, 973–74
14. *They Lived with God*, 165
15. MK, 197
16. *They Lived with God*, 237
17. SDA, 75
18. SDG, 108
19. SDG, 116
20. HMN, 92–93
21. SDG, 117
22. HMN, 91
23. SDG, 307
24. Swami Apurvananda, *Janani Sri Sarada Devi* (Udbodhan Office: Calcutta, 1988), 74–75
25. Chandra Shekhar Chattopadhyay, *Sri Sri Latu Maharajer Smritikatha* (Udbodhan Office: Calcutta, 1953), 260
26. SMA, 81
27. HMN, 93
28. Ibid., 94
29. MSS, 21
30. SDM, 125–26; AK, 67

Chapter 10
Pilgrimage

1. Swami Chetanananda, *How a Shepherd Boy Became a Saint* (Vedanta Society: St. Louis, 1980), 57
2. HMN, 96
3. Durga Puri Devi, *Sarada–Ramakrishna* (Saradeshwari Ashrama: Calcutta, 1967), 153–54
4. SDA, 78
5. HMN, 96
6. SDG, 114
7. *God Lived with Them*, 232–33
8. MK, 136
9. *They Lived with God*, 383–84
10. Ibid., 319
11. HMN, 99
12. MK, 319–20
13. Ibid., 136
14. *How a Shepherd Boy*, 59
15. Ibid., 58–59
16. SDM, 133
17. AK, 68

Chapter 11
Ordeals in Kamarpukur

1. AK, 68–69
2. SDG, 119
3. Ibid., 128
4. MJKB, 99; SDA, 76; SDM, 133; MK, 236
5. HMN, 104
6. MK, 236
7. Ibid., 237
8. SDG, 121
9. Abhay Chandra Bhattacharya, *Srimar Jivan Darshan* (Grantha Bharati: Calcutta, 1990), 320
10. HMN, 105
11. MJKB, 102–03
12. MK, 173–74; HMN, 106
13. DP, 302
14. SDG 127

Chapter 12
In and Around Calcutta

1. MK, 134–35; HMN, 107
2. MK, 135
3. HMN, 107–08
4. *God Lived with Them*, 458
5. SP, 3:611
6. *Udbodhan*, 108:795
7. MJKB, 112
8. HMN, 108
9. MK, 186
10. MJKB, 113–14
11. SDM, 144–45
12. MK, 193
13. MJKB, 118
14. Ibid., 119
15. Ibid., 119
16. RG, 808
17. Swami Chetanananda, *Girish Chandra Ghosh* (Vedanta Society: St. Louis, 2009), 221

18. MJKB, 122
19. SGW, 105–10; MD, 5–11
20. SDG, 273–74; Swami Omkarananda, *Sri Ramakrishna Swami Vivekananda O Dharmaprasanga* (Ramakrishna Vivekananda Ashrama:Howrah, 1974), 127
21. Swami Purnatmananda, ed., *Yugadishari Vivekananda* (Udbodhan Office: Calcutta, 2001), 333–34
22. MK, 293–94
23. Ibid., 238
24. HMN, 110–11; SDG, 136
25. HMN, 111
26. MK, 153
27. Ibid., 339–40; GHM, 293–94
28. MK, 15
29. MK, 102
30. GHM, 49
31. MJKB, 132–33
32. SDG, 141; SS, 7

Chapter 13
Holy Mother and Vivekananda
1. RSD, 307–10
2. HMN, 114
3. *Udbodhan*, 64:172
4. HMN, 257–58
5. RSD, 315
6. RSD, 316–20
7. MK, 190
8. *God Lived with Them*, 55
9. Swami Apurvananda, ed., *Shivananda Smriti Samgraha* (Udbodhan Office: Calcutta, 2005), 203; SS, 24
10. SS, 24–25
11. HMN, 115; SMA, 11–12
12. SS, 31
13. *God Lived with Them*, 601
14. SS, 27–28
15. Ibid., 24
16. GHM, 44–45
17. SDM, 307
18. Ibid., 43–44; MK, 44–45
19. HMN, 257
20. SDM, 308
21. MJKB, 159
22. Ibid., 159

23. MK, 262–63; GHM, 376
24. MSI, 230

Chapter 14
Holy Mother and Western Women
1. *They Lived with God*, 81
2. *Complete Works of Swami Vivekananda*, 6:389
3. HMN, 283
4. RSD, 149
5. Sankari Prasad Basu, ed., *Letters of Sister Nivedita* (Nababharat Publishers: Calcutta, 1982), 1:9–10
6. *They Lived with God*, 372
7. MK, 191; GHM, 96
8. SGW, 472
9. Transcribed and edited from Swami Krishnananda's tape, 27 December 1947, Hollywood
10. Linda Prugh, *Josephine MacLeod and Vivekananda's Mission* (Ramakrishna Math: Chennai, 2001), 352
11. Ibid., 346
12. Ibid., 347
13. SDA, 103
14. SS, 171
15. SS, 258
16. Ibid., 533
17. Ibid., 147
18. *Letters of Sister Nivedita*, 2: 630–31
19. MK, 308–9; BS, 142
20. SDG, 369; HMN, 237–38; SMA, 207–08
21. MK, 211
22. Pravrajika Atmaprana, *Sister Nivedita* (Sister Nivedita Girls' School: Calcutta, 1992), 258
23. *Complete Works of Sister Nivedita*, vol 1 (Sister Nivedita Girls' School: Calcutta, 1967), 106–07
24. HMN, 285; SDG, 217
25. *Complete Works of Sister Nivedita*, 1:105–06
26. HMN, 286
27. SDG, 302
28. SP, 3:686–87
29. RSD, 214
30. Ibid., 131–32
31. SGW, 289–90

32. SP, 4:1054–55
33. *Josephine MacLeod and Vivekananda's Mission*, 351
34. Ibid., 335–36
35. GHM, 121
36. Ibid., 67–68

Chapter 15
Holy Mother and Girish Chandra Ghosh
1. HMN, 271–72
2. Ibid., 272
3. *Prabuddha Bharata*, 1952:263–65
4. MD, 14–17
5. HMN, 272–73
6. Ibid., 273
7. Ibid., 123
8. Swami Chetanananda, ed., *Swami Brahmanander Smritikatha* (Udbodhan Office: Calcutta, 2003), 506
9. Hemendra Nath Dasgupta, *Sri Sri Ramakrishnadev O Bhakta–Bhairav Girishchandra* (Calcutta, 1953), 76
10. HMN, 274
11. SDG, 175–76
12. *Udbodhan*, 107:328
13. Ibid., 107:328
14. Ibid., 107:328
15. *Bhakta Bhairav*, 77–78
16. HMA, 193–94
17. MD, 30–32
18. Ibid., 74–75
19. *Udbodhan*, 107:330
20. MK, 39
21. Ibid., 197–98
22. Ibid., 9

Chapter 16
Holy Mother and Mahendra Nath Gupta (M.)
1. *Srimar Jivan Darshan*, 314–15
2. RG, 715–23
3. Ibid., 973–74
4. *Jivan Darshan*, 315–16
5. Swami Nityatmananda, *Srima Darshan* (General Printers and Publishers: Calcutta, 1972), 11:132

6. Ibid., 4:262–63
7. Ibid., 1:167
8. *Amritarup Ramakrishna*, 190
9. Ibid., 192; SDA, 119
10. *Udbodhan*, 108:795
11. Ibid., 108:795
12. Ibid., 108:797
13. Swami Chetanananda, *Mahendra Nath Gupta (M.)*, (Vedanta Society: St. Louis, 2011), 306
14. SP, 2:431–35
15. Ibid., 4:889–900

Chapter 17
Holy Mother's Caretakers
1. MK, 240
2. HMN, 259
3. Ibid., 259–60
4. RSD, 313–14
5. DP, 825
6. *Complete Works of Nivedita*, 1:104
7. SDM, 314; MJKB, 148
8. GHM, 171
9. SDG, 145
10. Swami Gambhirananda, *Bhakta Malika* (Udbodhan Office: Calcutta, 1963), 1:173
11. HMN, 266; MK, 240
12. *Jeman Dekhiyachi*, 34–36
13. *God Lived with Them*, 336–37
14. HMN, 267
15. SDG, 186
16. MK, 320
17. *Jeman Dekhiyachi*, 144
18. SP, 1:158
19. SDG, 183
20. Ibid., 183
21. HMN, 269
22. *Jeman Dekhiyachi*, 250–51

Chapter 18
Mahamaya's Maya
1. SDM, 354
2. MSS, 11–12
3. HMN, 119–20
4. SDG, 149
5. Ibid.,, 153
6. Ibid., 153

7. MJKB, 152
8. MK, 124
9. MSI, 29–30
10. MJKB, 151
11. HMN, 138–39; MK, 295–96
12. HMN, 139
13. Ibid., 116
14. SDG, 155
15. SMA, 39, 62
16. Ibid., 64
17. *Sarada–Ramakrishna*, 314
18. MK, 184
19. HMN, 162
20. HMA, 64–73; HMN, 163
21. HMA, 76
22. SDG, 164
23. HMN, 118–19
24. HMN, 118–19
25. MK, 255
26. *They Lived with God*, 374
27. Ibid., 374

Chapter 19
Radhu

1. *They Lived with God*, 183
2. HMN, 269
3. GHM, 21
4. MK, 20
5. Ibid., 366–67
6. SP, 1:99
7. SDG, 200
8. HMN, 140; SDG, 227
9. HMN, 140; SDG, 227
10. HMN, 141; SDG, 227–28
11. MK, 349
12. HMN, 144
13. MK, 343
14. Ibid., 316
15. Ibid., 246
16. Ibid., 246
17. Ibid., 124
18. Ibid., 318
19. MSI, 73
20. MK, 318–19; HMN, 130
21. MSI, 75
22. Ibid., 83
23. Ibid., 83–84

24. Ibid., 92–93
25. HMN, 144; SDG, 237
26. MSI, 91–92
27. Ibid., 94–95
28. Ibid., 95–96
29. Ibid., 97–101
30. Ibid., 101
31. Ibid., 101–02
32. Ibid., 105–06
33. SDG, 235; MSI, 108
34. MK, 321–22
35. SDA, 252; HMN, 145
36. HMN, 142–43; MSI, 150–51, 134–35
37. Pravrajika Vedantaprana, ed., *Janma-janmantarer Ma*, (Sarada Math: Dakshineswar, 2003), 317
38. Ibid., 317
39. HMN, 145

Chapter 20
Holy Mother in the Midst of her Family

1. *Teachings of Ramakrishna* (Advaita Ashrama: Calcutta, 1958), 93
2. RG, 165
3. Ibid., 165
4. Ibid., 428–29
5. Katha Upanishad, 1:2:23
6. MSI, 170
7. Ibid., 130–31
8. Ibid., 155–56; HMN, 121–22
9. HMN, 120
10. Ibid., 122
11. Ibid., 122
12. MSI, 98–99; HMN, 122
13. MSI, 145
14. SDG, 243–44
15. MSS, 53
16. SDG, 243
17. MSI, 159–61
18. SDG, 247
19. MK, 223
20. Ibid., 256
21. MSI, 154
22. HMN, 127
23. MK, 303
24. HMN, 130

25. SDA, 238–41
26. Ibid., 242–43
27. SMA, 100–01
28. Ibid., 252
29. Ibid., 242
30. Ibid., 250
31. MD, 67–68
32. MK, 175–78
33. Ibid., 241–42
34. SDG, 301
35. MK, 103
36. SDA, 245
37. HMN, 125
38. SDM, 437
39. MSI, 154–55
40. Transcribed and translated from 1986 cassette tape by Swami Chetanananda

Chapter 21
Pilgrimage in South India
1. MK, 97–98
2. SMA, 140–41
3. MK, 89–90
4. SMA, 147–51
5. Ibid., 145–46
6. SP, 1:212
7. HMN, 304
8. MK, 325
9. SMA, 161
10. MK, 265
11. Ibid., 209
12. *Nibodhata*, 13:81–82; HMN, 305
13. Swami Prabhananda, *Holy Mother in the South* (Ramakrishna Math: Chennai, 2005), 54–55
14. SDG, 195
15. *Yogakshema* (Calcutta, 1979), 100
16. *Holy Mother in the South*, 60
17. MJKB, 214
18. HMN, 304
19. MSI, 18–19
20. MK, 152

Chapter 22
Last Visit to Varanasi
1. MSI, 228
2. SS, 103

3. SDG, 200
4. MD, 38
5. SDG, 209–10
6. *Udbodhan*, 36:149
7. SDG, 210
8. *Swami Brahmananda*, (Udbodhan Office: Calcutta, 1955), 260–61
9. SDG, 211
10. Mahendra Nath Datta, *Master Maha-shayer Anudhyan,*(Mahendra Publishing: Calcutta, 1968) 26; MD, 53–54
11. HMN, 308
12. Ibid., 308–09
13. *Swami Brahmanander Smritikatha*, 16
14. MD, 40–41; *Shivananda Smriti Samgraha*, 12
15. MK, 232
16. MD, 39–40
17. MK, 233
18. Ibid., 310–13
19. Ibid., 313
20. MD, 29
21. MK, 315
22. MK, 312; SDTC, 230
23. Ibid., 235
24. SDTC, 178
25. MD, 50–51
26. SP, 3:540
27. *Latu Maharajer Smritikatha*, 444, and Swami Apurvananda's memoir
28. *Janani Sri Saradadevi*, 152–53

Chapter 23
At Belur Math and With Disciples
1. Chandogya Upanishad, 8:2:10
2. *They Lived with God*, 136
3. *Latu Maharajer Smritikatha*, 341–42
4. Swami Prabhananda, *Sri Ramakrishna Mather Adikatha* (Udbodhan Office: Calcutta, 2001), 222
5. Ibid., 221–22
6. SMA, 13–15
7. *God Lived with Them*, 57
8. Sharat Chandra Chakrabarty, *Swami Shishya Samvad* (Udbodhan Office: Calcutta, 1961), 2:140
9. *God Lived with Them*, 548

10. SDA, 228–29; SDG, 196–97
11. MK, 230
12. SDM, 332
13. MK, 231
14. SDG, 208–09
15. SP, 3:631
16. MK, 85
17. MD, 54–55
18. HMN, 242–43
19. MD, 54
20. SDA, 232–33
21. SP, 3:625–26
22. HMN, 243
23. SDM, 334
24. Anonymous, *Swami Brahmananda*, (Udbodhan Office, 1961), 290–93
25. Swami Mukteswarananda, *Smriti Katha* (Calcutta, 1970), 74–76
26. MSI, 76–77
27. MK, 347
28. Ibid., 119
29. SGW, 18
30. SDM, 285
31. SGW, 18; HMN, 259–60
32. MSS, 52
33. MD, 92–93
34. MSI, 77–79
35. Swami Apurvananda, ed., *For Seekers of God* (Advaita Ashrama: Calcutta, 1975), 205
36. Swami Apurvananda, *Mahapurush Shivananda* (Udbodhan Office: Calcutta, 1949), 208
37. *For seekers of God*, 206–08
38. SGW, 19
39. Swami Omkareswarananda, *Premananda Jivan Charit* (Ramakrishna Sadhan Mandir: Deoghar, 1966), 160–61
40. *God Lived with Them*, 209–10
41. Ibid., 210
42. SGW, 22; SS, 100
43. Swami Abhedananda, *Patra Sankalan* (Ramakrishna Vedanta Math: Calcutta, 1943), 1–2
44. SS, 106
45. Ibid., 111
46. SGW, 25–26

47. Swami Apurvananda, *Satprasange Swami Vijnanananda* (Ramakrishna Math: Allahabad, 1953), 111
48. Ibid., 151
49. SS, 85
50. SGW, 23
51. Ibid., 86
52. SP, 4:1007–09
53. SGW, 24
54. *Latu Maharajer Smritikatha*, 415–17

Chapter 24
Mother of the Ramakrishna Order

1. HMN, 241
2. *Complete Works of Swami Vivekananda*, 8:57
3. Ibid., 61
4. Ibid., 80–81, 91
5. SDG, 273
6. SB, 331
7. SGW, 33–36
8. HMN, 249–50
9. MSS, 20
10. HMN, 251
11. MSI, 27
12. SDG, 259
13. Ibid., 259
14. Ibid., 260
15. MSI, 24
16. SDG, 261–62
17. HMN, 250
18. MSI, 132–33
19. SDG, 263
20. HMN, 243–44; SDM, 392
21. SDM, 392
22. MSI, 50
23. MD, 26
24. *God Lived with Them*, 264–65
25. SDG, 264–65
26. Ibid., 265
27. Ibid., 265
28. MSI, 168–69
29. SDG, 268
30. Ibid., 268
31. MK, 202; SDTC, 153
32. SDG, 268–69
33. MD, 46–47

34. Ibid., 345
35. MSI, 173–74
36. Ibid., 112–13
37. SDG, 271
38. Ibid., 263–64
39. MK, 186
40. SDG, 272
41. Ibid., 272–73
42. Ibid., 274–75
43. HMN, 250
44. *For Seekers of God,* 210–11
45. Swami Nikhilananda, ed., *Vivekananda: The Yogas and Other Works,* (Ramakrishna–Vivekananda Centre: New York, 1953), 165
46. SP, 3:747
47. *Complete Works of Vivekananda,* 7:216, 214
48. Brahmachari Akshaychaitanya, *Swami Saradanander Jivani* (Model Publishing House: Calcutta, 1955), 186–87
49. *Udbodhan* (Swami Vivekananda's Centenary Number), 203
50. *Udbodhan* (Holy Mother's Centenary Number), 244–45
51. *Saradanander Jivani,* 189
52. Ibid., 56–57
53. SDG,260–61
54. Ibid., 261
55. Ibid., 264
56. Swami Abjajananda, *Monastic Disciples of Swami Vivekananda* (Advaita Ashrama: Calcutta, 2003), 228
57. MSI, 196
58. Ibid., 192–93

Chapter 25
Mother of All

1. Chandi, 11:5
2. SDTC, 120–21
3. SDA, 115; MK, 295
4. SP, 3:832–33
5. MJKB, 224
6. MK, 160–61
7. Gita, 9:29
8. SDG, 289–90
9. Ibid., 290
10. SP, 4:1225–26
11. MSI, 201–02
12. *God Live with Them,* 245
13. MK, 161
14. SP, 657–61
15. Swami Atulananda, *With the Swamis in America* (Advaita Ashrama: Calcutta, 1988), 10
16. SDA, 159
17. SP, 3:725–26
18. SDA, 117
19. HMN, 168–69; MSI, 53–54
20. MSI, 54
21. MK, 328
22. Ibid., 263
23. MSS, 165
24. HMN, 169; MSS, 165–66
25. MSI, 81; HMN, 236
26. Gita, 10:20
27. Chandi, 1:76
28. *Ramakrishna as We Saw Him,* 47
29. *They Lived with God,* 264
30. MSS, 54–56
31. MSI, 122–25
32. SP, 3:663
33. MK, 108
34. SDG, 292
35. SDA, 157
36. SDG, 281
37. SDM, 467; SDA, 157
38. MD, 76
39. MK, 402
40. SP, 3:653
41. MK, 244
42. MD, 183
43. SDG, 287
44. Ibid., 283
45. Ibid., 287
46. MSS, 50–51
47. MD, 214–15
48. MJKB, 197–98
49. SDG, 287–88
50. MSI, 117–18
51. SDA, 207
52. *Girish Chandra Ghosh,* 467
53. MK, 161–62

54. *Janmajanmantarer Ma*, 253; SDA, 207
55. SDA, 128
56. Ibid., 131–32
57. MSS, 48–50
58. Ibid., 36–41
59. Ibid., 61–63
60. Ibid., 41–47
61. SDA, 126
62. Ibid., 145
63. Ibid., 126
64. Swami Purnatmananda, *Chirantani Sarada* (Udbodhan Office: Calcutta,1997), 113–14
65. *Sarada–Ramakrishna*, 415–16
66. MSI, 50–52
67. SDG, 295
68. HMN, 161
69. *Jeman Dekhiachi*, 16
70. SDG, 294
71. Ibid., 294–95
72. Ibid., 295
73. MSI, 177
74. MSI, 177–78; HMN, 158
75. Swami Purnatmananda, ed., *Jugajanani Sarada* (Udbodhan Office: Calcutta, 2001), 61–63
76. MD, 139–40
77. SDG, 279
78. MK, 296–97
79. SDG, 284
80. Ibid., 284
81. Ibid., 280
82. Ibid., 280–81
83. SP, 3:680–81

Chapter 26
Holy Mother as a Guru

1. RG, 232–33
2. Katha Upanishad, 1:2:5
3. Shvetashvatara Upanishad, 6:23
4. Katha Upanishad, 1:2:7
5. Gita, 9:18
6. DP, 457–58
7. GHM, 157
8. RG, 210
9. SDG, 92
10. Swami Gambhirananda, *Holy Mother Sri Sarada Devi*, (Ramakrishna Math: Madras, 1969), 395
11. HMN, 165
12. GHM, 302; MK, 349
13. HMN, 154
14. Ibid., 151
15. RSD, 98
16. *Swami Saradanander Jivani*, 229
17. MK, 117; SDTC, 235
18. MK, 289; HMN, 173
19. MK, 88–89
20. MK, 296; GHM, 309
21. SDTC, 220
22. MK, 241; HMN, 171
23. MK, 210
24. Ibid., 210
25. HMN, 170
26. Ibid., 172
27. MK, 78
28. SDG, 306
29. Ibid., 307
30. Ibid., 307
31. HMN, 172–73
32. MJ, 36–38
33. MD, 101
34. MK, 291–92
35. Ibid., 95–96
36. SDG, 309
37. HMN, 159
38. MK, 334
39. SDG, 310
40. Ibid., 311
41. MK, 172–73
42. SS, 185–86
43. MK, 58–59
44. MK, 260; SDTC, 198
45. *Vedanta and the West*, 110:62
46. SDA, 201–02
47. MK, 184
48. MK, 259; SDTC, 197
49. Rammurty Mishra, *Yoga Sutras*, (Anchor Books: New York, 1973), 385
50. MK, 291
51. MK, 279–80; SDTC, 211–12
52. MK, 290; SDTC, 221
53. MK, 103; SDTC, 228

54. MK, 138–44; SDTC, 201–06
55. MK, 11
56. Ibid., 158
57. SP, 3:591–92
58. SDA, 161–63; SDM, 22–23
59. MK, 250
60. SDM, 223–24
61. SDA, 203
62. MK, 112–13
63. SDG, 318–19
64. MSI, 110–12
65. SDG, 320
66. SP, 1:126–27; HMN, 176–77
67. SDTC, 42–43; MK, 4–5
68. SDG, 317–18
69. MSI, 20–21
70. MJ, 39
71. MK, 118–19; SDTC, 233–34; GHM, 328–29
72. GHM, 24
73. HMN, 159–61
74. SP, 1:89–90; RSD, 261–62
75. SDA, 167–68
76. Ibid., 199–201
77. HMN, 239
78. Ibid., 215

Chapter 27
Ministry through Correspondence
1. RG, 185
2. Ibid., 839
3. *Mayer Chithi*, A Compilation (Rama-krishna Mission Institute of Culture: Calcutta, 2006), 9–10
4. SS, 171; Original in SP, 3:752a
5. Sister Devamata, *Days in an Indian Monastery* (Ananda Ashrama: California, 1927), 211
6. Ibid., 215
7. Ibid., 215–16
8. Ibid., 217
9. Ibid., 217–18
10. Ibid., 227–28
11. SP, 3:750–51
12. *Mayer Chithi*, 61
13. Ibid., 72
14. Ibid., 91

15. Ibid., 91–92
16. Ibid., 97
17. Ibid., 108
18. Ibid., 124
19. Ibid., 126
20. Ibid., 178–79; Original in SP, 3:816a
21. Ibid., 179
22. Ibid., 196
23. Ibid., 201
24. Ibid., 202–03
25. Ibid., 203–04
26. Ibid., 207
27. Ibid., 193
28. MSS, 93–97
29. SDTC, 163–64
30. HMN, 194–95
31. MK, 251–52; HMN, 195
32. HMN, 195–96; MK, 258–59
33. HMN, 198; MK, 260
34. SP, Original 3:784b
35. *Mayer Chithi*, Original 78a

Chapter 28
Untold Stories of Jayrambati
1. SDM, 393
2. Ibid., 394
3. Ibid., 394
4. MJ, 65–66
5. SDG, 214
6. MSS, 8
7. BS, 256
8. Ibid., 12–13
9. Ibid., 15
10. MSS, 38–39
11. Ibid., 64–66
12. Ibid., 16
13. MD, 143
14. SP, 1:15–16
15. Ibid., 4:950
16. Ibid., 4:949
17. MJ, 70
18. MSI, 39
19. Ibid., 43–44
20. Ibid., 45–46
21. MK, 162
22. *Mayer Chithi*, 121
23. Ibid., 214–226

24. MSI, 59–60; MSS, 169–71
25. MSS, 171
26. HMN, 169
27. MSS, 173–76; SDA, 141
28. SP, 4:1063–66
29. MK, 162–63; MSS, 157
30. SDM, 393
31. BS, 150–51
32. *Dictionary of Thoughts*, 652
33. MK, 271–72
34. SP, 3:693–99
35. Ibid., 3:720
36. MSI, 54–56
37. SMA, 210–11
38. MJ, 53–60
39. MSI, 10–11
40. MSS, 123–28
41. MK, 273
42. RG, 155
43. SDM, 411
44. MSI, 35–36
45. Ibid., 37–38
46. Ibid., 135–36
47. Ibid., 148–49
48. SP, 3:728
49. Ibid., 3:826
50. Ibid., 1:100–105
51. MSI, 62
52. Ibid., 64
53. Ibid., 68
54. Ibid., 70; *Jeman Dekhiachi*, 216
55. *Jeman Dekhiachi*, 216–17
56. MK, 293
57. MSI, 72–73
58. MD, 71–72

Chapter 29
Udbodhan: The Mother's House
1. *Complete Works of Swami Vivekananda*, 7:482–83
2. *Mayer Bati*, A compilation (Udbodhan Office: Calcutta, 1996), 25
3. *Sarada* magazine, 7:494–95
4. SDM, 369
5. SDG, 362–63
6. SMA, 189
7. *Sarada*, 7:177–79

8. MK, 34; SDTC, 74
9. MD, 34–35
10. MK, 153–54
11. MK, 32; HMN, 71
12. SDTC, 138–39
13. *Janmajanmantarer Ma*, 135
14. SP, 4:996–98
15. MD, 75
16. SP, 4:999–1001
17. *Brahmanander Smritikatha*, 193; MSS, 26
18. MSI, 79–80
19. MJKB, 181
20. MK, 7; SDTC, 46
21. MJKB, 182; MK, 31; HMN, 70–71
22. SP, 3:598
23. MK, 56
24. Ibid., 57
25. Ashu, *Srima*, 117
26. SDM, 388
27. MK, 12–13; SDTC, 51–52
28. MK, 46; SDTC, 90–91
29. MK, 52–53; HMN, 98
30. SMA, 199–200
31. MK, 31 32; HMN, 71
32. MJKB, 96
33. MK, 72
34. SDM, 387
35. Gita, 9:29–31
36. RG, 181–82
37. SMA, 177
38. MSI, 197–99
39. From Swami Dhireshananda's Diary
40. SMA, 209–10
41. Ibid., 214–15
42. SP, 3:627–28
43. SMA, 215–16
44. MK, 71–72
45. SP, 3:531
46. Ibid., 3:532
47. Ibid., 3:533
48 Ibid., 3:534–35
49. Ibid., 3:537
50. Ibid., 1:117–19
51. Leonard Roy Frank, *Quotationary* (Random House: New York, 2001), 794
52. SP, 1:120

53. Ibid., 1:125–26
54. Ibid., 1:122

Chapter 30
The Divinity of Holy Mother
1. Gita, 4:6
2. Chandi, 11:54–55
3. Brihadaranyaka Upanishad, 1:4:3
4. Gita, 10:12–13
5. Ibid., 9:11
6. HMN, 79
7. Ibid., 52
8. MK, 99
9. Ibid., 64
10. MSI, 140–41
11. SP, 3:615, 629
12. HMN, 187
13. MK, 350; HMN, 187
14. MK, 170–71; HMN, 207–8
15. MK, 175; SDTC, 125
16. MK, 92; HMN, 186
17. MK, 321–22; HMN, 187
18. BS, 92
19. Ibid., 287
20. MK, 331; GHM, 314
21. MK, 336; GHM, 343
22. MK, 349; HMN, 186
23. MK, 298–99; SDTC, 206
24. SDA, 172; SDG, 327
25. SDG, 328–29; HMN, 185–86
26. MSI, 179–83
27. MK, 159
28. HMN, 188–89; SMA, 147–49
29. SDG, 334
30. Udbodhan, 59:481–82
31. SP, 1:154
32. SP, 1:1–2
33. Ibid., 1:124
34. Ibid., 4: 1195–96
35. Ibid., 4:1199–1200
36. Ibid., 1:122–23
37. Ibid., 3:654
38. Ibid., 4:1130–34
39. SDG, 19
40. Sarada–Ramakrishna, 276–77
41. SMA, 31–32
42. Ibid., 78–79

43. SDA, 162
44. SDA, 163–64; SDG, 326–27
45. SDA, 165
46. Sarada–Ramakrishna, 418–19
47. Ibid., 420
48. SDG, 332–33
49. MJ, 41
50. MK, 49; HMN, 93
51. SDA, 142–43
52. SDG, 340
53. Katha Upanishad, 1:2:23
54. Gita, 7:25
55. SDG, 332
56. MJ, 40
57. MK, 132
58. MK, 68–69; HMN, 187–88
59. MK,85–86
60. Ibid., 317
61. Ibid., 347–48
62. Ibid., 353–54
63. Chandi, 1:81
64. MD, 163–66
65. SDG, 337
66. MK, 336–37
67. Ibid., 334
68. Ibid., 332
69. SDG, 338
70. MJKB, 195–96
71. RG, 178
72. MK, 185; SDTC, 135
73. MK, 202–03; SDTC, 153–56
74. Chandi, 11:4
75. MK, 85
76. Ibid., 86; HMN, 225
77. Ibid., 303
78. Swami Chetanananda's diary, Varanasi, 28 August 1982
79. MK, 88
80. Ibid., 294; GHM, 319–20
81. Ibid., 224–25; HMN,175
82. Ibid., 212
83. MK, 14
84. Katha Upanishad, 2:3:14

Chapter 31
The Human Aspects of Holy Mother
1. RG, 777

2. Ibid., 382, 782
3. MJ, 35–36
4. MK, 176; HMN, 126
5. MSI, 80–81
6. MJ, 88
7. MJ, 90
8. Bible: Matthew, 9:2, Mark, 2:19
9. MJ, 91
10. SMA, 90–91
11. SDG, 369
12. SS, 256
13. MK, 62
14. HMN, 295
15. *Sarada–Ramakrishna*, 324–25
16. MD, 74
17. MSI, 174
18. MK, 288
19. Ibid., 322
20. MSS, 148–49
21. MK, 187
22. Ibid., 56–57
23. Ibid., 34
24. SMA, 220–21
25. MK, 154–55
26. MSS, 74
27. Ibid., 117–18
28. Ibid., 74–75
29. Ibid., 159–60
30. RSD, 86–87
31. MJ, 30
32. SMA, 114
33. SS, 252
34. MJ, 49
35. MSS, 180–81
36. Ibid., 89
37. MK, 32
38. *Sarada–Ramakrishna*, 252
39. MK, 35
40. SDG, 186
41. MSI, 214
42. Ibid., 42
43. SDTC, 239
44. Ibid., 239; MK, 284
45. MSS, 100
46. SDG, 367
47. SP, 4:1016
48. MK, 34; SDTC, 74–75
49. SMA, 212–13
50. SDG, 356–57
51. Ibid., 368–69
52. GHM, 191–92
53. Ibid., 359–60
54. MK, 368
55. HMN, 128–29; SP, 4:1097–1101

Chapter 32
Two Flowers on One Stem

1. Shvetashvatara Upanishad, 4:3
2. RG, 310–11
3. Ibid., 311
4. SDG, 348–49
5. Ibid., 458
6. MJ, 142, 137
7. SDG, 343
8. MK, 249; SDTC, 189
9. MK, 319
10. MK, 23; HMN, 66
11. SDG, 343–44
12. MD, 100
13. SDG, 346
14. Ibid., 346
15. MK, 194
16. SDG, 347
17. Ibid., 344
18. Ibid., 346–47
19. MK, 321
20. SDG, 349
21. Ibid., 349
22. SMA,103
23. SDG, 349
24. Suresh Chandra Das and Jyotirmay Basu Roy, ed., *Pratyakshadarshir Smritipate Swami Vijnanananda* (General Printers & Publishers: Calcutta, 1977), 30
25. *Srima Darshan*, 11:132
26. SDG, 348
27. Ibid., 348
28. SS, 66
29. RG, 359
30. Ibid., 829
31. *Swami Vivekanander Vani O Rachana* (Udbodhan Office: Calcutta, 1964), 7:243

32. GHM, 167
33. SDG, 350
34. DP, 649
35. *Ramakrishna as We Saw Him*, 31
36. GHM, 77
37. RG, 943
38. MK, 208
39. Ibid., 208
40. Ibid., 248
41. SDA, 30
42. SMA, 84
43. HMN, 214–15
44. MSI, 133–34
45. Bible, 1 Corinthians, 7:9
46. SB, 233
47. MSI, 173–74; HMN, 181
48. MK, 116–17; SDTC, 231–32
49. HMN, 214
50. Ibid., 215
51. Ibid., 216
52. Ibid., 216–17
53. Ibid., 222
54. Ibid., 223
55. Ibid., 229
56. Ibid., 230
57. *Yogakshema* (Calcutta, 1979),164-65
58. SP, 3:599–600

Chapter 33
Further Glimpses of Holy Mother

1. Chandogya Upanishad, 7:23:1, 24:1
2. HMN, 287–88, 292
3. SMA, 194–95
4. Mundaka Upanishad, 2:1:4
5. Bible, John, 1:5
6. MD, 230–31
7. MK, 31
8. SS, 255
9. MSS, 158–59
10. SS, 255–56; RSD, 83–84
11. SMA, 197
12. SDA, 127; SS, 312
13. SDM, 451–52
14. SMA, 30–31
15. SDM, 445–46
16. Ibid., 447
17. HMN, 220

18. *Teachings of Sri Sarada Devi The Holy Mother*, A Compilation (Ramakrishna Math: Madras, 1985), 30–31
19. Ibid., 163
20. Ibid., 39
21. Ibid., 63
22. Ibid., 53
23. HMN, 159
24. *Teachings of Sarada Devi*, 141
25. Ibid., 75
26. HMN, 297
27. MK, 28–30
28. Ibid., 7; SDTC, 45
29. *Ramakrishna as We Saw Him*, 30; MK, 17
30. MK, 211; GHM, 121
31. MK, 335; GHM, 337
32. MK, 30
33. MK, 12; GHM, 11
34. RSD, 81–82
35. SMA, 86–89
36. Swami Nikhilananda, Bhagavad Gita (Ramakrishna–Vivekananda Centre: New York,1979), 52
37. MJ, 137–42
38. MSI, 228
39. MSS, 206
40. Ibid., 207–08
41. Ibid., 213
42. Ibid., 216
43. Ibid., 214–15
44. SP, 1:18, 21–22
45. MD, 102
46. SP, 1:96–98
47. RSD, 300
48. SP, 3:682–85
49. Ibid., 3:687–89
50. MD, 102
51. Ibid., 103–04

Chapter 34
Farewell to Jayrambati

1. MD, 79
2. Ibid., 80
3. Ibid., 80
4. Ibid., 81
5. MSI, 102

6. HMN, 104
7. *Saradanander Jivani,* 132–36
8. MJ, 69–70
9. Ibid., 70
10. Ibid., 73–75
11. MSI, 126
12. Ibid., 139–40
13. MJ, 75–79; MD, 115–16
14. MJ, 80
15. Mundaka Upanishad, 3:2:8
16. RG, 969
17. MJ, 83–85
18. Ibid., 90–91; SDG, 380
19. SDA, 292
20. MSI, 171
21. MJ, 94–95
22. SDM, 497
23. MSI, 172
24. MD, 124–25; MJ, 96–99
25. SDG, 383
26. MSI, 83–89

Chapter 35
Return to Her True Abode
1. MSI, 206
2. MSI, 199–200
3. SDA, 294
4. SP, 3:513–18
5. MK, 322
6. SP, 3:600
7. MD, 82
8. SP, 4:1190; SDA, 294–95
9. MSS, 196–97
10. SDM, 502
11. Ibid., 503
12. *Shivananda Smritisamgraha,* 196
13. *Janani Sri Sarada Devi,* 191–92
14. MSS, 192–95
15. MSI, 193–94
16. MJ, 100–101
17. Ibid., 111–12
18. SDM, 508; SDA, 295
19. SDA, 295; SDM, 508–09
20. SDA, 295–96
21. Ibid., 295
22. MSI, 222
23. *Jeman Dekhiyachi,* 257–60

24. Brahmachari Prakash, *Swami Saradananda,* 307
25. SDG, 389
26. MSI, 203
27. Ibid., 204
28. MK, 75–79; SDTC, 113–16
29. SP, 4:1173
30. RG, 631
31. SS.651
32. SDG, 389
33. Ibid., 389
34. MSI 204–05
35. SP, 3:518
36. SDG, 390–91; HMN, 315
37. MSI, 206–07
38. SDA, 297
39. MK, 167; HMN, 316
40. SDG, 394; HMN, 319; MK, 167
41. MD, 82–83
42. SDA, 297; MD, 83; HMN, 317
43. MK, 165–67
44. MSI, 208–12
45. MSS, 197–98
46. *Sarada–Ramakrishna,* 430
47. MSI, 212
48. SP, 3:518–19
49. HMN, 319
50. MSS, 200–201
51. MSI, 214
52. Swami Chetanananda, ed., *Swami Saradanander Smritikatha* (Udbodhan Office: Calcutta, 2006), 162
53. SP, 3:519
54. *Shivananda Smritisamgraha,* 196
55. MSS, 198–200
56. Ibid., 3:556
57. MD, 86
58. SP, 3:519–20
59. Ibid., 3:556–57
60. Prakash, *Swami Saradananda,* 201
61. SP, 1:26–27
62. Ibid., 1:27
63. MSS, 201–02
64. Romain Rolland, *The Life of Ramakrishna* (Advaita Ashrama: Calcutta, 1931), 314
65. SP, 3:845–46

66. *Prabuddha Bharata*, 1969:495
67. Swami Chetanananda's diary (Told by Swami Sridharananda in St. Louis on 23 May 2005)
68. MSI, 230–31

Epilogue
1. Bhagavata, 3:2:8–10
2. *Janmajanmantarer Ma*, 299–304
3. Ibid., 304–10
4. MJ, 127
5. *Janmajanmantarer Ma*, 313
6. MSI, 226–28
7. BS, 127
8. MSI, 228
9. BS, 130–32
10. MSS, 238
11. BS, 132
12. Ibid., 130
13. *They Lived with God*, 377
14. Ibid., 130–34
15. SP, 3:540
16. BS, 134–35

17. SDG, 401–04
18. SDA, 316
19. Ibid., 318
20. *Atmakatha* by Swami Tapananda, 134 [Quoted by Kalijivan Devasharma in *Sri Ramakrishna Parikrama* (Sri Balaram Prakashani: Calcutta, 2003), 17
21. MK, 22–24
22. BS, 25
23. Tarit Kumar Bandyopadhyay, *Sri Sri Ma O Dakat Baba* (Dev Sahitya Kutir: Calcutta, 1998), 88–96
24. SP, 3:830–31
25. HMN, 91
26. Prakash, *Swami Saradananda*, 206
27. SP, 3:626
28. HMN, 320

Appendix 1
1. Swami Chetanananda's diary
2. Hollywood Archives
3. HMN, 142
4. *Complete Works of Sister Nivedita*, 1:104

Index

Numbers in italics indicate photograph/illustration, n *is a footnote.*
RK=Sri Ramakrishna, SD=Sarada Devi (Holy Mother).

Sri Sarada Devi at Udbodhan House, 1909.

Quotes of Sarada Devi

As wind removes a cloud, so does the name of God disperse the cloud of worldliness.

One must be patient like the earth. What iniquities are being perpetuated on her! Yet she quietly endures them all.

Forbearance is a great virtue; there is no other like it.

Everyone can break down something, but how many can build it up?

Whatever you yearn for, that you will get.

God is one's very own. It is the eternal relationship. He is everyone's own. One realizes him in proportion to the intensity of one's feelings for him.

Don't be afraid. Human birth is full of suffering and one has to endure everything patiently, taking the name of God. None, not even God in human form, can escape the sufferings of body and mind.

The purpose of one's life is fulfilled only when one is able to give joy to another.

To err is human. One must not take that into account. It is harmful for oneself. One gets into the habit of finding fault.

I tell you one thing my child — if you want peace, do not find fault with others. Rather, see your own faults. Learn to make the world your own. No one is a stranger, my child; the whole world is your own.

I am the mother of the wicked, as I am the mother of the virtuous. Never fear. Whenever you are in distress, say to yourself, "I have a mother."